Kirkus
"Weisbrode's careful research and serviceable prose add light and dimension to a uniquely Eurocentric moment in American diplomatic history."

Brent Scowcroft, former National Security Advisor to presidents Gerald Ford and George H. W. Bush
"... reminds us how important the transatlantic relationship was during the twentieth century and of all the hard work that went into it on the part of many devoted public servants. This book also contains important lessons about diplomacy that remain highly relevant today."

Ernest R. May (†), Charles Warren Professor of History Emeritus, Harvard University
"A model for institutional history"

Klaus Larres, Richard M. Krasno Distinguished Professor of History, University of North Carolina at Chapel Hill
"Ken Weisbrode has written an outstanding book on America's diplomats and politicians who made and shaped the transatlantic alliance in the post-1945 era. The volume is highly readable and entertaining. The different personalities, their many idiosyncrasies and personal and political feuds and friendships vividly come to light. The reader is gently taken by the hand and presented with the fascinating manoeuvrings and visionary thinking of a plethora of leading statesmen that have shaped the contemporary world. This is a very important and enriching book. It helps us to understand the Atlantic world of the past and indeed the present."

David Mayers, Professor of History and Political Science, Boston University
"Weisbrode's book is bold in its sweep, covering the complex diplomatic interaction between American and European diplomats throughout the turbulent twentieth century. The book is grounded in thorough research conducted in multiple archives on both sides of the Atlantic. The analysis is astute. The judgments are judicious and persuasive. The concepts and interpretation are compelling. The elegance of the writing, the vivid portrayal of scenes and personalities, and the overall thoughtfulness make this book a treat for scholars and general readers alike. This impressive book repays careful reading while satisfying highest standards of scholarship."

Giles Scott-Smith, Chair of the Transatlantic Studies Association, and Ernst van der Beugel Chair in the Diplomatic History of Transatlantic Relations since WW II, Leiden University
"Few books have opened up new levels of diplomatic research as successfully.... This meticulous study interweaves the public and the private, the high and the low with an ease that belies the amount of scholarship that went into it. The result is an innovative and inspirational 'new look' at transatlantic politics, from the view of those at the coal face. All round, it is a major achievement in 20th century transatlantic studies."

Niall Ferguson, author of *Kissinger*
"... sheds fascinating light on the role of a key institution in the formulation of American foreign policy in the twentieth century. From World War I to the Cold War, the Bureau of European Affairs played a crucial part in bridging the Atlantic, sometimes leaning against the inclinations of the presidents and secretaries it supposedly served, always ensuring that Europe remained central to American grand strategy. Beautifully written and thoroughly researched, Weisbrode's book not only rescues four generations of diplomats from the condescension of posterity; it also delineates the crucial role of the State Department bureaucracy in shaping American foreign policy."

Martin Walker, *Internationale Politik*
"A gem of a book"

Edwina S. Campbell, *Foreign Service Journal*
"...quite simply, the finest, most balanced work of diplomatic history that I have read in many years.... Scholars of American diplomatic history and international relations will find themselves and their students well served by this book's archival and textual richness. And practitioners of American diplomacy will have the added pleasure of reading a work that recognizes the importance of their work, not only in EUR but throughout the State Department and around the world."

Alexander J. Groth, *Israel Journal of Foreign Affairs*
"The author has the skills of a novelist in presenting all his material about who the players really were, what they thought about foreign policy issues before them, and how they got along—or did not get along—with one another."

Andrew Roberts, *Commentary*
"It sounds a bit like the plot of a best-selling conspiracy theory novel: deep within the State Department there exists an elite group of largely Ivy League diplomats who, generation after generation, have been sedulously encouraging ever greater European integration... [a] well-researched and well-written book."

Andrew Moravcsik, *Foreign Affairs*
"Many books have been written about the presidents, secretaries of state, ambassadors, and 'wise men' who fostered the transatlantic partnership over the past half century. Weisbrode retells the story from the bottom up, focusing on the diplomats in the State Department's European Bureau. Until recently, many of the bureau's members viewed themselves as more politically astute and culturally refined than average diplomats... [a] carefully documented study..."

Choice
"Intriguingly nuanced, personality-driven narrative of how Atlanticism flourished as a result of individual efforts. Such perspective adds texture to the chronology of the Cold War. This expertly researched narrative offers insight into the minds of those 'small but powerful' actors who had the innate sense of place to create and maintain a framework of US diplomacy's finest hour. Recommended."

THE
ATLANTICISTS

Jean Monnet, David Bruce, William Tomlinson
(© Theo Mey, courtesy of the Fondation Jean Monnet pour l'Europe)

THE
ATLANTICISTS

A STORY OF AMERICAN DIPLOMACY

Kenneth Weisbrode

NORTIA
PRESS

2321 E. 4th St., C-219
Santa Ana, CA 92705
USA

An earlier edition of this work was published by Da Capo Press under the title *The Atlantic Century: Four Generations of Extraordinary Diplomats who Forged America's Vital Alliance with Europe.*

Includes bibliographical references and index. ISBN: 978-1-940503-07-3

1. Europe—Foreign relations—United States. 2. United States—Foreign relations—Europe. 3. Europe—Foreign relations—20th century. 4. United States—Foreign relations—20th century. 5. Diplomats—Europe—History—20th century. 6. Diplomats—United States—History—20th century. 7. United States. Dept. of State. Bureau of European Affairs—History.

Technical support by Russ Davis, Gray Dog Press (graydogpress.com)

Printed in the United States of America

Library of Congress Control Number: 2015941753

*For Rozanne L. Ridgway and
the late Andrew J. Goodpaster
Public Servants, Teachers, Atlanticists*

PREFACE TO THE PAPERBACK EDITION

IN THE SIX YEARS SINCE this book first was published, the short Atlantic Century it described—from the years just before the First World War to the end of the Cold War—has receded further in our collective memory. More than a dozen of the individuals I interviewed for it have died. The European Union and especially its currency, the euro, are under strain. It is not unusual to hear predictions of the failure of one or both. Anti-EU parties have gained support in several countries across Europe. Nationalism there is no longer taboo. The EU and the idea that underpins it, regional integration, appear today almost quaint.

The United States meanwhile has continued on an insular path—which is to say, a strange one, at once ambivalent and cyclical. In 2008 the American people elected Barack Obama to the presidency. He was, among other things, very popular in Europe. He soon announced that he was America's first Pacific president, while his new Secretary of State, Hillary Clinton, proclaimed the twenty-first century to be the Pacific Century. The announcements were accompanied by a policy called the Pivot to Asia. The Obama administration has since disowned the terminology but not the policy.

Presidencies rarely go as planned. Conflicts in the Middle East and a remarkable burst of revisionism by Russia's leader Vladimir Putin at the expense of his country's neighbors have occupied the attention of Obama and other Western leaders. The North Atlantic Treaty Organization—which has repeatedly snubbed theorists predicting its extinction—gained another lease on life. So has transatlantic diplomacy in other areas. The United States and the EU began negotiations for what, if they succeed, would be the world's largest trading bloc. And in his second term, Obama replaced Secretary Clinton with John Kerry, the francophone son of a foreign service officer whose career took place mostly in the State Department's Bureau of European Affairs.

Slogans notwithstanding, American policy has changed. It may or may not have fixed its gaze upon Asia, but it has acquired a different approach, characterized as "leading from behind." That might be consistent with the one this book has described: Atlanticism placed the collective unit, the West, in the foreground and individual nation-states, and their parochialisms, in the background. But I do not see this taking place today. From the outset of the euro crisis, for example,

ix

the rhetoric of nearly every major player was striking. Few proclaimed, we're all in this together. The language of solidarity that had become second nature to their late twentieth-century predecessors is used today mainly in the aftermath of terrorist attacks, not in any wider geopolitical or socioeconomic sense. Europe still looks like a beacon to some people but its leaders act more like the defenders of a fracturing fortress. Meanwhile American officials, including the president, keep insisting that Europeans are capable of handling their own crises.

Different things are probably said in private, but that is beside the point. The Atlantic Century really does look like it belongs to the ages. The concept it brought to prominence, collective security, has receded behind an older form of *Realpolitik*. Atlanticism's prestige has given way, on the one hand, to a global utopianism and, on the other, to a jaded and less creative orientation that touts itself as pragmatism. I distinguish here between actual policies—which may well be pragmatic—and declaratory ones, reflecting such an orientation in the spirit of our time. It has come to resemble, and may prove to be, another failed peace.

Just compare what took place in Central and Eastern Europe after 1989 with the response to the Arab revolutions of 2011. In both instances there was euphoria followed by tragedy. But in the former, tragedy—here I refer to the wars in the former Yugoslavia—brought forth a renewed commitment, in principle at least, to a region whole and free, whereas in the latter it has mainly led to retrenchment and resignation. There was no regional Marshall Plan on offer. No program of economic integration with one another or with neighbors across the Mediterranean. No mantra of shared responsibility, or mutual dependence. Europeans and Americans have been generous toward some Arab countries. They also continue to intervene militarily in this region. But the overarching sentiment is one of detachment: We wish you well; but this is your fate, not ours.

This is my principal reason for replacing this book's title. I have made no substantive changes apart from a handful of corrections. The subject remains the same: Atlanticism. But I now prefer to describe it explicitly as a story of individuals rather than of a particular epoch. I still hold to the judgment that there probably will not be another Atlantic Century, at least not in our lifetimes. The reason is more cultural than political; I do not see many signs that America and Europe will be as fashionably intertwined as they then were. Yet, I also retain hope that Atlanticism is not dead. For it to thrive again, however, its definition bears repeating: Atlanticism did not just mean being Eurocentric if you are American, or American-centric if you are European. It was not merely about having certain friends in the world, or favoring a particular geography. It meant something greater.

The Atlanticists were progressives who set out to improve the form as well as the substance of American diplomacy. They aimed to make Woodrow Wilson's ideal of a security community consistent with the reality of power rather than set the two at cross purposes, as he had done. They promoted a merger of the Old World and its diplomatic traditions with the New in a manner that served the interests of both, as well as their values. They advanced a diplomacy that respected the geographical diversity of its adherents but was united functionally in economics, society and politics. This included but was not limited to their collective defense.

Most of all, Atlanticists imagined a living map. The Atlantic Community was not fixed. There were diverging views over its boundaries, of course, but it was meant to grow and thrive. So, Atlanticists ought to be saddened by long and repetitive debates over who is a proper citizen of the West and by the zero-sum phobia that has again prevailed to the East and South. Most Atlanticists did not discriminate in this way. They not only spoke the language of allies and adversaries. They also spoke of institutions, interests, norms and goals; of structures and arrangements that could supersede national and other rivalries which struck them as more primitive than permanent or natural; and of the realistic appreciation of differences which called out for harmonization more than exploitation on "pragmatic" grounds. Their own pragmatism was directed against the posturing of the abstract, the formulaic and the dogmatic. William Howard Taft did not proclaim himself to be the first Atlantic president. But it was then that a generation of Atlanticists got to work and, among other deeds described in this book, fostered three more generations of diplomats who made something important in the world.

—K. W.
Ankara, Turkey
February 2015

PREFACE TO THE FIRST EDITION

THE ORIGINS OF THIS BOOK appear between the lines of its dedication. In 1992, just after the final collapse of the Soviet Union, I arrived in Washington, D.C., and began work as an intern in a small policy organization called the Atlantic Council of the United States. It was located in the Grange Building on H Street, where some of its members had offices. My own was tiny, barely as wide as my desk, with a view overlooking the slate roof of the old Decatur House next door. The internship turned into a job that lasted through the end of the decade. By then we had moved to the more spacious Barr Building on Farragut Square—although the quarters were still more shabbily genteel than grandiose, the Barr being the only building in the city with manually operated elevators run by kind old ladies who read Bibles and sold Avon cosmetics, and chosen for the council because its president insisted that we not be more than six blocks from the Metropolitan Club.

Like many Washington institutions, the Atlantic Council foundered after the Cold War. It struggled to find a new mission for itself and to retain financial backers. Today the organization is prosperous, but back then it just barely survived, thanks only to the reputation of its superannuated leadership. When I arrived, the council was chaired by the two people named above—the former supreme allied commander and White House staff secretary, General Andrew Goodpaster, and the retired ambassador and assistant secretary of state, Rozanne Ridgway. They were, as a council director once put it, the two most respected people in Washington among the still relatively intimate foreign policy nomenklatura. For a young person to learn the ropes from them and to be exposed daily to their circle of friends and like-minded colleagues was an education of which the value is impossible to measure. Not only did it open a window onto a fading world but it also conveyed a style of thinking—hard, lucid, self-confident yet practical, conscientious, consensual, and persistently creative—that itself came to seem like a relic of the past.

As those who experienced it will recall, Washington became a less happy place as the 1990s wore on. Demoralized, I moved, first to London and then to Harvard, determined to learn the craft of history so as to be able to record some of the things I had learned, too few of which appeared in the books I had read. But where to make the most useful mark? It was another teacher, Ernest May, who suggested in Sever Hall one cold November morning that I focus my dissertation on the Bureau of European Affairs in the State Department.[1] How did it prevail for so long? Tackling that subject seemed obvious. I had known or heard of many of its officers, but at a distance safe enough to assert objectivity and, of course, had never been one myself. I could sympathize, perhaps overly so, but not empathize. The latter would need to be done with the eyes of the trained historian I hoped I would become.

That this study came to be much more than an institutional history or an *éloge* was, I think, always the hope of Professor May. He and my other advisers—Waldo Heinrichs with his wise and subtle insight into the natural lives of bureaucracies, and Akira Iriye with his gentle yet compelling insistence upon an expansive view of international society—as well as my own interest in mental geography, dating back to my education at the hands of Professor Alan Henrikson at Tufts, gave it shape. Thus, in addition to being dedicated to two master practitioners, this book is also devoted to the hope that policy history and the study of the diplomatic art may be resurrected with a more symbiotic and multidimensional emphasis than has hitherto been the case. To understand these public servants and to see their world through their eyes, moreover, I pray will inspire others to discover, admire, and emulate their example, any and all warts notwithstanding.

I end here with a caveat lector. One of the frailer people interviewed for this book left me with a modest request: "Please don't write anything that won't sit easily upon my lap." The chronology covers nearly the entire twentieth century, but the main story centers on the period from the end of World War II to the early 1970s. The reader will note a tapering off at both ends, for reasons both thematic and logistical. The middle decades demonstrate the peak of Atlanticism in American foreign policy; the years that came before and after them are handled, respectively, as prologue and epilogue to the central action. Because this book is less a straightforward narrative than an episodic reconstruction of the collective mind and method of its subjects, I decided that it would be better to devote the bulk of attention to the period that typified their spirit.

As the story goes, the early 1970s saw the quiet reassertion of Atlanticism that put its adherents in an excellent position to seize upon the finale of the Cold War a decade later. Some, notably former Secretary of State James Baker, have urged that I take the story through the demise of the Soviet Union itself—that is, until 1992. Under ideal circumstances, this would have been the case. But at the time this book was researched, there was simply not enough material declassified, catalogued, and available to warrant an exhaustive analysis of those years. Any further treatment would have meant either a much heavier book or a more economical account of the most salient, middle period. So, the 1980s appear here as almost an Indian summer, just as the 1910s and 1920s present a tentative dawn before our subjects had planted their feet firmly in the bureaucracy. A full history of the transatlantic era and its political achievements, from the Balkan crises at the outset of the twentieth century to the wars of Yugoslav succession ninety years later, and written from the entire range of perspectives on both sides of the Atlantic, awaits its Gibbon. For now, I merely hope I have done a few of its American protagonists due justice.

—K. W.
San Domenico di Fiesole, Italy
February 2009

CONTENTS

1

THE SETTING

Early American ideas about Europe—nineteenth-century legacies of nationhood—old and new diplomats—shaping of the transatlantic mind—significance of Atlanticism

CALLED THE NEW WORLD into existence, to redress the balance of the Old." Those famous words spoken by Britain's foreign secretary, George Canning, in 1826 do not sound very American. America has generally suggested a departure, a renunciation, a "protest against Europe." The Old World ought to be left to its own devices. The New World was not made to be shackled to it, let alone become its source of salvation.[1]

The reality was different. Ever since Europeans gave America its name and colonized it, there could be no real or permanent separation—political, cultural, or intellectual—down the middle of the Atlantic. Whether they liked it or not, the transplanted Europeans now calling themselves Americans, as well as the people they conquered, brought, or otherwise enticed to settle with them in the New World, were linked by a large web of direct and indirect ties to the lands they left behind. As distinct as their civilization may have become after three centuries, it could not escape the burden of having originated in Europe.

This has been true to varying degrees throughout the Americas. The countries that appeared there following wars of independence were not cultural fictions: American states became nations in quick order, and differentiated themselves culturally from both one another and their former, European sovereigns. But since its earliest days as a modern, political idea, America had been a part of the European, or better put, Euro-Atlantic, world, and Europe a part of the American consciousness of itself and its historic mission.

Given its size and power, the United States of America has had an especially important role in defining the place of the Old World in the psychology of the New. "American exceptionalism" is an ideology with a predominant foothold in the United States, as is "isolationism." Both evolved chiefly with reference to Europe. Americans—here, and subsequently, the term is used to refer narrowly to inhabitants of the United States—therefore have been of two minds about the Old World. It could not be forgotten or written off; the more the children

1

of immigrants—especially recent immigrants—acted to put the ways of Europe behind them, the more they found themselves re-creating, imagining, and enacting them anew, if only to improve upon them by way of repudiation. America was not only, in William Penn's famous words, "a good poor man's country"; it was also a realm of imagined cultural possibilities with Europe very much in the background. And it was a particular, abstract notion of Europe that made it synonymous with every place "over there."

America's mental map of Europe became a derivative one during the course of the nineteenth century, pan-European first by default and then by conviction. As a bevy of social and economic norms, and as a political template, "Europe" emerged as an object of American thinking: whether as a place to flee, or as one to redeem. It had come to seem a beneficiary, rather than a primary generator, of culture.[2] The point at which the role reversal took hold was indeterminate. One of the commonplaces of American history has been that the earliest European settlers presumed their example to be redemptive for the Old World, as did their successors who established a viable modern republic in the Western hemisphere. But in American public discourse, that is, in the pronouncements, actions, and polemics of its political class, one does not find a clearly stated consensus over this particular mission until the middle of the nineteenth century. First with Young Americanism and then with the Civil War, American nationhood manifested itself not only as an exceptional phenomenon but also simultaneously as a competitive one: like Germany, Italy, and the other "new" countries promoting themselves at the vanguard of the modern world, the United States by now was singular, unified, centralized, dynamic, expansive. There was one American nation that could join the ranks of the great powers if it chose to do so. Seizing the mantle of Western civilization was another matter, however.

Americans remained ambivalent about both Europe and themselves for some time. "The trouble was that I did not care to look back, and I could not look forward," recalled the expatriate woman of letters, Mabel Dodge, upon her return to the United States in 1912. "The sea was all there was, and I did not like the sea. I felt nowhere—suspended 'between two worlds.'"[3] Europe still resided at the center of most maps, although the distance between Europe and North America remained great until World War II and the promulgation of the polar projection.[4] Nevertheless, during the latter decades of the nineteenth century and the early part of the twentieth, many leading Americans promoted the idea that the United States was a force the world had to reckon with, not only from the strength of its example but also by its sheer power, seemingly limitless. Hearts should follow in due course. "Remember, it is *ugly* in America," Dodge told her young son as they approached New York Harbor. "We have left everything worthwhile behind us. America is all machinery and money-making and factories—it is ugly, ugly, ugly! Never forget that!" The boy thought for a moment, cast a glance landward and replied, "*I* don't think it's so ugly." "And that," recalled Dodge, "was the end of that."[5]

THIS WAS THE MENTAL MILIEU of the first generation of America's professional diplomats. Many of their eighteenth- and nineteenth-century predecessors were gentlemen who knew Europe well; but many were not, and it did not seem to matter one way or the other. The practice of sending political opponents into diplomatic service did not originate in the United States, but the American political system—with its talent for proliferating rivalries and office seekers—took the practice to an extreme, as it continues to do. Europe received the highest number of such envoys. With just a handful of exceptions, the U.S. official representation in Europe was insignificant and unmemorable in addition to being amateurish. There was no "policy" for or about Europe apart from relative noninterference. The Americans who knew most about Europe resided professionally outside government: they were missionaries, artists, writers, expatriates of various sorts, merchants, bankers, and, by the turn of the twentieth century, social reformers, journalists, scholars of European history, society, and culture. And for the first time beginning in 1917, there were large numbers of soldiers. But there were very few diplomats.

For all of its great power pretensions, the United States only came around to establishing a professional diplomatic corps in the early twentieth century. Until then, most career diplomats were younger sons of rich families who, for one reason or another, found other careers unsuitable. Their positions were for the most part self-funded: Salaries were nominal while official duties, especially in Europe, required a large income. Professor David Jayne Hill, for example, who had the misfortune of succeeding the flamboyant Charlemagne Tower as Theodore Roosevelt's ambassador to Berlin, had to be recalled because the kaiser complained that Hill, despite having been president of Bucknell and Rochester Universities, could not afford to throw parties in a style to which the Germans had grown accustomed.[6] When they were not attending balls, coronations, and races, most American diplomats in Europe put in a few hours at their chanceries drafting formal correspondence to their counterparts in other ministries of similar working habits—"like the fountains in Trafalgar Square, [they] played from ten to four."[7]

By contrast, consuls were, by the time of the Taft administration, a professional caste with close ties to American expatriate communities. This was true mainly in Asia and Latin America, but even in Europe, a career as a consular officer was an honorable choice for middle-class Americans wanting to live abroad. To the chagrin of many consuls, the two services, diplomatic and consular, were combined in 1924. This was just the first of a series of mergers, culminating in the 1950s with the full integration of all foreign service officers—now including members of the civil service working in the State Department—into a single bureaucracy. These steps were meant in principle to promote executive harmony, and in many instances they did. But this was not the same thing as efficiency. The foreign affairs bureaucracy, both inside and outside the State Department, continued to grow, in both size and complexity, over the course of the twentieth century.[8]

THIS BOOK TELLS THE STORY of a small but powerful—probably the most consistently powerful—section of that bureaucracy: the State Department's Bureau of European Affairs, or EUR. My study has three aims: to trace the history of U.S. relations with the countries of Europe and, specifically, the rise of what came to be called "Atlanticism," through the eyes of the people who had the most to do with its spread and maturation on official grounds; to describe who they were, how they operated, and why they mattered; and to interpret the wider significance of their achievements and failures for the history of U.S. foreign relations and, by extension, for Europe.

The reader is right to ask why. Who ought to care about several hundred nearly anonymous bureaucrats mentioned only in the occasional back pages of official chronicles? Indeed, these people are footnotes to footnotes: Told from the beginning of their careers that getting one's name in the paper should only happen twice in one's lifetime (assuming one got married), most of them have disappeared, presumably happily, from mainstream and even most scholarly accounts. If any group has suffered from what the British historian E. P. Thompson famously decried as "the enormous condescension of posterity," it is surely this one. But why rescue them?

The answer is sheer success. America's transatlantic diplomacy during the twentieth century worked remarkably well, if one judges results by stated aims. Europe ended the century largely peaceful and prosperous for the first time in centuries, tied to the United States in the closest arrangement either has seen to a permanent alliance. Of course there were many other factors responsible for it, not least of which was the education imposed by three "world civil wars" and the vision, and struggle, of Europeans.[9] Indeed, it is often easy to understate the degree to which America's European relationships bolstered its own preeminence in the twentieth century. Success happened on both sides of the Atlantic, and there was nothing about it that was preordained or natural. Transatlantic harmony has always been the work of individuals and, it has seemed, more often than not, both fragile and reversible. In reconstructing its history from the perspective of the people whose job it was to promote it, we can see just how fragile it really was.

The Bureau of European Affairs housed one such group. It was virtually the only part of the American foreign affairs bureaucracy to remain unsullied by politics: Unlike so many other offices, there were never any large-scale purges of EUR, even though it had a hand in determining some of the most politically charged foreign policies.

EUR never had many officers who sought controversy, or many noteworthy ideologues. It was, in other words, one of the very few organizations at its level in the U.S. government whose prerogatives and views were almost always deemed essential yet which, apart from a brief moment in the early 1960s, remained immune to contagion from political fads. Contrary to popular myth, this is a rarity in American official life. EUR thus came closest to serving as the country's permanent foreign secretary, a kind of self-appointed guardian, conscience, or kingmaker, for nearly four generations. Yet it remains almost entirely unknown to the general public. One-time popular histories of the China hands and the Arabists made for gripping tales of adventure, failure, and disappointment.[10] A history of those on the State Department's European Desk, their fellow travelers, and even their competitors need not be any less compelling for being mundane, or happy.[11]

Of course there were many other groups, both inside and outside the U.S. government, who played important diplomatic roles in Europe. Chief among them were those in the military services, their civilian bosses in the Pentagon, and, also "across the river," the members of the Central Intelligence Agency (CIA) and its own vast network of agents, operatives, and collaborators. In many cases, one must admit, these people performed diplomatic roles equivalent to or, especially after the Korean War, even surpassing that of the rank-and-file foreign service. Several of them moved among the various organizations. But they appear in the following pages for the most part as supporting actors. The same is true for Congress, particularly the relevant committees and subcommittees in the Senate. All of these bodies struggled with many of the same problems. But none had anything like EUR in longevity, durability, and the unique combination of geographical and functional expertise, nor so formidable an overseas constituency. It may not have been the exclusive hub of European affairs from the beginning to the end of the twentieth century, but it was, to the extent there existed such a ranking among hubs, *primus inter pares*.

EUR emerged as a kernel of both regional and global thinking, and as the incubator of a bureaucratic method whereby professionals regularly co-opted the allegiance of political appointees, and vice versa, through the manipulation of alternating demands for specialization and generalization. This made it possible "to achieve the necessary professional footing without damaging the character of the Diplomatic Service," and counterbalanced the tendency of politicians and bureaucrats to disparage one another as unsound in the former case or unimaginative in the latter.[12] For EUR, the tension between the two groups was, on the whole, a creative one, as specialists found ways to convince generalists to embrace their causes while the regular influx of fresh blood, along with the periodic amalgamation of regional and functional experts, mitigated bureaucratic myopia. The elite of the State Department resembled less an aristocracy (although there were some elements of that passed down by generation) than a specialized corps with a sense of its own superiority. As will become clear, that was not entirely a bad thing—like any profession, diplomacy had standards, rankings, and rules, and sought to preserve and augment them. Yet in contrast to their public stereotype as effete, privileged snobs, it is important to recognize that most diplomats who specialized in Europe were in reality people of varied origins who deemed themselves a bit (or sometimes more than a bit) better than the others in the room.[13]

That also applied to many of the policies EUR promoted, because no other area of the world combined the various fields of regional and functional expertise more than Europe, particularly after World War II. Europe had long been the world's capital of multilateral diplomacy; the majority of international conferences, later called "summits," happened there. Most headquarters of international organizations were based in Europe. The educational opportunities for American diplomats there were vast. For all that America's own rise of globalism has been linked to its naval and financial power in Asia and Latin America, respectively, it was Europe that provided the breeding ground for its professional diplomacy. American diplomats learned to think and act globally through the eyes of Europe.

BESIDES PEOPLE AND INSTITUTIONS, this story is also about an idea: Atlanticism. In the twentieth century it came to mean more than an affinity between America and Europe, or a set of shared interests. Atlanticism had deeper roots, derived from the civilizing concept of the West that grew popular early in the modern period. As Americans came to see themselves as European-style nationalists by the mid-nineteenth century, the conviction became widespread that the fates of the United States and the nations of Europe were in reality more intertwined than separate.

Some Americans took nationalism a step further and announced that it was finally their duty to rule a large part of the earth in the name of the enlightened civilization that they had inherited and the federal experiment that they imagined to have global appeal.[14] There has been some debate over whether the Spanish-American War or World War I marks a better dividing line between the republic and the empire, so to speak, with the United States finally pulling its weight on the world stage as a powerful nation among nations. Proponents of the former have pointed to the imperialistic fervor that accompanied the war, the acquisition of overseas ("European") colonies in Asia and the Caribbean, and the navalist obsession with matching the other major world powers, namely, Britain and Germany, on the seas. Proponents of the latter have suggested that much of the rhetoric accompanying the Spanish-American War was aberrant; that, in fact, the political class of the United States had not properly thought through the global implications of so ambitious a policy. When the dust settled, they were only too happy to retreat, that is, until World War I posed a new set of challenges connected to the self-destruction of European power itself, which required that America—or, more precisely, President Woodrow Wilson—intervene in order to change forever the rules of international relations.

However, from the transatlantic point of view, the chronological distinction between 1898 and 1917 makes little difference. America's rise as a world power was long in coming and, in spite of the fad of great power navalism at the turn of the century and the fascination with Asia, had been directed mainly at Europe—not in seeking to become European or to supplant European power but rather to the extent that it presumed the United States to share a heritage, standard of conduct, and destiny with the great powers of Europe. Atlanticism meant that Europe and America were more alike than different. The twentieth century would prove, moreover, that the security, prosperity, and culture of each interpenetrated those of the other.

But there was more to it than all that. Atlanticism also invoked a diplomatic method, even an art form, that walked a fine line between pressing Europeans to do what Americans (and some Europeans) said was in their particular or joint interest, and convincing both Americans and Europeans of the need for common policies, responsibilities, and wisdom, that is, "to sketch the boundaries of an Atlantic consensus."[15] As the twentieth century wore on, consensus seeking became the norm, although in some instances it would compete with the urge to dictate. In 1980, for example, the British politician Roy Jenkins in his role as president of the European Commission recalled meeting the American ambassador, Thomas Enders, who "had nominally come to deliver a *démarche*, which the Americans were also sending to all the Community countries, in effect telling us to keep off the grass in the Middle East. In fact he did not deliver it, and merely asked what I thought about it, to which I said not much."[16] Atlanticism in fact was less about deference than about affinity, respect, and the common pursuit of goals, standards, and most important, institutions that all, at least in principle, obviated the need to come to the other's occasional rescue or to redress political imbalances.

In reality, there were multiple Atlanticisms. Several of the principal characters in this book—David Bruce, for example—were not Atlanticists in the strict ideological sense of the late 1950s and 1960s, but they shared and wielded many "Atlanticist" methods, particularly the more artful ones. They were, evidently, at home on both sides of the ocean. Atlanticism, like the North Atlantic Treaty itself, possessed just the right degree of ambiguity, which is probably responsible for its longevity in the twentieth, and perhaps the twenty-first, century. It is hard to imagine it being realized with a similar confluence of geopolitical, ideological, and bureaucratic success anywhere else. There has long been Pan-Americanism, of course, but this is a more romantic concept that lacks a diplomatic tradition and suffers from the heavy-handed reputation of the United States throughout Latin America. It is even harder to visualize the contours of a "Pacificism" or some form of American Eurasianism. Something important is missing in each, namely, a historical and cultural logic, although surely elements of Atlanticism were, and could be, applicable to other regions. The first task, however, is to understand the concept on its own terms.

THE "EUROPE, WHOLE AND FREE" that President George H. W. Bush toasted in May 1989 did not originate with the struggle against the Nazis or the Soviets. It dated several centuries back in time but would flourish politically only in the twentieth century when a number of leading Americans came to reimagine their place in the world, and their own position of leadership there, as combining the best of the traditional and the revolutionary. This was not, as Canning would have had it, an opportunistic negotiation between Old Europe with its American appendage but instead an altogether new, emblematic Atlantic world, bound together in mind and in deed. It did not come into existence—or thrive—absentmindedly.

2

A BEGINNING

*Professionalization of the foreign service—the Rogers Act—evolving ideas of Europe—
experiences with disarmament—blurring of private and public diplomacy*

THE ORIGINS OF THE BUREAU of European Affairs were humble and were found, curiously enough, in Asia. The credit went to a dandy of a man, the then thirty-year-old diplomat F. M. Huntington Wilson, who was recalled to Washington in 1906 from his first post in Tokyo on the orders of the secretary of state, the formidable New York lawyer Elihu Root, reportedly because Root was infatuated with Wilson's wife.[1] Having had much spare time on his hands in Japan, Wilson had devised a plan to reorganize the State Department. Among his many suggestions was the establishment of geographical sections to oversee all consular and diplomatic relations with their respective parts of the world, in line with the design of most established European foreign ministries. Root was reluctant to implement Wilson's plan, not because he was naturally very conservative—he was—and not because he was opposed to the idea—a longtime patron of administrative improvement, he was not—but rather because he reportedly disliked Wilson's character and "reputation ... of a bloodless machine."[2] Still, he was persuaded to allow the young man to establish a new Asian division on a trial basis, with two clerks at desks placed behind a screen in Wilson's office. One of them was William Phillips, who joined the department as a messenger but soon was inducted, thanks to various connections, into Teddy Roosevelt's Tennis Cabinet. Phillips would in short order be made head of the new Far Eastern Division, later becoming undersecretary of state, first in 1922 and then again in 1934.[3]

The experiment did not go badly, but went no further until Root's successor was replaced by Philander Knox, Roosevelt's attorney general, also known as "sleepy Phil" for his odd working hours, lugubrious disposition, and easygoing habits. Knox for some reason looked more favorably upon Wilson than Root had. He promoted him to the second-in-command position at State and gave him a free hand to remake the department. Hence were born additional geographic divisions—for Latin America, the Near East, and Western Europe.

8

The first chief for Europe was a nonentity named Chandler Hale, who got the job because his father, Senator Eugene Hale from Maine, demanded it as a condition for supporting the legislation for the 1909 departmental reorganization. In addition to Western Europe, the division was also responsible for the entire British Empire, Morocco, the Congo, and Liberia. But Hale's staff comprised only three clerks, one of whom doubled as the department's protocol officer.

Much would change with World War I. Billy Phillips recalled the surprise with which he and his colleagues in the department heard of President Wilson's request for a declaration of war against Austria-Hungary: It "came like a thunder-clap. No one expected it—not even the Cabinet; yet when he pronounced it the whole

Joseph Grew
Time & Life Pictures/Getty

assemblage rose to their feet and cheered."[4] Like Roosevelt before him (and another Roosevelt after), Woodrow Wilson wasted little time in chastising the meager bureaucracy at his disposal and in calling for a New Diplomacy. Partly in reaction, and partly due to the demands of the war itself, the bureaucracy grew both in size and complexity, and not for the last time. The European division staff quadrupled, while a separate Russia division was established, renamed in 1922 the Division of Eastern European Affairs and including the Baltic states, Finland, and Poland as well as the new Soviet empire.[5] The level and nature of work improved consistently, although most of the diplomatic initiative still rested in the hands of the president. "It is difficult to explain exactly the way in which business is conducted here," wrote the British ambassador, Cecil Spring-Rice, to his chief, Arthur Balfour, noting that "[t]he President rarely sees anybody....Mr. Lansing [the secretary of state] is treated as a clerk who receives orders which he has to obey at once and without question." Upon resigning, Lansing summed up his job in a quip written to his nephew, John Foster Dulles: "The question asked is, 'where is he to find a rubber stamp?'"[6]

At the Paris Peace Conference of 1919, the State Department seemed ill-prepared and underutilized. Nearly two years earlier, President Wilson and his top adviser, "Colonel" Edward House, had established their own team of specialists—mainly historians, geographers, and demographers—called the Inquiry. It produced 2,000 reports and 1,200 maps, and although disbanded soon after the war, it continued to vie with the department for influence by way of remnants who joined the American Commission to Negotiate Peace.[7] However, this latter group fell under the jurisdiction of the State Department, which had, through the "indispensable link" of the diplomat Joseph Grew, established a working relationship with House and his "troupe of performing professors." Grew, a Boston Brahmin drawn to public service in the Progressive Era push a decade before, had been in the Berlin embassy up to the outbreak of the war and witnessed the dramatic reversal of German opinion toward the United States during the course of 1916–1917; he would be on hand to burn the files and lock up the embassy, just as he would again nearly twenty-five years later as ambassador in Tokyo. But in Paris he enjoyed a respite of apparent peace, along with his newfound friends—the diplomat and adventurer Willard Straight, and a young philosopher and journalist, Walter Lippmann—despite all having contracted Spanish influenza.[8] Grew went on to Bern, the "department's pet Legation," where he oversaw relief efforts and prisoner repatriation, then served throughout Europe until his dramatic departure from Tokyo. In the meantime, as the "Cerberus of the Foreign Service," he set the standards and procedures for America's nascent diplomatic profession.[9]

As command of the bureaucracy improved, so too did pressure mount internally for reform and cohesion. "The result was," according to one chronicler, "that the State Department developed a professional cadre not moving about the field but in Washington, among, as the French call them, the *sédentaires*."[10] This was not entirely true. Professionalism advanced on both fronts. "To describe the system as bureaucratic would be only partially correct," noted Grew's biographer, the historian Waldo Heinrichs: "Working in small groups of their own nationality in an alien environment, diplomats were thrown upon one another and upon diplomats of other nations for companionship. Friendships and social groups arose that defied the hierarchical and status prescriptions of bureaucracy."[11] The diplomat had to invent and reinvent his own channels, practices, and networks in order to be effective. To some, this would count as cutting corners; but to the best foreign service officers, it was par for the course. In response, bureaucrats would continue to devise ways to call the shots, which usually involved the policing of information. Undersecretary William Castle, for example, recalled one ambassador who would ask the same question of several different officers, hoping "for contradictory answers." Castle subsequently ordered everyone in the department to coordinate their answers as soon as the ambassador was spotted nearby.[12]

Esprit de corps nevertheless helped to ease the endemically low morale American diplomats suffered from knowing that they had no substantial reputation among their countrymen and would disappear from public life when their careers ended. "There used to be a saying in England," recalled British expatriate and friend to many diplomats, Timothy Dickinson, "that American mastery is based on a foreign policy made largely by lawyers and generals—the people with the most experience dealing with the criminal classes."[13] Following the war, there were a great many more Americans, not all criminals, to cope with in Europe. By the end of the 1920s in Paris, there were 40,000 American residents, who spent, along with about 200,000 visiting American tourists, over $139 million there in 1929 and established, among other collective venues, numerous hospitals, schools, churches, newspapers, sporting teams, libraries, societies, and all sorts of businesses catering to American tastes, including ice cream and funeral parlors, along with a new embassy on the Place de la Concorde that the American ambassador, the former New Jersey governor, Walter Edge, struggled to convince his hosts would not be built as a skyscraper. Almost immediately after the Armistice in 1918, two dozen American students entered the University of Berlin; many other Americans there had never left.[14] The 1920s roared on both sides of the Atlantic in this, the first golden age of the overseas American. As to the diplomats, their orientation and career potential, as suggested by the following 1921 directive, sounded a great deal more modest:

Be American first, last and all the time.
Do nothing to cast discredit on your country.
Be neat in dress and appearance.
Be courteous to all.
Be discreet in speech and conduct.
Keep your temper always.
Be industrious, studious, thorough and punctual.
Be loyal to your chief.
Be as useful to your chief as possible.
Do not discuss your chief's official or private conduct with anyone.
Do not criticize your Government's policies or its high officials.
Never listen to anyone who speaks disparagingly of your country or your
    Government.
Avoid discussing American domestic politics with foreigners.
Suppress any partisan political feelings which you may have.
Remember that you are serving the present Administration.
Give no interviews to newspaper men at home or abroad.
Never write for publication without permission from the Department.
Remember that all Americans are your fellow citizens and treat them
    accordingly.
Observe carefully the social customs and confirm strictly to the etiquette
    of the country where you are stationed.
Do not give a false value to social position or be influenced by titles in
    monarchical countries.
Remember that in a monarchical country it is your official position rather
    than your personality which usually gives you social standing.
Do not permit your judgment, your ideas of life or your Americanism to
    be affected by the attentions of an aristocratic society.
Never permit society to interfere with your official duties.
Be guarded in your choice of friends and associates.
Avoid making confidences or repeating scandal.
Report to your chief information which you may consider of value to him
    or the Government.
Live modestly and always within your means.
Do not borrow or loan money.
Keep out of debt.
Remember that the Government is watching your conduct and career,
    and that merit always counts.
Remember that your future is in your own hands and not in the hands of
    your friends at home.[15]

Reform came presently with the Rogers Act, which merged the diplomatic and consular corps into a single foreign service, along with establishing a competitive examination and a promotion scale. Opposition came first from the consuls, whose professionalism overtook that of their diplomatic colleagues, albeit only recently, but the measure was generally regarded as being more favorable to the consular corps and a burden to diplomats. As one of the latter group recalled, "You don't have to be a coal miner to run a coal business."[16] Yet one of the act's main purposes was to extend more professional credentials to the diplomats, even though the two corps would remain provisionally autonomous within the same service because "nobody dares trust anybody else."[17] The new exams offered up a similar mix of earnest intent and practical making-do. Aspirants could prepare at the new foreign affairs schools at Georgetown or George Washington Universities, which offered degrees that took several years. Or they could go to Crawford's, where they could sit through a four-month crash course on such subjects as international law, taught as follows:

> The birds in the trees sing high, sing low.
> Trespass is always *ab initio*.

"Crawford's" referred to the residence and enterprise of an eccentric, "articulate, intolerant, and sedentary Buddha" named Angus McDonald Crawford at 3034 P Street in Georgetown. According to the diplomat Theodore Achilles, Crawford acquired "a stranglehold on admission to the Foreign Service," which frustrated the professionals back in the department, particularly Joseph C. Green, the former Princeton professor who oversaw the examinations with a meticulousness that was matched only by his wartime supervision of export controls. Achilles recalled:

> There was a duel to the death between Crawford and Joe Green ... who compiled the Foreign Service exams and took fiendish delight in making them as nearly impossible as he could. At that point Crawford had Joe on the ropes but a year or two later Joe concocted, and the Department adopted, a type of exam that proved to be cram-proof. Crawford died, it was said, of a broken heart and it may have been, but the heart had already been considerably damaged by whiskey.[18]

The written exams may have become progressively harder, but the oral exam remained the subjective means by which sitting members of the examinations board weeded out those who did not fit the mold. According to legend, they would look first at a candidate's shoes before determining whether or not there was something "a little too YMCA about him," as someone once recalled about the famously overachieving George Messersmith.[19] A well-known story put it that one examinee failed the exam even though he succeeded in naming the two most recent foreign ministers of Lithuania, while another, who, when asked to name where cloves came from, answered, "The left end of the bar," passed. If a man had the slightest "touch of the tar brush" about his appearance, he was in for trouble. This applied to other skin tones as well. Castle recalled:

We are inclined to pass anyone who is thoroughly American as we get so disgusted with the Smolevs and the Kardarshians. But of course to do that would be fatal. Some of the candidates are pathetic because they want so terribly to be in the Service and are so utterly hopeless. One man, aged 34, is a train despatcher in Georgia....There was nothing about his family life he did not tell us. In the war he rose gloriously so that at the end he was a sergeant-major—exactly the kind Bairnsfather could draw beautifully. His "formal education" consists largely in the hours he spent in museums. It was hard to keep from laughing, but the poor fellow was so frightfully in earnest that one was sad, too....Then there was Martin Tall, with a grade in the written of over 86, a Harvard graduate, a belligerent and dangerous Jew. We gave him 60 in the orals and shall undoubtedly hear from Congressmen and others in some detail....I have the feeling that some, at least, of the candidates are taking the examinations because of the hard times....The only serious dispute so far has been in the case of Kardarshian....I am in opposition to the rest of the Board, although to my surprise Doctor Edson joined me. I cannot see how we can keep the boy out unless we are willing to be entirely unjust ... if his name had been Smith he would have been given a high grade. He is a Harvard graduate with a couple of years at Oxford in addition. He is American-born and thinks and acts like an American....Carr and Byington are adamant....The Secretary says that to decide against Kardarshian would be to flout the Declaration of Independence and the Constitution of the United States.

How much easier it would have been, he cried, if everyone had been like Charles "Chip" Bohlen: "[A] thoroughbred" with "great charm" and "extraordinary intelligence ... [he] will go very far in the Service."[20] Or like Grew, who, despite himself having been hired because President Theodore Roosevelt was much impressed by his having shot a tiger in Africa, happily rejected a genial man from South Dakota who sought a position in order to "meet people" and "smooth over things."[21] Castle concurred:

Oh, for a few more people like Grew in our Service—keen, intelligent, first-rate Americans, who have been trained in the service of the Government just as other men are trained in business! Joe is wonderfully friendly about my being, in the opinion of the Service men really a part of the Service, but, in comparison with him, I feel myself a Tyro—in his class only so far as enthusiasm for the work is concerned.[22]

As time went on, autonomy gradually broke down, with foreign service officers generally beginning as vice consuls and moving their way up through the ranks. Grew, together with Wilbur Carr (mentioned above), the long-serving head of the consular service, succeeded in making the merger work. The diplomatic corps tended to be stronger in Europe, whereas the consuls' strengths were in Asia and Latin America, with the Middle East being something of a mix. Both groups had already begun to "reflect their clients."[23] The merger of the services, then, had the overall effect of making the foreign service more Eurocentric in outlook because

Europe was the most promising ground for career advancement within the diplomatic corps. Moreover, the Asia hands and Arabists who spent long careers in these regions tended to have prior credentials—many were missionaries' sons, for example—and so the foreign service became a recipient instead of a provider of regional expertise in these areas. Europe, by contrast, landed generalists and "after all, was the big stage most of them sought."[24] Yet many were still of two minds:

> American diplomats and consuls both admired and resented European diplomats. The Americans loved the Europeans' smooth practice of diplomacy and longed for the public respect the Europeans enjoyed, but they also believed that the aims of their European counterparts were inferior to American foreign policy goals. The Foreign Service reformers ... argued that the peculiar history of the United States, its lack of a plutocracy and a proletariat, its preoccupation with commerce instead of national glory, make its foreign policy more pacific than that of any European power.[25]

There was more to this transatlantic pattern than what outsiders occasionally regarded as mimicry. The European "great powers" still ruled the world, and that also meant they established the international codes of behavior, the rules of the game. Such were rated bankrupt—literally—after the culmination of World War I. The only presumptive great power still standing, with the partial exception of the Soviet Union, was the United States. It did not take long for people like Castle, a proud son of the Hawaiian planter class serving then as the department's head of the Western European Division (WE), to advertise that "the world must accept [America's] moral leadership because back of that leadership is power,"[26] adding:

> We must train men in the Department and in the Service ... not only to defend the country and advance its interest but to do both things in the best possible way. In other words we have to put across the American plan whether other nations like it or not and we must put it across in a way which will appeal to the largest number of Americans. Incidentally, if it does this, other nations are more likely to agree that we are right.[27]

This view was traditionally European. But many Americans—and Castle was no exception—regarded themselves and their own brand of power as different, perhaps incomplete but not inferior. "It was a novel observation for me to remark that European diplomatists were far less Machiavellian and far more like ordinary mortals than I had ever suspected," recalled another, Lewis Einstein. "In vain I searched for some hidden craft on their part, or for some secret illumination on my own, and failing to discover either I would ask myself if the fault was not due to my own obtuseness."[28]

ANOTHER IMPORTANT STRAIN running through the European sector of the State Department was multilateralism. It coincided with the conference diplomacy of the interwar years, which saw great power competition retreat, after 1919, to the consensual pattern of international relations that predominated before the Crimean War. Known earlier as the Concert of Europe, the post-1919 variety was distinct to the extent that it also spawned several supranational institutions, both within and beyond Europe, and alongside them, a renovation in diplomatic method. It was concert understood as community. The generation of American diplomats exposed to this change bought into it, claiming credit not only for its achievements during the interwar years but also for passing it on to their successors, thereby contributing to the so-called second chance for a liberal world order after 1945.[29]

Two elements of interwar multilateralism had lasting effect. The first was the conception of Europe as a geopolitical project. This was a normative rather than objective notion, to be sure. The project had undergone a contemporary renaissance at the hands of such pan-Europeanists as the French political figure Aristide Briand and the Austrian-Japanese pamphleteer Richard Coudenhove-Kalergi. To Americans who witnessed firsthand the great physical, moral, and political self-destruction of the Continent, it seemed to be the only way forward. No longer did it make sense to them to uphold "our aloofness from the affairs of European nations ... regarding each of these only as separate entities bearing little relation to each other." As the American diplomat Hugh Wilson pointed out, "[T]he continent of Europe cannot take punitive action against one of its own members so long as the most formidable nation in the world, ourselves, is running around loose and refusing to stay hitched."[30] The role of Americans, Wilson might have said, ought to be to perfect the ways and appearances of honest brokerage while encouraging Europeans to look beyond parochialism. "The only way to do the thing we want them to do," wrote another named Hugh—Hugh Gibson,

> is by bringing them into camp, and ... this can best be accomplished by something that is clearly based on the idea that we are the ... biggest and most important people in the picture at the present moment and the responsibility is on us for doing what is best for the rest of the world.... [W]e could justify the French in receding from their present rigid position by some action calculated to demonstrate to them that what we have done for Germany in the past has not been done for love of Germany and dislike of France, but that we have been working for our own good and that of the world in general.[31]

If multilateralism could be seen as the central, strategic element of American diplomacy, issue management was its primary tactic. It involved the pursuit of collective security through the promotion of transnational causes or "issues." The biggest at the time were disarmament and debt, which together represented two sides of the same evolving coin, namely, whether Europe would succeed or fail to devise a durable peace. We now know that it was probably destined to fail. But that need not diminish attention to the tremendous energy and occasional good sense that went into the effort. Both issues were complicated by the existence of "have" and "have-not" nations in Europe and elsewhere. Thus, Secretary of State Charles Evans Hughes launched the first round of disarmament talks in 1920 in

Herbert Hoover and Hugh Gibson
Time & Life Pictures/Getty

order to bring stability to the post–World War I power vacuum in Europe and the Pacific and to proscribe the resurgence of militarism among the "have-nots," while the debt negotiations, which began more or less simultaneously, were meant to underwrite a badly needed financial recovery. That the latter became commingled with the sensitive issue of war reparations, and subsequently with the contagion of the Great Depression, more or less doomed them by the middle 1930s, just as the cause of disarmament would find itself eclipsed by the counterreactions of the three principal "revisionist" powers: Germany, Italy, and Japan.[32]

At the center of much of this was the aforementioned Mr. Gibson. An early protégé of Grew, Gibson was proud, sardonic, and deeply loyal to his friends, among them Walter Lippmann, who once asked, "Can there be peace where you go? Has there ever been peace where you have been?" Remembered as "a great gentleman ... a sunny soul" and reputed originator of *bon mots* and a certain style of martini, Gibson also had a noticeable limp, the result of infection with polio, which he turned facetiously to his advantage. "Somebody once asked him why the President felt he could represent the United States at a military and naval conference on disarmament when he had no experience in this," recalled a friend. "And he said, 'Well, I don't know, but maybe the fact that I had a limp and looked as if I'd gotten it by pacing the deck on a warship might have something to do with it.'"[33] Another colleague, Gibson said, using a familiar line, was "the only diplomat in all history who can strut sitting down." And to the emissary politician Charles Dawes, who noted that diplomatic service "is easy on the head but hell on the feet," Gibson replied, "it depends which you use most."[34]

He used both, although the war found him sitting at a desk in Billy Phillips's office compiling lists of German abuses. But not for long. His career took off when, posted to Belgium, he took up the cause of the celebrated nurse Edith Cavell and gained brief fame as a gallant man of principle—not to mention a Belgian wife and an American patron, namely, Herbert Hoover, there overseeing Allied relief efforts.[35] Posted subsequently to Warsaw, Gibson acquired an acute sense not only of the tenuous quality of European peace, such that it was, but also of the importance of domestic interests back home and their capacity both to prompt and to impede diplomatic action. "I am convinced," he wrote in 1919, "that at any time we could, by perfectly plain warnings to the Germans and perhaps the adoption of threatening military measures, have brought about an orderly situation in these territories." But the Poles, at least then, did not carry sufficient political weight in Washington.

> If a Polish town is wiped out by German military fire, the matter is either dismissed as being a bit of Polish exaggeration or our communication on the matter is ignored. If one French soldier is killed in Berlin a heavy fine is put upon the Germans....If there is a Jewish beard cut off ... the newspapers scream and we send a mission to find out about it....But when a situation is developing which threatens the peace and economic security of the whole of Europe, we close our eyes to it.[36]

Gibson, largely on his own initiative, paired an American commitment to a peaceful and unifying Europe with intelligent participation in the disarmament negotiations in Geneva. This killed two birds with one stone: Not only did it suggest to his European counterparts that the United States would not match its isolationist rhetoric fully with inaction on the ground but also it had the added advantage of appeasing domestic opinion—some of it isolationist—by appearing to take seriously the popular cause of disarmament.[37] In fact, the purposeful and pragmatic methods of Gibson, the longest-serving American delegate to the various disarmament conferences, offset many ill effects of American failure at Versailles. That he did so by flattering the enthusiasts of the New Diplomacy was all the more remarkable, but Gibson had little choice. Their passions did not die easily. During disarmament talks in 1926, for example, he noted that "Geneva was crowded with celebrities, and the struggle to get into meetings was ferocious. More Americans clamored for tickets (among them no less than fifty professors) than citizens of all the nations actually belonging to the League put together."[38]

On the other hand, there were those who said, "You fooled me and I fooled you and Colonel [Edward] House bamboozled us both" at Versailles.[39] But Gibson did not dismiss the New Diplomacy outright. Instead he sought ways to make it work. "Wilsonian" in spirit but less idealistic and doctrinaire in practice, his efforts were more lasting and subtle than a mere repudiation would have otherwise been. Gibson and the men who followed in his footsteps—the rivals Hugh Wilson and Prentiss Gilbert—formulated a pattern of working with Europeans that would inspire at least two more generations of diplomatic entrepreneurs. Especially Gilbert, "the maverick consul," because he was "almost inhumanely efficient," became something of a one-man League encyclopedia before his untimely death on the eve of World War II. He tilled a breeding ground of top-

American diplomats in interwar Geneva
Private collection

flight European hands in the foreign service, including such men as Llewellyn "Tommy" Thompson, Jacob "Jake" Beam, and James "Jimmie" Riddleberger.[40]

Their approach would place the onus upon the Europeans to design and implement policies that were in the broader interest. The United States would provide the needed material and moral support, and would prod but not dictate. And so began the administration of the so-called light touch, so light, in fact, that it seemed almost deistic. "Mr. Gibson," recalled Allen Dulles, "indicated that the United States would not endeavor to impose its theories as to how the land armaments of Europe should be reduced. What we wished was to see reduction and if that reduction could be brought about by applying the principles [of others] ... this would be welcome."[41] For his part, Gibson, "work[ing] valiantly" but "always surreptitiously ... tickling his cheek with his tongue while putting on a brave, grave face," "emerge[d], perhaps somewhat ruffled inside, but with the poise and prestige of the Chairman of the American delegation intact."[42] It would not be the last time an American would appear in such a way coming out of a European chancery.

The diplomacy of the light touch often crossed the line into passivity, prompting a countervailing toughness and a hard realism. Americans were still prone to playing the dupe. Upon hearing of French plans to reoccupy the Ruhr in January 1923, for example, Secretary Hughes fired off a warning to the French ambassador only to hear the French government lie the next day about having received any such communication. He was outraged but did not succumb to pessimism.[43] Others less so. "Are the Germans repentant?" asked the international lawyer Paul Cravath: "My answer to this question is No."[44] Dwight Morrow, an old friend, added later, in 1931, "I have felt for a year or two that

Moses so that he could spread it on the *Congressional Record*. Being a little doubtful, I shall refrain.[57]

Such was the prestige of their profession. America's diplomats had only just begun to earn for themselves a respected place in American public life; they had yet to gain a permanent position of deference or establish a primary role in the formulation and exercise of policy. That would require at least three more decades of competition and collaboration with others in successive presidential administrations of both political parties. Meanwhile, two more world wars—one hot and one cold—would follow. The warring parties in both would regard Europe as the main prize; yet Europe itself would remain divided. For now, the image and reality of an Old World at peace remained confined to the diplomatic imagination.

3

SOME VERY LOVELY PEOPLE

Franklin Roosevelt's State Department—the ongoing struggle between consuls and diplomats—leading American representatives in Europe on the eve of war—their views on Fascism—the Welles Mission

I F ASKED TO NAME the best officer from among their ranks, a good many diplomats in the 1930s would have chosen J. Theodore Marriner: "Tall and courtly and possessed of great patience," "the best brains in the Service," as well as "the most photographed man in Europe." Marriner saw his career reach a high point in 1931 when, following yeoman's work on the disarmament negotiations, he became counselor of the embassy at Paris.[1] There he served under the popular Ambassador Edge, followed by the financier Jesse Straus, who turned out to be among the period's few political appointees respected by the professionals. Even before he fell fatally ill, Straus had already entrusted much of the embassy to Marriner, who presided over it in between assignments to the Geneva, London, and Lausanne Conferences. He impressed fellow countrymen and Europeans alike with his sincerity, dedication, and hard work. "Old Captain Ted, who sails the seven seas, disarmament or debts alike to him, he solves them with an almost faultless ease," sang one of them. And another:

> *For although the wily foreigner*
> *Has schemed to rule the sea,*
> *He overlooked the Marriner*
> *That comes from WE.*[2]

The balding, mustachioed Marriner gave a sophisticated, even fastidious, appearance; his tastes—particularly his obsessive interest in European royalty—recalled an earlier era; but his life and career adhered to the meritocratic vision of the founders of the foreign service noted in the previous chapter. "Beneath his disdainful manner was a real competence," recalled Ellis Briggs. "Although he looked and sometimes acted like a dilettante, he was in fact hardworking and conscientious and an astute and skillful negotiator."[3] Marriner was not rich, no scion of the plutocracy nor even the in-law of great wealth; the surname of this bachelor may have dotted the Maine coast for generations, but like many others it carried little with it besides its own past. Raised in Portland, Marriner was judged too sickly to fight in World War I and landed instead at Harvard, where he received a doctorate in medieval English in 1918. He joined the diplomatic corps soon after, was posted to Stockholm, Bucharest, and Bern, and then was named head of the Western European Division, the precursor of EUR, in 1927.

In the prewar department, a divisional directorship was important but ranked beneath the status of minister; still, Marriner made the most of the assignment and of Washington's social life. He lived at 1718 H Street, the home of "the Family" of

J. Theodore Marriner
Rare Books and Manuscripts Library,
Columbia University

diplomatic corps bachelors, where he took under his wing the young Chip Bohlen, then studying for his foreign service exam, and tutored him on the ways of the profession. Marriner's standards were as high as his devotion was to imparting them to younger officers.[4] He worked so hard that he suffered a string of health crises toward the end of 1928.[5] Yet his diary for these years reveals mostly news about trips to country houses, teas, and dinners with his closest friends in the department: the Castles and the Grews, S. Pinkney "Kippy" Tuck, James Clement Dunn—who will appear again momentarily—and Fred Dolbeare. His professional activities, which included, among other things, drafting and negotiating much of the Kellogg-Briand Pact, hardly feature at all.

Marriner's Paris embassy was the hub of Europe; to serve as the top diplomatic officer there under a well-placed political appointee almost guaranteed a minor, or even a major, European embassy posting soon thereafter.[6] Although he had caused a small stir by being misquoted by an American reporter to the effect that he understood the French better than his own countrymen, few doubted in 1936 that Marriner would get the usual reward.

It did not happen. Franklin D. Roosevelt had come into office three years earlier harboring a powerful distaste for those he and other self-described progressives called the "striped pants boys" of the State Department. The bias was widespread, both inside and outside government, and it was long-standing. Marriner, for example, had included in his diary back in 1919 a clipping from the *Congressional Record* in which Pennsylvania Senator Boies Penrose is quoted: "I have no sympathy with these young men. They are mostly Anglicized or Frenchified fops who get these appointments for the social distinction which it confers upon them," to which Marriner reacted, "It is great to be appreciated!" A decade later, he recalled a meeting with Charles Dawes, who had just been appointed ambassador to Britain:

[H]e came up to my office and, rather like a small boy, puffed and blew to the general effect that he knew all about everything there was to know ... and did not need to look at any papers, that he didn't like the Diplomatic Service anyway but still hoped to be able to get on with it and that after all he was not as indiscreet as he was painted. As I managed to take all this huff and puff very kindly, contradicting him on his wildest assertions, he suddenly decided apparently that he liked me very much and that even though I was a member of the Diplomatic Service, I was both intelligent and useful....He likewise said that one of his principal aims was to try to abolish the foolishness of presentations at court. I told him that this would be impossible....When he left, he said "you talk sense," and patted me on the back.[7]

Roosevelt was not the first president to serve as his own foreign minister, but he took the practice to new lengths in sowing so much confusion, redundancy, rivalry, and antipathy in the bureaucratic ranks that the young foreign service was very nearly nipped in the bud. The New Dealers he promoted in Washington were willing coconspirators in the emasculation of what many of them considered to be a heavily Republican State Department. What they did not erode through negligence they wounded by frontal attack. Supporting their cause were a few disappointed consuls and pedantic Congressmen who, nearly a decade after the passage of the Rogers Act, still sought to knock the diplomats down by a few pegs. The department hence required any officer in line for a ministerial appointment to serve first at a consular post.[8] The reaction of the leading diplomats was predictable. Bill Castle, having just been forced out of the government, asked,

Why should a man who is good at diplomacy be wasted in a consular office? Why should Beethoven be wasted teaching little girls how to play the piano? It is not that I am old-fashioned. I was in favor, and am in favor ... I am and always have been in favor of sending diplomatic officers to Calcutta and Sydney—but that would not prevent me from sending an utterly suitable consul to those places....The waste ... is intolerable.... The only way to run the Service is by exercising common sense and one's judgment....There is no other criterion. Oh, for a shot at it![9]

So, rather than gaining his European embassy, Marriner was named consul general to, of all places, Beirut. His friends in the French government made him a commander of the Legion of Honor and wished him well, holding a farewell dinner with "a tremendous mob of people," including multiple counts, marquises, princesses, and Rothschilds.[10] Marriner, following a long stateside leave, embarked on his consular assignment in the hope that it would be temporary and trouble free.[11] But that was not to happen, either. A few months later, an Armenian visa seeker named Mejardich Karayan waited across the street from the consulate and, upon seeing Marriner, fired six shots, killing him. The Armenian claimed to have done this in revenge for being denied a visa, though it later emerged that the visa application was approved but had never arrived because the applicant had failed to notify the consulate of a change in address. In any event, Karayan said he singled out Marriner for the simple reason that he was the first American to cross his path that day. His colleagues were anguished. For his part, President Roosevelt "said that he was sorry of his death and that 'Ted' had been doing a wholly good job. Of course, he added with a sigh, it is one of those things that can't be helped."[12]

LIKE OTHER PRESIDENTS BEFORE AND AFTER him, Roosevelt complained frequently about the State Department's stuffiness. Outgoing Secretary of State Henry Stimson recalled that the president-elect "alarmed" him by "indicating that he had been influenced by unfounded criticism of the results of the Rogers bill and that the members of the Foreign Service were wealthy young men who got entirely out of touch with American affairs in the course of their permanent service away from this country."[13] Also, like a few of his predecessors, including Stimson's own boss, Roosevelt occasionally entrusted his most important missions to special envoys rather than relying exclusively upon the professionals next door. The most important at this juncture were Sumner Welles and William Bullitt, who became locked in a bitter competition that would destroy the public careers of both men.[14] Welles would resign from his position as undersecretary of state in summer 1943 and drink himself to a slow and miserable death. Bullitt, forced out of his job as ambassador to France by the German conquest in 1940, was unable to convince Roosevelt to appoint him to a long list of jobs, each less prestigious than the last, until he finally ended his career in a failed run for the mayorship of his hometown, Philadelphia. As to the State Department, it was, according to one of its early stalwarts, Joseph Green,

> in a peculiar state, facing the uncertainties of the transition which may be very mild in its effects, but which may prove to be a cataclysm. Mr. Roosevelt has been giving us great aid and comfort during the past few weeks by assuring us, first in regard to one question of foreign policy and then in regard to another, that the incoming administration does not intend to deviate from the policies followed by the present administration. In this way, he has succeeded in lifting the atmosphere of gloom which has begun to settle on the Department. However, the deserving Democrats are swarming and they are very hungry.[15]

Another put it more starkly: "You have no idea of the White House control over foreign affairs now. To do so you must go back to the regime of the great Theodore."[16]

LET US FIRST MEET THE REST of the department. At the top sat Secretary of State Cordell Hull, one of the last log cabin legislators from Tennessee, a "gaunt inarticulate man" with no diplomatic experience and vengeful tendencies, complaining often of the "carefully laid plans to undermine and destroy me." Hull's tenure at State was long but it wore thin—he gave "an ill, tired and not very happy impression" with an "air ... of infinite patience and long suffering." As he would have been the first to admit, his sole interest in foreign affairs was the pursuit of tariff reductions. But Hull was a shrewd and experienced political infighter whom Roosevelt simply could not fire. Also, Mr. Hull "knows how to wait."[17]

Next down as undersecretary (preceding Welles) came William Phillips, who appeared in the previous chapter: A Brahmin from Boston's North Shore, onetime intimate of the first President Roosevelt and a senior member of the diplomatic service, Phillips was "the epitome of the handsome, well-traveled, polished ambassador, right out of central casting, whose Bostonianism was considerably mellowed by his wife." Caroline Phillips was an Astor and a Drayton from South Carolina as well as a close friend and frequent correspondent of Eleanor Roosevelt. By the mid-1940s, the two women would come to operate something of a back channel of influence upon their respective husbands.[18] Bill Phillips had served once before as undersecretary during the tenure of Secretary Hughes; he was regarded as a popular if somewhat spineless bureaucrat, although his soon-to-be predecessor, Bill Castle, had stronger feelings:

> W.P. is an almost completely vapid person....I should be personally angry if [he] succeeds me. I could have kept the job easily by coming out for F.D.R. when it became clear he was to be elected. That is all Bill did, and he has probably been more definitely Republican in the past then [sic] I have. Furthermore, Bill made a flop when he was Under Secretary before. There is no reason to think he would be any better now. Charley Adams amazed me the other day by saying you could not fool any Bostonian into thinking Bill Phillips was capable—a remark which enormously surprised me as coming from him. On the other hand, Bill knows the ropes....He would be a help to Hull on the routine—useless when it comes to any big decisions. Caroline would be splendid for Mrs. Hull, a thousand times better than Mrs. Sumner Welles.[19]

By most accounts, both Phillipses imparted an elegant veneer to the rough-hewn bureaucracy.[20] But when Phillips was named ambassador to Italy in 1936, the pot boiled over. The top candidate for his job was Welles. Not only was he considered to have one of the quickest minds in the foreign service but also he was very close to the ebullient president—as a child he had been the ring bearer at FDR's wedding—yet the two personalities could not have been more different. Welles was "dignified" and "distinguished ... both in appearance and in manners" but also dour, with few friends (Castle called him "detestable") and several clouds over his past. "He improves on acquaintance," wrote the British diplomat Alexander Cadogan, "but it is a pity he swallowed a ramrod in his youth."[21] Dean Acheson provided another memorable description:

> His manner was formal to the point of stiffness. His voice, pitched much lower than would seem natural, though it had been so since he was a boy, lent a suggestion of pomposity. Once, when a remark of my wife's made him laugh, he quickly caught himself and said, "Pardon me. You amused me."[22]

Hull's epithet for the man he came to despise was more direct: "That horizontal son of a bitch."[23]

Vying with Welles for the undersecretaryship was the septuagenarian lawyer R. Walton "Judge" Moore, a southern bachelor who had served in Congress and was close to Hull. Roosevelt postponed making a decision for many months until finally agreeing to a compromise: Welles would become undersecretary and Moore would occupy the new post of counselor. "I suppose," wrote Castle to Hugh Gibson, "they can only be asked together to houses which have folding doors wide enough so that Moore with his lady [sic] and Welles with his can walk abreast into the dining room. Then when it comes to sitting at the table, I suppose they will have to sit in each other's laps as the only way to avoid unfortunate precedence. It is one of the silliest rows that has ever afflicted the Department of State."[24]

Sumner Welles
Time & Life Pictures/Getty

The counselor position was defined vaguely, but in practice it came pretty close to the job of undersecretary without many of the administrative duties. So Moore would be Hull's deputy after all. For his part, Welles came to operate much as Castle had described: less as a deputy and more as a parallel secretary of state. "Apparently," Castle continued, "men in the Service are very much afraid of him."[25] Welles reported directly to the president and generally kept the rest of the department, including Hull, in the dark as to the substance of those and many other conversations. Moore got worked up over neutrality legislation but otherwise did little more than struggle to hold on to whatever diminishing prerogatives he could as his health, like Hull's, declined badly. Welles thrived. In his agile mind he carried—or was thought to carry—the secrets of the vast external realm.

Loyalties divided sometimes three or four ways; many senior officials were barely on speaking terms; clashes such as the one between Assistant Secretaries Dean Acheson and Adolph Berle, for example, became notorious inside and outside the department. Morale continued to suffer. Staff meetings of the "motley, long-winded group," recalled the diplomat Doc Matthews, "were productive mostly of long speeches, thinly veiled personal hostility ... and wide and varied disagreement."[26] Meanwhile, there was a war on the horizon.

Before getting to that, there is more to learn about another central character, indeed, one of the most talented diplomatic entrepreneurs the government had ever known: William Christian Bullitt.

A "fluorescent sort of fellow," Bullitt came to diplomacy by way of a career in journalism and the Hollywood film industry. His sense of the dramatic dated further back, however. Roosevelt's aide Admiral William Leahy noted Bullitt telling him about

> an interesting incident of his visit to Germany when he was 18 years of age. While present in the audience at an opera he was offended by the action of a young German officer who placed his sword in Mr. Bullitt's seat and upon a vigorous return of the sword to the seat of its owner Mr. Bullitt was challenged to a duel....He immediately accepted the challenge, choosing as weapons hatchets at a distance of toe to toe[,] which he informed the challenger's second was an accepted and usual form of duel among his American Indian ancestors....He heard no more of the incident ... and the duel was never held.[27]

Ten years later Bullitt had gone as Woodrow Wilson's emissary to Lenin; he then resigned publicly from the Peace Commission because of Wilson's refusal to deal seriously with the Bolsheviks and denounced Wilson before Congress; subsequently, he married Louise Bryant, the widow of John Reed, author of *Ten Days That Shook the World*. Bullitt therefore enjoyed a reputation for expertise in some matters Russian, although contemporaries regarded him as "a clever and quite unscrupulous intriguer, more or less of a communist" with frequent designs on other people's jobs.[28] Soon after his election, Roosevelt welcomed Bullitt into his inner circle, sent him to direct the American delegation to the London Economic Conference of 1933, and then appointed him to oversee normalization talks with the Soviets. Bullitt would be named, not surprisingly, as the first American ambassador to the USSR. There he would preside over one of the most interesting American missions anywhere, with one of the greatest collections of talent ever in the foreign service: George Kennan, Chip Bohlen, Loy Henderson, Elbridge Durbrow, Angus Ward, and a young West Point graduate named Charles Thayer.[29]

But Bullitt was far more than "Roosevelt's most recent crush." He acted as the president's eyes and ears in Europe, and was second only to Welles in advising the president on foreign affairs generally. The columnist Joe Alsop recalled that, "Bullitt had more inside information than all the rest of the American diplomatic service put together, and that he was one of the six or eight men in Europe who were [aware] of the different factors in the complete world situation ... [and] with his E. Phillips Oppenheim flavor and his vast fund of inside information has always tended to exaggerate the President's sense of international drama." Wilbur Carr put it somewhat differently: "Bullitt ... is a most dangerous person. Glad he is out of the country."[30]

Despite his own background, Bullitt was committed to improving the professionalism of American diplomacy, a campaign that blended nicely with his obsession to amass influence. The few ambassadorial appointments he did not generate were submitted for his approval; it was Bullitt who led the way, for example, in urging the president to fire Ambassadors Joseph Kennedy and William Dodd, and to appoint Hugh Wilson to take the latter's place.[31] His access to FDR and to numerous other statesmen was considerable, particularly in France, where he was treated like a member of the cabinet.[32] Finally, Bullitt's father had been a close law school friend of Judge Moore's; the rivalry of the Hull and Moore camp on the one hand, and Welles, on the other, therefore also had a prominent Bullitt dimension. It was only a matter of time before Bullitt and Welles would cross paths—there was just not enough room for both of them in the same department, or even in the multidimensional heart of Franklin Roosevelt.[33]

The clash reached its "sordid denouement" in early 1943 when Bullitt spread the word about Welles's homosexual liaisons, thereby forcing the hand of Hull, who was only too happy to insist that the president fire Welles. Both he and Bullitt would leave government service soon after.[34] The full story, involving Pullman car porters, deathbed promises, and some debauchery, was, of course, far juicier and more intricate, given the many intersecting loyalties and disloyalties. Its significance here, however, comes from its boost to the perception of an insubordinate, unmanageable, and lackluster

William Bullitt
Time & Life Pictures/Getty

State Department. John J. McCloy, then serving in the War Department as deputy to Henry Stimson (who returned to government service in 1940), noted that, "more thinking along political lines was being done and being asserted in the Munitions Building—this was before the era of the Pentagon—than in the old State Building."[35] Europe especially, it seemed, was too important to leave to the professionals. Therefore Roosevelt kept them at arm's length. Again, he was not unique in doing so; but Roosevelt and the burgeoning wartime bureaucracy would lay several additional layers of ambiguity (his detractors would say, intrigue) upon the conduct of foreign affairs, leaving many in the department and the foreign service bewildered and bitter.[36]

WITH ITS TALENT FOR KEEPING up appearances the European Desk managed to prosper in the mélange. "The Western European Division," observed a Washington hostess, "is the only one that is socially possible." It grew bolder in defending newly won geographic and functional prerogatives. By the time the real reformers came along—that is, in the immediate postwar years under Secretaries George Marshall and Dean Acheson—the bureau was already "a going entity, the predominant managing agency and trustee of State's policy formulation for relations with the great powers."[37] Other bureaus were debilitated by the wartime pressures, so the best, most ambitious young officers still gravitated toward

James Clement Dunn
Time & Life Pictures/Getty

Europe, where there was the most action and prestige.

There were two additional factors bearing on the European hands' capacity for creative self-promotion during this period: First, the department *grew*—approximately fivefold during the war, ending in 1945 with over 4,000 personnel in Washington and 8,000 foreign service officers. It was no longer "dominated by a group of worldly, hard-drinking, clever young snobs who went everywhere and knew everybody," according to a contemporary account. "Today they have vanished like the host of Sennacherib and an entirely different group ... [has] replaced them at the dinner tables and cocktail shakers of the capital."[38] Secondly, it broadened its authority. The department acquired some fifty-nine new principal functions—both wartime and permanent—and, after reorganizations in 1939, 1944, and 1945, went from thirty-two organizational units to twelve offices with sixty divisions. This was in keeping with New Deal tradition, to be sure; State was not unique in the U.S. government in expanding its reach.[39] But Roosevelt's disparagement made everyone seem more determined to reaffirm their worth. "It is interesting to hark back to the old days when we were fighting for a reasonable recognition of the Foreign Service as a permanent career," wrote Joe Grew to Hugh Gibson; "that's a great and most encouraging record, don't you think so? Drew Pearson and his ilk may still write facetiously about the white-spat career boys, but I think public opinion is now pretty well behind the new system and will demand its continuance."[40]

And so, faced with an uninterested and occasionally hostile president, dysfunction at its highest levels, badly thinned lower ranks, first by Depression-led budget cuts and then by the Selective Service, the State Department still found plenty of opportunities. Its European Desk did what it came to do best: It began polishing silver linings. The pattern of converting influence at the margins to steady positions at the center of foreign policy started then, as did the art of coopting political appointees. The war years thus marked the emergence of the European Desk as the most powerful of the State Department's various, semiautonomous fiefdoms—the "mother bureau."

TO UNDERSTAND HOW THIS TOOK PLACE, one must first get to know the man who had the most to do with it. James Clement Dunn was an Irish American builder's son from Newark, New Jersey. Although his father employed him in laying bricks, he also encouraged young Dunn to study architecture, which he did. This proved unsatisfying. Dunn joined the State Department in 1919, married an heiress to the Armour meatpacking fortune, cast himself as a would-be patrician, went to work for Billy Phillips, and bought a large house in northwest Washington, where he partook in the capital's social life and perfected his croquet game. The latter would come in handy, as Cordell Hull was so great an enthusiast that his inner circle would be dubbed by the aforementioned Pearson the "croquet clique."[41] Dunn had other skills as well. Appointed the White House director of ceremonies in 1927, he subsequently invented the department's Office of Protocol, becoming master of all things formal and acquiring a reputation for both fussiness and finesse, an "easygoing suavity [that] hid a terrific energy," with an uncommon ability to spend no more than a handful of seconds at a party while leaving everyone with the impression that he had been there all evening. A 1946 photograph of him reveals slicked dark hair, bushy eyebrows, and a long, solid nose, slightly too thick around the end to pass as classically Greek. His eyes and mouth each have a fine, deliberate curve, appearing at once focused and aloof. Another columnist would describe him as being "small, thin, sleek and suave ... with [a] well-bred quizzical look and precise, almost prim poise."[42] He could seem "tradition-crested" and did not have a great sense of humor; he was not shy but "reserved," except in matters of self-interest. To Castle,

> Jimmie ... is out for himself and that has my wholehearted endorsement.... [He] is, of course, always most cordial to me, knowing that the ways of politics are past understanding or prediction, but if I ever get back in the Department I shall remember everything he has done recently—not vindictively, of course, but as an indication of essential character.[43]

Dunn would exemplify the striped-pants diplomat so lampooned by the New Dealers, but it was an image he concocted rather than inherited. Along with a certain reputation for ultramontanism, his persona did not win him many friends among the more liberal members of the New Deal establishment, or among the press. Pearson, for example, regularly lambasted him as the leader of a cabal of Fascist appeasers. The caricature stuck and would come to plague the department's stances on wartime neutrality, especially toward the North African tangle described in the next chapter. But there is no evidence that it ever bothered him.

Lacking a strong deputy and uninterested in many topics himself, Hull came to rely upon Dunn both as his ambassador to the department and his chief source for information, appointing him first as head of international conferences and then as special political adviser, a position akin to today's undersecretary for political affairs, with operational control over everything from the geographic offices to liaison with other government departments. Dunn sat on the State-War-Navy Coordinating Committee, having replaced Welles as the State Department's representative after the latter's disgrace. Dunn's deputy and successor, Doc Matthews, later wrote that Dunn was "closer to Secretary Hull than any one else in Washington, and, of equal importance, one of the few who could interpret what the Secretary with all his circumlocutions and indirectness was driving at and wanted done."[44] The writer Martin Weil added,

> With Dunn as permanent chief of the Division of International

Conferences, the Europeanists had a sentry stationed at this vulnerable outpost, prepared to alert his colleagues to coming attacks on their monopoly control of American diplomacy. He could also use his position as "technician" to ensure a steady flow of briefing papers from the desk officers and to assign favored officers to staff positions. He thus found himself in a handy position to offer sympathy and instruction to Cordell Hull....Dunn became a surrogate son to his childless boss.[45]

This could not have happened were it not for Hull's anomalous relationship with the White House and the president's heavy use of diplomatic adventurers. Dunn made Hull's life more tolerable and himself indispensable. The four successive chiefs of the European Division—Jay Pierrepont Moffat, Ray Atherton, Doc Matthews, and Jack Hickerson—would lay, along with Dunn, the basis for a half century of organizational domination. They would capitalize upon military and political necessity in order to establish the primacy of Europe in nearly all matters of policy. Even though their predecessors were nearly all Eurocentrists, American diplomacy on the whole remained geopolitically ambivalent. They and the war would change that. They would, moreover, extend to the postwar period the particular approach to European problems rarefied in the 1920s, namely, the combination of honest brokerage among allies and deployment of transnational, or supranational, issues for collective regional and global ends. That was especially the case for the British, with whom American diplomats often found themselves in a delicate *pas de deux*, performing as both partner and foil of the Continent. In sum, the European Desk would seize the cockpit of foreign policymaking and would not give it up.

ON THE OTHER SIDE OF the Atlantic the situation was, to put it mildly, bleak. "In the state of utter cynicism and lack of regard for obligations existing in Europe today nothing should be unbelievable."[46] These anonymous words, reported by the diplomat Edwin Wilson, captured the powerful sense of many American diplomats, not to mention many Europeans, of moorings being cast adrift. Back "at the Department," reported the columnists Joe Alsop and Bob Kintner,

the diplomacy of the age of the ant-hill state and the terror from the air unroll somewhat incongruously, in a setting unchanged since the placid days of Chester A. Arthur. In those ornate, tesselated corridors, populated by an ancient race of Negro messengers, Lord Lothian hurrying to discuss the new Armageddon makes no more stir than Lord Sackville dropping in to protest the *Alabama* claims. But in the cable room, the nerve center of the Department, the instruments chatter ceaselessly, bringing word of the hopes of Chamberlain and Daladier, the intimations of the Wilhelmstrasse and the whispers of the Kremlin, the latest incidents along the Yang-tse, the latest pressures in the Balkans.[47]

If some of their European counterparts tried hard to convince themselves that war could be averted while others were resigned to its inevitability, American diplomats were torn between a justified paranoia over isolationism and the confusion of external events over which they had little control. Europe to them did "not present an edifying spectacle," nor did their countrymen seem up to anything but "struggle between faint hearts and foolish heads, hollow stomachs and woolly legs!"[48] Yet many of them, in spite of such doubts, saw where events were heading in the mid-1930s and were among the first to predict both the nature of the coming war and the role the United States would play in it. There was, to be sure, a good deal of fence-sitting and, of course, most people prayed for peace. Some, like Assistant Secretaries Berle and Breckinridge Long, succumbed to wishful thinking along those lines, while others, like Bullitt and the department's economic adviser and later historian, Herbert Feis, once known as the Jeremiah of the Hoover administration, were more pessimistic, and prescient. But many refused to expect too much of

Dunn at the office
Time & Life Pictures/Getty

American influence, or interests. Hugh Wilson wrote in June 1938, "twenty years ago we tried to save the world and now look at it....The older I grow the deeper is my conviction that we have nothing to gain by entering a European conflict, and indeed everything to lose."[49] Wilson claimed that he had never before "had such peace of mind" as he did while serving in Switzerland during the early 1930s, and he suspected that it would not last. He would presently replace William Dodd as ambassador in Berlin, serving there almost to the point war was declared. His dispatches and conversations are among the most striking examples of a sense of helplessness in the face of calamity, echoing Europeans in being "convinced there was no chance of separating Hitler and Mussolini, that Hitler would continue his movement eastward."[50]

The range of opinion about the future had much to do with the recent past. Fresh in the minds of people like Wilson, Feis, and Gibson surely must have been their bitter experience of trying valiantly but ultimately failing to secure the benefits of disarmament diplomacy. That was joined by the debacle of the 1933 London Economic Conference, ill timed to coincide with the brief, final chance for a breakthrough in the disarmament talks at Geneva. "First the Monetary and Economic Conference, then the Disarmament Conference, and then there was none!" recalled Feis.[51] Finally, there were the tortuous negotiations with Congress over neutrality legislation, which left many of them mistrustful of the so-called congressional wing of the department, that is, Hull and Moore, especially, who seemed to care more about the sensitivities of their former colleagues on Capitol Hill than about the deteriorating situation overseas.[52]

THE FRUSTRATION OF FEIS and his collaborators was compounded by Roosevelt's ambassadorial appointments. They were among the most outspoken

men that Europe had seen cross the Atlantic since the vogue of Young Americanism
in the mid-nineteenth century and, not surprisingly, were blamed for the "tragedy
and ... disgrace that American representatives abroad do not pull together as a
team for their country."[53] Few of them were professional diplomats. Contrary
to the stereotype, they were not, moreover, with the notable exceptions of Joe
Kennedy in London and Joe Davies in Moscow, big political donors.[54] Curiously,
most were self-proclaimed Jeffersonians. Bullitt, who fancied his reputation among
the French as rivaling that of Jefferson, if not his fellow Philadelphian Benjamin
Franklin, kept a portrait of the third president over his desk in Paris and earlier
had gotten into a well-publicized spat with the Soviets over their failure to agree
to the construction of a new embassy in Moscow modeled on Monticello. Another
leading member of this group was the ambassador to Spain during much of its
civil war, Claude Bowers, a journalist and historian who supposedly had declared
himself a Jeffersonian Democrat at age two. Bowers, who spoke hardly any
Spanish, would prove a disappointment, though he would have been hard pressed
to admit it: "I love Spain and the people here get that, and respond generously.
Frequently papers have made the point that I am the first man sent here since
[Washington] Irving with an appreciation of the cultural greatness of the country
and its history." But Bowers's mind was elsewhere, working "day and night" on
his book *Jefferson in Power: The Death Struggle of the Federalists*.[55] He was "the most
unambassadorial figure ever to present credentials," recalled Ellis Briggs, "with
bunions so painful ... he kept shoes with holes cut out ... and there were gaps
where lower teeth were missing. On one of the remaining stubs a dead cigar was
often impaled."[56] In any event, Bowers wasted little time in fleeing across the
French border to Saint-Jean-de-Luz soon after the first shots were fired in Madrid.
Roosevelt would face little choice but to dispense with him. His solution was to
appoint him ambassador to Chile, which he was led to believe Bowers would
refuse. Alas, Bowers accepted and continued to inspire the Spanish-speaking Left
for several more years. A not inconsequential side effect was the appointment of
the politician and former assistant secretary of state Breckinridge Long to head
the newly formed Special Division, about which more will follow, for it had been
Long whom Welles and the president had intended to send to Chile.[57]

Meanwhile in Berlin sat William Dodd: another historian, idealist, rural
sage, and hater of all things Fascist, including, he led one to suspect, significant
sections of the American foreign service. Unlike Bowers, Dodd was not close to
FDR or to any of his circle; it is not clear why the president appointed him to such
an important post, apart from the rumored possibility that Roosevelt thought
he had nominated President Harold Dodds of Princeton, a man he admired.
Still, William Dodd spoke good German—he had received his doctorate from
Leipzig with a thesis on Jefferson. He also had prominent backers—Secretary
of Commerce Daniel Roper, Harold Ickes, Claude Swanson, and especially
Roosevelt's old "chief" at the Navy Department and his ambassador to Mexico,
Josephus Daniels, who was also Dodd's friend and former neighbor in North
Carolina. A fellow historian, Charles Beard, wrote to him with encouragement: "I
am glad you are over there at the center of things. I do not see how it happened
that one of your spirit was put in Berlin, of all places. But history is a queer bird."[58]
And so was Dodd. Claiming that his staff was conspiring against him, he flooded
the department with memoranda criticizing their extravagance and laziness,

singling out for special animus one of his deputies, Orme Wilson, an Astor and a Vanderbilt by marriage who also happened to be the nephew of undersecretary Phillips, who, for his part, tried unsuccessfully to "soothe the situation" from a distance. It was reportedly Dodd who planted the idea in the president's head that all future ministers must undergo a period of consular purgatory. The objections of his diplomatic colleagues probably made him even less likely to change his mind. "Will knows everything," said his eighty-nine-year-old father, tracked down by a *Newsweek* reporter in Fuquay Springs, North Carolina. "You can bet your last dollar that whatever Will says about anything he knows what he is talking about. And furthermore, you might as well try to move the sun as to try to make Will tell anything that he's not a-mind to tell."[59] As suggested by his correspondence, portraits, and medical history, Dodd was a hard, stubborn, bitter, and sickly man.[60] He was not, by anyone's measure, a diplomat.

The refusal of the German government to grant him anything beyond the most superficial degree of access meant that he, too, could take time away from official duties, write his book *Old South,* and serve as president of the American Historical Association. The embassy functioned badly, with Dodd's various deputies—Wilson, Jack White, Ferdinand Mayer, and Prentiss Gilbert—carrying on independently, and most of the work being done by the team of Beam and Riddleberger, which had come with Gilbert from Geneva.[61] There was even a superannuated former ambassador, Jacob Schurman, on the scene, operating semiofficially and on his own with the German government. Marriner liked to tell the story of Dodd's explanation for why he never saw Hitler again after meeting him only twice: "Hitler does not know any history."[62] Or Dodd might have appreciated the word of a professional colleague, indeed one of America's foremost diplomatic historians, Bernadotte Schmitt: "I greatly admire your debut as a diplomatist," he wrote to him in 1933, "because seemingly you have not said a word about politics or diplomacy in a single letter which has been received from you since you sailed from these shores. If only all diplomatists followed your example the world might be a safer place."[63] Such a person might have been better suited to a more distant, more peaceful land: Chile, for example. But for Dodd, Nazi Germany was the wrong place and the wrong time. Phillips, who probably had no role at all in his appointment, struggled to control and educate him:

> You ask ... whether you ought to discuss publicly American views and convictions....There is a nice balance ... to be maintained which has to be worked out according to the conditions at any given post. Certainly the State Department could not lay down any rules and regulations in this respect....The old world has its habits and customs, which have been handed down through centuries. We do not like many of them, but, on the other hand, Europeans do not like many of our customs and habits.... Personally I have come to believe that comparisons between American and European viewpoints are useful only if they help one to understand the other's viewpoint.[64]

"Is there any chance of ridding ourselves of Dodd?" Pierrepont Moffat asked in October 1936.[65] It would take another year for Dodd to give up, but he had already grown forlorn in his German isolation. "How Europe drifts," he wrote back in March, "I think one can see now better than hitherto, France is doomed to fall into a second-power position, and ere long England must begin the decline which the Netherlands began in 1713....If Woodrow Wilson were alive he would be the most miserable leader in the modern world....I am almost compelled to retreat to my little farm on the eastern slope of the Blue Ridge Mountains and spend my days in complete retirement."[66] And that, apart from killing a girl while driving drunk, was what he did.

About the only bright spot in Dodd's ambassadorial career was his cultivation of a former consul for whom he helped secure an embassy in Vienna. George Messersmith was an interesting anomaly, one of the few consuls to rise to the top of the foreign service at that time. Known as "Forty Page George" because of his lengthy memoranda, which forced Secretary Hull to assign an assistant to provide special synopses, Messersmith fit the stereotype of the consul on the make. His "great merit was that he was always successful," wrote Willard Beaulac, who worked for him in Cuba; even Bill Castle rated him as "able," despite being "a rather conceited person."

The son of a Pennsylvania postmaster, Messersmith trained to be a teacher and began his career in a one-room schoolhouse in rural Delaware. Shortly thereafter he became a principal, and then an administrator. A few years later he lost a bitter battle to reform the state school system and decided upon a new career. While still a principal, he had roomed with the family of the famed jurist John Bassett Moore; he never met the man but decided to look him up after passing the exam for the diplomatic service. (Ironically, he had already failed the consular exam.) Moore dissuaded him from joining the diplomatic service on grounds of poverty; Messersmith retook the consular exam, and this time he passed. He entered the service in 1914. An early favorite of Carr, he rode the wave of consular preference in the late 1920s and early 1930s. His impression upon the older diplomats was predictable. Castle remarked further that he did "not like" Messersmith but had "to admit his ability and that he knows a lot. I think he goes a bit too far in his hatred of the Hitler Regime and that hatred is one of the things which has always made me wonder whether he had any Jew blood."[67] Historians, however, are indebted to Messersmith for the volume and perspicacity of his memoranda. Few members of the foreign service wrote more or more observantly about the growing Nazi menace.[68]

Meanwhile succeeding Bullitt in Moscow was Joe Davies, a Democratic crony from Wisconsin who landed the hand of Marjorie Merriweather Post in 1935 and, evidently, any embassy he desired thereafter. Four hundred people were invited to his oath-taking ceremony. Nearly all the professional diplomats regarded him with disdain, given his extravagances and puzzling defenses of Stalin. Elbridge Durbrow, for example, noted that the ambassador's residence, Spaso House, had to be rewired in order to accommodate the twenty-four deep-freeze chests that Davies (or Mrs. Davies) had sent from General Foods.[69] When he was transferred in 1938 to Belgium, the man he replaced—Hugh Gibson—was despondent:

[M]y whole heart is in the diplomatic service and I should get out only with the greatest reluctance. But I am sure you will understand that as between getting out or accepting a punitive assignment in order that Mr.

Joe Davies can enjoy the more congenial climate of Brussels, only one choice is possible for me.[70]

While Castle added insult to injury:

What has happened in the appointment to your post of that unutterable bounder Joe Davies, does not make me laugh—it simply makes me sick ... the wickedness of giving up the service of one of the most competent people we have for the sake of catering to an ignoramus who happened to marry a rich woman is just beyond my comprehension, or would be if I did not know the crowd in office....[Hull] is more or less of a coward in his relations with the White House ... so far as the Service is concerned Sumner Welles is supreme, and as he wants above everything else to be Senator from Maryland he will never do anything to offend Millard Tydings by way of Pap Davies et femme.[71]

A partial exception to this string of ambassadorial disappointments was found in Italy. Thanks to the urgings of his wife, the exhausted Bill Phillips was relieved of his undersecretaryship in late 1936 and was sent to Italy as ambassador, a long-sought-after post. He took up residence in the Villa Taverna, a former seminary built in the sixteenth century by Pope Gregory XIII on what then was a rustic hill dotted with pear trees. The large house and gardens were still owned by the Borromeo-Taverna family, which had renovated the interior in a modern style, with wrought-iron railings and animal door fixtures, softly colored yellow and green Vietri tiles in an interlocking pattern below walls of faux reliefs and inlaid fragments of Roman figurines obtained from nearby catacombs. There Phillips wandered among the "giant-like oak trees, the fountains and the quaint statuary" and "looked forward to many such happy and interesting days."[72] He sought to win the loyalty, or at least the neutrality, of the Italians, who, Jimmy Dunn had been insisting for some time, "may turn upon us the full force of their efforts to extricate themselves from the difficult position which they face."[73] But he had little to show for it, and would move presently to London and then to India.

Succeeding him in Italy after the war was his onetime deputy, Alexander Kirk. Known to his friends as "Buffy," Kirk was

Hollywood's concept of a successful diplomat. Tall, slender, dark, graceful in every movement, with a handsome hawk-like face, he was the last word in elegance as far as dress and bearing were concerned. He always spoke in a soft voice; he never seemed hurried, worried, or confused. To a casual observer he might have appeared to be detached from what was going on around him or in the world at large. Such an appearance was, however, deceptive. He was a keen observer of the international and local scene wherever he served. His mind was like a rapier in cutting through the nonessentials and the irrelevances to the core of a problem. Possessed of a huge personal fortune, pursued by social climbers and other hangers-on, he had a contempt for petty snobbery....[Nevertheless, h]e lived luxuriously. In Rome he rented a beautiful palace....In Cairo he had a

Alexander Kirk
Time & Life Pictures/Getty

residence out near the pyramids, and another one in the city....He also rented a large houseboat on the river which he placed at the disposal of members of the Allied Armed Forces.[74]

Kirk indeed was very rich; "Kirk's soap" had once been a household staple. His Egyptian excesses were hardly unique. George Kennan recalled that in Berlin, Kirk "kept, in the swank Grunewald district, an enormous mansion (selected ... because it was the only house he could find in Berlin with *only one* red room), where he maintained a staff of Italian servants and in which he gave a large buffet luncheon every Sunday noon"—although by his own account, he was "lying low as a Chargé." His house on the Via Nomentana in Rome, the Villa Blanc, had "indirect lighting up from the floor silhouetting flights of golden birds, little gold ballroom chairs and dozens of polar bear rugs on the floor. One wall of the dining room was all glass with a greenhouse of tropical trees beyond." Other idiosyncrasies included Kirk's insistence on wearing gray or silver, "with silver ballet slippers and thongs criss-crossed up the legs," never spending more than ten minutes at a reception, and serving color-coded meals—one day it would be all black ("caviar, black bean soup, overdone meat, truffles, ripe olives, chocolate ice cream"); another day, red ("borscht or tomato soup, rare meat, beets, strawberries"), and so on. He also adored his mother and sister (the wife of another diplomat), and reportedly never took his job seriously until the death of the former left him without any other motivation to live. Indeed, had he sought more fame, Kirk might be remembered more widely as "exactly the sort of American career diplomat of which the American philistine has always been most suspicious: elegant, overrefined, haughty and remote. It was a manner of enlivening life by playing the buffoon."[75]

Yet it was not obvious that Kirk liked the diplomatic profession—he infamously defended his choice of career by stating that he simply wanted to find a way to prevent his beloved mother from having her bags checked at customs—and threatened to quit several times when he did not get his way. Perhaps another reason, according to Bullitt, was "to wash off the smell of soap." Still, Kirk had real talent. His grandiose exterior concealed a deeply "subtle habit of mind." His memoranda were among the shrewdest and most lucid of his generation.[76] With the possible exception of Bullitt, whose vacillating zealotry and personality obscured much of his brilliance, no other American official displayed such mastery of the European situation in the late 1930s or close relationships with the leading Europeans. And yet Kirk seemed to have or seek few allies at home and complained often about his life abroad.[77] (Granted, anyone would if he were posted in Moscow or Berlin at the time.) What influence he did bring to bear came in the form of professional education. Many officers, including both George Kennan and Robert Murphy, who will appear in the next chapter, received training at the hands of Kirk. Kennan, who wrote that he "learned more" from Kirk "perhaps, than from any other chief," filled in the portrait:

> He never wrote anything if he could help it....His understanding was intuitive rather than analytical. His conversation consisted largely of weary, allusive quips....But behind this façade of urbane and even exaggerated sophistication there lay a great intuitive shrewdness and a devastatingly critical sense of humor....No one impressed him. He treated the most pretentious women like sluts....He despised the Nazis and held them at arm's length with a barbed irony. Even at the height of their military successes, he declined to entertain for a second the possibility that they might win the war. "They have undertaken," he would insist, "something they cannot finish....That is the cardinal sin: to start something you cannot finish."[78]

Perhaps for that reason there was a curious reluctance to put himself forward, to make full use of his talents, to take real risks beyond those for which he was so well suited but which, nevertheless, followed a predictable and secure career pattern. Kirk had joined the State Department in 1915 as Phillips's private secretary after earning degrees at Yale, Sciences Po, and Harvard Law School. He served with the Peace Commission in Paris and then in a variety of posts in Asia and Latin America before becoming deputy to Grew as well as vice chair of the Efficiency Ratings Board and executive secretary of the department, during which period he was charged with inspecting the various bureaus, thereby earning him the enmity of Castle, for one.[79] By the time he began nearly a decade of service in Rome in 1928, he was one of the most experienced officers.

From this point forward, Kirk's life was almost novelistic in its placing him in the right place at the right time: in Rome during the invasion of Abyssinia, then to Moscow and Berlin for the signing of the Nazi-Soviet Pact and the outbreak of war, then back to Rome, Algiers, Caserta, Cairo—where he gained notoriety as one of the few men to resist the extraordinary charms of Lady Diana Cooper—and Rome again. But Kirk often sounded frustrated. He was regarded as indispensable, which limited his freedom of movement, but his excellent advice often met resistance.[80] Upon retiring after the war, Kirk disappeared to adopt the life of a rancher in remote parts of Colorado and Arizona, consuming himself with soil conservation and his "beloved Angus cattle." He dropped off the map and claimed to forget the exceptional career he once had.[81]

One might ask whether such men, as extraordinary as they were, really merit a place in history. Overshadowed on the one hand by highly visible political appointees and on the other by departmental disarray, the officers in the field could only watch, worry, and wait until they were called upon to interpret events. That was, after all, what they were trained to do. But the interwar years were decades when they might have been more usefully assertive. As Kirk once put it, "[P]eriods of détentes are the worst because those are the times when preventive measures should be put into operation and nothing is done because everybody is too busy feeling relieved that chaos did not come."[82] In their circumspection and pessimism, they might have squandered whatever greater power they potentially had. This would not be forgotten by their successors after the terrible war was over.

BACK IN WASHINGTON, however, the European Desk continued to seed its bureaucratic garden. Roosevelt gave it a boost with his decision to normalize relations with the Soviet Union in 1933. This had been opposed for over a decade by the heavily anti-Bolshevik Eastern European Division (EE), but when normalization appeared imminent, its members did an impressive job in persuading Bullitt to drive a hard bargain. The head of this division was a legend in his day. Robert Kelley, from Somerville, Massachusetts, had won a scholarship to Harvard, where he nurtured an interest in the origins of the Crimean War, followed by a stint at the University of Paris and then back to Harvard, where he interrupted his graduate studies with army service, first in Germany and then as military attaché in Riga. In 1922, he joined the State Department and became head of EE in 1926. From his positions and memoranda, Kelley appeared to be something of a hardliner, but he was less ideologue than meticulous scholar. His views on the Soviet Union, and on its relations with the United States, came from the careful study of precedents, and were based upon the unlikely "existence of a government that is competent to discharge, and shows a disposition to discharge, its international obligations."[83]

Kelley may have derived some satisfaction knowing that after only a few months in Moscow, Bullitt was transformed into a passionate, lifelong enemy of the Soviets and would devote the rest of his career to denouncing anyone, including Roosevelt, who seemed the slightest bit agnostic about them. But in the meantime, Kelley would face not only the reversal of the line of policy he had long advocated but also the elimination of his division. In 1937, EE was merged with the Western European Division (WE) to form the new Division of European Affairs, known as Eu. Kelley was denied a promotion and sent to Turkey; his group of Soviet hands was scattered across Europe; its members' combined expertise in understanding not only the Soviet Union but also the effects of Bolshevism worldwide, diminished. They would all remain "in a sense Robert Kelley's heirs" but would not reconstitute themselves bureaucratically for another decade.[84] The effect was a certain degree of institutional ill-preparedness and a reticence to grapple with the longer-term import and trajectory of Soviet-American relations. Kennan noted a more immediate casualty—perhaps the most egregious of all: Kelley's precious collection of books, "the best library on Soviet affairs in the United States," was dissolved, with portions going to the Library of Congress, the remainder having been hidden by Kennan in the attic of the State Department.[85]

The merger or acquisition of EE did not necessarily mean a softening of attitudes toward the Soviet Union, however. One could argue that the reverse took place as former EE officers were folded into the larger bureau. Loy Henderson, for example, noted that almost everybody in Eu, at least during his time there from 1938 to 1943, "had no illusions with regard to the Soviet Union," even though many New Dealers were "inclined to look upon us in the Division of European Affairs as outmoded bureaucrats who were not able to adjust ourselves to the new world on the threshold of which we were standing and who could not see the light."[86] Rather, hostility toward the Soviet Union became less overtly ideological;

the generation trained by Kelley was too careful to allow any such biases to speak for themselves. By the late 1930s, their positions on the Soviets sounded more "pragmatic" and therefore more formidable than those of the previous generation, but they would prove no less rigid later on.

Heading the new combined division was Moffat, then forty-one years old, descendant of John Jay, one of three sons-in-law of Joseph Grew in the department, said to be the only European hand consulted by Secretary Stimson, and a well-liked member of the Union, Metropolitan, Alibi, and Burning Tree Clubs. Like Gibson, Moffat first served in Poland. Known for being extraordinarily punctual, "dependable," "unusually unexpressive," with "his precise mind, his instinct for protocol, his natural politesse, his serious feeling for precedent and the firmness of his diplomacy," Moffat was

J. Pierrepont Moffat and Cordell Hull
Houghton Library, Harvard University

> a tall man, rather heavy..., with a slightly nervous manner and a modest, inquiring expression[;] his whole appearance expresses dependability and orderly intelligence ... [and] a decidedly Victorian flavor.... He has a good brain which he suckles on European history. He is a man in all things moderate, courteous but never effusive, amiable but no back-slapper, sociable but no tea-hound. For him restraint is a virtue, but he does not carry restraint to the point where it becomes spectacular, as his superior Welles does.[87]

Like Dunn, Moffat had served as head of White House ceremonies, where "his friends dubbed him 'Pierrepontifex Moffaximus of Protocol.'"[88] He had headed WE in the 1930s and, following brief service in Australia (his consular purgatory being rather less onerous than Marriner's), took over Eu in 1937. His colleagues were overjoyed: "I can't tell you how pleased I am by the good news," wrote Hugh Gibson. "It isn't every day that things happen just as we would choose—but this time I feel that the Government is carrying out my mandate."[89] Castle likewise regarded the appointment positively as a tribute to himself: "I want officially to pat myself on the back for being convinced that you were the man to be Chief of W.E. and for exerting what little influence I had to bring about your appointment. It is a position, of course, which is very close to my heart since I held it for half my Departmental lifetime and I want it to be held by the best possible man."[90]

Many of Moffat's first days in the new job were spent in tying up the loose ends of the European disarmament talks on which he had collaborated closely with the two Hughs—Gibson and Wilson—but about which he had lately become disappointed: "It seems to me that we have deliberately put ourselves in the position occupied by England two years ago in the Ethiopian matter....Today, if the same thing happens in the Orient, it would be the United States and the United States alone that will bear the brunt. Once again Great Britain would have somebody to fight her battles for her." Wilson agreed: "It seems apparent that the idea of collective security was shattered," he wrote to Moffat in March 1938, "and it seemed to me the part of good sense to admit it."[91]

Moffat had earlier described the collapse of Credit Anstalt—the Austrian bank whose failure in 1931 precipitated the spread of the Great Depression across Europe—as a *"dégringolade."* The image stuck, and would extend presently to Europe itself. His views were consistent: War would come and America would be dragged into it, though that was not the way it ought to be. Traveling to Brussels for what would be the last of the disarmament conferences in October 1937, Moffat noted that Norman Davis, the head of the delegation, "would have liked to send me home for pessimism." He added a few months later: "Personally, I can see no cheer, though I expect that Germany will now mark time as far as other nations are concerned while continuing to burrow into Austria....The only real optimis[t] in Europe is Mr. Carr who has taken the position that Czechoslovakia is in no way threatened and is sticking to his story."[92]

Mr. Carr was Wilbur Carr, the civil servant whose long tenure as the department's head of the consular corps would end, ironically, with his appointment as minister to Prague, where he would serve until shutting the legation in 1939. "Quiet, dignified, affable, thoroughly schooled in all the intricacies of governmental and diplomatic procedure; accustomed to the frustrations of governmental routine and skilled in the arts of patience and of quiet persuasion by which alone that routine could be successfully assailed," Carr, the denizen of the consuls, supposedly was the only senior member of the State Department whom Franklin Roosevelt wanted to keep in his job.[93] But off to the epicenter of the European crisis he went, despite having almost no diplomatic experience overseas. There, recalled Kennan, he sat

> peacefully sleeping in an armchair. The servants stood respectfully behind the curtains of the dining room, not daring to wake him. The sight of the old gentleman, thus peacefully at rest in the solitary splendor of his heavily curtained salons while outside in the growing darkness a Europe seethed with fear and hatred and excitement danced its death dance all around us, struck me as a symbolic enactment of the helplessness of all forces of order and decency, at that moment, in the face of the demonic powers that history had now unleashed.[94]

Here again there was the multiple reversal of professional roles, with diplomatic officers serving in consular posts and vice versa, interspersed among political ambassadors and White House envoys. It was all, perhaps, well suited to the disorder of the late 1930s. Yet the *mot du jour* was "amalgamation"—referring initially to the ongoing fusion of the two halves of the foreign service. A decade since the passage of the Rogers Act, the adjustment continued to be knotty.[95] Luminaries such as Castle and Gibson would bemoan their fall from grace in favor of the Messersmiths and Murphys. Castle ridiculed the "new method of doing the same old things ... a lot of new and shiny labels to disguise the fact that the containers of the goods to be sold are a bit shopworn." Gibson wrote to his old comrade Norman Davis,

> While I don't want to do anything precipitate, neither do I want to mark time too long in the role of Mr. Micawber....The idea of being turned out to grass came as something of a shock, but as I have more time to reflect I am inclining more and more to the view that it may be a good thing.[96]

However, as he noted to Kate Wilson, the wife of his friend Hugh:

> Unfortunately our Government hasn't many facilities for expressing its gratitude for long years of service. Of course, in England they can make you a Grand Duke, and in France they can give you a Grand Cordon. But our people have to take it out in thoughtful kindness and commendation. I got mine in the form of a telegram which I shall hand down to Michael [his son] and his descendents, in the following terms: "It will not be necessary for you to return to Geneva!"[97]

In the hands of Moffat and his generation, amalgamation might have stood for something better, but such hands were full with a European crisis and an ever-larger piece of the bureaucratic pie. The new division by now stretched from the Atlantic to Siberia and retained jurisdiction over some thirty-two governments and multiple colonial (or quasicolonial) territories in Asia, Africa, and the Western Hemisphere, including "the Dutch East Indies ... Antarctica..., the League of Nations, the International Institute of Agriculture, the International Labor Office, and the World Court."[98] Although its members did not enjoy the level of access they would come to have in the 1950s, they more or less dominated the State Department. With the exception of the Latin Americanists, in whom Welles took a parochial special interest, the European Division was the only geographic bureau that got the undersecretary's consistent attention. Moffat, his fellow Grotonian, earned Welles's trust just as Dunn had done with Hull. This seemed to please nearly everyone, except Bullitt, of course, whose bureaucratic allies by now had dwindled to a few consuls.

The final straw for the turf-obsessed Bullitt was Roosevelt's decision to send Welles on a "peace mission" to Europe in the winter of 1940. Moffat accompanied the undersecretary to London, Paris, Rome, and Berlin and then back to Rome again. "Everybody was agog" but nobody seemed to know the real aims of the trip.[99] Welles and Roosevelt hinted at a diplomatic intent, probably the last of several "peace feelers"; others viewed it as a fact-finding mission or, more cynically, as a political stunt.[100] Little apparently came of it besides a few rather colorful conversations and a clearer sense of Europeans' conviction of America's detachment from European problems. Nevertheless, Welles formed a few definite opinions of his own. Meeting with Italian foreign minister Count Ciano, for example, in a tapestry-hung grand hall in the Quirinal Palace, Welles found Mussolini's son-in-law "agreeable" and "modest," and only witnessed the "chest out, chin up" persona upon being met with the movie cameras. Neville Chamberlain impressed and surprised him with his physical strength. David Lloyd George amused him and "spoke of President Wilson with respect, but with no particular enthusiasm, and of French statesmen with neither respect nor enthusiasm." Ernst von Weizsäcker confided *sotto voce* that Hitler was bent on war and there was nothing anybody could do about it; Hjalmar Schacht went a step further and sounded out Welles on possible American support for an anti-Hitler coup, noting in passing, "I cannot write a letter, I cannot have a conversation, I cannot telephone, I cannot move, without it being known....If what I am going to tell you now is known, I will be dead in a week." Joachim von Ribbentrop struck Welles, who made much of the man's previous career as a champagne salesman, as possessing "a completely closed mind ... also a very stupid mind. I have rarely seen a man I disliked more"; and Hermann Göring had an "incredibly ugly house." As to the great dictator himself, Welles recalled entering

with a very slow and measured tread ... a tremendously long red marble hall, of which the walls and floor are both of marble; then up a flight of excessively slippery red marble steps into a gallery which, also of red marble, has windows on one side and tapestries on the other. The gallery is lined on the tapestry side by an interminable series of sofas, each with a table and four chairs in front of them....I went with Kirk into the adjoining room, a very long drawing-room furnished with comfortable upholstered sofas and chairs, and overlooking the garden of Bismarck's old residence, in which Hitler now lives....He greeted me very pleasantly, but with great formality....

I said that the Chancellor would, of course, understand that it was the belief of my Government that if some way could be found towards a stable and lasting peace which promised security to all peoples, no nation could have to "go down," let alone all of them. For that reason I earnestly trusted that such a way and such a peace might still be found....Hitler looked at me, and remained quiet for a moment or two. He then said, "I appreciate your sincerity and that of your Government, and I am grateful for your mission. I can assure you that Germany's aim, whether it must come through war or otherwise, is a just peace." I replied by saying that I would remember the phrase the Chancellor had used. The interview then terminated.[101]

Welles had no proposals to offer, or at least there is no evidence of any. Otherwise, the trip served merely to open a few doors for the less privileged, for neither Kirk in Berlin nor Phillips in Rome had been granted visits with the respective heads of government there until Welles arrived.[102] "Diplomacy," however, was "as dead as a door nail."[103]

WELLES'S MISSION NEVERTHELESS marked a certain turning point. Within six months, France would be defeated, Bullitt would be out of a job, as would Kennedy, Bowers, and Dodd; by the end of the year, the United States itself would be preparing for war, and Welles's own days in government would be numbered. From that point on, as Bullitt acknowledged: "Harry Hopkins really ran FDR's foreign policy."[104] Welles's last great contribution was to assist in the drafting of the Atlantic Charter; the only contribution of Dunn and Eu to its recognition was later to suggest removing a quaint reference to the "Indies, the thatched villages of the South Pacific."[105] Moffat, for his part, stepped aside as soon as the action began. "1940 will rank as a pretty grim twelve months," he wrote in his diary, "but for me personally the two bright features will always be the glimpse we had together of Europe—at war to be sure but not yet irrevocably locked in the death struggle—

John Hickerson
Courtesy of Harry S. Truman Library

and of course my appointment to Canada." He took over the embassy in Ottawa in June and died shortly thereafter of a pulmonary embolism. His passing was mourned with even more sadness than Marriner's had been a half decade earlier. Welles, for one, said it was the "greatest loss the State Department could have."[106]

Replacing Moffat was Ray Atherton, another onetime architect who was known in his Paris student days as the "beau of Beaux Arts."[107] Joining the service in 1917, he had a less august lineage and was not as beloved as his predecessor, but he still did well for himself, marrying a Coolidge and then a Hunnewell, and receiving several choice posts, including Tokyo, Athens, Sofia, Copenhagen, and London, where he ran the embassy as counselor until he was recalled, reportedly, because the king complained that American diplomats should act more like Americans. But Atherton, like Moffat, was no blind Anglophile. One Briton reported, "Ray Atherton is terrified he will be put on the spot as an appeaser, and very sore with us, who, he thinks, led him to support food for France....[He] is incredibly lazy, and they all moon about gossiping ... while our civilization burns[;] ... the Atherton gang are ... defeatist."[108] By now, he, like the rest of Eu, was anything but. Most of his tenure there was spent in haggling between various cliques in the State and Treasury Departments over interpreting U.S. neutrality in ever more creative ways and in urging the division to include, for the first time, a permanent economic section. He also fought several battles with the Far Eastern Division and the Office of the Legal Adviser over jurisdiction for British and French colonies in Southeast Asia, which had begun while he was in London.[109] Atherton would staff the post until August 1943, at which point he too was sent to Canada but, unlike Moffat, lived on. He was followed in Eu by a man of much greater substance, and one who would come to rank among the most venerated founding fathers of the postwar department.

Harrison Freeman "Doc" Matthews came from an old Baltimore family. He joined the service in 1924 after graduating from Princeton and toying with a career in the navy. The nickname "Doc" derived from a college friend's satiric remark about the particular style of eyeglasses he favored. Unlike many of his colleagues, his career did not rest on a splendorous lineage or a marriage, at least not in the fiscal sense, even though his first wife, "Frisk," would prove to be a source of strength for many years. Rather, Doc got ahead by mastering his brief better than anyone else, and by getting along with them. He had been a protégé of Jefferson Caffery, a foreign service stalwart whom he considered a great judge of character, and the tradition continued downward.[110]

Doc's deputy was the son of a cotton farmer from Crawford, Texas, named John "Jack" Hickerson. Some in the department called him "Texas Bill," others, "Mr. Canada." (Hickerson was secretary of the Joint American-Canadian Defense Board.) He carved out a niche in the British Commonwealth that few dared to trespass. Yet in contrast to his later role as institutional guardian, Hickerson's reputation during these years tended toward the insecure. Castle, for example, regarded him as "fairly poisonous ... conceited," a loud talker with an "awful" wife. Even worse, Hickerson "annoys by watching closely to see whether one laughs at the proper moments and that is awkward because one sometimes prefers to cry."[111] But Hickerson, like so many others, evolved fast and far during the war, cultivating a ruthlessness beneath a genial, wry, and occasionally irreverent demeanor, particularly toward Europeans. As his close friend Ted Achilles recalled, "When Jack twists their arms, they stay twisted."[112]

Matthews and Hickerson built the wartime bureau into a formidable machine that withstood inroads from the recently bolstered wartime "functional" (i.e., nongeographic) offices and other departments. Chief among the latter were the Treasury, War Department, the Office of Strategic Services (OSS), and the Office of War Information. They also managed to mitigate the decimation of their lower ranks by sending frequent appeals for deferments of military service. The inclusion of the foreign service in the draft caused a great deal of anxiety, especially after early 1944, when deferments were handled almost entirely on a case-by-case basis. That year, only 57 percent who applied for deferment got it. It was not necessarily a blessing; some officers in Europe were caught up in the fighting and sent to internment camps, while others endured public scorn for draft dodging. One internee, Woodruff Wallner, supplied an apt motto: "On the bench as on the field."[113] Many officers had been used to what they deemed to be unfair treatment during the Depression—exams, raises, and promotions were all frozen—but the war was another matter. The department's overall appropriation in 1942, for example, rose by some $1.4 million. But this did not stem the complaints about understaffing, particularly in Eu.[114] The burdens of office had swelled more than any of them could have imagined.

4

ON THE BENCH AS ON THE FIELD

Wartime roles of diplomats—impact of the war on the State Department—dramatic successes of the "Vichy gamble" and Spanish policy—meetings of the Big Three—the refugee tragedy—postwar planning

B OB MURPHY ONCE recalled being asked by a major general, "Will you please tell me what in the hell the State Department has to do in an active theater of war?" Murphy, whose memoir carried the title *Diplomat Among Warriors*, replied that "the State Department is interested in and responsible for foreign policy.... [I]t was directly concerned in the political decisions inevitably to be made during the military operations and would have to deal with the post-war political effects of the operations."[1] But military service during World War II would prove to be a burden for many foreign service officers; again, they were eligible for the draft. Among the younger members of the service who transferred to the army were several who will figure in later chapters: Sam Reber, Julius Holmes, Jack Tuthill, Walter Stoessel. For many, wartime also presented a temptation. David Bruce, Allen Dulles, and Robert Joyce, for example, volunteered for work in the Office of Strategic Services, just formed by the Republican lawyer "Wild Bill" Donovan. A few senior members got into the act. William Phillips and Hugh Wilson both went to work for Donovan and set up the various geographic divisions of the OSS along the same lines they had once done at the State Department. Another volunteer was Bullitt, still desperate to play a role in the drama. Unsatisfied with the desk job he had been given in the War Department, Bullitt asked Donovan for permission to serve in the commandos. Denied, Bullitt then wrote to Charles de Gaulle, offering his services to the Free French. This was accepted, and Bullitt found himself back in Paris in time to enter the recently liberated American embassy, seizing the opportunity to make a speech from the balcony.[2] For his part, Bill Castle offered to help in a "behind-the-scenes capacity." Even old Huntington Wilson sent several designs for posters and stickers to the Committee to Defend America by Aiding the Allies, only to receive a polite rejection.[3]

By now there was a new senior team in the field: In London, Joe Kennedy—who

reportedly broke down once he heard that the "Germans marched into Poland....
We're afraid those God-damned Poles are going to fight, and then the fat really
will be in the fire"—left with the permanent taint of appeasement. Replacing him
was the former governor of New Hampshire, John Gilbert Winant, "a strange,
disorderly, inarticulate man," "a loner," and "an intense, melodramatic theorist,"
but, unlike Kennedy, an ardent backer of the British whose best-known line was,
"What can I do to help?" Kirk left Italy, Hugh Wilson left Berlin, and relations
with the Soviet Union were left in the capable hands of Ambassador Laurence
Steinhardt. Bowers had left his redoubt in the Pyrenees when the American
mission was reconstituted, first by Matthews and then by Alexander Weddell,
another veteran diplomat, who stepped in until 1942.[4] Meanwhile, paralysis back
in Washington had been repaired somewhat by the departure of Welles in mid-
1943 and his replacement with the director of the Lend-Lease Administration,
the steel executive and future secretary Edward Stettinius Jr. Remaining in place
were Long and Berle, joined now by Dean Acheson. Taking over for Carr after
brief service by Messersmith was G. Howland Shaw, a protégé of Castle who
was rumored to have once sought a career in the priesthood. Shaw was also a
trained sociologist and future member of the Harvard Board of Overseers. He
would remake the Division of Personnel into an incubator for analysts as well as
operators, thereby raising the intellectual bar of the foreign service: His "influence
on the younger men entering the Service was magnificent."[5] Shaw would stay
in the job until December 1944, when he quit in order to devote himself fully
to social work or, as he liked to say, "Mr. Shaw has gone back to his juvenile
delinquencies!"[6]

The mission of the department was no longer to preserve the peace but to
help win the war, which was another thing entirely. It meant several complex
strategies designed to divide or otherwise isolate the enemies of the Allies. If
victory in Europe by 1945 was partial proof of the strategies' success, so too was
the cohesion of a wartime alliance that would extend—albeit also partially—
to the postwar period. As to the war itself, there were three interrelated policy
questions to settle: What position to take toward the European dictatorships in
light of official neutrality? What response to make to the fall of France? And
what to do about the persecution of the Jews? The department's handling of the
first was reasonably successful, though it came with a price; the second was a
stupendous achievement; the third was a tragic failure.

These questions gave rise to four operational priorities by the beginning of
1942: managing the neutrals, particularly Spain, in order to ensure that they
would not enter the war on the side of the Axis; neutralizing French military
assets in North Africa, the so-called Vichy gamble; the caring and feeding of
the Anglo-American alliance; and appeasing Josef Stalin. As to the latter two,
the professional diplomats were subordinate to special envoys Harry Hopkins
and Averell Harriman as well as the president. Other government departments,
especially the military services and the Lend-Lease Administration, also played
an important diplomatic role, one too vast to recount here. With regard to the
former two missions, however, the European Desk was at the front and center.

THE END OF THE SPANISH CIVIL WAR in 1939 with the victory of Francisco

Franco's Nationalists presented a challenge for the United States. The United States had been officially neutral in the Spanish conflict, but vocal groups of Americans, including several volunteers and Ambassador Bowers, favored and assisted the Republican, or loyalist, side. "Spain is a special case, excitedly argues the *New Republic* school of professors and preachers, but back in 1917 our drum-beaters said the same thing," wrote a young Martin Hillenbrand.[7] Not so the European Division. It, and Dunn in particular, tended to favor the Nationalists. He worked hard to prevent modifications to the neutrality laws that would help their enemies, although this policy was in conflict with the presumed preferences of his superiors, including Hull and the president.[8]

Given Bowers's own tendencies, the president still probably thought it prudent to replace him with the aforementioned Weddell, a Virginian with long experience, most recently in Argentina. Weddell, however, was somewhat past his prime. A British observer described him as "behaving in a[n] ... idiotic way. He stands there, as my Nannie used to say, 'looking dazzed [*sic*] and acting silly.' He won't go and see Franco. He's frightened, the old sheep."[9] Roosevelt presently sought yet another replacement, again from the well of historians. This time he chose one of a different color. Columbia University's Carlton J. H. Hayes was a scholar of nationalism, a specialist in European, not American, history, and a devout convert to Catholicism. Hayes neither spoke Spanish nor expressed interest in the country or the job. But Roosevelt gave him little choice. Arriving in Madrid in May 1942, he set out to cultivate a fruitful relationship with Franco with two aims in mind, the first being to move Spain from a position of nonbelligerency to "benevolent neutrality" and the second to enlist Franco in a campaign of strategic denial of critical materials, namely wolfram, to the Axis. He achieved both.[10]

Hayes ran a tight ship in Madrid. He demanded the loyalty of his staff, which he usually got, and fought bitterly against the activities of outsiders, namely, propagandists in the Office of War Information and the OSS, whose contingent in Madrid included fifteen "petroleum advisers," only one of whom knew anything about the subject. Hayes was finally able to get rid of them in 1945 by using the excuse of a budget crunch.[11] Then there were the British. Hayes and his Foreign Office counterpart, Sir Samuel Hoare (of Hoare-Laval fame), detested one another.[12] The animosity flowed down the ranks. The British diplomat Frank Roberts, for example, who would soon develop a close friendship with George Kennan in Lisbon, reported his embassy's frustration with the Americans and with Lord Halifax, then British ambassador in Washington, who would not take up the Spanish problem with the president. "Generally speaking," he added, "the Americans have refused to realize that the best way to handle the Spaniards is to take great trouble and even do the Spaniards' work for them, as our Embassy have done so successfully."[13] But Hayes counseled a different approach:

> I hold no brief for the existing Spanish régime. It is not a régime with which I have any personal sympathy or under which I would wish any nation to live permanently. I feel, however, that we can afford to be patient with it for some time to come. For, if we are impatient and apply sanctions against it, we shall, in all probability, be faced with the worst kind of factional squabbling.... This, in turn, would increase, rather than diminish,

the opportunities for German intrigue in the Peninsula and might well necessitate our armed intervention.... On the other hand, if we remain patient, we can confidently expect a gradually quickening evolution of the existing régime and its domestic policy, and under present circumstances, evolution seems greatly preferable to revolution.[14]

Hayes endured considerable criticism for his attitude toward Franco, but he was adamant in seeking to "favor leaving Spain to the Spaniards so long as its government (Franco's or any other) pursues a foreign policy benevolently neutral towards us." Both Dunn and Matthews supported him steadfastly.[15] The ambassador, meanwhile, placed his faith in

the large majority of the Spanish people [who] greatly desire (1) to stay out of the international struggle, (2) to avoid recurrence of civil war, and (3) to be friendly with the English-speaking democracies, especially with the United States.... [T]hey are no menace to the peace of the world, and they are a people whose tradition and temperament are stubbornly opposed alike to domestic regimentation and to interference from abroad.[16]

His job done, Hayes would return to Columbia at the end of the war, and would never enter official service again.

IN SPAIN THERE WERE about 20,000 refugees who arrived after the "drab, undignified, and painful" fall of France.[17] While ambassador, Bullitt made desperate efforts to rally his friends in the French government and argued until almost the last minute that the French Army would prevail—indeed, he was in the middle of such a conversation with the French minister Édouard Daladier when news arrived that the Germans had breached French defenses. He presently found himself calling Dunn and Welles to report a recent aerial bombardment over Brussels: "One of the bombs dropped three hundred feet from the American Embassy...." Welles replied, "We'll put in a call to you every two hours or so.... Good luck to you, Bill."[18] Citing the precedent set by Ambassador Herrick in 1914, Bullitt took the controversial move of remaining in Paris, even though the government itself had fled to Tours and then to Bordeaux. Bullitt stood his ground long enough to serve as temporary mayor of the city in order to hand it over to the invading Germans.[19]

Doc Matthews and his family had arrived nearly three years earlier. They took a small house on the Left Bank at 14 rue Vaneau that was owned by the countess sister of the cosmeticist Elizabeth Arden. It was "beautifully proportioned ... decorated with stone heads of women, dogs and other animals protruding over the door" and with a "well-equipped kitchen ... fine library ... modern plumbing ... and one of the best chefs in Paris," who came cheap because his job prospects were limited by having been gassed in the previous war. Life at home was as good as life at work. Matthews could not have been more "pleased to belong to our beautiful embassy, with its outlook on the Place de la Concorde and its large roomy offices; and especially pleased to be in Europe, where, as they say, the action was."[20]

He was right. Having sent his family back to the States well before the final onslaught, Matthews fled with the French government to Bordeaux. Its environs were in chaos, with "thousands sleeping in the streets, all roads jammed, food scarcity," and Matthews endured what he said were the "busiest two weeks of my life—so far." He and some others, notably Douglas MacArthur II (nephew of the general) and Woody Wallner, were joined there by Anthony Drexel Biddle Jr., the "nice, genial playboy" who had been ambassador to Poland and then had moved to become Bullitt's deputy because of the latter's insistence upon remaining in Paris. (Biddle was already in France at the time as representative to the exiled Polish government.) According to Matthews, Biddle "was the last person in the world to succeed in the task" of representing American interests in such circumstances, and "the effort to keep Tony on the proper track—or any track at all—was not the least of my

American mission, Vichy
Manuscripts Division, Library of Congress

problems. At least, however, he was glad to have me write all his cables." The group hid under their desks during bomb raids and endured a number of other privations. One small perk, thanks to Biddle's reputation in certain circles, was excellent food at the Chapon Fin. Open only to special prewar clients, the owner permitted Biddle to reserve a table every night where he and his colleagues drank, soon before leaving the city, the last bottle of Château Latour 1904. Matthews's own contribution, at the request of a colleague in the French Foreign Ministry, Henri Hoppenot, was to steal away for safekeeping the original copies of the Treaties of Westphalia and Versailles. "Since Hitler had announced he would publicly burn" the latter, Matthews wrote, "I was happy to deprive him of that pleasure.... Such was my contribution to history!"[21]

Matthews and company proceeded to Vichy, where they spent a year and a half in not too unpleasant circumstances, although their boss rated the embassy second only to Moscow in being "more difficult and less promising of success."[22] They occupied a small, art deco–style building and lived at the Villa Ica instead of at the Hôtel Des Ambassadeurs in order to avoid their "chers collègues ... [who] had nothing to do but sit in the lobby, bow up and down to each other ... and to buttonhole our embassy officers in search of news or gossip. They knew quite well that we were the only ones who knew what was going on." Biddle had moved on to London, where he continued to serve as representative to the various exile governments; Bullitt, after a brief visit to Vichy, had departed for the United States in pursuit of a cabinet position; and Admiral William Leahy, later top assistant to Presidents Roosevelt and Truman, arrived as ambassador after a two-day journey from Spain through mud, snow, "chickens and vegetables" to present his credentials to Marshal Pétain. Leahy served through the middle of 1942, with orders to persuade the marshal of the Nazis' lost cause, but in reality that meant to keep Vichy as cooperative as possible. In this he more or less succeeded, probably because so many Frenchmen, including Marshal "Popeye" himself, were agreeable. Leahy's deputy, the diplomat and old comrade of Ted Marriner's, Kippy Tuck, later told the story of informing Pétain of the forthcoming North African invasion and requesting the passive response of local troops.

> The Marshal delivered a long speech referring to the historic friendship between France and America, Lafayette, etc., and protesting against the attack.... [I]t was monstrous that the United States should launch such an aggression when France was occupied and helpless. When he had finished this tirade, the Marshal accompanied Tuck to the door and shaking him by the hand said, "What I have just said represents my official attitude. But speaking as a private individual I am *delighted* by your news."[23]

Despite losing his wife to illness and enduring "constant surveillance" Leahy did his best to keep open the channels of diplomacy.[24] Out of this situation came what would be known as the Vichy gamble. It signified the refusal of the United States to break relations with the French government in the expectation that it would facilitate the North African invasion and, ultimately, military control of the Mediterranean. As with Hayes's courting of Franco, the policy brought Roosevelt and the State Department tremendous criticism, not to mention the deep distrust of Charles de Gaulle and, to a lesser extent, of his British backers. But wartime had made many converts, even the usually moralistic Cordell Hull, who said that "if he were attacked by a thug on the street and someone came to his assistance he would welcome [it] ... but he would not cease to fight and ask his unexpected collaborator to tell his name and antecedents."[25] The Vichy gamble was judged on balance to be both a military and political necessity that would be finessed politically at some later date.[26] For when American forces finally landed in North Africa, the French offered only a minimal defense; the formidable French Navy never made it into the hands of the Germans, even though much of it would have to be sunk. Some British were quietly supportive of the policy, as was the European Division. Indeed, it had originated neither in the Allied planning councils nor in the mind of the man who eventually got most of the credit, Bob Murphy (see below), but in a series of conversations Matthews had in August 1940 with Robert Marjolin and Emmanuel Monick, two French officials in Morocco who would each go on to play important roles in postwar Europe. They persuaded Matthews that the United States could offer several types of assistance to the North Africans—oil, tea, sugar, and the like—in order to gain their loyalty and occasional reciprocation, for example, in selling some cobalt before the Germans could seize it. At the time, the British and the U.S. Treasury were heavily opposed to the move, but the gamble went ahead and, according to Matthews, "paid off handsomely at the time of our North African landings."[27]

Matthews would leave Vichy in November 1941 for London, then would return to Washington to run the bureau (as noted at the end of the previous chapter) before being named ambassador to Sweden at the end of the Truman administration. His place in France would be filled by Sam Reber and Kippy Tuck; but by then the most active diplomacy was taking place in Algiers, where Bob Murphy reigned as political adviser to General Eisenhower.

Murphy has been compared to his fellow consul Messersmith in that he was one of the very few to reach the highest levels of the foreign service. But, whereas the latter was a workaholic scholar *manqué*, Murphy was in a class by himself. The grandson of German and Irish immigrants to Milwaukee, he joined the civil service in 1917, and soon attracted Carr's attention. This got him appointed to the Paris consulate. Ambassador Bullitt simply adored him. Second only to Carmel Offie (another fixer and improvisationalist extraordinaire

H. Freeman Matthews and William Leahy
Manuscripts Division, Library of Congress

plucked from the bowels of the consular corps), Murphy was Bullitt's right-hand man.[28] Murphy was subtle, quick on his feet, and extremely resourceful, confounding even the shrewd Felix Frankfurter, who recalled him as a "soft-spoken smoothie with easy charming manners, but lack of deep understanding of the forces at play."[29] Murphy would go on to serve as ambassador three more times, and then as assistant secretary and deputy undersecretary before retiring from public service at the end of 1959 and joining the Corning Glass Corporation.

Murphy moved to Algiers in early 1942, where his job was to be the political eyes and ears of both the department and Eisenhower.[30] The first task was to maintain a working relationship with the British, who mistrusted him for obvious reasons. As in Spain, they adjusted with some difficulty to being the "junior partners," although their representative in Algiers, the future prime minister, Harold Macmillan, came to get along well with the Americans.[31] Murphy bore the brunt of the mission on the ground. The experience would influence him to a degree that few others would during his long career. His deputy in the 1950s, Robert Blake, recalled that Murphy was so marked by Vichy and the unpleasant side of the French, particularly the French military, that he would never again count himself a Francophile, although one could argue that he had acquired some of their attributes: "He was not at all pro-French but also not anti-French." That was characteristic of the "mildly devious" man.[32]

The main task was to strike a deal with the French commander in North Africa and de facto French premier, Admiral Jean-François Darlan. Matthews, who "probably knew Darlan better than any other American," considered him "a complete opportunist.... He was not an admirable man; he was sly, tricky, very ambitious and power hungry and he certainly hated the British. On the other hand he had built the prewar French fleet into a highly effective well-armed and well-disciplined navy.... He was also a patriotic Frenchman."[33] With a combination of appeals and threats, the Americans pushed Darlan to do their bidding. The effort paid off, as Matthews later wrote to historian William Langer:

> Had we not fought ... at that time so vigorously at Vichy, I believe our North African expedition of 1942 would have found the Germans already installed at Bizerte, Algiers, Oran and Casablanca.... I disagree strongly with your apparent feeling that Ambassador Leahy's exhortations and warnings in the first half of 1941 did not do much good.... It was not only the good will and patience that we counted on to restrain the marshal and his advisors. It was the threat of a break in our relations which [they] so much feared and dreaded.[34]

Dealing with the opposition—especially de Gaulle—was trickier. Both Matthews and Murphy shared Roosevelt's dislike of him. Of all the American officers working on France at the time, the only one who was reported to be even the least bit open to cooperation with de Gaulle was Reber.[35] For the others, both civilian and military, the preferred candidate to lead France after the war was Henri Giraud, a less colorful but eminently more agreeable figure, the "bridegroom," as Roosevelt put it, to de Gaulle, "the temperamental bride."[36]

Supporting the Giraud camp was one more important person in the mix: Jean Monnet, the future father of the European Community, longtime collaborator of the aforementioned Marjolin and tutor to scores of Americans. Monnet's relationships with them dated back decades. As will become clear in the next several chapters, Monnet made optimal use of these relationships as a gardener would nurture a prized plot over the years. For now, suffice it to say that Monnet, in addition to setting up the joint Allied purchasing mission in Washington and convincing the Roosevelt administration to build far more planes than it ever imagined the United States could produce, successfully bolstered the resolve of his American confrères to the point where an outright choice for de Gaulle became almost inconceivable.[37] Thankfully for the bureaucrats, Roosevelt was of the same mind, although even he could not prevent, by 1943, inclusion of the Free French leader in semipartnership. Here then, for all their diplomatic successes with France in the short term, the European hands fell short on another account; de Gaulle's disaffection with Americans would reverberate for another thirty years.[38]

IF WARTIME DIPLOMACY MAY be regarded on balance as a success, the department's consular record, in spite of enormous demands, must be seen as a failure because of a permanent stain on both its reputation and that of the entire U.S. government. This was of course the resistance, both active and passive, to saving the lives of the European victims of Nazism, mainly Jews. The extensive literature on the subject has laid blame on a few individuals at higher levels of the Roosevelt administration, and rightly so, even though those occupying the next few levels down were hardly blameless.[39] Typical were stories like the one about the well-known consul Jack Erhardt, "a big, kind-hearted, hard-boiled

Brooklynite who had been a top sergeant in World War I and still spoke out of the side of his mouth," who denied a visa to a particularly insistent Rothschild, telling him on the way out to remember not to "lose his vial of cyanide."[40] Here, then, one may add another possible culprit—the policy of amalgamation mentioned in the previous chapter. There is some anecdotal evidence of a "quiet subversion" among a few low-ranking officers in the various embassies to help Jews to escape. The Berlin embassy was such a "madhouse," for example, with refugees "found in every nook and cranny" that such a bending of the rules may have been possible.[41] But the fact that so many other consuls stood in the way of so many desperate people must come down to something other than cowardice or cruelty in the face of standing orders. Whatever their inner convictions may have been, it cannot have helped the cause of heroism that so many diplomatic officers were both inexperienced and unhappy with having to perform consular duty. Ted Marriner was surely not the only one rolling over in his grave.

In ostensible charge of the refugee problem was the newly formed Special Division (1939), later called the Special War Problems Division, which had been under the direction of Messersmith and then passed to Assistant Secretary Long in September. The division also handled matters relating to enemy assets, the bulk of congressional relations, and displaced Americans and espionage cases. Long came from the Missouri gentry and had previously served in the department during the Wilson administration, making something of a name for himself in securing rights to the Pacific island of Yap in 1918.[42] During the interwar years he remained a force in the southern wing of the Democratic Party, ultimately securing in 1933 a three-year posting to the embassy in Rome, where he served until Phillips arrived after having caused a small crisis over launching a peace over- ture to Mussolini entirely on his own. Other ambassadorial possibilities having fallen through, Long reluctantly agreed to take on the job of assistant secretary, then complained repeatedly about its burdens. He found himself the target of great hostility or, as he put it, the most favored "bull's eye" of the press, especially the radical press. The publication *PM*, in a long exposé, called him "stupid and bumbling, old, narrow, limited and rich." He was also said to be inattentive and frequently absent.[43] To put things more charitably, one might note simply that Long, despite his best efforts, was not an enlightened character. "A true reading of my actual thoughts as regards both Communism and Hitlerism," he confided to his diary on the morning Germany invaded the Soviet Union, "would not be a decoration to these pages." Nor, one suspects, would be his praise for Mussolini's peaceful aims, the stabilizing effect of the *Anschluss*, and the eloquence of *Mein Kampf*, all of which appear in his diary for 1938. Long worried a great deal more about the domestic effects of ideological warfare and its capacity to place power in the hands of the wrong sort of people: "Personally, I would feel much easier about the future if we could get rid of *all* groups, blocks [sic] and special interests."[44]

In spite of his professed patriotism—he was another self-declared Jeffersonian, once calling the Destroyer-Bases deal, for example, the greatest episode of international illegality [sic] since the Louisiana Purchase—Long's wartime actions would give his country and himself a very bad name. At the top of the list was his handling of the refugee question. He raised three principal objections to a more liberal policy: that it would violate current immigration law; that the "Herculean" problem would overwhelm the capacity of the State Department and

other agencies to keep dangerous persons from entering the United States; and
that it would threaten the fragile stability and status of the remaining neutral
states through which many refugees would seek to flee. The final argument
would be buttressed from the field. Ambassador Hayes, for example, wrote as
late as May 1944 that while he "sympathized fully with the humanitarian purpose behind the establishment of the War Refugee Board," he felt "most strongly
that regardless of the importance of its work it should not be permitted to operate
in a manner which would jeopardize objectives of more immediate importance
in our war effort." Dodd meanwhile ran into trouble when one of his embassy
employees with a Jewish surname, who happened to be a sister of the prominent
journalist Herbert Bayard Swope, raised eyebrows with the Nazis, as did an officer,
Ferdinand Mayer, who turned out not to be Jewish but nevertheless caused Dodd
to question his transfer to Berlin because a Jew with the same name had recently
been dismissed from the German Foreign Ministry and Dodd feared provoking
a "racial incident."[45] Among the many other anecdotes, this one from Kennan's
Prague diary is particularly revealing of prevalent attitudes:

> At home for breakfast, I found that I myself had a refugee, a Jewish
> acquaintance who had worked many years for American interests. I
> told him that I could give him no asylum, but that as long as he was
> not demanded by the authorities he was welcome to stay there and to
> make himself at home. For over twenty-four hours he haunted the house,
> a pitiful figure of horror and despair, moving uneasily ... smoking one
> cigarette after another, too unstrung to eat or think of anything but his
> plight. His brother and sister-in-law had committed suicide together after
> Munich, and he had a strong inclination to follow suit. I pleaded with
> him ... not to choose this way out, not because I had any great optimism
> with respect to his chances for future happiness but partly on general
> Anglo-Saxon principles and partly to preserve my home from this sort of
> an unpleasantness.[46]

Wilbur Carr, who posted a guard down the road from the Prague Legation in
order to keep away visa seekers, wrote, simply, "[T]here is nothing which the
United States can do to alleviate the [Jewish] condition."[47] Carr, incidentally, was
a Christian Scientist.

The position of the State Department was that strategic, political, and even
legal priorities trumped all others, even moral ones. The only consistent objectors
to this argument in the department were the administration's assiduous refugee
envoy, the lawyer George Rublee, along with Herbert Feis and a middle-ranking
official, Robert Pell, who was charged at the time with preparing the positions at
the 1938 Evian Conference and worked tirelessly under Rublee and Roosevelt's
and Truman's envoy to the Vatican (and delegate to the conference), the former
head of U.S. Steel, Myron Taylor. Pell, whose career began as the Paris embassy's
public relations officer in the 1920s, would only find himself eased out of a job and
a marriage. Others like Bullitt and Messersmith would propose various resettlement plans, with destinations ranging from Madagascar to Alaska, Rhodesia to
the Dominican Republic, Guiana to Kenya, Paraguay to Ethiopia. None received
the enthusiastic support of Long.[48] By 1940, he would complain repeatedly about

the "assiduous" efforts of American Jews. Then in June of that year came his notorious directive:

> We can delay and effectively stop for a temporary period of indefinite length the number of immigrants into the United States. We could do this by simply advising our consuls to put every obstacle in the way and to require additional evidence and to resort to various administrative advices [sic] which would postpone and postpone and postpone the granting of visas.[49]

It would be too simplistic to ascribe this callous policy merely to deep prejudices, as widespread as they may have been. Castle's diary, for example, is riddled with nasty remarks about Jews and many other groups.[50] But prejudice alone could not sustain it. One must look deeper and ask why Roosevelt himself, known in some quarters for his philo-Semitism and having been anything but discriminatory toward Jews in his administration, would go along with turning a blind eye to the horrors. Feis, who agonized over the tragedy more than most, provided a clue in his papers. There one finds without comment a diagram of "Roosevelt's Supreme Council," a Jewish star with each point marked with the head of a network: Felix Frankfurter, Louis Brandeis, Frances Perkins, Bernard Baruch, Lincoln Filene, and Henry Morgenthau. Listed under each name are several others, including Bullitt (whose mother was Jewish), David Lilienthal, Samuel Rosenman, Fiorello La Guardia, Ben Cohen, and so on.[51] Dodd was not alone in urging various Jewish leaders to tone down their pleas for help, even going so far as to ask Colonel House to intervene with them, which prompted the wise old man to reply, "I feel certain that if Hitler is reasonable the Jews will be equally so." And Ambassador Laurence Steinhardt, one of the few of that faith in the diplomatic service, seemed obliged to denounce, according to Long, the "unfit ... lawless, scheming, defiant ... unassibilable [sic]" "Eastern Europeans," who are "just the same as the criminal Jews who crowd our police court dockets ... in short [who] have a philosophy entirely foreign to our standards of government and proper conduct in public and private life."[52] One therefore should not underestimate the pressure the president must have felt to minimize any appearance that he was taking the country to war on behalf of the Jews. In the back of his mind there probably was this fear, the notion that there were people looking under every rock in Zeeland in order to prove the Hebraic origins of the Roosevelts. And there were more recent, though ironic, memories. As late as the 1930s, it was well known that many Jews played a leading role in organizing pro-German sentiment on the eve of World War I. Finally, there was the New Deal's persistent emphasis on the competitive nature of American society: It was all about redistribution, not growth; thus Jews were the upsetters, the rootless cosmopolites, the threat to the republic. Those backing the restrictive refugee policy for whatever reason might have taken refuge in these sorts of presumptions when evidence of fifth columnists—the ostensible rationale for the greater restrictions after 1940—proved unsubstantiated. For most of these people, Feis admitted, the question really was not one of moral or philosophical debate but rather a practical matter of managing expectations amid "slightly varying degrees of caution."[53]

How much blame does the European Desk deserve? Its members were not the primary architects of the policy, but they acquiesced in it. And it happened almost entirely on their home turf. Whether they had the ability to change or subvert it meaningfully is another question. But their wartime reputations would have gained considerably in having had made a more conspicuous attempt.

FEW DIPLOMATS TOOK THE durability of the Grand Alliance for granted. Official memoranda are full of gripes, petty and not so petty, regarding the British and Soviets. Keeping the Allies happy was not the sole responsibility of the European Division, of course; it fell first to Roosevelt and his military commanders, who professed to give little thought to the postwar life of the alliance apart from their frequent mention of the Atlantic Charter as the basis for a new world order. To the extent the Allies had any precise, official war aims besides defeating the Axis, this was it.

Lower down, however, a good deal of thinking took place about what would follow the war. In the United States, it took shape in several postwar planning committees dating back, remarkably, to the autumn of 1939. By 1942, however, the "immense machine of committees and subcommittees" with its "tyranny of words" had evolved into something of a bureaucratic football between the Hull and Welles camps in the department, with Dunn shuttling between the two and an obscure economic adviser, Leo Pasvolsky, carving out an ever-expanding role for himself as planner in chief.[54] Having split, reproduced, reconfigured, and split again, the committees ultimately produced little in the way of real policies or permanent results, apart from the United Nations Charter, drafted mainly by Pasvolsky. But the process kept many people busy for many months, and it helped to refine some thinking about competing regional and global approaches to world order as well as clarifying a few war aims, particularly with regard to approaching decolonization.[55]

Henry Stimson described the scene in November 1945: "Now that the war is over, the U.S. has reached a position of power and prestige in world affairs it has never before known.... I see now, however, a tendency for us to dissipate our power and prestige perhaps from our somewhat piecemeal approach to the complexity of problems.... The nations of the world, are, at present, in an almost psychopathic state of suspicion and unease resulting from the unprecedented destruction of the war."[56] It would be Stimson, McCloy, and the War Department that took the lead in opposing Henry Morgenthau's pastoralizing plans for postwar Germany and oversaw the actual nature and timing of the surrender. Feis, by now retired from governmental service, would lend a hand, and Doc Matthews would play a critical, eleventh-hour role in securing French participation in the German occupation. The official vehicle for this and related planning was the European Advisory Commission (EAC), originating in a London meeting between Gil Winant, Anthony Eden, and the Soviet diplomat Ivan Maisky, with Kennan serving unhappily as Winant's deputy. Perhaps the only thing worthwhile that emerged from it was the Declaration on Liberated Europe, presented at Yalta and drafted largely by Dunn and his staff.[57]

Back home, more changes were happening in the department. It undertook two reorganizations in 1944 and another in 1945 in order to free hands at the higher levels from administrative duties and, according to some observers, to streamline the exercise of power on a global basis. The geographic divisions were elevated to "offices," now to be headed by assistant secretaries. The legislative and economic offices under Dean Acheson and William Clayton, the cotton magnate who had transferred over from the Office of War Mobilization, grew as well, but without the corresponding establishment of new divisions. Acheson and Clayton had a combined personal staff of sixty-three, but the latter oversaw only nine divisions, and the former, none. Dunn, by contrast, controlled fourteen divisions. The adjustment was not easy—"[E]verything is confusion here compounded with paralysis," noted Livingston Merchant, then a young economic officer—but the postwar State Department, and EUR, were born. "All of us were delighted," reported Hickerson:

> There was considerable excitement ... but everything came out all right....
> Jimmie [Dunn] is moving to the room on the second floor directly under
> one he now has. Will Clayton is taking Jimmie's rooms, plus Doc's
> room, Paul's [Culbertson] and Jamie's [Bonbright]. Doc is taking Stanley
> Hornbeck's old room (Yes, we finally got it). Hugh Cumming prepared
> fourteen different floor plans for the Office of European Affairs before
> he finally got one which would stick. Practically everybody in the Office
> moved somewhere except Old Man River Hickerson who made a lone but
> successful fight to be left alone.

"Even the walls," he noted, "were painted four new shades of green."[58]

Such small steps accompanied bigger ones abroad. Much of Europe, of course, lay in ruin, yet many Americans expected what later came to be known as a "peace dividend," and many Europeans knew it. Others probably wondered if the Americans would stay indefinitely as conquerors. Despite the victory celebrations, the time was unsettled and confused. In this respect it is worth quoting at length from one of the more thoughtful British observers of the United States, the diplomat and future ambassador in Washington, Roger Makins. Like many of his countrymen, Makins married a well-off American (the daughter of Dwight Davis, Calvin Coolidge's secretary of war and founder of a certain tennis tournament). Makins counted himself a loyal friend of the United States, especially during the intense months in Algiers, where he served as Macmillan's deputy. Yet he feared the effects of Americans' "feeling their power in the world as they never have in the past.... Superior or equal on the sea, in the air, on land, and in technical achievement, they are still conscious of inferiority in negotiation and diplomacy.... The State Department is therefore on its mettle ... constantly on guard against accusations that they are reactionary, undemocratic and, in matters of policy, merely following in the British wake."[59] Greater power brought greater obligations, particularly toward allies, but Makins would have known better than most about the dangers of familiarity breeding contempt. "There is a growing tendency" he added,

> to what might be called dotted-line diplomacy. It is probably that many
> Americans are beginning to think that British powers are waning, and
> that it is time for the heir to take over most of the estate, while keeping,

George Kennan
Holton Archive/Getty

Charles Bohlen
Time & Life Pictures/Getty

of course, the whole thing in the family as far as possible. But American actions are often due to inadvertence, lack of experience, and insufficient coordination of policy.... In a phrase, they are the actions of [a] large but unusually amiable Newfoundland dog in a boudoir full of bric-a-brac.

The Americans were not the only ones responsible, of course. For the "waning" British power,

the consequences are more serious. The subconscious awareness of dependence on American power ... sets up in the Government and the bureaucracy a permanent condition of irritation.... The result is that in Whitehall the approach to the U.S.A. and to the handling of particular questions with the Americas are too often misjudged. We are apt to select the wrong point to argue about, the wrong place to argue in, and then to use the wrong arguments. This is a pity because by the right treatment (which includes firmness at the right time) the Newfoundland dog can still be led almost anywhere we want to go.[60]

If this foreshadowed the 1956 Suez crisis, which happened immediately after Makins's term as ambassador, it was not entirely accidental. Managing the British relationship during the war had been enormously difficult. As with de Gaulle, old resentments died hard. And yet each side seemed to realize that it had little choice but to persevere—if anything, the interwar years had taught the allies that national security was no longer divisible.

The same could not have been less true with regard to the Soviet Union. Nearly everyone in EUR was clear-eyed about cooperation with the Soviets. That is, they were cynical and unenthusiastic about it. Nobody there, so far as one can tell, spoke up in favor of Stalin's request to be included in the occupation of Italy in 1943; few expressed great sympathy for his repeated pleas for the launching of the long-promised cross-channel invasion; many shared Bullitt's diagnosis that "Stalin intends to eat like a cancer into Europe so long as the war goes on, and that he hopes in the end that Germany will go Bolshevik, and that he will then be able to 'bolshevize' France and England also.... [The Soviet Union] acts to spread the area in which it can murder persons whom we regard as decent, and extend its form of tyranny."[61] Even though their office had never been reconstituted fully since its dissolution in 1937 and the Moscow mission remained a shabby "stepchild," the Soviet hands continued to set the tone in the department regarding their subject country. When it became clear that their views were not fully shared by the president, they sought to influence others, notably Hopkins and Harriman. Relations between them and the rank-and-file members of the division were good and, in Harriman's case, increasingly intimate, but it remained the case that the two groups moved in different ideological and professional orbits.[62]

An exception was Chip Bohlen. Serving as Roosevelt's interpreter at Tehran and Yalta, and then as principal adviser to both Hopkins and Harriman, Bohlen was probably the only professional Soviet hand who shared the president's determination to strike a postwar bargain with Stalin.[63] This put him at odds with his old friend Kennan and launched what would become a famous exchange in the winter of 1945 on the occasion of the latter's latest announcement that he intended to resign from the department. Kennan wrote:

> Six weeks of most intimate contact with Russian affairs have not changed anything in my conviction that Soviet political aims in Europe are not, in the main, consistent with the happiness, prosperity or stability of international life on the rest of the continent.... I fail to see why we must associate ourselves with this political program, so hostile to the interests of the Atlantic community.... We must bury Dumbarton Oaks [the United Nations, etc.] as quickly and as quietly as possible.... We should accept as an accomplished fact the complete partition of Germany.

Bohlen replied:

> As you know there is a very great deal in your exposition that I agree with ... but have you ever seriously thought through the alternatives. The constructive suggestions that you made—are frankly naïve to a degree ... as factual suggestions they are utterly impossible. Foreign policy of that kind cannot be made in a democracy. Only totalitarian states can make and carry out such policies. Furthermore, I don't for a minute believe that there has been any time in this war when we could seriously have done very differently than we did.... [T]he very simple fact remains that if we

wanted to defeat Germany we could never have even tried to keep the Soviet armies out of Eastern Europe and Germany itself.

Almost three decades later, he added:

> We went into World War II very much the way we went into World War I. If you follow our policy during World War II, you will see that almost without exception we gave priority and preference to measures which would help win the war and win it more quickly against other pressures which might have been more salutary for the future peace of the world. This, I think, was one of the expressions of our isolationist tendency.... During [Yalta] Roosevelt made a statement which I think has been very much overemphasized by some historians but nevertheless which apparently impressed Winston Churchill very much.... [H]e gave the opinion that American troops would remain in Europe only about two years.... He did not see the United States permanently having troops in Germany.... [H]e felt this was the business of the Europeans.[64]

Thus having won the war, many thoughtful Americans remained ambivalent about the peace. Here were the department's two best Soviet experts—the first trained in Germany, the other in France—reaching the end of the war with dramatically different mental maps of postwar Europe. Some people like Kennan seemed to doubt whether the United States, or the world, would be any better off with America remaining a European power; others like Bohlen fought their pessimism with the ghost of Woodrow Wilson at their side. More trustful of collective security and international institutions than some of their colleagues, they still seemed to be staring into the unknown: Would the Anglo-American alliance survive, and in what form? Would the Soviets prove worse than the Nazis? Would Europe resume its leading place in the world? Would America stay committed to Europe? Nobody knew for certain. But, as usual, Bill Bullitt had seen the vision of a European "house divided against itself," and had done so well in advance. He had written from Paris eight years before:

> I enclose herewith a photograph taken from my bedroom window. It is as good a description of Europe as any dispatch could be. You will note on the left, the eagle of the Nazis; on the right the cross of the Pope, and in the middle, the Bolshevik's hammer and sickle.[65]

There, with one eagle having supplanted another, stood matters at the end of 1945.

5

MASTERING EUROPE

Postwar recovery—onset of the Cold War—Europe as the prize—new bureaucratic constituencies—Marshall Plan—Monnet method—Atlantic movement—North Atlantic Treaty—European Defense Community

THE POTSDAM CONFERENCE, code-named "Terminal," took place in the Cecilienhof Palace outside Berlin from July 17 to August 2, 1945. It was meant to settle the unfinished business from the war, namely that concerning the postwar occupation of Germany. The conference, however, was just the beginning of a long and arduous postwar adjustment that would last, according to several accounts, into the 1960s, and one that had begun, by other accounts, as early as 1943.[1] There were some new protagonists. Harry Truman had assumed the American presidency; Winston Churchill presently would give way to Clement Attlee in Britain. But in the background there was a familiar cast of characters. Among those accompanying Truman from the State Department were Doc Matthews, Chip Bohlen, and Jimmy Dunn.

These three toured Berlin together and noted the destruction, the worst they had ever seen, according to Matthews, who also mentioned traveling in Hermann Göring's old railroad car and Bob Murphy's occupation of Ribbentrop's house. Admiral Leahy's attentions were drawn to the "fat, sloppily attired and unattractive" women who nevertheless "did perform beautifully on their violins."[2] Bohlen meanwhile, on hand to interpret for his third Big Three Conference, took time to write to his friend Isaiah Berlin about how much he missed him there.[3] Accompanying them were Ben Cohen, a bright but temperamental New Dealer who was amanuensis to the new secretary of state, former judge and legislator from South Carolina James Byrnes; undersecretary for economic affairs Will Clayton, who would go on to invent the Marshall Plan; Ambassadors Joe Davies and Averell Harriman; and a young diplomat already known as the department's best mind on Germany: James Riddleberger.

"Loyal, rather self-effacing, though sociable," "inclined not to argue against top reactionaries even when he knows they are wrong," and "worth any six men you may lose," Riddleberger was raised in Woodstock, Virginia, tended farm, laid

James Riddleberger
Courtesy of Harry S. Truman Library

bricks, painted houses, and then joined the State Department as a tariff expert in 1929 following his education at Randolph-Macon and Georgetown Universities.[4] He had served in Geneva and Berlin, as mentioned in previous chapters, overseeing, along with Jake Beam, nearly all reporting under the tutelage of Prentiss Gilbert. He, too, was struck by the decimation of the German capital in 1945: "Don't worry about being hard on the Germans," he wrote to his wife, Amelie, a Dutchwoman raised in Switzerland and Indonesia who suffered more than her share of transatlantic voyages in steerage on account of the Riddlebergers' strained finances.[5] He, Dunn, and Bohlen drafted the basic outlines for postwar Germany, including the settlement over its eastern boundary, which would be a long-lasting source of tension, and not only for Germany and Poland.[6] After all, it was Riddleberger who spent weeks before the Potsdam Conference in Washington's Shoreham Hotel briefing Byrnes, who had chaired the State Department committee on the postwar occupation of Germany and who, with Doc Matthews, had intervened unsuccessfully with the War Department to lay a stronger political foundation for the occupation zones and to forestall their hardening into new spheres of influence by having them "converge upon Berlin like slices of pie." When accused of "not having any faith in Soviet intentions," Riddleberger replied that this was "exactly right."[7]

Keeping Germany viable from one crisis to another took a heavy toll on Riddleberger's career and health. He had a serious heart attack and suffered from diabetes. He would spend so much time working obsessively on Germany that by the mid-1950s, his superiors would insist on a transfer, although that generally proved more difficult than anyone had wanted. Riddleberger really was regarded as indispensable.[8]

Planning for the postwar occupation, as noted at the end of the previous chapter, had been an extensive and disorganized process, involving multiple governments and departments, most acting separately. According to Herbert Feis, who drafted a long plan of his own, it took place without "any certain knowledge" about territorial adjustments, restitution, or the interests and policies of other Allies.[9] Providing a veneer of joint consultation, again, was the European Advisory Commission in London. But the American representative, Gil Winant, got few instructions and was not privy to the planning under way back home, despite the frustrated pleas of his deputy, Kennan, to make the ends meet between the State and War Departments. Having met 111 times for 520 hours over nearly two years, the EAC reached the tautological conclusion that "[a]ll this work has been justified by the work accomplished."[10]

Confusion also prevailed back in Washington. The various interdepartmental postwar planning committees churned out one report after another, but there was never a system in place for implementing a single set of recommendations at the wartime conferences. To the extent this took place, it happened informally through talks between Dunn, McCloy, and Matthews, but there is little evidence that they took the other planning seriously. If they did, it probably would have had less to do with substance and more with its role in keeping the various bureaucracies busy. Neither Matthews nor Bohlen, the State Department's principal delegates to the wartime conferences, was intimately involved in the planning committees. There was only Leo Pasvolsky, but then his contribution was confined to work on the United Nations. He had very little to do with the postwar settlement in Europe, especially with territorial questions. These were handled piecemeal, as it were. Harry Hopkins, who remained the top emissary to Stalin, found himself by the middle of 1945 seriously at odds with the British, with whom President Truman had failed to consult before sending Hopkins abroad to reach a Polish agreement. Nevertheless, he handled the Polish question "extremely shrewdly," at least according to Harriman.[11]

The postwar settlement would take at least another decade to iron out, whereas the most central issue—Germany—would take another two. In the meantime, the delegates at Potsdam would go through the motions of Allied consultation while voicing suspicion that the Soviets would renege on promises to permit their new client states any semblance of real autonomy, let alone independence.[12] Riddleberger, who had witnessed firsthand the effects of the Molotov-Ribbentrop Pact while serving in Berlin, was among the most pessimistic: "I didn't anticipate that there would be a high degree of cooperation, never did." Matthews for his part would blame Byrnes and especially Cohen for relying upon vague and inconclusive legalisms.[13] It would fall to Riddleberger and his colleagues in EUR to devise a basis and continuity for America's German policy that would extend from military to civilian occupation and then to vassalage. In practice, this meant acquiescence to a postwar division of the country that few of them foresaw with any precision but nonetheless became devoted to in practice once the Federal Republic had been constituted as a Western ally.

The hopes of Riddleberger and his fellow German hands for peace were always there, to be sure, but there was also the deep fear of losing German allegiances, and that must have been primary in their thoughts. For the most part, he and other German hands came to accept by the middle of 1946 that some division of the country would have to happen. It was, in spite of their initial preference, necessary because "we need Germany and the Germans desperately; but they betrayed civilization and had to be destroyed. It is with that situation which we must now contend as best we can." Indeed, "God had broken Germany across his knee—at the River Elbe." It would remain so for the foreseeable future.[14]

MATTHEWS, DUNN, AND RIDDLEBERGER stopped in Frankfurt to see General Lucius Clay on their way back from Potsdam, and they told him in direct terms that the Soviets had no intention of cooperating with their fellow occupiers. Potsdam had underscored as much. But of course the trio, particularly Riddleberger, hardly needed to be convinced. Second only to his colleagues on the Soviet Desk, he and his fellow German hands became the most ardent Cold Warriors.[15]

Who were these German hands? They comprised roughly two generations: the diplomats whose experience dated back to before World War II and the next generation of consuls who came to Europe either as military or civilian agents of the occupation, along with another group of roughly the same age (late twenties to early forties) that provided legal, economic, and other forms of technical advice to the occupation authorities. This mixture mirrored the postwar configuration of EUR itself and its various subcultures. Each of the groups, moreover, had strong ties to the U.S. military and would contribute to the militarization of American foreign policy that would accompany the Cold War. And each would be forced into further amalgamation with one another, following the prewar bureaucratic pattern, only now to an even greater extent. The effects of such mergers will be discussed momentarily; first, there is a bit more to say about the initial generation of diplomats—those who experienced directly in *their* late twenties the decline and destruction of bourgeois Europe—and to note its effect upon their postwar attitudes.

One of them was Loy Henderson, an Arkansas minister's son whose twin brother, Roy, died as a teenager. After completing his studies at Northwestern University, Henderson went to Europe to help repatriate German prisoners for the Red Cross in 1918. From there, he joined the foreign service, married a Latvian woman, and took up Russian. A few years older than Kennan and Bohlen, he became something of an elder brother to them in Moscow, where, as embassy counselor, he was the only member of Bullitt's staff whom the perfectionist ambassador did not criticize behind his back. Like nearly all the early Russia hands, Henderson transmitted wisdom and certainty about the nature of the Soviet Union. Yet he was transferred out of his bailiwick to Iraq and then to Washington to serve in the Bureau of Near Eastern Affairs, which then held jurisdiction over Greece and Turkey. On February 21, 1947, at 3:00 P.M., he received two notes, one pertaining to each country, from the counselor of the British embassy. He called Jack Hickerson and the two went immediately to see Undersecretary Acheson (Secretary Marshall having left for the weekend) and showed him the notes, which stated the cessation of British aid to these two frontline states. "I want you to get your staff together and work like hell over the weekend," Acheson told them. And so, a few steps removed from EUR, the Truman Doctrine was born.[16]

Was this really how the Cold War began? There are two myths, now largely discredited by historians but still present in the minds of many people who read about the United States and the world at mid-century. The first is that President Roosevelt and his left-leaning advisers betrayed the Poles and other Central Europeans, and thereby brought about an unnecessary rupture by a premature (or criminal) appeasement of Stalin. To the extent the State Department participated in such acts, namely, at the conferences of the Big Three, it was culpable in their outcome. Or at least so claimed the McCarthyites and their supporters, who spent nearly a decade destroying many foreign service careers. The second myth came predictably from the other side of the ideological spectrum, namely, that reactionaries in the State Department, particularly in EUR, obstructed the good-faith efforts of Roosevelt to strike a durable settlement with Stalin, and then, along with fellow travelers in the Pentagon and Congress, brainwashed a gullible Harry Truman into bringing on a costly fifty-year conflict that might otherwise have been avoided.

The point in recalling these myths is not to launch a new round of Cold War revisionism on the backs of some nearly forgotten bureaucrats. Rather, it is to underscore the historical consequences of both sets of charges. They—and the fears accompanying them—preyed heavily on the minds of many officials who grappled with the problems of the postwar years. Despite their having seen the Cold War coming, there was little they could do to stop it.[17] Their purpose then, as Matthews noted when he asked Kennan in early 1946 to draft what became famous as the Long Telegram, was, first and foremost, to understand and adapt to it.

Asking how this or that diplomat on the ground changed the course of Cold War history therefore does little to illuminate the central significance of EUR during these years. Its role was to redirect thinking and to defend its priorities. Accordingly, EUR made three main contributions: First, it kept the focus of policymakers on Europe and helped to transform the "loss" of China and the Korean War into advantages in Europe; second, it retained a role for the State Department in the implementation of the Marshall Plan and related programs and, in the process, helped to ensure that European integration remained bound to Cold War imperatives; and third, it helped to minimize the distraction of non-European questions, particularly decolonization, and, notably, the ill effects of the Suez adventure, thereby solidifying the Atlantic Alliance, so that few would question its existence by the time Dwight Eisenhower left the White House in 1961. All the while, it would cultivate the ranks of its devoted officers and their reputation of first among equals. They, in turn, would become ever more "transatlantic" in their lives and outlook, much as Europeans would themselves.

At the same time, prevailing views toward the Cold War and the rebirth of "Europe" seemed to stand in opposition to one another. Within the department, the Cold War was seen as a fact of life that demanded the full commitment of the United States.[18] This opinion was held particularly strongly by old-line officers such as Sam Reber and Jimmy Dunn, then serving in Rome, and Bob Murphy, Jimmie Riddleberger, and Jake Beam in Berlin, who watched it unfold (and nearly explode) on the ground.[19] Few could foresee it ending anytime soon; yet few regarded it as permanent; most said it would end somehow, someday. The unity of Europe might result, but many of them were less enthusiastic about that. Of course Western unity was essential to winning the Cold War; and to the extent it furthered European unification, neither was a bad thing. But the inherent value of unification was less evident. There was no guarantee that a united Europe, especially if it came to resemble a single political unit like the United States, would remain a permanent ally or even a friend. Stated differently, the official mind of EUR was "Atlanticist" before it was "Europeanist," placing transatlantic over pan-European solidarity while casting the latter as subordinate to the former.[20] Many in EUR, especially the German hands, began to warn over the course of the 1950s that the pace and appeal of European integration, especially political integration, could vitiate the Western unity needed to win the Cold War because European unity implicitly meant all of Europe, including the East, but not necessarily the United States and Canada. The vision the Atlanticists inherited from the previous generation was of a free and democratic Europe, without divisions and wars. They cast the Cold War, like the two world wars before it, as a dire but still temporary condition that had to be endured and eventually surmounted rather than be allowed to redraw the map of Europe forever. Europeanists, however, had a different aim: that is, of a strong, united, and peaceful Europe, allied with other nations or groups of nations, but not necessarily as part of a single community with North America. To the extent the demands of the Cold War abetted the rebirth of Europe, the Europeanists were all for waging it. But the way they related geopolitical ends to means was very much the reverse of that endorsed by the Atlanticists.

Of course, there were Atlanticists and Europeanists on both sides of the Atlantic; the distinction was more political than purely geographic. And few people in either camp worried seriously about it during the salad days of the late 1940s and early 1950s. As Chapter 7 will reveal, it only became a serious source of intramural warfare after 1958. Within EUR itself, however, the lines were drawn as soon as the bureau took over primary responsibility for tracking and furthering both European federalism and the North Atlantic Alliance. They would play out in a series of turf battles between and among foreign and civil services, and country and functional specialists. A number of such battles were caused by the institution-building frenzy of the immediate postwar years, and the accompanying rise to prominence of this latter group of diplomatic *arrivistes*, which came to include German as well as non-German hands, as will soon become apparent. The functionalists, as one member of EUR recalled, soon were "all walking around looking like cats fairly stuffed with canaries."[21] The story did not end there. Just as it had during the war, EUR moved to exploit the opportunities afforded by such cleavages, positioning itself repeatedly as the most trusted repository of institutional wisdom and common sense, and which also happened to have jurisdiction over one of the most important parts of the world. Even self-important functionalists could be co-opted. If amalgamation was to continue, EUR would be only too happy to lead it.

The German hands were at the center of that story. Before the war, there was no established German Desk or corps of experts, and most of the bureau's talent gravitated to France. During the war, of course, the State Department drew on the few German specialists it had to plan for the aftermath, although, again, most of the initiative for running German affairs rested elsewhere, primarily in the War Department. The few specialists at State were men like Riddleberger and Beam, who had served in Germany before the war. Kennan, whose spoken German was reported to be the most fluent in the department, was also considered a specialist, but more by inclination than vocation. He, like Murphy, had grown up in heavily German Milwaukee and, as noted in the previous chapter, his Russian training had taken place in Germany, as Bohlen's had in France, and so Germany retained a special, formative pull on his mind, just as Bohlen, despite family ties to the Krupp dynasty, had reserved a special spot in his heart for the French since childhood.

Following the war, the army named General Clay as head of the occupation forces in Germany and acceded to the appointment of Murphy as his political adviser. Accompanying Murphy at various points were Riddleberger, Beam, Reber, and another well-liked German hand, Perry Laukhuff. They helped Clay to fix occupation policies upon a combination of leniency toward the Germans and rigidity toward the Soviets.[22] Their relationship with the occupation authorities, and to their bosses in State, was complex and often tense. Clay was known to disdain diplomats and to go out of his way to exclude them from decisions. But the bias never seemed to apply to the individual diplomats with whom he worked, particularly Riddleberger; nor were they known to put Clay's staff on the defensive or to seek to undercut him. Indeed, there appeared at times to be more tension between the economic and political sections within the State Department than between either and the military authorities, if only because it was clear who ultimately was in charge.[23] The institutional division of labor in Germany also meant that the diplomats led and oversaw working relationships with the middle-tier German bureaucrats and rising politicians like Willy Brandt as well as with the other occupation authorities. Riddleberger, who spoke good French as well as German, worked especially hard with his French counterparts, who otherwise found Clay difficult.[24]

In 1949, the occupation transferred to the civilian control of High Commissioner Jack McCloy, otherwise known as "Herr Commissar to Deutschland." Under him, the relationship with the State Department would become even closer, despite McCloy's long-standing distrust of its imaginative capacity. The shift of authority from Clay to McCloy therefore might have seemed like moving to "the Republican Party from the Democrats after a victorious presidential campaign"; but Riddleberger would remain in place.[25] This meant his promotion to ministerial rank, rare for the mere head of a political affairs department in an embassy but necessary because Riddleberger was the senior career officer on the spot, and his British and French opposite numbers carried such rank.[26] Back at the department, the "set-up to handle German affairs ... look[ed] like a Rube Goldberg cartoon. The fact that it has worked so well as it has is due to Jimmy's knowledge of Germany, his patience and his firmness."[27] The burden of the "curious amalgam" of German affairs eventually grew so heavy that a new bureau, nominally separate from EUR, was established, headed initially by a military officer, Hank Byroade. He had been the Pentagon's "leg man" on Berlin, working side by side with his counterpart in State, Bohlen. Following the establishment of the new bureau there, Byroade would shed his uniform to run German affairs during these critical years.[28]

GER, as it was known, did for the German hands what Robert Kelley's old shop once did for the Soviet experts. By the time GER was reintegrated into EUR in 1952, it had launched a corps of officers who would keep vigilant watch over German policy throughout the 1950s and into the 1960s. GER mirrored EUR in the sense that it had parallel political and economic offices, the former run by Laukhuff and the latter by Jacques Reinstein, a member of the Miriam Camp circle (see below). Like their Soviet counterparts, the German hands were a tightly knit group. One could leave for occasional service in Eastern Europe or in one of the major EUR capitals, but few outsiders could ever get in unless they were handpicked at the very beginning of their careers.

The next two generations of German hands got their start here, either in GER itself or in occupied Germany.[29] Jock Dean, who will reappear in Chapter 9, for example, was among the initial group of foreign service officers taking over occupation duties from the army, a turnover that happened in the course of a single week. Officers like Dean were posted in small villages and charged with everything from helping to get the sewer systems to work, to hunting down Nazi officials, to keeping watch on the political activities of local Communists. The impact such power and authority had on these young officers—many just out of the war and serving in their first posts—cannot be emphasized too heavily. Like the subsequent generation of young officers sent to remote villages in Vietnam, many emerged from the experience with "large chips on their shoulders." They acted as though they could do just about anything. But in contrast with those of the Vietnam generation, the experiences of these officers had been over-whelmingly positive, if tough. They had, after all, helped to convert the largest country at the heart of Europe into a loyal, democratic, and prosperous American ally. There seemed little else they could not accomplish. They were, therefore, a supremely confident and even idealistic group of people.[30]

A SIMILAR CASE COULD BE made for another noteworthy cohort that arrived on the European scene soon after the war. This was the staff and representatives of the European Recovery Program—the Marshall Plan, known formally as the European Cooperation Administration (ECA). There were surprisingly few German hands in this "glamour agency"—Riddleberger (briefly) and the young foreign service officer Russell Fessenden being the only notable ones. Those who had not fought in the war served in wartime agencies like the Strategic Bombing Survey, the Office of War Mobilization, and the OSS. Most were well educated, well connected, and very keen—in every sense the best and the brightest of their day. Their counterparts in the State Department, especially those who had remained in the foreign service during the war, were initially aghast at the *braggadocio* of these people. Arthur Hartman, who dropped out of Harvard Law School to join them, recalled the shock of some diplomats upon hearing of Marshall Planners calling up ministers on the telephone or staying out until all hours with students, journalists, and trade unionists. "[T]hey got into the habit of working with Europeans," recalled George Ball, "and they found it ... very congenial, and they began to develop a certain sympathy for the people they were working with."[31] It was only a matter of time before regular foreign service officers were regarded as irresponsible if they did not jump on the bandwagon:

Our Uncle which art in America
Sam be thy name
Thy navy come, thy will be done
In London as 'tis in Washington
Give us this day our Marshall aid
And forgive us our un-American activities
As we forgive your American activities again.
And lead us not into Socialism,
But deliver us from Communism,
For thine is our Kingdom
The Atom-power and the Tory
For ever and ever
G-men[32]

The reaction of EUR to the Marshall Plan was mixed. The idea for it did not originate there but in Will Clayton's economic bureau and in Kennan's new policy planning staff, which Secretary Marshall established in 1947. EUR made almost no contribution to it, initially, and was kept at arm's length from its operations. The impetus and support for the plan came from higher up: from Clayton, Marshall, Acheson, Harriman, and Robert Lovett, the former Brown Brothers banker and colleague of McCloy's in the War Department, now at State as undersecretary. But EUR was not wholly uninvolved or unsupportive. It backed the rest of the department in arguing that the ECA remain nominally independent and in resisting the effort of the Budget Bureau to combine offices, but still sought to maintain some control over the new agency.[33]

Zeal could still be contagious, and disorienting. Several in the bureau got so caught up in it that they were uncharacteristically slow to anticipate Soviet hostility to the program, which raised eyebrows elsewhere. The columnist Joe Alsop reported, for example, that there was "no spadework, no education.... Everyone in the Department, including Chip, expected Soviet overtures for some sort of settlement after passage of the Marshall Plan.... But now they are all really frightened."[34] Over time, fitting a Cold War truss onto the Marshall Plan fed the uncertainty of people like Bohlen over the extent to which the United States should take the lead in shaping European affairs as well as doubts over what the proper balance between national and regional policies should be. A forward, regional approach, so long as it appeared to place the heaviest emphasis on German recovery, risked inducing the very resurgence of German domination it sought to prevent by failing, according to Bohlen, to press the British to integrate more deeply with their European neighbors. This, in turn, was thought to impede European recovery.[35] Postwar Britons still entertained the idea that parts of their empire could survive alongside a preferred role for itself (and Canada) in the pantheon of America's relationships. The prospects of an Anglo-American condominium toward, if not over, Europe worried Bohlen considerably and provoked another one of his instructive jousts with Kennan. Here is Bohlen in October 1949:

> The Washington talks with the British and Canadians, the manner in which the British devalued [the pound], and a number of other things have caused the French to feel that while we are still giving lip-service to ... the general unification of Europe, in reality, we are as a matter of basic policy envisaging future developments more along the line of Anglo-American partnership, with the continent ... as a sort of junior partner.

The problem with this, as Bohlen stated it, was not simply one of national preferences but also one of regional cohesion. He continued:

> If ... we come to the conclusion that realistically it is impossible to effect any real economic integration of Great Britain with Western Europe, then we will be confronted with the fundamentally artificial task of attempting to separate the economic from the political and military.... I can only tell you my strong conviction that if it becomes evident that we are creating an Anglo-American-Canadian bloc as a political reality in our European

policy we will not be able to hold on to the nations of Western Europe very long.

To that, Kennan replied:

> You say now that the French would have to be sure that the U.S. special economic relationship with the U.K. does not put the latter in a favored position regarding the continent. I really do not know what can be meant by this. Would the French prefer to have the British dollar drain progress *more* rapidly than it is progressing? Do they think that the continent has something to gain from the blows which are going to fall upon the entire non-communist world within the coming months from the disintegration of the British financial system?

For Kennan, therefore, the question had everything to do with practical necessities. Yet he came to the opposite conclusion about the triangular relationship between America, Britain, and Europe:

> [Y]ou say the French will want to be sure that Germany will not be the American pet in economic matters to the detriment of France and other western neighbors. Again, this sort of suggestion leaves me with a feeling of helplessness.

Bohlen, sounding annoyed at being tarred again with the brush of Francophilia, rejoined:

> I think we would greatly clarify the issues if we would recognize that [European integration] does represent a departure from previous policy and that there is a very important and fundamental difference of opinion between us as to the wisdom of such a departure.... [T]here may lie one of the sources of our difference in opinion: that is, the difference between intention and result. Regardless of the intention, I think the result of the full implementation of the concept outlined ... would inevitably be a further weakening and even "desolidarization" of the U.K. from the continent.

Thus, to Bohlen, it was not so much a question of balancing the interests of the various European powers but more a problem of altering the entire nature of their relationship with one another, and with the United States. For this, the full commitment of Britain to the Continent was essential. He added:

> There is, however, a much more fundamental fallacy which brings us to the ... thesis that there can be a feasible European integration without British participation to the maximum degree possible.... There is not enough potential economic and military strength on the continent alone to counter-balance in the future the power of a revived Western Germany and certainly not of a revived and unified Germany.

The *Realpolitiker* Kennan would remain unconvinced:

> You refer to the fallacy in the belief that without the U.K. the Continental countries would go more rapidly and farther in the direction of integration. I think you are probably right; but is that the question? The point is whether with the U.K. they *could* go farther? ... The British and French are peripheral military powers of Eurasia.... Without the Germans on our side ... we will not succeed in creating an adequate military balance to support our political policies.... [T]he U.S. is someday going to end up in a cruel dilemma with respect to the complex of Russia, Germany and western Europe.... I am afraid that what you are recommending, and what we are going to do, will engage our responsibility to an unsound approach and will tie our hands for the future in ways that we may bitterly regret.[36]

This exchange, like the one excerpted in the previous chapter, appeared to confirm a State Department truism: If you wanted a first-rate analysis of a problem, you would go to Kennan; if you wanted to know what to do about it, you would go to Bohlen.[37] But beyond that, it spoke to an important, larger question, namely, to what extent was the Marshall Plan a self-conscious agent of European unification, of Cold War alliance—of either or both? Historians have been asking and answering that question for a long time. From the point of view of the State Department, and especially EUR once it became a loyal convert, the Marshall Plan was the means to an end—recovery, peace, and stability in Europe, and an insurance policy against Communism. Its specific utility for European integration was important but secondary. "It was only in the second year of the Marshall Plan," recalled one of its staffers, the former Harvard Business School professor and later ambassador Linc Gordon, "that interest shifted to more far-reaching economic integration in Europe.... [E]ven at this stage there was no overt appeal for supranationality or federation."[38] The latter was regarded as premature, which reinforced EUR's opportunistic attitude toward European unity and an approach to "be largely one of obtaining clarification rather than making positive suggestions ... [and] limited to matters of broad importance."[39] This, rather than a deterministic, almost messianic pan-Europeanism, was the legacy handed down to EUR from the interwar period, which it passed on to the newly acquired proconsular role of the U.S. government in Europe. One recalls the advice of Hugh Wilson from the 1930s (referring to, of all things, *Mein Kampf*): "As a matter of fact, few people in the world have 'ultimate objectives'. The great mass are opportunists to seize the next possible step."[40] The latest strategy was, in other words, more temporal than ontological, and not nearly as self-evident to those on the ground as it would appear to later chroniclers. To most at the time, the policy just seemed to be heading in the right direction.

Relations between most embassies and the Marshall Planners were generally positive, but rarely intimate and occasionally resentful. Tom Finletter in London and James Zellerbach in Rome were both strong personalities, but each managed to devise an acceptable division of labor with their respective ambassadors, Lew Douglas and Jimmy Dunn, as with Selden Chapin in the Netherlands.[41] Chapin claimed he had no problems at all with the ECA people but, like Dunn, acquiesced

William Tomlinson and Jean Monnet
© European Commission, courtesy of
the Fondation Jean Monnet pour l'Europe

to the view (attributed to the historian Basil Rauch), that the "pen that hovers over Uncle Sam's checkbook is mightier than the striped pants." Others did not adjust as easily. In Paris, Ambassador Jefferson Caffery, nearing the end of his career, seemed to want to have little to do with the ECA and all the other acronyms sprouting through his turf. His relations with David Bruce were notably cool, and it was Bruce, then heading the Marshall mission in Paris, not Caffery, whose approval was solicited each time the French formed a new cabinet. "I saw [Prime Minister Robert] Schuman a few minutes ago on his way to a Cabinet meeting," Caffery reported dismissively; "Schuman observed: 'Everything hinges on reducing prices.'"[42] So much for high politics. Will Clayton, for whom prices, high or low, mattered a great deal, noted the differences in personality:

Caffery was tight as a knot on a log! It's a shame to have a fellow like that, putting on such a show. I had an office in the American Embassy when I was in Paris and when I'd ask Caffery to come see me about something he would send in his Military Guard to me ahead of him to announce that he was coming, although we were in the same building! Also he always kept in tow two or three minions who'd salute you at the front door as you came into the Embassy ... so that when he came out of his office one would hand him his hat and the other his cane.... His residence was something out of this world—six lackeys clicking their heels at his orders, 4 butlers for 6 people at lunch.... If anything went on in C's head you'd never know what it was, all he does is nod acquiescence.... Some fellows think that as long as they don't stick their necks out they're all right in the diplomatic service.... Jean Monnet told me that the French didn't appreciate, didn't approve of the style Caffery put on.[43]

For his part, Harriman, now head of the ECA in Europe, was said to insist upon being accorded ministerial rank everywhere he went.[44]

From the perspective of EUR, the depiction of the Marshall Plan as a masterful intersection of economic self-interest and Cold War logic at a fortunate conjunction of the more salient points of the Bohlen and Kennan debate is rather ahistorical. It combined elements of both, but again was designed mainly to boost the confidence of the Europeans and to reintegrate their countries, someday, into a prosperous world economy. For this reason, a great part of the Marshall Plan's emphasis—and this, too, tends to be overlooked—was on the deference it paid to European wishes, demands, and political arrangements; that is, it was less propaganda per se than "adult education on an international scale."[45] The emphasis was as much on the adult as it was on the education. That it succeeded to the extent it did was due not only to financial largesse, political nous, and hard work but also to the pragmatic, and occasionally skeptical, prodding on the part of the department's European hands to tailor the effort to European realities and practices, or simply to play it slow and cautiously, allowing form to shape substance.[46] This made it possible for the otherwise disruptive injection of new blood, enthusiasm, and expertise—especially in economics—to the foreign representation of the United States to proceed successfully. Several leading members in EUR would emerge from this group of "colonels."[47] Their approach to European affairs was, accordingly, more proactive than that of their predecessors. Europe would remain a field of creative potentialities as well as a source of concern; now for the first time it also was manifest as a joint project. To some this was nothing less than Europe's "spiritual salvation."[48] To EUR, it became business as usual.

BOTH THE GENESIS AND IMPLEMENTATION of the European project passed as much from above as from below.[49] Here something should be said about the man who probably did the most to inspire the particular vision of transatlantic solidarity that came to dominate the postwar period. He was Jean Monnet. The literature on this fascinating French cognac merchant is vast. Most of it has focused justifiably on his role in giving birth to the European movement, resulting eventually in the European Community, later Union. Less is known, at least in the United States, about his important role in reinventing the methods and outlook of American diplomacy. He did this through the clever, strategic cultivation—one is tempted to say manipulation, or as the German statesman Walter Hallstein once put it, the "co-conspiracy"—of individuals and groups of like-minded people in important positions. And he did it with gentle but clever and persistent persuasion. The "Monnet method," according to one acolyte, Stanley Cleveland, "was quite special." "Monnet never wrote anything in his life," he recalled. "He developed his ideas and let other people write them up for him. But whenever Monnet attacked a new problem he would gather a bunch of people around him.... He would begin a sort of nonstop *Kaffeeklatsch*." Then ideas and policies would take on lives of their own. The origins of his technique have long been speculated upon, but several people who knew him well attributed it to his early wanderings as a salesman around North America at the beginning of the century. In some respects, then, Monnet was as much American as European, and for that reason his long-standing friend, lawyer, and co-conspirator, George Ball, had the band play the "Battle Hymn of the Republic" at his funeral.[50] Of his many talents, Monnet's instinct for targeting the right person at the right time was the most vital. As Cleveland put it, "[T]he people who allowed themselves to be used by Monnet are almost legion." For others he had little time. Ball, for example, often tried to get him together with Adlai Stevenson; Monnet was not interested.[51]

Monnet's real skill, however, was that he just "made so much sense."[52] During World War I, Monnet gained American backing for the joint supply mission he led for France and Britain. Following a stint in the League of Nations, he went into business in San Francisco and on Wall Street, where he grew close to the Dulles and Dillon families, and several other future collaborators. He was especially friendly with McCloy. The two had similar entrepreneurial tendencies and trajectories: McCloy had worked his way through Amherst and Harvard Law, and then fell under the wing of Paul Cravath in New York, where he was advised by his patron, George Wharton Pepper, to practice law there rather than in his hometown of Philadelphia because family connections, which McCloy lacked, counted for too much in the city of brotherly love. (McCloy's father had died when he was a boy and his mother became a hairdresser to support the family.) Monnet's longtime friend, the brilliant lawyer Donald Swatland, also worked at Cravath, whose Paris offices at 3 rue Taitbout were run by McCloy. Nearby was Allen Dulles, who had left the foreign service and joined his brother's firm, Sullivan & Cromwell. McCloy's network grew wide and deep. By now he had married Ellen Zinsser, whose sister married Lew Douglas, his Amherst roommate and later Congressman and ambassador; the Zinssers had extensive family in Germany; one cousin was married to Konrad Adenauer. McCloy himself became an expert on Germans, particularly German spies, through his work investigating the "Black Tom" sabotage case from World War I (the main culprit of which, Paul Hilken, was the uncle and namesake of Paul Nitze). That effort led ultimately to his hiring by Henry Stimson to work alongside his friend Bob Lovett in the War Department. Together the two were known there as the "imps of Satan."[53]

For his part, another war led Monnet back to Washington and to Harry Hopkins and Felix Frankfurter, with whom he coined the term "arsenal of democracy" and, as mentioned already, provided critical encouragement and assistance with wartime production and the tangle of the French in exile. Following the war, he enlisted the political and financial support from America for the nascent European Coal and Steel Community, which he headed, and for the other institutional kernels of European integration. Behind all of these, and so many other efforts, was a simple idea. That idea—a united Europe—was many centuries old, of course. In the United States it dated back to George Washington. As noted in Chapter 1, there were many more recent promoters of the European Movement—Winston Churchill and Richard Coudenhove-Kalergi, for example, but none had the enduring influence of Monnet.[54]

Of all the prominent Americans whom he considered intimates, none (with the possible exception of Ball) was closer to Monnet than David Bruce. Bruce may not have been, as his biographer claimed, "the last American aristocrat," but he was, nonetheless, an exceptional figure: "a Virginian with a beautiful voice and superb presence ... immensely shrewd, very experienced, a person of enormous cultivation and knowledge, with perfect manners ... as skilled a diplomat as one could ever hope to meet."[55] The only American to serve as ambassador to Bonn, London, Paris, and NATO—as well as heading up the first liaison office in Beijing—Bruce also, it is important to note here, was the first American delegate to Monnet's High Authority, the office directing the Coal and Steel Community. Previously, he had been the Paris representative of the Marshall Plan before becoming ambassador there in his own right. Throughout this period he met and corresponded with Monnet almost daily. Without Bruce, Monnet later wrote, "I should never have succeeded."[56]

France had been Bruce's first love even though he was known to joke that his greatest ambition was to end his government career where it had begun—

David Bruce with the Confrérie des Chevaliers du Tastevin
U.S. Information Service, courtesy of Bertrand Celce

as vice consul in Rome. Of Bruce's original foreign service class of fourteen, only four remained by late 1940s, the rest "whittled down by death, drink, and disillusion."[57] But this diplomat's diplomat did not remain a career foreign service officer, despite having been encouraged early on by Billy Phillips, who called him "as fine a type of young American as could be found."[58] He had fought in France during World War I ("One sees mud, thinks mud, and, if the rain continues, will eat mud"), then joined the department in 1926 soon after marrying Ailsa Mellon, the daughter of the treasury secretary and said to be the richest woman in America. She turned out to be both unfaithful and unstable; Bruce divorced her in 1945 but remained on good terms with the family, especially with her brother Paul. Bruce himself was not lacking for money; he came from the Chesapeake gentry; his father was a senator and landowner. He grew up at Staunton Hill, the family estate in Virginia, and in Baltimore, where he rode to school in a horse-drawn "barge" with a young Doc Matthews.[59] After just a few years in the foreign service, Bruce went to Wall Street to work for Averell Harriman, and not for the last time.

There were many qualities about Bruce that impressed people, but high among them had to be his taste in food and drink. "You have asked me to select my favorite dish," he once was asked:

This is ... a crafty question. So much depends on one's mood, one's companions, one's physical condition.... I can recollect very well at one time living for ten days on tins of Portuguese sardines, with a ration of one can each day. Nothing since, in retrospect, has ever seemed as delicious.... On another occasion I subsisted for a week on a diet of highly-spiced, dry, cold sausages, thoroughly impregnated with garlic and accompanied by a rough Spanish wine carried in puncheons which flapped along the flanks of a sweating mule.

His favorites also included American dishes: "Virginia ham ... diamond-back terrapin ... a wood duck, fed on acorns ... creamed kidneys, resting on golden waffles ... stewed chicken livers, with rich brown sauce and hot buttered rolls ... Shrimps Norfolk, and the innumerable ways of preparing crabs, open up vistas that perhaps are best, for the moment at least, forgotten."[60] A typical diary entry for 1949 reads: "We arrived back late for dinner, and found Piggy Warburg and Lew Douglas waiting for us. The Achesons, Harrimans and ourselves were the others who tasted what the Chef, Robert, apparently considered a simple Sunday night dinner—onion soup, a timbale of Lobster with thick wine sauce, chicken, salad, cheese, peach melba, cocktails (before), Clos des Mouches 1945, Grand Échezeaux 1937, magnums of Moët and Chandon 1941, Mirabelle, Cognac, Armagnac, cigars, etc." Bruce's own wine cellar held over 4,000 bottles and supposedly set the record for allotted space at his Washington, D.C., storage company. And there were the visual pleasures, particularly those afforded by the wives of his deputies. He recalled the face of Elsie Lyon, wife of Cecil and daughter of Joseph Grew, for example, as "one of those international affairs of bones so well coordinated she might be an aristocrat of any occidental race."[61] Above all, Bruce, like Alexander Kirk, was cultivator of his own refined character. No man looked so much the representative of a great republic as Bruce did. Yet he, also like Kirk, lacked what most Americans counted as ambition; to be a truly formidable figure one must be prepared to live with failure, and Bruce was not, at least in his public life. As Isaiah Berlin once put it, "He emerged from the water dry" because he never really stepped in.[62] He spent his whole life avoiding disappointment; he was well rewarded.

When war broke out Bruce went to London, serving with the Red Cross and then with the OSS. According to legend, Bruce and Ernest Hemingway were the first to liberate the Ritz Bar in 1944.[63] It was also at this time that Evangeline Bell, a sophisticated and stunning Anglo-American adventuress, got a job with Bill Phillips, who had recently left the State Department to open the OSS office in London. Bell's father, Ned, had been a diplomat; her godfather was Hugh Gibson. Soon after Phillips left for India, Bell was assigned to be Bruce's secretary. The two fell in love and had three children, one of whom was later murdered only a few years after Bruce's daughter from his prior marriage had been killed in a plane crash.

Judging from the few letters from his children interspersed in his diary, Bruce's family life was far from happy. Private sorrow juxtaposed with public glory. Here, however, one must regard the "private life" of the Bruces and their ilk as being distinct from their family life.[64] For "Vangie's" transatlantic salons in Georgetown and Paris, and their socializing, gossip, letters, affairs, holiday trips, and so forth were just as public as the Addisonian-styled cables Bruce sent routinely from various capitals. This was how business was done, how this particular transatlantic network held itself together, and how it advanced the project of Europe. There was very little about it that was genuinely private.

Bruce was not a EUR man, strictly speaking. His only time in the department was a brief stint as undersecretary at the tail end of the Truman administration.

Evangeline Bruce
Lichfield Archive/Getty

Despite many rumors over the years, he had never been a serious candidate for the secretaryship. Administration, management, and committee work were not his forté, nor an area of interest. Bruce prided himself on nonchalance and efficiency; he excelled in not looking busy and not using up the time of others unnecessarily.[65] But despite everything he did, it mattered just as much who he was. Here came into play his special relationship with Monnet. For all of the latter's reputation as a man of action, he was, in Bruce's words, primarily a philosopher or, as Charles de Gaulle famously sneered, *l'inspirateur*. He still needed loyal and effective American backers, especially ones like Bruce who could at once encourage and charm the right people on both sides of the Atlantic to support his various initiatives. Bruce more than any other American lent prestige and *élan* to the European project; he spent a great deal of time with journalists and genuinely enjoyed them (and they, him), which gave consistently good press to it; he set the standard for what an American ambassador should do and be; he held up the morale of hundreds of foreign service officers and their families; he made, in a word, a pro-European policy orientation highly fashionable from the late 1940s until the middle 1960s. It did not take someone as shrewd as Monnet to see the advantages in such a person.

WITH ALL THAT HAPPENED IN Europe during these years, EUR had its hands full. It responded in the usual way: It got bigger, subdivided, and got bigger again. In addition to its geographic coverage—still including, for the time being, most of the repatriated British and French colonial possessions in Africa and Asia— it also took over responsibility for the various supranational arrangements and organizations beginning to emerge in Europe itself. The result was a new desk— soon to become an almost impossibly large office—called European Regional Affairs (RA). RA became a clearinghouse for Europe as well as an official check on the imaginative and operational excesses of the department's growing cabal of Euro-mavens.[66] Although its remit was multilateral affairs, RA "operated in a jungle"; its officers often found themselves having to decide which country desk had to be kept informed on which issues and oversaw the ever-critical forwarding of memoranda thereto, much as Jimmy Dunn once had done. Its best-known officers—Doug MacArthur, Jeff Parsons, Jamie Bonbright, Ben Moore, Edwin Martin, Jack Tuthill, and especially the indomitable workaholic Benson "Lane" Timmons—were unknown to the public but became memorable figures inside the walls of government. RA as the watchdog on European regional policy housed some of the most astute and creative thinkers about European integration.[67] One of them was a prim, earnest-looking trade specialist, Miriam Camp. The daughter of a mathematician, Camp studied history at Mount Holyoke and Bryn Mawr, and went to work during the war in the Office of Price Administration, where, among other things, she set the wartime price of bread and managed the "bread moguls ... no doubt all male, aggressive ... and hardly likely to be impressed by a slip of a girl."[68] She won them over with her self-confidence and the trust placed in her by her then patron, John Kenneth Galbraith. This led to a job in the Bureau of Economic Warfare, which landed her in London. There she recalled the first meeting to establish what would become the Economic Commission for Europe. It was like a Grade B film ... a naked light bulb on a string, and ... peeling pink wallpaper on the wall, and there was a round table. Eight of us sat around the table, and the head Russian looked at me and said, "You are one of a kind ... you must be our chairman." Then they passed these little glasses of liquid around—colorless liquid ... and I was busy chairing and steering things where I wanted them to go, and knocking back these little glasses from time to time. We had a very successful meeting. The next day ... this was the first evidence I had that there was an Eastern bloc. Because at that reception, the Russians, the Byelorussians, the Poles, the Czechs and the Yugoslavs all came up to me and said: "We hear you are a very good vodka drinker."[69]

Miriam Camp
*Mt. Holyoke Archives
and Special Collections*

Her opposite number there was a Cambridge classicist named William Anthony "Tony" Camps. The two married in 1953; Miriam's surname gained an "s," but she lost her job: Women were not allowed to be married at the time, especially to foreign citizens, and remain employed by the State Department. She went on to write for *The Economist* and wrote several books about Europe. By the early 1960s, however, she was back in the department as a consultant to George Ball, becoming, in 1968, the first female vice chair of the Policy Planning Staff.[70]

From the beginning of her career Camp struck some of her colleagues as an intense perfectionist with an "exceptional power of concentration," but there was a good deal more to her, with a rare gift for both synthesis and salesmanship; in other words, she was a quieter and less imposing (in some ways) female American version of Monnet. She "divided her world," said her colleague Robert Asher, "into two categories—good draftsmen and bad draftsmen," and was herself a "great condenser ... packing a great deal of meaning into each term and idea." Recalled another colleague, William Diebold, "When the discourse was oral, matters were different.... Persuasion—or at least explanation—was the task that came most naturally." She seemed to have unlimited time for that, even though she also devoted great energies to her small group of friends and their families, with a precise, rigorous sense of balance. Indeed, there was almost nothing that was "accidental or unconsidered" about Miriam.[71]

While in London, Camp continued to draft the terms of reference for the new Economic Commission for Europe and attended its first meeting in May 1947, which led to a central role in the design of the Marshall Plan. This took place in William Clayton's former office, now headed by Assistant Secretary Willard

Thorp, who had replaced Clayton when the latter moved up to become the first undersecretary for economic affairs, occupying Jimmy Dunn's old space.[72] One day in July 1947, Thorp said to Linc Gordon, "There is a very bright young woman in the European Bureau who worked in London with the emergency economic committees set up in 1944 to plan [the] postwar reconstruction of the Continent. Her name is Miriam Camp and she might have some useful suggestions for you."[73] Gordon did as he was told, and the two, in just a few weeks, drafted the first blueprint for the ECA. Also working under Thorp were C. Tyler Wood, General "Tick" Bonesteel, and Paul Nitze. Harriman, meanwhile, would take with him to Europe three professors: Gordon, Richard Bissell, and Milton Katz. Completing the picture were two other economists, William "Tommy" Tomlinson and Robert Nathan. Nathan, a leading New Deal economist, was part of the old Frankfurter network—indeed, Dean Acheson had first met Herbert Feis in his New York apartment in 1915—and, after leaving the War Production Board, went to work directly for Jean Monnet. Tomlinson, born in Idaho, was a brilliant and much beloved prodigy of Harry Dexter White. As the Treasury Department's representative in Paris, he became, alongside Bruce and Ball, Monnet's closest American confidant. The two appeared as almost surrogate son and father. "If it goes on," noted the industrialist Clarence Randall, not a particular fan, "there will come a time when all steel production in Europe will be priced by one man."[74] Tomlinson struck his colleagues as superhuman. Some said his vast energy came from knowing he was dying of a heart ailment; others merely marveled at his talent. Art Hartman recalled:

> So this guy Wood said to me one day, You know, I'm a Ph.D. in economics, and I go through all the calculations, and when I explain problems to Tomlinson, the conclusion he reaches, he's reached without all the calculations, he's decided that the way to get at this inflationary problem is to take this amount out, and he looks—because he knows that it must be found inside of the agricultural sector, or he knows that there's something happening on the collection of customs duties.... So here he is, a twenty-eight-year-old kid, by this time, or twenty-nine, spoke practically no French, from Moscow, Idaho! An absolute workaholic.[75]

Life for most of these people in postwar Paris was not uncomfortable, apart from their cramped quarters in the Hôtel Talleyrand, where offices "had been put together out of wallboard in various, ungeometric shapes" and where some secretaries worked in washrooms with typewriters set up on bidets.[76] "But Paris," recalled the journalist Ben Bradlee, who worked in the embassy, "had great cachet." One could live very well; real estate was so cheap that Carmel Offie, for example, "an utterly shameless wrangler" who seemed to turn up everywhere all at once during these years, bought dozens of Paris apartments, which he lent to friends while finding time to jet over to Germany to act as tour guide for "about half of Congress."[77] The Marshall Planner Ty Wood found himself living in the Septième Arrondissement, in what a photograph shows to have been an elegant, chandeliered apartment with Empire furniture, twenty-foot-tall Ionic columns leading to a dramatic cornice, late-afternoon winter light filtering through silk draperies, all suggesting a timeless sense of grandeur, apart from the small, disheveled Christmas tree awkwardly counterposed against the statue of Apollo in the garden.[78]

"Well, these agencies are like human beings," Wood later recalled. "They are born, they go through a very vigorous youth, manhood, then age and senility."[79] Like human beings, they also thrived from proximity to one another. A visitor to the sixth floor of the new State Department building at Twenty-first and C Streets in Washington would have found the various EUR offices situated together, surrounded by an outer layer of related geographic and functional offices, much as they had been in the old War, Navy, and State Building, even though that "friendly and old-fashioned and tranquil" pile bore almost no resemblance to its successor, an "atrocity ... apparently designed by some architect who thought diplomacy was a disease and should be housed in an up-to-date hospital."[80] The geography of American representation in Europe also fused the old with the new. It remained concentrated in Paris, only by now that headquarters competed with bolstered British and German outposts for resources and attention as well as with the bevy of new ECA offices, military, and other missions. The constellation of American officialdom in Europe seemed to expand like crazy. Still, Bruce, upon arriving at his embassy residence—the mansion built in 1885 by President Grévy and purchased by Bruce's predecessor Myron Herrick—retained not only an old Cadillac (which Bruce disliked) but also an even older embassy doorman, a Spanish-American War veteran who had gone to Europe with the Buffalo Bill ensemble and had gotten lost, but who eventually found employment with the State Department, for which he worked forty-five years.[81] Just further to the east, across the Place de la Concorde, was the chancery; then slightly to the west, facing the Place itself, was the former headquarters of the Inquiry and the American Commission to Negotiate Peace, the Hôtels Crillon and Talleyrand, the latter occupied by the Marshall Planners. Further to the west near the Bois de Boulogne was the Château de la Muette, to be the site of the Organization for European Economic Cooperation (OEEC), a magnificent building that Ambassador Caffery refused to buy for a bargain price at the end of the war, much to the later dismay of Bruce. To the south were Monnet's offices in the rue de Martignac, which later moved, once he left government, back west to the Avenue Foch.

The influx of important people and positions carried with it a predictable amount of duplication. Several officers inside and outside EUR began to complain about the overlapping channels and relationships, and the fact that there were just too many American ambassadors in Paris.[82] The problem would not go away soon. The abundance of prerogatives and flowcharts bothered some traditionalists, who saw in them too much sloppy thinking. Kennan later noted:

> This proliferation of organizational forms, all differing in membership, naturally raised the question as to how, if we really wished to see European union become a reality, we envisaged it as proceeding: within what circle of countries, that is; through the development of which, if any, of these existing organizational forms; and to what degree of merging of sovereignty. These were problems in which there was need for clarification of American opinion, not just because we were pressing the Europeans in the direction of unification and therefore had a duty to explain to them

just what we had in mind when we used those words, but also because the questions at issue were ones bound to affect at many points our own determinations of policy.[83]

Clarification would take time, but better coordination could not wait. The job would fall to Camp and to Jeff Parsons, an officer whose career began as Joseph Grew's personal secretary in Japan and ended several decades later as deputy head of the delegation to the Strategic Arms Limitations Talks. They would draft the outlines for the bureaucratic management of Europe, giving economic affairs a permanent, if nominally separate, place in EUR.[84] RA, for its part, became the "bridge between the political and economic sides of the State Department dealing with Europe" and refined the distinctions among self-help, light touch, and "hands-off" approaches. "There is already an excessive tendency," Camp later wrote, "to regard the development of the Schuman Plan and European Political Community as things which the Europeans are doing because the U.S. wants them to be done rather than because the European countries concerned believe in them."[85] To Camp and her collaborators, the challenge was to make the most of American influence without appearing to flaunt it—a task well suited to such serious-minded and unobtrusive people. Although their devotion and intelligence earned the support of their European colleagues, the great salesmen—Bruce, Monnet, and Harriman as well as the Washington head of the Marshall Plan, former Studebaker executive Paul Hoffman—won over legislatures and public opinion on both sides of the Atlantic. Integrating the integrationists, cultivating the light touch, and keeping the public on board were all part of the same mission.[86]

They would be helped considerably by two additional figures, close friends since their college days at Princeton: Livingston Merchant and Henry Labouisse. "Livie" was one of the most beloved officers in EUR's history, "most impressive, elect and pleasant," one of the few men whom John Foster Dulles supposedly said could do no wrong. For that reason, Merchant became instrumental as a go-between with Dulles and the career service in the 1950s. His closeness to Dulles and his popularity among the rank and file, bolstered by his habit of sending frequent thank-you notes to line officers, allowed him to rise to the top of EUR ahead of his unspoken rival, Riddleberger. He also helped to keep many career people in place who otherwise would have left in the nasty political climate of that decade.[87] Earlier during the war he worked under Labouisse in the so-called Eastern Hemisphere Division, which dealt mainly with blockaded materials and supply, a position that put him into direct contact with Monnet on the Allied Purchasing Commission.[88] This division merged in October 1944 with another, called the Liberated Areas Division, and Merchant moved over to EUR itself. Following the war, Livie went to the Paris embassy as economic counselor, and soon thereafter joined the staff of the Marshall Plan to help sort through the economic impact of the new North Atlantic Treaty. He too found himself in tight quarters in the Talleyrand, crammed into a small office next to the men's toilet, facing the courtyard. Lacking the reticence of his colleagues, at least on this occasion, however, Merchant complained that his assignment sent a poor signal about the new alliance. "Livie," his colleague Fisher Howe recalled, "was modest and unpretentious but the force of his character came through always."[89] He got his new office in short order. He would go on to establish the headquarters of the U.S. mission to NATO, then modestly called the "U.S. Regional Office" whose "tri-cephalous chief," General William Draper, was simultaneously representative to NATO, the U.S. special representative in Europe, and European head of the Mutual Security Agency, the successor to ECA.[90] Brought back to EUR by Doc Matthews in 1953, Merchant was, according to Eisenhower, the leading candidate to replace the ailing Dulles as secretary, had it not been for the clean bill of health given to Dulles's deputy, Christian Herter. Under Livie, EUR had nearly one-half the entire budget of the State Department and processed 16,000 documents per week. He had passed, as Bruce put it, from the "frying pan into the fire."[91]

Livingston Merchant
Courtesy of Harry S. Truman Library

His friend Henry Labouisse (pronounced "Lah-bow-eeze") came from a large, distinguished yet troubled New Orleans family (his father had committed suicide), but was also descended from New England Puritans, a heritage that meant much to him, as did his sense of himself as a great humanitarian.[92] Labouisse was as beloved a figure as Merchant, though he was less of a careerist, remembered more as a generational emblem than for any set of policies he championed during his service to the U.S. government. He inspired nearly everyone he met with his gracious disposition, endearing himself to the French almost as much as Bruce had, and later to the Greeks while ambassador there.[93] After replacing Nitze as Thorp's deputy in the department and overseeing relations between it and the ECA, he moved to Paris to head the ECA mission. Then, after leaving his Parisian townhouse to Bruce, Labouisse went on to work for the United Nations, dealing with the resettlement of Palestinian refugees and later, as the longtime head of UNICEF, became known as the "world's grandfather."[94] He was equally at home in European capitals with his second wife, Eve, a daughter of Madame Curie, as he was in desert tents with the Bedouin, feasting upon the eyeballs of sheep. The two were a most popular couple: "[T]hey combine[d] unselfishness with grace, talent with modesty, and character with charm," Bruce recalled.[95] Recruited to public service from Wall Street by his childhood friend Walt Butterworth, Labouisse took to government work like a natural. Butterworth, incidentally, also came from Princeton, worked tirelessly to keep Spain (and the munitions and other valuables on its territory, as noted briefly in Chapter 4) out of the war, went on to follow Bruce as U.S. representative to the European Coal and Steel Community, and then became, in 1961, the first U.S. ambassador to the European Communities, where, to the surprise of many who knew him as a well-tailored and deeply Anglophile diplomat of the old school (attributable in part to his membership in the club of former Rhodes scholars), he became a passionate convert to European unity.[96] Butterworth was also one of the very few officers to serve in both EUR and the Far Eastern Bureau, and one of the very few senior officials of the latter (besides Livie Merchant, who served there briefly as well) to escape the full onslaught of Senator McCarthy. "We rejoice in your indestructibility," Labouisse once told him, presciently.[97]

Such personalities made the postwar bureaucracy work. Just as Labouisse smoothed edges between Washington and the field, so continued Miriam Camp, once the work of the Marshall Plan began to wind down, to bridge various constituencies with a combination of respect, openness, and esteem. "We really were a triumvirate," recalled the future assistant secretary of EUR, John Leddy, of himself, his deputy, the economist Ray Vernon, and Miriam. He and Vernon worked together in the Bureau of Economic Affairs (E), laying the institutional groundwork for the new General Agreement on Tariffs and Trade (GATT) as well as establishing the first Cold War export control system. Camp, who remained in EUR, had to make sure that these efforts took European economic integration and recovery fully into account. She was as much a member of their office as her own. Indeed, her initial foray into the work of the Economic Commission for Europe in 1946–1947 happened in large part because her boss at the time, Will Clayton, was preoccupied with the GATT negotiations.[98]

Camp's other main contribution besides the ECA was to launch the OEEC, later OECD, as a viable entity. In Europe it was yet another outgrowth of the Marshall Plan, and carried a dual function of coordinating the economic policy of the various European governments while keeping the United States partnered with them. It never became, despite some early attempts, "the focus of a European customs union," as the British had feared. They tried repeatedly to weaken the organization and scuttle nominations, notably of its first proposed chair, Belgian politician and later NATO secretary-general Paul-Henri Spaak, the top choice of the United States and many other Europeans to run the OEEC. Finally it was Camp who reportedly convinced Anthony Eden of its virtues.[99] To the extent, then, that the European Common Market took over the former function, the OEEC emerged as an important economic forum for the North Atlantic Alliance. Like Camp, it became the bridge of two orientations and networks, and an important vehicle for bringing the British into the tent of an integrating Europe.[100]

This was not entirely successful. Too many suspicions remained about American designs on the OEEC as the economic arm of NATO, on the one hand, and British schemes to reduce it to an insignificant talking shop, on the other. By the end of the 1950s, it had become clear that the OEEC had to be replaced, especially when the British had advanced their latest competitor to the Common Market, the "Free Trade Area." Jack Tuthill, another acolyte of Monnet in the foreign service, joined with John Leddy, C. Douglas Dillon (the ambassador to France and future treasury secretary), and Randolph Burgess (the ambassador to NATO), and pushed for the establishment of the Organization for Economic Cooperation and Development (OECD). This organization eventually grew to include nearly all of the NATO countries as well as Japan, Australia, New Zealand, and others.[101]

Until this happened, however, the OEEC lived on in organizational limbo, despite the long-standing American position that OEEC and NATO "should be regarded as complementary rather than competing organizations." Moreover, the OEEC was meant to be an economic forum that transcended Western Europe, encompassing (to date) most of the "Atlantic Community." But it was not, to be clear, "the economic organization of the Atlantic Community." Casting it in such a way was the fault of the British, who continued to dislike "our somewhat ambiguous position in the OEEC" that "enables us to stimulate action on the part of other countries without necessarily having to undertake the same action ourselves."[102] That would prove harder to do by the end of the decade, and would result in a serious crisis over trade and tariffs by the early 1960s.

The ambiguity and ambivalence over the orientation of the OEEC mirrored the aforementioned divide between Atlanticists and Europeanists. Here were people backing "integration" against those backing "unification."[103] Monnet and his more ardent disciples were lodged firmly in the unification camp. They were, in other words, their generation's partisans for "deepening" in what would later become known as a debate against "widening," although at the time, the question seemed more like one between "inadequacy" and "unrealism."[104] The Harvard law professor Robert Bowie was an influential interlocutor on that question. He was recruited by McCloy to draft much of the early legislation for the German Federal Republic and the European Coal and Steel Community. (He, too, was extremely close to Monnet.) In his long career, as will be learned in the next two chapters, he stood firmly for the Europeanist view and for the determination to tie Germany to a number of European institutions. The American role, following this concept, was to uphold and underwrite the arrangement, but not necessarily to become a permanent, political part of it.

Many of the Marshall Planners, by contrast, were also firm supporters of integration but less for its own sake than for the potential it held for both regional and global economic growth. Perhaps for this reason, a few of them like Linc Gordon, Miriam Camp, and Harriman himself had carried with them a trace of Anglophilia. Several of the people Harriman hired had been Rhodes scholars or, like Camp, had other long-standing ties to Britain. But below the surface was a more complex mixture of proclivities.[105] In reality, their thinking was less predetermined emotionally or biographically than it was the result of a self-conscious historicism, unlike that of the Francophiles or many of the German hands. They did not view the world through British eyes, necessarily, but rather sought to recast the United States and its allies in what was by then an obsolescent British role in underwriting the international order. Thus, many of them did not use the term "unification" in either the Atlantic or European senses; they preferred Camp's favored term, "integration," and retained an open mind regarding the territorial boundaries of Europe.[106] They sought the greater involvement of the United States (and Canada) in European political, economic, and institutional life and were impatient for the British to do the same. (On the latter point it must be noted that Monnet also argued very strongly in favor, but for somewhat different reasons.) And they supported a steady opening toward the Soviet bloc by way of trade negotiations and other forms of economic exchange. Therefore, while favoring stronger integration on many levels, they were backers of a European concept that would nevertheless retain the character of a community,

Theodore Achilles
Atlantic Council of the United States

rather than a union, of nations.

Here is how they also differed from the Atlantic unionists led by the journalist Clarence Streit (described further in Chapter 7), notwithstanding his "successive tailoring down of his comprehensive union to smaller sizes."[107] At the other end of the Atlanticist-Europeanist spectrum, Streit and his allies sought to do for the Atlantic region what Monnet and company had set in motion for the Continent: that is, to merge sovereignties into a single, tightly knit Atlantic Community, a term that incidentally had not originated during the most recent war, as is commonly understood, but was celebrated by Walter Lippmann as far back as 1917.[108] Camp and her colleagues were not federalists in the Streit sense and never suggested that Europe and America dissolve national borders. As Jack Hickerson once put it, the difference between the various approaches lay essentially between those who regarded European unity as an end in itself and as an alternative to consolidation of the Atlantic Community, and those who regarded it as a stage on the way to a larger synthesis.[109] As already mentioned, this meant both a strategy and bureaucratic configuration that combined in parallel the development of the political, military, and economic elements of transatlantic affairs. EUR became the official hub of so many spokes, making it possible for free trade universalists, European regionalists, and Atlantic federalists all to work together for the same result, which best approximated Camp's integrationist model somewhere near the middle of the spectrum. Where they sat in EUR defined, to some extent, where they stood, and many came with intellectual and professional biases already in place. There were innumerable struggles among them, but in the end, the particular postwar structure of EUR made it possible for them to function together more than the sum of their parts would otherwise suggest.[110]

"By the end of 1950 or early 1951," Camp noted, "the attitude of the United States Government was much better defined than it had been."[111] EUR had come to accept the need for special trading relationships with Europe so long as the latter evolved in a way that augmented global free trade. It had determined that the OEEC would perform a role reflecting the one Lord Ismay later famously ascribed to NATO—keeping the Germans down, Russians out, and Americans in; only it would do so in this case by helping to promote German prosperity within

Europe and occasionally by inviting Russia's client states into closer contact. And finally it had struck a balance between the Atlantic and European "animal[s]," proving, as the British diplomat Frank Roberts once claimed, that it was possible to be both, at least for the time being.[112] The glue holding it all together turned out to be NATO itself.

IF THE MARSHALL PLAN WAS a stepchild adopted (and co-opted) by EUR, the North Atlantic Treaty was its legitimate offspring. The idea emerged out of the wartime alliance and was articulated initially by British foreign secretary Ernest Bevin in the spring of 1947 as an outer ring of a series of concentric military circles. The treaty, later regarded as having established the closest thing the United States had to a permanent alliance, began very much as a "crash operation." It was the work primarily of two men: Hickerson and his deputy, Ted Achilles, a well-regarded foreign service officer whose laconic exterior concealed a high operational intelligence. William Castle, who credited himself with persuading the young Eastman-Kodak heir to join the service in 1931, once regarded him as "a nice enough boy but he is rather hard sledding. I had to do all the talking, which really was not fair as he had asked me to lunch with him."[113] Achilles had decided long before that meeting—on a trip to the League of Nations at age seventeen, actually, accompanying his Christian Scientist mother on frequent trips to Europe after his father had deserted the family—that "the foreign service was my destiny."[114] That conviction notwithstanding, Achilles dabbled in journalism (in Japan) and talked about becoming a playwright, then eventually landed a job in WE on the League of Nations Desk because Stanley Hornbeck, the chief of the Far Eastern Bureau, did not like his appearance, whereas Jack Hickerson, who had corrected Achilles's papers at the Foreign Service Institute, apparently liked his brain. "At that time," he noted, "I had two long-range ambitions—one to be Under-Secretary of State, the other to be a member of the Alibi Club." The second of the two, at least, was helped by his working for Moffat, Matthews, and Hickerson, and, during the war, in Winant's London embassy as an American representative to several governments in exile.[115] A great "back channel man" who was "more influential than any job he held would lead you to believe," Achilles's semiprofessional involvement with transatlantic relations would last until the 1980s.[116] But the winter of 1947 was his moment in the sun:

> Somehow, the North Atlantic Treaty will always be associated in my mind with fishhouse punch. The Metropolitan Club in Washington always holds open house on Christmas Eve and New Year's Eve. Christmas Eve they serve free drinks and charge you for lunch and New Year's Eve they charge you for drinks and serve free lunch. Between the two they make a tidy profit. But, having just come back from abroad, I forgot to go to either of them. On that New Year's Eve [December 31, 1947] I was sitting at my desk, slightly drowsy in the middle of the afternoon, when my immediate chief, Jack Hickerson, Director of the Bureau of European Affairs, came into my office, well mellowed by fishhouse punch and said, "I don't care whether entangling alliances have been considered worse than original sin

ever since George Washington's time. We've got to negotiate a
military alliance with Western Europe in peacetime and we've got
to do it quickly."

I said, "Fine, when do we start?"

He said, "I've already started it. Now it's your baby. Get
going."[117]

Together with John Foster Dulles, then working as a State Department
consultant, Hickerson convinced Secretary of State George Marshall and Senators
Arthur Vandenberg and Tom Connally that Bevin had the right motives in mind,
but that a better model for the alliance would be the Rio Treaty of 1947, that is,
a regional collective defense pact falling under Article 51 of the UN Charter. As
late as 1953, the British still noted that Americans were uncomfortable with the
term "alliance."[118] The process here was as important as the substance: Hickerson
took special care to involve Republican members of Congress from the outset, so
successfully that they ultimately regarded the treaty as their own, while Achilles
spent much of his time at the Pentagon and in secret meetings with the British
and Canadians, keeping a single draft of the treaty locked in his safe at night.
Once the negotiations began, the first of many "working groups" of the various
future signatories, modeled on the wartime committee work of the Allies, met
daily to iron out the details. In doing so they fathered not only the "NATO spirit,"
which to Achilles basically meant changing instructions if they did not work, but
also at least two generations of NATO hands who claimed, much as the Marshall
Planners did before them, that far more diplomacy was accomplished by such
procedural interactions than by the pieces of paper that resulted from them,
including this one, written for an "Omaha milkman" and signed in a ceremony
in the Department of Commerce building on April 4, to the tune of Cole Porter's
"I Got Plenty of Nothin'."[119] Their influence, then, came less from what they produced than from the way in which they eased policies along in a quiet, friendly,
but persistent way over time, *festina lente*, allowing consensus to be forged from
within or, as Eisenhower famously put it, "Where, among partners, strength is
demanded in its fullness, unity is the first requisite."[120]

Outside EUR there was less support for the treaty. Bohlen and Kennan both
argued that the effort would backfire because Congress would never sign on
to a peacetime military alliance. But neither had much to do with the actual
negotiations.[121] Bohlen cautioned restraint, arguing that a Western military
alliance would be premature. Although he was perceived to have convinced
Bob Lovett of the need for delay, his "blockade" would prove unsuccessful, as
Lovett, an especially critical player as undersecretary of state and confidant of
Vandenberg, would become a strong supporter of the pact.[122] The opposition from
Kennan had deeper roots and became the main reason, apart from his personality
and the difficulties it caused him in the department, for his leaving government
service at the end of the Truman administration. His views on the relationship
of the United States to Europe, as noted above, were out of step with those of
his government and, on balance, with political realities. His wish, as expressed
in 1955, "to see this country learn to mind its own business, to adopt toward
others policies similar to those of the Swiss ... and to cultivate, with dignity and
humility, the art of self-improvement" must have struck his colleagues as the

last hurrah of a midwestern isolationist, just as the idea, conveyed in the same document, to restrict the defensive perimeter of the United States to the Atlantic and Pacific littorals bore very little utility in the missile age.[123]

To a great extent, NATO gave the older generation of European hands— particularly those who rose up in the foreign service like Hickerson and Achilles—a focus and a source of prerogatives to match those of the European functionalists, even though NATO, too, would breed its own semipermanent crop of technical experts. They were, on balance, a more conservative group, skeptical but not entirely dismissive of European integration, drawn more toward the British, Dutch, and Germans than to the French, and among the more doctrinaire Cold Warriors in the department. They attracted people of similar outlook—from Averell Harriman, who occupied himself mainly with Alliance affairs after 1950, to Livie Merchant, who contributed the necessary expertise in economics.[124] The "inevitable" Alliance became for them the bedrock of America's European policy: Nearly every other initiative, whether it had to do with trade, the Third World, arms control, and so on, came to be viewed through a NATO lens.[125]

The NATO hands were of course fervent Atlanticists. That is, they were promoters of the Atlantic Community and broadly sympathetic to Streit's ideas; they disparaged the notion of a separate (even a separate but equal) European union; as Chapter 7 will show, they would launch a rearguard action in the 1960s against the Europeanists who reigned within George Ball's State Department.

However, like Camp, they too were not, as has been often charged, uniformly pro-British. Just as Dean Acheson, Walt Butterworth, and other reputed Anglophiles were more British in style than in substance, the NATO hands regarded themselves as being no more favorable to the British than was necessary. Here again, they could be seen as wanting American power to improve upon (albeit by way of imitation) the British, insofar as it would uphold the balance of interests among France, Germany, and the smaller European countries while pressing them all to make the Atlantic Community an open one. NATO, by the weight of its political and military strength, and its ever-expanding network across the Atlantic, helped to paper over the differences. With the exception of Kennan, who left government soon after the treaty was signed, very few people opposed the idea of the Alliance or its institutionalization. But German rearmament—an extension of the latter—would be more difficult to finesse. The effort to do so would bring about the first serious postwar crisis for EUR.

IN THE STATE DEPARTMENT, recalled Martin Hillenbrand, few were worried about a resurgent Germany in any military sense. By contrast, most had seen how truly devastated the country was. But most recognized both the necessity and the sensitivity of rearmament.[126] Squaring the circle meant the invention of something called the European Defense Community, or EDC. The idea for it first arose, it was said, in parallel conversations on the one hand between Monnet, Bruce, and Tomlinson, and, on the other, between Hank Byroade, McCloy, and a few more people, including Bob Bowie and Dean Acheson, in the spring and summer of 1950. Out of the first set of discussions came the kernel of what would be known as the Pleven Plan, named after the French defense minister, later prime minister, and long-standing Monnet associate, René Pleven, announced in October of that year. By the spring of 1951, Bruce and Monnet had persuaded Eisenhower, then the Alliance's first supreme commander, to back it, their task made easier by Adenauer's having thrown a "bombshell" in the form of a moan about German soldiers being treated as second-class citizens.[127] German rearmament could take place through the invention of a European army, which would have the added virtue of augmenting regional integration, even though some Allies (notably the British and Dutch) did not take the latter rationale very seriously, while others regarded the plan as "a cumbersome, unworkable, organizational swamp."[128] The American role, however, seemed straightforward: Convincing the Germans to support the EDC was not difficult; this McCloy and Bowie did with relative ease, although for extra assurance Bruce hired Riddleberger, whose sister-in-law was a close personal friend of the German negotiator Albrecht "Teddy" von Kessel.[129] Persuading the French was another matter; negotiations with them were in the hands of the Atlanticists' old nemesis, the diplomat Hervé Alphand, who "pushed it ably" even though he "couldn't have liked the idea less." In truth, both Frenchmen and Germans gave EUR cause for concern—indeed, that was the point of the EDC to begin with. Byroade put it well in October 1949: "[W]e were doing a lot of things right in Germany, but in general we were doing them too late.... [W]e must somehow find the means of convincing the French that for their own good and the good of Europe they should take the lead in the German problem."[130] Although they were complacent for the time being, it was conceivable that the Germans would not remain so forever, particularly given the uncertainties inherent in the nuclear arms race. The NATO allies, led by the United States, therefore had to come up with some preventive medicine.

It would be a mistake, however, to cast the EDC as primarily an American initiative. It began as anything but. Most of its early support had been in France, but France was in the middle of a nasty war in Indochina. Tomlinson, Labouisse, and Dunn worked hard to assuage concerns about the EDC at lower levels of the French bureaucracy, while Alfred Gruenther, Eisenhower's successor at NATO, lobbied the British by way of his good friend, NATO secretary-general Lord Ismay. Lending a hand later on was another person with long-standing ties to France, although more on the Gaullist side of the aisle: Senator Henry Cabot Lodge Jr.[131] For his part, Acheson recalled that

> [t]he negotiations in Paris about this had become so involved that the only two Americans who claimed to understand them were Ambassador David Bruce and a Treasury attaché named Tomlinson.... Neither of them could impart understanding of the negotiations to the rest of us; indeed, Bruce would not try. The Europeans, he said, liked to do things in a way that seemed to us like beating up a soufflé of generalizations. It would come out all right, if we would leave it alone and worry about something else. I accepted the first but not the last part of his advice and, therefore, worried alone and in the clarity of ignorance.[132]

The smaller European states got behind the EDC once their governments imagined there was little to do to stop it. So when the French National Assembly voted it down in August 1954, many people were shocked. The vote may have said more about the state of the French government, particularly its foreign minister Georges Bidault, "a weak man who wanted to be taken for a strong one," than it did about the EDC itself.[133] Why did this happen? One must recall that the vote took place in the wake of the defeat at Dien Bien Phu and the lackluster Berlin and Geneva conferences happening at the time. Livie Merchant was the American note taker at both. At Berlin, for example, amid guards, large crowds, eighteenth-century crystal chandeliers in a green and gold room with silk brocades, "modernistic glass," pink, marbled Corinthian columns, and a "tremendous stained glass window of the Kremlin" sat "Chip reading *Pravda* during translations ... B[idault] surrounded by his advisers looking like a Rembrandt ... Eden ... beginning to look very badly around eyes," and everyone, especially Secretary Dulles, bearing the "brunt of Molotov" as "we," according to Merchant, who wrote nearly everything down in his tiny notebook, "were accorded the chief villain's role," even though "the chief villain was, in a real sense the Germans." The air was "electrical" but the conference was a "fraud."[134] He also noted that the large portraits of Stalin and Lenin in Dulles's borrowed office there were each apportioned with hidden microphones, one placed in Stalin's decoration, the other in Lenin's vest pocket. Dulles might have avoided a similar inconvenience if he had taken up Hugh Gibson's offer of a Geneva lodging, a quiet house on the lake. Alas, Gibson died soon thereafter.[135]

Both conferences saw a new aggressiveness on the part of the press, and an obsession with it by the delegates. But that was about all. Berlin brought little about besides the realization that Soviet policies had not changed significantly after the death of Stalin; Geneva led to an inadequate half solution for Indochina, paving the way, ultimately, for American intervention.[136] Thus, for all of Dulles's "lucubrations" and threats or, as some have argued, "bluffs" to undergo an "agonizing reappraisal" should ratification fail, there was little he or anyone else could do to secure French opinion in the EDC's favor. To him in any case, "[t]he arrangements relating to the EDC Treaty were extremely complicated. I never studied them as carefully as I should have. They represented a pile of printed documents nearly a foot high."[137] Other American officials—particularly Achilles, then the Paris embassy's deputy chief of mission—seemed so exasperated with the French government, it almost seemed that they wanted the EDC to self-destruct, or that they somehow knew it would. Merchant, when placing a bet on when the EDC would become a reality, voted "never," and strutted about the Geneva conference with his head in his hands. "The French are a most talented people," Woody Wallner noted, "and they show an almost supernatural talent in getting under one's skin.... [N]ever has 'la cuisine' given off more varied and pungent odors than it is doing now."[138] And Art Hartman, still working for David Bruce, was sent by him to watch the assembly debates. There he witnessed Bidault nursing an ailing stomach with mustard, bread, and champagne. "As soon as I saw the condition of Bidault," Hartman said, "I knew it was never going to come off."[139]

Bruce for his part agonized over it almost constantly during the winter and spring of 1953–1954. He was one of the last to claim that it would pass, having said at the outset that the French people would endure German rearmament so long as significant numbers of American and British troops remained in Europe. It was said that failing to do so would be a crisis not only for France and Europe but also "for the whole free world."[140] The EDC became his obsession. At the same time, he acknowledged the abnormality of France's "anarchistic" attitude and its policy of procrastination:

[T]he hope persists in France that its citizens (because of a favored geographic position which will force the United States to continue to keep overflowing the cornucopia of foreign aid, and to maintain France as one of the three great Western powers) can preserve domestically a government which ... does not govern, in the hopeful expectation that a fine day will arrive when these troublesome concerns of war ... will be settled by men of good will.... Under such circumstances, individual nations, and particularly France, would be able to afford the continued luxury of an asocial, confused, ineffective, unstable, unrespected, uncooperative, sensitive, economically-isolated system of government.

Simply put, he added, "the combination of Candide and Cassandra is almost inevitable in dealing with this problem."[141]

"By the summer of 1954," recalled another experienced observer, "France was like a man flayed alive."[142] The EDC was defeated at last. There was "unmitigated gloom"; it was "the greatest lost opportunity in modern Western European history." Monnet reportedly had had a stroke right before the vote and had gone into seclusion. Tommy Tomlinson's weak heart finally gave out and he died at age thirty-six. Lane Timmons was on the verge of physical collapse but remained for the time being in Paris, as did Art Hartman and Marty Hillenbrand; Hervé Alphand, the French diplomat identified most with the EDC, in spite of his own presumed lukewarm feelings about it, was exiled to his country's embassy in Tokyo. But others were more sanguine. Dulles described the defeat, without irony, as a mere setback resulting from Dien Bien Phu: "She is not dead but sleepeth," implying, perhaps, that it had been something of a foil all along. Meanwhile, the Messina Conference and then the Common Market followed in a pattern that would be repeated after Suez with the European Atomic Energy Community.[143] Integration would forge ahead. For his part, Monnet, who came to hold great misgivings about the EDC despite having helped devise it, left his position with the High Authority and went on to establish the Action Committee for a United States of Europe, which would extend his influence over the European movement for another two decades. Bruce would also leave government, but only briefly. He would be recalled two years later following Eisenhower's reelection to be ambassador to the Federal Republic. Meanwhile, Merchant and others in EUR regrouped and took off the shelf the planning they had already done for ways to strengthen the nonmilitary aspects of the Alliance as well as other alternatives to the EDC. "We didn't go through an agonizing reappraisal," recalled Marty Hillenbrand. "We ha[d] other things on our mind[s]."[144]

Why had the EDC become such a focus? A good deal of it had to do with the general atmosphere in Europe. In France, especially, the emotions surrounding the EDC recalled nothing less than the Dreyfus Affair.[145] One could not remain aloof or dispassionate. This was less true elsewhere, although it would be difficult, even for pragmatists like McCloy, to stay immune, given their deep, emotional attachment to the European project. Like many other grand initiatives—such as the Multilateral Nuclear Force (MLF), described in Chapter 7—proponents tended to get carried away by their own rhetoric. To convince skeptics, they had to sound sincere and passionate; but it is hard to imagine that such clearheaded people really believed all that they were saying. Like the MLF, the campaign for the EDC became something akin to a Machiavellian theology, if such a combination is possible. In successive reports, Ted Achilles and his political staff in the Paris embassy noted that there was more psychology floating about than met the eye. They were very well informed and "worked closely together" with their French counterparts, "as if we were colleagues in the same office."[146] In their version, French premier Pierre Mendès-France, whose cynicism was widely blamed for the defeat, was never really set on killing it, nor was he committed entirely to playing the anti-American. Yet he could not figure out how to "put toothpaste back in the tube."[147] His actions suggested that he thought—or was led to think—that the German Army would be reconstituted one way or another, with or without the EDC. At the same time, the French as well as the British were given a particularly hard sell—more extensive than Dulles's single leaked speech, the one that included the notorious mention of the "agonizing reappraisal," in December 1953, the effect of which was more confusing than salutary. Bruce was reported to be "completely puzzled by Dulles."[148] Was he committed to the EDC? Was he trying to manipulate, or merely confuse, the French? And then there was the president. One found Eisenhower, who had once been dubious, telling Lord Ismay also in December that failure to ratify the EDC would lead not only to stagnation of America's policy initiatives but also to a resurgence of isolationism in Congress. "In these circumstances," Ismay noted, "the President suggested that EDC should be the battle cry of NATO agencies and personnel, both civilian and military. Any member of either of those agencies who cast doubts upon it should be fired."[149]

Back in Washington, however, there was more confusion than conviction, notably outside EUR. The leadership of the Pentagon, for example, sounded determined to see a German army but mistrusted "jerry built" schemes like the EDC. The reporter Cy Sulzberger recalled asking "why in the hell we could not stop this nonsense of pushing German arming until the French had an army?" only to be told that, according to the Defense Department, doing so would be futile in any case because "the Pentagon thinks the Germans are better soldiers. They had a high regard for German troops during the war."[150] Many in EUR, however, were more likely to speak of the issue, in Paul Nitze's terms, as the "nigger in the woodpile."[151] Failing to finesse German rearmament might have dire consequences, so something, whether it was the EDC or some other plan, was needed. Their case was not helped by Kennan, whose outspokenness, culminating in his infamous BBC Reith Lectures in 1957, sealed the door on whatever influence he may still have had with his former colleagues. In these lectures he reversed himself on earlier positions and called, essentially, for a reunified and neutral German state, a remedy for what he came to regard as the mistake of German partition.[152] The reaction this so-called Bismarck option provoked among the Atlanticists was predictably hostile. Acheson emerged from retirement to issue a strong rebuke of the "very pernicious doctrine," mainly to reassure the European, especially German, public that no such model could ever be taken seriously. In truth, Kennan's appeal never resonated worldwide; few people took it at its word; some even regarded it as a British-inspired plot. EUR's concern was principally that too many Germans would begin to dream along those lines. But there, too, they need not have worried as much as some of them did.[153]

Could EUR have done a better job with selling the European army? Probably not.[154] The officers who counted most on European defense—namely, Hickerson and Achilles—were early opponents and failed to preach with the conviction of the converted, even though they claimed, in fact, to have been in favor following the decision of the Dutch government to switch sides midway through the negotiations.[155] But EUR was still sufficiently concerned about the doings of the Bruce mission to send both Merchant and Ridgway Knight, a true-blue foreign service officer, to keep watch. Knight, incidentally, was the French-born son and grandson of American artists. Bruce regarded him, along with William Tyler, another European-born officer who will appear later in this book, as the two best-informed Americans about France. Both were also noted for their rather un-American mannerisms. Hartman, for instance, recalled that his mimicking young children always pronounced Knight's nickname as "Ehrridge" with a French "r."[156] Their nominal support for the EDC, as well as the uncharacteristic passion of Dulles and Eisenhower, do not altogether make sense. But then neither did the actions of the French.[157] If the French people were so against the idea of German rearmament, how could the French government sign the Paris Agreements only a few months later, effectively agreeing to what Byroade and McCloy had proposed in 1950? In order to answer that question, one must also know why the French really came to kill an initiative they had the most to do with proposing in the first place. Perhaps the Americans who knew them so well also knew best when it mattered to play along with a charade.

Again, it would be easy to overstate the American role in the entire drama and to understate, again, the detrimental psychological effects on French national prestige of the war in Indochina. As to German rearmament, there is evidence to suggest that it had always been taken for granted in one form or another. Perhaps the EDC folly was not taken as seriously as it ought to have been as bucking the prevailing trend of Atlanticism.[158] What if Bruce had adhered to the same light touch to the EDC that Camp and others used in pursuing economic integration? Certainly that is what he seemed to think he was doing. His diary entries describe him bristling many times over accusations of meddling in French politics; he went to great pains to hide and even dispel his proper role as advocate; if anyone could have pulled off the light touch, Bruce was the man to do it. But even he lost patience and became overinsistent.[159] Tougher to explain is the hard salesmanship of the skeptics, namely Achilles, Merchant, Dunn, and Dillon, not to mention Dulles and Eisenhower. Were they merely doing their duty, or was something more conspiratorial under way? Unfortunately, the entire episode lends itself to too many plots—for years it was alleged, for example, that Mendès-France had made a secret deal with the Russians to trade an EDC defeat for help with extricating French troops from Indochina. But a secret deal between the French and the United States to move forward with German rearmament in the guise of a four-year-long, abortive melodrama? Even the "old fox" Achilles would have been hard pressed to manage that.[160]

Whether the EDC crisis could have been handled any better, therefore, is less significant than its outcome: a rearmed West Germany in NATO and, later on, an American military commitment in Vietnam that turned out to be doomed, but in the end still served to reaffirm the primacy of the transatlantic commitment. In the short term, the crisis also meant patching up things with the British, who led temporarily in rescuing the rearmament cause.[161] It also meant, for EUR, an even greater role for the NATO hands within the bureau. But it marked the first serious miscalculation of the Euro-mavens—an early crack in their fragile foundation. In spite of the damage the EDC drama leveled on their idealism, the channeling of their energies into more practical directions was nevertheless useful. Cautious and conciliatory officers like Livie Merchant would rise to fill the temporary gap in leadership in the department. The failure of the EDC, according to him, "made possible a better solution, all things considered, than otherwise would have been conceivable." Indeed, by the spring of 1955, just a decade since the end of the war, one could read about NATO's supreme allied commander, General Gruenther, standing next to a German general while "Deutschland über alles" was played outside NATO headquarters.[162]

6

WINDS OF CHANGE

*Reactions to the decolonization—secretaryships of Acheson and Dulles—
effects of Wristonization and McCarthyism—retirement of the first generation of foreign
service officers*

VIETNAM AND, to a lesser degree, Algeria, would have much unhappier endings than the European Defense Community. As one would expect, EUR generally opposed the wishes of Americans, including Franklin Roosevelt, to promote the quick decolonization of the European possessions in Asia and Africa after World War II. Its case became even stronger as the Cold War progressed in the 1950s: No longer was it a question of the viability for self-government of the various independent movements and the extent to which an apparent rush to decolonization would upset important constituencies in Europe; by now there was also a life-or-death struggle with the Soviet Union (and China) for the souls of millions of fence-sitters, many of whom seemed sympathetic to Communism and to Communist-inclined independence movements. The irony in all this was not lost on the British, whose files are full of hand-wringing over contradictory American attitudes. Ivone Kirkpatrick wrote to his friend Roger Makins in November 1955: "It is of course an old anomaly that the unthinking anti-colonial Americans should be admonishing the civilised nations to lay down sovereignty and abandon nationalisms—whilst they excite the barbarians and cannibals to nationalism and imperialism."[1] But most people in EUR were hardheaded: Third World nationalisms were not to be condoned if they set themselves against Europe. Few in EUR called for the preservation of colonial empires, but many were confirmed gradualists—and the more gradual the better—even though this position put them at odds with their colleagues in other bureaus, particularly Far Eastern Affairs (at least before the McCarthy purges).

The resistance to decolonization, either passive or, where Communists were visibly involved, active, carried tangible and intangible costs the United States seemed unhappy to have the Europeans pay by themselves. Prolonged anticolonial struggles would ultimately imperil the commitment to the security of Europe, particularly for France. One officer who took the problem especially seriously was the man who replaced Chip Bohlen as the department's counselor, Doug MacArthur, who appeared earlier in the Vichy drama. He remained known for his French expertise, having won the trust of Ambassador Caffery while also getting along with most of the latter's detractors. Only one other person, besides Caffery's protégé Doc Matthews, was reported to succeed in doing so in French affairs, and this was a popular foreign service character right out of a Noël Coward play, Elim O'Shaughnessy. A second-generation diplomat, Elim, also known as "The Turtle," acted the part of the striped-pants man better than almost anyone, with affected accent, "protruding fish eyes," long cigarette holder, elegantly tailored suits, and lank hair. He did it so well, in fact, that he failed his foreign service oral exam several times until he was told the reason: He did not present a sufficiently American appearance. So he moved to St. Louis and got a job as a gas station attendant. The result was mixed: O'Shaughnessy was admitted to the foreign service but had not changed much. However, a visitor to the St. Louis gas station later noted that nearly everyone there used a long cigarette holder.[2]

In any event, having barely weathered the EDC crisis, the intense MacArthur had "gone native" following a few trips to Asia, describing, "with throbbing voice, glowering looks, and with minatory overtones," America's NATO allies as "millstones around our necks."[3] For the time being, however, the United States had "swallowed its scruples" and instead urged Europeans to do all they could to prepare their colonies for viable self-government.[4] It was the beginning of another period of ambivalence toward Europe and the countries soon to be labeled "Third World"—an ambivalence bred of the incompatibility at one level between the morality and necessities of foreign policy, a choice that did not seem so stark in Europe itself thanks to the successes of the Marshall Plan, and, on another level, between the conflicting strategic imperatives of deterrence and containment. Where NATO was ill disposed to fight directly (that is, on the European continent), it had to resort to what seemed to be a limitless arms buildup; yet where the United States and other European states decided they must intervene (that is, beyond Europe), deterrence functioned in reverse: namely, interventionists were deterred by the risk of what came to be called "escalation" in the act of containing, rather than defeating, the Communist threat. Here, too, diplomats stood more frequently behind the soldiers. As the 1950s wore on, then, the temptation among both groups to cloak ambivalence in moral self-righteousness rose considerably. No doubt it caused a good deal of grief for EUR and its European counterparts, especially when their careers advanced by virtue of their close ties to one another. British undersecretary of state Douglas Dodds-Parker chided Makins, by now the latest in a string of highly popular postwar ambassadors to Washington, that much of America's own history and practices south of the Mason-Dixon line, as well as abroad, "reminds me of the great American children's game of Cowboys and Indians, or what my—and perhaps your—half American children refer to (at least in the absence of their mothers) as Cowboys and Americans." He went on to lay blame on a popular source:

> Hollywood's up-to-date glorification of sex, violence and alcohol, have in my personal experience in the past twenty-five years done more to eliminate the horrors of colonialism than any other single factor. They

have more than offset the century of endeavor by Christian missionaries with the sole unfortunate effect that the locals are unable to distinguish between a European and North American skin pigmentation now that the indigenous Americans have been virtually eliminated.... All this is largely irrelevant to the pure doctrine of anti-colonialism as preached by the keen and semi-initiated.[5]

Makins would go on to serve in Washington right up to the eve of the Suez crisis. The timing of his departure was fortuitous, at least for him, but not for his large band of American fans, to the growing annoyance of his superiors.[6]

Gradualism would be put to rest, if not in the jungles of Vietnam, then in the warm waters of the Nile. The Suez crisis of October 1956 capped a difficult three years during which the United States was forced to take a stand against its British and French allies and, ironically, join with the Soviet Union and its incipient client, Gamal Abdel Nasser, right on the heels of the violent Soviet crackdown in Hungary. If the failure of the EDC was seen as a tactical victory but a strategic defeat for the Soviet Union, Suez appeared to signify the opposite for the West. In France, bizarrely, flags flew at half mast, but for the victims of the Hungarian crackdown, not for Suez. "The French are jubilant," wrote the wife and daughter of diplomats, Susan Mary Patten, later Alsop: "[they] don't care two pins for U.N. or world opinion, and are united in applauding the landings." "But," she added, "we talk Suez constantly and NATO is in pieces.... Bill [her husband] and I are for Eden and disgusted by the smugness of the Administration. Who forced Nasser to nationalize the canal? Dulles, of course."[7]

Two things resulted: It became clear to even the most romantic latter-day Victorians that "empires [were] going out of style"—everywhere; and that almost no place in the Third World, even the vital Suez Canal, was worth a schism in the Alliance. After it was all over, the Europeans still knew that "we loved them."[8] Next, sanctimony toward the Third World would give way to redoubled attempts to cultivate direct ties to those blowing in the winds of change, especially in the Middle East, where President Eisenhower was said to prescribe more "molasses, not starch."[9] But the problems of decolonization continued to rest precariously upon widening cracks in the bureaucracy. Subsequently, it was not unusual for young foreign service officers, and others, to begin to wade directly into the internal politics of such places, much as they had done a decade before in Europe.[10] EUR then spent the rest of the 1950s mending fences, while the fence-sitters continued to waver—only now it would become harder to play the Europeans and Americans off one another. As the British journalist Henry Brandon confided to his journal, the synthesis of two competing orientations—of "those who believe [foreign policy] must revolve around the Atlantic pact" and "those who believe that [the] US must pursue a strong anti-colonial policy"—was only temporary, with the result of "say[ing] we need to preserve the alliance in Europe and play the rest by confusion."[11]

In the end both the EDC and Suez crises seemed to be brief setbacks with their own silver linings. Both shored up the power of EUR against would-be rivals. The only major negative side effect, at least in Europe, was the decision taken by the French to develop an independent nuclear force, although that probably would have happened anyway.[12] The West Germans would rearm and join NATO as full members in 1955. The Middle East would grow more divided by the Cold War but would not divide the West again until the 1970s. Decolonization would proceed, by fits and starts, and with further crises, but also would not, apart from Vietnam, pose serious challenges to Atlantic solidarity. By the end of the 1950s, the Alliance was without a doubt in fine shape; and so too were the prospects for European integration, now that Europe's anticipated economic boom had arrived. The people who ran EUR took conscious advantage of these crises much as their predecessors had during the war and their successors would after the nadir of the 1960s. They had been sufficiently "infiltrated" by integrationists at this point to succumb to the allure of the European project; even Livie Merchant and Ted Achilles were now nominal supporters.[13] But so too were the integrationists brought around to the idea of an Atlantic Community and to NATO as its central pillar. Moreover, as will become clear in the next chapter, there were by now several important nongovernmental support groups that had come into existence, each promoting similar agendas.[14] An important constituency had taken root, of course diverse and variable, but with significant reach into officialdom. It embedded a certain idea of the American commitment to Europe—both military and political—so well that it came to be taken for granted by most opinion makers. It was a surprise to very few of them, for example, that President Eisenhower rejected out of hand Charles de Gaulle's proposal of a transatlantic triumvirate in 1958.[15] Such a thing was no longer conceivable, just as going it alone would be unthinkable after Suez; and from then on, at any rate, personalities seemed to count for less. "It was clear," according to a later account, "that de Gaulle did not believe that Eisenhower understood what he was talking about."[16] Institutions and collective arrangements, however nascent, mattered most of all.

THERE WERE, ALAS, two more crises to weather. The first was the collapse of State Department morale at the hands of Joseph McCarthy. The second was something few people remember today, but it was on everyone's mind in EUR at the time: the folding into the foreign service of many of the Marshall Planners and other personnel in a process called "Wristonization." The name derived from the plan of Henry Wriston, president of Brown University and head of the commission that prescribed the personnel changes. EUR survived both ordeals, not without some pain, but again, better than any other section of the department and in a manner that once again brought out its talent for transforming crisis into opportunity.

Some saw Wristonization as redemptive. "I believe that this new committee which has been set up under Dr. Wriston ... may be productive of good effects," Bob Murphy wrote to Jimmy Dunn in March 1954. "I feel reasonably confident that the low point has been passed for the Service."[17] He spoke too soon. Most people in the department reacted to the wholesale entry into their ranks of so many unwashed with a distaste that had not been seen since the days of the Rogers Act. Many of the "Wristonees," as they were called, had served in the army or in the occupation, and none had taken the foreign service exam, which remained highly competitive, with only 18 percent having passed the written test in 1948–1950.[18] Many of the newcomers, as it happened, were economists or administrative experts. They were depicted, in other words, as impostors and enthusiasts, "imbued with an evangelical zeal" and lacking the formation and common experience of the line officers.[19]

The postwar reforms did not stop there. In 1949, the latest in a series of State Department reorganizations finally completed the last of the great mergers—that of the department and its civil service employees, whose ranks and pay scales had risen substantially during the war, whereas the foreign service had shrunk badly, apart from the establishment of the Auxiliary Foreign Service. Now there would be a single foreign service with one exam, one set of promotion standards, and one large bureaucracy, with a continued effort at greater coordination, at least in theory, between operations and policymaking.[20] The results were not altogether negative, but they were no doubt disorienting. George Kennan regarded it typically as the "final liquidation of the old Foreign Service we knew."[21] In a long colloquy with Wriston reprinted in the *Foreign Service Journal*, he noted that when he had joined, "one could rely on the uniformity and stability of the conditions in which, from then on, the competition for advancement and recognition would proceed." Lest there be any doubt, Kennan added, "These hopes and expectations, as experience was to prove, were largely unfounded." He went on to bemoan the further decline of the diplomatic corps, attributing it alternately to Wristonization and the ingrained incapacities of his country, which he noted, quoting Jules Cambon on democracies, would always "have diplomacy" but never "diplomatists." Wriston responded in kind. "Some, [Kennan] says, 'would think it more important to have 25 really superior officers than to have 2,500 mediocre ones.' Would he object to 2,500 superior officers, or is he convinced the American democracy could not produce—or use—so many?" Wriston's plan was meant to provide them. For his part, Paul Nitze, in one of his few instances of agreement with Kennan, termed the Wriston report "dishonest in its facts, illogical in its reasoning, politically biased in its tone." He was not the only one to say so.[22]

It was a curious coincidence that the man Dulles charged with implementing these changes was none other than Kennan's old Moscow colleague, Loy Henderson, who had reemerged from his Middle Eastern exile to become deputy undersecretary. He initially opposed the recommendations of the Wriston report, but he enacted the mergers with all the meticulous fairness he could muster and would leave behind a long legacy of admiration in the department, despite being disliked in some quarters. "There were two State Departments in those days," recalled Jake Beam's wife, Peggy, "one under Henderson and one under Bob Murphy."[23] In general, however, the diplomats fell in line behind the reforms. As with the Rogers Act, they claimed there was little to fear from amalgamation: The department's mandarins retained most of their power, at least over policymaking. Their "grip" on the personnel process and on their department, at least as seen from the outside, remained firm.[24]

The 1950s was a volatile decade for the State Department despite all outward appearances of conformity and consolidation. General Marshall, who became secretary in 1947, brought a long-overdue sense of order and pride to a war-weary group of bureaucrats. He and his deputy, Bob Lovett, brought the department into policymaking to a degree it had not had seen, arguably, since the days of Herbert Hoover, and probably even beyond that.[25] That position was cemented by Dean Acheson, later regarded as among the most formidable secretaries of the twentieth century, despite the considerable hostility directed against him at the time, which had more to do with the Republican insurgency in the Congress and the press against President Truman than with Acheson's direct mishandling of either.[26] In the words of British ambassador Oliver Franks, whom Acheson reportedly saw more often than all other ambassadors combined, the secretary "combine[d] an eighteenth-century style of personal taste with the moral conscience and austerity of a seventeenth-century puritan.... He is profoundly American in this regard."[27] Likewise for Acheson, Europe remained the supreme prize of the Cold War. Moreover, Acheson had established a relationship with the president that was closer, perhaps, than any other before or after him. Harry Truman relied upon him entirely, and with few exceptions, deferred to his judgment.

For those in EUR, then, it was the best of all possible worlds: They had a brilliant and engaged boss who not only had the full attention of the president but also cared deeply about their part of the world and viewed its problems more or less in the same way they did. Acheson did not always use the bureaucrats as much as he could have; they were, in his lawyerly mind, primarily aides for deliberation, that is, "second chairs." Perhaps this was also because he made very few of his own appointments. With the exception of his counselor, Philip Jessup, almost all the senior officials, including his deputy James Webb and the assistant secretary for European affairs, a former Merck executive, George Perkins, were appointed to satisfy either Truman or some member of Congress.[28] Apart from Webb (to whom Acheson was not close), most proved amenable and supportive, particularly Perkins—even though he was a registered Republican.

Few senior members of the department would survive the transfer of power in 1953. John Foster Dulles was a different kind of lawyer, corporate and more ostensibly methodical. Whereas Acheson strove to evoke the views of others in order to maneuver them into sharing and enforcing his own, Dulles simply kept all but the most trusted people away.[29] And whereas Acheson, the son of an Episcopal bishop, let his core principles show only in moments of exasperation or—as will be seen in the next chapter—crisis, Dulles, the Presbyterian elder, wore his on his sleeve almost all of the time. The French diplomat and later foreign minister Maurice Couve de Murville, a Calvinist himself, noted the distinction:

> I would say that the two men were almost exactly the opposite. First, in their behavior. While Acheson ... is ... very British ... in the way he speaks and the way he behaves ... [h]e's a little difficult, of course.... He has certainly a sense of his intellectual and social superiority.... Foster Dulles was very different because he was much more simple. I wouldn't say more modest, because I don't know. But the *appearance* was more modest. Probably he was, just as much as Acheson (and that is not critical; it is normal), convinced that he was *right*.... But he showed his conviction in a different way.... [I]t is very much the difference between an Episcopalian and a Presbyterian ... [b]etween..., in England, you would say an Anglican and a Nonconformist.[30]

It is amusing to think of Foster Dulles the schoolboy debating whether Washington or Lincoln was the greater president: "A man's right to honor," he said, "rests on two things: his character and his achievements, and it seems to me that Lincoln excelled Washington in both these respects."[31] The diplomat Coburn Kidd suggested that times called for nothing less: "[W]hen [Dulles] tells a *Life* reporter that we were ready 'to smite them hip and thigh' ... [t]hat is not optimism, but a cheerful lucidity of purpose in taking on the Devil.... This is what, I feel, is at bottom wrong with Kennanism: it is not tough enough to be Machiavellian; it is an artist's conduct of diplomacy, and diplomacy is too serious to be treated as an art."[32] And yet Dulles seemed, unlike Acheson, willing to alter his views if a better argument presented itself. His mind was at once more recalcitrant and less fixed than his predecessor's.

As the grandson and nephew of secretaries of state and a foreign policy authority in his own right since the 1920s, Dulles was seen as having been born to the position, in contrast with Acheson, who came to Washington as part of the Frankfurter migration, and despite becoming a leader of the "little hot dogs," never really fit in fully with the permanent bureaucracy until he made it to the top. Dulles was always the heir apparent, although Eisenhower was reported to favor McCloy for the job and only chose Dulles after having been persuaded by General Clay that Dulles would have an easier time with Congress, particularly with Senator Robert Taft.[33] Accordingly, Dulles entered into office with a clear sense of how things should be done, even though, again in contrast with Acheson, he had never previously held any formal office in the department.[34]

His relationship with the president was also very different from the one Acheson had with Truman. If the latter was an almost textbook study of the bond between lawyer and client, the former was more akin to a good cop–bad cop pantomime. For by the time he was "drafted" to the presidency, Dwight Eisenhower was far more surefooted than Harry Truman ever could have hoped to be in 1945. He was also a good deal more devious. In crafting his so-called hidden hand presidency, Eisenhower almost always let others take the credit, and the blame, for the administration's actions. The histrionic Dulles was practically typecast for the part of foreign policy guru; yet there is little sign that he ever let himself forget who was in charge. This put the State Department in an odd position. The bureaus were consulted far less than they had been under Acheson; often they claimed to be embarrassed by Dulles's speeches and his obsequiousness toward members of Congress. Their interactions with the hatchet men of the front office—hired to appease Senator McCarthy and his backers—were unpleasant, to put it mildly. Yet with regard to Europe, the advent of Dulles did not present an altogether unhappy prospect. Dulles was personally closer to Monnet, for example, than Acheson had ever been, and was regarded by EUR especially as a dyed-in-the-wool Europeanist.[35] By his own account, Dulles's closest affinity was to France, but he was also very experienced with Germany from his service on the Reparations Commission after World War I, when he became known for his lenient stance on payment conditions. Throughout the 1920s, Dulles worked extensively on German banking and other industrial cases.[36]

At the top of the list of the few people to whom Dulles listened regularly as secretary were Livie Merchant and Bob Bowie. Doug MacArthur, as already noted, was his counselor, and he enlisted David Bruce, a loyal Democrat, to be special representative to the EDC negotiations and to the Coal and Steel Community.[37] But almost everyone else from the Truman years, including the "Thursday lunch" group of Marshall Planners—Paul Nitze, Linc Gordon, Dick Bissell, Harlan

Cleveland, and nearly all the rest—were cast to the political wind.[38]

EUR, however, survived the purges. Hugh Gibson, Joe Grew, Norman Armour, and Doc Matthews were called upon to pass judgment on ambassadorial appointments, and Matthews, as already mentioned, selected Merchant for the job of assistant secretary. Dulles pointed out in the same breath that Merchant was a "solid Republican" and that he, Dulles, would never let EUR be run by anyone who was not a fully trained foreign service officer. Merchant, for his part, replied, "In all my life no comparable bolt ever came from so blue a sky."[39] Merchant became assistant secretary for Europe for the first of two tenures that lasted, apart from a two-year interruption in 1957–1958, until the end of the decade. Together with MacArthur and Bowie, Merchant formed a European triumvirate that went by the name MacMerBo. It was immortalized in the following ballad by a deputy, Phil Trezise:

High Noon in Abazu or
Robert R. Bowie Rides Again

Breathes a man with pulse so slow
As not to feel an inner glow
When scribes recount and bards sing, O
The ancient glories of MacMerBo?

Whose memory's so far arrears
As fails to call back from the years
Those stirring days when 'gainst the foe
Stood ranged the phalanx, MacMerBo.

When marched this tiny, happy band
With vision of a Promised Land
Each day into the Secretary's sessions
Prepared to put the harder questions,

Control of arms, aid for the Indian,
Think twice of Matsu, hear out the Russian.
No cause so long, no hope so slight
MacMerBo ne'er eschewed the fight.

So welcome, Bowie know our esteem
Even while off in Academe
Tell us, though, do thoughts e'er go
Back, back to times of MacMerBo?[40]

But the times were not so happy. From Dulles's first week on the job—when he gave a notorious speech in the parking lot of the new department building about "positive loyalty"—he offended and frightened the staff, which, along with a few European counterparts, came to mock him in ways unimaginable since the days of Ed Stettinius. "Even the good Lord only saved the world once," went a well-known saying. "The trouble with Foster," went another, a play on nuclear brinkmanship, "is that he has such a weak head—three brinks and he's brunk."[41] Acheson had had his own managerial hatchet men—namely, Carlisle Humelsine and John Peurifoy—but neither provoked the kind of animosity raised by Dulles's "domestic appeasement" and two notorious deputies: Scott McLeod and John Hanes. McLeod was especially offensive: a vengeful, "roly-poly," former FBI agent and member of the staff of Senator Styles Bridges, he was assigned to terrorize the foreign service. Many of his attacks were nakedly political, such as lowering the efficiency rating of Willard Beaulac, Carlton Hayes's former deputy in Madrid, because he had made a campaign contribution to Adlai Stevenson. Doc Matthews, who, amazingly, was interviewed by the FBI about Dulles's own loyalty, regarded McLeod as the most "despised person" ever to be visited upon the department.[42] He performed with gusto until nearly being fired after passing personnel files to Senator McCarthy. He was subsequently named ambassador to Ireland. Hanes— of the underwear dynasty—had a softer touch and reserved much of his passion for birds. Both he and his colleague Roderic O'Connor—who replaced McLeod— had served briefly in the CIA and might have been deemed necessary to protect the department against excessive congressional pressure.[43]

It is important to recall here that despite the steep drop in morale, the State Department's main problem with the McCarthyites was more managerial than ethical; that is, it had to do with security, not with loyalty per se. Too often its enemies in Congress conflated the two. The security problem was a long-standing one: Cordell Hull's State Department had been known especially for leaks, missing files, and disorderly procedures. The loyalty issue also predated McCarthy. President Truman's Loyalty Order came in March 1947, and a little over two months later, Secretary Marshall established a Personnel Security Board. In the first five years of its operation, the board had 745 cases, of which it passed along only 77 to the FBI, and it made only 3 "adverse decisions" relating to loyalty. (There were 30 for security.) Of the 205 Communists appearing on Senator McCarthy's imaginary list (which the senator eventually narrowed to 61 actual names from the State Department), only 2 ended up being rated as "ineligible" on security grounds—the celebrated cases of John Carter Vincent and John Service. Neither came from EUR.[44]

Yet the climate of persecution provoked and exploited by the McCarthyites was another matter entirely. Some government workers committed suicide or disappeared to assume new identities after the mere hint of an investigation. Kennan once described McCarthyism as "a struggle of the industrial civilization— technocracy and semi-educated against old liberal educated civilization." Acheson called it simply, "the attack of the primitives."[45] It hit the department hard. McCarthy's campaign began as an assault for the "loss" of China; it decimated the Far Eastern Bureau, drove both it and the Latin American Bureau to the conservative fringes for nearly two decades, and scared away many of the more talented Wristonees who were likely to have had dubious, New Deal connections.

EUR as a whole, however, remained comparably unscathed. Hickerson and his NATO group were solidly anti-Communist, even though Hickerson himself had moved to the U.S. Mission to the United Nations—a favorite target—and had once even supervised Michael Straight, the owner of the *New Republic* who was later revealed to be a Soviet spy. The German hands similarly were too important to destroy en masse. Almost none of the Soviet hands could be regarded as pink—despite Roosevelt's earlier attempts to cleanse EUR of the old Kelley network. In general, the department's postwar succession of undersecretaries—particularly Grew, Acheson, Lovett, and Bruce as well as Doc Matthews, Bob Murphy, and Loy Henderson, who served as deputy undersecretaries—worked hard to defend the service as best they could against its domestic enemies. But they and other senior members of the department seemed to regard the direct attacks on their organization more as a nuisance than a threat, and appeared mostly concerned with the negative effects McCarthy and others had on America's image, particularly in Europe.[46]

A few tragic sacrifices ensued nevertheless. Some, such as Julius Holmes, one of the most talented officers in the department and an old acquaintance of Eisenhower, fell victim to the terrible state of the relationship between the State Department and Congress. Accused (most likely falsely) of corruption, there was little he could do to salvage his nearly destroyed career, in spite of numerous appeals on his behalf.[47] Similarly, Sam Reber, regarded as a brilliant, cultivated, and extremely conscientious officer, not only for his work in Italy (where he had served under Breckinridge Long and William Phillips), France, and North Africa during the war but also as deputy high commissioner in Germany, retired from the service mysteriously in June 1955. He was, by most accounts, "an inherently decent sort," even if he was "occasionally made the goat for unpopular moves worked out by his superiors." It was rumored that McLeod had hit on something incriminating about his private life (Reber was another confirmed bachelor), but if it ever existed, it never surfaced in public.[48] Other, lesser-known figures took the same route out of government, either scared or threatened by the inquisition. A few tried their best to react less seriously than was otherwise advisable. Ben Bradlee, who left the U.S. Information Service post in Paris for *Newsweek*, recalled the infamous European tour of McCarthy's lackeys, the lovers Roy Cohn and David Schine, during which they purged embassy-run libraries of books and provoked as many officers as they could. According to Bradlee, the trip provided great amusement to the embassy and press corps, which conspired to embarrass the duo at every turn.[49] Another who seemed to take the terror in his stride was Walt Butterworth. One day when headed to Capitol Hill to testify, his assistant noticed he was wearing his usual homburg and advised him to think about removing "that symbol of a diplomacy McCarthy was trying to vilify." "This hat has been loyal to me for many years," Butterworth replied after a brief moment's thought. "I am not going to leave it now."[50]

As suggested above, one would have expected McCarthy to select the Soviet hands for the harshest treatment. He did not. Most had such a solid anti-Communist record that attacking any of them would have been difficult, even for him. But there was one notable exception: Chip Bohlen. When Eisenhower named Bohlen to be ambassador to Moscow, the McCarthyites on Capitol Hill and in the press geared for battle. Here was the man who had been Roosevelt's interpreter at Tehran and Yalta, who had roomed with Alger Hiss, and who, for years, had urged a pragmatic and flexible policy toward the USSR. And there were other rumors: For some reason, Bohlen's secretary had become convinced he was a homosexual; he was said to drink too much and have loose friends, and so forth. There was even an allegedly incriminating tape, which Senators Sparkman and Taft listened to surreptitiously while lying on the floor of Dulles's office. The secretary took it all most seriously: "Now, it's been said that this Bohlen case is an acid test. I think it's an acid test of the orderly processes of our Government."[51] But Bohlen proved too smart and resourceful to be brought down. Dulles did not put up a great fight for him, but Eisenhower ultimately did, and the Senate confirmed his nomination. The "small group of 'willful men'" was defeated; the "shame that must rest on all Americans who cherish the moral dignity and intellectual freedom for which their country stands" remained.[52]

Less fortunate than Bohlen was his brother-in-law and close friend, Charlie Thayer. Unlike Bohlen and Alger Hiss, Thayer was both "a little guilty and a little innocent."[53] To borrow from the conspiratorial thinking of the McCarthyites, one might say that Thayer became the necessary scapegoat for Bohlen. Thayer was, to be sure, an unusual diplomat, though he regarded himself an expert on the subject and even wrote a book about the profession modeled on Harold Nicolson's.[54] A graduate of West Point, where he excelled mainly in polo and in fastening pup tents, Thayer left the army and made his way to Moscow, where he was appointed to the staff of Ambassador Bullitt and where he met Bohlen, to whom he became so close as to introduce him to his sister and Bohlen's future wife, Avis. Bullitt's memoranda are full of complaints about the duo and their high jinks, most of which are described comically in Thayer's two short memoirs—*Bears in the Caviar* and *Hands over the Caviar*.[55] Slightly more irreverent and somewhat less brilliant than Bohlen, Thayer served in Russia and in Afghanistan, and then went to Yugoslavia as the U.S. military adviser to Tito and his partisans, eventually landing in Germany, where he became a first-rate political reporter and one of the first foreign service officers to socialize frequently with German politicians in Bonn during the earliest days of the High Commission when such contacts were still limited. There he married the daughter of Jimmy Dunn and began to work on advancing a more conventional career as, among other things, one of the founders of Radio Free Europe. But being the misfit that he was, Thayer not surprisingly had a raucous private life. McLeod and company alleged that he was homosexual, and strung together a good deal of rumor to that effect, without ever proving their case. Thayer had fathered an illegitimate child with a Russian woman. He was threatened with publicity unless he resigned, which he did, and went on to live quietly and, for the most part, unhappily as a part-time journalist and novelist in Mallorca and Bavaria.[56]

Thayer's case angered many in the government, particularly his long list of close friends. One was Bob Joyce, a foreign service and OSS veteran who subsequently suffered what seemed to be a mental breakdown, deciding to leave government service for the warm Greek skies of Spetsai.[57] He resembled Labouisse and others of that generation—well loved, well educated, and well networked, and included Hemingway and Cy Sulzberger among his friends and acquaintances, with a wife, Jane, who was one of the handful of women who reigned over Georgetown society. He spoke for many of his colleagues when he noted at the time that "if the present process continues we are certain to find that Gresham's law of bad money driving out good will increasingly apply to the Foreign Service and that ... we will acquire a Foreign Service designed to serve a hagridden totalitarian state rather than a liberal and self-confident democracy."[58] For his part, Charlie Thayer may well have consoled himself with the lines he copied from William Ernest Henley's "Invictus":

Out of the night that covers me,
Black as the Pit from pole to pole
I thank whatever gods may be
For my unconquerable soul.

In the fell clutch of circumstance
I have not winced nor cried aloud.
Under the bludgeonings of chance.
My head is bloody, but unbowed.

Beyond this place of wrath and tears
Looms but the Horror of the shade,
And yet the menace of the years
Finds, and shall find, me unafraid.

It matters not how strait the gate
How charged with punishments the scroll,
I am the master of my fate:
I am the captain of my soul.[59]

Apart from these unfortunate cases, the impact of the McCarthy tragedy upon the State Department and its ability to do its job in Europe mainly had to do with morale. The "poison blows across the Atlantic like some horrible prevailing wind," recalled Susan Mary Patten; few could avoid breathing it.[60] The excitement and drama of the immediate postwar years seemed to crash. Where the influx and competition of nondiplomats energized the ranks of Americans serving abroad, McCarthyism in its various manifestations made them more cautious, even afraid, to take risks, speak their mind, and cement relationships. With few exceptions, they began to look inward, became defensive of their country and eager for opportunities elsewhere. Others tried their best to toe the line, with varying degrees of plausibility. In one such example, an opportunistic Doug MacArthur advised Dulles to mention more often the numbers of war veterans in the foreign service in order to counteract the impression of "cookie-pushing panty-waisters."[61] Still, McCarthyism was not the only source of poor morale. Dean Acheson's former assistant, Jeffrey Kitchen, griped, "Little Rock and *Sputnik* have cost all that we gained through the prestige of the Marshall Plan effort and the humanitarian implications of [the] Salk vaccine."[62] The postwar years were turning out to be less sunny than anticipated.

The disruptions leveled upon the foreign service by Wristonization and the political purges of the 1950s, one by addition, the other by subtraction, also meant that other aspects of professional advancement would remain stagnant. The department made only superficial progress in building a more representative officer corps, although it had professed the desire to do so, even hiring a special "consultant on minority problems."[63] Perhaps its worst showing was in recruiting

C. Douglas Dillon, Christian Herter, Robert Murphy
Time & Life Pictures/Getty

women. The appointment in 1953 of Frances Willis as the first female foreign service officer to head the Swiss embassy was only small comfort. There were only a handful of them, never reaching more than 10 percent of any incoming class and given a career expectancy of six years.[64] Although the wartime rule against marriage to foreigners had begun to be relaxed for men—gradually, and provided they were the right kind of foreigners—women were still not permitted to marry at all. This is not to say that women did not play an important diplomatic role. Wives certainly did. Efficiency reports included ratings for the quality of one's wife, her social talent and alacrity. It was nearly impossible to become an ambassador if one did not have a wife. When Selden Chapin's wife became ill and had to return to the United States from their post in The Hague, Chapin's teenage daughter had to step in to help run the embassy and oversee all social events. Not doing so would have been unthinkable, especially when one's father had been a scion of the foreign service, indeed its first director-general.[65] The ambassador's wife was nothing less than the deputy ambassador for all things social and cultural. It was a full-time job. Upon arriving at a new embassy, a foreign service officer's wife would report immediately to the ambassador's wife and be given her duties. She could not opt out. Some were truly notorious—"Wahwee" MacArthur, wife of Doug and daughter of Vice President Barkley, and Elise Henderson, Loy's Latvian wife, for example. Many an officer found his diplomatic skills stretched to the fullest in avoiding assignments to their embassies, not only for his wife and family's sake but also for his own.[66]

IN MAY 1959, one month after the tenth anniversary of the North Atlantic Treaty, John Foster Dulles took ill and died. His funeral was probably the most momentous of its kind since Roosevelt's and featured a well-rounded Cold War ensemble: In attendance were Adenauer, Andrei Gromyko, Joseph Luns, Dag Hammarskjöld, Madame Chiang Kai-shek, Heinrich von Brentano, Selwyn Lloyd, Spaak, and Couve de Murville, in addition to most senior members of the Eisenhower administration, the cream of Wall Street, and several prominent clergymen. Among the honorary pallbearers, Jean Monnet was the only foreigner. The band played four ruffles and flourishes and a strain of "God of Our Fathers," and then John Foster Dulles, as Dean Acheson supposedly said, was underground, thank God.[67]

Replacing him was his deputy, Christian Herter, the former Massachusetts governor and Congressman whose committee shepherded the Marshall Plan through Congress. Herter was known as the "high priest" of the Atlanticists and is an underrated secretary of state. His tenure was brief and his health was not good; his relationship with Eisenhower was not anywhere near as close as Dulles's; he was perceived, not inaccurately, as a kind of caretaker. But he cut an impressive figure, not as intellectually formidable as either of his two predecessors, but nevertheless as "a man of impregnable honor, which is much rarer and more important than brilliancy."[68] He certainly was less controversial and far less devious than Dulles. Like Dulles, Herter had been at Versailles in 1919, and was for many years a member of the foreign policy establishment; but unlike Dulles, Herter seemed to get along well with most people, a talent he honed during his years in state politics. Moreover, he really looked and sounded the part: tall, borderline lanky, with a high forehead, angular jaw, a perpetually worn bow tie, and a deep, patrician voice. He was, according to his friend Christopher Emmet, the "ideal appointment": "He had many friends and no enemies."[69] The bureaucracy, especially EUR, could not have been more delighted. Herter had been a quiet but popular undersecretary and was regarded as one of them: He had joined the diplomatic service in 1916 after having studied architecture. His grandfather was an 1848 refugee from Germany who became a successful muralist. Herter himself had been born in Paris. With the possible exception of Henry Kissinger, he was perhaps the most European of secretaries, and though the influence of the State Department probably declined under his watch, Herter proved to be a happy transitional figure. Bohlen noted that under him, as under Marshall, the department had never been in better shape.[70]

Herter's disposition and his diplomacy—simple, quiet, straightforward— delivered a dignified end to a dramatic decade and a half, in spite of the U-2 affair in 1960 that scuttled the Paris conference, for which both he and the president had prepared so carefully. By the end of Eisenhower's second term, Europe and the transatlantic relationship had begun, as Dulles was heard to say, accompanied by a swoop of his hand, to "all come together."[71] The ground for an Atlantic Community had been tilled and planted, and partisans inside and outside the department had begun the weeding. Many of the loose ends from the war—too detailed to be described here, but including, among others, the settlement of the Trieste and Saar disputes and the rehabilitation of Spain—were resolved.[72] The bipartisan consensus on foreign policy, damaged by McCarthyism and Dulles's occasional, odd insistence that the Atlantic Alliance was just one of several such arrangements around the world, was resumed, with NATO moving again to the head of the pack. Europe and America started to resemble Eisenhower's image of "an expanding spiral of strength and hope and confidence," while the unraveling of America's influence elsewhere in the world had yet to begin in earnest.[73]

A respite for EUR was long overdue. The Cold War had already begun to take a toll on many people, especially the German hands. German policy underwent reviews so constant that they seemed to last the whole of the 1950s. But Jimmie Riddleberger had departed for the embassy in Greece and then to head the International Cooperation Agency. Perry Laukhuff grew fed up, transferred to Vietnam, and later ran the Dag Hammarskjöld Foundation. Another lesser known but beloved German hand, Arch Calhoun, ended up in Chad. Elwood Williams, despite his worsening muscular dystrophy and chain smoking, continued to preside over an exhausted but still formidable German office, reserving what remarkable, remaining energies he still had for the meticulous nurturing of talented officers, more impressive in mind than in appearance, in contrast, say, to the department's specialists on France.[74]

One member of the latter group who finally left the foreign service in 1962 was Doc Matthews: The father of the Vichy gamble, the State Department's senior delegate to Yalta and Potsdam, the interim undersecretary, and, along with Dunn, Murphy, and Henderson, among the first class of foreign service officers to earn the new rank of "career ambassador."[75] His final embassy was in Vienna, where he was on hand to observe John F. Kennedy's disastrous meeting with Nikita Khrushchev. Soon afterward, he decided to retire. A younger colleague, William Harrop, recalled Matthews's last day at the office:

> I saw him in that second corridor on the "C" Street side, where the Personnel area, the Foreign Service Lounge, the Leave and Retirement Office, and Accounts are located. He was walking around all alone, a little dazed. I said, "Ambassador Matthews, how are you? What are you doing?" He answered, "Well, I'm trying to retire. I'm going around here. I've got to find a Mrs. So-and-so. What is 'PT4L2'? I've got all these papers to sign, and I don't know where to take them." He was wandering about. No one was helping him, no one was advising him.... It is a poignant moment in a man's life to end a 40-year career. You just feel completely isolated, alone, and rather forlorn, walking around and slipping away. You hand in your identity card and slip out the side door for the last time you'll be in the Department. It's a rather difficult experience, which everyone must go through.... It's a very different style altogether in the armed forces.[76]

This was the paradox of America's "heroic age," as Louis Halle called it. It featured diplomatic giants, both inside and outside the foreign service, people who wrote the rules of the Cold War, who established structures and patterns for a half century of international affairs, who led "a remarkable record of involvement in getting us plugged into the world." Yet, with only a few exceptions, they did so collectively and nearly anonymously, less as conquerors than as subtle missionaries, eager to muffle with so many institutions and committees the slightest hint of self-interest in their actions and prescriptions.[77] It was their manner, or what Henry James once called a tone-standard—the combination of the Marshall Plan's mantra of "self-help" and EUR's cautious balance of multiple national and regional interests—that made it all work.[78]

To sum up, the record of the bureau during its golden years came down to three sets of components that would transform both it and American diplomacy for the remainder of the twentieth century. To borrow some terminology from the military, they were as follows:

Strategically, there was the solidarity of the Atlantic Alliance, with the ultimate aim of constructing an Atlantic Community.

Operationally, there were NATO and European integration within a wider, global program of economic liberalization.

Tactically, there was the continuous pursuit of political, economic, and military measures that harmonized the two operational aims, both with one another and with the overall, strategic aims stated above.

This was the system that EUR devised in 1950–1951 that would survive, albeit with ups and downs, to the end of the 1980s. It was not as self-conscious an approach as one may like to think. Indeed, there often appeared to be an inverse relationship between the success of an initiative, as shown by the case of the EDC, and the outward conviction with which it was advanced. EUR's approach, then, was a good deal more complex in practice, alternately deistic and Panglossian, claiming both victory and defeat while continuously serving, as Roy Jenkins once put it with reference to himself and European unity, as more "buttress" than "pillar."[79] Along the way it also acquired the most durable institutional memory in the department; indeed, it became its center of gravity. One is tempted to view the decade and a half as a kind of apotheosis, even though, again, few people would have said so at the time, or later. But there can be little doubt that EUR became more sophisticated in the 1950s. Not only did it preserve America's commitment to Europe, but it also took the wartime recasting of its bureaucratic self as *primus inter pares* to new levels. It was both the enforcer of its own, seemingly permanent, supremacy at home and the unchallenged guardian of the transatlantic relationship. It would, moreover, reinvent the contemporary practice of diplomacy, and do so globally, showing by example the benefits of institution building, collective security, and the mutual reinforcement of an alliance and a community. It also demonstrated, though less voluntarily, how diplomatic professionals, technocrats, and political appointees could collaborate by accentuating one another's better talents. The people and the policies did not fit well all the time; but on balance the arrangement worked. Indeed, some promoters of Europe would get so carried away with success that they would nearly wreck the whole effort in the 1960s. This is the subject of the next two chapters.

7

THE AMBIVALENCE OF
DEAN ACHESON

The activist National Security Council—policy muddle—Atlanticists versus Europeanists redux—nongovernmental networks—Berlin, Skybolt, the Multilateral Nuclear Force, offset, and balance of payments

N THE SPRING OF 1962, Ted Achilles ended his thirty-year career in the foreign service. After the riveting years in London, Paris, and Washington, he served briefly as ambassador to Peru and then as counselor of the department, still an undefined and unpredictable job. For some, like Achilles, it was little more than a professional holding cell. He finally concluded, as Jean Monnet had in 1954, that

> [t]he present administration is moving toward goals, such as that of an expanding and deepening Atlantic Community and a new relationship with other American republics based on identification of the United States with the aspirations of the common man which many of us have for years been urging.... Having fought bureaucracy for over 30 years in efforts to have these ideas adopted as goals ... I am confident that the wealth of talent which exists in all ranks of the Foreign Service can make steady progress toward their realization.... I have decided that in [the] future I can contribute best toward the realization of these goals as a private citizen....

Attached to his letter is a short message noting "a very interesting and sincere letter, which, I think, illustrates understanding, sensitivity and encouraging dedication to the concept that 'the old order changeth, giving place to new.'"[1] But it would not be the last time they heard from Mr. Achilles.

John F. Kennedy's assumption of the presidency did not spare the State Department the changes he, or rather his most enthusiastic partisans, advertised for the country. "The Cold War in Europe has lost its old meaning," wrote the future national security adviser Zbigniew Brzezinski, only a few years later. "There was a vitality and a passion to it.... Neither condition truly exists today."[2] But what would replace it? And where?

Reading the tea leaves was not difficult. For the first time in recent memory, the department had a secretary whose formative foreign experiences were not European. Dean Rusk was an Asia hand who rose quietly up the ranks of the State and War Departments, leaving government in 1952 to head the Rockefeller Foundation. Unlike his three predecessors, Rusk was not a typical member of the establishment. He had been poor, from rural Georgia, and so undemonstrative that the Kennedy administration's in-house chronicler, Arthur Schlesinger Jr., described him as Buddha-like.[3] "Having conversations with Rusk was like talking with someone through a very thick glass window," Bob Bowie reportedly said of the "odd, shy, meticulously public-spirited and honest man," who "had the highest integrity."[4]

Rusk was not Kennedy's first choice for the job. Chester Bowles, the idealistic Connecticut politician and favorite of Kennedy's rival, Adlai Stevenson, posed as the Democratic heir-in-waiting, much as John Foster Dulles had once been for the Republicans. But Kennedy kept his distance from many of the Stevenson men, as he would from Stevenson himself, another presumptive secretary of state, relegated to the United Nations.[5] As to Bowles, he would get the number-two job in the department. He would last there only a year.

According to Schlesinger and others, Bob Lovett was Kennedy's top pick for State. But Lovett was both hypochondriacal and content with private life. He turned down the job as expected, along with the Pentagon and the Treasury, which also were offered to him. Then he played kingmaker. Lovett convinced Kennedy to appoint Robert McNamara, whom the president had never met, to head the Defense Department and the Republican C. Douglas Dillon to lead the Treasury.[6]

Another person Kennedy turned to for help was Dean Acheson. Acheson told him "to get all the rest you can while you can" because "you will find no lack of advisers ... but you will need all your good judgment to disregard most of their advice."[7] Nonetheless, he urged Kennedy to choose David Bruce as an interim secretary in order to pave the way for Paul Nitze, his former director of policy planning, widely known as resourceful, discreet, and, in Joe Alsop's words, "one of the strongest Don't-tell-the-boobs men I've seen in government," but who, according to Acheson, was still too unknown a figure to fill the job.[8] Neither Bruce nor Kennedy seemed amenable to the arrangement, so Kennedy offered Nitze the White House position that eventually went to the Harvard dean, McGeorge Bundy. Nitze demurred and went across the river, where he became assistant secretary of defense in the Pentagon's small policy office—International Security Affairs—which continued to evolve under his direction as the "mini-State Department."[9] As to Bruce, he got word that he could have any embassy he wanted. He chose London.[10]

How Rusk became secretary of state, then, remains something of a mystery. It was most likely Acheson who swayed Kennedy in his favor, a move Acheson would later regret. But Kennedy was already predisposed to pick a weak figure: When he asked the various, presumptive candidates—Stevenson, William Fulbright,

Bowles, Lovett, McCloy, and so forth—whom their ideal choice for deputy would be, nearly all said Rusk. It became clear that the president intended to be his own secretary of state.[11]

Kennedy's views about the department were mixed. He had made much of opportunities afforded by his father's appointment to the Court of St. James's by Franklin Roosevelt, and he came to like the foreign service officers who facilitated his European encounters. (An especially enthusiastic one in Paris was Carmel Offie.) During Kennedy's career as a legislator, he had gotten to know various State Department officials, endearing himself with his curiosity, irreverent humor, and iconoclastic, almost cynical, cast of mind.[12] As president, Kennedy became well known for disregarding hierarchy and calling desk officers whenever he wanted an answer to a question. It was not the conventional way to establish bureaucratic loyalty, but it tended to have an effect. Livie Merchant recalled once picking up the phone and being asked how he was doing. "I'm fine," Merchant replied, "but who the hell are you?" "This is the president" was the reply.[13] Back at State, though, hierarchies remained in place, even extending to gradations in the thickness and color of the office carpet.[14]

Like Roosevelt and later both Lyndon Johnson and Richard Nixon, Kennedy relied upon his own staff for handling big problems and complained regularly about the lack of imagination and toughness (a favorite Kennedy quality) at State. He was impatient, pushing often to demand a quick, clever response. He seemed to like or trust very few ambassadors, with Chip Bohlen (in France), Tommy Thompson (in the USSR), and, to a lesser extent, David Bruce being the only major exceptions. Some responded in kind. Bruce wrote in his diary:

> What a charming man the President is, in or out of his rocking chair. It sounds as if one were talking of a Schweppes tonic advertisement, or a fashion model, when one speaks of his sense of style.... Monnet, with austerity, makes guests and auditors feel they are being regaled with nectar and philosophy; Kennedy, with the panoply of luxury at his disposal, makes one feel everything is cordial, simple, and that caviar is for the general.... He is a chic egghead.... I find nothing in him unpraiseworthy.[15]

Kennedy's relationship with Rusk, however, never became anything like the one Truman had with Acheson or the very different one Eisenhower had with Dulles. For example, Rusk was the only person Kennedy addressed as "Mr. Secretary."[16] By contrast, Bundy as special assistant for national security, was among the top "marshals around Napoleon"—in essence, the president's alter ego on foreign policy. Bundy, recalled president-watcher Richard Neustadt,

> is an accomplished juggler of many balls at once. He juggles while he skates, and skates so fast that even in a close-up ... he himself remains a blur—which is as it should be with a staff officer. But sometimes one ball or another crashes through the ice; recovery is costly. One wonders whether Bundy might not need a Bundy of his own.[17]

It was Bundy, not Henry Kissinger under President Nixon, who first established the National Security Council (NSC) and its staff as foreign policy and national security operatives in their own right.[18] A similar thing happened with Robert McNamara's Pentagon, particularly among its civilians. Whereas for Eisenhower, the White House staff coordinated the various institutional views presented for decision (even after the president had already made up his own mind), Bundy acted more like an academic adviser, synthesizing problems himself and talking them through with Kennedy in order to reach a decision. Bundy had become a public figure, a not-so-gray eminence for Kennedy. He was already an academic star, having been the youngest dean of Harvard's Faculty of Arts and Sciences and a familiar face in foreign policy circles, following an apprenticeship to his father's former boss, Henry Stimson, and his direction of various study groups, notably one in 1949 at the Council on Foreign Relations chaired by Dwight Eisenhower about the future of the U.S.-European relationship. The language of the many drafts of the group's reports is classic Bundy: brisk, precise, firm, and skeptical (especially about European federalism), bold about American power but otherwise conservative. "Europe is important ... ," he wrote, "[but] cannot Europe fend for herself? The evident answer is NO.... [I]f the Germans cannot become partners, they must become wards." Berlin, he went on in a less plausible vein, "is a liability to the western allies.... [W]e should cut our losses and start fresh."[19] How concretely Bundy held these views fifteen years later is difficult to say, but his memoranda and actions as special assistant to Kennedy give a picture of a man with an astonishingly clear and wide-ranging mind, and a level of self-confidence so high it was difficult to imagine him as anything but superior. David Bruce, apparently without irony, remarked that Bundy was nothing short of "the kind of civilized human being I would like to have been."[20]

In September 1962, Bundy left on an official trip to Paris, Bonn, Berlin, Copenhagen, and London, which was covered widely in the press. His memo to the president advanced a short list of items he planned to discuss "unless you object."[21] No staff assistant to Eisenhower would have done such a thing, or used such language. A new style meant different results. Accordingly, the cumbersome Eisenhower apparatus for decisionmaking was replaced with the more permissive system of Kennedy, for which Bundy received his share of criticism.[22] How much of the State Department's eclipse during the 1960s may be attributed to this system, as opposed to personalities, especially the unassertive Rusk, is difficult to measure. But eclipse was undeniable.[23] Relations between the White House and the State Department, never easy, fell to a new low, with some notorious breakdowns in communication, both large and small. There was the six-week delay over the reply to a Soviet note on Berlin in June 1961, with the White House and State Department each blaming the other for losing the relevant memoranda.[24] There was the dinner for the French writer and minister of culture, André Malraux, at which only a few diplomats were seated, thanks to another misplaced piece of paperwork. Assistant to the First Lady Letitia Baldrige complained in exasperation, "It is *typical* of our relations with the State Dept!"[25] The department would not recover its preeminence in policymaking until Kissinger went there as secretary in 1973; meanwhile, the foreign affairs bureaucracy continued to swell across departments and agencies, with functional units both inside and outside the department amassing ever-greater influence. The 1960s saw the creation of the Arms Control and Disarmament Agency,

George Ball and Dean Rusk
Courtesy of Lyndon B. Johnson Library

the Office of the U.S. Trade Representative, and the Agency for International Development, all with responsibilities previously housed in bureaus at State. The Pentagon grew increasingly assertive as well, with Nitze's foreign policy shop and a longer list of expert officers on the military side. Similar steps were taken elsewhere, for example, in the Treasury and Agriculture Departments. The size of embassy staffs swelled accordingly, with foreign service officers beginning to look like minority populations. Bruce noted in December 1962 that there were 1,163 State Department employees throughout Britain: 688 were in the embassy itself, but only 152 were "working on State Department programs."[26]

To bring about some order, the Johnson administration, following the advice of General Maxwell Taylor, established in March 1966 the so-called SIG/IRG system, which stood for Senior Interagency Group and Interagency Group, the head of which was nominally the undersecretary of state. Each group was meant to combine the efforts of all the relevant officers throughout the government on a given issue or problem, and was matched overseas by "country teams" in each embassy. Over time, the system began to work better, but at first it disappointed many people and did not bring any real additional authority to the State Department under whose auspices it ostensibly lay.[27] Policymaking remained diffuse, unclear, itinerant. The beneficiary was the National Security Council.

EUR had an additional problem. Although it had survived the Dulles years comparably unscathed and saw, Undersecretary Herter, a very brief but happy moment, its most formidable leaders—the first and second generation of EUR hands like Matthews, Dunn, and Hickerson—had all retired or were about to retire by the end of the 1950s. Their successors were for the most part well-respected gentlemen, but they stood further from the center of power. The one who came closest, Livie Merchant, was too identified with the outgoing regime to rise any further in the department, although he, along with Herter himself, would provide yeoman service to the Kennedy administration. A new team, full of confidence and fervor, ruled the town. Among them was one of the strongest and most self-consciously "European" personalities ever to set foot in Foggy Bottom—George Ball.

Ball was the son of an English immigrant, a Midwesterner, a graduate of Northwestern University, and a law partner of Adlai Stevenson's in Chicago. He was a complicated and contradictory man: a heavy drinker and reputed womanizer, yet very "buttoned up, tall, formal," a "powerhouse" and extremely energetic, "with a freshness and an originality about him that could be very appealing, along with a genuine modesty."[28] To Bruce, his "ability to concentrate on whatever demands decision is really astonishing. Habitually overworked, his attention never seems to flag, even when he yawns and eructates." "To sum up," recalled another colleague, he was pragmatic, cautious, and a loner who, "on every issue ... just wanted to be the piano player."[29] Ball had served with the Lend-Lease Administration and the Strategic Bombing Survey during the war, being first on the scene in Germany (with Nitze and John Kenneth Galbraith) to interview the captured Albert Speer. In Washington, he lived on Woodley Road, across the street from Nitze and Walter Lippmann. He had admirers. Roy Jenkins once said he "has been more nearly right on every major foreign policy issue of the past forty-five years than anyone else I know."[30] And he had one especially favorite client: Jean Monnet.

Ball had gotten to know Monnet well during the war and then moved with him to Paris, where he became Monnet's principal American lawyer. Like Monnet, Ball was an obsessive draftsman, generally thinking out loud, subjecting documents to endless revisions, and driving staff members to exhaustion.[31] By 1961, Monnet need not have worried that his influence over the Americans—once so great with Foster Dulles—was in jeopardy. His most devoted disciple was in the State Department with a critical portfolio—economic affairs. Following the dismissal of Bowles, Ball would rise even higher—to the number-two position and the role of de facto secretary of state for Europe.[32]

Dean Rusk, despite having been a Rhodes scholar, was neither an Anglophile—after having served with the British in Asia during the war, it would have been difficult to remain one—nor especially interested in Europe. His main interests, to the extent he revealed them, lay elsewhere, especially as the Vietnam War came to take up everyone's attention. So Ball took charge of the European portfolio. This did not make everyone happy. The journalist Henry Brandon later noted that "Rusk ... does not provide leadership," while "on Europe you only have the doctrinaire approach of Ball[,] who builds a dream house, but has no sense for politics and wants to impose his solutions.... [He] is courageous, articulate, but out of line." And, one might have added, disorganized—even Monnet once urged him to stop "diffusing your energies."[33] Although Ball and Rusk insisted that they had a trusting partnership, worked hard to demonstrate fairness and respect toward one another, and were conscious of the need to avoid a repeat of the Hull-Welles "fiasco," there may have been less faith there than met the eye.[34] EUR, for its part, suddenly found itself subservient to a tough, brilliant, and powerful intermediary who was not, strictly speaking, a member of their sect. Art Hartman, who has appeared in previous chapters and who will figure again later when he became assistant secretary for EUR in the 1970s, went upstairs to work for Ball. EUR's chief at the time, the diplomat Foy Kohler, made sure to tell

Hartman on his way out, "Remember who your friends are."[35]

KENNEDY, HOWEVER, WAS unlikely to rely upon a single person for anything, let alone a man once so close to Adlai Stevenson. He turned again to the man of "intimidating superiority," Dean Acheson.[36]

The Dulles years had not served Acheson's humor well. His letters, articles, and speeches became hostile, sarcastic, even angry. His quick, fluent voice began to sound shrill. Having ended his term as secretary on bitter terms with Congress and the general public, Acheson spent much of the 1950s seething at the damage he determined Dulles to have wrought upon the fragile new transatlantic relationship, leading one diplomat to wonder whether Acheson's perpetual "bloody-mindedness was partly an attempt to épater ... les clercs harvardiens or essentially a negotiating tactic vis-à-vis those whom he regarded as the 'softies' in the administration."[37] In 1960, he endorsed Lyndon Johnson, not Kennedy, but did all he could to support the latter once his nomination became certain. Acheson refused any kind of official appointment, citing his ongoing law practice, but agreed to serve informally as much as the new president wanted. To start, Kennedy put Acheson in charge of a Berlin study.[38] If the president had any doubts about where the old man stood, his imagination was soon put to rest. Acheson by now was an unmitigated hawk.

If only things had been that simple. This depiction of Acheson, coming largely from the positions he took during the Cuban Missile Crisis and in the early years of the Vietnam War, all strident to be sure, tended to mask a deeper set of doubts that he passed along to the new administration. On the one hand, vying with him for influence were the "Europeanists" described in Chapter 5, now flourishing under Ball's auspices. These were the Monnet partisans of a unifying Europe who imagined the United States serving as its primary underwriter, financially and militarily. In the early 1960s, this group came to espouse something George Kennan once called the "dumbbell" theory, which became official policy following Kennedy's July 4, 1962, speech in Philadelphia announcing a "Declaration of Interdependence" that cast America and Europe as separate but allied geopolitical units.

On the other hand, there was the older generation of Atlanticists, whose ideas were rooted in the diplomacy of the interwar years and whose postwar masterpiece, the North Atlantic Alliance, seemed to be entering a period of adolescent (or perhaps early midlife) crisis. The Atlanticists deplored the dumbbell idea, insisting rather that Europe and America were members of a single, growing community, centered on the Alliance itself. But they had a tendency to preach to the converted.

Europeanists and agnostics alike were dubious. "What is meant by the Atlantic Community?" asked Miriam Camps in 1960. "I do not feel closer historically, economically, politically, or culturally to a Turk than I do to a Swede or to a New Zealander. Quite the contrary."[39] Dumbbellists, as they were known, argued that the transatlantic relationship would remain imbalanced so long as the European nations cohabited with an overpowering United States. "There was something rather touchingly narcissistic" in this belief, noted one longtime observer: "Europe is to be sort of transatlantic Jane for the American Tarzan."[40] In their view the transatlantic relationship would be more equitable, and thereby stronger, with a united Europe; a dumbbell was more stable than a large ball surrounded by little balls; and there would be only a single, strong bar between the two, rather than many spokes or a sphere.[41]

Atlanticists remained skeptical about the prospects and desirability of European unification. To them, such abstract thoughts about the balance of power distorted recent history and missed the larger point about the need for solidarity against the Soviets. Achilles stated it in this way:

Acheson & Kennedy
Bettmann/Corbis

In the first place I do not think that "Europe," even the Six, will ever be able to speak with one voice in the sense that the USA can. Secondly, I think that if it did it would become merely another large nation-state and that this would be anything but a good thing for the US or Canada or any country in Europe not a part of the new nation-state. Thirdly, I do not think we should sit back and wait for a part of Europe to develop greater unity before getting on with the job of developing that greater non-national unity of the advanced democracies which is so badly needed....

One of the basic problems which must be solved is how to develop a form of unity which will avoid either a US-satellite relationship or a flimsy bilateral partnership between two sovereign "equals...." No one in this country fears domination by anyone, even Texas. In the long run we will probably have something like New York—"built by the Italians, owned by the Jews and governed by the Irish."[42]

The old guard of Atlanticists appeared moreover to resent their successors in government. They had not reared the people who dominated foreign policy making in the 1960s; for all that they moved in the same social circles, the New Frontiersmen were just a bit too flamboyant and self-confident to qualify as full members of the club. Now they were the club that supplanted what had been there before. To a few old cave dwellers like Joe Alsop, the change was to be embraced at full throttle. But to other members of the postwar establishment, especially its reigning master, Dean Acheson, there was something awkwardly contradictory about Camelot-on-the-Potomac, especially when it came to the part of the world they cared about the most. Europe was too important to rebrand. The New Frontiersmen had other priorities, in any event.

This presented a problem for Acheson on two levels. Intellectually, there was his desire to keep policymaking focused, to educate—in one of his favorite sayings of Justice Oliver Wendell Holmes Jr.—in the obvious rather than investigate the obscure. Personally, there were the psychological effects of being the perpetual "wise man": At once flattered and underappreciated, solicited and rebuffed, Acheson did not seem to know where he stood. His doubts spread. One recalls the infamous line he spoke at West Point in 1962—"Britain had lost an empire but has not yet found a role"—and wonders whether he might not also have been thinking on some level of himself. Acheson had too many parts to play consistently; he could not bring himself to withdraw from the action, even in his new capacity as chief naysayer. He still cared too much.

Debates over such things as dumbbellism tend to strike us today as ridiculous. But this kind of existential exercise had an impact. With Ball holding the reins at State, the Atlanticists reverted to a rearguard effort to tie his hands, both within EUR and through unofficial channels, namely by way of several newly formed Atlantic support groups, to be described momentarily. Somewhere in the middle stood Acheson with his own set of bureaucratic allies, particularly in the Pentagon. He was himself neither fully in nor out of government, nor fully loyal to the Kennedy and Johnson administrations he pledged to advise, nor fully trusted by either.[43]

If any single group suffered from the diverging worldviews and agendas, it was EUR. Even though it had spent a decade finessing them, and was still recognized as the premier bureau in the department, the most ambitious young officers now sought posts in African, Asian, and even Latin American hotspots, while the White House seemed in any case to prefer the leadership of superannuated ex-officials from the Roosevelt and Truman administrations when it came to Europe, Ball notwithstanding. The attention of the press, and therefore of the administration, was transfixed upon such places—Congo, Cuba, Vietnam; a best-selling book of the decade written by a onetime foreign service officer referred to "the Atlantic mirage."[44] Within the department there was a kind of dissembling, "a constant tug-of-war between those who attached overriding importance to America's posture with the Afro-Asian world and those who attached it to America's relationship with ... NATO."[45] Assistant Secretaries Foy Kohler and Bill Tyler, both talented public servants, found themselves bogged down by one transatlantic crisis after another while being overshadowed by their superiors and competitors, notably Ball and Bundy, whose own putative rivalry (at least to Ball's camp) ended with the victory of the latter and the attendant loss of the Europeanists' most formidable partisan.[46] Ball's allies and appointees, first Bob Schaetzel (who served as deputy to Tyler) and later John Leddy (who succeeded Tyler), were not particularly intimate with the White House. Neither of them was a traditional foreign service officer. Leddy was a trade expert whose career began with the Pan American Union and then continued under C. Douglas Dillon in setting up the new OECD, Dillon having described him as "the best civil servant [he] ever met."[47] Schaetzel also began his government career as a civil servant in the Bureau of the Budget, at the European Atomic Energy Community and with the State Department's Bureau of Economic Affairs, where he supposedly invented Truman's Point Four program. Given those ties and a yearlong sabbatical at the behest of the Ford Foundation to study European integration, Schaetzel was a natural acolyte to Ball. Along with Art Hartman and George Springsteen, the trio was known as the "Ball boys."[48]

The tangled decade of the 1960s therefore featured several views about Europe. The New Frontiersmen asserted that the real action was elsewhere. Although they acknowledged that Europe remained important for all the usual Cold War reasons, they did not have any clear ideas about what should replace a set of policies regarded by them as stale and outdated. Into the breach came Ball and the Europeanists, with their reinvigorated partnership, a "Grand Design" for transatlantic relations that took into account Europe's new prosperity.[49] Into *that* breach, as shall become apparent, came Charles de Gaulle, who was perfectly willing to embrace a renunciation of the Atlantic Community but was hardly on the side of the dumbbellists.[50] Indeed, de Gaulle, by rejecting British admission to the Common Market in 1963, signing a separate Franco-German treaty soon thereafter, and withdrawing from the unified NATO military command in 1966, seemed to confirm the worst suspicions of the Atlanticists about the risks of experimenting with alternative approaches. Into *this* breach, then, they came from their perches outside government to defend the idea of Atlantic Community inherited from the late 1940s and to act as its self-appointed policy guardian. They had become, in other words, a kind of European Desk in exile.

Meanwhile there was still Acheson. Nobody had stood more firmly by George Ball in denouncing de Gaulle "as the enemy of the kind of Europe I believed in."[51] Yet the Atlanticists—men like Ted Achilles and Jack Hickerson—had served under Acheson, endorsed his strong stand over Berlin, and considered him, particularly during his more iconoclastic moments, a spiritual ally. Other allies working in both the State Department and the Pentagon fought hard against the Ball clique at State, whose members, especially Bob Schaetzel, nevertheless counted Acheson a good friend. He may very well have supported European integration, but his real affinity, they must have told themselves, was Anglo-centric, or better, Atlantic-centric. A united Europe was simply impractical for the foreseeable future.[52] But Europe remained the "hinge of fate," whose condition was far simpler than met the eye: "The division of Eastern and Western Europe ... is the chief result and manifestation of the collapse of the wartime alliance with the Soviet Union," he wrote in 1966. "De Gaulle's solution is to revive the Triple Entente against Germany, unite a neutralized Germany and have Europe assume a satellite position to the USSR—although he does not see the inevitability of the last stage."[53] But what to do about it?

Ironically, it would be a few staff members of the National Security Council, along with Achilles and his fellow conspirators inside and outside government, who would join forces to save policy from the worst excesses of the Europeanists. This would make it possible for Atlanticism to resurface in the 1970s in ways essentially determined toward the second half of the Johnson administration. That, in turn, would pave the way for its triumph with Reagan. But for now, their vision—the same one that Dean Acheson signed on to during his time as secretary—was very nearly lost in the strange, exhilarating, and confused decade of the 1960s.

THOSE WHO NEVER LIVED through the years of Camelot find the emotional texture of those years hard to grasp, but to say that it had a powerful magnetic effect upon these protagonists would hardly be inaccurate. For many in or connected to EUR, Washington was again the place to be. Susan Mary Patten, for example, ended her fifteen-year Parisian exile following the death of her foreign service husband, Bill, and moved to Georgetown, which meant marrying her deceased husband's former roommate, the homosexual newspaper columnist Joe Alsop. It was to Alsop's house on Dumbarton Avenue that Kennedy made one of his most memorable visits on inaugural night. Within a few blocks along the "P and Q Street Axis" lived the Wisners, Harrimans, Bruces, Achesons, Bradlees, Joyces, and Grahams.[54] The quarters were not as tight as they had been for the Marshall Planners in Paris, but the same set seemed just as concentrated on the other side of the Atlantic a decade or so later. Everybody's favorite ambassadors were there, too. The neurotic and familiar Hervé Alphand, whom Achilles described as a "devious, unprincipled, charming or despicable at will, supremely able French diplomat," had replaced the dour Maurice Couve de Murville, though he too had once been "all on our side."[55] David Ormsby-Gore, the Kennedy family intimate, replaced the cerebral Harold Caccia. Among the many other lights, greater and lesser, only the dull German ambassador Wilhelm Grewe left an unpopular mark on Georgetown. All had been much better when Dulles was alive, he, and only he, later noted.[56]

This was the world of the New Frontiersmen and their wives. Some, like the Bundys, Galbraiths, McNamaras, and Schlesingers, fit especially well. Despite their attraction to the Third World, they, like Kennedy himself, had tastes, personalities, and friends that recalled an American hybrid of Tom Wolfe's "Mid-Atlantic Man."[57] A few others—for example, the Rusks—did not mingle as well, but then they were not really New Frontiersmen. Bruce noted, for example, that Schlesinger's famous description of Rusk as a Buddha in cabinet meetings was apt because Rusk probably assumed that whatever he said would be repeated that evening across the Georgetown cocktail circuit, a world of which he did not consider himself part.[58] But that hardly mattered to the in-crowd. "There was an almost sexual charge about realizing that you know these people who are running the world," recalled the longtime Georgetown inhabitant Timothy Dickinson. "If it hadn't been for Vietnam it probably would have survived another twenty years."[59] Another resident, Margot Lindsay, concurred. Georgetown died "dramatically with the suicides of Phil Graham [1963] and Frank Wisner [1965]." But until then it was "a closed and very supportive circle ... all peas out of the same pod ... an endless party and so competitive."[60] The proliferation of salons proceeded on both sides of the Atlantic, although most, like Vangie Bruce's and Pamela Berry's, and even Jane and Bob Joyce's in Spetsai, featured many of the same people.[61] The consensus forged in such places, as in Washington's clubs like the Alibi and Metropolitan, is impossible to measure, of course, but they must be acknowledged as significant para-diplomatic milieux, lending both tone and substance to the quality of transatlantic relationships as well as a fair share of appointments and promotions.

There was another important "unofficial" sector that came to the fore in the 1960s. This was the collection of nongovernmental groups that concerned themselves with transatlantic relations, with most playing a role ranging from lobbying to what the British like to call a talking shop, which formed soon after the establishment of NATO as an unofficial support network. The best known were the American Council on NATO, headed by Christian Herter, the American Committee on United Europe—a more Cold War–orientated outfit under Wild Bill Donovan and Allen Dulles—the National Committee for a Free Europe and the Atlantic Union Committee, an offshoot of Clarence Streit's federalist "Union Now" movement. Streit, mentioned briefly in Chapter 5, was a former Rhodes scholar and journalist from Montana who was one of the first to gain the League of Nations beat after the war, where the "proverb of Geneva" held that "Streit will be Streit!" There, watching the promise of the League wither from lack of commitment and consensus, "he saw its motion slowing to a stop like an unwound phonograph," when suddenly "the germ for the federation idea incubated in his mind ... like a flash of light." But his failure to distinguish between governments and communities rubbed many, even fervent Atlanticists like Walter Lippmann and Ted Achilles, who called Streit the "Atlantic John the Baptist," the wrong way.[62]

By the mid-1950s, the Atlantic Union Committee had "field representatives" in nearly every state and several dozen national members.[63] There was also the Declaration of Atlantic Unity group, affiliated with the AUC and an almost one-man show of another former journalist, Walden "Wally" Moore, who was so persistent with promoting the agenda of Atlantic federalism, he and his frequent "Walligrams" would appear to be a nuisance even to the most dedicated Atlanticists, not to mention to officials like George Ball, who evidently refused to answer Moore's letters.[64] The differences between these organizations might appear minute, but they reflected diverging mental maps of the Atlantic and took up considerable energy. The Atlantic Union Committee and the American Committee on United Europe, for example, negotiated extensively in 1951 over a common agenda, and agreed to disagree over whether European integration or transatlantic integration should take priority.[65] Then there was the U.S. Committee for the Marshall Plan and the American Council on Germany, headed by Christopher Emmet, the publicist who was formerly the mainstay of the Committee to Defend America by Aiding the Allies.[66] In Europe there was its sister organization, the Atlantik-Brücke, the Atlantic Treaty Association (with chapters in all NATO members' countries), and Monnet's Action Committee, formed in 1955, bringing together integrationists across national and party lines in Europe and functioning as an almost quasi-institutional overseer for the European Communities. The activities of these organizations ranged from consensus-building exercises to public information. The American Council on NATO, for example, circulated radio kits and placed over 400,000 lines of newspaper advertising in 1958.[67]

None of these American groups was as formidable as Monnet's Action Committee. Perhaps for that reason in 1961, one of Rusk's first steps as secretary was to convene a meeting of the various "Atlantic organizations" to discuss ways to consolidate their efforts. Present at the meeting on July 24 were Christian Herter, William Foster, Henry Cabot Lodge Jr., Randolph Burgess, Robert Murphy, Michael Ross of the AFL-CIO, Paul Gordon of the Ford Foundation, and Ed Cooper of the Motion Picture Association. Bill Tyler, Russ Fessenden, and W. J. Lehmann from the State Department joined Rusk.[68] The result was the formation of the Atlantic Council of the United States, a private, nonprofit, and ostensibly nonpartisan group of advocates for close transatlantic relations. Upon taking the helm of the new group in 1963, General Lauris Norstad, who had just stepped down as NATO supreme allied commander, Europe, proclaimed, "A strong Europe is, thank God, a fact of life."[69] Accordingly, the council

> was formed in the conviction that the nations of the Atlantic area are parts of one community and are dependent on each other for their mutual freedom and prosperity in the foreseeable future as in the recent past. Our economic well-being and military security, as well as the political exigencies of the nuclear age and the orderly evolution and welfare of the developing countries demand the creation of a true Atlantic community suitably organized to meet the political, military and economic challenges of this era.

But its inspiration went further back. The statement continued:

> Free societies are based on the supremacy and dignity of the individual, respect of law, and the conviction that human endeavor, whether economic, aesthetic or spiritual, is best conducted in freedom and diversity. Together the Atlantic peoples are heir to a magnificent civilization whose origins include the early achievements of the Near East, the classical beauty of Greece, the juridical sagacity of Rome, the spiritual power of our religious traditions, and the humanism of the Renaissance. Its latest flowering, the discoveries of modern science, allows an extraordinary mastery of the forces of nature.[70]

Apart from the Council on Foreign Relations, the best-known U.S. foreign policy organization (which had its own active program on Atlantic studies in the 1960s), the history of these groups has yet to be written. With the exception of the CFR and a few smaller groups like the Foreign Policy Association, they were mainly a Cold War phenomenon, even though most were set up to promote particular regions, issues, or political orientations, and many have survived to this day as semi-official auxiliaries. As with the social salons, their historical significance is hard to determine because evidence for it is primarily anecdotal but nonetheless striking in the frequency with which it is suggested by their members' appointment books, diaries, memoirs, and letters.

Some, like the Bilderberg Group or Le Cercle, have maintained an air of secrecy and exclusion, serving as small, intimate retreats for the transatlantic elite; others like the Munich Conference, the Atlantic Treaty Association, or perhaps the best known of more recent such groups, the World Economic Forum, held at Davos, Switzerland, have been more public.[71] Their aims have varied, but their power has tended to come more by the relationships they further than the demonstrable results they have produced. That they proliferated in the mid-1950s and 1960s was no historical accident: As diplomacy itself grew more attuned to the mass media and bureaucracies became more complex, there arose a related need for alternative, "unofficial" purveyors of elite consensus and continuity, in what one frequent participant, Monnet's collaborator Richard Mayne, described as "a walk-in-the-woods sort of policy."[72] This was something more subtle and powerful than their ostensible roles as policy talking shops and cheerleaders. They were at once alternative spaces for policymaking and policy planning as well as important catalysts and incubators of political consensus among a diversifying and increasingly contentious bevy of leaders. Of course they had their detractors—Bruce, for one, distrusted "citizens groups, the direction of which ultimately seems to devolve on the loudest blowhard"—but these nevertheless supplied much of the propagandistic infrastructure of the postwar years. Similar initiatives included a festival of Atlantic Community Culture, an Atlantic Foundation, an Atlantic Institute of Technology, an Atlantic Award (first given to Averell Harriman), an Atlantic Economic Union, and an Atlantic Congress, which later became the Atlantic Assembly.[73] That so many were focused on Europe spoke to Europe's continued centrality in American foreign policy and the related demand for persistent "needling."[74]

Some were ostensibly educational organizations as well. The Atlantic Council sought to appeal to the general public for support and endorsement of the ideas it put into circulation through its in-house journal, the *Atlantic Community Quarterly*, which began publication in 1963 and appeared with its blue-and-white cover for nearly thirty years. The first few issues featured mainly reproduced speeches and articles from other publications, but it soon came into its own as a repository for "Atlantic minded-ness."[75] The Atlantic Council, along with the Paris-based Atlantic Institute, established a Committee on Atlantic Studies with about a dozen members, including Bob Bowie, the historian Hans Kohn, and political scientists Arnold Wolfers and Robert Strausz-Hupé, which oversaw exchange programs and curricular reviews and even helped to establish an Atlantic College. The children of David Bruce and Martin Hillenbrand were among several Americans who were enrolled there.[76] The Atlantic Institute was a rather unique organization. The brainchild of a young, former civilian in the German occupation, Jim Huntley, it was the first transatlantic and pan-European organization of its kind devoted to analyzing the two intersecting communities.[77] Following Huntley's departure, the organization became more Europeanist in line with the prevailing attitudes of the Kennedy administration, but then lost its way by the end of the decade, so that by 1968 it had proposed doing away with the "Atlantic" moniker altogether.[78]

Meanwhile, within the State Department, Bob Schaetzel oversaw the establishment of a program to train a corps of "Atlantic Specialists."[79] Nearly all of the efforts were sponsored by the Ford Foundation, headed, incidentally, by McGeorge Bundy after 1966. Under the careful stewardship of Shepard Stone, a close friend of Schaetzel, Ball, Monnet, and McCloy, for whom Stone had worked in Germany, the foundation gave about $33 million to various Atlantic projects between 1950 and 1963, including the lion's share of support for Monnet's Action Committee, the Atlantic Council, and the Atlantic Institute, which it backed through Henry Cabot Lodge Jr.'s deputy, Pierre Uri, "almost a genius and [an] almost impossible" man who had written much of the Treaty of Rome. At the institute, however, Uri was less productive, though he insisted, in protesting what would be the first of two salary cuts, that his lunch breaks were short and that he stayed late in the evenings. Rather, the fault, he claimed, lay with the lackadaisical board, including its two "lady governors." Should any more be allowed to join, Uri concluded, "they must present at least one of the following features ... : the looks, or the brains, or the money.... Barring these ... they are not entitled to representation without taxation, and the Institute is not the vehicle for buying flowered hats in Paris."[80]

The Atlantic fervor of the early 1960s had a good deal to do with the perceived counterpredilections of the New Frontiersmen and with the fact that so many foreign policy figures from the Truman and Eisenhower years remained active in public or semi-public life. And yet there was a sense that the demand for their ideas had ebbed as the ways of making policy had changed. "U.S. leadership no longer is possible on the basis of our ability to aid others in material ways," wrote Jack Tuthill to Ball in early 1961.[81] Thus, in spite of Rusk's best efforts to consolidate the Atlantic chorus into a single, nonpartisan whole, the Atlantic Council found itself cast in the role of the loyal opposition. As was often the case, it was part political, part personal. Soon after the council was formed, its new chair, General Norstad, along with Ted Achilles, who, as resident vice chair until the mid-1980s, ran it as "his personal plaything," proposed to launch a special commission on European policy, a sort of Action Committee for the West and a quiet back channel to de Gaulle.[82] The administration demurred, with a dismissive Rusk telling Achilles, "I don't think we need to be too worried about losing our virginity on this one."[83] For his part, Schaetzel took the challenge more seriously, noting that "it cannot be ignored that the initiative being proposed by the Council amounts to an implicit attack on the President's European policy."[84] Achilles and the more doctrinaire Atlanticists on the council's board came to depict the administration's rhetoric of partnership as a betrayal of the community spirit upon which the postwar transatlantic relationship was founded. "The twin pillar approach," wrote Achilles in 1967, "seemed to many of us in the ACUS a completely dead duck." The unifying goal of the Europeanists, in other words, was laudable, "*provided* that it was outward-looking and contributed toward Atlantic, or even wider, unity."[85] By this point the two sides had coalesced into warring camps, as suggested by the following exchange of letters between Monnet and Wally Moore:

MONNET: I think our objective is common: the unity of the West. I think that our ways to reach it are very different. I, for one, believe that the reality of the Atlantic unity can only be reached by the way of creating the unity of Europe and an effective partnership between Europe and the United States....

MOORE: I certainly agree that we have a common objective but I am not sure whether or not "our ways to reach it are very different."

MONNET: On one point I should like to comment straight away. In your letters to Sponsors, you say that "The US Sponsors agreed with the unanimous advice of the above (and of Jean Monnet) that we should continue this year our all-out offensive to bring about a 'true Atlantic Community'...." A "true Atlantic Community" is generally understood by most people as a system of relations between the United States, U.K., and the various *separate* nations of Europe. I do not believe this will work— as I told you and many of our friends—I believe that the transformation of relations must be between the USA on one hand and a European federation—including the U.K.—on the other hand, a relations of equal partners....

MOORE: You may recall that during our talk in your office last November we did not discuss *how* Atlantic relations should be arranged although your own views on that question were, of course, well known to me.

Actually the text of the Second *Declaration* ... does not deal with the form of Atlantic organization but only with the substance. [Monnet's red exclamation point appears here in the margin.] Some of our signers prefer the system of Atlantic relations which you ascribe to us. But others, on both sides of the Atlantic, prefer the arrangement of "equal partners" which you yourself advocate....

While the *Declaration* ... has never addressed itself formally to the precise form of "the true Atlantic Community..." we have, over the past years, conducted a dialogue with some of our signers....

Meanwhile, it seems to us unwise to adopt too rigid a position with regard to the ultimate organization of the Atlantic Community....

MONNET: ... let me say just this. The term "Atlantic Community" well describes the Community of interest and civilization that binds the West. But it seems to me and to many other Europeans potentially misleading in so far as it suggests that Atlantic problems are likely to be settled by the same procedures as those at work in the European Communities. And I particularly do not believe that "political integration" is possible "on an Atlantic basis" unless there is not only equality of status but also something closer to equality of size between the participants. This can only be achieved by the unification of Europe....

MOORE: While, for understandable reasons, you declined our invitation to sign the "Statement" we think that you will be interested in the attached list of those who did sign it.[86]

It was no wonder then that people on each side termed one another "theologians."

IN THE MEANTIME THERE WAS Europe to deal with. The first crisis happened, not surprisingly, in Berlin—that "navel in the human body, cut off with contact with the mother, ugly in itself, but without it one would lose face."[87] Following Nikita Khrushchev's emergence as the Soviet leader after 1956, tensions began to worsen. Nearly two years later, Khrushchev issued an ultimatum for the end of the city's military occupation. In 1959, the Western powers proposed a new peace plan based in large part on work that had been done by the U.S. State Department.[88] If the German hands then had moderated Dulles's propensity to negotiate over Berlin—for despite his tough rhetoric, Dulles, who considered himself as knowledgeable about Germany as anyone, was more likely to make concessions over Berlin than his Democratic predecessors—they would do the same thing for Kennedy, only in reverse, in order to ensure that the door of diplomacy remained open. When the new president met Khrushchev in Vienna in June 1961, the latter would make a notoriously aggressive first impression as soon as the conversation moved to Berlin. Then came construction of the "monstrosity" of the Berlin Wall in August, followed by the missile crisis in October 1962, ostensibly about Cuba but really, according to the official consensus at the time, about Berlin. As Kurt Birrenbach later put it, "the Berlin Crisis practically ended with the Cuba Crisis, where your country showed that you were ready to use force, if necessary."[89] Next there was Kennedy's 1963 trip to Germany that "immensely moved" him. Bill Tyler recalled their visit to the Cologne cathedral, hearing

> that rhythmic, almost hysterical scanning of his name: "Ken-ne-dy, Ken-ne-dy." They all shouted and stamped their feet and pronounced those syllables with enormous enthusiasm, and you felt that the popularity of the President was something which went far beyond anything that could be accounted for by an act, or policy, or by the fact that he was President.... We were nearly crushed to death.

Later when Kennedy gave his famous speech at the Berlin Wall, his sister, Eunice Shriver, said, "Oh, John, you're the champion," and the president turned to Tyler: "It's quite something, it's really something, isn't it?"[90]

Matters had not seemed so glorious two years earlier. Paul Nitze asked, "Shall we venture war rather than yield? If not, shall we acquiesce through a negotiation?" This was the critical question facing the Kennedy administration when it came into office.[91] It could not have been more focused on Berlin, even though many of its leading lights chose, especially in retrospect, to interpret Khrushchev's Viennese *démarche* as a bluff.[92] Those with experience on the ground did not do so, and continued to fear the worst. Typical was the warning from Bill Tyler:

> [R]esponsible circles in the Dept. [assume] that Kruschev [sic] doesn't set great store by Berlin really, and that he would be prepared to live and let live, were it not for the perpetual goading to which the GDR subjects him, and the ensuing necessity of making a show of positive effort to hold [Walter] Ulbricht in line.... This trend, of course, is playing K's game to the hilt.[93]

In addition to commissioning Acheson's report, as already noted, the president reconstituted the State Department's Berlin Working Group in 1961. At its head he put Assistant Secretary of State for European Affairs Foy Kohler, an Acheson ally. A "wizened little man, sharp as a whip, with much resolve and diplomatic skill," Kohler was a well-regarded Soviet hand, "a team man" who would go on to replace Tommy Thompson as ambassador in Moscow. His career was nearly derailed in the 1950s by an arrest for drunk driving, during which the police found classified documents in his car, but Kohler survived, thanks in large part to Loy Henderson's and Livie Merchant's patronage.[94] Following Kohler's move in 1962 the group was headed by Marty Hillenbrand. Hillenbrand, as will become clear in Chapter 9, was a professional who, more than any other German expert, filled the shoes of James Riddleberger as the dean of this small guild. Hillenbrand's task force, later broadened with members of other departments and agencies, continued its work through the missile crisis well into 1963. It produced a stream of proposals out of which came the basis of what would, by

1971, become a four-power Berlin agreement formalizing the status of the city and the end of the occupation.[95]

Germany thus dominated EUR's attention. Going above and beyond the Berlin crisis, it involved a deeper set of questions about collective defense, both nuclear and conventional. NATO by now was a decade old and the Americans could no longer afford to carry so much of the burden. Western Europe, and especially Germany, meanwhile, had undergone an economic boom. The Kennedy administration, prodded by Acheson to bolster the "conventional deterrent" and to dispense with what he and others had derided as the previous administration's doctrine of "massive retaliation," now found itself, with Vietnam on the horizon, short of both troops and cash.[96] So the Kennedy and Johnson administrations came to urge the Europeans to pay more, resulting, ultimately, in protracted negotiations between John McCloy and the Germans over what came to be called "offset." Like most questions of political economy, it involved complicated domestic questions and messy arithmetic. "In this case it wasn't even two plus two equals five," recalled Johnson's assistant, Francis Bator, "but two plus two equals an elephant."[97] The case against Germany was pushed hard by the Defense and Treasury Departments, raising concerns on the part of EUR over the political fallout, concerns that proved justified when German chancellor Ludwig Erhard lost his job in December 1966. Many in the press blamed Lyndon Johnson for undercutting him with too much pressure at the moment when he was most vulnerable. Johnson was sympathetic but less willing to budge than others in his administration. To McCloy, he summed up the problem in characteristic fashion: "Jack ... I'll try to hold this Alliance together longer than anybody else will ... but they have got to put something in the family pot. I can't do it alone." To Bator he was even blunter, recalling old neighbors from Johnson City, Texas: "I know my Germans ... they are great people; but by God they are stingy as hell."[98]

But this is getting ahead of the story. Retooling the Alliance involved two additional problems that would dovetail with offset and balance of payments, which Ball called "a kind of King Charles' head. It just intruded into every kind of argument."[99] Both addressed the long-standing question of how best to integrate the Anglo-American Alliance into the wider transatlantic relationship, involving not only NATO but also Britain's own halfhearted movement toward closer ties, and eventually membership, in the European Community. The first problem was that for the British, it meant accelerating what had been regarded by many people as an inevitable process of pulling back their "east of Suez" security presence for lack of access to foreign exchange.[100] Only a few Americans and British Tories argued that this was not inevitable, someday. But it need not have happened so fast, with all the predictable consequences for a new, unfamiliar, and politically tricky American position as the gendarme of a most difficult part of the world. "Goddammit," Harriman reportedly quipped to McNamara. "This is what you brought on us, insisting on the British maintaining their larger full Army on the Rhine."[101]

The second, related problem was the long-standing and seemingly paradoxical desire of the British and French to become full members of the nuclear club. In practice, however, this was consistent with their desire to limit the conventional buildups being urged upon them by the United States. Both had traveled far down the nuclear path by the mid-1960s, but it, too, enacted far more collateral damage than might otherwise have been necessary. The first stumbling block was called Skybolt. This was a weapons system promised to the British as the centerpiece of their national deterrent. McNamara, however, had become convinced that Skybolt was neither cheap nor effective.[102] He subsequently canceled it. The British were predictably outraged. Kennedy and Prime Minister Harold Macmillan patched things up in December 1962 at their meeting in Nassau, but only after the latter secured a shiny substitute, the Polaris missile, and threatened to blame Kennedy with the fall of his government and the United States as the "outside destroyer of the British deterrent."[103] Yet, it should be recalled that "it was not the American President who was bounced into giving Britain something he did not want to, it was the British cabinet which was bounced into accepting something it was not sure it wanted."[104] Those in EUR were displeased not only with the outcome—they had earlier opposed assisting any British national deterrent—but also with the poor handling of the whole matter, including the most meager conference preparations in recent memory. Bill Tyler recalled sitting around, having cocktails in the "chintzy," Bahamian country club atmosphere with the smell of roses drifting in through the windows, feeling "underwater" from the poor communication between himself and Rusk, who did not go to Nassau but assured him that he had cleared everything about Polaris with McNamara ahead. That was not evident on the spot. At one point Kennedy got up, went for a walk with Macmillan, and came back with the stunning announcement about Polaris. It was, Tyler recalled, "a drama out of scale—like being in a girl's bedroom with something going on that shouldn't happen there."[105]

There was more to it than sloppy summiteering. The French had not been part of the discussion. Kennedy only subsequently made an equivalent offer to Charles de Gaulle, which de Gaulle predictably rejected. Tyler had been right when he warned that neither the Joint Chiefs nor the White House had "grasped the de Gaulle connection in all this."[106] If they had, it was with something less than good faith, a "strange way," noted the journalist Nora Beloff, "to treat a man widely known to suffer from an acute persecution mania, amounting almost to paranoia, about the 'Anglo-Saxons.'"[107] Delivering the offer in person was none other than the new American ambassador to France, Chip Bohlen, who reportedly embellished it, but to no end. De Gaulle would proceed with his nuclear *force de frappe*, with or without American help.[108]

And then there was Germany. It had no nuclear weapons of its own, nor would it seek them. But the topsy-turvy negotiating at Nassau did little to allay persistent fears about German nuclear ambitions. Namely, if Macmillan could gain an advanced system through political blackmail, who could say the others might not do the same? Modest nuclear capabilities for the British and French were one thing; nuclear weapons falling into the hands of Germans was quite another, not merely for their Western neighbors but also for the nervous Soviets, with whom the United States was finally beginning, with the partial test ban treaty in 1963, to forge a realistic path of arms control.

Reenter the dumbbellists. They had expropriated an all-out solution to the problem, which brings us to another, even bigger obstacle to squaring the complex circle of alliance readjustment and strategic reposturing, to echo the language of the day's defense bureaucrats. No matter that the European Defense Community had once proved to be such a lightning rod; they would make something similar toward what came to be called the Multilateral Nuclear Force, or MLF.

"Who came up with this nutty idea?" asked Senator Henry "Scoop" Jackson. The prospect of NATO deploying a nuclear force operated on ships and submarines staffed by multiple nationalities did seem far-fetched and hardly genuine—essentially, it meant letting the Europeans "have a finger on the nuclear trigger, even though that fingers would be a little finger, and the American big finger would still be there."[109] It originated in parallel with one of General Norstad's ideas, while still at NATO, to introduce a new generation of medium-range ballistic missiles and deploy them to Europe, but this met resistance from the State Department, then as well as later.[110] In response, Secretary Herter in 1959 asked Bob Bowie, by now back at Harvard, to draft an alternative, which Bowie included in a seminar report published at the very end of Eisenhower's second term.[111] Bowie, who later returned to government as counselor of the department in 1966, along with his friends Henry Owen of the Policy Planning Staff and Gerard Smith, another former Eisenhower official, saddled the administration with the MLF, despite its being vitiated by Kennedy's improvised formulation in Nassau. Bowie noted that the Polaris decision "pretty well derailed any possibility for having a multilateral force," while Owen threatened, "We're going to wreck our policy in order to preserve the Macmillan Government." Still, they succeeded in getting the MLF mentioned in the final communiqué at Nassau and in enlisting the support of Rusk.[112] Thereafter, they persisted with a passion that had not been seen in a decade. Hence it was Smith and Owen, along with allies Schaetzel and Ball, whom Bundy first termed the "theologians."[113] But apart from being devout Catholics (Owen was in fact a convert) and abhorring the existence of nuclear weapons, there was little that was theological about the former two, despite, in Owen's case, having been known as "egregious as well as ubiquitous and inevitable."[114] Their obsession with the MLF was essentially political and came from a conviction that it was the right answer for the problem of German and European security, and only needed a persistent fight to overcome the parochial obstacles in its path.[115] "Every now and then, official American psychological processes go through a peculiar cycle," recalled Hillenbrand:

> We perceive a need, itself largely psychological, on the part of our European allies for some new weapons deployment. We then devise some way to fill this need and offer it to the Europeans. Their response may be muted, but gradually the American side builds up a head of steam and begins to employ the hard sell. In the end, what started out as a favor becomes an American cause and a test of European loyalty to the alliance.[116]

The MLF has proved to be one of the odder episodes and projects of the 1960s. The idea that a few nuclear ships or submarines could serve as the basis for a Europe-wide nuclear deterrent seemed somewhat insane, and it spawned predictable jokes about the crossing of signals among French engineers, Turkish cooks, Italian navigators, and so forth. To help influence European opinion and stimulate the bureaucratic process back home, Kennedy recalled Livie Merchant from semiretirement and asked him to lead a mission to the various NATO countries to sell the MLF. Merchant was not enthusiastic but he did so loyally, describing his mission as a "reconnaissance in force." It had the opposite effect. The Merchant mission was "so large ... traveled in such style, and was treated with such deference by American ambassadors as to be criticized for leaving the impression that MLF was what Washington wanted."[117] Others got into the act. Schaetzel urged his friend Art Hartman, then serving in London, to try to use Monnet's associate and later biographer, François Duchêne, to plant favorable articles in *The Economist*. He asked the strategist Thomas Schelling to say good things about it at the annual conference of the Institute for Strategic Studies, a new and important British think tank.[118] Reactions to the MLF in Europe, however, were mixed. The Dutch and Germans were said to be for it, assuming the proposal was probably serious, while the Italians and Greeks were less so. The French were opposed, while the others were said to be at best "indifferent."[119] As Hillenbrand noted, "Until we can make up our own minds on doctrine, we have little possibility of persuading the Europeans."[120] Ultimately the opponents of the MLF—residing primarily in the State Department's new Bureau of Political-Military Affairs (PM) and in the Pentagon itself—would coalesce around Bundy, while Ball would fight for it with all the influence he could muster.[121] Neither Kennedy nor Johnson was impressed. With an echo of what would come later with Vietnam, only in reverse, the latter told Ball, "When you're trying to save your face ... you'll lose your ass."[122]

Finally, in December 1964, Johnson rejected the hardware solution put forth by the MLF in a single meeting. It coincided with a difficult visit with British prime minister Harold Wilson. The British diplomat Nicholas Henderson recalled the moment:

> L.B.J. listened. He listened silently for a long time doing a samba backwards and forwards in his anglepoise chair. He hardly spoke, to the British delegation at any rate, though he carried out whispered consultations behind the back of his hand with his own Ministers. However, from the time of that meeting, we never heard anything more about US insistence on the MLF. L.B.J. killed it at that conference.[123]

Urging him to do so were Bundy and Neustadt, then serving as an emissary between the White House and the British government. Neustadt was "euphoric":

> [Johnson] not only made a *free* choice ... but the *right* choice for a President to make at this juncture. I'm impressed, and proud of him, and I'm *not* joining the chorus ... of Achesonians (to-lead-is-to-lead) or of British Foreign Office spokesmen.... Those guys think rulers exist to be *used*. But we're the king's men, so the hell with that. The FO professionals want an Anglo-German entente ... but if *they* have to use *our* king to make *their* move, their reasoning is flawed as fatally as that of our "cabal...." So please don't let anybody's Foreign Office types depress you! To cheer you up I offer "Neustadt's law" for policy planners: what governing politicians don't find serviceable won't be feasible. MLF is a classic case. I hope we'll soon have heard the last of *it*.[124]

There were no dire professional consequences for anyone, and the immense quantity of paper devoted to defending the MLF would land in the archives, largely untouched since. The episode was over. Did it matter? Indeed, it did. It added to the accumulation of tension between the White House and the Europeanists, especially Ball, who, in addition to becoming something of a "hate figure" to the British, spent considerable bureaucratic capital with both Lyndon Johnson and his subordinates in the State Department.[125] And it raised further doubts about the logical consistency of the transatlantic agenda itself, since, strictly speaking, the MLF on its face would have seemed to be more of an Atlanticist-inspired project than a Europeanist one, but it was the latter group that fought hardest for it. Nobody really seemed to understand why, apart from there being a sense that they had to fight hard for something new and important.

Why did these very intelligent men become so obsessed with what the British called the "multilateral farce"? And why did it take so long for their skeptical bosses to kill this "phony answer to a nonproblem"?[126] The answers rest mainly in the volatile bureaucratic politics and the conceptual fog of the Kennedy and early Johnson years. It was not simply a case of fanatics waging war against pragmatists. On the one hand, the MLF debacle was a symptom of a foreign affairs system in flux. There was then a much greater, direct role for the Pentagon and the White House in diplomacy than there had been in the past, and the division of labor had not yet settled into a familiar pattern. So there may have been something to the suspicion that the State Department overstepped itself in search of a cause. On the other hand, personalities really did matter. The "outrageous tale" only lasted as long as it did, according to Bundy's assistant David Klein, because "George Ball lent his prestige to it and the White House ... never blew the whistle."[127] Added Neustadt: "I do not share the view that Henry Owen and Company are 'bad guys.' On the contrary, they are dedicated 'good guys' with valid 'hunting licenses' from this Administration. The President and they don't seem to read those licenses alike. But a lot of things in the President's mind don't show on the printed page."[128] Thus, it was the old Roosevelt problem all over again, only now the roles were reversed, with the most enthusiastic policy entrepreneurs residing in the State Department rather than in the more cautious White House.

Nevertheless, the concern over national nuclear deterrents, particularly the French and German, as either boons to proliferation elsewhere or destabilizing agents in Europe, was genuine, if overblown, and would take some time to dissipate, even if the theologians had no evidence that the French or Germans would be any worse nuclear proliferators than the British, Soviets, Chinese, or their own American compatriots. The putative German desire for a nuclear capability was based on an American generalization about nuclear "satisfied nations" more than on German political realities. There was, finally, a bit of good old imperial insecurity at play. Bowie later admitted as much: "Our basic analysis was that it was not awfully healthy for the United States to be so predominant and others to be such small fry"—especially if the small fry come to trust the U.S. nuclear deterrent less and less.[129] When it became clear that there were different ways to deal with the problem, namely, with the Nuclear Non-Proliferation Treaty (NPT)—a document that Adenauer once called, in referring to the World War II plan for German pastoralization, "a Morgenthau plan raised to the 2nd power" but whose successors were won over—the task became one of convincing the

Germans to put their money where their mouths were on nonproliferation rather than continuing to offer them a fig leaf of a nuclear program. The United States meanwhile would continue to negotiate reductions on its side of the defense balance sheet. The successful conclusion of the offset negotiations therefore made possible both the NPT and the subsequent replacement of the Bretton Woods–era fixed exchange rates by the Nixon administration in 1971.[130] The Germans would accede to the NPT, and the NATO nuclear planning group, a more informal coordinating body for the nuclear inventories of the various members of the Alliance, would satisfy nearly everyone that there was no need to have mixed-manned nuclear submarines. In the end, as Bundy's replacement at the NSC, Walt Rostow, reminded everyone, "Bonn's heart still belongs to Daddy."[131]

Yet Bowie had a larger point—the MLF proposal succeeded in underscoring the basic question of whether an entity called Europe, either as partner or as a set of community members, would have important military assets of its own, and, if so, which kinds. Would Europe and America pursue the common defense as a single force, in parallel, in concert, or separately? The fact that such questions were still being asked suggested that NATO was on thinner ice than it would have liked to admit. The longer-run defense posture of a unifying Western Europe remained imprecise. Thus, the aims of the MLF were indeed far more political than military, serving as the latest litmus test for adherence to the European idea—"the talisman for enlightened Atlantic policy."[132] Once enveloped into the Europeanist agenda, it suggested Americans could trust Europeans with nuclear weapons and Europeans could trust Americans to share them. To be opposed to this plan was to be opposed to the whole idea of partnership. It therefore made sense that someone like Schaetzel, who had made his career in being the ideological enforcer of dumbbellism, would embrace the MLF with the passion of a convert almost immediately after de Gaulle announced his decision to reject British membership in the Common Market.

David Bruce was not the only one who wished Schaetzel "could be less impetuous and hasty, and more calm and orderly." Ted Achilles regarded him as a mere tyrant.[133] His zeal recalled not only a famous line by Talleyrand but also the words of Lord Acton, as quoted by Acheson: "The pursuit of a remote and ideal object, which captivates the imagination by its splendor and the reason by its simplicity, evokes an energy which would not be inspired by a rational, possible end, limited by many antagonistic claims, and confined to what is reasonable, practicable and just."[134]

This was a moment for reason to prevail. But drama and distraction would overtake the doomed Kennedy and Johnson presidencies. The big questions Schaetzel and his fellow theologians had gone so far to flaunt would go unanswered.

8

LA PÉRIODE TEXANE

De Gaulle's NATO withdrawal—who's who revisited—Lyndon Johnson's approach to Europe—the Kennedy Round—bridge building and the acceleration of détente

TOMMY THOMPSON, who first appeared several chapters ago in interwar Geneva, had just begun his second tour as ambassador to the Soviet Union. By the early 1960s, he had risen to occupy the heralded place of Loy Henderson as the senior Soviet hand in the department and, if the White House transcripts of the Cuban Missile Crisis present an accurate picture, the one to whom nearly everyone deferred on all such matters. He characteristically saw through the fog to the essence of the problem in 1963. Europe, he wrote, would remain unstable so long as Berlin was unresolved, and that was not in the cards anytime soon. The only way de Gaulle could prevail in his aim to reinvent France as a great power would be to decouple the United States and European nuclear deterrents. That would mean tying "Germany to France through a French nuclear capability not possessed by Germany," something the Germans were unlikely to endorse if push came to shove. Nearly everyone else in Europe appeared to accept the American military umbrella, just as they were "unwilling to provide conventional forces adequate to United States strategy [and were] highly suspicious of [American] efforts to force them to do so." Thus the Multilateral Nuclear Force, if it ever had a chance of succeeding politically, would not have made much of a difference on the ground. Thompson may have supported it for political reasons, but only while also urging that France be given nuclear technological assistance, the price for that being the admission of the United Kingdom to the Common Market.[1] Apart from the MLF, all of this would happen by the middle of the 1970s. It may not have been a grand design, but, eventually, it seemed like a good bargain.

De Gaulle, however, was in no mood to wait. He announced in March 1966 that France would leave NATO's unified military command. Few people in EUR were shocked. "It would be amazing," wrote one longtime observer of France, "if the withdrawal of France from NATO had not been taken in the United States, and especially in governing circles in this country, very badly indeed. Indignation, anger, regret, variously mingled and intense, are natural responses; surprise is

137

not."[2] De Gaulle had waxed unfavorably about NATO (the organization, but not the treaty or the alliance—an important distinction) for several years.[3] During the summer and fall of 1965, French foreign minister Couve de Murville had warned that de Gaulle planned to take a step of this nature, although most people expected it to come in 1969 with the treaty's twenty-year renewal.[4] It came earlier for various reasons, namely, that de Gaulle was worried about the upcoming 1967 parliamentary elections and the likelihood of an end to his tenure in office.[5]

Just as significant from the point of view of EUR as the "Gaullist disruption" was the American reaction to it. For most in the bureau, de Gaulle and his methods were a fact of life, whether one liked him or not. But for Ball, Acheson, and, by extension, the higher levels of the State Department, the de Gaulle affair proved to be something of a crucible in their strained relationship with Lyndon Johnson. Although the Vietnam War continued to affect that relationship—to Acheson's favor and to Ball's disfavor—it was the determination of both men to "take de Gaulle to Coventry" that threatened whatever momentary standing they had with the president on European affairs.[6] Johnson would hear none of it. At an infamous meeting on May 19, 1966, the two sides came to verbal blows. "It is never difficult to ignite the Acheson powder magazine," Bruce noted in his diary, "and the President's spark set off an explosion." While Rusk and McNamara tried to calm things down, "Acheson visibly seethed in silence; LBJ looked like a human thundercloud."[7] Acheson, finding himself "in the middle of a whole series of intra-USG vendettas—Defense vs. State, White House vs. State, JCS vs. McNamara, Semitic-Gaullists vs. European Integrationists, and LBJ-turn-the-other-cheekism vs. DA-let-the-chips-fall-where-they-mayism," let loose: "I lost my temper.... Rusk and McNamara dove for cover while Ball and I slugged it out with Mr. Big. Dave Bruce was a charmed witness. It was exhilarating."[8]

Soon after, Acheson upbraided Francis Bator at a dinner party (hosted by the British, no less): "[Y]ou know what you did? You made the greatest imperial power the world has ever known kiss de Gaulle's arse!"[9] But Johnson held firm to the line set down earlier by Kennedy: as much as de Gaulle's attitudes and actions could infuriate, the United States still needed to do business with him. Where flattery did not work, patience just might. "Hostility to General de Gaulle is not a policy," Bundy once wrote. "He is a most difficult man, but these problems existed before him and will continue after him."[10]

For most people on the sidelines, however, being anti-Gaullist was synonymous with being anti-French. There were very few well-known American devotees of de Gaulle apart from Walter Lippmann and Senators Frank Church and William Fulbright.[11] Many of their contemporaries regarded the general as a romantic figure out of the ruin of France, an almost exotic brand of nationalist and, perhaps less charitably, "a twentieth-century Don Quixote," "an aging mongoose" surrounded by "sickly cobras." At root he was aloof, insecure, prickly, and ambivalent; an older, more bitter version of the child who had been shunned as "the asparagus."[12] Accordingly, reaction to de Gaulle's latest rebuff ranged from the annoyed to the hysterical, with most people in EUR landing cynically closer to the former. Many took de Gaulle at his word, recognizing that there did in fact exist alternative conceptions of transatlantic order but that, as John Foster Dulles phrased it long ago, "we shall not always agree with France any more than France will always agree with us, but I trust that throughout it will be recognized that

Francis Bator and Lyndon Johnson
Courtesy of Lyndon B. Johnson Library

the differences are of economic rather than moral origin."[13]

Well, not quite. De Gaulle's vision was political and differed from dumbbellism on philosophical as well as practical grounds, and in substance though not in form: As Christopher Emmet noted, "The theory is O.K. as an ideal to strive for, but its effect in giving the Gaullists their *only* respectable argument was unfortunate."[14] De Gaulle promoted a strong, united Europe, not in the Monnet sense of mixed sovereignties but rather as a traditional alliance of nation-states, ideally under French hegemony. "Like Hitler," de Gaulle "thought we should leave Europe to him," only his Europe would not be a "Third Force" but "a Second Force in the West."[15] Or, as *The Economist* put it succinctly in December 1962, this was a clash between "unity" and "parity," and "the two may in the end prove irreconcilable."[16]

De Gaulle's American opponents rightly saw his challenge as providing an affront to their vision of transatlantic cooperation and an opening for neutralism. But his defenders had something of a point: de Gaulle had been snubbed at Nassau; his quest for a national deterrent was a legitimate expression of *Realpolitik*, particularly given suspicions that the United States and the Soviet Union would negotiate arms reductions over his head or, alternatively, might go to war, dragging his nation and the rest of Europe in with them. Thus, he made it clear that his decision did not apply to the Alliance itself but merely to the hierarchical sharing of military resources and control within NATO; he preferred that only French officers command French troops, and this extended naturally to France's new nuclear weapons. Otherwise de Gaulle, as his behavior during the Cuban Missile Crisis demonstrated, could be a loyal ally when it really counted. That he had defeated the Communists at home, extricated his country from Algeria, and continued to inspire the French people with national pride should have reassured his American allies. But then there was the man himself. Officials on both sides of the Atlantic who were able to see past his personality and rhetoric wasted little time in making sure that the NATO baby was not thrown out with the bathwater.

By the early 1970s the various NATO ambassadors treated their French colleague like any other representative. The Gaullists back home to whom he reported did not express the slightest degree of annoyance.[17]

THE TUSSLE OVER DE GAULLE capped a period of estrangement between the White House and the more ideological Ball group in the State Department.[18] At each point the White House asserted a more cautious plan of action. The interesting thing about this was that EUR, apart from Schaetzel, who served as deputy assistant secretary during most of this period, did not subscribe to the Europeanist ideology or the policies they were meant to defend; indeed, the views of most people in the bureau were closer to those of the NSC than to those of Ball and his small group of allies. Supporting EUR and the White House was Acheson's own tribe of acolytes in the office of the undersecretary of State, U. Alexis Johnson, especially Jeff Kitchen and Sey Weiss. In league with Paul Nitze's office in the Pentagon, they helped to mount the rearguard action against the MLF.[19] Aligned with them was David Klein, Bundy's shrewd assistant on the NSC who also happened to be a foreign service officer and veteran of EUR. Bundy had decided he needed "a stuffy foreign service officer with some Soviet/German experience" following the construction of the Berlin Wall. Bill Tyler recommended Klein.[20] Bundy hired him after a single meeting.

The bureaucratic map was therefore more complicated than nameless flowcharts might otherwise suggest. Individual policy positions adhered less to office stereotypes than to networks of patronage and "like-mindedness," including those that extended back and forth outside government, and to coalitions on the inside. Labeling which official stood where, therefore, is less relevant historically than knowing that EUR lost considerable influence over foreign policy for the first time since World War II. This was because the political leadership of the department, namely, Ball, presumed itself to be both more knowledgeable and imaginative than the diplomatic professionals. That had happened before, particularly with Dean Acheson in the Truman years, but the effects on the institution this time were the opposite, mainly because Acheson, unlike Rusk, had enhanced the department's standing through a close relationship with his president. Kennedy and Johnson, by contrast, reposed little faith in State. Where they did not neglect it outright, they infiltrated it with critics. One such person was the former attorney general Nicholas Katzenbach, who became undersecretary in 1966. Miriam Camps's old colleague, Jeff Parsons, noted that Katzenbach "couldn't care less about the senior officers.... [H]e implied that good men could as well or better be found outside so why have a stuffy old and unnecessary prof Service anyway[?] ... K has a congenital dislike for anyone who dresses neatly, washes, combs hair and brushes teeth."[21] Katzenbach's problems were not entirely of his own making. Rusk, for instance, forgot to tell him that he had hired Walt Rostow's brother Gene, a Yale Law School professor and onetime Acheson protégé "who had been waiting for the call since 1948."[22] Unfortunately, Rostow had fired Katzenbach from the law school's faculty; the two spent a good deal of time avoiding one another on the seventh floor. This story was typical. For all his virtue, diligence, and decency, Rusk was not a very good manager. Unwilling to stick his neck out, overworked by Vietnam and other crises, and overly submissive to the White House and Pentagon, Rusk left EUR and most other bureaus of the department little choice but to wither.

Bureaucracies, as we know, abhor a vacuum. Enter Francis Bator. Intense, quick on his feet, resourceful, and occasionally audacious, Bator was a Hungarian immigrant who served in the army and worked for Max Millikan at the Massachusetts Institute of Technology, having received a Ph.D. there in economics with a minor in Central European diplomatic history done under the direction of Karl Deutsch. In 1961, he was working at the RAND Corporation; this led to a job with the Agency for International Development and then to one on Bundy's staff.[23] He was well liked. His boss said of him, "He has the sophistication of the Central European, the good manners of the Grotonian, the intellectual acuteness of the Institute [MIT], and the splendid combination of human qualities for which all residents of Cambridge are noted."[24] He also had an important ally in Walter Lippmann, for whom he did occasional research and writing. When Bundy left the NSC, Bator established a parallel relationship with Bundy's replacement, Walt Rostow, similar to the one Rusk had with Ball: Though nominally his deputy, Bator oversaw all matters pertaining to Europe and international economics, and reported directly to the president.[25]

Bator's counterpart at EUR was Leddy, regarded by one former subordinate as "the most knowledgeable economist ever to serve as Assistant Secretary of EUR." After some skirmishing over who was in charge of European policy, he served Bator quietly as a back channel and deferred to him, not only because frequent back problems kept him away from work but also because the star of his patron, Ball, had fallen so low.[26] It was Bator then, who, by his account, singlehandedly brought focus to the "inescapably decentralized way of handling relations with Europe" shaping the president's decisions.[27]

Another disadvantage for Leddy was that he succeeded a man known as "perhaps the most cultivated person in the department": Bill Tyler. He was not a favored choice but got the job because he was Kohler's deputy and there had been no consensus on a successor. Still, Tyler earned points with the White House after serving especially well as interpreter with de Gaulle.[28] "Amiable, a bon vivant, highly intelligent, an expert linguist [fluent in French, German, Spanish, and Italian, with] a pleasing personality and sound judgment, a thoroughly exceptional man," Tyler had been born in France to an American expatriate, Royall Tyler, and his Italian wife. Tyler *père* was also a displaced American: he had grown up in Biarritz, where his mother moved after the death of her husband. He was an old friend of Allen Dulles's and had helped him set up the OSS station in Bern, then went on to direct Red Cross efforts in Europe and had many close friends in the foreign service.[29] His wife, Elisina, had emigrated to England with her sister, who went on to become the first woman to hold a chair in Italian at the University of Birmingham. There Elisina married the publisher Grant Richards, whom she later left for Tyler. The two moved in an elegant circle of friends, including Robert and Mildred Bliss, Bill Tyler's godparents, who donated Dumbarton Oaks to Harvard and made him its first director, as well as Edith Wharton, which is how Tyler became Wharton's literary executor. Wharton's chauffeur lived at the Tylers' château at Antigny until he died.[30] Like his father, Tyler was educated at Harrow and Oxford, and was, also like his father, an amateur historian, authoring a book about the dukes of Burgundy. He was in his twenties before he visited the

United States, where he went in 1932 to work in a bank, even though he had really wanted to pursue a career in the fine arts. His godparents meanwhile tried to get him a job in the State Department. When war broke out, Tyler found himself in Boston, making short-wave propaganda broadcasts for the station WRUL under the name l'Américain-Bourguignon. From there he was seconded to the Office of War Information in North Africa, where he got to know many leaders of the Free French. After the war he joined the foreign service, serving under Jefferson Caffery, David Bruce, and Jimmy Dunn in Paris. To Bruce, Tyler was "serene, humorous, witty, scholarly ... the most superior man in the Foreign Service. He is modest, unselfish, unassertive, but through character, ability and personality captivates one's interest and affection."[31]

With Ball over him and Schaetzel under him, Tyler had a tough hand to play. Like Bruce, he was not wont to assert himself, preferring to be asked for advice and almost always giving it, cautiously. Above all, he was keen to preserve the appearance of influence and the prerogatives of office. He later recalled, in referring to the orientation of Ball and company:

> One thing I did not do and could not have done would have been ... in anything I said or wrote, to appear to be deviating from our position and our policy goals. If I had felt that a matter of principle was involved, I would have resigned. But I didn't feel my integrity was at stake, because I was entirely in sympathy with the objective, but not with the means pursued. But I kept this to myself. It was just not a realistic position for us to take, and I feared the effect it might have on our relations with certain other European countries, in addition to France, if we pressed so hard that it seemed as though we were completely and unremittingly beholden to the prospect of somehow using our power and our political clout to try to impose European political integration when Europe itself was not ready for it.[32]

Thus, Tyler worked in league with Bundy and against the spirit of both his boss and deputy. Tyler was certainly not a Europeanist in the Monnet mold, but neither was he a Gaullist, the occasional suspicion notwithstanding. If asked, he probably would have said he was just doing his job and had no such allegiances one way or the other. Like Bruce, he preferred the cultivation of trust behind the scenes in the usual formula: "[W]e ought to take our foot off the European accelerator pedal and ... leave it to the Europeans to work out when and how they propose to organize themselves into an entity which would constitute a basis for partnership."[33] It was this judgment that drew them together, along with Bohlen and Klein, into a subtle but effective source of influence upon Bundy and Kennedy. As a result, the latter two were predisposed to reject Ball's and Owen's insistence that Europeans were "inexperienced teenagers" who would "never do anything by themselves."[34] On each issue—the MLF, de Gaulle, Skybolt—they tended to keep their thoughts to themselves, as Tyler put it, trying to follow the policy line while casting doubt and plotting alternatives.[35]

His career would appear to have suffered little from his isolation at the top of his bureau. When Bohlen began to hint that he was ready to give up the

Paris embassy, Tyler would have been an obvious candidate to replace him. But Tyler insisted on being named ambassador to the Netherlands. His reason was a mystery to most people, apart from the few who knew that his mother was rumored to be the illegitimate great-great-granddaughter of Napoleon Bonaparte's brother, Louis, the king of Holland. It seemed therefore a fitting place to end one's diplomatic service.[36]

THERE WERE TWO IMPORTANT achievements in transatlantic relations that would ultimately overshadow the crises and setbacks in the 1960s. These were the completion of the Kennedy Round of multilateral trade negotiations and the so-called bridge building initiative that laid the basis for a political and economic opening to Eastern Europe. Their success was a repudiation of dumbbellism and marked a return to the traditional goal of an expansive Atlantic Community. Bator, whose fingerprints were on both, depicted the alternatives a bit differently: There were actually "three visions" at play: Monnet's, the Atlanticists', and a third, not de Gaulle's but some other formula involving a "scheme of U.S.-Soviet disengagement in Europe which would allow the unification of Germany," which in reality meant a kind of growing out of the Cold War. If the focus on the first two was primarily on the West, the third placed the burden of change upon Central and Eastern Europe.[37] But first the Western half of Europe needed to get its house in order.

This began with a reconfiguration of the trading relationship with the Common Market. The Kennedy Round began in 1964 under the leadership of Treasury Secretary C. Douglas Dillon, a Republican and Eisenhower's ambassador to France, who appeared here in Chapter 5.[38] Because it involved core economic relationships between the United States and Europe, EUR, or specifically, the new office within EUR—a spin-off of RA called Regional Political and Economic Affairs, or RPE—was heavily involved alongside the Bureau of Economic Affairs (E) and the undersecretary for political affairs, who was then the aforementioned Gene Rostow. Rostow was a talented but abstract-minded lawyer, about whom Bator's assistant Ed Hamilton once was heard to say, "[T]alking to him was like watching a great big wool ball float above four feet off the floor, passing slowly by."[39] He was supportive, but the nominal protagonist of the Kennedy Round was none other than Eisenhower's former secretary of state, Christian Herter, who would barely live beyond the end of the negotiations. Herter agreed to lead them, and hired two deputies: Mike Blumenthal and William Roth, who later replaced Herter as the U.S. trade representative. Things got off to a slow start, but ultimately came to a head in 1965 with Roth and Blumenthal shuttling back and forth to Geneva and the "Bator command group" overseeing the coordination back in Washington.[40] They were supported by RPE's Deane Hinton and E's Thomas Enders—who became known as the Kennedy Round's dueling duo, a loosely rendered Doppelgänger of Blumenthal and Roth. Hinton and Blumenthal were salty, street-smart operators; Enders and Roth were more urbane, although just as tough, especially Enders, whom Roy Jenkins rated as "an impressive, self-confident, over-tall Yale man, who I think is probably very good."[41] In the 1970s, both men would end up as ambassadors to the European Community and as assistant secretaries for economic and business affairs. Enders, in particular, was known for "plugging everything in the right sockets" and had his own political ambitions. With their help, Blumenthal and Roth reached a deal in Geneva after more than two years of tortuous negotiations and following a critical intervention on the part of President Johnson, who ordered that agriculture was not equivalent to industry and so sealed the deal.[42] Dean Rusk wrote to the negotiators, "Warmest congratulations on a superb job beautifully done." To Bob Schaetzel, Acheson noted that the result was "better than I dreamed possible."[43] It was a comparably unsung example of successful bureaucratic cooperation, although it might not have seemed so harmonious at the time.

In order to grasp the political import of the Kennedy Round and why EUR veterans like Hinton regarded it as having so long-lasting a success, one must take a step back and note that the trade negotiations culminated a decade of difficult external and internal readjustments toward and within Europe.[44] Largely, this had to do with the effort—strongly endorsed by Monnet—to bring Britain into the Common Market and with the related need to ensure that the market itself would evolve in a way that would not prove injurious to American national and global interests. Here they were joined by Acheson, who asked Adenauer to urge de Gaulle to approve the British application, as did Ball.[45] It was Ball, "amazed" at his own "directness," who told the British entirely on his own that the United States would support their application unwaveringly. Soon after, a previously skeptical Macmillan took him aside and said, "[W]e are going to do this thing." Ball proceeded, again largely on his own initiative, to lobby Walter Hallstein and other concerned Europeans in favor of British admission.[46] But the economic team in EUR was not fully on board. Joe Greenwald, one of its top officers, warned back in 1961 against moving too fast, urging instead that American rhetoric "seriously and scrupulously follow our announced policy of leaving the decision up to the UK." An interagency committee on the "tangled affair" of British entry was chaired by Bill Tyler and reached similar conclusions, as did Bundy, who sounded perplexed by Ball's activism. Walt Butterworth, then the American representative to the European Communities, even insisted that the United States raise the stakes with the British: "Given the entire record of recent years, we must take a hardheaded, objective view of new overtures from London.... If they want in, they will have to pay a political price in the form of a genuine commitment to the Continent. They full well know what the alternatives are, and nothing is to be gained by our acting as agents to communicate to the Europeans their feelings of puzzled or outraged innocence."[47]

Macmillan and de Gaulle met at Rambouillet just days before Kennedy met with Macmillan at Nassau to sort the Skybolt mess. We now know that de Gaulle told Macmillan that the British application would be rejected, as indeed it was that January. "What hit us?" many a Briton asked. Monnet might have wondered something similar; it was the only time he was ever seen drinking a martini before dinner, recalled Jack Tuthill. But the question was not whether it would be done, but how. "At Rambouillet," de Gaulle was said to have recalled, "Mr. Macmillan came to me to say that we ought to unite our two forces. Several days later he went to the Bahamas. Naturally, that changed the tone of my press conference."[48]

To add further insult to injury, this was followed by the Élysée Treaty, a Franco-German pact that solidified an alliance of the two countries outside the nascent European Community, causing, as one European observer recalled, "profound distress" in the State Department.[49] But Ball pushed ahead, even though he might have suspected that Macmillan was being less than forthcoming about his own conversations with de Gaulle when he earlier told Bundy that "our noises are not the same as your noises," regarding de Gaulle's reported resistance to the British move.[50] Now the question became one of how to avoid an overreaction from the British and other European nonmembers of the Common Market. There was the possibility that the British and others would establish a competing trading bloc and force the United States to play favorites; or that protectionism would spread throughout the Atlantic region. Jean Monnet seemed especially desperate to keep the various issues from interconnecting, and so brokered, by way of Ball and possibly others, the inclusion of critical revision language in a preamble to the Franco-German treaty that reaffirmed the central place of the United States, the United Kingdom, and the Atlantic Alliance for Europe.[51]

Miriam Camps at this juncture reentered government service. Her attention was focused almost entirely on the British effort to join the Common Market, and the related harmonization of relations between the so-called Sixes (the EEC) and Sevens (the British-led European Free Trade Association, or EFTA), a subject about which she contributed what remains one of the most authoritative books.[52] Camps and her close network of fellow trade specialists—among them Leddy, Tuthill, Greenwald, and Reinstein, a group described by EUR's Abe Katz as "the clan"—continued to work quietly in favor of an active American role in European integration by using traditional methods. Here is Camps writing earlier in October 1959:

> I am just back from a few days in Brussels where I talked to all our old friends and some new ones: [Robert] Marjolin, [Jean] Rey, [Max] Kohnstamm, [Jean-François] Deniau.... I am accredited to no one and yet pretty well steeped in everyone's views ... having listened for x years on both sides of the Channel convince me of the purity of their intentions and the justness of their views.... I think the U.S. should now say something like this to the U.K.: if the U.K. is prepared now really to take a decision to give its European relation primacy and to work out its relationship with the U.S. primarily although not exclusively in that context, we will use our influence with the Six to see that a sensible negotiation on association is conducted on their side.[53]

The only problem with this plan was that it lacked the consensus of the other European governments, and Ball's freelancing did not help. There had been the hope that the problem of harmonization could be solved by pushing for closer European integration within the OECD, which, as noted, was founded in part to replace the obsolescent OEEC; to coordinate European and American trade and other economic approaches toward the developing world; and, according to a few cynics, to "kill the Free Trade Area," an anti–Common Market group established by the British in 1958.[54] The era of infighting acronyms was well under way. The story of such maneuverings is long and complex, even for many trade specialists to follow. Nora Beloff has simplified it:

The Americans, Mr. Dillon said, could not lie down and let the Europeans get together and discriminate against them just at the moment when they were making their first acquaintance with Britain's old friend, the balance of payments problem. Like all good Americans, Mr. Dillon did not question the right of the Europeans to merge their sovereignties and establish a United States of Europe on the American model. For political reasons, Mr. Dillon was personally all in favour of the Community experiment even if it was commercially disadvantageous to his own country. But he certainly could not support a purely commercial arrangement with no political component, which would bring Britain in and America out.[55]

Moreover, the OECD might have had the additional advantage of raising the European Commission's diplomatic profile, which could have allowed for a "marriage of interests," in this one instance, between some Europeanists and the Atlanticists.[56]

For her part, Camps was skeptical about the successor organization she helped to set up: "I do not believe that the OECD offers the neutrals enough to satisfy them for two reasons," she wrote to Bob Schaetzel in October 1961. "They are prepared for free trade with the Community; we are not.... Second, I think past examinations have shown that it is not possible to attack the problem by isolating items that are of particular interest[;] ... it is not a problem that can be dealt with on the basis of woodpulp, watches and a handful of other stuff."[57] Yet such things mattered, politically as much as commercially. "Americans tend to oversimplify matters and to take extreme positions," noted one liaison officer for the European Communities in Washington. "They are enthusiastic at the beginning but expect spectacular or concrete results from the 'Grand Designs.' ... [W]hen progress is not obvious ... they become extremely negative."[58] Although in the case of the Sixes and Sevens, the Americans had a point: The United States would find it difficult to defend trade discrimination against NATO allies in favor of members of the Common Market who were not in the Alliance.[59]

Camps and her colleagues would eventually come around to the determination that the Common Market was the only way forward, and that the United States had to help it both grow and liberalize. "It is our judgment," conceded C. Douglas Dillon back in 1959, "that the best way of dealing with European and world trade problems would be for all of us—the U.K., the continental European countries outside the Six, the United States, Canada and others—to accept the Common Market as an accomplished fact."[60]

The intensive, retail diplomacy by members of the "clan" as well as the Kennedy Round team did away with the perception among the British and neutrals like the Austrians and the Swedes of a conspiracy by the United States to overlook their interests in its role as the "keeper of the faith" on integration, and thereby established a decade-long relationship of trust between Americans and Europeans on trade and related economic matters.[61] The British would join the Common Market in 1973 and would prove wrong the prediction that "a little England going into Europe is likely to favor a policy of little Europe once she is in."[62] Meanwhile, the OECD would evolve in ways that transformed it into today's global organization, but one not too different from what Ball once described as another "umbrella in which Europe could get together."[63] The various pieces of the puzzle still, amazingly, continued to coalesce in fits and starts. To the extent an American contribution to European integration succeeded at all, then, it was because of the behind-the-scenes work of people like Camps in remaking institutions, chief among which was her old shop, the OEEC.

IT WAS IN THESE CIRCUMSTANCES, ironically, that the term "bridge building" became known in Europe. Initially it referred to the various efforts by the British to establish "halfway houses" like the Free Trade Area. The State Department, especially EUR, regarded them as dubious attempts to "undercut" the Common Market and opposed them at nearly every turn.[64] As much as American policy favored trade-liberalizing schemes on principle, its priority remained strengthening the European movement and the Common Market, specifically. In the neat formulation of the economic expert and later ambassador to Italy and Spain, Richard Gardner, "the idea was to get the external tariff of the six EC members low enough to facilitate British entry in a way that would minimally impact our relations with them."[65] But EUR was "so concerned" about the Common Market negotiations, wrote one of its most thoughtful officers, Richard Vine, "they wouldn't let themselves think about it." Vine argued that the British were mainly to blame for failing to integrate their Common Market, nuclear and East-West policies, as some British Europeanists, for example the Tory prime minister Edward Heath, later admitted.[66] It seemed up to the Americans to recast the balance between them and the other Europeans, much as the MLF crowd vainly sought to do in its sphere. However, it appeared that they, or EUR at least, did little besides provide a sympathetic ear for Europe within the U.S. government, and to make sure the Europeans knew it, which may have mitigated what otherwise might have been a far more contentious period in transatlantic economic relations, as indeed the early 1970s would become. EUR restricted its role, in other words, to early warning identification and process management. Any more ambitious agenda carried several risks, not least of which was the mutual dependence of the trade talks upon progress with European integration, which is why, again, those in charge said the Kennedy Round just had to succeed.[67]

The larger point to all this was that, like dumbbellism, the above set of priorities had an almost exclusive focus on *Western* Europe. It followed Monnet's program for consolidation, first of Western Europe, and then of transatlantic partnership. But bridge building presently acquired a much different meaning, which takes us to Bator's third model. Détente was well under way by the mid-1960s. There had been Kennedy's 1963 American University speech, but it was really more about an overture to the Soviet Union than an opening to the East per se, and spoke against the recurring fear of the Western Europeans, particularly Adenauer, that the superpowers would reach agreements over their heads. Indeed, the German question lay not too far from the surface; it would be Germany, or rather policy toward Berlin and not a separate Franco-German alliance, that would eventually supply the second pillar of partnership, if such a thing existed.[68] Again, it should be recalled that Germany required some of the hardest economic and political choices for the United States; German ambivalence fed American fears about de Gaulle's true aims for Europe, and the suspicions that he and a senile Adenauer, or a more left-of-center German successor, would pursue an alternative path to reunification; or that he would sign some kind of pact independently with Moscow. Also, Germany and presumed German sensibilities remained the most vexing obstacles to an integrated, European defense. Kennedy put it succinctly: "If the pressure comes back in Berlin, then you will find unity in the Alliance. If it is off Berlin, then we are going to have to recognize that we are going to deal with a lot of problems ... particularly ... with the General."[69]

An interim answer to these various questions—and the closest thing to a grand design the 1960s would produce—came with a speech Lyndon Johnson gave in October 1966. In it he put forth the logical synthesis of both détente and what would come to be called *Ostpolitik*, stating that German reunification could only occur hand in hand with a relaxation of the Cold War standoff and an opening of the Soviet bloc to the West.[70] That simple idea was to "shift from the narrow concept of coexistence to the broader vision of peaceful engagement" in order to build "a surer foundation of mutual trust."[71] The speech foreshadowed a good deal of the "linkage" diplomacy of the 1970s, which, as the next chapter illustrates, laid the basis for the "Europe, whole and free" that would be proclaimed another decade later by President George H. W. Bush. Yet Johnson's 1966 proposal was self-consciously modest, with

> goals defined not in terms of a concrete, architectural outcome, but rather in terms of maximizing piecemeal movement in broadly indicated directions, as opportunity presents itself. It is a vision exceedingly flexible in both structural outcome and tempo. It allows for political integration in Europe but does not require it, and emphasizes the practical arrangements and the increasing closeness needed for efficient problem solving. It allows, but only at the end of a very long process, for some sort of growing together of the two parts of Germany, but in the meanwhile calls only for a further opening of relations between Western and Eastern Europe.... It calls for increasing East European independence of the Soviet Union, but only at a pace which keeps down the risk of backlash. It allows for increasing autonomy in Western Europe's relations with the United States, even in defense, but only in step with the European capacity to manage a credible deterrent of its own.... It allows for some institutionalization of Atlantic politics, but looks mainly to increasingly close ad hoc cooperation on specific problems.[72]

The bureaucratic tale behind the speech is significant. Mainly the work of Bator, the speech made the rounds of the various bureaus. Henry Owen's Policy Planning Staff took a special interest, contributing several early drafts written by Owen's assistant, the Columbia University political scientist Zbigniew Brzezinski. Brzezinski, who would go on to achieve fame as Jimmy Carter's national security adviser, later claimed credit for having written the entire speech.[73] Bator pointed out that this was not only incorrect but also detrimental to its goals, since Brzezinski had the reputation of a hawk and, as some would allege, a Russophobe. At any rate, he was not known for his open mind toward détente, particularly in the Soviet Union. A Polish refugee, he was not seen as being very pro-German, either. Bator and his coauthors, Leddy and Bowie, took pains to cast the speech in the most positive possible terms; but as soon as Brzezinski claimed credit for it, the Soviet press jumped on the speech as a resurrection of the "rollback" policy of the 1950s. Even though the State Department had stopped using terms like "Communist bloc" and "satellites" in favor of geographic ones like "Soviet Union and Eastern Europe," the speech would have less of an immediate impact than its backers might have liked.[74] But it nevertheless marked the official end of the crisis era and the beginning of what Richard Nixon would come to label the era of negotiations.

THE STORY OF BRIDGE BUILDING takes us full circle to the beginning of the decade, which featured a mental map of Europe centered somewhere near the Elbe, with concentric circles expanding in three directions: toward the East with the beginnings of superpower détente, toward the West with a steady program of economic and political integration, and toward the South with the emergence of a transatlantic consensus over decolonization.[75] Then came another series of crises: First Berlin and Cuba, then Skybolt, then de Gaulle, balance of payments, and finally, Vietnam. Although each one has not been fully described here, all were to one degree or another interrelated and drove those in EUR nearly to distraction. The bureau seemed to have lost its way, sounding confused, abstract, overzealous, and defensive. Why did this happen? There were several reasons. There was the aura of the Kennedy ascendancy with its passion for the new, the different, the exciting. There was Europe itself—more prosperous and, apart from Berlin, a bit more dull and insular. And there was the passing, or better put, mutation, of a generation of diplomats. Elspeth Rostow, Walt's wife, once made the now infamous point that the principal architects of foreign policy were nearly all junior officers in World War II, all eager at last to prove their worth to their collective fathers. There was something to the notion. Men in their forties and fifties like Ball, Owen, and Schaetzel were old enough to have witnessed the triumph of the transatlantic commitment in the immediate postwar years and yet, with the partial exception of Ball, were not among its central players, most of whom by then had gone on to achieve notoriety—or infamy—elsewhere in the world. So now it was someone else's turn.

But the 1960s called for stability and consistency, not for new conquests. The mission to remake Europe was too self-conscious, too explicit, too buccaneerish, and, thanks to M. Monnet, too exclusively wedded to the Western half of the continent. Even dumbbellism's presumed proponents began to have second thoughts. Gene Rostow wrote to Ball in January 1962, "I am more inclined than ever to think that the 'dumbbell' debate is about a chimera.... I suppose it will be as absurd to expect the Prime Minister of Norway to have a policy about Laos as it would be to expect as much from the Governor of Wisconsin.... [N]o one ... expected to reach the height of pure dumbbellism for another ten years at best."[76] That would never happen, in good measure because their great initiative—the MLF—obviated the basic, separate but equal, tenets of partnership. If de Gaulle had not pointed out the contradiction and used the dumbbellists' rhetoric against them, someone else almost surely would have.

Ultimately, ideologues canceled one other out like bouncing billiard balls falling into their respective corner pockets. Left on the table were the good sense and pragmatic enterprise of people like Bundy, Bator, and Tyler, who worried about the "generally unsatisfactory and, I fear, deteriorating relationship between Europe and ourselves"; yet others recognized that the relationship still rested "upon certain abiding and fundamental realities ... the hard facts of life."[77] The question was, as noted above, less of competing or "irreconcilable" grand designs than of the concrete against the abstract, or what Tyler once called the "empirical" over the "doctrinal."[78] By the middle of the decade, their understated approach to the various transatlantic problems would prevail, suggesting a variation on the traditional life cycle of bureaucracies, with "zealots" having overtaken "conservers," to be followed again by the latter as against the general rule that the larger the bureaucracy, the greater its tendency toward insularity and resistance.[79] Although EUR's ranks had indeed been infiltrated by Europeanists, it was able to draw on a range of allies in other departments, in other governments, and beyond—particularly in the expanding network of Atlantic advocacy groups—as well as among the more pragmatic members of the Europeanist tribe—people like Art Hartman, John Leddy, and even, on his better days, Ball himself. Ultimately, they all shared the goal of keeping Europe, and European questions, in the foreground of policymaking. They had begun to see it institutionalized with all the strains and imperfections that this entailed.

Weary of playing the devil's advocate for Vietnam, Ball resigned in 1966 and went to work for Lehman Brothers, where Bruce reported that he was very happy, with "an office, apartment, car and chauffeur." He returned only briefly to government service as ambassador to the United Nations in 1968 but probably would have gone on to become Jimmy Carter's secretary of state were it not for his controversial positions on Israel. Schaetzel meanwhile lingered on in Brussels until 1972, after which he retired to found the American Council for Jean Monnet Studies and wrote a nasty book for the Council on Foreign Relations: *NATO—The Unhinged Alliance*. Owen remained active in the Johnson administration, followed by a long tenure at the Brookings Institution and then back in government as President Carter's chief of economic summits. But by the time Richard Nixon came to office, the few remaining theologians were barely heard from.[80] The same was almost true for EUR. But, as will be seen in the next two chapters, it would regroup and begin to repair the damage of midlife crisis.

The decade of the 1960s, as complex and confusing as it was, proved to be neither salutary nor lethal to the Atlantic Community. It was, as Acheson's latter-day career appeared, a glass both half full and half empty. Although Atlanticism had not fully "ground to a halt ... out of inexperience, overconfidence, or a combination of both," it was not exactly ironclad.[81] Another new team, arriving with Richard Nixon, would determine its fate.

9

THE ORDEAL OF
HELMUT SONNENFELDT

Resurgence of EUR—Ostpolitik and détente—Berlin Quadripartite Agreement—
Conference on Security and Cooperation in Europe, and Helsinki Final Act—
"Sonnenfeldt Doctrine"—beginning of the end of the Cold War in Europe

NINETEEN HUNDRED AND SIXTY-EIGHT—that dramatic year with
its loud crack in the bipolar world—passed quietly in EUR, at least in
comparison with what was to come. The transatlantic crises of the 1970s—the
oil shocks, the post-Vietnam deterioration of America's position in Europe, and
the public phenomenon of Henry Kissinger—were still around the corner. More
immediately visible in EUR were the first real signs of middle age among the
postwar generation of Atlanticists. Their mission, enthusiasm, and vital force
were sidetracked badly in the 1960s, not only by the Vietnam War and Charles
de Gaulle's exhibitionism but also by the putative refinement of Atlanticism in
the guise of the Grand Design—a typical shooting star of the era and by now
well extinguished. The *période Texane* was over.[1] By 1968, EUR, like much of U.S.
officialdom, was weary and petulant.

Assistant Secretary Leddy would hang on for another year before decamping to
a quiet retirement. Nobody in the bureau seemed to have been excessively nettled
over the Soviet annihilation of the Prague Spring that August; as elsewhere, the
reaction to it was as something "unprecedented but not unexpected."[2] The usual
post–Kennedy Round tussles with the Common Market would continue at a slow
boil, nearly all forgotten later except by veterans of EUR's Office of Regional
Political and Economic Affairs. Meanwhile, the Alliance remained strong, at least
outwardly, and a new president announced that his first foreign trip would be to
Europe.

Accompanying Richard Nixon was Kissinger, the "self-described Europeanist,"
indeed, the first European-born national security adviser and, with the partial
exception of Christian Herter, the first foreign-born U.S. secretary of state in the
twentieth century.[3] The legend of Kissinger begins, in this period, with his skillful

Helmut Sonnenfeldt
Courtesy of Gerald R. Ford Library

marginalization of Secretary of State William Rogers, alongside his reinvention of the National Security Council as the preeminent agent of foreign policy. We now know both to have been exaggerated, in part by Kissinger himself but also by his many biographers. The primacy of the NSC was already well established by Bundy and endorsed by Nixon, who chose Rogers for his loyalty and legal skills but had never intended to entrust him with a heavy policy role. Nixon, like Kennedy, disliked and distrusted the State Department and came into office determined to run foreign policy out of the White House. Kissinger, then, made the most of a fortunate situation. He did not invent the system in which he flourished, but pushed it to its outer limits of effectiveness.

This was not necessarily a bad arrangement from the point of view of the professionals, even before Kissinger became secretary of state in his own right in 1973. But elsewhere the mood was bleak. Kissinger's initial step of transferring operational oversight over foreign policy from the State Department to the NSC was viewed by some in the upper and middle echelons as sacrilege, and the secretive methods he and Nixon used deemed indecent if not unforgivable.[4] Lower down, the mood was brighter, at least at the beginning. It was not necessarily the case that the foreign service liked the new regime but rather that it respected (or feared) and even took pleasure in the shrewdness of its new leaders. Jim Sutterlin, a foreign service officer then assigned to Kissinger's Center for International Affairs at Harvard, noted that despite the "personal jealousies and antipathies I think most people here are genuinely relieved and impressed by Nixon's choice. Certainly I am."[5] Kissinger co-opted the department to a remarkable extent, not simply by recruiting some of its most talented officers onto his own staff but also by treating them seriously as fellow conspirators. Or, as he said to the wife of one of them, "I am so happy with putting career people in jobs because they are so easy to get rid of."[6] This led a few of them to the not entirely self-serving belief that co-optation could happen in reverse. Thus, it was true that

Kissinger succeeded in outmaneuvering the State Department both intellectually and politically, imposing his own tactics—and occasionally concepts—on foreign policy. But he was also capable of changing his mind, and worked harder and more tenaciously than nearly anyone else in the administration. It was also the case that Kissinger had a firmly held, academic vision of the world that, rightly or wrongly, made a habit of rationalization that freed bureaucratic hands from his micromanagement.[7] Therefore it was no accident that, apart from only a handful of exceptions, most of them being former Harvard associates and his military aides, nearly all of Kissinger's inner circle came from the foreign service. This had not been the case in the Kennedy or Johnson White Houses.

One of the bright lights to join Kissinger's staff was forty-three-year-old Helmut Sonnenfeldt, otherwise known as Hal. A short, somewhat bulbous man, Sonnenfeldt had a disposition that combined extremes of intensity and insouciance amid fits of thoughtful restlessness. Like his new boss, Sonnenfeldt was a refugee from Nazi Germany. Born in Berlin, he escaped soon after the beginning of the war, making his way to England, where his physician parents left him in a boarding school. He attended the University of Manchester and joined his parents in the United States, then became an American citizen after a year in the army (where he got to know both Kissinger and Kissinger's patron, Fritz Kraemer). He went on to receive a master's degree from the Johns Hopkins University in 1951. Soon after, he married Marjorie Hecht, a local department-store heiress, and landed a job in the State Department.[8]

Sonnenfeldt spent most of his early career in the department's Bureau of Intelligence and Research (INR), rising to head the Office of Research and Analysis for the Soviet Bloc by November 1961.[9] His particular area of expertise was nuclear weapons, and he advised Harold Stassen and John McCloy in the 1950s and early 1960s on disarmament. At this time, there was a fairly rigid line separating political and intelligence officers; in Soviet affairs, the former were known at times to look down upon the latter, knowing that most had never set foot in the Soviet Union. Sonnenfeldt seemed to have escaped the burden of that prejudice because of his evident intelligence and strong defense of prerogative.[10] His reports from the period are workmanlike and confident.

Sonnenfeldt's job as an analyst brought him into contact with academics on the transatlantic circuit of conferences and seminars. He took a year off in 1959 to teach at his alma mater, Johns Hopkins, and was invited by Kissinger in 1965 to take a sabbatical at Harvard's Center for International Affairs. The correspondence between the two is friendly, revealing of a certain alignment of character and, more implicitly, of interests.[11] Sonnenfeldt wrote, "I do want tell you though how much I appreciate your proposal; in fact I am quite touched by it.... I find much that is attractive in the possibility of a year with you and I am most reluctant to let the opportunity pass lightly," to which he added, in a confidential coda,

> I want to raise separately and for your eyes only the one further problem, the others had been logistical.... I have some difficulty visualizing myself happy and contented—and creative—in the presence for a year of your Director. While I have always had the most agreeable personal relations with him I am nevertheless distinctly uncomfortable in his company and

find it virtually impossible to maintain a fruitful intellectual association with him.[12]

The director was Bob Bowie, with whom Kissinger himself was barely on speaking terms.

The Bureau of Intelligence and Research was known for its good sense or, in Washington parlance, "getting it right." Sonnenfeldt was a typical INR man, full of intellectual beans. His political views were also stridently held. While accompanying Stassen to disarmament talks in London in 1957, Sonnenfeldt portrayed the Minnesota Republican as stubborn and misguided on the Soviets with views about Central Europe resembling, in a phrase he would use some years later, the "dubious aspects of Kennanism."[13] Sonnenfeldt was one of the few people in the U.S. government to have predicted accurately the crackdown on the Prague Spring, claiming later that it was a "big mistake" for the Soviets and that it demonstrated the inherent weakness of their system.[14] By 1968, however, he had grown frustrated with his place in the bureaucracy. Writing to his boss, Thomas Hughes, he complained:

> Twice in the past week I have been told that our judgments on certain aspects of Soviet policy were useless because they are not based on all the available information.... Even with only partial access to information, it is clear that current Soviet diplomatic actions on several fronts cry out for integrated analysis.... I have told you this before, and I know you think it is merely histrionic, but I seriously question how we can justify some three-quarter million dollars of public money a year for this office (and $28,000.00 for myself) if we are literally precluded from having a meaningful say on the most crucial issues of Russian-American relations.[15]

Sonnenfeldt was ready to move out, and up.

HE WAS NOT THE ONLY one who spent the latter years of the 1960s feeling restless and underappreciated. The new president seemed the most unlikely of men to soothe a war-weary nation. But Nixon won the presidency by a small margin, just enough to capitalize upon divisions among the Democrats, and came into office promising to be a peacemaker and unifier. His decision to take a European journey at the end of February 1969 marked a different sort of change: Presidents usually began their terms of office by venturing somewhere in the Western Hemisphere. Nixon and about 300 retainers would spend eight days in Brussels, London, Paris, Berlin, and Rome, appearing keen to set transatlantic relations on a new footing and to reassure America's allies that he wanted their support to end to the Vietnam War.[16] The feeling on the ground was less cheerful. David Bruce wrote in his diary:

> I doubt whether State is being consulted as it should be by lower levels at the White House.... I begin to suspect that Dr. Kissinger does not find this a difficult task. His German—not fine Italian—hand appears discernible

in trying to bring his personal friends abroad, even though some are comparatively obscure politically ... Kissinger is not as well known in public circles here [London] as is the President of the United States, a fact of which Kissinger ... is not fully conscious.[17]

For his part, Kissinger welcomed "returning to the continent where I was born" with "eagerness" and deep interest in the "geopolitical realities and historical ties between countries sharing similar histories, values, and institutions." Sonnenfeldt did not accompany them on Air Force One, probably the first of many moments when, according to the journalist Seymour Hersh, Kissinger did not "think too many Jews should be around."[18]

The impression one gains from Kissinger's memoir is of a humble neophyte thrust into the diplomatic limelight. But he had long sought, and ultimately thrived upon, fame and admiration. "Nixon respected me; and he envied me because he thought—not wrongly from his point of view—that I skimmed the cream of the glories of power while he had to suffer the continuing social ostracism that resulted from the mutual distrust of the old Nixon acolytes and the Washington Establishment."[19] Kissinger had grown svelte and alluring during his rise to intellectual stardom during the late 1950s and 1960s. For all that he had lost the friendship and trust of former academic colleagues during his years in government, at one point saying that the only thing "Harvard wants from us" was "failure," he would continue to serve as Nixon's principal ambassador to Georgetown, which for the most part did not hesitate to cast him in the role of courtier and eventually welcomed him as one of their own. Joe Alsop, for one, wasted little time. On February 29, 1969, he wrote to Kissinger to invite him to a party for the socialite Brooke Astor: "I must say I send you my congratulations on the progress on the European trip to date. It all seems so well arranged and, above all, so well prepared. And the President was so wise to avoid the kind of traveling circus effect that characterized the foreign forays of Eisenhower, Kennedy and Johnson."[20]

Nixon's trip to Europe therefore served a dual purpose: It underscored the president's staged gravitas on relatively safe ground; and it introduced Henry Kissinger as the éminence grise, the European who had not quite renounced his Old World origins but who had, apparently, advanced to a superior realm of global power. The Europeans and the European Desk were put on notice: This was a man who required attention—and on their home turf.

Better known than the man himself at this point were Kissinger's views on foreign affairs. He made his first big mark with a critique of the Eisenhower administration's nuclear strategy; almost a decade later, his The Troubled Partnership (1965) appeared, promoted by the Council on Foreign Relations as "a re-appraisal of the Atlantic Alliance." Kissinger assumed the familiar tone of the debunker of postwar assumptions grown stale. He credited the foresight of the Atlanticists in building a foundation for a Western European order that was able to withstand the challenges of the late 1940s and 1950s, and the successive stabs in the back by de Gaulle during the 1960s. But the times had changed. In one of the most quoted passages of the book, Kissinger asserted:

European unity is not a major cure-all for Atlantic disagreements. In many respects it may magnify rather than reduce differences. As Europe gains structure, it will be in a better position to insist on differences whose ultimate cause is structural rather than personal. Phrases like "indivisible interest" are correct when applied to the defense of Europe or East-West relations; they come close to being platitudes in other parts of the world. A wise Alliance policy will not gear everything to the expectation that common positions can be developed on a global basis; it will also take account of the fact that the interests of Europe and America are not identical everywhere ... Our European Allies will almost certainly consider that their vital interests are not at stake in Asia, Latin America. If Atlantic policy is completely centralized, it may grow stagnant. The Alliance will be able to agree only on doing nothing.[21]

In other words, a European-American relationship resting on the twin pillars of European unity and trans-Atlantic solidarity should no longer be taken for granted. Kissinger issued a moratorium on the intramural debates over the shape of the transatlantic relationship described in the previous four chapters. So far as he and Nixon were concerned in 1969, such talk was a waste of time. The United States still needed the military alliance, to be sure, but only as leverage against the Soviets and to keep the Europeans compliant. They in turn no longer depended on the United States as heavily as before. If they were going to be partners elsewhere in the world, or even within the European economic and political orbit, they were going to have to prove their worth. "When all is said and done," noted one American Gaullist, Chip Bohlen's son-in-law, David Calleo, "Europe is not America's front porch, but somebody else's house."[22]

Kissinger probably would not have accepted that his effort to recast American power as an instrument of global order by discarding the "old" notion of an Atlantic Community in favor of a more flexible, and conditional, relationship with Europe would take the idea of dumbbellism to its logical—and perverse—extreme: It replaced the Western European side of the dumbbell with one centered in Moscow. Such went counter to the geopolitical realism upon which his thinking purportedly was based. Europe was not an abstraction but a piece of the same interconnected landmass at whose other end sat the Soviet Union and that remained, at least in the minds of a few people, the desired object of its expansion. As the Atlantic Council was compelled to repeat in 1974, "[S]ome in Europe claim that Europe must choose between the concept of a 'European Europe' and that of an 'American Europe.' Europe faces no such choice. The only feasible course for Europe is that of an Atlantic Europe, just as the only feasible course for the United States is that of an Atlantic America."[23] Yet Nixon's and Kissinger's version of détente, which really resembled a traditional entente, or condominium, with the Soviet Union, had the effect of dividing Europe further against itself and subjecting it to a hierarchical order that neither the United States nor the Soviet Union could sustain. Meanwhile, the genuine détente that EUR had worked so hard to cultivate since the Cuban Missile Crisis was put at risk. It should have been no surprise, then, that Kissinger placed Sonnenfeldt, a Soviet analyst, in charge of European policy. His views were summarized well in a 1972 speech to the National War College:

We want to enlist the support and the contribution of the Soviet Union in the building and maintenance of a stable world order.... As regards Western Europe, let's face it: we have a serious problem. We have with the West Europeans a fundamental community of interests in regard to basic values, their physical security and political vigor.... Our interests with respect to them are not markedly different from how the British perceived their interests with respect to the Continent for a long time. And the Atlantic is approximately as wide as the Channel was in those days—maybe not quite as wide.... So we have a simple interest in throwing our weight into that balance on geopolitical grounds, even apart from values, historical attachments and all the other things that make us more like Western Europe than any other part of the world.

He continued with a retrospective:

In participating in this process in the forties, fifties, into the early sixties, we did not think through some of the other implications and particularly the implications in the economic area.... In a situation where East-West relations become more stable, the political and security interests that we share with the Europeans tend to become more remote and less tangible and more the subject of learned discussions at war colleges and academic writings than in the sense of immediacy and urgency of citizens, Congressmen, and Senators....

I am afraid we have reached a situation where if we let economics dominate our relationship with the Western Europeans, the concrete character of the economic problems, the effect on the livelihood of real, living, voting people on both sides of the Atlantic will be such that these larger commonalities of interest ... are likely to be drowned out.[24]

At the root of the Atlanticists' concern with the above assumptions about Europe was the usual confusion of means and ends, which may refute the truism—attributed to General Alfred Gruenther—that "military strategy and prostitution are the only two professions where the amateur is better than the professional."[25] To Nixon, Kissinger, and Sonnenfeldt, the Alliance was now a source of leverage, no more, no less. The Europeans, whom Kissinger especially came to regard with a mixture of annoyance and exasperation, seemed to miss the point in depicting transatlantic solidarity and their own process of building unity as important ends in themselves. That was especially true for their American supporters, who finally seemed to have found a way to harmonize the opposing doctrines of Atlanticism and Europeanism into a workable combination of principles and policy. To Kissinger, it all seemed to be a case of denying the vanished supremacy that was Europe.[26] From him, it merited little more than condescension.

Atlanticism, however, had survived the crises of the 1960s and the innovations applied to it by the various American administrations. That it continued to flourish had as much to do with the people who believed in it as with the external circumstances that demanded its preservation. So, the new team just had to be converted in the ways EUR had practiced before. This was not entirely a lost cause, for despite their intellectual arrogance, Kissinger and Sonnenfeldt were also inherently flexible; they may have held strong opinions, but a tough appeal to their intelligence often worked. The following exchange with Art Hartman from April 1974 is a typical illustration:

> KISSINGER: Can we now hear about [the] Bilderberg .[Conference?] ... [General Andrew J.] Goodpaster was under the impression that the American delegation told the British that they should seek their destiny inside the Common Market and not hanker after a special relationship....
>
> SONNENFELDT: We did not.
>
> KISSINGER: It is not our policy....
>
> SONNENFELDT: What I said on the subject was that bilateral relations and relations with whatever European entity there was were not mutually exclusive, and we are not going to make any statements regarding the existence of special or bilateral relationships....
>
> HARTMAN: ... I think that if you eliminate totally any reiteration of our view as to support for European unification, even with the qualification of what kind of unity we are talking about, it is a significant change in position which I think will involve us in the debate....
>
> KISSINGER: Why do we have to take any position? ...
>
> SONNENFELDT: I don't think we should shout a position from the rooftops unasked....
>
> KISSINGER: Sure—because the Europeans have the unbelievable nerve, after harassing us for a year and trying to organize Europe on an anti-American basis, and shipwrecking themselves on the basis of their economic difficulties, their domestic weakness—now they are asking us to put European unity back together.... We are not that crazy—not while I am here.
>
> HARTMAN: Yes. But there is a difference between capitalizing on what we have succeeded in doing, which is making the issue of what kind of European unification we can support, and now changing our policy completely and saying we do not support—
>
> KISSINGER: Our policy used to be a greater advocate of European unity than the Europeans. George Ball was more outraged at the exclusion of Britain from the Common Market than the British were.... The Europeans have this built-in tendency ... of fighting for trivial objectives.... Brandt has a vapid mind.... Brandt doesn't have the guts for ultimate confrontations. At any rate, we are not going to fight European unity. But we are not going

to put the Europeans back together, either.... The only disagreement they have with us on détente is that they didn't do it themselves.... It is the same sort of irresponsibility they had last year.... One way or another they are sticking us with their problems. And one way or another, we are going to force them to stand on their own feet.

SONNENFELDT: That is exactly right....

HARTMAN: All I am saying is we can stay out of the debate by repeating our past position and making the point again that we will not stand idly by if Europe is going to be made in opposition to the United States....

KISSINGER: That I am in favor of. But I don't think that is how it is going to come out.... When EUR starts operating, and our ambassadors start running loose, the proclivities of the fifties—they are going to listen to Jean Monet [sic] and not to me....

HARTMAN: What I propose to you is contingent enough, and also defines what we are talking about enough....

KISSINGER: I have to see it. But I just want to make clear that the only support we give to European unity at this moment is ritualistic. We are perfectly willing to say that we have not changed our policy....

HARTMAN: I would begin with a quote from Emerson—about consistency....

SONNENFELDT: If you come to the conclusion that you did in the *Troubled Partnership*, that the only kind of unity ... is a unity hostile to the United States—

KISSINGER: I didn't say that, either. That is a quote taken totally out of context. What I said was it was senseless to speak of a unified Europe not being a third force to some extent, because the reason it is being unified is to make it a third force.... That is the part they always leave out....

SONNENFELDT: That is a different quote....

KISSINGER: We are all for it as long as they are doing it on their own. But we are not going to permit them to use whatever prestige we have left in Europe to build a Europe that then can be exploited against the United States....

SONNENFELDT: That is completely right.

KISSINGER: So if they want our help, let them define an organic relationship between the United States and Europe that removes the danger of a hostile Europe. I have no objection. In fact, on the available choices, my first preference would be a unified Europe cooperating with the United States—not cooperating by grace, but in some organic way. My second choice would be a divided Europe. My third choice would be a unified Europe opposed to the United States...

HARTMAN: I think the debate is now on the right issues. And that is where we have to keep it.[27]

If Kissinger entertained such hostility toward the European project at the outset of his term in government service, he held it closely. Back in 1969, he and the president were saying all the right things about the Alliance and, in a funny way of proving them, sought to win over EUR's *bête noire*, Charles de Gaulle. The older generation was not pleased. Acheson told his former aide Lawrence Eagleburger (who was about to join Kissinger's staff and suffer a famous break-down) "not to let Nixon make an ass of himself with de Gaulle" and wondered about the consequences of cozying up to the French leader with a "nuclear bouquet" just as he was preparing to give up power.[28] John McCloy complained to Monnet "that Kissinger is all for a 'Let's be friendly with de Gaulle' policy but how far it goes or whether it will extend with nuclear understanding, I do not know. If it went that far, I would greatly fear for the Alliance and the future direction of the Federal Republic."[29]

This was precisely what was in the works. As described in the next chapter, the U.S. and French governments were about to launch a secret program of nuclear cooperation. During his many moments of exasperation with the French, Kissinger would wonder aloud about the value of the program, but it would continue. In the meantime, there were others in the U.S. government who saw this trip as a unique opportunity to gain concessions from the French, convinced that Nixon should rush to exploit the relationship with de Gaulle for all it was still worth.[30] Their French colleagues perhaps regarded things similarly, although they tended to rate the expertise of Nixon much higher than that of his top adviser. For his part, Nixon seemed determined to control the exchange personally, keeping Kissinger away as far as he reasonably could.[31]

The early focus on France, and on de Gaulle, signaled less a reaffirmation of Atlanticism than a repudiation of the Ball integrationists and an important change in outlook toward Europe that was consistent with the Euro-skepticism of Kissinger and Sonnenfeldt, almost as though they wanted the old general, in a supreme final act of irony, to anoint them as his successors on the other side of the Atlantic. Yet they overlooked the crux of the dispute between de Gaulle and Monnet, namely, the United States and its European vocation. Whether Europe would resemble more a "plate of fried eggs" or an "omelette" was another, less pressing, matter.[32] It was de Gaulle, as mentioned earlier, whose proposal for a global directorate was rejected by Eisenhower in 1958; it was now Nixon whose view of world order (expanded to include China and the USSR) resuscitated that earlier concept, which would, if implemented, overtake the Atlantic Community. The Gaullist architecture, in other words, was neither circum-Atlantic nor trans-Atlantic but rather anti-Atlantic, with a more fixed, hierarchical, and conservative view of global order that vitiated the whole principle of collective security. Most

Hans-Dietrich Genscher and Henry Kissinger,
Martin Hillenbrand in the middle
German Press and Information Office, courtesy of Hal Jones

of all, it was nationalist and in every sense a throwback to Kissinger's romantic notions of Europe's Old Diplomacy.

Caricatures of Kissinger as a Jewish-American Metternich (or, more accurately, Bismarck) have ill served students of international history. If anything, he and Nixon were Gaullists: willing to make the most of supranational assets when they availed themselves, but wedded nonetheless to the primacy of the nation-state and the freedom of executive maneuver. They valued institutions and norms less than concepts and techniques of power, which, for better or worse, they were thought to have in great supply.

TAKING OVER THE HELM OF EUR in 1969 was a very different man. Martin Hillenbrand, it will be recalled, was a professional reared in EUR at the peak of its postwar prestige. He was the son of German immigrants and had once worked as a chemist in the Ford Motor plant in Dearborn. He joined the foreign service in 1939 after winning fellowships to Columbia University (where he got a doctorate) and Fordham Law School. His scrapbooks present a portrait of a thoughtful, diligent, and self-protective man—a kind of intellectual Eagle Scout, who seemed to subordinate almost everything to his career.[33] Apart from brief service in Burma during the war and later in Africa, Hillenbrand made his home in Europe. His first post was in Switzerland; after the war, he joined the occupation of Germany and then, after a brief fellowship at Harvard, moved up the ranks of the German hands before landing in Paris under David Bruce, who noted little about Hillenbrand besides his "delightful and pretty wife, Faith," who suffered five miscarriages, and who, like her husband, "ask[s] for no favors whatever."[34]

Hillenbrand was known for being calm, unassuming, professional, and restrained but not overly formal, with a wry sense of humor: simply put, "an ornament to our Foreign Service."[35] He was, according to his younger colleague David Klein, "probably the best German hand the State Department had ... and practically raised a whole cadre of so-called German experts loyal to him." But he was not entirely enthusiastic about taking the job of assistant secretary. For obvious reasons, "his biggest problem was ... Kissinger who saw in Hillenbrand another source of political wisdom about our relations with Germany, the kind of competition Kissinger did not enjoy having. Although he needed Hillenbrand more than he admitted, theirs was a tempestuous relationship." Bob Schaetzel reflected on this in a February 1969 letter to Acheson:

> [T]here is a sharpness in relations between [Secretary of State William] Rogers and Kissinger, apparently—and foolishly—abetted by the latter.... [T]his is not a fight that Henry can win [sic], but while the battle goes on a great deal of damage can be done.... Being an innocent in this business, Rogers really has to rely on the staff and yet the Department has hardly ever been weaker.... The one happy note is Marty Hillenbrand.[36]

The relationship between Hillenbrand, on the one hand, and Sonnenfeldt and Kissinger, on the other, was by most other accounts professional but not intimate. In memoranda, Hillenbrand's tone was passive, probing, and for the most part respectful. Kissinger's toward him was businesslike, lacking either the friendliness he extended toward his successor, the elegant Walter Stoessel, or the provocative jousting with Art Hartman, who followed next. Although Hillenbrand would later excoriate Kissinger in his memoirs and characterize his time in EUR as unhappy, he did not leave behind much evidence of problems and gave the new administration the benefit of the doubt, noting that "[Nixon] sincerely wants to extricate us from this morass [Vietnam]; ... 1970 could be a sort of watershed year."[37] He was rarely upbraided or insulted. Rather, it was Kissinger's "amplifier," Sonnenfeldt, who bore the brunt of the man's temper.[38]

Another person caught up uncomfortably in the mix was Larry Eagleburger. Eagleburger's career in the foreign service took a leap when he got the job of staff assistant to Dean Acheson during the latter's consultancy in the 1960s. Acheson, following the suggestion of Francis Bator, recommended him to Kissinger as a smart and loyal aide; that Eagleburger was one of the few known Republicans in the foreign service was probably an added boost to his candidacy, as was the fact that he did not look the part, but rather more "like the Michelin man with a cane."[39] Eagleburger, who would later have one of the most impressive careers in the foreign service and would become the first secretary of state to rise from its ranks, barely survived his White House tenure, having become so consumed by Kissinger that he became known as his alter ego.[40] Whether or not he actually suffered a nervous breakdown in 1969 matters less than the fact that the "man with a first-rate, second-rate mind," as Kissinger was once overheard describing him, survived along with those under his watch.[41]

Hillenbrand would work quietly to satisfy his new masters while preserving as much continuity with the past as possible. Given the departure from Atlanticism on the part of Nixon and Kissinger, it is striking to read that the assistant secretary of state, after little more than a year in the job, would state his bureau's outlook as follows:

> We are so involved in Europe, politically, militarily and economically, that it would be impossible to extricate ourselves even if we or they wanted to do so.... The future form of the Atlantic relationship cannot be specific now as it depends upon how Europe develops.... Nixon is much more Atlantic-oriented than previous Administrations, and this will be reinforced by the visits to Washington of Prime Minister Wilson and President Pompidou this month and next.... We still favor European integration—the new aspect is that Nixon is not going to pressure them.[42]

There is no mention, apart from the final line above, of redefining, let alone discarding, the transatlantic relationship. May one conclude that the Nixonian redefinition was already a historical fact? It is possible to view EUR, like much of the State Department, in semiconscious isolation, churning out long reports that nobody at the higher levels ever read and certainly never implemented. There was a good deal of that kind of activity; Kissinger was notorious for assigning such work after a policy had already been decided upon.[43] But that verdict would obscure a more complex story. The White House, and later Kissinger and his seventh-floor staff at State, did not remake the world over entirely. The relationship of personalities to geopolitics also operated the other way around. No matter how formidable the Kissinger phalanx was, it could not overturn so many decades of work, particularly with Europe, which had by this time far too many constituencies to be dismantled or redirected by any single administration. The self-assurance and faith in continuity that one finds in the memoranda from EUR during this period appear in notable contrast to the bureaucratic hand-wringing over diminished prerogatives that continued from the previous decade. The two were not necessarily contradictory. Hillenbrand stated it well:

> Prophets of doom were always seeing the alliance as in a state of crisis—a theme periodically stressed by journalists and the uninitiated within governments. In my experience, NATO was usually alleged to be passing from one crisis to another. What the naysayers did not realize was that, as long as the Soviet military threat seemed to exist, the glue that held the alliance together was far stronger than the centrifugal forces working within it. Certainly American leaders had to say the right things and to provide the needed assurances, but self-interest in the continuation of a common defense regularly overrode the discontents with American unilateralism and emerging economic weakness.[44]

And so the superficially quiet tenure of Hillenbrand as assistant secretary from 1969 to 1972 would prove to be one of the most fruitful periods in the history of the bureau. Although morale fell to perhaps its lowest point since the 1950s, EUR worked to launch the final diplomatic push of the Cold War, and did so in spite of its outward emasculation in the organizational pecking order. In retrospect, that pecking order would appear to be far more fluid, and far more susceptible to the fates of personalities, than the memoirs of a few disgruntled ex-officials would have us believe.[45]

TWO CRITICAL THINGS BESIDES the arrival of Martin Hillenbrand took place in 1969. The first was Willy Brandt's election in West Germany, and the second was the advent of a human rights agenda at NATO. Both would lead—despite many twists and turns—to the culmination of détente by 1975 and, ultimately, to the fall of the Berlin Wall a decade and a half later. The role of the U.S. government in both episodes would be central. The diplomatic successes of the 1970s—the Berlin Quadripartite Agreement of 1971, the Strategic Arms Limitation Treaty of 1972 (SALT), and the Helsinki Final Act of 1975—were not brought about by Nixon and Kissinger *contra mundum*. With the exception of the second, to which EUR contributed relatively little, these achievements were made possible by the adherence of the bureaucracy to an orientation handed down from earlier generations of Atlanticists, that is, détente plus *Ostpolitik*. According to EUR, the two trends were not mutually exclusive, nor was it a mistake to defer to Europeans to shape and lead them. Like so many other accomplishments, it was less a victory of a single office over the rest than another case of mutual, interbureaucratic accommodation. That it was possible to ease relations with the Soviet Union while diminishing the Soviets' own control over their European satellites was a success second to none. That it happened amid the worst climate in transatlantic relations since World War II, and with a White House staff (and later a Secretariat) hostile to many of the policies on the table, was nothing short of miraculous. It would be ironic if future historians come to consider these achievements to have been even greater than Kissinger's shuttle diplomacy in East Asia and the Middle East. But from the vantage point of EUR, there was little doubt that this was the case.

Let us begin with Brandt. Part of the rationale behind Nixon's push for rapprochement with France was dialectical. That is, Nixon and Kissinger claimed that French policy emerged as a logical reaction to Germany's shift eastward, and vice versa. As Kissinger's assistant Peter Rodman later wrote, "The invasion of Czechoslovakia and Germany's persistence with *Ostpolitik* have caused France to drop the Eastern game until brighter opportunities appear."[46] Hillenbrand took a less severe view. In an April 1969 memorandum sent under Secretary Rogers's name to the president, he wrote that in spite of a "moderate" and "prudent" approach, "any successor government [in France] will probably be interested in pursuing the possibility of improved East-West relations." However, he concurred that in the meantime, "the Germans are likely to play an increasingly important role in Europe now that the dominating presence of de Gaulle is removed."[47]

In State Department jargon, playing a bigger role often meant receiving greater attention from Washington. Thus, France might be weaned westward as Germany looked eastward. EUR, however, tended to resist dialectical appeals and failed to see why American policy could not capitalize upon both trends at once. It was probably fortunate that the bureau was now under the command of an old German hand and an accomplished political officer. Hillenbrand took charge of an interagency group on European policy at the National Security Council that now moved the agenda back to the center of Europe. The first task was a return to talks over the status of Berlin.

The conventional view of this episode, based largely on Kissinger's memoirs, is of a chaotic and incredibly complex negotiation that was overtaken by *force majeure* in the shape of a high-level "back channel." Actually, there were several back channels: The primary one was between Kissinger and Soviet ambassador to the United States Anatoly Dobrynin; predating this was one between Kissinger's counterpart in Bonn, Egon Bahr, and a KGB colleague, Vyacheslav Kevorkov, as well as one between Bahr and Kissinger; there was also an independent channel to the White House between the U.S. ambassador to the Federal Republic, Kenneth Rush, by way of his friend Attorney General John Mitchell. Without minimizing the significance of the channels, the impetus for movement from the perspective of the State Department lay elsewhere. As Hillenbrand later wrote, "[D]espite sporadic and sometimes unpredictable White House involvement, the hard slogging, the sustained thinking and drafting of memorandums and instructions and participation in both intra- and multi-governmental meetings would have to be handled by the Bureau of European Affairs."[48]

The relevant point was not so obvious. The Berlin agreement might not have been reached without the use of the various back channels.[49] But it almost certainly could never have been made by them alone. Consensus among the bureaucracies of the four powers and the Germans was just as important as any secret deal at higher levels. Without such consensus, the agreement probably would not have lasted, and more importantly, the 1975 Helsinki Conference on Security and Cooperation in Europe, described below, would never have come about. Not only was the American willingness to proceed with a European security conference made contingent on a Berlin agreement, but the insistence on conditionality itself was made to work both ways in order to ensure that any success with the Soviets had Allied support.[50] Therefore, the Berlin talks had to bear result.

Soviet premier Aleksei Kosygin wrote to Nixon in May 1969 that his government would not object to a new round of negotiations over Berlin. For Nixon, who had made the offer in March, and for Kissinger, all roads led to SALT—that is, to the goal of bilateral arms control with the Soviet Union and with it a global "equilibrium."[51] For the Soviets and the Germans, linkage meant more than that. So far as Europe was concerned, it meant a comprehensive formalization of the security order, that is, a final peace settlement on the Continent. As we shall soon see, Kissinger in particular expressed fears that the Germans under the mercurial Brandt would move out of control, leading ultimately toward a unified, and ostensibly neutral, Germany—in other words, Rapallo all over again.[52] Such a view was not entirely irrational nor held solely by Kissinger. Bob Schaetzel, for example, railed from Brussels with cries of doom for the European movement. Dean Acheson concurred with customary terseness: "[O]ne cannot make a silk purse out of Brandt."[53]

However, a more junior group of foreign service officers in Germany, Washington, and the NATO mission in Brussels did exactly that. They were more sensitive to the potential for the kind of linkage the Europeans had in mind, thereby redirecting the nascent Soviet-American entente, which Kissinger seemed to promote as an end in itself, or at least with a global, rather than European set of objectives, into a genuine policy of détente throughout Europe. None of it could

Berlin Quadripartite meeting. *Courtesy of Richard B. Russell Library, University of Georgia.*
Andrei Gromyko and William Rogers in foreground. Ken Rush at center, first row behind Rogers.
Martin Hillenbrand and David Klein to Rush's left. Jonathan Dean behind, to his right, second row.

have happened without the successful conclusion of the Quadripartite Agreement in September 1971.

Leading the American team was Rush, a political appointee who had been on the faculty of Duke Law School when Nixon was a student there and who would go on to have a lucrative career at Union Carbide Corporation. Rush was stentorian and formal but quick on his feet; Kissinger's later portrait of him was glowing, naming him the "linchpin" of the talks.[54] He had earned the loyalty of his subordinates in Bonn and Berlin as well as Hillenbrand's. Yet Kissinger treated Rush as little more than a conspirator, serving on the German end of the back channel and carrying the bureaucracy along with decisions already reached with Bahr and Dobrynin. Of course, Secretary Rogers existed nowhere in this picture, nor, for that matter, did German foreign minister Walter Scheel. Kissinger even boldly suggested that the source of all this duplicity was Bahr's mistrust of his own bureaucracy; thus one back channel begat another.[55]

The flowchart became even more complicated further down. Rush was based temporarily in Berlin and negotiated with British, French, and Soviet counterparts. The negotiating positions, however, were prepared for them by the Bonn group, a standing arrangement in the West German capital among representatives of the four powers, plus the German Foreign Office, with the United States represented by foreign service officer Jonathan "Jock" Dean. Dean in turn received instructions from Hillenbrand by way of the German Desk under James Sutterlin. Both Dean and Sutterlin were in regular contact with David Klein, the old mainstay of the Bundy White House, who had since become the political counselor in West Berlin. Klein oversaw liaison with German counterparts there. Because of the unique division of responsibilities, the group of foreign service officers could exert tremendous influence.[56] Again, personalities mattered. Dean, recalled by one deputy as "the greatest EUR man of the postwar era," occasionally rubbed others somewhat differently. According to another colleague, he was "intelligent, highly motivated" and "idealistic ... prepared to pursue his own path to secure the realization of his ideas with, or without, authorization."[57] He was the workhorse of the negotiation, the primary drafter of the treaty language, proving himself indispensable both to Rush for his expertise and to the German Desk in Washington for being their principal source of information in Bonn, although both sides were also aware of the various back channels.[58] Finally, he served as an important interlocutor with several German politicians, particularly with the Christian Democrats, who mistrusted Brandt and Bahr and worried over where the talks would lead. Meanwhile, Dean would prove to be the most intrepid and indefatigable of negotiators.

As noted in Chapter 5, Jock had been among the first group of foreign service officers who took over from the U.S. Army immediately following the occupation in 1949. He was based in Limburg, in the Rhineland, where he was put in charge of de-Nazification and, subsequently, tracked the political involvement of Communists. Proconsular work was heavy for someone still in his twenties; but, as mentioned, the generation of foreign service officers who helped to rebuild Germany rose quickly up the ranks with enormous confidence. Dean was a typical member of this group. Gruff, street smart, and magnificently devious, he was not deterred by his propensity to offend and allegedly would do things like revise cables after they had been sent to reflect conversations in the way he preferred.[59]

Dean moved to Bonn, where he worked for John Paton Davies, and then on to the German Desk under its legendary head Elwood Williams. After an interruption in the Congo—where he was sent because State wanted a "nasty" person there—he returned to Bonn in time for the Prague Spring and the brief ambassadorial tenure of Henry Cabot Lodge Jr.[60] As the embassy's political counselor, he credited himself with a minor role in "preventing World War III" because he heard that the commander of the U.S. European Command (EUCOM) was about to hold a big exercise on the Czech border on the day of the Soviet invasion. Dean urged him to call it off. "Some say this was wrong," he recounted with a slight grin.[61]

Dean's main job in Bonn was to feed the substance of the negotiations while striving, in Hillenbrand's words, "to placate the British and the French and to assure them ... that they were not the victims of a gigantic shell game with an unpredictable outcome."[62] Dean had a formidable aptitude for the minutiae of negotiations, and he knew the German scene intimately, but the Berlin problem, in the words of Kissinger's former aide W. R. Smyser,

> resembled a World War I battlefield. It had been fought over many times. All knew the strategically sensitive points that might provoke a violent counter-attack. All knew, or thought they knew, the other side's contingency plans. All knew they could not win except at unacceptable cost. But they did not dare to lose.... Diplomats had learned that, as on a World War I battlefield, they could be safer by remaining in the trenches than by moving forward to try a breakthrough.[63]

It would take the better part of eighteen months, but a breakthrough would happen. The four parties had agreed to guarantee Western rights to the city, permanent and unhindered access, and a formalization of inter-German ties leading ultimately to international recognition of the East German state with abandonment of the claim that the city was "an integral" part of the Federal Republic. Berlin would never again be the trigger for major war.[64]

The real importance of the Berlin negotiation lay in the basis it provided for a broader settlement. Dean wrote to Rush in July 1970, "[W]e are in practice engaged in the political equivalent of peace treaty negotiations for Germany." Indeed, both Dean and Hillenbrand, who had drafted similar plans for twenty years, finally saw them reach fruition.[65] Although many people, including Dean at times, seemed worried about how far the rapprochement would go, most in EUR sounded determined to secure the Berlin agreement as a necessary precondition for moving forward, ultimately, with German reunification in circumstances that would not pose a threat to the unity of the West.

For all of their subsequent insistence, one can never know for certain whether Bahr and Brandt shared this view; they were certainly suspected of being neutralists, or at a minimum, of being willing to grant more concessions to the Soviets than their allies, especially the Americans, would do in pursuit of what the latter most likely assumed to be their primary aim: reunification. But the ambivalence of the 1960s persisted and was itself occasionally confused with both neutralism and ambiguity, which often was "a diplomatic necessity, the lubrication of government." Indeed, it could be hard to distinguish between a "plight of clarity seeking irrational support," and "the plight of ambiguity seeking clear-headed acquiescence." People like Schaetzel and Chip Bohlen therefore continued to deplore both the style and the substance of *Ostpolitik*, probably against their better judgment.[66] Others like George Ball tried to see positive elements but did so with great skepticism, even sarcasm.[67] All the while the State Department worked at cross-purposes with the White House, with the latter accusing the former of being too pro-Brandt. Within each group there were significant differences of opinion as well. Sonnenfeldt would find himself accused by Alexander Haig, then Kissinger's military aide and later White House chief of staff, of being too soft on the Germans.[68] Hillenbrand and another deputy, Robert Gerald Livingston, would come to see Brandt and Bahr as being both inseparable and too close to the Soviets, and would occasionally join outsiders like Dean Acheson in urging a harder line.[69] Even Jock Dean, Ken Rush, and Jim Sutterlin would disagree brutally, and there was constant tension between the Bonn and Berlin missions. In one memorandum from December 1970, Dean reported pressure from Bahr on Rush to refrain from leading a "cavalry charge" and deviating from a pre-existing agreement to be "firm on substance and flexible on method."[70] The tone of the memorandum suggests that Dean shared Bahr's view. At other times, Dean could sound more hawkish. To Sutterlin in June of the same year, he wrote, "I do not follow what appears to be a more general inclination on your part not to risk Soviet negative statements. To me, we are in a negotiation. It is normal to hear all kinds of statements in a negotiation, including a lot of negative ones."[71] Alas, Dean's devious reputation would appear to catch up with him. Larry Eagleburger, assigned by then to NATO, wrote to him in October:

> [W]e do have a real—and growing—problem. Many of the non-Bonn Group here are increasingly concerned about what the Four are doing in Berlin. They argue—with some justice—that what is going on there has a substantial effect on NATO business.... There are several possible ways to handle these pressures, but one of the easiest is to pay careful attention to *form*, even if we have to be light on *substance*.... Jock, despite appearances—and whatever others may say—we love you dearly.[72]

The negotiations, disagreements, and deceptions would continue throughout 1971 until the agreement was signed that September. It almost did not happen. Kissinger told Rush, "[N]o one will believe what we did here."[73] For his part, Jock Dean recalled:

> I have an unforgettably vivid picture in my mind of the four ambassadors of France, Britain, the Soviet Union and the United States, meeting in that big room in the Berlin *Kommandatura*, about to toast each other on their success and about to sign this hard-won agreement, when at that very moment Ambassador Rush received a telegram from Washington instructing him to refuse to sign and to negotiate further.
> He did not miss a beat, but said, with a grin, "tell them we're going to sign anyway."[74]

Hillenbrand noted in his diary that "the State Department, one would think, had done little or nothing. So be it. If this agreement fails or turns out to be a travesty, then blame will soon be shifted to us."[75]

In spite of tactical differences that filled hundreds of memoranda, the Berlin negotiations were remarkable for their underlying clarity. "There was never a lack of understanding," Sutterlin and Klein wrote in their 1989 memoir, "never a time when arguments could not be made or clarifications obtained through regular channels of communication." Credit, they argued, went mainly to the State Department:

> Kissinger and Rush did not depart substantively from the basic negotiating position defined and coordinated in the Department of State and approved by the president...No new substantive element was introduced then or later by the National Security Council or by Dr. Kissinger personally. The only suggestion of difference was a cautionary suggestion from Dr. Kissinger's office (Sonnenfeldt to Sutterlin) that the Department of State might be too enthusiastic in supporting Brandt's Eastern policy.... But in terms of negotiating objectives and the principles of the Western negotiating position there was consistent agreement.[76]

Then why the multiple back channels? And why the bitter, and contradictory, recollections of the Berlin episode in Hillenbrand's and Kissinger's memoirs? Sutterlin and Klein concluded that the main reason behind the deception was to "enhance the ego and power" of Kissinger, although they conceded that he may have had other aims in mind.[77] He had. For him and Nixon, the Berlin negotiation was wrapped up in a larger agenda with the Soviet Union, as well as with the Vietnam peace talks and the diplomatic opening to China. Hillenbrand, Sonnenfeldt, and several others at both State and the White House were almost certainly aware that "linkage" could exist in several varieties; and though they may have disagreed deeply over diplomatic priorities, one must suspect that the constant to-and-fro, suspicion, and bureaucratic contestation led, paradoxically, to a rise in mutual awareness and a refinement of objectives. It may go too far to apply Egon Bahr's famous phrase from the period, *Wandel durch Annäherung*, to the American bureaucracy, but that is nearly what happened.[78] As Kissinger and Sonnenfeldt came to accept the inevitability of change in Central Europe through the seriousness and persistence of inter-German diplomacy on the ground, their counterparts in EUR and elsewhere came to adapt, refine, and bolster their own priorities *vis-à-vis* Kissinger's notion of détente.[79] The story, again, was not so much one about the triumph of one part of the U.S. government over another in the cause of peace but rather the maximum pursuit, and tentative achievement, of several sets of goals within multiple confines and openings. Nowhere would this phenomenon be demonstrated more clearly than with the struggle over the Conference on Security and Cooperation in Europe (CSCE).

THE BERLIN AGREEMENT WAS NOT greeted with uniform praise. Many Atlanticists were uneasy. Kurt Birrenbach, for example, wrote to his friend Eleanor Dulles, "I must confess you [sic] that I am not as happy as you at the

Berlin Agreement.... We remain dependent on the good will of the Soviet Union.... I, of course, know that détente without an equilibrium of power is not thinkable. But ... my fear is the future Finlandization of Europe."[80]

We now know that such a fear would not come to pass. But it was real in the early 1970s, and there was more to it than the concern that Brandt and Bahr would double-cross their Western allies. For all of their mistrust of the new German leadership, Kissinger and Sonnenfeldt were realistic about the risks of heightened hopes. They were not alone. The Atlantic Council, which convened a study group to examine the "problems, prospects and pitfalls" of the CSCE, came up with a mixed bag of suggestions. Ted Achilles appended a sharp dissent: "The conclusion of such an agreement [here referring to the nonuse of force] at the CSCE in the absence of justified confidence that no party might violate it, could be positively harmful by contributing to unjustified euphoria."[81] To suggest, then, that Ostpolitik would have set in motion a train of expectations that might have been hard to contain was not too far-fetched. Sonnenfeldt commiserated with Berndt von Staden, soon to become German ambassador to Washington:

> I said that no one I knew questioned the firm intentions of Brandt and the FRG's government to remain strongly committed to NATO and to European integration. Yet one could foresee a point down the road, where many of the benefits that the Germans anticipated from Ostpolitik had failed to materialize and where the Russians would take the line that any such benefits could only accrue to the FRG if it changed its relationship with the West. At this point there would be some bitter arguments and anguished soul searching....[82]

Ambivalence went even deeper than that. Just as there was never a single definition of Ostpolitik, there were several understandings of détente.[83] Yet in contrast to their generally healthy skepticism regarding the former concept, Kissinger and Sonnenfeldt were strident in the defense of their version of détente with the USSR, which they defined as "a way of regulating competition, not a way of disarming the West," again, one more akin to entente than détente.[84] That may have been because they saw themselves as its originators, whereas Ostpolitik predated them in the shadows of their birthplace. Their passion for selling détente, or perhaps their overselling of it, made possible such a personalization to begin with. But to officers who had spent much of their careers mastering the kleine Schritte, or small steps, that would ease the burdens of the Cold War in Europe, Kissinger's détente posed a far greater threat than Ostpolitik because it froze or possibly even negated progress on the ground in the name of peaceful coexistence. This placed Kissinger at odds not only with the prevailing views of the State Department but also with the Pentagon and its counterparts at NATO, who ultimately would coalesce in a powerful movement against his policy direction.[85] Whatever global rationale it may have had, its more serious critics pointed out that if it did not make sense for Europe, it was hard to see how it could work anywhere else, thereby reducing it to "an elaborate program of tranquilizers-for-everyone in the West."[86] General Andrew Goodpaster, then serving as NATO's supreme allied commander in Europe, put it this way:

Genuine détente, a meaningful and durable détente, must be based on reducing and removing the *causes* of tension, rather than merely the *symptoms* of tension, while at the same time preserving the security, the integrity, and the values of our societies. A reduction in tensions, if it is to be meaningful, must be coupled with a reduction in the dangers that beset us.[87]

For many in EUR especially, there was too little emphasis on the latter and far too much enthusiasm for the former.

BECAUSE AN AGREEMENT TO proceed with the European Security Conference was made contingent upon a Berlin settlement, it would take some time for the conference to get off the ground. The preconditioning was more than a White House delaying tactic; Russ Fessenden, serving in Bonn as Rush's deputy chief of mission, described it in more probationary terms: "We believe that in our own American interests, we should support the German effort to make improvement in the Berlin situation and the regularization of relations between the two parts of Germany for the desirability of a European Security Conference," adding, "[I]f we can bring our NATO allies to consider Berlin improvement and the regularization of FRG-GDR relations as a valid test of Soviet intentions, even failure to make progress on the sounding may be useful specific evidence of the undesirability of a purely propaganda conference."[88] As this modest foreign service officer had done so many times during the previous two decades, Fessenden would contribute a sensible voice to a tumultuous set of circumstances, in this instance, while holding down the fort in Bonn in Rush's absence. His memoranda and letters from the period were guardedly optimistic about Brandt's initiative.[89] Like the above statement, they suggest that, for all its determination to turn the new era of negotiations to Western advantage, EUR would take a tentative position, perhaps overly so.

This was certainly true when the Soviets first proposed the European Security Conference in the mid-1950s. Since then, nearly everyone in Washington regarded it, in Sonnenfeldt's words, as a "ploy" in order to formalize the post–World War II boundaries in Eastern Europe. Christopher Emmet, the perennial, self-appointed conscience for all matters German, posed the obvious trade-off: "In short, if we are to actively help the Soviets keep their Empire we should at least get something substantial for it for the cause of peace."[90] For his part, Kissinger was openly hostile to the idea well beyond the point when he could do anything to stop the conference from going ahead. His well-known references to it range from the patronizing to the scornful: "I couldn't care less what they do in the European Security Conference. They can write it in Swahili for all I care."[91] Earlier, he put it more diplomatically to French foreign minister Michel Jobert: "[F]rankly our attitude toward the Conference is one of great indifference, that it doesn't do too much damage."[92]

How then did the U.S. government come to support, even shape, the CSCE? Actually it had been the French who first conspired with a few like-minded Americans in EUR to transform the conference into an initiative that the White House could not ignore. They did this in two ways: by working closely with midlevel American officials and those of other allies, principally at NATO, to devise the basic cultural and humanitarian components of the conference's Final Act; and by serving as the principal interlocutors with the Soviets, at least until Kissinger became involved directly in late 1974.

French motives were unclear, but one suspects they had as much to do with keeping alive de Gaulle's old notion of Europe from the Atlantic to the Urals as they had with ensuring some dynamism to their diplomacy in light of the aforementioned eastern shift of focus accompanying *Ostpolitik*.[93] There may also have been some latent jealousy of the heavily American flavor of détente. Rightly or wrongly, the French had come to pride themselves on their alleged rapport with the Russians; by 1969, the Franco-American rapprochement also suggested that France was in a splendid position to lend an Atlantic spirit to the conference.[94]

It was the resignation of de Gaulle in April that really moved things forward—leading one Nixonian to quip that the United States now had "a solution and no problem."[95] De Gaulle had resisted the Soviet idea for a conference; his successor, Georges Pompidou, reversed the policy and embraced it, which coincided well with renewed efforts of others, particularly the neutrals like Finland, to proceed. EUR wasted little time in jumping on the bandwagon. In mid-April, it issued an instruction to its mission to NATO to participate actively in these consultations. They continued throughout the summer and fall, resulting in the first-ever mention of "freer movement of people, ideas, and information" in a NATO communiqué that December. But Hillenbrand was hardly sanguine: "This includes ... a ceaseless round of lunches and dinners ... a declaration and a communiqué ... and ... the usual drafting crisis. But so it has been and so it is. All will more or less come out all right in the end—and life will go on."[96]

Between then and the beginning of the conference in November 1972, EUR held the line in the U.S. government in favor of a commitment to the "counter-proposal" of freer movement. This was not easy. On the one hand, the department remained weak under an ineffectual and marginalized secretary. It also had to cope with a White House that was largely uninterested in the subject. On the other hand, the conference's American proponents feared that the Europeans, who had begun to run with the idea, would lose sight of the human rights aspects in their zeal to reach agreement with the Soviets on other questions.

The U.S. government had "always considered CSCE as an event essentially of, by, and for the Europeans."[97] But at the same time, EUR insisted heavily in the face of Soviet pressure on a place for both the United States and Canada in the conference. The role would be a modest one soon after the talks got started but would become more pronounced to the point where Henry Kissinger himself would make the key breakthrough on the language over frontiers in late 1974. It was not so much the case that Kissinger had been converted by a determination to see CSCE succeed. Rather, and as in other instances, the views and positions of the White House and the department had outflanked one another to such an extent that all opposition seemed to dissolve in as many machinations. In contrast with the EDC and MLF, however, the project moved forward in good part because EUR's determination to hold its ground on freer movement was matched by its relatively quiet promotion of the conference itself. In the meantime, American negotiators facilitated a common position among the NATO allies and many of the neutrals, thereby giving to Kissinger, who had hitherto viewed the CSCE as little more than a weak bargaining chip, a much sharper arrow in his quiver of détente.

EUR and diplomats at NATO made three principal contributions. First, there was the initial setting of the agenda to include a human rights component. Next, there was the discrete but vital hand-holding during the negotiations themselves—the bridging of differences among Europeans. And finally, there was the insistence on a program of implementation—regular follow-on meetings and what came to be called "Helsinki Watch" groups. The effort succeeded on all counts, also for three reasons. First, there were the tactical benefits to détente already mentioned. Next, there was the intense interest of several European allies in the conference. Both factors made it impossible for Kissinger to kill American participation in it. Last, there was the commitment to freer movement, and to the overall success of the conference, that took root within, and later beyond, the bureaucracy.

There were moments, even in EUR, when it appeared that the CSCE had bogged down or was not worth the time and effort. Larry Eagleburger wrote to Kissinger in January 1970:

> We have already slipped into a relatively dangerous position on the Soviet proposal for a European Security Conference.... [T]he immediate point is that—by focusing on the Soviet proposal, talking about it, and trying to shape it into something we might be able to live with—we have agreed to play in the Russian ball park. We probably should have ignored the ESC proposal ... [and should] stay away from anything that the Brandt government can use to blame us for an Ostpolitik failure.... If, as I believe, you and the President are presiding over the partial dissolution of the American Empire (a process I believe to be essential), then the crucial question is how to do it with as much imagination and as little damage as possible.[98]

Sonnenfeldt put it more succinctly:

> We ought to end it.... [Y]ou must not expect the Russians to sign on the dotted line to ratify a transformation of their system.... And the longer it goes on, the less likely it is that expectations will be met.[99]

Both would be proven wrong, although few people could have known in the mid-1970s how powerful a force of change the "Helsinki process" would prove to be. There were just a few hints of its potential. Walt Stoessel, who had replaced Jake Beam as ambassador in Moscow following his tenure as assistant secretary, suggested that the CSCE would help to "foster a more humane society" in the Soviet Union. White House aide Peter Rodman also noted, "[T]he CSCE turned out to be the biggest propaganda beating the Russians have taken in a long time," while Secretary Rogers stated what became the received wisdom, reminiscent of President Johnson's 1966 speech:

> [I]n general, we take a positive attitude toward a CSCE which is carefully

prepared, emphasizes substance over atmospherics, deals with underlying causes of tensions and not merely their superficial manifestations, and holds prospects of meaningful results. We see such a conference in dynamic rather than static terms, as a modest step in a broader and long-range process intended to lead toward a more stable situation in east-west relations in which causes of tensions are reduced, contacts are freer, and the present political and social divisions of Europe are being overcome in a manner that best serves allied interests.[100]

Of the three reasons given above for the success of that policy, the third—bureaucratic tenacity—is the least known and understood. The so-called reaction to *Realpolitik*, the resumption of a moral, humanitarian, or ideological foreign policy, has been explained mechanistically by way of trends that follow one another according to a hidden logic of historical evolution or, in language favored by international relations theorists, a structural transformation of the world system. But the bureaucratic—and historic—success of the CSCE mainly came down to personalities, will, and luck.

Eagleburger's boss in Brussels was a tall, laconic Kansas politician named Robert Ellsworth. Ellsworth was courtly and could be, on occasion, mildly eccentric. He would later hold an important post in the Defense Department and act, along with Goodpaster and Paul Nitze, as one of the American mainstays of Alastair Buchan's International Institute for Strategic Studies. He got the job heading the NATO mission after nominating Pennsylvania governor Bill Scranton for it. Ellsworth had been close to Nixon during the campaign and the transition; he had been one of the people to propose the 1969 trip to Europe; once Kissinger joined the team, Ellsworth's correspondence with them became respectful, almost deferential.[101]

Ellsworth would prove to be an early convert to the CSCE. What brought him around to it is not clear. A hint is provided in the same November 1968 memo in which he suggested Scranton for the job of NATO ambassador:

Another way [to show concern for Europe] would be to send as Ambassador to NATO a prestigious figure who was known to be close to Nixon.... In fact, the U.S. Ambassador to Moscow ... , together with the Ambassador to NATO ... , and RN, should think of themselves as a three-way system in this context, with a need for close communication between the NATO man and the Moscow man, and the need for the NATO man to understand his particular responsibility in handling the Europeans being of particular importance.[102]

That the NATO man became Ellsworth himself did not necessarily compromise the diplomatic point. Indeed, Ellsworth's stature provided important cover for the NATO political staff to keep their work on CSCE alive inside the bureaucracy. Given the nature of his job and his own tendencies, Ellsworth was also very close to the military, both at Supreme Allied Headquarters and back in Washington, and to a few counterparts at NATO, particularly François de Rose, with whom he "just clicked."[103] His position on the CSCE, then, was as much a matter of official prerogative as intrinsic commitment. This was not as true for the three other officials who had the most to do with championing the cause of the conference: George Vest, James Goodby, and John Maresca. All three were Atlanticists with strong ties to NATO, having served at either the U.S. mission or in the NATO Secretariat. All three were, by their own accounts, ardent supporters of the conference and the ideas behind it.

Ellsworth was known to think the world of Eagleburger, and the latter may not have been as bearish on the CSCE as some of the memoranda to his former colleagues at the White House indicated. In any case, neither he nor Ellsworth seemed determined to kill it; if anything, they allowed it to proceed, even if at times it seemed they wanted to slow its progress. Before long they would ally with EUR in an effort to put the U.S. government's commitment to the negotiations on a sustainable course.[104]

Succeeding Eagleburger at NATO was Goodby, a midlevel official in EUR who would later serve as the principal American delegate to the Stockholm Conference on Confidence Building Measures, perhaps the most successful of the CSCE follow-on conferences, and would go on in the 1990s to negotiate the various "Nunn-Lugar" programs for the safe and secure dismantlement of the former Soviet nuclear arsenal. A quiet, resolute New Englander, Goodby had been involved in similar multilateral negotiations for nearly two decades, having been responsible for some of the earliest test-ban proposals. He delivered most of the conceptual legwork and, in particular, devised a set of options from which the Soviets could "not dine *à la carte*."[105] It followed efforts by his colleagues, both at EUR and in the NATO mission, to keep alive the idea of CSCE as a viable proposition. This represented a different kind of linkage: The conference really was a substitute peace treaty for World War II; it was the best chance the Allies had for establishing a basis on which an integrated Europe could supersede the divisions of the Cold War. Therefore, linking the frontier settlements, the language of peaceful change and freer movement, and the institutional underpinnings of all three would put *Wandel durch Annäherung* into practice. It seemed in retrospect to be nothing less than the application of Jean Monnet's ideology to the whole of Europe, including the Soviet Union.

If Goodby supplied an intellectual basis for the CSCE, George Vest gave it operational and tactical life. Vest was a minister's son from Virginia, a genial and extremely charming man—"one of nature's princes" and the "possessor of one of the most subtle diplomatic minds in the contemporary U.S. Foreign Service."[106] He had also been a NATO stalwart since the mid-1950s, having once worked as the chef de cabinet to Secretary-General Dirk Stikker. Vest now had the job of leading the U.S. delegation in the preparatory talks and striking a delicate balance between resoluteness and the appearance of indifference, lest the White House and the Soviets grow too suspicious. There was also the problem of managing the Allies or, as Vest once put it, "having one hand on the French shoulder and the other on the German."[107] And there was one additional fact: Vest had no instructions.

Keeping the Allies together was not easy. On the one hand, most Western European governments sought the veneer of taking the conference more seriously than the United States did, yet they did not necessarily move as quickly as the Soviets wanted.[108] On the other hand, almost none of the Allies held identical views on CSCE. The British were reported to consider it harmless, being more worried about the consequences of the Mutual and Balanced Force Reduction Talks, or MBFR, described in the next chapter. The French, as noted, promoted CSCE as an important opportunity but were also apprehensive about MBFR. The Germans, however, were thought to be unshakable on MBFR and merely went along with CSCE as the price for gaining further concessions from the Soviets on the former.[109]

There were also important distinctions between American perceptions of allied positions and the positions themselves. Most British were indeed dismissive of the CSCE and regarded it as an unavoidable bit of "détente atmospherics." But they expressed greater concern about the ambivalence toward both the CSCE and MBFR in Washington and the mixed signals this sent to the other Allies, much as they had during the MLF debacle.[110] The Quai d'Orsay, by contrast, did indeed seem to take the CSCE far more seriously than both Whitehall and the White House, but it also appeared most concerned over the Soviets' losing interest or dividing European public opinion.[111] West German governments acceded to the conference once they were given sufficient assurances on Berlin and MBFR, again much in the same way they had vis-à-vis the MLF. But going along with a policy for the sake of the Alliance or for the sake of placating the Americans is too simplistic an understanding of the pressures at play. Rather, Germans agonized most about being blamed for failure no matter who was responsible.[112] Kissinger seemed to take delight in the opportunities multiple European positions provided for obfuscation. To Austrian chancellor Bruno Kriesky, he wrote in November 1974: "The problem is not us but Western Europe. Each European leader wants to show a success to its Parliament. If we could get a consolidated European position, we could get some Soviet concessions. If you would help us on this." Later, in August 1975, he reported to the Cabinet upon his return from Helsinki:

> CSCE was never an element of U.S. foreign policy. We never pushed it and stayed a half step behind our allies all through the process. But we didn't want to break with our allies or confront the Soviets on it.... Our relations now with our allies are better than ever since the early Marshall Plan days.[113]

But for Vest, who "likened the Conference to a team of mules," the self-defined task was to make

> the most of the "low profile...." NATO solidarity thus substituted for Washington instructions and was used by the U.S. delegation in its communications with Washington as justification for positions taken in the absence of instructions.... The Western consultation process was the principal device for ensuring unity, and in spite of the U.S. low profile it worked fairly well. The NATO caucus, in which the United States participated, was effective sporadically. Probably the EC-Nine caucus was even more useful. Ironically, the Nine were able to come to joint positions largely because of U.S. disinterest.... An informal two-tiered allied consultation process emerged, under which the Nine consulted first, then

took their positions into the NATO caucus.

At one point, Vest asked, "How am I doing?" There is no record of a reply.[114]

For Vest personally, the negotiation was arduous, but it was "the most fun I ever had." Exchanging his house in Brussels, complete with family and servants, for a small duplex in Helsinki attached to a Tunisian nightclub, Vest spent the next several months negotiating the agreement nearly autonomously, apart from one "horrendous episode" in which Vest recalled hearing from his various counterparts that Kissinger had instructed all the ambassadors in their respective countries to "forget all this business about human rights." Vest confessed to a rare loss of equanimity: "I was flabbergasted, of course, and angry, and ... to each of them I said, ' ... we are supporting a strong human rights activity in the CSCE.'"[115]

By the middle of 1971, Ellsworth had been replaced in Brussels, first by outgoing Treasury Secretary David Kennedy, whose brief and inexplicable tenure there was followed by that of Donald Rumsfeld. Vest served as chargé for nearly nine months in the interim, while Goodby had moved in as political counselor and later deputy chief of mission. The conference by now had taken on a life of its own, although very much below the radar of high politics, then or later. The second volume of Kissinger's memoirs, covering this period, barely mentioned it.[116] The fight to keep the CSCE on the agenda had fallen to Maresca, who ranked even lower in the bureaucracy but whose dedication at Geneva bordered on the obsessive. His bosses, notably Art Hartman, occasionally found the subject, and Maresca's commitment to it, tedious.[117] But Maresca hung on and sustained the bureau's attention until the end, shortly before which his work was given a tremendous boost by a sudden resumption of attention from the top.

By this time Kissinger had moved to the seventh floor of the State Department and Sonnenfeldt had gone over with him as counselor. There is no evidence that the views of either man on the CSCE had changed. They remained preoccupied with more urgent issues, namely, coping with the aftermath of the Vietnam War and with preventing the escalation of another crisis in the Middle East. The strategic agenda with the Soviet Union had moved from SALT to SALT II, although by now détente, especially in the shape of tighter nuclear arms limitations, had given birth to a formidable opposition in Congress led by Senator Jackson. Jackson and his two principal staffers—Dorothy Fosdick and Richard Perle—would make opposition to détente, and to Kissinger personally—a *cause célèbre*; it would not take long for them to fuse the two into an intellectual and political campaign against what they touted as Kissinger's immoral and dangerous version (or perversion) of *Realpolitik*. Human rights, particularly those of Jews and other dissidents behind the Iron Curtain, figured prominently in the campaign. Jackson's power in Congress meant the State Department had to comply with his wishes, however inconvenient or petty. Typical of the latter was the order to fire the staff of the Bureau of Political-Military Affairs as a price for ratifying SALT.[118]

In late 1974, Kissinger finally focused his attention upon Helsinki and, in a dramatic breakthrough with Andrei Gromyko, negotiated the compromise "peaceful change" language that made possible the consensus on frontiers, and hence, the final agreement.[119] It was a masterful bit of linkage—or to use Timothy Garton

Ash's term, the "horizontal synchronization"—of several efforts leading to the same revolutionary goal in Europe.[120] Conditioning American agreement to accede to the European security conference upon completion of the Berlin Quadripartite Agreement, itself conditioned on both the MBFR talks and SALT, made sense to all sides. From the Soviet point of view, conditionality worked because the Americans wanted SALT, MBFR, and Soviet help elsewhere in the world—that is, détente across the board. Giving them the CSCE on their terms, that is, a conference along the lines of the Warsaw Pact's Budapest Appeal of March 1969, which mentioned only frontiers and a divided, non-nuclear Germany, seemed like a good deal. To both Kissinger and the Soviets, then, CSCE would be little more than a throwaway, although each would differ over the value of what was gained in return.[121]

To EUR and the foreign service officers on the ground, however, the picture looked significantly different. The Budapest appeal was just another in a series of Soviet calls for a security conference going back to the mid-1950s. What made this one distinct was its following in the wake of the crackdown on the Prague Spring. The Soviets' prestige had suffered; they both wanted, and needed, détente, if only to buy some time to recover. Moreover they, and not the United States, seemed prepared to concede a great deal—not only on arms control, both nuclear and conventional, but also on Berlin. In fact, they seemed so desperate to restart the engine of détente in the wake of Prague that they might have been willing to grant further concessions, even if it meant losing control of a conference whose initiative they had long promoted as their own.[122] So EUR took the baton from Budapest and ran with it all the way to Helsinki.

Other groups got into the human rights act. After 1975, the attention of the State Department to humanitarian provisions of the Helsinki Final Act often came at the behest of vocal demands from Congress and an array of nongovernmental organizations. But this was not so much the case in 1969 and 1970, when the critical steps on CSCE were taken in Brussels. So to whom were the diplomats listening? Who inspired them to push forward with an agenda at odds with the preferences of their superiors?

"Believe it or not," Goodby later recounted, "diplomats have minds of their own!" To him, the CSCE "was an obvious riposte to a Soviet ... surrogate peace treaty that would ratify the postwar borders in Germany and Europe generally. If they should not be awarded that prize (as Kissinger appeared ready to do), then you have to demand a quid which projects western influence into Soviet-dominated territory."[123] One could also argue that they were being foresighted and saw the longer-run potential for a human rights agenda. But the more likely explanation was their desire to use the conference as a negotiating lever that had the additional advantage of reasserting the appeal of the Atlantic Community under Western leadership. Because the French in particular pushed so strongly for it, a successful conference might also have solidified their reintegration with the Alliance, thereby advancing the very unity that the Soviets ostensibly had sought to weaken over the previous two decades. That this could be accomplished in combination with a settlement over Berlin, a meeting of the minds with the Soviet Union, *and* a relaxation of restrictions between Eastern and Western Europe was just too good an opportunity to pass up.

One could draw the speculation back even further to represent Helsinki as a kind of postwar apotheosis, even if it fell short of being a master plan. Certainly, it accorded with the approach to Europe embedded in EUR since its very beginning; here again the United States used its leverage and low profile to induce the Europeans to come together, to bridge divisions on the basis of universal standards and on behalf of global interests. But such arguments carried little weight with Kissinger and his staff. He found the whole thing quite "ridiculous":

> Now, I know we are in a madness where the intellectuals around the world are not content with messing up foreign policy and now have to get involved in the domestic policy of other countries ... [but] why can't we give them that? ... [E]ither these changes and human contacts are going to come about or they are not. If they are not going to come about, they don't need an excuse.... I don't believe that a bunch of revolutionaries who manage to cling to power for fifty years are going to be euchred out of it by the sort of people we have got negotiating at the European Security Conference.[124]

Even so, he would not relinquish the opportunity such people presented to him, however much, in the words of one veteran Washingtonian, "Henry opposed the opening of any forum unless it was a forum of one."[125] Whether or not he was manipulated into that position by the bureaucracy against his instincts is less important than recognizing its potential benefits: Kissinger's disdain for the conference may in fact have helped to convince the Soviets that the human rights provisions were not going to be taken seriously over the long term, which may have eased any serious resistance they were inclined to put up. But one way or another, the Final Act made its way onto paper. It never really needed détente's full blessing.

THE DIPLOMATS WHO TOOK part in the CSCE negotiations over the years became accustomed to rooms filled with "gesticulating Italians, ruddy-faced Irishmen, a phalanx of smiling, handshaking Russians, Vatican priests in round collars, oddly clothed East Germans, elegant Spaniards, and slouching, casual Americans." This was the assemblage President Gerald Ford would encounter when he took the controversial trip to Helsinki at the end of July 1975 for the final proceedings. Kissinger said it would be the most "unbelievable circus."[126] There in Finlandia Hall on August 1 at 5:05 P.M., following a sober welcome by Finnish President Urho Kekkonen, Ford and thirty-four other heads of state and government signed the Final Act. Following the farewell dinner, Maresca reported the following conversation between three diplomats:

> "Well, they signed it," said one.
> "And now it will be buried and forgotten," said another.
> "No," replied a third, "you are wrong. We have started something."[127]

The Final Act's provisions would make possible the proliferation of several nongovernmental organizations throughout Eastern Europe, culminating in historic demands for "civil society" that most historians now credit with giving the final push to the monopoly of Communist rule. For all that civil society came to matter during the 1980s, particularly in the three vanguard states of Poland, Czechoslovakia, and Hungary, it could not have flourished on its own in a diplomatic vacuum.

In addition to regular follow-up meetings, the first of which took place in Belgrade in 1977, the CSCE also provided for standing monitoring groups in nearly every country. These "Helsinki Watch" organizations publicized human rights abuses and concerns, compared notes on the state of individual freedom across Europe, and generally exerted pressure on their host governments. In the United States, a CSCE Commission was established on Capitol Hill under the leadership of Representatives Millicent Fenwick and Dante Fascell. The Ford administration was initially aghast at the idea of having a permanent eye looking over its shoulder, but eventually the CSCE Commission would become an important ally of the State Department as the latter amassed greater resources for human rights monitoring during the 1980s.[128]

Again, EUR wrote the program for implementation.[129] An important component was the compliance effort that took place both at the review conferences as well as bilaterally. Goodby, promoted to deputy assistant secretary of state under Vest, traveled with his deputy, John Kornblum, throughout Eastern Europe in the late 1970s, along with a few members of Congress's CSCE Commission. Their journeys took them to Warsaw, Budapest, Sofia, East Berlin, Belgrade, Prague, as well as to a few non–Warsaw Pact capitals. There they covered with their foreign ministry counterparts all the components of the CSCE, not just human rights, although they also brought along specific lists of people whose cases deserved attention. Goodby would depart in 1980 for Finland as ambassador, but he would continue the practice later in the Reagan administration once he moved on to head the delegation to the Stockholm Conference. According to him, the Americans were "well received everywhere," with only one exception being the reaction of a certain Hungarian minister, who, upon being given a letter from Secretary of State George Shultz, "gave such a dusty, snotty answer that my escorts noticed my anger and told me, 'the mills of the gods grind slowly but they do grind.'"[130]

With his signature at Helsinki, Gerald Ford possibly did more for the sovereignty of the various Eastern European states than any American president since Woodrow Wilson. It was ironic, perhaps, that Ford went on to lose the 1976 election to Jimmy Carter, in part because of a disastrous televised debate in which Ford misspoke, saying that there was "no Soviet domination of Eastern Europe." Carter jumped on the error; Ford sacrificed swathes of the East European ethnic vote across the Midwest.[131] But those voters need not have worried; the peaceful demise of the Soviet empire had already begun to take shape.

THERE WAS ONE ADDITIONAL event in 1976 that would put an end to grand designs and seal the perception of détente as appeasement in the minds of its critics. This was a short-lived but intense drama over something called the "Sonnenfeldt Doctrine," named after this chapter's protagonist. In fact such a thing never existed, and Sonnenfeldt quickly repudiated the rumor of it, although he was said secretly to be pleased that something so important as a doctrine should be named after him.[132] Here are the facts:

In December 1975, Sonnenfeldt attended a regular meeting of American ambassadors to Europe, held in London. The discussion was informal, broad, and ruminative. At one point near the end of a long discourse about the ebb and flow of relationships in Eastern and Central Europe, Sonnenfeldt, speaking in master geopolitician mode, termed the current situation "inorganic, unnatural," and continued, "[S]o, it must be our policy to strive for an evolution that makes the relationship between the Eastern Europeans and the Soviet Union an organic one ... [without] an excess of zeal." Warren Zimmerman, a foreign service officer who later became a celebrated ambassador to Yugoslavia, took notes. The notes made their way into a classified cable that followed the usual rounds back in Washington.[133] One copy went customarily to the Defense Department. There it landed in the office of Don Rumsfeld, who had moved from NATO to become White House chief of staff, and then secretary of defense, after engineering the infamous Halloween massacre (actually on November 4, 1975) that led to the dismissal of James Schlesinger and the clipping of Kissinger's wings at State.[134] Working for Rumsfeld was a "hot shot, a real hot shot," who conspired to leak the cable to the columnists Rowland Evans and Robert Novak.[135] On March 22 their column, "A Soviet-East Europe 'Organic Union,'" appeared in the *Washington Post.* Sonnenfeldt's Doctrine was now an official footnote in the history of the Cold War.

It seemed far more explosive at the time. Cables streamed in from embassies around the world, begging for precision on the new turn in détente and the apparent confirmation of the Soviet-American condominium over the captive nations. Kissinger, weary from his battles over the years with the Pentagon, the press, and the Congress, barely defended his aide. For his part, Sonnenfeldt saw little point in trying to explain what he considered "a simple smear."[136]

The scapegoating of Hal Sonnenfeldt was ironic on several levels. Not only had there been the dual success of the Berlin treaty and the CSCE, the details of which disabused any notion of there being a narrow Soviet-American condominium. There was Sonnenfeldt himself—a well known anti-Communist from his earliest days in the U.S. government, whose role in the Nixon and Ford administrations had been as Kissinger's hatchet man on the Right. Soviet officials were well aware of it and took frequent opportunities to poke fun at him. A transcript of an October 1974 meeting in the Kremlin records Leonid Brezhnev saying, "There is always good and evil in the world. I am the epitome of good. Gromyko and Sonnenfeldt are the epitome of evil," at which moment he pointed a toy artillery piece, first at the secretary of state, then, after loading it with a shell, at Sonnenfeldt.[137] And there was the irony of language. A natural, or organic, relationship between the Soviet Union and its neighbors in both Eastern and Western Europe was precisely what the CSCE was meant to bring about. Indeed, it was the sense of integrated wholeness that Kissinger and Sonnenfeldt professed to subvert, or, to be more charitable, stall indefinitely, in the name of a global equilibrium. So in a way Sonnenfeldt was caught with his hands in the cookie jar; the critics of his so-called doctrine were correct if the man's inner motives matched his rhetoric in most memoranda and meetings. However, if one is to believe his defense of "organic" as having a meaning consistent with the one backed by the State Department, then we are faced with a hypocrite getting his just deserts on the eve of leaving office. It was either that, a subconscious snub of his boss or merely a self-destructive statement from someone who did not always consider the full measure of his words. He would pay a price. Sonnenfeldt's official career was more or less over by 1976; he would never get an embassy; and he would spend the next several decades as a fellow of the Brookings Institution, writing very little but continuing to speak a good deal.

The strange story of the Sonnenfeldt Doctrine was a loud but brief distraction from the saga of détente. One is given to wonder, however, whether it was not bound to happen at some point because détente, as stated at the beginning of this chapter, had mangled the ends and means of policy so badly.[138] It may have made perfect sense to strike a deal with the Soviet Union over Berlin and the respective Eastern and Western European spheres of influence. For such a détente to have been an end in itself, however, would have flipped the idea of Atlanticism on its head by narrowing the scope of its power in space and time, just as dumbbellism had tried to do. Europe must not remain divided between superpowers on either end. The aim of American policy had to be the emergence of a "Europe, whole and free," without permanent spheres of influence or divisible sovereignties. The tactics and operational strategies may have varied a good deal. But the central policy remained the same one that had been designed two generations earlier.

Ambassador and Mrs. Cooper and guests, East Berlin, 1976
Courtesy of the Schlesinger Library, Radcliffe Institute, Harvard University

10

FRAYED EDGES

Nadir of the transatlantic relationship—GLOP—Nixon Doctrine—Mansfield amendment and MBFR—nuclear rapprochement with France—Eurocommunism—October War and energy crisis—Year of Europe

THE ERA OF DÉTENTE SAW a few interesting events besides arms control negotiations and presidential visits. One finds, for example, amid memos on the 1974 Nixon-Brezhnev summit, an invitation from the wives of Ambassadors Dobrynin and Stoessel to the first joint U.S.-Soviet film coproduction, *The Blue Birds*, starring Elizabeth Taylor, followed by an ice cream social.[1] Another especially notable happening was the July 4, 1976, celebration in East Berlin. The United States had only recognized the GDR eighteen months before and sent as its first ambassador the courtly Kentuckian senator, John Sherman Cooper. He was an unlikely choice for so bleak a post. But he proved to be a popular appointment, despite being nearly deaf and having had no prior experience in Germany. One important source of his success was his wife, Lorraine. Daughter of a California real estate magnate, she had had two husbands before Cooper, one the son of Woodrow Wilson's secretary of the Treasury, the other a film actor. Her third marriage in 1955 came just as Georgetown society ascended its peak. Lorraine Cooper, with charm that "just oozed from every pore," reigned as hostess and presumed power behind the throne, yet like her fellow social mavens, Vangie Bruce, Kay Graham, and Joe Alsop, she would see her world spiral downward by the late 1960s.[2] Graham's star would be the only one that would continue to sparkle, thanks to her part in uncovering the Watergate scandal; Bruce would presently endure the murder of a daughter and the end of her husband's storied career; Alsop, by then "a bit of a bore these days in his role of the roaring Jeremiah," would devote himself almost entirely to art collecting following a final stand in support of the Vietnam War.[3] For people like the Bruces and the Coopers, a period of exile seemed tasteful and timely, one final chance for "carrying their country's flag into hostile, unexplored territory."[4] Vangie Bruce conspired to secure David's appointment to Beijing to open the new American liaison office there; Lorraine Cooper would follow in due course, pressing Henry

184

Kissinger at every opportunity to grease the wheels of the senator's appointment to the new post in East Berlin.[5]

There Mrs. Cooper set about remaking one of the drabbest residences in the diplomatic service, covering it from ceiling to floor in red damask. Ever confident, she was once overheard saying to the embassy's deputy chief of mission, Brandon Grove: "Mr. Grove, some people have bad taste, some have no taste and some have good taste. You have no taste." She was in charge of the bicentennial celebration. Under a red-white-and-blue *shamiyana* tent sent specially from Pakistan, several hundred guests drank champagne and ate a faux-simple meal of scrambled eggs with vermicelli, Kentucky ham, white and yellow cheese with crumbled bacon, and strawberries with cream. Each table for eight was draped with a white tablecloth and narrow, crossed red and blue runners. Carnations dyed red, white, and blue were arranged in clear vases packed with strawberries; miniature American flags stuck out from these centerpieces in all directions, giving the appearance of small, spiky explosions. Lorraine Cooper herself wore a Parisian evening dress with sheer black chiffon sleeves and bodice overlay, diamond bangles, and a Dior diamond necklace festooned with enormous sapphire pendants; the ambassador appeared in a dark suit completed by his usual, thick horn-rimmed glasses, and conservative tie with matching pocket square. His Soviet opposite number, Piotr Abrasimov, who had been Ken Rush's stubborn counterpart during the Quadripartite Talks and the Soviet Union's representative in Berlin since 1962, was seated at the head table across from Lorraine. He reached over toward her and said, "[L]et's start the dancing."[6]

THE 1970S WAS A DECADE of such semiconscious juxtapositions. The lines between East and West had blurred with détente. The Atlantic Alliance had survived a generation of challenges but had begun to fizzle as economic disputes began to undercut strategic consensus. Responses to crises in the Middle East and Asia appeared to take transatlantic solidarity for granted, but many Europeans and Americans suddenly found that it rested on thinner ground than anyone had imagined. Did it? The central irony of this decade was that the transatlantic consensus still held, not because, but rather in spite, of the exercise of a *Realpolitik* whose ostensible goal was to bring stability to the Cold War.

Yet if the center—that is, the web of institutional relationships that underwrote the transatlantic order—remained viable, the Atlantic Community itself began to fray badly at the margins by the early 1970s. The misplaced rhetoric of détente was largely to blame. For all that American leaders spoke about the need to put the Cold War on a new footing with strategic arms control, the routine relationships that had matured during the previous three decades took a bad beating. Their tone had deteriorated during the latter Vietnam years, and now it sounded bitter, occasionally hostile or sarcastic, and ever more personal, much like Kissinger's way of doing business. The future secretary of state George Shultz complained to him in 1973: "[T]he climate is bad for everything." Kissinger replied: "They said it would improve after Vietnam." Shultz objected: "[I]t has never been worse!"[7] During this time, NATO faced the prospect of having one, perhaps even two Communist governments within its ranks while two of its other members nearly went to war with each other. And in the background came the dismantling of the Bretton Woods economic system, with all the anxiety that entailed. If détente really did represent a conservative reordering of a world torn asunder in 1968, then it was tentative and imperfect, reminding one of Bob Schaetzel's comment on the Nixon administration's opening to China: "like an amateur playing chess whose second move is for checkmate."[8]

And yet there was, as there always seemed to be, a brighter side. Beneath the surface of apparent chaos and halfhearted stability was a steady reassertion of American influence in Europe. The best-of-times, worst-of-times quality of the 1970s did not spare the State Department. Beginning its slow rebound during the Nixon administration, EUR did all it possibly could to remain relevant to foreign policy. That it did so largely without descending to the devious depths that were then typical of its bosses, however, did not diminish the contagion of "malaise" that had afflicted the department and so many other areas of American life, as Jimmy Carter later notoriously diagnosed it.[9]

Kissinger, as noted, became secretary in his own right in September 1973, remaining in the job until 1977. State—or some parts of State—would find itself presumably back at the center of the action. Some center it was. Kissinger's treatment of the professional foreign service and the department did not improve once he became its head. His testiness may have seemed even more pronounced once he no longer had so important a need to reflect the institutional and personal biases of the president. That is, the rancor was genuine and mutual. To him, the foreign service remained "Kennedy liberal," an indiscreet, self-interested, and occasionally disloyal breeding ground of intellectual competition and personal sabotage.[10]

Yet what made Kissinger unique compared to other foreign policy entrepreneurs like Harry Hopkins and McGeorge Bundy, who also kept the careerists at arm's length, was a strong, albeit idiosyncratic, devotion to the diplomatic profession. Although he succeeded in marginalizing his predecessor as secretary of state perhaps to a greater degree than any other national security adviser had, and frequently disparaged the department, he did so less as a bureaucratic competitor per se than as an independent foreign minister. It seemed only natural for Kissinger to make the move to Foggy Bottom (or rather, at first, to merge his two positions), something that would have been unthinkable, even for Bundy or Hopkins. And though the latter two men brought in deputies from the outside and confided in only a few inside professionals, Kissinger, as also noted above, relied heavily on the latter group, cherry-picked from the ranks.

Once he became secretary he professed to care little for the views of the foreign service. His relations with the assistant secretaries were another matter. In his conversations with Hillenbrand, Stoessel, and Hartman, Kissinger could be terse or sarcastic, but he listened to them, often changed his mind in response to their arguments, and appeared, at least implicitly, to respect their judgment. He would continue to use Sonnenfeldt to discipline the lower ranks, while favoring his lieutenants, including several future well-known diplomats such as Thomas Pickering, L. Paul Bremer, James Dobbins, and Robert Blackwill.

Kissinger's professional sense as secretary was as hierarchical as his rhetoric was pragmatic. Indeed, the two were interchangeable. One finds him, for instance, complaining in 1974 to Art Hartman about poor discipline: "[T]he morale of the Assistant Secretaries is my problem.... If the subordinates of the Assistant Secretaries have low morale, it is their fault, not my fault. I am not in the business of holding the hand of every subordinate Foreign Service Officer who is in this building."[11] That would have been impossible. By then the State Department (including the foreign service) already had about 11,000 officers at home and abroad, including approximately 4,000 members of the civil service. EUR itself had about 130, not including the several hundred posted in Europe.[12] Within the department, the geographic bureaus still held sway; most officers sought career advancement through specialization, moving between the country desk and the field.

To remedy such insularity, Kissinger inaugurated the "Global Outlook Program," or GLOP, which appeared at the beginning of 1974. According to legend, the idea came to Kissinger when he was visiting Latin America and had to respond to a cable about the SALT negotiations; the foreign service officer on the spot whom he asked to pursue the question evidently had never heard of them. Designed by Soviet hands with long experience in serving around the world and overseen by Larry Eagleburger, who described it "as a way to beef up the Foreign Service for Kissinger," it meant the regular transfer of specialized officers to unfamiliar places.[13] This had worked well for the Soviet hands who were assigned to track the activities of their Cold War opposites across the globe, but for others it was not a total success. Like Wristonization, GLOP became both process and outcome. One was "glopped" or became a "gloppee." To those who did not appreciate being sent halfway across the world to terra incognita, and this included most European hands, the program was a deliberate effort to weaken the power of the desks and regional bureaus.[14]

But there is little evidence that it proved damaging to EUR to any meaningful extent. Much of the credit must go to Assistant Secretary Hartman, who caught the helm of the bureau in 1973 after being recommended to Kissinger by Donald Rumsfeld, whom Hartman had known in Brussels. He followed the brief tenure of Walt Stoessel. Stoessel had been ambassador to Poland and would go on to head the embassies in Moscow and Germany, ending his career as undersecretary and deputy secretary of state. A handsome midwesterner, Stoessel had grown up in Beverly Hills and had considered pursuing a film career. He looked every part the old-school gentleman diplomat, but Stoessel was also a thoughtful and judicious analyst, and Kissinger appreciated him. He was known to be a "gentle manager," never raising his voice and often using phrases like "I wonder, do you think we might consider ..." to mean that he wanted something done by the following day.[15] His life would end tragically, according to many friends, after he suffered a terrible bout of cancer that many thought to have been the result of the radioactive waves aimed at the Moscow embassy by the Soviets during his time there. In one of his few known battles with Kissinger, then desperate to conclude arms negotiations, Stoessel fought tenaciously against the extent of Soviet involvement in the construction of the new embassy, judgment that would be vindicated when the embassy was found riddled with listening devices.[16]

Art Hartman was cast from a different mold. His manner, though perhaps less cool than Stoessel's, was similarly elegant and wise, but underneath he was "hard as steel."[17] Hartman's true love was France. Paris was his first choice when offered an embassy by the Carter administration; upon retirement, he would spend several months each year in his Provençal manor house. He had joined the Harriman mission in Paris in 1947 and was intimate with the group around

Jean Monnet. Subsequently Wristonized into the foreign service, Hartman rose quietly up the ranks of EUR, specializing primarily in the arcana of European integration, and later worked, as noted in Chapter 7, for George Ball and David Bruce, who rated him "a rarely superior human being."[18] By now Hartman had come to epitomize the bureaucratic rectification, in both form and substance, of Europeanism and Atlanticism. There was also a kind of edge to him, a savvy and more nimble air that most foreign service regulars like Hillenbrand and Stoessel lacked or possibly repressed behind a thick wall of disinterested expertise. Hartman was equally professional yet seemed able to put himself in the minds of Kissinger and Sonnenfeldt, to adapt to their temperaments and to grapple with them on their own terms. Along with George Shultz, as will become clear later on, Hartman deserved a good deal of the credit for holding both the bureaucracy and the transatlantic relationship together during an exceedingly troubled period.[19]

Much of the trouble dated back to the very beginning of the Nixon administration, despite the president's grand tour at the outset. Nixon continued to fight perceptions that he cared little for Europe or for Europeans and, like Johnson, thought the Europeans should foot more of the bill for the defense of the West. The corresponding policy that came to be known as the Nixon or Guam Doctrine was first announced in July 1969 by the president, who applied it initially to Asia. To suggest that America's allies bear the primary burden for their own conventional defense, however, had clear implications for Europe. The dumbbellists were unhappy. Here is Ball, imploring Acheson to join the indignant chorus:

> The endlessly repeated theme of the "Nixon Doctrine" or the "Guam Doctrine" or the "Doctrine of the Low Profile" ... is scarcely the lesson to be derived from Vietnam. What we should have learned from Vietnam is not to abdicate leadership, or stay out of other people's affairs, but to be more selective in the use of our power....
>
> In line with these principles, I would close half our embassies in Africa, or at least greatly reduce their size, stay out of such adventures as the Katanga invasion, etc. On the other hand, where our interests are real and important, as in our relations with Western Europe or Japan or the Soviet Union, I think we should stand as tall as possible, exerting our leadership and exercising our influence wherever it is needed.[20]

Was Nixon's foreign policy that implicitly isolationist? There is little evidence that EUR worried about a hasty retreat. Many there probably welcomed the lower profile in Asia because it meant, by contrast, a greater, or at least more balanced, commitment to Europe. The test would come by way of the so-called Mansfield resolutions and their diplomatic corollary, the Mutual and Balanced Force Reduction talks. Ball added:

> By harping on the "Nixon Doctrine," the President risks giving hostages to the growing number of damn fools on Capital [sic] Hill who are yammering for a drastic reduction of our forces in Germany. Nothing could be more stupidly timed; a Senate move ... would strongly reinforce

the growing German feeling that they may have to make their own security arrangements with the Russians. Moreover, it would immensely weaken our total position if we were pulling troops out of Germany just at the time when the Middle East were to boil up....

I mention all this to you, since Henry made it clear that your counsel carried weight with the President, and I do think you should press him to redesign the "Nixon Doctrine".... I find talk about America lowering its "profile" an absurdity.[21]

Democrat Mike Mansfield of Montana was the longest-serving Senate majority leader and, by the late 1960s, a vehement opponent of the Johnson administration's Vietnam policy. He would become a quiet confidant of President Nixon's after 1969, having been assured that a Vietnam withdrawal was imminent.[22] Yet beginning that same year, Mansfield introduced a series of resolutions, and later amendments, that called for dramatically shrinking the U.S. troop presence in Europe. The Nixon administration fought very hard against them, and none passed.[23]

James Lowenstein, a worldly New Yorker who had once been Eagleburger's companion in misadventure in Yugoslavia, and who later became Hartman's deputy in EUR, worked on Capitol Hill during the late 1960s on the Senate Foreign Relations Committee. He averred that Mansfield was never truly serious about passing the legislation, intending instead for it to be an "educational exercise"—otherwise the cuts he demanded would not have been so drastic and unfeasible.[24] Also likely was the possibility that Mansfield used the legislation to satisfy domestic constituents while gaining additional leverage with the administration. For in providing a regular challenge to conventional deployments, Mansfield made it possible for Kissinger to threaten the Europeans and the Soviets with tough consequences. It was a regular tactic the new secretary picked up from his counterpart up Sixteenth Street, Ambassador Dobrynin: Confide in me in order to protect our relationship from the fanatics back home.[25]

The specter of the Mansfield resolutions made possible the third component of the détente troika—MBFR—the other two being CSCE and SALT. The MBFR talks got started when Jim Goodby and Elliot Richardson (briefly undersecretary of state in 1969) decided to test the Soviets' willingness to discuss conventional arms control. The response came from Leonid Brezhnev in a speech at Tbilisi in which he suggested it was time to "come taste the wine." Goodby then drafted a cable to Ambassador Jake Beam in Moscow to speak with Gromyko about talks, and he went with Richardson to the Senate to say that they had approached the Soviets.[26] MBFR served two purposes: to take the bite out of the Mansfield legislation by demonstrating to its supporters a commitment to reduce NATO troop levels; and to gain an additional card to play *vis-à-vis* the Europeans and Soviets on European security. Whenever the Soviets insisted on a European security conference, this being before the human rights provisions were formalized, the United States would insist on MBFR talks; each time the Germans and British expressed concern that the French and the Russians were about to redraw the strategic map of Europe, the United States would reassert its commitment to a viable MBFR.[27]

But MBFR was not a serious negotiation, at least during this period. It would drag on for over a decade until overtaken by Conventional Forces in Europe talks in 1989–1991. MBFR's lead American negotiator was none other than Jock Dean. Dean admitted later that the talks were never meant to succeed but were aimed merely to deflect the appeal of Mansfield.[28] If he thought so at the time, he had many people fooled. Dean devoted his usual obsessive energy to them, mastering the esoteric details of weaponry so well that his several requests for a transfer were denied. He was particularly known for sending very long, intricately written cables that nobody could reasonably be expected to read, although he would often call ahead and tell the recipient to reply to only a few key sentences on a given page.[29] In a way, the cables resembled the negotiations themselves. "Day after day they went on," recalled Dean's deputy, Reggie Bartholomew, "and day after day Jock and I would go to these talks in the wet, cold winter air, and we would say a, b, c, and the Soviets would say d, e, f, and the thing would start all over again." To cheer him up, Dean took Bartholomew to the Vienna opera, but it did little good. "How much longer will this go on?" Bartholomew finally demanded. The ever-patient, shrewd Jock Dean merely smiled.[30]

Whatever their aim, the MBFR talks accomplished two things: They trained a generation of conventional arms controllers, and they advanced Allied unity, particularly among the British, Germans, Dutch, and Canadians, which underscored the important role of NATO's Senior Political Committee and afforded, for the first time since Hugh Gibson had graced the halls at Geneva, a prominent place for conventional arms control in Europe. For all its intended domestic impact in the United States—pacifying the Senate so that the United States could appear serious about conventional force reductions while simultaneously assuaging the Pentagon that nobody was giving away the store on European security over détente, particularly at the CSCE—the MBFR talks, like George Vest's diplomacy, had the added advantage of laying a foundation for a more genuinely European defense within the system of the North Atlantic Alliance and its nuclear umbrella.[31] It was a circuitous and complicated path, to be sure, but the Nixon Doctrine made it to Europe after all. Meanwhile in the shadows, another reconfiguration took place. This again had to do with France.

DE GAULLE'S REBUFF to NATO in 1966, as discussed earlier, was more show than substance and, thanks in good part to President Johnson's instincts, did not lead to a permanent rupture. Military cooperation would continue quietly and continuously.[32] By 1973, this had taken on a deeper dimension as France and the United States established a significant program of joint cooperation in nuclear weapons technology. According to political scientist Richard Ullman, who broke the story in 1989, the deal originated in talks between Nixon, Kissinger, and French foreign minister Michel Jobert soon after Georges Pompidou entered office. Its principal aims were to underpin Nixon's policy of rapprochement with something tangible and to help offset residual European fears of a Soviet-American nuclear condominium as well as a countervailing concern in the United States that the British and French might cooperate too closely behind American backs.[33] But Kissinger was never a great fan of the program and was often given to doubts. For one thing, his relationship with Jobert bordered on the dismal: "[Y]ou have always chosen me as your foil from the beginning," he told him in December 1973. And he appeared to worry that the program would take on a bureaucratic life of its own, not only moving beyond his control but also serving the interests of rivals in the Pentagon and the intelligence agencies.[34] He complained in late 1975, "We paid ten years for McNamara. He wanted all nuclear weapons under U.S. control. He is in part responsible for de Gaulle."[35] The only thing worse, at least for the dumbbellists, would have been a tilting of the balance too far in de Gaulle's favor.

More interesting than the popularity of the program was the way it evolved and, like MBFR, the procedural precedents it set. At the time, it was called "negative guidance": The French would pass along the kinds of techniques and designs they were advancing, and American officials would "wink and nod," while subordinating responsibility for most of the actual exchanges to technical teams under the combined direction of nuclear experts Johnny Foster and Jean-Laurens Delpech. A similar method was used to retain the participation of French troops in NATO under the guise of informal talks and visits by American commanders.[36] If this was not disengagement, it certainly was a different, more *sotto voce*, style of engagement reminiscent of Gibson, Camp, and Bruce. Again, as in the MBFR negotiations, the French nuclear deal was an imperfect arrangement of convenience that came from a mixture of motives. It bought time, and some good favor, but did not transform the transatlantic relationship in any drastic way. Yet it had the paradoxical effect of affirming the post-MLF displacement of major military questions from bilateral agendas, converting them into lower-level political, or even administrative, issues. When Art Hartman went to France as ambassador in 1977, he was told, without being given any details, that the "agreements" were still in place and that he should merely alert the French accordingly.[37]

For better or worse, then, Kissinger's détente diplomacy and its indirect results served further to regularize the military relationships that had dogged the Alliance since the mid-1950s. Whatever one thought of his motives, he was a master of disaggregation—the Paris peace talks ending the Vietnam War were not the only case of a settlement being forced by ostensibly separating political objectives from military ones. In Europe, the latter would reappear presently with the Euromissile controversy, described in the next chapter; but for now such matters were quiescent, suggesting a tactical pause in the Cold War, at least over military questions per se.

From EUR's perspective, however, the mid-1970s was not merely a period to regroup or to nurse Vietnam-inflicted wounds to American prestige. It was also a time, again, to polish silver linings. With both the MBFR and the French nuclear arrangement, American diplomacy succeeded in partially satisfying multiple constituencies while gaining strategic advantage over the Soviet Union, however much critics of détente charged the opposite. It was up to lower-ranking diplomats to derive what longer-term benefits of cooperation they could from the putative freeze in military competition. In the meantime, they would have their hands full with much hotter conditions on the political and economic fronts.

SOON AFTER TAKING THE JOB as assistant secretary, Hartman found himself seated next to a Congressman running for reelection. The Congressman told him the campaign was going well, apart from his two southernmost counties, which never ceased to cause him problems. Hartman replied, "[M]e too!"[38]

He was referring to a mess over Cyprus that he had inherited in full eruption when Kissinger transferred jurisdiction over Greece and Turkey from the Bureau of Near Eastern Affairs to EUR. But the same could also be said about politics throughout Latin Europe.[39] The problem was something called Eurocommunism. It was less a movement than a temporary force that propelled the popularity of Communist parties in France, Italy, and Portugal to higher-than-usual levels during the mid-1970s. In the latter two cases, the parties appeared on the verge of taking over the governments, which would have presented an interesting question for the Alliance. The problem finally came to a head in April 1974, when the army of Portugal overthrew the civilian government of Marcelo Caetano. Within the army was a group of pro-Communist or Communist officers that sought to seize full control of the country; they were resisted with uncertain conviction by the incoming president Francisco da Costa Gomes and the head of the Socialist Party, later prime minister, Mário Soares.

Because the prime minister, General Vasco dos Santos Gonçalves, was suspected of being sympathetic to the Communists, and both Costa Gomes and Soares were considered weak, the political situation seemed dire.[40] NATO had long looked the other way during the dictatorial rule (ending finally in 1968) of Antonio Salazar, and it had important assets in Portugal, especially in the Azores, which proved essential during the 1973 Middle East war. Indeed, Portugal had been the only European country to assist with the supply of vital American arms to Israel. Now the entire Western orientation of the country seemed to be in jeopardy.

Kissinger's reaction to the situation was decisive and firm. Soares, he famously declared, was another "Kerensky"; Gonçalves and Costa Gomes were even worse. Nothing could save the situation but a "strong action" on the part of NATO or a Chilean-style coup. Barring any or all of that, Kissinger wondered if the United States should "attack Portugal ... and drive them from NATO."[41]

EUR did not share that view. Although it concurred that the global prestige and credibility of the United States appeared to be on a slippery slope, mainly because of Vietnam, the Portuguese situation did not present a simple choice between resistance and resignation.[42] In the first instance, it was not absolutely clear that a Communist government in Europe would ally readily with the Soviet Union. As ridiculous as it might have sounded to some, a principal tenet of Eurocommunism was independence, a different path, so to speak.[43] Today, one may dismiss the potential for a proliferation of Titos in 1970s Europe; yet one must still acknowledge that the rhetoric of independence was taken seriously by many people there at the time. Moreover, Communist parties were popular, notably in Italy and apparently among a significant portion of the Portuguese Army, which had seized power. An overt policy of resistance on the part of the United States would probably have only strengthened and emboldened the true ideologues among them. There had to be an alternative.

EUR argued that a Portuguese crisis could be averted proactively with a mixture of above-the-board talks and the occasional salami tactic. Rather than issuing regular threats in the distant hope that Portuguese leaders would be intimidated into renouncing the Communist sympathizers in their ranks, it seemed in EUR to make more sense to work with them directly in order to divide the various leftist groups against each other, including several to the left of the

Communists.[44] Close cooperation with the non-Communist Left was a policy that had proved successful throughout the Cold War. Why abandon it now? The problem then was to find a way to convince Kissinger, or at least to minimize his opposition to what had to be done.

That burden fell to the new ambassador to Portugal, Frank Carlucci. Carlucci had joined the foreign service in the early 1960s and was part of the same celebrated group of Congo enlistees that included Jock Dean, Monteagle Stearns, and Raymond Seitz. Born into a family of modest means in Scranton, Pennsylvania, Carlucci's early foreign service career also took him to South Africa and Zanzibar. In the 1960s, one could make a name in such places: They called for "FSO's who didn't faint at the sight of blood," recalled Stearns, later to marry the daughter of Jimmie Riddleberger and, like him, to be ambassador to Greece.[45] Carlucci moved fast. After less than a decade, he left the foreign service to become, in 1971, the number-two person in the Office of Management and Budget (OMB), and then, one year later, the undersecretary of the Department of Health, Education, and Welfare (HEW).[46]

Innate ability was not the only engine behind Carlucci's rise. He also had important friends, namely, Donald Rumsfeld, with whom he had been close at Princeton, and Caspar Weinberger, under whom he worked at HEW. Back in the State Department, Carlucci would prove to be a tough opponent for Kissinger. He had independent political ties to the White House, where Rumsfeld was now chief of staff, and to other executive departments. He also had the support of EUR.[47]

Carlucci and Art Hartman spent many hours on the latter's back patio in late 1974 plotting how to "get Henry to lay off" the Portuguese.[48] They chose a direct assault. In a few dramatic meetings, Carlucci confronted Kissinger and told him the situation did not merit so much pessimism. He could work with Soares; the politics on the ground were not so dire. Kissinger would not be convinced, that is, until President Ford, most likely pressed by Rumsfeld, sided with Carlucci. Although Kissinger never explicitly endorsed the change in policy, he allowed the ambassador to proceed, telling him he was on his own in public.[49]

Meanwhile, Carlucci enlisted the support of another Princeton classmate, Ed Streator, who was the number-two official in the NATO mission under David Bruce, then serving out his final diplomatic assignment. The Alliance henceforth backed Carlucci's position. The Germans were particularly helpful in this regard, the German Social Democratic Party (SPD) and the German embassy in Lisbon having played a critical, quiet role with their sister socialists, girding them against Communist intimidation and sending funds.[50] The policy succeeded. Soares won his election, the Communists never prevailed, and Portugal, according to Henry Kissinger, was "saved, either from the communists or from Kissinger, [I am] not sure which."[51]

The Portugal story suggested a few more interesting points about American diplomacy in the 1970s. It affirmed that for all the concentration of foreign policy at the top, a diplomat on the ground could still make a world of difference, even when his policy advice was in direct opposition to that of the secretary of state. Next, it demonstrated that bureaucrats in EUR often had a better sense of global priorities, in spite of the presumed "localitis" of their colleagues overseas. In his memoirs, Kissinger praised Carlucci's tenacity but cited the latter's rather diplomatic admission that he did not hold Kissinger's opposition against him. After all, the secretary of state had global priorities; the ambassador obviously had more parochial ones.[52] Here Kissinger missed the larger point: Carlucci had been *right* about Portugal. Imagine if the United States had taken a harder line toward Soares, demanding a tough repudiation of the Communists and other leftists? Imagine what the global consequences would have been if Portugal really had collapsed and a Communist government, however short-lived, had taken over in 1976? The Global Outlook Program notwithstanding, there were times and places when national priorities called for a local expert who knew best. Portugal was such a case.

Carlucci's actions in Portugal reaffirmed in the topsy-turvy climate of détente the value of the traditional Cold War practice of backing the European non-Communist Left. A few years later, Jimmy Carter's new ambassador to Italy, Dick Gardner, would pursue a nearly identical policy, reversing the harder-line of his Republican predecessor, John Volpe, and with similar success.[53] Here, too, an American ambassador with connections (Gardner had long-standing ties to the Democratic Party and was close to both National Security Adviser Zbigniew Brzezinski and Secretary of State Cyrus Vance) was able to circumvent bureaucratic rivals back home in order to pursue a more moderate, and pragmatic, policy of splitting ranks on the ground. Gardner's rival in this instance was the department's executive secretary, Peter Tarnoff, a former aide to Henry Cabot Lodge Jr. and a reputed Francophile who intervened with his boss, Secretary Cyrus Vance, at the behest of French Socialists François Mitterrand and Jean-Pierre Cot, then allied with the French Communist Party in upcoming municipal elections. It was Tarnoff's view, it was said that the Fifth Republic would collapse if Mitterrand could not hold together his coalition of the Left, which led Tarnoff to rewrite a critical speech in a manner that favored the French situation but obviated most of what Gardner was trying to do in Italy.[54] Gardner succeeded in undoing much of the damage, and the Italian Communists lost significant votes in every subsequent election.

Both the Italian and Portuguese cases suggest that the American policy of "differentiation"—referring to the differential treatment of varying Soviet Bloc states based on their openness to the West, a policy that dated back, paradoxically given its stance on "neutralism," to the Eisenhower administration—could be applied to Western as well as Eastern Europe.[55] To Kissinger, however, the logic of détente negated these differences in the name of geopolitical *force majeure*. His passionate opposition to Eurocommunism—unusual for a man who prided himself on a rarified yet sober ear for political reality—was perhaps less purely ideological and more calculated, on two interrelated grounds. To begin with, there was the fear that the Soviet-American entente that Kissinger had in mind could not tolerate political openings or deviations in client states. The Soviet outcry over the success in countering Communist gains in the polls in Western Europe was lukewarm, even though some of these parties took their orders directly from Moscow. If Western European governments began allowing Communists to win control of more ministries, who could say Eastern European governments would not be compelled to do the same for non-Communists? So there had to be limits to differentiation.

One must also remember that Kissinger was deeply fearful of the political

Right in the United States, which had never forgiven him for the nature of the Vietnam settlement, and had now begun to mobilize heavily against détente as well as against him personally.[56] The last thing he wanted to give them was a political victory for the Left anywhere on his watch. One could say, then, that in addition to saving Portugal, Carlucci saved Kissinger from himself.

Like détente, differentiation was a policy that was more virtual than systematic, yet EUR managed to transform it into something both equitable and effective. The benefits would be felt not only in Portugal and Italy but also in Spain, which was about to face a difficult transition from forty years of Francisco Franco's rule. There were fears that the Spanish political class was not sufficiently prepared for the succession, and that Communists might gain a foothold there as well. This did not happen, and efforts to integrate Spain with transatlantic institutions, particularly NATO, would be well advanced by the time Franco finally died in 1975. Staffers in EUR, the Office of Political-Military Affairs, and the NATO mission in Brussels had been working actively on this since the mid-1960s. Even so, Nixon sent General Vernon Walters on a secret mission in February 1971 to find out exactly what the plans were. Franco told him not to worry.[57]

CERTAINLY A BIGGER MENACE than Eurocommunism was the 1973 Arab-Israeli War and the subsequent world energy crisis. These events, in combination with the 1971 decision to take the United States off the gold peg, sent transatlantic economic relations into a tailspin. American balance of payments deficits by the end of the Vietnam War had become so severe that Nixon faced little choice but to opt for devaluation. Yet his administration took the decision evidently with almost no prior consultation with America's European allies.[58] It would take another half decade to undo the damage.

EUR's economic shop, the office of Regional Political and Economic Affairs, was then headed by a onetime Soviet specialist named Abe Katz. He held the job for nearly a decade and became a critical arbiter among the State Department's Economic Bureau (E), the Treasury Department, and the Europeans. A small, bullish man, Katz was tough but amiable. He took his job seriously.

Like its larger predecessor, RPE was an anomaly, a cross between a regional and a functional office. Its mission, on the one hand, was to ensure that relations with NATO and the European Community took proper account of the effect on the American economy. On the other hand, it often found itself squaring the circle between the more strident views of E and the Treasury Department and the interests and desires of the Europeans. In the 1960s the "clan" of like-minded economic experts reached its zenith across Europe, with Joe Greenwald in London, Stanley Cleveland and Jacques Reinstein in Paris, and Jack Myerson and Deane Hinton in Brussels. Most would remain active in various capacities during the 1970s, but without equivalent support in the bureau. Katz was there, more or less, on his own.[59]

Such status seemed only to embolden him. Katz initiated the first regular meetings between the head of the Council of Economic Advisers, Paul McCracken, and his counterparts at the OECD, often paying for the lunches himself. He established a quiet but close friendship with Georges Pompidou's top economic deputy, Jean-René Bernard, which served as a kind of back channel linking transatlantic talks on trade and monetary affairs, not yet tied to one another formally.

And he convinced Kissinger, still waffling over how to react to the Arab oil boycott, to turn to that old mainstay, the OECD.

Following the Middle East war in October 1973, the Arab nations of the Organization of Petroleum Exporting Countries (OPEC), along with Egypt and Syria, announced an oil boycott affecting all states that had backed Israel in the recent conflict. Apart from leading to the first major postwar energy crisis and worsening an already bad recession in Europe and the United States, the oil shock drove a wedge across the Atlantic. European governments were also divided against one another once the French government decided to renege on an agreement to let its currency float against the dollar.[60] Leading the anti-American camp was the implacable Michel Jobert. Jobert's prejudices may have been unexpected because he had an American wife and was working for a government that was ostensibly devoted to redressing the damage of the de Gaulle years. Yet as foreign minister, he was almost "violently anti-American," and many observers blamed the "petty, unhappy" visit he mismanaged for French president Pompidou in early 1970.[61] Kissinger, having failed to anticipate the embargo and being a self-described economic illiterate at odds with much of his own bureaucracy over a response, lost a good deal of the momentum to Jobert, who insisted that the whole producer-consumer problem be handled by the United Nations with heavy French direction.

This would be reversed in the weeks leading up to the infamous Washington Energy Conference of February 1974, infamous because Kissinger credited it with driving the final nail into the coffin of Jobert's attempt to wrest the leadership of European diplomacy away from the United States. Kissinger's version of the story left out the State Department almost entirely, probably because he had been furious with it for seeming to cater too much to the Europeans.[62] Yet Katz had been the one to suggest to Kissinger that he convene the energy committee of the OECD with himself in the chair. This scuttled Jobert's attempt to use a multilateral forum in order to isolate the United States as leader of the consumer nations. The forum was indeed multilateral, but now the French, rather than the Americans, were isolated because Kissinger controlled the agenda. Together with Helmut Schmidt, he manipulated the procedural debates at the OECD toward an outcome resulting in the establishment of the International Energy Agency, a new organization meant to provide emergency oil supplies and to coordinate responses to future crises. It did not initially include France. The United States also succeeded in striking an agreement with the oil producers that proscribed the French fondness for cartelization.[63]

Repairing the damage of 1973–1974 was beyond the sole capacity of Abe Katz, however. Kissinger ultimately turned to a Republican loyalist who had been secretary of the treasury and secretary of labor as well as the first director of the OMB. He was Ronald Reagan's future secretary of state, George Shultz. Shultz had weathered the OPEC storm and left government service in March 1974 for a lucrative post at the Bechtel Corporation. Soon thereafter, Kissinger asked him if he would reactivate an informal arrangement he had established a year earlier in order to cope with the turmoil in international capital markets. During the 1973 annual Washington meetings of the International Monetary Fund and the World Bank, Shultz, together with Valéry Giscard d'Estaing, Helmut Schmidt, and the British chancellor of the exchequer, Anthony Barber, met in the White

House library to review the range of international economic problems and to derive some quiet consensus. These meetings, dubbed the Library Group, were the kernel of what would later become the G-5, G-6, and eventually the G-8, summits of industrial countries.[64]

It appeared that de Gaulle's old proposal of a transatlantic directorate had finally become a reality. That may have been true; there was little doubt that both Nixon and Kissinger favored such arrangements, having had little time for the bureaucrats in the European Commission or for Bob Schaetzel, still lingering on there as American ambassador, ignored so much by Washington that he could pander to European audiences at will, even at the expense of his own government.[65]

Conference diplomacy, notably at Martinique in December 1974, and at the first G-6 summit at Rambouillet in November 1975, again became the favored means for tackling economic problems. Yet the record of high-level summitry does not give the whole story. It is certainly true that such arrangements produced consensus more readily than months of lower-level negotiations with the European Commission generally did. But the latter negotiations were nonetheless critical now that the British had finally joined the Common Market. Further attempts to set up a halfway house for the British had been nixed, primarily by Katz and British collaborators, each working on occasion against their own political leaders. In crafting responses to French and German efforts to enlist American support for such attempts, Katz was careful to link the benefits of British membership in the Common Market to U.S. support for Europe on all levels. Katz noted, "[W]e're not buying trade discrimination without the political benefits of European integration. If the American people and Congress should perceive that Europe was going to discriminate against our economic interest, then they might begin to rethink the troop commitment there. This made the Germans apoplectic."[66]

And so while *directoires* came and went, EUR maintained in place the remnants of policies and organizations that were formulated earlier by Miriam Camp and friends in the 1950s. The British did join the Common Market; the GATT trade agreements held; American troops remained in Europe; and a new, post–Bretton Woods consensus on monetary policy took shape without forfeiting or otherwise injuring core transatlantic political relationships. None of that happened on its own, or fully in spite of the reintroduction of economic summitry.

THE COMBINATION OF SHREWD TACTICS on the part of Kissinger and an adherence to a policy vision on the part of the bureaucracy were at the root of the diplomatic successes of the 1970s. But such successes were still barely detectable where Europe was concerned; the next chapter describes their blossoming to full flower. In the meantime, transatlantic relations only seemed to go from bad to worse. Adding considerable insult to injury was, neither last nor least, Kissinger's curious 1973 initiative, the "Year of Europe."

In Kissinger's first formal speech in public on April 23, he repeated what Nixon had said the previous February: that 1973 would be the Year of Europe because "the era that was shaped by decisions of a generation ago is ending. The success of those policies has produced new realities that require new approaches." These included the usual menu of détente, negotiations with the Soviets, and embracing the emergence of new, important actors such as Japan—which Kissinger now included among the "Atlantic" powers. It also called for a new "Atlantic Charter" and, finally, the *pièce de résistance*, a favoring by America's European allies of their regional interests, in contrast with the global responsibilities of the United States.[67]

The final point really did make the Europeans apoplectic. Jobert reacted with outrage; a few British upper lips became loose, especially because they were being led into the Common Market by their most Eurocentric (and anti-American) prime minister since Anthony Eden, Edward Heath, who said he might as well have proclaimed a "Year of the United States." They were not alone.[68] Throughout Europe, many people still regarded their nations as world leaders; many at the same time promoted the Atlantic Alliance as the bedrock of global stability. Did they really think that the world had entered an era with Europe and America standing as competitors, even rivals? Was that not paying too much notice to the usual French pretensions? Or was Kissinger's initiative really meant to be, to use a Chinese Communist term, "a rectification campaign"?

Whatever its intellectual or political rationale, the Year of Europe became, in Kissinger's apt words, "the year that never was."[69] So, too, did the new Atlantic Charter. Approved finally in mid-1974, this "Atlantic Declaration" accomplished little besides recognizing the value of French and British nuclear forces for Western deterrence and, perhaps, providing an implicit green light for the secret assistance to the French already under way. The rest of it has been lost to posterity. Former French foreign minister Maurice Schumann put it best when, asked in 1990 for his thoughts on the Year of Europe, he replied, "I must say I've forgotten all about that, and the very act that I have forgotten it just shows how important it was."[70]

Still, for all his condescending flattery of the European and American "old guard," including the octogenarian Jean Monnet, to whom he paid an obligatory visit and awarded a prize soon before making the Year of Europe speech, Kissinger had something of a point about entering a new era. Art Hartman's deputy, Wells Stabler, put it nicely:

> I recall some years ago attending a staff meeting at the State Department's Bureau of European Affairs when one of the senior officers turned to the head of policy planning ... and asked, "What are you going to do? You've got Adenauer who's 80 [sic]; you've got de Gaulle who's way up there; you've got Tito who's in his 80s; you've got Franco who's in his 80s; and you've got Salazar. What are you going to do with all these old men? What are your contingency plans?" The head of policy planning thought for a few minutes and replied, "Well, we are in touch with the local undertakers."[71]

Most men in power in the 1970s had been teenagers or in their early twenties during World War II; they would reach political maturity during a very different type of global conflict; they were perhaps more cynical, less bold, more self-consciously tactical in their thinking and action, and certainly less visionary, than their predecessors. Nixon once called his European counterparts a "bunch of ward heelers"; Kissinger termed his "all idiots."[72] To a lesser degree, the generational parallel held true in the U.S. government, where the men who had reached the highest levels of the bureaucracy—and they were still mostly men, as the gender revolution was slow to arrive—were nonconfrontational, prudent, competent, and almost entirely forgotten, in notable contrast to their Marshall Plan–era forebears.

The 1970s was also a time for loosening ends and letting go. "Sometime in the late 1960s the so-called post-war era ended," wrote Marty Hillenbrand. "We are clearly in an era of transition."[73] Tommy Thompson got cancer and died. David Bruce, after opening the liaison office in Beijing, returned to serve one last tour abroad as ambassador to NATO, then passed away in 1977, to the dismay of many friends who had watched him decline rapidly after the murder of his only surviving daughter, Sasha, the previous year. Chip Bohlen left the embassy in Paris in 1968 and died five years later. His successor was Sargent Shriver, the husband of John F. Kennedy's sister and founder of the Peace Corps, but a man without much of a diplomatic reputation.[74] General Lyman Lemnitzer, the last of the World War II generals, would leave NATO the same year, replaced by Dwight Eisenhower's former aide, General Andrew Goodpaster. Goodpaster would serve there until 1974, when, desperate to remove Alexander Haig from a Watergate-plagued White House, Kissinger would convince Ford to name Nixon's former chief of staff to the NATO post.[75] Bill Tyler left the State Department, becoming director of Harvard's Dumbarton Oaks. Lorraine and John Sherman Cooper would return to the United States soon after their July Fourth party. Ken Rush, disappointed that he had been passed over for the secretaryship, eventually left government to become chair of the Atlantic Council of the United States, where he served until 1985, when he was replaced by Goodpaster.[76] The Declaration of Atlantic Unity had run out of money by 1971; few would hear much more from Wally Moore, although he would continue to work occasionally on a voluntary and part-time basis. Jim Huntley, however, found that he was no longer able to do so. In a letter to a benefactor, he wrote:

I believe that I am an asset and we simply have to work to find the necessary formula to keep me fruitfully working away at the long-range goal: an effective Atlantic federation.

My personal situation, Schmitty, is this: I have an equity in a house in Guildford, a car, and additional assets in the amount of about $4,000. At the moment, with all my freelancing, enough is coming in to cover essential expenses, but there is no margin. I work 60 hours a week or more. Practically everything I do has "Atlantic" content and value—whether lecturing students at Leiden, IBM executives from all over Europe, environmental planners in Paris; or writing articles about U.S. troop withdrawal for a teachers' magazine or acting as secretary of the new "Mid-Atlantic Club"; or preparing a pamphlet ... for NATO. I have a lot of other irons in the fire and some may well help to meet ongoing expenses, but they are not a long-term solution.... Within two or three months, we are going to have to decide whether or not to go back to the States and accept some pedestrian employment, quite off the "Atlantic" track.

If I were to do this, I believe it would be a substantial loss to the Atlantic Movement.[77]

Huntley would go on to work for Rush as president of the Atlantic Council, also until 1985.

And so the Atlanticists began to disassemble, but they did not disappear. It was one thing for Kissinger and Nixon to coddle the old guard, to flatter its members while self-consciously setting out in new directions.[78] It was quite another to enforce a lasting change in orientation throughout the network of Atlanticists. That never took place. There were three reasons. The first had to do with personality. Those closest to Kissinger during his time in government generally found it hard to remain loyal. He could be cruel, dismissive, and abusive toward the people around him, even once saying to Sonnenfeldt, "[A]mong the many State Department rules is one that no one with an IQ higher than sixty is allowed to get close to me."[79] But, as noted, he still respected many of them. He did not impose his views strictly as Dulles or even Ball had; he had a tyrannical personality, but he was not uniformly tyrannical in practice. He rather was a survivor, keener to use the bureaucracy to his advantage than to destroy all rivals for his own sake. His greatest exertions, meanwhile, were directed toward the tactical manipulation of perceptions—"framing the problem"; he never expended any real effort, or expressed any serious willingness, to effect a permanent transformation of the machinery of foreign policy. More buccaneer than imperialist, Kissinger would have little choice but to defer to those in the bureaucracy in the areas they cared about the most, which coincided rather fortuitously with the governments he least cared for, namely, those in Latin America and Europe.

Second, one cannot forget that Kissinger and, above all, Nixon never publicly forswore the fundamental basis of Atlanticism.[80] For all their displeasure with Europe, they never really undermined NATO. They may have taken the Europeans far less seriously than the Europeans took themselves and their various initiatives, particularly *Ostpolitik*; and they may have found the Europeans' and EUR's insistence on the global primacy of European issues and problems both frustrating and debilitating to the extent it was seen to interfere with more urgent centers of attraction. But they never reverted to becoming doctrinaire Asia-firsters or isolationists.

The final and most significant reason was the flexibility of EUR. It succeeded, much as it had done in the 1940s and 1950s, in coopting the talent and loyalty of others. Kissinger and Sonnenfeldt watered at the same wells, read the same papers, and took part in the same seminars on both sides of the Atlantic, as the leading lights in EUR. The two refugees may have promoted their tenure in power as truly special, and they did what they could to adapt to larger changes in the international system. But where Europe was concerned, they had become more the objects of fascination than the protagonists of revolution; their imagination in the realm of policy was as limited as their social and personal appetites were insatiable. Both had come to take for granted the benefits of the Atlantic Community—in every sense—while denying, or at least obscuring, the responsibility for cultivating it. This they left to the rank and file in EUR.

EUR helped to prevent the Berlin talks from dividing the Alliance. It helped to transform the CSCE from a Soviet propaganda exercise into a subtle yet powerful agent against the perpetuation of Soviet power. It crafted a response to Eurocommunism that did not play into the hands of those it most sought to defeat and helped to prevent any genuine enemies of the West from gaining control of any Western European government. And it did what it could to restore the primacy of transatlantic relations after the Vietnam War, to include a largely successful adjustment to an enlarged Common Market and the political and economic crises of the early 1970s.

Nearly all of its efforts were opposed in varying degrees by Kissinger and his staff. But that was not the point. EUR did not always prevail. On balance, though, it managed to find a way to elicit autonomy and, ultimately, support, from above. This became something more than the traditional art of exercising influence at the margins. By the middle of the decade, the twin projects of Euro-Atlantic integration and a peaceful winding down of the Cold War had seen EUR move back into the visible center of American diplomacy. The dramatic *dénouement* was now set to occur.

Paul Nitze and Rozanne Ridgway, Tom Simons in background
Time & Life Pictures/Getty

11

THE LAST DANCE

Jimmy Carter versus Helmut Schmidt—Euromissiles—George Shultz and Europe—
Geneva and Reykjavik Summits—intensification and dénouement of the Cold War—
Indian summer of Atlanticism—fall of the Berlin Wall

I N NOVEMBER 1989, a delegation of the Atlantic Council was visiting Taipei for talks with counterparts in various research institutes and with several government officials as part of an unofficial exchange program. It was there—on the anniversary of Monnet's birth and de Gaulle's death—that the group learned about the fall of the Berlin Wall. Leading the delegation was the council's chair, General Goodpaster, and the organization's new president, Rozanne Ridgway, a foreign service officer who had just retired from a thirty-year government career, culminating as assistant secretary for European and Canadian affairs. She would go on to preside over the bureau during the surprising, "transformational" administration of Ronald Reagan that followed the underachieving presidency of Carter, moving from the last battle with the Soviets to a series of events that brought about a peaceful end to the Cold War. EUR and its allies were again at the center of that story.

Ridgway's career had both typical and atypical qualities. First of all, she was a woman. As noted in previous chapters, women were not entirely invisible in the foreign service or the State Department, although they rarely made ambassador, and never assistant secretary of one of the major bureaus, with Ruth Shipley, the longtime head of passports and visas, and Miriam Camps being only partial exceptions.[1] Ridgway grew up in St. Paul, Minnesota, the daughter of a onetime school teacher and tire salesman, and a French Canadian homemaker; in addition to Roz and her parents, the household included two brothers, two uncles, an aunt, and a grandmother. Exceptionally intelligent, bookish but highly practical, with a clear mind and an ability to communicate in crisp, clipped sentences, she decided at a young age (after reading an article in *Life* about American diplomats) that she was destined for neither school-teaching nor nursing, and so took the foreign service exam, which she passed easily. Her career began with a clerical post in Washington, followed by a stint as a personnel officer in Manila; then she went to Italy, Norway, and back to the department, where she worked on NATO affairs under George Vest and Ron Spiers, a well-regarded political officer. Spiers, under whom Ridgway later served in the Bahamas, and Vest determined to promote her no matter what.[2]

There was resistance, of course. EUR never looked favorably upon tokenism, and Ridgway's mid-career coincided with "equal opportunity's" halfhearted popularity throughout the government. But like Camps, she was so professional, intelligent, conscientious—in department parlance, "very, very good"—that her gender became seen as almost incidental. Ridgway, who probably wanted to keep it that way, refused to join a discrimination lawsuit filed by several female members of the department in the early 1970s. She nevertheless was a pioneer; she suffered penalties, particularly early in her career, and her fair share of bureaucratic limbo—as when the Carter administration, "determined to have a woman's face on the flowchart," named her counselor but gave her almost no duties or access. She later concluded:

> The job that most people think was the beginning of my career—they forget the years in administrative and consular affairs that, in fact, inform so very much of my view of the Service—had its desk in an area of EUR shown on the Department architectural plans as reserved space for a prospective third elevator shaft on the fifth corridor. Luckily, I was not lost, never to be found.... It was not so long ago that the junior officer rotation program in Manila stopped when I arrived to join the ranks of the junior officers there. It was not so long ago that an American Ambassador in Buenos Aires refused to include me in a stag luncheon honoring the American fishing delegation of which I was a member.... It was not so long ago that a senior Administration official forgot who was negotiating the joint statement for the Reagan-Gorbachev Geneva summit and allowed as how women knew nothing about throw-weight and Afghanistan. Unfortunately, it was too long ago that a woman Foreign Service Officer was able to reach the top of the Service ladder. In 1962 Frances Willis was named a career Ambassador—the first and so far the last woman to reach that rank. So to the women of the Service, I do believe I leave a Service vastly altered—positively altered from the one I joined. I leave plenty of opportunity for new firsts, and, in the path of Frances Willis, a too-long-delayed important second. And I leave a Service whose women officers include in their ranks all the talent needed to make it to the top. Giving advice is not my habit, but I would use this occasion to give just one bit of it ... don't take a token job unless you have a token mind.[3]

Ridgway's career break came in 1973, when, as the Ecuador Desk officer, she was handed a messy negotiation over Pacific tuna. She became so proficient on the subject, and proved so tough and effective a negotiator, that she soon was known around the department as "tuna Roz" or "fish Roz." This led, following her assignment as deputy chief of mission in the Bahamas, to an appointment as deputy assistant secretary and ambassador for oceans and fisheries, and then to a posting as ambassador in Helsinki. Following her next job as counselor, she became ambassador to East Germany, and it was there that the new secretary of state, George Shultz, tapped her to return as assistant secretary. They got along famously well. The two would develop a relationship that seemed a cross between an older brother–younger sister and general–top lieutenant.[4] Ridgway had all the diplomatic qualities that Shultz liked: She was shrewd, clearheaded, and strong; her background was in Europe, and her training was at the hands of "the very best" officers in EUR; and finally, she "listened to George Shultz, whereas many other senior advisors in the State Department didn't, because they wanted him to do what they wanted ... she actually listened, as he did with Ronald Reagan."[5] Under Shultz and Ridgway, EUR would experience something of an Indian summer, much as the transatlantic relationship would in the early 1980s. It was well primed.

BUT THIS WOULD NOT BE a second golden age, at least not yet. First there was the Carter interlude. By now, of course the bureau was back in the hands of professionals. Following the restorative tenures of Assistant Secretaries Hillenbrand, Stoessel, and Hartman, the direction of the bureau passed to Vest, its most beloved chief since Livie Merchant. Serving as his deputy was Jim Goodby.

The new team in the White House replicated the pattern of previous administrations by allowing a rivalrous relationship to develop between it and the department. National Security Adviser Zbigniew Brzezinski fought just as hard as Henry Kissinger for the control of foreign policy. He may have been less offensive than Kissinger, but he probably was no less ambitious or brutal. He, too, was something of a Gaullist. His opponent, Cyrus Vance, proved almost as pliant as William Rogers had been, even if Vance probably entered the job with more bureaucratic allies, having occupied important positions in government since the early 1960s: "A skillful negotiator, probably a very good manager ... [but] probably not enough of a conceptualizer" was the postelection assessment by Brzezinski, who realized, "after putting down the telephone receiver ... that I had in fact recommended Cyrus Vance ... as Secretary of State."[6]

Brzezinski's education was every bit as Eurocentric as Kissinger's. But like his predecessor, a fellow political scientist to whom he was often compared, Brzezinski emphasized a broader international experience and similarly found his official tenure dominated by relations with China and a series of crises—Ogaden, Afghanistan, Nicaragua, Iran. His summary list of foreign policy priorities for the newly elected president never mentioned Europe or NATO by name.[7] This was somewhat ironic, given that Brzezinski had made his reputation, as discussed in Chapter 8, as a Cold War specialist in European, primarily Eastern European, affairs and had catapulted himself from academia to the heights of the policy world by running David Rockefeller's Trilateral Commission, a job, incidentally, that made it possible to endear himself to Carter from the mid-1970s as the organization sought to broaden its national base, especially to up-and-coming southern governors.[8] In the meantime, he had become a favorite of the Democratic establishment (especially of Pamela and Averell Harriman, with whom he lived for some time), perhaps eager—as overdrawn and stale as the comparison was and is—for its own Kissinger figure. Like him, Brzezinski's Eurocentrism took

James Lowenstein, Frank Carlucci, Zbigniew Brzezinski, and Jimmy Carter
Courtesy of Jimmy Carter Library

on a more global hue during the course of the 1970s, and so, while appearing to generalize about policy priorities in the "inner core" of the Alliance, Brzezinski had in fact translated a European, or Euro-Atlantic, conception of power politics on to the entirety of American foreign policy.[9]

In the National Security Council, Brzezinski delegated most European matters to his deputy, David Aaron, a foreign service officer whom he first met when Aaron was assigned by EUR to keep an eye on him during the Johnson administration.[10] Despite that earlier connection, many people perceived Aaron to have been a token appointee of the Walter Mondale wing of the Democratic Party, and a liberal voice in the White House. In fact, Aaron had not been exclusively close to Mondale, or to Senator Ted Kennedy, another person to whom he was linked.[11] He was appointed and was evidently trusted by Brzezinski. He did not have the personal relationship with the president that Bator once had with Johnson, but he would become just as tenacious a guardian of European policy, even though he found himself occasionally siding with the State Department in Brzezinski's absence.[12]

This combination left EUR playing second fiddle on most issues, namely, nuclear arms control, which was at the top of the Carter administration's agenda. As with the Kennedy and Johnson administrations, creative leadership in EUR managed to seize the occasional opportunity from the intersection of rivalries, but that was often difficult. For example, there was the Bureau of Political-Military Affairs (PM), now under Les Gelb, a political appointee who had been in Robert McNamara's Pentagon and would later achieve renown as a newspaper columnist and president of the Council on Foreign Relations. Gelb genuinely did represent the liberal wing of the Democratic Party and was particularly keen on SALT II. Gelb controlled this issue carefully. When Goodby proposed that the NATO mission oversee the upcoming Euromissile negotiations (see below), Gelb insisted it be managed by his office directly with the European capitals rather than leave it to the professional diplomats. He labeled the still ongoing MBFR talks, with some derision, a "negotiation with tradition."[13]

THESE WERE RELATIVELY QUIET, glum years in EUR that, like much of Europe itself, suffered from a "feeling of relative helplessness." "The early '70s were a high which was not borne out by events," noted one of its officers. "For most of the period since, Europe has been in a psychological trough."[14] The list of the Carter administration's initiatives and accomplishments in Europe pales in recent memory against its shortcomings, chief of which was Carter's dismal relationship with the German chancellor, Helmut Schmidt. Vest tried hard to mitigate the terrible conflict that had developed between the earnest Hamburger and the "extremely pedantic" president, to little avail. The tone of Carter's various letters to the condescending, exasperated Schmidt was dismissive, almost nonchalant, in spite of the chancellor's addressing Carter as "Dear Mr. President, dear Jimmy."[15] Schmidt was overheard in a moment of frustration: "I am very pro-American. I am much more pro-American than I am pro-British, and I have never really been pro-French. But Valéry [Giscard d'Estaing] is my only real friend."[16]

The two most contentious issues between them—the old, now reinvigorated, balance of payments problem and the East-West military balance—each played to Schmidt's intellectual strengths, for he had been both defense and finance minister, but also pointed to his country's relative dependence upon the United States. It was rather like a poorly drafted second act of the Kennedy-Macmillan relationship, only this time neither antagonist had a great deal of charm, or history, on his side. The more Carter seemed to give the appearance of deferring to Schmidt, the haughtier and more annoyed Schmidt would become with him. There was little anyone else could do about it, not least Brzezinski, who was probably just as poorly regarded by the German leader, though for different reasons.[17] Along with Brzezinski's hard-line views about the Soviets—which, to his but not to Carter's credit, proved justified—the Schmidt problem gave, if nothing else, the impression of a Polish foreign policy: anti-Russian, anti-German, and pro-French.[18] The effect it had upon transatlantic relations at this point in the Cold War was threefold: It puzzled and unnerved the Soviet leaders, who were also confronted in the strategic arms (SALT II) negotiation with some of the most accommodating American policies they had ever seen; it played for time, with MBFR and most Western economies lingering on unproductively; and it reserved the initiative on Europe to Margaret Thatcher, Ronald Reagan, and, eventually, Mikhail Gorbachev, while dissipating, one could argue, the energies of poor Helmut Schmidt.

EUR had little to do with any of it meaningfully until the very end of the 1970s. Vest was too much of a gentleman to wade deeply into the interoffice fray, prompting one subordinate to say, "George, it's great that we all love each other, but we need to win a few, too."[19] There was another reason for the bureau's imbalanced hand: staffing. The bureau's Soviet and German hands had long been respectful rivals. Since the 1950s, they resided in offices across the corridor from one another on the fourth floor, with the German office facing C Street overlooking the Lincoln Memorial and the Soviet hands facing inward. The Eastern European specialists tended to come from either one group or the other, and with the partial exception of Yugoslavia and Poland, each of which had its small group of experts, most of the rest "began babbling panslavic" after a while.[20] The effect of this, and the related need to liaison with more vocal ethnic lobbies in Congress, tended to blur their expertise, which, combined with the preeminence of Brzezinski and his staff, reduced their influence at the higher levels of the government until the 1980s. To a lesser extent the same was true of the Soviet hands, who nevertheless began to undergo something like a Renaissance. The majority of their German counterparts were posted in the field. Stuttgart, Düsseldorf, Bonn, Munich: These were all important, well-staffed posts. In EUR, however, the German Desk was tiny by comparison; it had only a handful of officers. By contrast, the Soviet Desk had at least three times as many officers in Washington, and their tours in Moscow tended to be short. Two Soviet hands in particular—John Evans and Sherrod McCall—took recruiting very seriously, modeling it either consciously or unconsciously on the tradition of Elwood Williams and Martin Hillenbrand in German affairs. "They put together a first-rate group," recalled one of the beneficiaries, E. Wayne Merry, "the finest cadre you can imagine ... that took us through the end of the Cold War into the post–Cold War world ... with the vision to make this all work."[21]

THERE WAS ANOTHER CRISIS on the horizon that would resurrect the ghosts of the European Defense Community (EDC) and Multilateral Nuclear Force (MLF). This was the saga of the so-called Euromissiles. In 1975, the Soviets deployed SS-20 intermediate-range missiles whose targets were exclusively European, a move that would ultimately prove "particularly disastrous" for the Soviets.[22] At first this did not provoke alarm in the United States—"[W]hat difference did it make if Paris was hit by an SS-20 or an SS-18?" asked Gelb's deputy and later successor in PM, Reggie Bartholomew—but it most certainly did in Europe, where leading politicians still reeled over Carter's dramatic reversal on the development of the neutron bomb.[23] In what would be a seminal speech at the International Institute for Strategic Studies in October 1977, Schmidt laid down the line: The SS-20s represented something altogether different.[24] Schmidt was "fed up with Brzezinski and Carter who had told [him] that the Russian SS-20s did not matter at all.... [T]hey did not understand that the SS-20 was a political threat, political blackmail against Germany most of all and later on against others in Europe.... Carter talked a lot of nonsense."[25] However, the Carter administration cared most about strategic arms control, notably the SALT II agreement and its ratification by the Senate, which turned out to be doomed, in good part because of its mishandling of other political-military issues like the SS-20s. So, after some hand-wringing, the Carter administration responded: NATO would install its own intermediate-range weapons in Europe, even though many experts, particularly in EUR, discounted their utility. "Under Kennedy, it was the multilateral force," wrote Jock Dean, "under Carter the INF deployment. But the basic mistake was to believe in a hardware fix." He continued:

> The new U.S. INF missiles are no more and no less likely to be used
> in the event of a Soviet attack in Europe than existing forward-based
> systems.... [T]o the contrary, the real basis for transatlantic coupling is
> the continued maintenance of equality with the Soviet Union in strategic
> nuclear forces, the maintenance of a close political relationship between
> U.S. and European leaders, and the retention of ground forces in Europe.[26]

Determining when, where, and how these Euromissiles were to be deployed was
another matter.

Negotiations among the NATO allies over that question would resemble the
earlier battles for the EDC and MLF, to the extent that American diplomacy
was mobilized in support of demands made, at least initially, by Europeans—
although the calculus of challenge and response was somewhat different in this
case. In the previous two instances, the call for a political-military program was
framed in terms of what would be best for the Alliance, with the Americans being
the primary boosters; here, the Europeans urged the Euromissiles upon their
disinterested American ally, but once the latter jumped on board, the Europeans
(again led by Schmidt) attached several conditions, namely, the so-called dual
track policy, requiring that deployment and arms control negotiations happen
simultaneously.[27] Here again, the "Americans said all right, we shall go along
for the sake of the alliance." Bartholomew, who led the team at State, "crossed
the Atlantic I don't know how many times" and ultimately succeeded in getting
NATO to agree in December 1979 to the dual track policy, even though it would
take nearly four years for the deployments to occur, during which period the issue
became highly politicized throughout Europe.[28] These years were a real "turning
point in East-West relations," not only because they reaffirmed the fact—which
had been overshadowed and underrecognized by SALT II—that the interests of
the Western European allies still counted but also because they gave the to-date
"infirm" American administration a renewed sense of purpose in Europe, thereby
setting the stage for the triumphs to come.[29] Reassuring the Europeans was
therefore critical, which forced through the most proactive, pro-European policy
since Helsinki. "[W]e gave in because the Europeans wanted it," Bartholomew
recalled, but "this was an American-driven effort ... with American weapons that
were being deployed."[30]

THE COLD WAR HAD BEEN reignited in Europe, not only militarily but also
politically, economically, and, above all, ideologically, by the time the Carter
administration left office. Enter Ronald Reagan. His language of rollback—not
heard to such an extent since the days of John Foster Dulles—worried many
members of the transatlantic establishment. To reassure them, perhaps, Reagan
named Nixon's former chief of staff and later NATO supreme allied commander,
Alexander Haig, as his first secretary of state. Haig knew many Europeans and
they knew him.[31] He seemed eager to surround himself with EUR loyalists. He
brought in as his undersecretary for political affairs none other than Walt Stoessel
and the department's old Republican protector, Larry Eagleburger, who replaced
Vest as assistant secretary of EUR. As soon as Stoessel moved up to the number

two position in the department the following year, Eagleburger replaced him as undersecretary. And so, for all that the Reagan administration—speaking mainly of the White House and Pentagon—were imagined to be fearsome foreign-policy radicals, the State Department seemed to rest in good, Atlanticist hands.[32]

If only it were that simple. Also lurking slightly offstage—in the restless Bureau of Political-Military Affairs, to be precise—was another figure. Richard Burt was a onetime journalist who had replaced Les Gelb as top national security correspondent at the *New York Times*, in which capacity Hodding Carter supposedly termed him the "open mouth on the running sore of the Brzezinski NSC."[33] He was a recognized expert on arms control, having once worked at the International Institute for Strategic Studies (where he edited its annual yearbook). Burt was tall, elegantly dressed, and bordering on the flamboyant; with the possible exception of Stoessel, nobody at State looked more debonair.

Burt gathered around him in PM and subsequently in EUR a group of officers known for their brilliance and tenacity: Jim Dobbins, Bob Blackwill, John Kelly, Richard Clarke, Arnold Kanter, Rand Beers, Richard Haass, and later Mark Palmer. They "were cocked and loaded, and could have taken on any bureau."[34] All would go on to have prominent careers. Nearly all were European hands, but of a different generation and disposition than Vest and his predecessors. Most had cut their teeth in their twenties and thirties working for Kissinger, Eagleburger, or Sonnenfeldt. Like their bosses, they were impatient, self-confident, resolute. To a certain extent they reminded one of Jock Dean and his generation of proconsuls close to power; but they were more overtly ideological and more attuned to the emerging media politics of the 1980s than their more workmanlike predecessors. To capture the genre of officer they represented, one thinks less about proconsuls, brooding analysts, or patient mediators, and instead is drawn back to someone like Bill Bullitt or forward to President Bill Clinton's troubleshooter, Richard Holbrooke. Within the department, such people were called, simply, "the elbows."[35]

They were remarkably effective. Vest, about to leave for Brussels as the U.S. representative to the European Communities, was among some in EUR who "did not cotton to Rick Burt."[36] Burt would carve out a near monopoly over political-military issues during the first half of 1981, leaving the others feeling rather frustrated on the sidelines, but also earning the respect of a few old hands like Goodby. At first, Eagleburger had gotten Haig's assurance that he, and not PM, would have the lead on NATO strategy, with the former taking charge only of its principal "client"—the Pentagon. Burt "took it like a man," recalled Bartholomew's former deputy, David Gompert, who went to work for Eagleburger, and the two offices functioned well together from then on. "Differences over turf are always bloodier than those over substance," Gompert added. "The latter are decided in a gentlemanly way."[37]

Alas, Eagleburger would move presently to the front office. Burt would go over to EUR and bring along his team "of barbarians on [their] shag ponies." For the first time in its history, the bureau had a nontraditional chief—a journalist! Not surprisingly, this was viewed by some in EUR as a "hostile takeover," recalled Avis Bohlen, the daughter of Chip and an arms-control specialist in RPM. For his part, Jim Dobbins noted that "moving to EUR with Burt was like the scene in the *Magnificent Seven* when the bandits ride out of town and then ride back in again."

In reality, the bark was worse than the bite. The rivalry between EUR's NATO office, RPM, and PM—the "elite within the elite"—seemed considerable at the time, but all were fundamentally on the same team. Burt may have been seen, in other, more pointed, words, as "an unmitigated schmuck on the side of the angels" but mainly because he had worse rivals, namely "Scoop's troops," led by the "other Richard," a man known then and later as the "Prince of Darkness": Senator Scoop Jackson's protégé, Richard Perle. Perle was all for the arms buildup but cared nothing about the Allies; indeed, he "loved to badger them."[38] Burt may also have "imagine[d] a grander role for himself," but for now he had to redouble efforts to assuage European concerns about the divisions within the American government.[39]

This meant, first and foremost, a successful negotiation of the Euromissile deployments. It was much harder than the decision itself; as Burt was known to joke with his predecessor at PM, Reggie Bartholomew, "you got the decision made but I got it done." For both men, the deployments had more value as a catalyst for "alliance management" (a term popularized by Burt) than they did intrinsically because, as Burt recalled, "[T]here was a need for constant psychotherapy."[40] His deputy, Jim Dobbins, recalled it similarly: "[O]ur job was to stay sensitive to [the Allies'] political needs while not skewed by our own. The bureaucracy was totally mobilized around this issue."[41] Ironically, the person who led most efforts to persuade the Europeans to embrace the Euromissile deployment had been one of its greatest skeptics, the perennial Washington presence, Paul Nitze. Nitze earlier had resigned as Nixon's top arms-control negotiator and then, after a public falling out with the Carter administration, became a committed opponent of SALT II, a role that culminated in Nitze's founding, with Gene Rostow, the Committee on the Present Danger, an important, informal brain trust for the Reagan ascendancy.[42] This would lead to a job as Reagan's top arms-control negotiator and an Indian summer for Nitze as well. (He was by now in his late seventies.) Yet Nitze, according to Burt, never really thought the Germans would deploy the Euromissiles—which accounted for Nitze's determination to reach an arms-control agreement with the Soviets as soon as possible and was probably why he took seriously the so-called zero option—stipulating the abandonment of such weapons on both sides, announced in November 1981.[43] The tactical and strategic elements of Nitze's mind were often difficult to disentangle; nobody will ever know what he really sought or why.[44] But the effect of all his ambiguity, at least for EUR and Burt, was to bolster their determination to get the European diplomacy right. In an almost poetic counterpose to Hugh Gibson's stance at Geneva sixty years before, rearmament would proceed as a collaborative effort among Europeans and Americans. Doing so would bring them that much closer together and would set the stage for the final confrontation, rapprochement, and drawdown with the Soviet Union. As to the actual negotiations—the "bizarre," "disordered puzzle"—they would culminate in December 1987 in a treaty that brought about the dismantling of all intermediate and shorter-range land-based weapons on all sides.[45] Zero was no longer just an option.

Whether this had been the conscious aim of Burt, Schmidt, or any of the other proponents of the dual track is difficult to prove. But it is more or less what happened. Meanwhile, a new secretary entered the scene. Haig, having opposed the zero option and mishandled his relations with the White House, proved an early victim of the Reagan administration's backbiting. After nearly a year of unpalatable and unflattering distractions—over the Falkland Islands, the Soviet pipeline, and a would-be presidential assassin—he was replaced by Shultz. Shultz's public service dated from the Eisenhower administration; in addition to his two cabinet posts, he had also been the director of the Office of Management and Budget (OMB). With the possible exceptions of Elihu Root and George Marshall, no man would come to the secretaryship with so much prior experience in the executive branch. Yet Shultz, in addition to being a marine veteran and college football star, was also an academic economist, dean of the University of Chicago Business School, and a corporate chief executive, which taught him the importance of an effective structure and training. He was, in a word, not only smart and capable but also uncommonly wise and well rounded. Few in his position were ever so trusted by the president, beloved by the bureaucracy, and versed in the ways of administration.[46] Even the physical premises looked brighter. The seventh floor of the State Department "had just been completely rebuilt in grand colonial style," overseen intermittently by Shultz himself.[47] He went so far as to solicit Joe Alsop's views on the right books to display in a new diplomatic library and had his assistant, Charlie Hill, rearrange the office portraits, replacing Acheson's with that of "the unrecognized greatest Secretary of State ... of all: William Henry Seward."[48]

Shultz's thinking favored Europe; his hierarchical mind had a strongly geographical cast, so for him the Cold War in Europe, and the superpower relationship, always mattered most, followed by the cultivation of cooperation among the most developed economies (basically Europe plus Japan), which had been a priority since his founding the Library Group, mentioned in the previous chapter. Indeed, Shultz's preferred metaphor for diplomacy was the one used by Marshall and Kennan: gardening. Less self-conscious a tactician than Kissinger or Shultz's successor, James Baker, Shultz was, at least implicitly, more strategically minded and ostensibly diligent. He could be quiet, at times impenetrable, but he was never devious. His staff saw him as trustworthy, straightforward, and lucid. Those who knew him best also recognized that he could be very firm.[49]

EUR was a special beneficiary of his tenure. Once again it had a secretary who carried weight with the president; Reagan came to trust and listen to Shultz more than anyone besides the first lady, whom Shultz cultivated skillfully. And he came at precisely the right time: Europe was in need of attention, the Cold War was shifting into a higher gear, and Reagan was about to lead the infamous "turn" away from confrontation and toward assertive diplomacy. How much of it came from his (and Nancy Reagan's) inner convictions will long be a subject for historical speculation. To some people at the time, Reagan's interest in negotiations appeared at first to be poorly thought out, even insincere. From the point of EUR, however, there was more continuity than change in Reagan's position, so long as it was understood as combining elements of both strength and the willingness to negotiate. Since virtually the beginning of his first term, Reagan stated a faith in the power and promise of a negotiated "solution" with the Soviets.[50] A boost came from Margaret Thatcher when she said, famously, that the West could do business with Gorbachev. This disarmed the ideologues in the Reagan administration who insisted that allies and negotiations were indicators of weakness.[51] By the end of 1983, then, Shultz was able to conclude that

our moves in arms control negotiations had been well timed. Our INF
[Euromissile] deployments had begun. Our allies were with us. The
Soviets had suffered a severe propaganda defeat throughout Europe.
Now it was time for us to try to resume a dialogue with the Soviets if we
could.... With deployments under way, our position was one of strength.
We had started the year 1983 with Soviet threats and efforts to decouple
the United States from our European allies. We ended the year with our
alliance stronger than ever, forged by a common effort that proceeded
under conditions of enormous tension.[52]

Planning began in earnest during the fall of that year. Shultz convened at
Reagan's behest a secret "Soviet Core Group," also called the Saturday Group,
including himself; Vice President Bush; Robert "Bud" McFarlane and Jack
Matlock from the National Security Council; Burt, Eagleburger, and Art Hartman
from the State Department; Robert Gates from the CIA; and Brent Scowcroft,
then out of government. The group's discussions were characterized by their
conservatism about the Soviet Union: Eagleburger and Burt, for example,
stressed in discussions that "our dialogue is like ships passing in the night" and
that little progress should be expected with strategic arms talks. At the same
time, "forcing collapse of the Soviet system (as distinct from exerting pressure
on Soviets to live up to agreements and abide by civilized standards of behavior)"
was an intentionally "missing element" from the policy. So much for Reagan's
resuscitation of rollback.[53] The new three-part approach to the Soviets—"realism,
strength, dialogue"—was premised on the Soviet "threat" lasting for a very long
time; yet the thrust of the new thinking in the Reagan administration was all
about making progress, even on the margins, and gaining advantage. "We have
arrested U.S. decline and are in strong negotiating position," one paper noted.
"Soviets are on diplomatic defensive and have growing problems at home."[54] But
there remained many doubts about the best approach.

Overseeing the process on the National Security Council was "Jumping Jack"
Matlock. Matlock was a foreign service officer with long experience in both the
Bureau of Intelligence and Research (INR) and on the Soviet Union Desk (SOV),
and a well-versed scholar of Russia. Born in modest circumstances in Greensboro,
North Carolina, Matlock had been interested in Russia from a very young age,
although his attempts to learn the language then foundered because "there was
no one in Greensboro to tell me how to pronounce the letters, so I could not
even memorize the alphabet." He did not give up. After arriving at Duke and
finding himself "stirred" by Crime and Punishment "as no other book," Matlock
went on to Columbia, studied for a doctorate in Russian literature, and published
a book, an index to the collected works of J. V. Stalin. After a brief teaching job at
Dartmouth College, he joined the foreign service and rose up through the ranks
of Soviet hands following service in Africa.[55] Brought to the NSC to succeed the
purged hard-liners and to educate Reagan, Matlock wasted little time in taking
charge. He would later insist that nearly all the policy direction came from the
White House; EUR was, according to him, "insufficiently appreciative of the
pressure to change," but once change began to happen, "they were enthusiastic
implementers."[56]

THE NEW SOVIET GENERAL SECRETARY greeted Shultz and Vice President George H. W. Bush following the funeral of Gorbachev's predecessor, Konstantin Chernenko, in March 1985. There, in St. Catherine's Hall at the heart of the Kremlin, "a stunning reminder of past grandeur, with three gilded bronze chandeliers, green malachite columns from the Ural Mountains and replicas of the emblem of the Order of St. Catherine," Shultz took measure of the "confident but not overbearing" Russian leader. According to an aide's notes, Gorbachev seemed "businesslike and bright ... can be provoked but keeps control ... not just an empty guy but full of content. Very different kind of person from others."[57] Shultz was similarly pleased by the new Soviet foreign minister, the unknown Georgian, Eduard Shevardnadze, who replaced the ancient Andrei Gromyko that July and gave a different, livelier impression right away. No longer would Shultz have to wonder if there was not "something better I can do with my life than meet with that son of a bitch"; at long last "Mr. Nyet" was gone.[58]

The climax came in two superpower summits in 1985 and 1986. The first, in Geneva's Maisons Fleur d'Eau and de Saussure, resulted in a tentative agreement to work toward reducing strategic nuclear arsenals by 50 percent, and a joint statement, negotiated by Ridgway, that signaled, in her words, "a very deliberate change in language and content to get away from paragraphs covering fundamental disagreements and different definitions of invented phrases; you will not find 'peaceful coexistence' or 'détente' thereafter." Shultz may have affirmed his prediction that Gorbachev would "blink," but Reagan seemed mainly interested in getting Gorbachev to like and trust him. With regard to their predecessors, "they had little practice, since they had never done it before," Reagan noted after dinner on the second night. "Nevertheless, having read the history of previous summit meetings he had concluded that those earlier leaders had not done very much.... 'To hell with the past,' we'll do it our way and get something done."[59]

The second, at Reykjavik, went even further. At these meetings, Ridgway approached the negotiations with her counterpart, Alexander Bessmertnykh, vertically, lining up American interests in succession rather than trading one off the other, which had been the custom at previous summits. The Soviet side would occasionally attempt to attach additional items to the agenda (e.g., an aviation agreement), prompting Ridgway to threaten to walk out and forcing Shultz to intervene directly with Gorbachev to keep his team in line. It was this kind of methodical discipline, in contrast with the freewheeling tactics of Kissinger, that Ridgway credited with solving the range of issues, large and small. "Maybe because I was in fish I knew that the last small fish really mattered," she later recalled. "There is *never* a small issue. They always come back to haunt and become big issues, and they can kill an agreement."[60]

Expectations for Reykjavik had been low. Even Nancy stayed home. Donald Regan, the president's chief of staff, said that it was only a preparatory meeting and would "be considered successful if no more was accomplished than agreement for a Reagan-Gorbachev summit in Washington." This failed to acknowledge how truly desperate Gorbachev was for an agreement. Indeed, the planning papers for the meeting appeared to make the opposite assumption.[61] Working parallel to Ridgway on the military side was Nitze, upon whom Shultz relied heavily because he was probably the only senior official trusted by both arms-control skeptics and

the Soviets. The negotiations took place at Hofdi House, a stark white building
that had once been a French and British consulate (established, incidentally, to
assist fishermen). Nitze and his Soviet counterpart, Marshal Sergei Akhromeyev,
worked on one floor, Ridgway and Sasha Bessmertnykh on the other. The
talks there culminated with a tense back-and-forth exchange between Reagan
and Gorbachev that resulted in a proposal—far too serious, it would seem—to
eliminate *all* nuclear weapons, although Gorbachev insisted that Reagan's pet
project, the Strategic Defense Initiative (SDI), also be confined to the laboratory.
Here the drama ended. Reagan was firm and walked away. Matlock's reaction was
typical: "I rushed to the car assigned me in the motorcade and sank into the rear
seat in a blue funk. How could Shultz have let that happen? ... Why had Shultz
been so obtuse?"[62]

How indeed? But Shultz, like his chief, was steadfast. He told the press,
"[S]ound policies got us to the results evident in Reykjavik and so we will
continue with the policies." The "administration," he added, "entered office with
its eyes open regarding [the] Soviet Union.... [T]he outcome was extraordinary
... the Soviets learned [that the] President won't compromise his conscience
or U.S. security for a quick deal." As to public perceptions, particularly in Europe, one administration official noted with apparent pleasure back in Geneva
that "Gorbachev's evident determination to restrain SDI reinforces Europeans'
impression of SDI as a useful prod, if not an outright bargaining chip." Shultz's
aide Charlie Hill put it even more bluntly: "1. It failed. 2. It achieved a lot. 3. Oh
no! It achieved a lot."[63] Nonetheless, Ridgway and Nitze were "very lonely at Reykjavik," having received little support from Washington or from the Allies, who
were in "deep desperation."[64] Nearly everyone criticized the summit, prompting
Ridgway to say, much later, that one simply needs to wait around long enough
"until your own version of history is written." Reykjavik would eventually be rated
a resounding success. Looking back, she concluded modestly, "It is hard to say
how much of a role EUR had in getting us to 1989. The EUR view was always, to
my knowledge, one of favoring dialogue and seeking opportunities to weaken the
hold of the USSR over Europe.... But at the end of the day it was determined by
Reagan, Gorbachev, Thatcher and Shultz.... [E]ach piece made it possible; it would
not have happened if any of the pieces had been missing."[65]

TWO MORE OF THOSE PIECES deserve mention. Francis Bator's old program of
bridge building—described in Chapter 8—finally got going in earnest. Under the
direction of Deputy Secretary of State John Whitehead (formerly of Citibank) and
Ridgway's deputy, Tom Simons, the administration paid regular visits to Eastern
Europe and raised the profile of reformers there, including support for Poland's
Solidarity and related movements. These efforts—and the principle that underlaid
them—followed on the earlier visits of Goodby and John Kornblum under CSCE
auspices noted in Chapter 9 and had been given a particular boost by Brzezinski's
deliberate efforts in the Carter years to redefine détente as a "mixed" policy
that "combines elements of both competition and cooperation" and is "both
more comprehensive and more reciprocal." To skeptics who suggested that such
actions would vitiate the Reagan administration's other aims, Shultz defended the
maximalist position with a strategy of "build[ing] the walls brick by brick, and the

roof comes later."[66] Ridgway once described the approach similarly:

> [I]n any negotiation, if you're going to do it as a card game, you not only know your cards, you pretty much know the other guy's cards. It's like a master level bridge thing. You know where the cards are on the table. You practically play the game with the cards face up, because after enough encounters you know what they are. And the difference is that in the diplomatic game, after the cards are played, if one party takes all the coins off the table, that's a bad outcome. You sort of have to end up as a tie at the end of overtime and you split the pot, because otherwise you can't take it home.[67]

A related effort was the Committee on Disarmament in Europe (CDE) negotiation in Stockholm, where the United States was represented by Goodby.[68] These talks, also an outgrowth of the CSCE described in the previous two chapters, involved a range of "confidence building measures" that the Soviets "seem[ed] to prefer" over the MBFR and the strategic arms negotiations, which by now had moved from limitations to reductions (SALT to START). CDE formalized things like joint notification of maneuvers, limitations on their size and location, and provisions for inspection and observation.[69] The CDE, like the less successful MBFR, served, in a quiet, instrumental way to establish a common denominator of dialogue across Europe, which helped to offset the unpredictable character of the summits and strategic arms negotiations, particularly for the Eastern Europeans. The short-term result of both efforts was to hold the Soviets' feet to the fire, which gained time, built trust, and raised expectations for liberalization in Eastern Europe and in the USSR itself. The longer-term impact was to bolster the attainment of a unified, peaceful continent with an American presence. Ultimately, it was an indirect but effective policy. Gorbachev, possibly realizing where things were headed, exclaimed in 1986, "Who do you Americans think you are ? ... [You] won't allow us to have the same global role that you have. The world can't be just the way you want it to be ... there are other people in it."[70] The diplomatic record of these years suggests that even he had become fatalistic. But few at the time understood how desperate his situation really was.[71]

The scene was set, as we now know, for the end of the Cold War, meaning the reunification of Germany and the demise of the Soviet Union itself. The two events were not necessarily coterminous in the eyes of EUR. Ridgway, for example, rated German reunification a longer-term possibility before she left office; she certainly did not consider it to be desirable, or likely, anytime soon.[72] Virtually nobody expected the Soviet Union to collapse as quickly as it did; if anybody had in EUR, it is almost inconceivable that they would have endorsed the outcome as being in anybody's immediate interest.

Ridgway would retire from the foreign service soon after the first Bush administration took over. During the previous couple of years, the foreign policy machinery had come to perform exceptionally well. Shultz had carved out a role for himself akin to Acheson's as the president's top foreign-policy lieutenant. Frank Carlucci (the hero of Portugal discussed in the previous chapter) was national security adviser and later secretary of defense; Colin Powell, an army officer and future secretary of state, was deputy to Carlucci and then replaced him as national security adviser. "The Carlucci-Powell-Shultz team worked excellently," recalled Simons, who, along with Matlock, was the principal notetaker at Reykjavik and had also once been a deputy to Jock Dean. "The line went directly from Reagan through the NSC to Shultz to me. It was a straightline hierarchy ... [although] it took some work to keep even that straight."[73]

Baker subsequently dismantled not only that hierarchy but also the close relationship between the bureaus and the Secretariat. His council seemed less an "inner circle" than "a trapezoid," according to EUR's chief, Ray Seitz, yet the gap between the seventh floor and the bureaus was greater than it had been at any point since the Dulles years.[74] Baker was a Texas lawyer who came to State by way of the White House, where he had been Reagan's chief of staff, and the Treasury Department, where he had been secretary. Accustomed to a different set of practices than Shultz, he centralized policymaking in his office with his own small group of deputies, who worked very closely with counterparts at the National Security Council. They would prove a remarkably effective team in managing diplomacy during the climactic days of 1989 and the dawn of a "Europe, whole and free."[75]

But those events open another story. Just as the precise origins of the Cold War will be debated for a long time to come, so too will its termination. Competing chronologies—1962, 1975, 1989, 1991—have much to do with debates over the nature of the conflict itself in all its military, political, ideological, socioeconomic, and "structural" dimensions.[76] On the ground, however, the end of the story was more immediate. When the Wall fell, it finally seemed conceivable, even likely, that Germany, and Europe itself, would come together. This represented something more than a Cold War victory; to those with a sense of history, it was nothing less than the culmination of nearly a century of American and European efforts to forge a united, peaceful continent, "the apotheosis of everything we'd been striving to achieve."[77] Even George Kennan was roused from his long semi-retirement at Princeton to reaffirm that, at long last, the age of Wilson was finally upon us.

Cold War triumphalists have argued that it was Reagan's shrewdly administered brinkmanship, followed by his manipulation of Soviet vulnerabilities, that "won" the Cold War. Others have argued persuasively that it was Mikhail Gorbachev who simply forfeited, and that he joined with Reagan to bring it to a peaceful end in a manner that reminded Art Hartman (present at the summits in his capacity as ambassador to the USSR) of Jean Monnet's favorite tactic of having one's adversary move from across the table to the same side, with the two solving the problem together.[78] Both renditions, however, minimize the critical role of other Europeans. It was the Poles, Hungarians, and their neighbors who pushed Soviet prestige and power to the brink of collapse in the early 1980s, emboldened no doubt by the dramatic flourishing of "Helsinki Watch Groups" mentioned above; it was eventually the Russians themselves who brought about the final end of the Soviet Union little less than a decade later. And, of course, it was the Germans, sitting at the heart of Europe and the Cold War, who tore down their own wall in 1989.

And it was EUR that held the line within the U.S. government in favor of keeping the Europeans and their concerns at the forefront of superpower diplomacy during this critical time, which shaped the circumstances that made all the rest possible. It was plain that the Soviet Union could not divide the West against itself as it had done so successfully elsewhere in the world, and nearly got away with doing in Europe until the early 1960s. It was also clear that no European settlement could be imposed from above; superpower diplomacy made it possible, but it could not happen unless Europeans took part as willing participants. This was why alliance management in the 1980s was so important and why the publicity given to Rick Burt's efforts, despite the ill taste it may have left in the mouths of his many detractors, was so well suited to the times. The Europeans had to be and feel part of the process; they had to subordinate their individual interests to the general interest, or at least come to see them as mutually consistent; and they had to lead, as Gibson, Bruce, Camps, Goodby, and many other European hands had long insisted.[79] This was the essence of Atlanticism. In this instance, finally, it brought forth an exceptional result.

Arthur Hartman and George Shultz with Ronald Reagan
Bettmann/Corbis

12

CODA

S INCE THE FALL OF THE BERLIN WALL, Europe has come together
politically and culturally, yet it remains, in the apt description of historian
Tony Judt, "a Europe of the mind ... this hyper-real Europe, more European than
the continent itself."[1] There is still no consensus, either within Europe or beyond,
over its boundaries and its role in the world. To those Americans who helped
to devise NATO's post–Cold War accommodation of the former Warsaw Pact—
which went by the unfortunate name of "Partnership for Peace"—the idea of
Europe was decidedly aterritorial, and in some respects harkened back to the
earliest American notions of the Old World noted at the beginning of this book.[2]
Europe was simply everything over there; whichever country met the criteria and
wanted to join its ranks ought to be free to do so.

No doubt many Europeans saw the issue differently, not least those who
suffered most from the wars of Yugoslav succession in the 1990s, in which, after
its own prolonged period of hand-wringing, the United States intervened in
the form of NATO's first armed action in its fifty-year history. Indeed, bombs
were falling on Belgrade as the scaled-back anniversary ceremonies began in
Washington.

In the meantime, the Alliance admitted several new members, not only every
former Warsaw Pact country (minus some of the Yugoslav successors) but also
the former Baltic republics of the former Soviet Union. To those who recalled
the promises made to Gorbachev in order to see through a peaceful but rather
tumultuous and quick process of German reunification, NATO's enlargement
was something of a shock. The full set of reasons for it, and their effects, await a
decent historical interval to be understood. But suffice it to say, by the end of the
first decade of the twenty-first century, Europe, although its center was no longer
"disenfranchised and unstable," was neither whole nor entirely free.[3]

EUR ITSELF SOLDIERED ON through the Bush I, Clinton, and Bush II administrations. Midway through Clinton's, it lost Canada to a new Western Hemisphere Bureau and gained nearly all the states of the former Soviet Union because Senator Jesse Helms, the recalcitrant chair of the Senate Foreign Relations Committee, announced that Russia should be treated like any other European country and therefore should no longer have its own special "ambassador-at-large." Once the desk officers for the other former Soviet states protested that being in a separate bureau from Russia would make their jobs nearly impossible, the department decided to establish a new Bureau for European and Eurasian Affairs. Thus, Iceland sat within the same bureaucratic unit as Kyrgyzstan, or at least it did until 2001 and the second Bush administration's focus on Central and South Asia led to yet another redrawing of the map.[4]

Back on Western European desks, the twentieth century seemed like a long time ago indeed. European integration by now was an arcane topic for technicians. It appeared to interest almost nobody else. Marty Hillenbrand wrote in 1994 to his old colleague and occasional jousting partner, Bob Schaetzel:

> I share your impression that no one in the State Department or the White House, at least at the policy-making level, has much regard for or even interest in the European Union and all it symbolizes. As current fashions go, Europe is definitely at the bottom of the heap. In post-modern academic circles, white European males and their history are regarded as anathema. I fear that some of this academic disparagement of Europe in the pursuit of multiculturalism has rubbed off on the Clintonites just as it has been reflected in the appointment record of the administration.[5]

Both would die less than a decade later.

IF SUCH GRUMBLING WAS reminiscent of the 1960s, it was not entirely accidental. The so-called sixties generation had reached maturity and the peak of its power; it was, again, the new establishment during a period of great prosperity when the potential for American leadership seemed limitless. Clinton's second secretary of state, Madeleine Albright, herself a refugee from Europe and one of the most fervent backers of NATO enlargement, declared at this time that the United States was the world's "indispensable power." Maybe so. Europe, whatever its state of flux, remained ambivalent about its global role and seemed to suffer from a "want of will."[6] All too often willpower came down to a certain clarity of vision. There still were some who imagined Europe's role to be that of an incipient competitor to America; others, such as the popular writer Robert Kagan, cast it in a more romantic but not necessarily flattering light, as Venus to America's Mars. Of the various contending abstractions, the old Atlanticist notion of a single community of like-minded states seemed to be the least headline-grabbing and most remote as the nostalgic residue of an orderly, manageable, and vanished world.

There will probably never be another Atlantic Century. But old habits, institutions, and relationships die hard. The achievements of four generations of very talented people have not been lost forever.

AMERICAN DIPLOMACY nonetheless appears less Eurocentric than it did even a decade ago. Understanding the reasons for this poses a tougher set of questions. Have the ways we measure the geopolitical proclivities of those in power changed? Or have we gone full circle back to America's westward (as in Pacific) orientation of the nineteenth century? If we look at trends in tourism, in cultural exchanges of various kinds, in commercial relationships, and so forth, we can make a strong case for a Janus-faced turn to the Pacific, beginning sometime in the 1980s and accelerating since. But Europe has hardly disappeared from the American consciousness.[7] Nor has it metamorphosed into a caricature of its literary past as the American secretary of defense, Donald Rumsfeld, in a more controversial incarnation than he had earlier in this volume, notoriously labeled it in 2003 as "old" and "new" Europe. Such so-called structural explanations for the rupture of relationships oversimplify and exaggerate the reality of human experience, and too often depict international politics as more akin to physics than chemistry. That is not how most diplomats are trained to think, nor how most people live. Whether Atlanticism will survive, let alone thrive, for another century is unknowable; its present and future value should not be dismissed in the name of historical inevitability.

Some will suspect from such language that this story is meant to be Atlanticism's epitaph. I pray not. Its future still depends as much on the people who aim to sustain it as it does on their leaders and the conditions of the world. Of course it has a great deal to do with the future contours of Europe itself. Should NATO, for example, finally succumb to the predictions of several decades and cease to exist with its current geographical delimitation, either by evolving into the world's peacekeeping agency of last resort or by a more sudden disappearance, then "Europe" in the form of the European Union will face two especially well armed yet insecure neighbors—Russia and Turkey—as well as a number of tough adjustments at home. How long can it realistically expect to survive as prosperous and united while nominally excluding both powers from its inner councils? Perhaps more to the point, how much longer can the leaders of the EU, along with those in the United States, NATO, and Russia, continue to delay the long overdue post–Cold War redefinition of their mutual relationship?[8]

AT SUCH MOMENTS OF DOUBT it is tempting to recall the opening lines of Garrett Mattingly's great life of Catherine of Aragon, written during the bleak days of 1940: "Some characters appear to triumph with history; some to be overwhelmed by it."[9] EUR certainly found itself in the former category, which leads us to a somewhat different question: Who most shapes success? The people, the policies, or the events that demand attention? It is good to recall that there are several ways to write history: from the bottom up or top down, or from the inside out, or outside in, or in some combination thereof. The historian, moreover, may focus upon what social scientists call "outcomes": the decisions, actions, and their effects; or upon the "inputs": the sources of intelligence, pressure groups (both foreign and domestic), public opinion, calculations of perception and misperception. These subjects have been at the center of inquiry ever since Leopold von Ranke established diplomatic history as a professional field of study in the mid-nineteenth century. However, the preponderance of this work, like most historical inquiry, hovers over the impossibility of knowing the real motives and motivations for action. The temptation to conclude what this or that person "believed" is particularly strong for diplomatic historians. The written record is simply enormous. It teems with justification and refutation. Yet the first lesson to learn for any civil servant or historian is that no single document has significance outside of the setting in which it was written, just as events have no historical meaning apart from the people who produce them.

In the preceding pages, I have made the case that EUR and its networks of influence had much to do with its accomplishments. They came down to more than multiple instances of being in the right place at the right time, for as much as that mattered (as many from Jimmy Dunn, Alexander Kirk, and Doc Matthews to Miriam Camps, David Klein, and Roz Ridgway would attest), it was a necessary but not a sufficient causal factor. The most important factor of all was the more nebulous one called orientation, persuasion, creed, or, to use the French cultural term, *mentalité*—in other words, the ineffable yet powerful force of Atlanticism itself. Having originated with the American historical consciousness as both stepchild and savior of the Old World, it spread throughout the body politic at the turn of the last century and came to thrive in the cauldron of war. It left deep roots that are no less significant for being less visible than leaders or less measurable than political and economic trends. For America's common cause with Europe, once a mere preference, rated, by the end of the century, nothing less than an axiom.

It would not go unchallenged, of course, and began, by century's end, to dwindle. But it has still proved remarkably durable. One reason is that its proponents mastered the machinery of diplomacy so well—not only the office flowcharts and budgets but also the informal alignments and allegiances, mentorship and patronage networks, and interwoven personal and professional relationships that defined the transatlantic world. The link between such networks and the collective, geopolitical mind was more organic than dialectical.

In other words, the innate sense of place, of rootedness, and of fluency—cultural, familial, social, spiritual—fed the kinds of associations and relationships these diplomats sought, which in turn defined and redefined the manner by which they situated themselves in the world. International networks—even virtual ones—did not negate a sense of territory; they reinforced it. Boundaries and borderlands did not disappear; they were redrawn.[10] The sense of territory wove together the professional and personal elements of their history and underwrote their common culture. Of all the motivational factors speculated upon in this book, the territorial imperative drove them the hardest: the fulfillment of a certain geographic destiny, not merely in serving where they wanted but also in seeing their desired geopolitical ends emerge through their own efforts over time in what for many of them was a lifelong crusade.

EUR therefore came to resemble something greater than a club—even a meritocratic club, although it certainly had its exclusionary tendencies. Rather, it was a society. Like most social organisms, it had its high and low elements, its outcasts, its environment or "turf," its pecking order, its fluctuating standards. In this respect, that society is no longer with us. Today's government and diplomatic corps are both very different than they were even a mere generation ago. Whereas the opportunities for public service have grown more diverse in both form and substance, much continuity has been lost to political turnover. Of course this sort of thing has long been a feature of American official life, but it was only during the Dulles years that it became more or less the norm at State. Today, nearly everyone down to the level of deputy assistant secretary, even office director, is a political appointee. Many come from the semipermanent class of Washington policy artists whose priorities, almost by definition, are drawn in contradistinction to those of their immediate predecessors. Meanwhile, the full-time "professionals" have become ever more specialized. John Kornblum, one of the last of the storied twentieth-century German hands, foresaw its coming:

> Since the more traditional skills of analysis and reporting were identified with the *old* elitest [sic] concept of the foreign service, they were consciously downgraded in favor of the more modern approaches, i.e. management and various "technical" specialities. For several years, young foreign service officers have been warned that there is no future in being a purely substantive officer, especially in the political field and especially in the more developed countries.[11]

Some diplomats, it must be admitted, will always be burdened with a snobbish reputation, and EUR has been particularly susceptible. Indeed, one longtime China hand suggested this book be entitled "Ingrown Tweed."[12] The stereotype contains an element of truth. It was not merely the result of bureaucratic prestige and priorities having been directed toward Europe. (The effect of that on other areas of the bureaucracy and upon the diplomatic record is a related, but different, question.) Many European hands were snobs, and proud ones. Roz Ridgway liked to say, "I suppose we are arrogant but I think we've earned it."[13] That was the point. They had high standards of conduct and judgment, and worked hard to pass them on to successors. This is the common element revealed in their histories. Many mention this or that great event they happened to witness or partake in, but most emphasize the continuity of their careers—that is, how one kind of assignment prepared them for another—and their education at the hands of older, more experienced officers. Recalling that the first generation of professional diplomats only got going in the late 1920s, one cannot overestimate the salience, and the overlapping, of legacies. Even as late as the 1980s, very few European hands were more than one or two generational steps removed from the founders. Ridgway, for example, joined the foreign service while Doc Matthews and Livie Merchant still walked the halls. Hugh Gibson remained professionally active (working for the United Nations) until the mid-1950s. John McCloy, who first made a name for himself investigating sabotage by German agents during World War I, was called upon several times by Alexander Haig for advice. The list of examples goes on. That may be true for most professions. But few have had so illustrious a history in so brief a time as EUR. Its legacy from the twentieth century is of a more refined, more creative, more dexterous era. Its commitment and contribution to Europe mark our diplomacy's finest hour.

ONE OF THE MORE ACTIVE recent promoters of "Atlantic history," the historian Bernard Bailyn, has taught that the field owes much of its prominence to contemporary political imperatives.[14] The same may be true of this conclusion.

And yet today's use of the term "Atlanticist," which has come merely to signify pro-American Europeans and their American abettors, oversimplifies the idea's political dimension and overlooks many of its important cultural and social tenets, particularly those having to do with the tone, texture, and nuances of diplomacy. The Atlantic is a special kind of community; its character derives from a blend of the past and future, the regional and global realms of national power, and the European and American traditions. One can recall the advice of Russell Leffingwell at the beginning of this book; it appears again and again, here, for example, in the words of John Foster Dulles, explaining why "we do take a special interest in Europe":

> What is it that Americans want? [Not] world mastery.... [Not] a place ... to dump our surplus goods.... American hopes as regards Europe are precisely the opposite of those which unfriendly sources impute to us. We want Europe to have so much political strength that neither the United States nor any other power whatsoever will ever be able to use Europe for purposes alien to the free development of Europe itself.... We want Europe to be sufficiently unified so that, practically, we can work with it.... We want a Europe which will again produce great literature, music, and art and such religious movements as have, in the past, inspired and enriched the world.[15]

Back to this story's protagonists. It has become fashionable again since the end of the Cold War to speak of transformations in history and politics. These diplomats and civil servants made possible one of the most momentous of such transformations—amounting to the near merging of continents and centuries—but succeeded precisely because they did not proclaim, or even fully recognize, the extent of their accomplishment. There was always another problem to manage, another aggrieved party to assuage, another job to do. Grand strategies were better left to politicians or generals, as Lord Salisbury once noted, with maps of too small a scale. If diplomats knew anything, it was that the world would remain, for the foreseeable future, a large, complicated, difficult place. The twentieth century saw it grow smaller, to be sure, but it would not be one world for a long time to come, probably never. To presume otherwise would be to commit the diplomatic professional's greatest sin: the confusion of means and ends. For them, the ends were the same as they had always been: to serve their country, and to preserve peace.

APPENDIX

I. POLITICAL CHRONOLOGY

1909   Geographic divisions founded
        Western European Affairs: Great Britain (including Canada, Australia,
        New Zealand, and all British colonies); Portugal, Spain, France, Morocco,
        Belgium, the Congo, Switzerland, Norway, Sweden, the Netherlands,
        Luxembourg, Denmark, and Liberia
        Secretary of state: Philander C. Knox
1917   United States enters the Great War
        Secretary of state: Robert Lansing
1919   Division of Russian Affairs founded
        President Wilson travels to France for Peace Conference
1920   Secretary of state: Bainbridge Colby
1921   Secretary of state: Charles Evans Hughes
1922   Russian Affairs becomes Division of Eastern European Affairs; given
        jurisdiction over Russia, the Baltic States, Finland and Poland
        Western European Affairs also now includes Austria, Czechoslovakia,
        Germany, Hungary, Irish Free State, Italy, international organizations
        based in Europe, and European possessions in Asia (until 1974, the Balkan
        states remain in Near Eastern Affairs, as do Greece, Turkey, and Cyprus)
1924   Dawes Plan unveiled
        Disarmament commission meets in Geneva
        Rogers Act passes
1925   Secretary of state: Frank Kellogg
1927   Naval disarmament talks begin
1929   Secretary of state: Henry Stimson
        Young Plan unveiled
1932   Disarmament talks restart at Geneva, last through 1937
1933   Secretary of state: Cordell Hull
        Normalization of diplomatic relations with Soviet Union
        London Economic Conference
1936   Spanish Civil War, through 1939
1937   Eastern and Western Divisions united under new Division of European
        Affairs
1939   Invasion of Poland
1940   Welles mission
        Fall of France
1941   Lend-Lease begins
        United States enters World War II
1942   North African invasion; "Vichy gamble"
1943   European Division renamed Office of European Affairs
        Bullitt/Welles purge

1944	D-Day invasion
	Secretary of state: Edward Stettinius Jr.
1945	Yalta and Potsdam Conferences
	First meeting of the Council of Foreign Ministers, last sporadically until 1959
	Secretary of state: James F. Byrnes
1947	Truman Doctrine and Marshall Plans announced
	Secretary of state: George Marshall
1948	Organization for European Economic Cooperation (OEEC) founded
	Berlin airlift
1949	Office renamed Bureau of European Affairs
	North Atlantic Pact signed
	Secretary of state: Dean Acheson
1950	Korean War begins, lasts until 1953
	Plans for European Defense Community initiated
1951	European Coal and Steel Community established (Treaty of Paris)
1953	Secretary of state: John Foster Dulles
1954	Berlin and Geneva Conferences
	European Defense Community rejected by the French National Assembly
	Wriston Report released
1956	Suez, Hungary crises
1957	Treaty of Rome
1958	Berlin crisis begins anew
1959	Secretary of state: Christian Herter
	Planning begins for Multilateral Nuclear Force
1961	Berlin wall constructed
	Secretary of state: Dean Rusk
	Atlantic Council of the United States incorporated
	OEEC becomes OECD
1962	Cuban missile crisis
	Rambouillet/Nassau meetings
1963	De Gaulle rejects British application to Common Market
1964	Kennedy Round of trade talks begins in earnest, through 1967
	Lyndon Johnson kills the MLF
1965	United States escalates military involvement in Vietnam
1966	De Gaulle withdraws France from NATO military command
1968	Soviet Invasion of Czechoslovakia
	Nuclear Non-Proliferation Treaty signed
1969	Budapest appeal
	Berlin quadripartite talks begin
	NATO December communiqué mentions "free movement"
	Secretary of state: William Rogers
1971	Berlin quadripartite agreement signed
	Smithsonian monetary accord issued
1972	SALT I signed
1973	"Year of Europe"
	British join the Common Market
	October war and Middle East oil crisis

Secretary of state: Henry Kissinger
1975   Helsinki Final Act signed
1976   "Sonnenfeldt doctrine" promulgated
        Mário Soares wins Portuguese election
1977   Secretary of state: Cyrus Vance
1979   NATO dual track decision
1980   Secretary of state: Edmund Muskie
1981   Secretary of state: Alexander Haig Jr.
1982   Secretary of state: George Shultz
1983   Intermediate range nuclear missiles deployment begins in Europe
        EUR renamed Bureau of European and Canadian Affairs
1985   Geneva Summit
1986   Single European Act signed
        Reykjavik Summit
1987   INF treaty signed
1989   Berlin Wall dismantled

II. Three Careers in the Foreign Service

1. Hugh Gibson

1883	Born, August 16, Los Angeles, California
	Attended Los Angeles Military Academy
	Attended Pomona College
1907	Graduated, École Libre des Sciences Politiques, Paris
1908	Took the Diplomatic Service Examination
1908-1909	Secretary, American Legation, Tegucigalpa, Honduras
1909-1910	Second Secretary, American Embassy, London
1910	Private secretary to the assistant secretary of state
1911	Clerk, Department of State, Washington, D.C.
1911-1913	Secretary, American Legation, Havana, Cuba
1913	Observer, elections for Constituent Assembly of Santo Domingo
1914-1916	Secretary, American Legation, Brussels
	Liaison between Herbert Hoover and the Belgian Government for the Commission for Relief in Belgium
1916	First secretary, American Embassy, London
1917	Assigned to State Department, War Missions
	Aide to Lord Balfour, British minister of foreign affairs, during visit to the United States
	Attached to Belgian War Mission during visit to the United States
1918	First secretary, American Embassy, Paris
	Advisor to General Pershing
1918-1919	Member, Interallied Mission to Countries of former Austro-Hungarian Empire
1919-1924	Envoy Extraordinary and Minister Plenipotentiary to Poland
1924	Attended Temporary Mixed Commission for the Reduction of

	Armaments, League of Nations, Geneva
	Maintained as ambassador-at-large, League of Nations
1924-1927	Envoy extraordinary and minister plenipotentiary to Switzerland (Bern)
1925	Vice-chair, American Delegation, Arms Traffic Conference, Geneva
1926-1930	Chair, American Delegation, Preparatory Commission for the Disarmament Conference, Geneva
1927	Delegate, Conference on Private Manufacture of Arms, Geneva
	Chairman of American delegation and conference, Conference for the Further Limitation of Naval Armaments (also called Tripartite Naval Conference or the Three Power Conference), Geneva
1927-1933	Ambassador extraordinary and plenipotentiary to Belgium and Envoy extraordinary minister plenipotentiary to Luxembourg (Brussels)
1930	Delegate, London Naval Conference
	Observer, Conference of Experts for a Moratorium on Intergovernmental Debts (also called the London Conference or the International Conference of Ministers), London
1932-1933	Acting chair, American Delegation, General Disarmament Conference, Geneva
1933-1937	Ambassador extraordinary and plenipotentiary to Brazil (Rio de Janeiro)
1935	American representative, mediatory group to end the Chaco War between Bolivia and Paraguay, delegate, Chaco Peace Conference, Buenos Aires
1937-1938	Ambassador extraordinary and plenipotentiary to Belgium and envoy extraordinary and minister plenipotentiary to Luxembourg (Brussels)
1938	Retired from foreign service
	Vice-president, Belgian American Educational Foundation
	Chair, A.R.A. Association
1940	Escaped from France during German occupation
	European representative for the National Committee on Food for Small Democracies
1940-1941	Director general for Europe of the Commission for Polish Relief and the Commission for Relief in Belgium
1946-1947	Member, Herbert Hoover Food Mission (Herbert Hoover, Chair)
1947	Member, Investigatory Committee for postwar German economic policies
1952	Director, Provisional Intergovernmental Commission on Movements of Migrants from Europe (ICEM)
1954	Died December 12, Geneva

2. Robert D. Murphy

1894	Born October 28, Milwaukee, Wisconsin
1917-1919	Clerk, American Legation, Bern, Switzerland
1920	LL.B., George Washington University
1921	Vice consul, Zurich, Switzerland
1921-1925	Vice consul, Munich, Germany
1925	Consul, Seville, Spain
1928	LL.M., George Washington University
1926-1930	Department of State, Washington, D.C.
1930-1940	Consul, Paris, France
1940	Chargé d'affaires, Vichy, France
1940-1942	Presidential envoy to French North Africa
1941	Concluded economic accord with General Maxime Weygand
1942	Effected preparations for Allied landings in North Africa
1942-1944	Chief civil affairs officer and political adviser on staff of supreme commander
	Cochair, North African Economic Board
1942-1943	Member, Advisory Council, Allied Control Commission for Italy
1944-1949	U.S. Political Adviser, Germany
1949	Director, Office for Germany and Austria, Department of State
1949-1952	Ambassador to Belgium
1952-1953	Ambassador to Japan
1953	Assistant secretary of state for United Nations affairs
1953-1959	Deputy undersecretary of state
1959	Undersecretary of state for political affairs
	Retirement from government service
1960-1978	Successively president, chair of the board, and honorary chair of the board, Corning Glass Works, Corning Glass International
1968-1969	Member, Presidential Transition Committee
1973-1975	Member, Commission on the Organization of the Government for the Conduct of Foreign Policy
1969-1976	Member (chair, 1976), Intelligence Oversight Board
	Member, President's Foreign Intelligence Advisory Board
1978	Died January 9, Washington, D.C.

3. Arthur A. Hartman

1926	Born March 12, New York, New York
1944	A.B. from Harvard University
1944-1946	U.S. Army Air Corps
1947-1948	Attended Harvard Law School
1948-1952	Economic officer, Economic Cooperation Administration, Paris
1952-1954	Economic officer, U.S. Delegation to the European Army Conference
1954-1955	Politico-military officer in Paris
1956-1958	Economic officer, Saigon

1958-1961	International affairs officer. Economic Organization Affairs Section of the Bureau of European Affairs
1961-1962	Staff assistant to George Ball, undersecretary of state for economic affairs
1962-1963	Special assistant to the undersecretary of state
1963-1967	Chief of the Economic Section in London.
1967-1969	Special assistant to the undersecretary of state and staff director of the senior interdepartmental group
1969-1972	Deputy director for coordination
1972-1973	Deputy chief of mission and minister counselor to USEC in Brussels
1974-1977	Assistant secretary of state for European Affairs
1977-1981	Ambassador to France
1981-1987	Ambassador to the Soviet Union
1987	Retired from public service
2015	Died March 16, Washington, D.C.

(Sources: Hoover Institution; Carter Presidential Library)

NOTES

All boxes and folders were numbered as they were at the time the documents were consulted. Interviews were with the author unless otherwise indicated.

Preface

1. Ernest May died while this book was in press.

1. The Setting

1. Alfred L. P. Dennis, *Adventures in Diplomacy, 1896–1906* (New York: E. P. Dutton and Company, 1928), p. 12; Anthony Pagden, *European Encounters with the New World*. (New Haven, CT: Yale University Press, 1993), pp. 8, 117–118.

2. Tiziano Bonazzi, "Constructing and Reconstructing Europe: Torture of an American Prometheus or Punishment of a New World Sisyphus?" in Maurizio Vaudagna, ed., *The Place of Europe in American History: Twentieth-Century Perspectives* (Turin: Otto Editore, 2007), pp. 16ff.; Walter Lippmann to Robert Brand, December 20, 1947, in Walter Lippmann Papers, Sterling Memorial Library, Yale University (hereinafter WL), Reel 48.

3. Mabel Dodge Luhan, *European Experiences* (New York: Harcourt, Brace and Company, 1935), p. 452.

4. Susan Schulten, *The Geographical Imagination in America, 1880–1950* (Chicago: University of Chicago Press, 2001), pp. 3, 30.

5. Luhan, p. 453.

6. Hill to Root, March 12, 1909, Elihu Root Papers, Library of Congress, Washington, D.C., Box 55, f.4; Waldo H. Heinrichs, *American Ambassador: Joseph C. Grew and the Development of the United States Diplomatic Tradition* (Boston: Little, Brown and Company, 1966), p. 14; Joseph C. Grew, *Turbulent Era: A Diplomatic Record of Forty Years, 1904–1945* (Boston: Houghton Mifflin Company, 1952), p. 64. Grew, who went subsequently to Vienna, complained that he had had "five posts and *not once* have we been under a chief and chéfesse who could teach us how to do things right ..." ibid., p. 98. Cf. Hugh Gibson to Gilchrist B. Stockton, December 12, 1929: "Diplomacy is the one thing that interests me. There never has been so much that can be accomplished by trained diplomats and never has there been such a need for them. But failing an assured financial future I can't see what there is to justify a decision to stay on indefinitely in diplomacy...." Perrin G. Galpin, ed., *Hugh Gibson 1883–1954* (New York: Belgian American Educational Foundation, 1956), pp. 42–43.

7. Frederick Leith-Ross, *Money Talks: Fifty Years of International Finance* (London: Hutchinson, 1968), p. 20.

8. The department in 1926 comprised about 700 people; in 2006, the number was about 19,000, not including the 38,000 foreign nationals employed overseas. Harry W. Kopp and Charles A. Gillespie, *Career Diplomacy: Life and Work in the U.S. Foreign Service* (Washington, D.C.: Georgetown University Press, 2008), p. 40; Ellis O. Briggs, *Proud Servant: The Memoirs of a Career Ambassador* (Kent, OH: Kent State University Press, 1998), p. 12.

9. These refer to World War I, World War II, and the Cold War. The phrase is Salvador de Madariaga's from *Victors, Beware* (London: Jonathan Cape, 1945), p. 11.

10. See Robert D. Kaplan, *The Arabists: The Romance of an American Elite* (New York: Free Press, 1993); E. J. Kahn, *The China Hands: America's Foreign Service Officers and What Befell Them* (New York: Penguin Books, 1975).

11. There is an additional, academic reason to revisit the lives and careers of these public servants. For nearly thirty years, international historians have urged students to give priority to subjects other than the rise and fall of states and statesmen. That has all been for the good, mostly. Many impressive works of history have been written about

subjects ranging from commodities to diseases to sports competitions to the proliferation of ideas, art forms, and cultures—both elite and popular—across the globe. "Nonstate actors" now hold a place equal to, perhaps even above, that of heads of government, soldiers, ministers, kings, and even emperors, in the historian's pantheon. This has left the hundreds of diplomats and other bureaucrats whose professional (and in most cases, personal) lives were devoted literally to the conduct of international relations appearing lonely in the historiography. Daniel Rodgers's magisterial work of 1998, *Atlantic Crossings*, for example, never mentions them, and makes only contextual reference to political events. The objection is not as parochial as it may sound. Of course, one need not preface every social or cultural history with a kowtow to politics. Yet one must know that the world Rodgers described so beautifully never could have existed absent a diplomatic or political foundation. There would have been far fewer Atlantic crossings. Thus, our subjects may lack the notoriety of major public figures yet they remain, strictly speaking, "state actors" or, in their preferred terminology, "practitioners." Inhabiting the causal middle ground, they have fallen through the cracks of scholarship. But no honest historian, let alone anyone who has ever had direct experience with waging war or peace, can deny that these people matter a great deal. How to reconstruct their world is a more difficult problem. One solution may to be make use of a genre used by ancient and medieval historians called prosopography. It combines biography with sociology, analyzing the public and private lives of people in time as well as their underlying social patterns, habits, norms, and institutions. This book aims to do something similar. It is part prosopography, part pageant. Like the best biography, in the words of the historian Jacques Revel, it "stylizes experience" and derives general value thereby. It blurs the lines between state and nonstate actors, showing their combined actions to have been complementary in the shaping of an organic community and a set of ideas more than establishing a causal hierarchy of people and deeds. Indeed, it does away with the official/nonofficial distinction altogether, for these officials, despite being state emissaries, stood at the political and, in some cases, cultural, vanguard of a movement that traversed many borders and, on the whole, abjured solitary allegiances. Few described their professional lives as functioning apart from those of friends, relatives, and all manner of other social contacts. Their historical significance is found more in the reification of a regional, and ultimately global, consciousness than in any list of material achievements, despite the policies and institutions they did so much to sustain. At the same time, it was their mastery of an official bureaucracy that made so much of this work possible. What follows therefore is also part chronicle, part reflection or, as the historian Herbert Butterfield once urged, both a story and a study, and derives in large measure from the firsthand accounts of its subjects, who guided subsequent forays into archives and secondary sources. A reverse method no doubt would have brought different results, perhaps adhering more closely to the historical record of senior statesmen and outside observers, but would be, in my view, a less plausible depiction of the times of the European Desk as it lived them.

12. Heinrichs, p. 95; see also Daniel P. Carpenter, *The Forging of Bureaucratic Autonomy: Reputations, Networks, and Policy Innovation in Executive Agencies, 1862–1928* (Princeton, NJ: Princeton University Press, 2001), pp. 3–5, 14ff.; Hugh Heclo, *A Government of Strangers: Executive Politics in Washington* (Washington, D.C.: Brookings Institution, 1977), pp. 15–19, 22ff., 46–49, 128–133, 142–148; Kopp and Gillespie, p. 7; interview with David Acheson.

13. Based on the author's compilation of biographic and professional data from a sampling of 160 foreign and civil service officers mentioned in this book. See also the previous note and Mary Douglas, *How Institutions Think* (Syracuse, NY: Syracuse University Press, 1986), pp. 53ff.; cf. T. G. Otte, "European Nobility and Diplomacy," in Markus Mösslang and Torsten Riotte, eds., *The Diplomats' World: A Cultural History of Diplomacy, 1815–1914* (Oxford: Oxford University Press, 2008), pp. 26ff.

14. See, for example, John Fiske, "Manifest Destiny," *Harper's New Monthly Magazine*

70, no. 418 (March 1885). I am grateful to Professor Frank Ninkovich for help with the formulation of the ideas in this section.

15. Kai Bird, *The Chairman: John J. McCloy, the Making of the American Establishment* (New York: Simon and Schuster, 1992), p. 472.

16. Roy Jenkins, *European Diary, 1977–1981* (London: Collins, 1982), p. 640.

2. A Beginning

1. Martin Mayer, *The Diplomats* (Garden City, NY: Doubleday, 1983), p. 197. Lucy James was the closest friend of Hugh Gibson and godmother to his son. Background from Hugh Gibson Papers, Hoover Institution on War, Revolution, and Peace, Stanford University, Stanford, CA (hereinafter HG), Box 44, f.54.

2. Hugh Wilson (no relation), *The Education of a Diplomat* (London: Longmans, Green and Co., 1938), p. 10; Richard Hume Werking, *The Master Architects: Building the United States Foreign Service, 1890–1913* (Lexington: University Press of Kentucky, 1977), pp. 127–130; F. M. Huntington Wilson, *Memoirs of an Ex-Diplomat* (Boston: Bruce Humphries, 1945), pp. 160–161.

3. Interview with Christopher Phillips; William Phillips, *Ventures in Diplomacy* (Privately printed, 1952), pp. 33–37. Huntington Wilson, according to his memoir, had received a similar invitation but foolishly told Roosevelt that he preferred golf (p. 162).

4. William Phillips Diaries, MsAm, 2232 Houghton Library, Harvard University (hereinafter WP), December 4, 1917, Box 1, f.6.

5. Pierre deL. Boal to Iris Shuford, May 6, 1931, 111. 24/43 and Departmental Order No. 691, June 15, 1937, State Department Central Files, RG59 250 111.24/96, National Archives and Records Administration, College Park, MD (hereinafter NARA), Box 224, f.1.

6. Lansing to Dulles, February 19, 1920, John Foster Dulles Papers, Department of Rare Books and Special Collections, Princeton University Library, Princeton University (hereinafter JFD), Reel 1; Cecil Spring-Rice to Arthur Balfour, December 22, 1916, Balfour Papers, ADD 49740, British Library, London; Castle to Dresel, February 15, 1920, Papers of Ellis Loring Dresel, MsAm 1549, Houghton Library, Harvard University (hereinafter ED), Box 68, f.8; and Dennis, p. 361, for the Theodore Roosevelt precedent.

7. Lawrence E. Gelfand, *The Inquiry: American Preparations for Peace, 1917– 1919* (New Haven, CT: Yale University Press, 1963), pp. x, 157ff.

8. Grew to House, June 22, 1915, Edward M. House Papers, Sterling Memorial Library, Yale University, New Haven, CT (hereinafter EH), Box 52, f.1655; Heinrichs, pp. 37, 40: "Grew was thus buffeted from all sides"; Dresel to Fred Dolbeare, July 23, 1919, ED, Box 106, f.1; Grew, pp. 142–143, 206, 356–357.

9. Grew diary, March 15, 1925, Joseph C. Grew Papers, MsAm 1687, Houghton Library, Harvard University (hereinafter JG), Series I, Vol. 29; Grew to Dresel and Wilson, July 5, 1917, f.1, ED, Box 160.

10. Mayer, p. 139.

11. "Bureaucracy and Professionalism in the Development of American Career Diplomacy" (1971), reprinted in Marc Gallicchio and Jonathan Utley, eds., *Diplomacy and Force: America's Road to War, 1931–1941* (Chicago: Imprint Publications, 1996), p. 17. See also Heinrichs and Hugh De Santis, "The Department of State and Foreign Policy," in Zara Steiner, ed., *The Times Survey of Foreign Ministries of the World* (London: Times Books, 1982), pp. 579–581; "Diplomat" (William Castle), "Our Diplomatic Service," *Weekly Review*, December 15, 1920, pp. 579–580.

12. Castle, "The New Diplomacy," June 1934, William R. Castle Papers, Herbert Hoover Presidential Library, West Branch, IA (hereinafter HHPL), Box 29.

13. Interview with Timothy Dickinson; Martin Hillenbrand, "The Foreign Service: Ten Years from the Outside," n.d. (1986), pp. 4–5 in Martin J. Hillenbrand Papers, Richard B. Russell Library for Political Research and Studies, University of Georgia Libraries, Athens,

GA (hereinafter MJHH), Series II, Box 4, f.25.

14. Frank Costigliola, *Awkward Dominion: American Political, Economic, and Cultural Relations with Europe, 1919–1933* (Ithaca, NY: Cornell University Press, 1984), pp. 78–79, 173ff.; Liaquat Ahamed, *Lords of Finance: The Bankers Who Broke the World* (New York: Penguin Press, 2009), p. 256; Walter Evans Edge, *A Jerseyman's Journal: Fifty Years of American Business and Politics* (Princeton, NJ: Princeton University Press, 1948), pp. 168, 182.

15. Memorandum, January 3, 1921, J. Butler Wright Papers, Department of Rare Books and Special Collections, Princeton University Library, Princeton University, Princeton, NJ (hereinafter JBW), Box 1, f.4. Wright was an early scion of the service: From the Hudson Valley, he went to Lawrenceville and Princeton, then worked in banking and in cattle ranching in Wyoming before joining the department in 1909. "Biographical Sketch of J. Butler Wright," in Cordell Hull Papers, Library of Congress (hereinafter CH), Box 40, f.98. Cf. Phillips's advice (according to Castle) to Hugh Gibson: "[T]here were three things especially to remember—that he must not indulge in any propaganda, that he must be very careful never to be humorous with Congressmen as they did not like it, and that he must think out the proper answer to the question, 'What is the difference between a diplomatic secretary and a clerk?'" William R. Castle Diaries, Houghton Library, Harvard University, MsAm 2021 (hereinafter WRC), Vol. 4, December 4, 1923.

16. Quoted in Briggs, p. 26; Werking, p. 103; Castle diary, WRC, Vol. 5, May 14, 1924, notes that it was "considered a consular affair [until Grew] and Gibson came out as its champions."

17. Ibid., June 10, 1924.

18. "How Little Wisdom: Memoirs of an Irresponsible Memory," unpublished memoir by Theodore Achilles, p. 146; Briggs, pp. 1ff.

19. Interview with Waldo Heinrichs.

20. Castle diary, October 14, December 27, 1930, WRC, Vol. 17; Achilles, p. 158. Castle himself was considered by Hoover as "altogether the best man in the Department" for the job of undersecretary, although one suspects that Stimson did not share the opinion. Stimson diary, March 30, 1931, Henry L. Stimson Papers, Sterling Memorial Library, Yale University (hereinafter HLS), Reel 3, Vol. 15.

21. Grew address to the Foreign Service School, April 20, 1925, and Grew diary, January 14, 1925, JG, Vol. 29. For the Roosevelt conversation in which the president told him, "I have put you in the Service because I believe in you, but I can't recommend it as a permanent career," and to which Grew replied, "Mr. President, I'll take the chance. We *must* develop a career...." See Grew, p. 13.

22. Castle diary, November 11, 1922, WRC, Vol. 3.

23. A later observer summarized the stereotypes: "AF [Africa] is full of missionaries. NEA [Near East] is devious, throws sand in your eyes. EA [East Asia] is mandarin ... EUR is suave and sophisticated. And ARA [Latin America] ... *mañana*" (quoted in Mayer, p. 205); Norman Armour to Hugh Gibson, July 2, 1924, HG, Box 13, f.70.

24. Heinrichs, p. 96.

25. Robert D. Schulzinger, *The Making of the Diplomatic Mind: The Training, Outlook, and Style of United States Foreign Service Officers, 1908–1931* (Middletown, CT: Wesleyan University Press, 1975), pp. 6–7.

26. Quoted in Costigliola, p. 60.

27. Castle diary, July 20, 1928, WRC, Vol. 13.

28. Lewis Einstein, *A Diplomat Looks Back* (New Haven, CT: Yale University Press, 1968), p. 24.

29. The line of argument is traced in Patrick O. Cohrs, *The Unfinished Peace After World War I* (Cambridge: Cambridge University Press, 2006), pp. 81ff. Cf. David E. Kaiser, *Economic Diplomacy and the Origins of the Second World War: Germany, Britain, France, and Eastern Europe* (Princeton, NJ: Princeton University Press, 1980), and Robert A. Divine, *Second Chance: The*

Triumph of Internationalism in America During World War II (New York: Athenaeum, 1967).

30. Hugh Wilson to Walter Lippmann, June 13, 1933, WL, Reel 99; Lewis Einstein to Hugh Gibson, n.d., HG, Box 22, f.29; Hamilton Fish Armstrong, *Peace and Counterpeace, from Wilson to Hitler* (New York: Harper and Row Publishers, 1971), p. 133.

31. Gibson to William Castle, October 7, 1931, HG, Box 18, f.3. Gibson moved temporarily to London as an observer to the international debt conference. He would return to Geneva the following year.

32. The conflation of the issues was resisted strongly by Presidents Coolidge and Hoover, but acknowledged by nearly everyone on the ground. See, for example, Stimson diary, December 30, 1930, HLS, Reel 2, Vol. 10, and June 15, 1931, ibid., Reel 3, Vol. 16, noting Castle's indiscretion in saying so to the press.

33. Donald C. Blaisdell Oral History, October 29, 1973, Harry S. Truman Presidential Library, Independence, MO (hereinafter HST); Lippmann to Gibson, April 16, 1919, WL, Reel 11.

34. Tribute, Bohemian After Glow Party, October 30, 1955, HG, Box 5, f.5; Grew to House, April 12, 1919, EH, Box 52, f.1657; Charles G. Dawes, *Journal as Ambassador to Great Britain* (New York: Macmillan, 1939), p. 247. In Dawes's case it was rarely both: He once hired a group of jugglers to serve at a diplomatic dinner, resulting in many tossed plates and shocked British guests. Leith-Ross, pp. 84–85.

35. Background from Phillips diary, March 1, 1917, WP, Box 1, f.1; Gibson to Lippmann, December 28, 1921, WL, Reel 11; Hugh Gibson, *A Journal from Our Legation in Brussels* (Garden City, NY: Doubleday, Page and Company, 1917).

36. Gibson to Dresel, August 18, 1919, ED, Box 146, f.6.

37. Castle diary, March 16, 1926, WRC, Vol. 9.

38. Gibson quoted in Armstrong, p. 346.

39. Bullitt to Lippmann, January 21, 1920, WL, Reel 6.

40. Armstrong, p. 403. Others working in Geneva at the time included Sam Reber and Ted Achilles. Achilles, pp. 223–225; Castle diary, October 22, 1931, WRC, Vol. 19. Gilbert was unpopular among the more stalwart members of the diplomatic corps, particularly Hugh Wilson, who resented his standing in Geneva, and J. Butler Wright, who once said of him, "[T]he great trouble with Mr. Gilbert is that he will never be able to reconcile theory with fact." JG, Vol. 29. For background on Gilbert as "maverick consul," see J. B. Donnelly, "Prentiss Gilbert's Mission to the League of Nation's Council, October 1931," *Diplomatic History* 2, no. 4 (1978): 373–388. See also Stimson diary, October 16, 1931, HLS, Reel 3, Vol. 18.

41. Dulles speech to the National League of Women Voters, June 7, 1929, HG, Box 22, f.3; Wilson to Hull, March 21, 1934, JPM, Vol. 7; Phillips diary, August 29, 1923, WP, Box 1, f.17; Achilles, p. 238.

42. Ray Atherton to Gibson, May 27, 1929, HG, Box 14, f.6; Castle diary, May 13, 1925, WRC, Vol. 7; cf. Norman Davis to Moffat, October 18, 1933, Allen Dulles to Moffat, May 2, 1933, and Fred Mayer to Moffat, June 24, 1933, J. Pierrepoint Moffat Papers, Houghton Library, Harvard University, MsAm 1407 (hereinafter JPM), Vols. 2–3. Castle added, "At least Hugh Gibson is enough of a politician and a black enough Republican to know that the Administration needs a few flags of victory to wave before the women voters." WRC, ibid.

43. Phillips, p. 114; Phillips diary, January 9, 1923, WP, Box 1, f.10.

44. Paul D. Cravath, "Impressions of Germany," *Philadelphia Public Ledger*, September 5, 1920; for Hughes's views, see Hughes to Dwight W. Morrow, September 19, 1924, Dwight Morrow Papers, Amherst College Special Collections (hereinafter DM), Box 26, f.26; cf. Cravath to Dresel, November 8, 1920, ED, Box 79, f.2, and Dresel to Lithgow Osborne, June 3, 1920, ED, Box 306, f.2. For irritation with the French, see Melvyn P. Leffler, *The Elusive Quest: America's Pursuit of European Stability and French Security, 1919–1933* (Chapel Hill: University of North Carolina Press, 1979), p. 36.

45. Morrow to S. Parker Gilbert, September 11, 1931, DM, Box 24, f.12.

46. I am grateful to Dr. Jessica Wardhaugh for this point. Cf. Leffler, pp. 160–161; Arthur Krock, *Memoirs: Sixty Years on the Firing Line* (New York: Funk and Wagnalls, 1968), p. 139, for the longer-term effect of this pattern, notably in James Dunn's framing the Council on Foreign Ministers conferences of the post–World War II period as a more gradual effort, following suggestions by Hoover and Gibson in 1942. There were a few recent precedents— notably the engagement by Theodore Roosevelt and his administration in the Portsmouth and Algeciras conferences. An instructive account of the latter is found in Einstein, pp. 3ff.

47. Castle to Gibson, November 13, 1920, HG, Box 17, f.4; for Gibson's independent tendencies, see Gibson to Castle, on having to rely on French and German diplomats for reports on Laval's conversations in Washington, n.d., ibid., Box 17, f.2; and Gibson to Grew, October 31, 1925, on Gibson's single-handed mediation of the Greek-Bulgarian dispute, ibid., Box 42, f.46.

48. Gibson to Grew, October 31, 1925, HG, Box 42, f.45; Grew, p. 639; Edge, pp. 212–213, suggesting that the Americans were being manipulated by the British; cf. Hugh Wilson: "The struggle to build up a machinery for the maintenance of peace, a machinery for the prevention of war, a machinery to make warfare too hot for the aggressor, is all concentrated within this Continent.... It is in this Continent only that there is a conscious effort to arrive at what they call 'the organization of peace.' It does not exist in Asia, it does not exist in the Americas, and, as far as I know, it does not exist in Africa." Outside Europe, he concluded, the burden fell almost entirely upon the United States. Wilson to J. P. Moffat, March 29, 1933, JPM, Vol. 4. N.b.: this diary, as well as Grew's, circulated frequently among members of the department.

49. Castle diary, November 5, 1924, WRC, Vol. 8; "Conversation with Colonel House," May 19, 1919, William C. Bullitt Papers, Sterling Memorial Library, Yale University, New Haven, CT (hereinafter WB), Box 40, f.928; Huntington Gilchrist to Gibson, April 30, 1928, HG, Box 42, f.4: "During those years, the half-dozen Americans in the Secretariat have done their utmost to see that people at home, either in the Government or outside, obtained an accurate idea of how the League was developing, and I only hope that the many progressive leaders of political thought who have continued to support the ideas for which the League stands realise how much their constant interest has encouraged those who have been trying to express American opinion inside the official League organization...." Cf. Dexter Perkins, "On the Sidelines: The Department of State and American Public Opinion," in Gordon A. Craig and Felix Gilbert, *The Diplomats 1919–1939*, Vol. 1 (New York: Athenaeum, 1963), p. 292. Gilchrist is today an obscure figure but traces of him appear in several collections as one of the most knowledgeable Americans about the League. He later worked for the United Nations in Pakistan and in Brussels as director of the Food and Agriculture Organization. Gilchrist to Dulles, April 9, 1955, JFD, Reel 35; Gilchrist to Eric Drummond and reply, March 23, 28, 1928, Gilchrist Personnel File, Archives of the League of Nations, Geneva.

50. Profiles in Kenneth Paul Jones, "Alanson B. Houghton and the Ruhr Crisis: The Diplomacy of Power and Morality," in Jones, ed., *U.S. Diplomats in Europe, 1919–1941* (Santa Barbara, CA: ABC-Clio, 1981), pp. 25–39; T. Bentley Mott, *Myron Herrick: Friend of France* (Garden City, NY: Doubleday, Doran and Company, 1929). Of the three, Herrick left the scene first, dying, as Raymond Poincaré noted, "as he would have liked, in harness and in France." Armstrong, p. 436.

51. Gibson to Phillips, July 16, 1923, HG, Box 17, f.7; Grew to Gibson, February 14, 1924, HG, Box 42, f.46; Heinrichs, p. 104; Grew, p. 409.

52. Castle was wary of Cotton at the outset, having considered himself the best candidate for the number two job. Castle diary, May 21, 23, 24, 27, June 7, 11, Sept. 7, 1929, WRC, Vols. 14–15. Stimson, however, noted that he "could not have two more loyal friends" than Cotton and Morrow. Stimson diary, September 29, 1930, HLS, Reel 2, Vol.

10. The origins of the special financial envoy "approach" are described in Leffler, pp. 60, 70ff., and are attributed mainly to the skittishness of Secretary Charles Evans Hughes, and subsequently, Henry Stimson and Herbert Hoover, over the prospect of becoming too diplomatically involved in European recovery, and the concomitant bureaucratic struggles and failures to coordinate between the State and Treasury Departments. For additional differences between the Morgan bankers and the envoys, see ibid., pp. 106ff., 192–193, 206–207. For his part, Hughes may have come to regret the appointment of so strong a personality as the former vice president, Charles "Hell and Maria" Dawes. Following their meeting in Hughes's office, Phillips found his chief in a "state of exhaustion, covered with perspiration. He scarcely had voice enough to do more than gasp 'I pity those French'. I could not help roaring with laughter." Phillips diary, December 11, 1923, WP, Box 1, f.30. Castle diary, December 11, 1923, WRC, Vol. 4; see also Drew Pearson and Constantine Brown, *The Diplomatic Game* (London: Lovat Dickson and Thompson Limited, 1935), pp. 87, 96, 133, noting Dawes's fist shaking and gusto, and that Morrow "became spearhead of the drive for greater American political cooperation with Europe." For later concerns about Dawes as "an admirable figurehead ... and a very fine fellow for spasmodic work," see Stimson diary, December 14, 1931, HLS, Reel 4, Vol. 19.

53. Dulles to Dresel, February 2 and May 18, 1921, ED, Box 113; Castle diary, March 23, 1926, WRC, Vol 9; Heinrichs, letter to the author.

54. Morrow to Charles Dawes, July 3, 1921, DM, Box 17, f.61; Paul Cravath to William McAdoo, May 4, 1917, Papers of Russell C. Leffingwell, Sterling Memorial Library, Yale University, New Haven, CT (hereinafter RL), Box 6, f.119; Costigliola, p. 35; Leffler, p. 26.

55. "Address by R.C. Leffingwell on 'America's Interest in Europe' before the National Association of Credit Men, Indianapolis, June 8, 1922," RL, Box 9, f.182. Cf. Stimson to a group of journalists: "I pointed out to them that this was the difference. We were not interested, for example, in what the boundary between Germany and Poland shall be. We expressed no opinion on that. But we are interested in having that boundary and its problems settled in a peaceful way and not by war, because every nation in the world is concerned in not having war in Europe. War is a prairie fire which spreads to everybody." Stimson diary, September 10, 1931, HLS, Reel 3, Vol. 18.

56. Phillips diary, January 11, 1918, WP, Box 1, f.7.

57. Castle diary, March 30, 1929, WRC, Vol. 14.

3. Some Very Lovely People

1. Charles E. Bohlen, *Witness to History, 1929–1969* (New York: W. W. Norton and Company, 1973), p. 6; J. Pierrepont Moffat to Ray Atherton, October 12, 1937, JPM, Vol. 12; "Marriner Filled Difficult Posts," *New York Times*, October 13, 1937, p. 18; Stimson diary, December 14, 1931, January 1, 1932, HLS, Reel 4, Vols. 19–20. Castle was in the minority in rating him a "willowy person." Castle diary, October 25, 1922, WRC, Vol. 3.

2. Marriner diary, May 1, 1930, J. Theodore Marriner Papers, Columbia University Rare Book and Manuscript Library (hereinafter JTM), Box 3; "Verses read by Mr. Norman Armour at the Farewell Dinner given at the Embassy in Paris on August 31, 1932, by Ambassador Edge, in honor of Mr. and Mrs. Armour," Walter Edge Papers, Department of Rare Books and Special Collections, Princeton University Library, Princeton University (hereinafter WEE), Box 1, f.2; and for the relationship with Straus, who fought hard on his behalf, see Phillips diary, August 14, 1934, WP, Box 3, f.6; Irma Straus to Marriner, September 10, 1936, JTM, Box 2, f.53; cf. letters from Henry Stimson and Alexis Léger, f.62; on Straus, see Wilbur Carr diary, April 29, 1935, Wilbur J. Carr Papers, Library of Congress (hereinafter WJC), Box 5, f.2; Castle diary, April 26, 1935, WRC, Vol. 28.

3. Briggs, p. 49.

4. Marriner diary, July 6 and December 18, 1928, JTM, Box 3; additional background from JTM, Box 5, including photograph; lecture by Marriner on correspondence, n.d., in

W. Walton Butterworth Papers, George Marshall Foundation, Lexington, VA (hereinafter WWB), Box 4, f.10; Bohlen, p. 6; Briggs, p. 106. "The Family" was an informal circle of mandarins, including Marriner, Gibson, and about a dozen others. Mildred Bliss noted that Phillips's earlier appointment, inter alia, marked "the triumph of 1718 H." Castle diary, March 29, 1922, WRC, Vol. 3. See also Ahamed, pp. 133ff.

5. Grew to Marriner, September 2, 1928, JTM, Box 2, f.37.

6. Carr to Bullitt, November 23, 1936, WJC, Box 13, f.3.

7. Marriner diary, May 15, 1929, JTM, Box 3; Marriner to Dwight (?), April 15, 1919, JTM, Box 2, f.8.

8. Castle blamed William Dodd for the policy; Marriner attributed it directly to the president. Marriner diary, September 11, 1935, JTM, Box 3. Consuls-general were also granted diplomatic status following the 1934 "Messersmith report." WP, Box 3, f.10. Others in the department blamed Sumner Welles for Marriner's particular demotion. Joseph Green to Moffat, January 9, April 22, 1936, and John Hickerson to Moffat, November 24, 1935, JPM, Vol. 10. See also the note below.

9. Castle diary, June 6, 1936, WRC, Vol. 31; Carr, memorandum, December 2, 1935, WJC, Box 11, f.5; see also Castle diary, April 2, 1935 (Vol. 28), suggesting that Carr "may ... get a good bit of sadistic pleasure out of this sort of thing ... he has always had a chip on his shoulder so far as diplomats are concerned," October 17, 1935 (Vol. 29), and January 9, 1936 (Vol. 30). For his part, Marriner noted that most of these people opposed the policy, including George Messersmith, who was "outraged." Marriner diary, November 21, 1935, JTM, Box 3. The latter may have been meant ironically, given that Messersmith, a former consul and Carr favorite, had been sent earlier to Paris to keep a watch on Ambassador Straus. Carr diary, April 29, 1935. For his part, Carr wrote, "I am tempted to get out as the only way out of this disagreeable mess. As for F.D.R., the less said the better. Phillips got his finger burned ... and now regrets it. Thinks he will stay out and I have advised him to do so." Diary, August 14, 1935. Carr confirmed that Welles—"that crook"—played a critical role. See Carr to Marriner, May 12, 1934. WJC, Box 11, f.5, and an apologia directed at Phillips, October 28, 1935, Box 12, f.4: "No one sees the arguments for and against such transfers more clearly than I do." In the same letter, Carr noted that since 1933, forty-five officers had been transferred from the diplomatic to the consular service, and sixty-five in reverse, or a total of one-sixth the total officers in three years. The size of the consular service itself, however, had diminished considerably—by 1940, there were less than half the number of separate consulates there were in 1900. Elmer Plischke, *U.S. Department of State: A Reference History* (Westport, CT: Greenwood Press, 1999), p. 333. Castle concurred regarding the role of Welles: "I hear from all sides in the Department that the diplomats who are being most savagely punished for being good diplomats, such as Marriner, for example, are people who were not followers of Sumner Welles in the old days. He is on the Personnel Board and he is apparently paying off old scores." Diary, September 4, 1935, Vol. 29; Moffat to Wilson, January 31, 1933, JPM, Vol. 4.

10. "J.T. Marriner Honored by France," *New York Times*, April 9, 1936, p. 4; Marriner diary, April 1, 1936, JTM, Box 3.

11. Straus to Marriner, June 6, 1936, JTM, Box 2, f.57; diary December 2, 1935, and January 4, 1936, noting Phillips's advice. Ibid., Box 3. Marriner's leave involved visits to "15 countries, 17 States of the United States, 24 different cities of which 10 were capitals ... 14 nights on trains, 13 days on boats, 2 part days in planes ... also ... talked to, and remembered ... 1,174 different people, including some 120 Colleagues in the State Department ..." Diary, follows April 27, 1937; see also Castle to Hugh Gibson, June 12, 1936, HG, Box 8, f.5.

12. *New York Times*, October 13, 1937, p. 1; *Time*, October 25, 1937.

13. Stimson diary, January 9, 1933, HLS, Reel 5, Vol. 25.

14. Bullitt had blackmailed the president into forcing Welles's resignation following allegations that Welles had propositioned some train porters in Alabama. The story of the

debacle is told in Irwin F. Gellman, *Secret Affairs: Franklin Roosevelt, Cordell Hull, and Sumner Welles* (Baltimore: Johns Hopkins University Press, 1995). Much of the rivalry was waged by proxy, with columnists Drew Pearson backing Welles and Arthur Krock backing Hull and Bullitt, with Joe Alsop being fed commentary from the trenches by Adolph Berle, whose diaries were the source of Alsop's and Robert Kintner's infamous *American White Paper: The Story of American Diplomacy and the Second World War* (New York: Simon and Schuster, 1940). Dunn was also reportedly close to Krock: The latter noted that Edward Stettinius Jr. once quoted FDR: "You must watch your step with Jimmy Dunn.... You know he and Arthur have long talks together all the time." Krock, p. 181.

15. Green to S. Pinkney Tuck, January 26, 1933, Joseph C. Green Papers, Department of Rare Books and Special Collections, Princeton University Library, Princeton University (hereinafter JCG), Box 37, f.15; see also Green's Oral History, Oral History Transcripts, HHPL, pp. 29ff.

16. Moffat to Wilson, April, 22, 1933, JPM, Vol. 4.

17. Hull to Phillips, July 11, 1933, and clipping attached to letter from R. H. Whaley to Hull, November 3, 1933, CH, Box 34, f.62 and Box 35, f.65, respectively; Henry Brandon diary, December 22, 1941, Henry Brandon Papers, Library of Congress (hereinafter HB), Box 1, f.1; Herbert Feis, *1933: Characters in Crisis* (Boston: Little, Brown and Company, 1966), p. 74, quoting Raymond Moley; Carr diary, March 22, 1935, WJC, Box 5, f.2.

18. Caroline Phillips diary, February 24, 1933, Box 6, Caroline Phillips Papers, Schlesinger Library Archives, Radcliffe Institute for Advanced Study, Harvard University (hereinafter CP). See also Caroline Phillips to Eleanor Roosevelt, February 28, 1933, Box 2, f.1; interviews with David Acheson and Christopher Phillips. The Acheson and Phillips families were close; Christopher and David were each other's oldest friend.

19. Castle diary, October 3, 1935, WRC, Vol. 29, and February 25, 1933, ibid., Vol. 22. Stimson had similar, although more generous, qualms. Diary, March 3, 1933, HLS, Reel 5, Vol. 26.

20. Castle diary, August 18, 1935, WRC, Vol. 29; William Phillips to Caroline Phillips, April 9, 1936, CP, Box 3, f.5. See also, for example, Green to Marriner, January 13, 1934, JCG, Box 37, f.15; Moffat diary, August 25, 1937, JPM, Vol. 38. For a favorable view of Phillips from a curious source, see Messersmith to Feis, July 21, 1936, Herbert Feis Papers, Library of Congress, Washington, D.C. (hereinafter HF), Box 21, f.11, and Feis, *1933*, p. 99; a critical account of Phillips's tour in Italy is in John P. Diggins, *Mussolini and Fascism: The View from America* (Princeton, NJ: Princeton University Press, 1972), pp. 278, 352ff.; cf. a report by the State Department's Italian Desk chronicling the efforts to keep Mussolini out of the war, in WP, Box 14, f.11.

21. *The Diaries of Sir Alexander Cadogan O.M., 1938–1945*, ed. David Dilks (New York: Putnam, 1972), p. 399; Galeazzo Ciano, *Diary, 1937–1943*, trans. Robert L. Miller (New York: Enigma Books, 2002), p. 323. Welles's view of Ciano, in fact, may be said to approximate himself: "a creature of his times, and the times in which he had his being are the least admirable mankind has known for many centuries" (from Welles's preface to the same volume, p. xxi). Castle diary, June 7, 1924, WRC, Vol. 5; see also W. Phillips diary, September 23, 1941, WP, Box 14, f.8. For Welles's infidelities, see Benjamin Welles, *Sumner Welles: FDR's Global Strategist—A Biography* (New York: St. Martin's Press, 1997), pp. 52ff., 83ff.

22. Dean Acheson, *Present at the Creation: My Years in the State Department* (New York: Norton, 1969), p. 12.

23. James Bonbright Oral History, Association for Diplomatic Studies and Training, Arlington, VA (hereinafter ADST).

24. Castle to Gibson, May 3, 1937, HG, Box 18, f.5. All was not harmonious before this, of course. Stimson, for example, had a difficult relationship with both President Hoover, with whom he often disagreed and whom he accused of micromanagement, and with senior

members of the department such as Castle. E.g., Stimson diary, June 18, 1931, HLS, Reel 3, Vol. 16, May 16, 1932; Reel 4, Vol. 22, November 29, 1932; Reel 5, Vol. 24.

25. Castle diary, October 5, 1933, WRC, Vol. 21; Feis to Bullitt, July 2, 1937, HF, Box 12, f.7; cf. C. Phillips diary, April 20, 1933, CP, Box 6.

26. H. Freeman Matthews, *Memories of a Passing Era* (Washington, D.C.: Privately printed, 1973), p. 258; for more on the bitter Hull-Welles rivalry, see Feis, notes, January 14, 1938, HF, Box 126, f.3. For the Acheson-Berle feud, which required nearly all memos meant for both to see to be sent in duplicate to each separately and marked "approved in draft," see Achilles, p. 669.

27. William D. Leahy diary, September 4, 1946, William D. Leahy Papers, Library of Congress, Washington, D.C. (hereinafter WDL), Reel 4.

28. Carr diary, July 3, 1936, and February 10, 1937, WJC, Box 3, f.3 and f.4; Castle diary, WRC, Vol. 22; Feis, p. 104.

29. The biographical literature on this group is vast. See, for example, Hugh de Santis, *The Diplomacy of Silence: The American Foreign Service, the Soviet Union, and the Cold War* (Chicago: University of Chicago Press, 1983), esp. pp. 31ff., and two humorous accounts: Charles Thayer, *Bears in the Caviar* (Philadelphia: Lippincott, 1951), and Anabelle Bucar, *The Truth About American Diplomats* (Moscow: Literaturnaya Gazeta, 1949). Both books were written by people who worked in the American embassy at the time, the latter on behalf of the Soviets.

30. Carr diary, September 2, 1935, WJC, Box 3, f.2; Castle diary, July 6, 1936, WRC, Vol. 31. Carr endorsed the widespread rumor that Bullitt had carried on an affair with the president's secretary, Missy LeHand. Alsop's information was based on a conversation with "H.F.," probably Herbert Feis. Memorandum, March 8, 1939, Joseph and Stewart Alsop Papers, Library of Congress (hereinafter JA), Box 32, f.11. Feis implied that Bullitt's European cachet was somewhat exaggerated and that he always desired to "make a clean breast of what he was up to" but was encouraged by Roosevelt to perform the role of *éminence grise* later ascribed to him. Bullitt's own correspondence with both the State Department and the president tended to support Feis's view on the whole.

31. Bullitt to FDR, May 10, 1937, President's Secretary's Files, Confidential, Franklin D. Roosevelt Presidential Library, Hyde Park, New York (hereinafter FDR), Box 30, f.4; Wilson to Kirk, September 2, 1939, Hugh R. Wilson Papers, HHPL, Box 3.

32. Bullitt arrived in Paris as ambassador after three difficult years in Moscow, where he found life barely tolerable. He later advised Alexander Kirk: "[T]he solution for life ... is easy. Install by the side of your bed one large lamp of the latest model which provides ultra-violet rays and another large lamp which provides infra-re rays [*sic*], turn them both on at once; take a drink of Polish *Zubrowka*, and imagine you are on the Riviera!" Bullitt to Kirk, February 13, 1939, WB, Box 45, f.1076.

33. Or, for that matter, with Kennedy, the other great "prima donna," in Europe. John Cudahy to R. Walton Moore, February 11, 1939, R. Walton Moore Papers, FDR, Box 4, f.2.

34. Long diary, August 29, 1943, Breckinridge Long Papers, Library of Congress, Washington, D.C. (hereinafter BL), Box 5, f.3.

35. John J. McCloy, "The Challenge to American Foreign Policy," The Godkin Lectures, John J. McCloy Papers, Amherst College Special Collections (hereinafter JJM), Box SP1, f.57.

36. N.b.: Stimson was in office for over three months before he met with the assistant secretaries and other department heads, and relied almost exclusively upon his own inner staff, at least during the first year of his tenure. See his diary, November 17–18 and December 10, 1930, HLS, Reel 2, Vol. 10: "[T]he foreign policy of this country now would really have to be guided, or initiated rather, so far as the State Department was concerned, by [Cotton] and me...." Cotton would die the following March.

37. Heinrichs, letter to the author; Briggs, p. 46.

38. Jay Franklin, "Main Street on the Potomac," *Vanity Fair*, March 1933, quoted in Robert Gottlieb et al., eds., *Katharine Graham's Washington* (New York: Knopf, 2002), p. 25.

39. By 1934, for example, there totaled some 124 interdepartmental committees, boards and commissions, 224 interdepartmental subcommittees, and 348 interdepartmental arrangements. W. Phillips diary, December 11, 1934, WP, Box 3, f.17; Records of the War History Branch, Drafts of Chapters for an Overall History of the Department of State During World War II, 1945–50, chap. 1, RG59 Lot Files, NARA (hereinafter HLG), Box 1, f.2.; G. Howland Shaw, "The State Department and Its Foreign Service in Wartime," Address to the Thirtieth National Foreign Trade Convention, New York, NY, October 26, 1943, BL, Box 189, f.10.

40. Grew to Gibson, February 2, 1934, HG, Box 43, f.1; cf. Grew: "American diplomacy has come into its own at last." "The New Diplomacy," n.d. (1925), JG, Vol. 29; Herschel V. Johnson to Dunn, June 10, 1944, Herschel Johnson Papers, HST, Box 3, f.1. On budget freezes, see Katherine Crane, *Mr. Carr of State: Forty-Seven Years in the Department of State* (New York: St. Martin's Press, 1960), pp. 314–316.

41. Drew Pearson and Robert S. Allen, "Washington Merry Go-Round," *Washington Times-Herald*, December 20, 1940; Matthews, p. 258. Another frequent player was the chief of the Far Eastern Bureau, Stanley Hornbeck. For a portrait buying into Dunn's personal myth, see Robert Bendiner, *The Riddle of the State Department* (New York: Farrar and Rinehart, 1942), pp. 184–185. Additional background in W. Phillips diary, March 24, 1924, WP, Box 2, f.4.

42. Frank O'Brien, "Dunn Proves Two-Fisted Envoy," *Washington Post*, August 3, 1947, p. M13; "James Dunn Named Our Envoy to Italy," *New York Times*, July 23, 1946, p. 7; Martin Weil, *A Pretty Good Club: the Founding Fathers of the U.S. Foreign Service* (New York: Norton, 1978), pp. 79ff. One of Dunn's daughters would marry a Belgian count; the other, Charles Thayer, the brother-in-law of Chip Bohlen and his comrade-in-arms in Moscow; Achilles, p. 228.

43. Castle diary, March 16, 1935, WRC, Vol. 27; Interview with David Acheson; Chester H. Opal Oral History, ADST; for Welles's reputed hostility toward Dunn, see Long diary, April 20, 1940, BL, Box 5, f.2. Dunn reportedly knew no languages other than his own. *Ambassador Dodd's Diary, 1933–1938*, ed. William E. Dodd Jr. and Martha Dodd (New York: Harcourt, Brace and Company, 1941), p. 240.

44. Matthews, p. 257. The proposal to merge the divisions under Dunn's authority was urged initially by Charles Taft. Taft to Hull, March 30, 1944, CH, Box 95, f.401.

45. Weil, p. 81. Cf. Gosnell, "International Conference Administration," in HLG, Box 2, f.10; John J. McCloy Oral History, October 15, 1957, George Marshall Foundation, Lexington, VA; Charles Taft's unpublished book on the State Department, chap. 11, pp. 150–151, in Melbourne L. Spector Papers, HST, Box 2, f.2.

46. Wilson to Secretary of State, March 5, 1937, 852.00/4872, in *Foreign Relations of the United States* (hereinafter *FRUS*) *1937*, Vol. 1, p. 250.

47. Alsop and Kintner, p. 2.

48. David Eccles to Roger Makins, May 24, 1941, Roger Makins Papers, Bodleian Library, Oxford University (hereinafter RM), Box 518. He added: "The U.S.A. are coming in ... Bill Donovan's house, where I live, is a sort of heart hospital.... The S.D. don't understand how to make a man's mind up for him, because their own is uncertain. So I went off to the War Department and did a pretty warm piece of work (but it won't get into the history books), the result is that Stimson has told F.D.R. he's ready to send *men* as well as *materiel*"; Philip Noel-Baker, "The United States and the League" (1930), Philip Noel-Baker Papers, Churchill Archives Centre, Churchill College, Cambridge University, NBKR 4/840; cf. Ben Nicolson to Isaiah Berlin, November 13, 1938, Isaiah Berlin Papers, Bodleian Library, Oxford University (hereinafter IB), f.117–118, and Berlin to Alsop, February 11, 1944, f.8.

49. Wilson to Welles, quoted in Wilson, *A Career Diplomat, the Third Chapter: The Third*

Reich, ed. Hugh R. Wilson Jr. (New York: Vantage Press, 1961), p. 39. See also Wilson to Hull, September 22, 1934, CH, Box 37, f.78; Wilson to Dunn, November 16, 1936, Wilson Papers, HHPL, Box 1 ("As to how the League can be reformed, the Lord only knows!"); Feis to Frankfurter, July 15, 1931, HF, Box 16, f.12; Lord Lothian to Hull, October 12, 1937, CH, Box 42, f.101; Bullitt to Dodd, April 19, 1937, William E. Dodd Papers, Library of Congress, Washington, D.C. (hereinafter WED), Box 50, f.7; J. B. Donnelly, "Prentiss Bailey Gilbert and the League of Nations: The Diplomacy of an Observer," in Jones, ed., p. 105. Examples of those who got it wrong include: Cudahy to Roosevelt, December 27, 1933, John Cudahy Papers, FDR, Box 1; Moore to Bowers, December 12, 1936, Moore Papers, FDR, Box 3, f.6; Kellogg to Marriner, April 5, 1935, JTM, Box 1, f.56; Memorandum by Harry Hopkins, July 20, 1934, Harry Hopkins Papers, Georgetown University (hereinafter HH), Box 1, f.29; Long to Dodd, April 7, 1936, WED Box 49, f.6; Tracy Kittredge to Sydnor H. Walker, March 25, 1938, Tracy Kittredge Papers, Hoover Institution, Stanford, California (hereinafter TK), Box 19, f.1; Sosthenes Behn to Frank Pace, January 24, 1940, Welles Papers, FDR, Box 155, f.2; and Dodd to Stephen Duggan, July 24, 1934: "I am inclined to think there is no more danger to Americans here than in Chicago.... The European situation seems to be rather more settled than at any time during the last eighteen months." WED, Box 44, f.1. For those who got it right: John Wiley to Robert Kelley, February 26, 1938, Robert F. Kelley Papers, Georgetown University Archives and Special Collections, Washington, D.C. (hereinafter RFK), Box 4, f.11; Kennan to James W. Riddleberger, November 20, 1941, George F. Kennan Papers, Department of Rare Books and Special Collections, Princeton University Library, Princeton University, Princeton, NJ (hereinafter GK), Box 28, f.4; J. Butler Wright to Dunn, February 8, 1939, JBW, Box 1, f.2; Feis to Robert Brand, April 22, 1940, HF, Box 11, f.17, and Feis to Hull, May 20, 1936, HF, Box 19, f.8; Long diary, June 7, 1940 (reporting views of Alexander Kirk), BL, Box 5, f.2; Moffat to Norman Armour, September 8, 1937, Vol. 12, JPM; Castle diary, March 19, 1935, WRC, Vol. 27, and esp. Matthews, pp. 151ff. See also Luther to Foreign Ministry, April 8, 1935, 8595/H603535–43, No. 18 (629), *Documents on German Foreign Policy, from the Archives of the German Foreign Ministry* (hereinafter AA), Series C, Vol. 4, pp. 23–27 (dissecting various official and unofficial American opinions).

50. Feis, Notes, March 16, 1938, HF, Box 126, f.3; see also Wilson to Roosevelt, March 4, 1936, President's Personal Files, FDR, f.4157; cf. Castle diary, July 10, 1926, WRC, Vol. 10, representative of an earlier, more favorable view of *Il Duce.*

51. Feis, p. 302; Castle diary, May 30, 1933, WRC, Vol. 23, and Hugh Wilson, *Disarmament and the Cold War in the Thirties* (New York: Vantage Press, 1963), p. 29; and by the same author, *Diplomat Between Wars* (New York: Longmans, Green, 1941), p. 327; see also Feis, "Washington: An Important Station in the Circuit of Indecision," *Seen from E.A.: Three International Episodes* (New York: Knopf, 1946), pp. 218ff. Feis was hired by Stimson as the department's first economic adviser following Stimson's reading of Feis's book, *Europe: The World's Banker,* and was the only senior State Department official to make the transition from the Hoover to Roosevelt administrations; indeed, he served along with Frankfurter and Stimson as unofficial transition liaison. In addition to becoming a notable historian in his own right, he married the granddaughter of President James Garfield, thereby granting him a foot in Washington circles. The other foot was planted firmly in the New York–Cambridge turn-of-the-century intelligentsia—Feis had once been a protégé of Louis Brandeis. Stimson diary, April 14, 1931, Reel 3, Vol. 15 and December 24, 1932, HLS, Reel 5, Vol. 25.

52. Then again, that might have been the reason Roosevelt appointed them in the first place. Green to Feis, December 2, 1938, HF, Box 126, f.3; Bonjean et Burin des Roziers, Note, September 6, 1939, Série Correspondance politique et commerciale 1914–1940, Amérique 1930–1940, États-Unis 319, Ministère des Affaires Étrangères, Paris (hereinafter MAE); Luther to Foreign Ministry, February 15, 1937, 1993/586511-26, No. 207(217), AA, Series 6, Vol. 6, pp. 438–445; Dodd, p. 211. For Roosevelt's own ambivalence at the time,

see Dominic Tierney, *FDR and the Spanish Civil War: Neutrality and Commitment in the Struggle That Divided America* (Durham, NC, and London: Duke University Press, 2007), esp. pp. 28ff.; cf. Roosevelt to Hull, June 29, 1937, CH, Box 41, f.99A.

53. Norman Davis quoted in Davis to Hull, April 13, 1937, CH, Box 41, f.98A.

54. The following jingle, reported by Felix Frankfurter, summed up the reputation of the former: "Joe, Joe/Kennedy, Kennedy/Went to the Court of St. James/Where he liked to be seen/With the king and the queen/at cricket and other games/.... But when hell was popping/and bombs were dropping/All over London town,/Said Joe, Joe,/'I've got to go,/ the British have me down...,'" President's Secretary's Files, Confidential, FDR, Box 135, f.7. For more of Kennedy's sarcasm, referring to his "beautiful silk room" surely designed by a "fairy" and the portrait of "Joe Choate looking down at me in a red gown and" saying, "Call me a cab," see Kennedy to James Roosevelt, March 3, 1938, CH, Box 42, f.104; William W. Kauffmann, "Two American Ambassadors: Bullitt and Kennedy," in Gordon A. Craig and Felix Gilbert, eds., *The Diplomats, 1919–1939* (Princeton, NJ: Princeton University Press, 1953), pp. 649–681.

55. Bowers to Hull, May 4, 1936, CH, Box 39, f.90.

56. Briggs, p. 145.

57. Long diary, May 11, 1939, BL, Box 5, f.1; Hull and others planned to send Long to Berlin or Mexico. Long diary, December 18, 1939, BL, Box 5, f.2; Roosevelt to Long, November 29, 1944, President's Secretary's Files, Confidential, FDR, Box 71, f.6; FDR to Hull, April 5, 1937, CH, Box 41, f.98A, notes that another plan had Gibson going to Spain and Bowers to Belgium. Bowers's account of his ordeal is in Claude G. Bowers, *My Mission to Spain: Watching the Rehearsal for World War II* (New York: Simon and Schuster, 1954), pp. 253ff. and pp. 410–421, for his treatment back home. See also Douglas Little, "Claude Bowers and His Mission to Spain: The Diplomacy of a Jeffersonian Democrat," in Jones, ed., pp. 130–131.

58. Beard to Dodd, April 12, (1935), WED, Box 46, f.3. The dubious story about Harold Dodds appears in Matthews, p. 129. The author was an old acquaintance of H. Dodds's and had previously recruited him for State Department work. Briggs, p. 98. There was also a rumor that Roosevelt had confused him the prominent lawyer, Walter F. Dodd. For William Dodd's speculations as to the source of his appointment, see his diary, p. 4.

59. *Newsweek*, May 22, 1937; for his obsession with embassy expenses and the problems with his staff, see Dodd's reports on White and Wilson, August 1, 1934, WED, Box 44, f.3; Dodd to Moore, October 5, 1934, WED, Box 45, f.1, and Dodd to Moore, April 26, 1935, WED, Box 47, f.2; Dodd to Long, February 20, 1936, WED, Box 49, f.6; Dodd to Phillips ("for you alone"), December 14, 1933, WED, Box 42, f.6; W. Phillips diary, June 25, 1934, WP, Box 3, f.4; Dodd to Carr, June 1, 1934, WED, Box 43, f.9; Dodd to Moore, August 17, 1936, Moore Papers, FDR, Box 5, f.3; and Dodd diary, pp. 195, 276–278; Dodd to Hull, October 19, 1933, CH, Box 35, f.64; translated clipping from *Das Kleine Journal*, May 31, 1934, in CH, Box 36, f.76; Dodd to Hull, March 25, 1933, CH, Box 34, f.58, for Dodd's complaint on there being too many anti-Wilsonians in the service.

60. *New York Times*, April 15, 1934; Thomas R. Brown, M.D., "Regimen for the Honorable William E. Dodd," WED, Box 46, f.2; Messersmith to Dodd, October 24, 1939, CH, Box 45, f.120, noting a "mental disturbance." The Germans were aware of Dodd's problems with his staff. See, for example, Dieckhoff, memorandum, April 10, 1934, 5747/H03500-501 5747/H03504-05, No. 395, AA, Series C, Vol. 2, pp. 738–739.

61. As noted in the previous chapter, Gilbert, Beam, and Riddleberger had served together in Geneva, along with Tommy Thompson. Beam and Riddleberger supported Gilbert's widow, Charlotte, financially for many years until her death. Interview with Antonia Stearns. Of the group, Gilbert regarded Thompson as the best. Gilbert to Moffat, August 16, 1937, JPM, Vol. 12. Other notable officers who served in Berlin during these years were Alfred Kliefoth, a former associate of Kelley's in the Eastern European Division

who had supposedly known both Hitler and von Neurath well; Raymond Geist, the consul whose contacts among the Nazis were second to none; and George Messersmith. W. Phillips diary, June 13, 1935, WP, Box 4, f.5.

62. Castle diary, April 26, 1935, WRC, Vol. 28.

63. Schmitt to Dodd, August 25, 1933, WED, Box 43, f.1. Additional problems for Dodd were created by his two misbehaving children, particularly his daughter, Martha, who had affairs with many leading Nazis, although she herself later became a Communist. Her romantic liaisons reportedly gave her "the best intelligence network in the embassy." Interview with Margaret Beam; W. Phillips diary, December 20, 1933, WP, Box 2, f.9.

64. Phillips to Dodd, November 27, 1933, WED, Box 42, f.6; cf. Dodd to Dieckhoff, December 23, 1934, WED, Box 43, f.10.

65. Moffat to Green, October 19, 1936, JCG, Box 37, f.17. He noted in the same letter that he did not mind Bullitt so much; indeed he rather liked him; Carr diary, March 26, 1934, WJC, Box 5, f.1; March 22, 1935, ibid., Box 5, f.2. Welles informed the German government at the beginning of October 1937 that Dodd would be recalled. Dieckhoff to Foreign Ministry, October 1, 1937, 2422/511393, No. 410, AA, series D, Vol.5, p. 632. See also Dieckhoff telegram, January 14, 1938, 2422/511432-33, No. 432, same volume, pp. 679–680.

66. Dodd to Long, March 23, 1936, WED, Box 49, f.6.

67. Castle diary, April 14 and 26, 1935, WRC, Vol. 28, and September 11, 1923, Vol. 4; Willard Beaulac, *Career Ambassador* (New York: Macmillan, 1951), p. 148. Beaulac noted that Messersmith once told him "he never had time to write a short letter"; examples of summaries appear in memoranda from WE to Hull, September 16, 1936, CH, Box 39, f.92, and November 14, 1936, CH, Box 40, f.95. See also Kenneth Moss, "George S. Messersmith and Nazi Germany: The Diplomacy of Limits in Central Europe," in Jones, ed., p. 115. Information on Messersmith's early life comes from Jesse H. Stiller, *George S. Messersmith: Diplomat of Democracy* (Chapel Hill: University of North Carolina Press, 1987), pp. 2–7. Cf. Briggs, pp. 157ff.: "Humorless, opinionated, and sly ... a puny creature, forever contemplating the wonders that lay beneath his navel."

68. Examples of his vivid correspondence are in *FRUS 1934*, Vol. 2, pp. 35ff.; Messersmith to Phillips, November 23, 1933, 862.0/3417, reprinted in U.S. State Department, *Peace and War: United States Foreign Policy, 1931–1941* (Washington, D.C.: Government Printing Office, 1943), pp. 194–195.

69. Elbridge Durbrow, unpublished memoir, Durbrow Papers, Hoover Institution Archives (hereinafter EDD), Box 40, f.1, p. 94; Castle diary, December 2, 1936, WRC, Vol. 32; a curious exception was Henderson. Henderson to Martin Wishnatsky, March 18, 1972, Loy Henderson Papers, Library of Congress, Washington, D.C. (hereinafter LH), Box 15, f.3.

70. Gibson to Welles, February 18, 1938, HG, Box 8, f.2. Gibson was packed off to the embassy in Brazil, not a happy post for him, and then, following a brief return to Brussels, to retirement from the foreign service. He would work as an editor at Doubleday for some time thereafter. Cf. Drew Pearson and Robert S. Allen, "Who Killed Hugh Gibson?" *Daily Washington Merry-Go-Round*, December 20, 1936. See also Galpin, ed., pp. 13ff.

71. Castle to Gibson, May 8, 1938, HG, Box 18, f.5.

72. W. Phillips diary, September 24, 1936, WP, Box 6, f.5. The house was only sold to the U.S. government after the war, during which it was designated as a hospital under the protection of the Knights of Malta in order to spare it from German bombing following the intervention of Col. Louis Wickersham, whose cousin, the Count Nasalli Rocca di Corneliano, was a member of the order. History from a brochure distributed on site.

73. Dunn to Wilson, November 12, 1935, Wilson Papers, HHPL, Box 1. See also letter of November 22, ibid. For Phillips's condition, see Green to Moffat, January 9, 1936, JPM, Vol. 10; Phillips to Charles Evans Hughes, January 5, 1934, WP, Box 2, f.10; Castle diary,

November 8, 1932, WRC, Vol. 21.

74. Loy Henderson, draft memoir, LH, Box 19, f.2; W. Phillips diary, September 12, 1942, WP, Box 14, f.15.

75. George F. Kennan, *Memoirs, 1925–1950*, Vol. 1 (Boston: Little, Brown and Company, 1967), pp. 113–114; Kirk to Hugh Wilson, May 21, 1939, Wilson Papers, HHPL, Box 4; Achilles, p. 198.

76. E.g., on the Nazi-Soviet Pact, see Kirk to Secretary of State, 761.6211/156, August 31, 1939, *FRUS 1939*, Vol. 1, pp. 345–346. Other descriptions of Kirk are from Makins to Orme Sargent, June 6, 1944, RM, Box 521; James McCargar Oral History, ADST; Bullitt to Roosevelt, August 31, 1938, WB, Box 71, f.1797; Wilson, p. 179.

77. E.g., "And so, dear Pierrepont, I say to you, and say it with all the emphasis at my disposal, that no one, literally no one, whether he be janitor or Ambassador, should be sent here unless, in the first place, he knows more about his job and can work harder at it than those already on the spot, and unless, in the second place, he is reconciled to taking things as they are without insisting on disrupting the working machine in an attempt to live in a state to which he is unaccustomed or to give a party that's a flop to a bunch of bored oldtime diplomats or a group of frightened natives who come for fear of being shot if they don't and then get shot for coming." Kirk to Moffat, May 29, 1938, JPM, Vol. 13.

78. Kennan, p. 114; cf. Carr memo, December 20, 1934, WJC, Box 11, f.5.

79. Details of Kirk's career from Presidential Official File, "Alexander Kirk" F4180, FDR; Castle: "[I]t was funny to see [Spencer] Phenix and Kirk at tea yesterday.... They came in together, talked together and left together—for all the world like conspirators in a farce.... [Kirk orders the building's fireplaces bricked up to give more space. The fireplaces] gave dignity to the room and ... ventilation—one thing which Kirk has no use for." Diary, January 5, March 14, June 28, 1928, WRC, Vol. 12.

80. See, for example, Phillips to Welles, May 31, 1940, Welles Papers, FDR, Box 63, f.15; Kirk to Welles, January 27, 1943, Welles Papers, FDR, Box 93, f.6; William L. Langer and S. Everett Gleason, *The Challenge to Isolation, 1937–1940* (New York: Harper and Brothers Publishers, 1952), pp. 494–495; for Cairo, see Simon Ball, *The Guardsmen* (New York: Harper Perennial, 2004), p. 251.

81. Kirk to Feis, December 4, 1952, HF, Box 20, f.9.

82. Kirk to Moffat, October 28, 1938, LH, Box 16, f.4; cf. Castle diary, August 22, 1935, WRC, Vol. 29.

83. Kelley and Evan Young, memorandum, June 2, 1924, RFK, Box 3; Biographical detail from Box 1, f.9; "Memorandum by Chief of the Division of Eastern European Affairs, July 27, 1933," *FRUS 1933*, Vol. 2, pp. 782–788. Backing Kelley were Bullitt and Phillips. See Feis, notes September 22, 1933, HF, Box 123, f.11, and W. Phillips diary, August 15, October 31, November 6, 8, 18, 1933, WP, Box 2, f.5–6. For the argument against normalization, see Gibson to House, February 17, 1933, HG, Box 46, and Earl Packer to Castle, August 15, 1936 (misdated in original), Office of Eastern European Affairs, USSR Section, 1917–41, Lot Files RG59 A1 370–373H, NARA, Box 3, f.17. Another critical player in the normalization talks was Secretary of the Treasury Morgenthau. See Feis, p. 308. Stimson's private views in favor of normalization are noted in his diary, January 9, 1933, HLS, Reel 5, Vol. 25.

84. Henderson, eulogy of Kelley, LH, Box 5, f.1; Castle diary, December 27, 1933, WRC, Vol. 23, on Bullitt becoming "hard boiled" and Bullitt to Roosevelt, December 19, 1939 (last page), WB, Box 72, f.1806; on embassy move see K(?) to Carr, July 25, 1934, WJC, Box 11, f.4; Bullitt to Hull, July 19, 1937, CH, Box 41, f.99A.

85. Kennan, pp. 84–85; Carr memorandum, June 3, 1937, WJC, Box 13, f.5; Carr memorandum, March 2, 1937, WJC, Box 13, f.6; Davis to Henderson, January 22, 1978, LH, Box 2, f.7.

86. Henderson to Mark Stoler, August 1, 1970, LH, Box 15, f.4; a typical, hardline

position is in *FRUS 1941*, Vol. 1: "Policy with Regard to the Soviet Union in Case of the Outbreak of War Between the Soviet Union and Germany," 740.0011 European War 1939/19382, pp. 766–767. Cf. Hugh Wilson: "If a spirit should develop in Europe which would permit a cessation of hostilities in the west to allow Germany to take care of Russian encroachment, I for one should enthusiastically applaud and believe sincerely that the ends of civilization would be furthered thereby." Wilson to Kirk, December 4, 1939, Wilson Papers, HHPL, Box 3.

87. Joseph Alsop and Robert Kintner, "The Capital Parade," *Washington Star*, April 17, 1939; Feis, *1933*, p. 88; Briggs, p. 61; Stimson diary, January 21, 1933, HLS, Reel 5, Vol. 25. Moffat was also the brother-in-law of John C. White, one of the counselors Dodd disliked in Berlin and the son of Henry White, the token Republican at the Paris Peace Conference and ambassador to France, Italy, etc. Moffat to Pierre Jay, February 15, 1941, JPM, Vol. 19; Castle diary, June 7, 1932, WRC, Vol. 20; Dresel to Castle, April 21, 1921, ED, Box 68, f.4.

88. *The Moffat Papers: Selections from the Diplomatic Journals of Jay Pierrepont Moffat, 1919–1943*, ed. Nancy Harvison Hooker (Cambridge, MA: Harvard University Press, 1956), p. 3.

89. Gibson to Moffat, June 27, 1937, JPM, Vol. 12; see also in same volume, Gilbert to Moffat, August 16, 1937.

90. Castle to Moffat, March 3, 1933, JPM, Vol. 2.

91. Wilson to Moffat, March 7, 1938, Hugh R. Wilson Papers, HHPL, Box 3, f.25; *Moffat Papers*, October 5, 1937, p. 154. Cf. Armstrong, p. 371, quoting Allen Dulles.

92. *Moffat Papers*, February 18, 1938, p. 189. See also diary entries for November 5, 1937 (p. 172), November 13 (p. 182), February 15, 1938 (p. 189), September 9 and 11 (p. 199); Moffat to Wilson, October 5, 1938, Wilson Papers, HHPL, Box 126, f.4. Feis noted that Moffat argued at this time that Italy was merely trying to force a negotiated settlement between the British and Germans. Feis notes, August 28, 1939, HF, Box 126, f.4; the Credit Anstalt reference appears in Feis, *1933*, p. 5. The official line on Munich, of course, was that the United States would "remain completely aloof." Memorandum of Conversation by the Under Secretary of State (Welles), March 14, 1938, 760F.62/1471/2 FRUS 1938, Vol. 1, pp. 485–486; a more perspicacious view is in Einstein to Hull, May 10, 1938, CH, Box 42, f.106. Cf. Moffat on U.S. public opinion (760F.62/718), in same volume, pp. 572–573. For his part, Phillips reacted to Munich with "indescribable relief." Phillips to Hull, September 30, 1938, CH, Box 43, f.108.

93. Carr diary, November 15, 1932, WJC, Box 4, f.4; Kennan, pp. 89–90.

94. Kennan, ibid.

95. See, for example, Daniels to Dodd, September 19, 1935, WED, Box 46, f. 5; George Gordon to Dodd, January 31, 1935, and April 4, 1935, and reply, March 8, 1935, WED, Box 46, f.8.

96. Gibson to Norman Davis, December 27, 1937, HG, Box 8, f.2; Castle quotation from "The New Diplomacy," n.d. (1934), HHPL.

97. Gibson to Kate Wilson, April 24, 1933, HG, Box 54, f.12. Cf. Einstein, p. 207, on his similar dismissal by Hoover.

98. "Office of European Affairs and Its Predecessors," p. 6, HLG, Box 4, f.2; Moffat considered the amalgamation "unwieldy" but made the best of it. Moffat to Marriner, August 13, 1937, Vol. 12, JPM; Moffat diary, July 20, 1937, Vol. 39, ibid.

99. Douglas MacArthur II to Carmel Offie, February 21, 1940, WB, Box 54, f.1312; Saint Quentin to Ministry, February 10, 1940, No. 235–237, Amérique 1930–1940, États-Unis, B-9-1 319t MAE; Bullitt to Moore, April 18, 1940, WB, Box 58, f.1442; for views on Moffat's role, see J. Simon Rofe, *Franklin Roosevelt's Foreign Policy and the Welles Mission* (London: Palgrave Macmillan, 2007), pp. 150–151, 161, and Hooker, ed., *Moffat Papers*, esp. March 12, 1940, pp. 299–300, for his cynical views of the British.

100. "Admiral Stark's Comments on U.S.-British Naval Cooperation and Combined Planning," Box 21, f.1. Cf. Welles's later mention, leaning more to the fact-finding

explanation but allowing for another. Ciano, pp. xvi and 331. For the aims of the mission, see Rofe, pp. 3ff., 70–71.

101. Welles report, February 26, 1940, et seq., CH, Box 95, f.406.

102. Phillips to Hull, March 1, 1940, CH, Box 46, f.127.

103. Phillips to Welles, June 25, 1940, Welles Papers, FDR, Box 63, f.15.

104. Bullitt quoted in Jordan A. Schwarz, *Liberal: Adolf A. Berle and the Vision of an American Era* (New York: Free Press, 1987), p. 192; Hull to Roosevelt, March 29, 1944, CH, Box 53, f.166.

105. Pell to McDermott, August 1, 1942, President's Secretary's Files, Confidential, FDR, Box 1, f.7.

106. Welles to Mrs. Pierrepont Moffat, January 24, 1943, State Department Decimal Files, RG59 250 (1940–44) 123 M 723/414, NARA, Box 507, f.7; Records of the Office of European Affairs (Matthews-Hickerson File), 1934–47 Lots 54D394–395 M1244 (hereinafter MH), Box 1, Reel 2 and Box 2, Reel 8; Moffat to Welles, December 21, 1940, Welles Papers, FDR, Box 63, f.2; for Moffat's happiness in Canada, see Moffat to Hickerson, June 14, 1940, NARA, ibid.

107. *New York Times*, March 17, 1960, p. 33.

108. David Eccles to Roger Makins, April, 3, May 16, and June 4, 1941, RM, Box 518; for Bullitt's alleged change of heart about Atherton, see Henderson to Orville Bullitt, February 9, 1972, LH, Box 6, f.6; the story about the king appears in Weil, pp. 82–83; see also W. Phillips diary, March 14, 1934, WP, Box 3, f.1; Castle diary, January 30, 1935, WRC, Vol. 27; photo of Atherton in *Washington Post*, June 25, 1942, shows heavily lined eyes, a double chin, short mustache, and a crooked mouth.

109. For example, Hornbeck to Hackworth and Atherton, May 6, 1942 (one of several letters in this file on the subject), Stanley Hornbeck Papers, Hoover Institution, Stanford University, CA, Box 59, f.2; for interdepartmental tussles over neutrality and with the British and French, see Feis to Butterworth, August 28, 1936, HF, Box 12, f.11; Feis to Frankfurter, July 11, 1956, HF, Box 16, f.12; notes, November 16, 1942, Box 127, f.6; Culbertson to Murphy, July 17, 1943, and August 23, 1943, Robert D. Murphy Papers, Hoover Institution (hereinafter RDM), Box 44, f.20; Feis, *Seen from E.A.*, presents a detailed account of three such episodes. For Atherton's alleged inattention to detail, see Gosnell, "Memorandum of Conversation with Miss Clara Borjes," September 27, 1949, HLG, Box 44, f.4.

110. Matthews, p. 117; interview with H. Freeman Matthews Jr. Caffery was known for "a pragmatic and aggressive style" as well as a talent for dispensing patronage. Over two dozen protégés became ambassadors—a State Department record. Briggs, p. 104, and "Jefferson Caffery," *Dictionary of American Biography, Supplement 9, 1971–1975* (New York: Charles Scribner's Sons, 1994).

111. Castle diary, March 15, 1936, and May 16, 1936, WRC, Vol. 30; interview with Lucius Battle; Bonbright Oral History, ADST; Messersmith notes Hickerson as being "a good No. 2 man." Messersmith to Hull, May 28, 1940, CH, Box 47, f.132. Hickerson's calling Churchill's famous description of Lend-Lease ("the most unsordid act") an "unstinking remark" was indicative of his brand of humor, noted in Achilles, p. 308.

112. Ibid., p. 339; interview with David Acheson.

113. Wallner to Matthews, December 30, 1942, MH, Box 3, Reel 13. He later escaped. Additional information about his career, especially his involvement in intelligence work in North Africa, is in his personnel file, State Department Decimal Files RG59 250 (1940–44) 123/Wallner Woodruff, NARA, Box 628, f.2; cf. Cissy Patterson, "Some State Department Boys Who Do Not Choose to Fight," *Washington Times-Herald*, July 14, 1944; Matthews to Berle and Hull, September 16, 1944, MH, Box 2, Reel 10; Hull to Roosevelt, February 9, 1944, President's Secretary's Files, Confidential, FDR, Box 72, f.4; and Shaw to Rosenman, March 16, 1944, ibid., Box 72, f.6; Murphy to Dunn (on transfer of Sam Reber), August 10, 1943, RDM, Box 44, f.25, and Murphy to Matthews (on Bob Joyce), April 15, 1944, RDM,

Box 44, f. 30; and the following exchange between Dean Acheson's then assistant, Eugene Rostow, and Patrick Hurley, reported by Drew Pearson: "If you were a real man, you'd have a uniform on now. I'll bet you're one of those deferred diplomats." Pearson continued, "Naturally this got back to the White House. Some time later the President was talking to a friend about the State Department and remarked: 'Too much hurly-burly.' Presumably, he referred to his friend Patrick and Assistant Secretary Berle." *Washington Merry-Go-Round*, May 20, 1944. Cf. Briggs, pp. 110–111.

114. Shaw address in BL, Box 189, f. 10, p. 4; Atherton to Erhardt and Shaw, April 6, 1942, MH, Box 1, Reel 2; on Depression cutbacks, see Green to Marriner, January 13, 1934, JCG, Box 37, f.15; Carr memorandum, n.d. 1932, WJC, Box 9, f.8; Carr to Shaw, March 30, 1933, WJC, Box 10, f.1; Carr to Sayre, March 19, 1934, WJC, Box 11, f.3. By contrast, the State Department had grown by nearly 20 percent during the Hoover administration but by 1936 had decreased by 12 percent. Carr, "Administrative Achievements of the Department of State during the Present Administration," April 27, 1931, WJC, Box 9, f.7; memorandum to Hull, January 21, 1936, CH, Box 95, f.401. For the proliferation of wartime agencies, see Luther Gulick, *Administrative Reflections from World War II* (Birmingham: University of Alabama Press, 1948), esp. chap. 2.

4. On the Bench as on the Field

1. Robert Murphy, "The Role of the Political Adviser to the Military Governor," speech at the National War College, October 17, 1949, RDM, Box 30, f.26. Murphy subsequently asked General Patton "what he was doing about the control of prostitution. 'None of your so and so business,' he exploded, 'The State Department can stay out of that one!'" Cf. Policy Committee, July 15, 1944, "Survey of Principal Problems in Europe," CH, Box 53, f.169.

2. The first people to arrive there were Douglas MacArthur II and a former cleaning lady. See MacArthur, Oral History, ADST for the emotional story; Bullitt notes, April 29, 1942, WB, Box 73, f.1823.

3. Roger S. Greene to Wilson, April 9, 1941, Committee to Defend America by Aiding the Allies Papers, Department of Rare Books and Special Collections, Princeton University Library, Princeton University, Princeton, NJ (hereinafter CDAA), Box, 1, f.13; Castle to Hull, January 28, 1944, CH, Box 53, f.165.

4. Matthews, p. 229; Long diary, February 15, 1941, BL, Box 5, f.2; William Strang, *Home and Abroad* (London: Andre Deutsch, 1956), p. 207. Winant later committed suicide following the failure of his marriage. Achilles, pp. 243, 260, 287, noting that nearly everyone on the embassy staff celebrated when Kennedy left; Bernard Bellush, *He Walked Alone: A Biography of John Gilbert Winant* (Paris: Mouton, 1968), p. 27.

5. Castle diary, September 30, 1930, WRC, Vol. 17; Carr memorandum, November 14, 1936, WJC, Box 13, f.2; Carr to Tom Wilson, March 25, 1937, WJC, Box 13, f.6; Carr to Welles, January 18, 1937, WJC, Box 14, f.1; Waldo Heinrichs, letter to the author; Ellery C. Stowell, "The Appointment of Assistant Secretary of State G. Howland Shaw and Our Foreign Service," *American Journal of International Law* 35, no. 2 (April 1941): 340–345.

6. Shaw to Murphy, December 31, 1944, RDM, Box 59, f.30.

7. M. J. Hillenbrand, "American Muddle," n.d. (1937?), MJHH, Series II, Box 1, f.17.

8. Valuable accounts are in Herbert Feis, *The Spanish Story: Franco and the Nations at War* (New York: W. W. Norton and Co., 1966 [1948]); Ernest K. Lindley and Edward Weintal, "How We Dealt with Spain," *Harper's*, December 1944. For earlier statements of policy, see Bowers, pp. 410–421; Paul Culbertson, memorandum, October 10, 1936, JCG, Box 12, f.1; Green to Dunn et al., January 15, 1945, JCG, Box 12, f.1; John Morgan, "United States Policy During the Spanish Civil War, July 1936–April 1939," JCG, Box 12, f.2; Hugh Wilson to Dunn, November 29, 1935, and enclosure ("Jimmy, there ain't no such thing and the sooner we all realize that neutrality is the merest legal act and has no moral side to it,

the sooner our thoughts will be cleared up.... Misunderstanding occurs in the prevalent assumption that 'neutrality' and 'impartiality' are synonymous. Such is not the case ... we cannot legislate impartiality into human beings ..."), Wilson Papers, HHPL, Box 1, f.36; Sumner Welles, *The Time for Decision* (New York: Harper and Brothers Publishers, 1944), pp. 58ff.; Bowers to Dodd, September 10, 1936, WED, Box 48, f.7; Department of State, Press Release No. 561, December 28, 1940, CH, Box 48, f.141; Beaulac, pp. 160ff. Tierney challenges this view, pp. 39ff., 71–74, 95–109, 117–119, 158. The official who initially handled most of the neutrality talks with Congress was Judge Moore. A sample of his thinking on the subject is in Moore to Hull, May 5, 1938, CH, Box 42, f.106.

9. Eccles to Makins, November 18, 1940, RM, Box 518. This was not entirely Weddell's fault; see Carlton J. H. Hayes, *Wartime Mission in Spain, 1942–1945* (New York: Macmillan Company, 1946), p. 80.

10. Hayes to Hull, June 3, 1944, Carlton J. H. Hayes Papers, Columbia University Archives, New York, NY (hereinafter CJHH), Box 1, f.7; Hayes to Murphy, May 4, 1944, RDM, Box 45, f.5; Hayes, pp. 3–7, 16–17. See also Anthony Cave Brown, *The Last Hero: Wild Bill Donovan* (New York: Vintage Books, 1984), pp. 224ff., 345–348; Feis, *Spanish Story*, pp. 148ff., 215–262 (on wolfram, etc.); Hayes, chap. 7, esp. pp. 220ff.; David L. Gordon and Royden Dangerfield, *The Hidden Weapon: The Story of Economic Warfare* (New York: Harper and Brothers Publishers, 1947), pp. 105ff. All of it was at some cost to later relations with Stalin. See Hugh Wilson to Walter Lippmann, May 24, 1943, WL, Reel 99. Another even longer-term side effect, according to Drew Pearson, was the animus of the "Georgetown Jesuits" toward Dean Acheson for his determination to enforce the embargo. Drew Pearson, *Diaries, 1949–1959* (New York: Holt, Rinehart and Winston, 1974), p. 314.

11. Hayes to Beaulac, October 2, 1944, CJHH, Box 1, f.5; Hayes memorandum no. 991, June 16, 1943, CJHH, Box 1, f.18; Berle to Hayes, March 26, 1943, Adolph Berle Papers, FDR, Box 36, f.5. Henry Labouisse from Eu ultimately went to Spain to oversee the petroleum purchasing program. Feis notes, March 7–14, 1943, HF, Box 60, f.5. Of the OWI group, Hayes reserved particular venom for Perry Winner, noting in particular the number of Jews in Winner's shop. To take over many of the propaganda duties, Hayes brought in Emmet Hughes, his former student, who later achieved renown as a spokesman, then opponent, of the Eisenhower administration. Other officers who worked in Spain during this time were Walton Butterworth, Outerbridge Horsey, and William Smyser, whose son would also have a notable career in the foreign service as a German specialist and aide to Henry Kissinger on Vietnam.

12. Hayes to Welles, December 29, 1942, CJHH, Box 1, f.15.

13. Roberts, "Economic Relations with Spain," November 18, 1942, RM, Box 517; for his relationship with Kennan, see Frank Roberts Papers, Churchill Archives Centre, Churchill College, Cambridge University, Box 2, part 2, f.2, and Roberts, *Dealing with Dictators: The Destruction and Revival of Europe, 1930–70* (London: Weidenfeld and Nicolson, 1991), p. 65. Other views of Hayes, including those of the Spanish, are noted in Paul Preston, *Franco: A Biography* (New York: Basic Books, 1994), p. 459, 38n.

14. Hayes to Hull, December 27, 1943, CJHH, Box 1, f.11; see also Hayes, pp. 34ff., 110.

15. Beaulac to Hayes, June 16, 1944, CJHH, Box 1, f.7; Beaulac to Hayes, June 27, 1944, same folder; Perry George to Hayes, December 14, 1943, CJHH, Box 1, f.11; Matthews to Hayes, October 23, 1943, CJHH, Box 5, f.7; Hickerson to Beaulac, January 11, 1944, MH, Box 1, Reel 4; Hayes to Hull, December 27, 1943 (on the "impatience" of the State Department), MH, Box 2, Reel 9.2. Matthews appears to credit himself with the origin of the policy. Matthews, pp. 140ff. Eu's overenthusiasm seemed to earn it a rare rebuke from Welles. Welles to Atherton, December 3, 1941, Welles Papers, FDR, Box 166, f.4. Roosevelt's views—consistent but tepid—are summarized in his letter to Norman Armour, March 10, 1945, White House Central Files, Confidential Files, HST, Box 37, f.2.

16. Hayes, "Memorandum on the Spanish Situation with Special Reference to Relations

between Spain and the United States," February 1945, CJHH, Box 1, f.3; Hayes to Roosevelt, May 3, 1943, CJHH, Box 3, f.1; Hayes to Hull, December 27, 1943, CH, Box 53, f.164.

17. Bullitt to Hull, July 3, 1940, Moore Papers, FDR, Box 3, f.13.

18. "Transatlantic telephone conversation between Mr. Dunn and Amb. Bullitt [and Welles]," May 10, 1940, CH, Box 47, f.132.

19. A summary of the controversy is in Langer and Gleason, *The Undeclared War, 1940–1941* (New York: Harper and Brothers Publishers, 1953), p. 525, esp. n.59. Hull's view is in his *Memoirs*, Vol. 1 (New York: Macmillan Company, 1948), pp. 789–791.

20. Matthews, pp. 131–132.

21. Matthews was otherwise known as "a red burgundy man." David Bruce diary, December 10, 1954, Diaries of David K. E. Bruce, 1949–1974, State Department Lot Files, RG59 Lot 64D327, NARA (hereinafter DB), Box 2, f.24. Other details from Matthews, pp. 151ff. In the Chapon Fin, they also secured the short-lived liberty of the minister Georges Mandel, "the cold-blooded Jew," and rumored illegitimate Rothschild son who became a hero of the resistance (pp. 194–195); see also Matthews to Rev. Thomas Luke, August 14, 1940, MH, Box 3, Reel 13. Another good account of this and related stories is in Douglas MacArthur's Oral History, ADST.

22. Leahy diary, February 10, 1942, reporting the views of Admiral Standley, WDL, Reel 3.

23. Leith-Ross, p. 302; Matthews to Leahy, December 10, 1942, WDL, Reel 3. For Leahy's touching letter to the marshal following the latter's request for a character reference during his postwar trial for treason, see Leahy to Pétain, June 22, 1945, WDL, Reel 4; diary January 3, 1941.

24. Roosevelt to Leahy, n.d. (December 1940); Leahy to Roosevelt, May 26, 1941; Leahy to Roosevelt, January 25, 1942, WDL, Reels 2–3; Matthews to MacArthur, March 28, 1962, and enclosures, Records of Douglas MacArthur II 1951–62 RG59 Lot Files UP-253, NARA, Box 1, f.2.

25. Memorandum of Conversation, Hull, Tixier, D'Argenlieu, Atherton, December 8, 1942, CH, Box 28, f.209.

26. See William R. Tyler, "Memorandum on the Role of the French Committee of National Liberation in Liberated France," December 31, 1943, C. D. Jackson Papers, Dwight D. Eisenhower Presidential Library, Abilene, KS (hereinafter DDE), Box 1, f.4; Matthews to Leahy, December 10, 1942, WDL, Reel 3. For Hull's particular enmity toward de Gaulle, see Stimson diary, June 20, 1944, HLS, Reel 9, Vol. 47.

27. Matthews, p. 205. Two people who also had a great deal to do with this behind the scenes were Felix Cole, the consul in Algiers, and William Eddy of the OSS. "The Role of the Department of State in the North African Economic and Political Program from Its Inception to the Invasion," HLG, Box 19, f.9, p. 15; Kenneth Pendar, *Adventure in Diplomacy* (London: Cassell, 1966 [1945]), pp. 78ff.; Brown, p. 238ff.; Langer and Gleason, pp. 92–93. The Near Eastern Division also took credit for dreaming it up. See "Memorandum of Conversation by Acting Chief of Division of European Affairs (Atherton)," January 27, 1941, 740.00112 European War 1939/2161½, *FRUS 1941*, Vol. 2, pp. 247–250. Matthews, p. 208; William L. Langer, *Our Vichy Gamble* (New York: W. W. Norton and Company, 1947), pp. 44, 106–107. Others in the department were less supportive. Feis notes, November 16, 1942, HF, Box 127, f.6; Long diary, January 10, 1943, BL, Box 5, f.3; Long to Matthews, May 31, 1944, BL, Box 192, f.13; cf. HLG, Box 1, f.5, p. 24. French reaction in the United States is summarized by Henri Hoppenot's memorandum, November 15, 1942, Hoppenot Papers, Nos. 547–550, MAE. For the secretary's early obsession with the fleet, see Hull, pp. 771ff. Monick's own relations with Americans, including Roosevelt, dated at least as far back as the London Economic Conference of 1933, when Monick was French financial attaché in Washington. Marjolin, a protégé of the economist Charles Rist, had been an exchange student at Yale in the early 1930s and was married to an American. See Leffler,

pp. 325–326, and Robert Marjolin, *Le travail d'une vie: Mémoires, 1911–1986* (Paris: Éditions Robert Laffond, 1986), pp. 36ff., 102–112. For prevailing misconceptions about the Darlan deal, see Lippmann, "Memorandum on Our Relations with Darlan," November 17, 1942, WL, Reel 77.

28. On Offie, see Burton Hersh, *The Old Boys* (St. Petersburg, FL: Tree Farm Books, 2002), pp. 56ff., 140–143, a rare portrait of this colorful figure.

29. Felix Frankfurter, *From the Diaries of Felix Frankfurter*, February 25, 1943, (New York: Norton, 1975), p. 197; cf. Harold Macmillan, *The Blast of War, 1939–1945* (New York: Harper and Row Publishers, 1968), pp. 145, 176, 188–189; Pendar, pp. 19–20.

30. His orders are in *FRUS Europe 1942*, Vol. 2, pp. 379–381: "Directive by President Roosevelt to Mr. Robert D. Murphy," September 22, 1942, 123M956/4771/2.

31. Macmillan to Arthur Salter, January 29, 1943, Harold Macmillan Papers, Bodleian Library, Oxford University (hereinafter HM), f.102, and Macmillan memorandum, February 6, 1944, f.283–284. For Murphy's reputation with the British, see Eccles to Makins, May 22, 1941, RM, Box 518, and Matthews to Atherton, December 17, 1942, MH, Box 2, Reel 9. For more of Matthews's reaction, and his determination to "educate" the Foreign Office, see Matthews to Murphy, June 18, 1942, RDM, Box 45, f.25; interview with François de Rose.

32. Interview with Robert Blake; cf. Leahy to Welles, March 12, 1941, WDL, Reel 2.

33. Matthews, pp. 207, 248; Matthews to Murphy, May 16, 1944, MH, Box 2, Reel 9.2, where Matthews referred to the agreement struck between General Mark Clark and Darlan as the "Clark-(Murphy-Holmes-Matthews) Darlan agreement." See also Leahy diary, February 11, 1942, Roosevelt to Leahy, n.d. (February 11), Leahy to Welles, July 18, 1941, WDL, Reel 3. Darlan was murdered in December 1942. Cf. Churchill to Roosevelt, April 6, 1941, CHAR 20/37/53–55 Churchill Papers, Churchill Archive Centre, Churchill College, Cambridge University; Henri Michel, *François Darlan* (Paris: Hachette, 1993), pp. 105ff.

34. Matthews, p. 218; cf. Matthews to Langer, January 17, 1945, MH, Box 3, Reel 13; Leahy to Hull, July 18, 1941, CH, Box 49, f.145. The Algiers story inspired a few notable tales of "intrigue, American style." See Wes Gallagher, *Back Door to Berlin: The Full Story of the American Coup in North Africa* (Garden City, NY: Doubleday, Doran and Company, 1943), and Pendar, who was a participant.

35. Makins to Strang, April 7, 1943, RM, Box 520. N.b.: Reber's British counterpart was Makins's replacement, Harold Caccia, who would also become an ambassador to Washington. Various views on de Gaulle are found in Leahy's diary, November 18, 1942, WDL, Reel 3; Moffat, "Memorandum of Conversation with Messrs. Walter Lippmann and Norman Robertson," December 8, 1942, MH, Box 1, Reel 2; Matthews to Atherton, June 25, 1943, MH, Box 2, Reel 9; MacArthur to Matthews, September 6, 1944, MH, Box 2, Reel 9.2; Wilson to Matthews, November 10, 1943, Records of the Office of Western European Affairs, Records of the French Desk, 1941–51, RG59 Lot 53D246, NARA, Box 1, f.1; McCloy to Dunn, June 27, 1944 (attaching a report by Julius Holmes, "What is de Gaulle asking for?"), same collection, f.12; For Dunn's position, see his "Memorandum of Conversation with Jean Monnet," May 20, 1944, MH, Box 3, Reel 13; Dunn to Hull, June 17, 1944, same reel; and Hoppenot memoranda, November 15, 1942, and March 11, 1943, Hoppenot Papers, MAE; cf. Winant to Roosevelt, July 9, 1943, Map Room Files, FDR, Box 30, f.6; Dunn to Murphy, August 10, 1943, RDM, Box 44, f.25; *Frankfurter Diaries*, June 17, 1943, p. 260 (for Hull); Kittredge diary, January 12, 1944, TK, Box 20, f.1 (for FDR); Strang, pp. 71–74; Wallace Murray to Hull, November 19, 1942, CH, Box 50, f.152 (for Marshall); Bohlen to Reber, Atherton, and Dunn, January 7, 1943, 740.0011 European War 1939/26973 *FRUS 1943*, Vol. 3, pp. 497–498 (for the Soviet dimension).

36. Paraphrase of a message from Roosevelt to Hull, January 18, 1943, CH, Box 51, f.153.

37. Monnet to Harry Hopkins, March 8, 1943, AME 29/2/1 Jean Monnet Papers,

Fondation Jean Monnet pour l'Europe, Lausanne, Switzerland (hereinafter JM). See also Marjolin, pp. 119–122, and François Duchêne, *Jean Monnet: The First Statesman of Interdependence* (New York: W. W. Norton and Company, 1994), pp. 81ff.; cf. Burin de Roziers and Roger Makins oral histories, Archives of the European Union, Florence (hereinafter EU). Other key figures in helping Monnet achieve his ends in Washington were Harry Hopkins, Felix Frankfurter, David Bruce (then working for the Red Cross), John McCloy, and John Foster Dulles. See Bullitt to FDR, October 4, 1939, PSF France/Bullitt (from the Roosevelt Presidential Library) in JMDS/16, EU.

38. Whether or not it could have been prevented is beside the point; that option was never entertained. For more on Monnet's wartime activities, see *Frankfurter Diaries*, February 5, 1943, p. 183; and John McVickar Haight Jr., *American Aid to France, 1938–1940* (New York: Athenaeum, 1970).

39. The standard account is David S. Wyman's *Paper Walls: America and the Refugee Crisis, 1938–1941* (Amherst: University of Massachusetts Press, 1968). See also Moffat to George A. Gordon, April 4, 1933, JPM, Vol. 3.

40. Achilles, p. 272.

41. William Russell, *Berlin Embassy* (London: Michael Joseph Ltd., 1942), pp. 11, 23, noting similar conditions in "all of our consulates"; interview with Antonia Stearns. Cf. John Wills Tuthill, *Some Things to Some Men: Serving in the Foreign Service* (London: Minerva Press, 1998), pp. 36–38, 153–165; Kirk to Wilson, June 4, 1939, Wilson Papers, HHPL, Box 3; Wilson to Kirk, July 11, 1939, ibid.; Gilbert to Moffat, December 18, 1937, JPM, Vol. 12.

42. Long to Pasvolsky, January 25, 1943, BL, Box 198, f.21; Charles Thayer to Loy Henderson, January 11, 1940, Charles W. Thayer Papers, HST, Box 3, f.9.

43. Castle diary, December 22, 1933, WRC, Vol. 21; Long diary, December 16, 1940, BL, Box 5, f.2; see September 4, 1943, January 1, 1944, July 13, 1944, all in f.3, and also profile of Long in *PM*, February 11, 1941. Long's clipping was sent by a reader with the note, "How is your conscience? If you have one." Box 202, f.13; W. Phillips diary, September 20, October 15, 1935, WP, Box 4, f.9, f.13.

44. Long diary, June 22, 1941, BL, Box 5, f.2; Long to Hull, "Nationality Groups, Appeals to Them as Groups and the Effect of Them on Our National Unity," May 1943, BL, Box 192, f.15; diary, February 6, 18, 1938, Box 5, f.1; indeed, Long was accused of endangering the welfare of others besides Jews. An investigation found that he also hindered timely prisoner exchanges, for example. Miscellaneous Papers, Special Division 1941–45, JCG, Box 16.

45. Mayer to Dodd, May 27, 1935, WED, Box 47, f.2; Dodd to Moore, October 16, 1935 (not sent), WED, Box 47, f.3; n.b.: Mayer was an old friend of John Foster Dulles and later held rather right-wing views. Hayes to Hull, May 26, 1944, CJHH, Box 1, f.7; see also "Memorandum for the President on the Refugee Problem in Spain," May 3, 1943, CJHH, Box 3, f.1.

46. Kennan notes, March 21, 1939, WJC, Box 10, f.2.

47. "Measures Considered with Respect to the Attitude of the United States toward the Jews in Germany" (Carr), WJC, Box 10, f.2; cf. Memorandum of Conversation (Atherton and Irving Goff), February 1, 1941, BL, Box 192, f.10, and Memorandum of Conversation (Hoyer-Millar and Long), June 5, 1941, Box 192, f.8.

48. Roosevelt to Phillips, January 10, 1939, President's Secretary's Files, Confidential, FDR, Box 9, f.1; Feis to Bullitt, May 18, 1938, and reply, June 1, 1938, HF, Box 12, f.7; Feis to Frankfurter, April 4, 1938, HF, Box 16, f.12; and Ruth Feis, diary, May 6, 1933, HF, Box 123, f.6; Memorandum of Long and Lithuanian minister, May 8, 1940, BL, Box 192, f.7, and Pell to Long, February 20, 1941, with attachment, BL, Box 202, f.15. For Hickerson's view, similar to the above, see Hickerson to Berle, February 26, 1940, MH, Box 1, Reel 1: "I am in full sympathy ... [but] find myself in complete agreement with Mr. Long's memorandum to you on February 23, 1940." The officer handling the issue under Moffat was Ted Achilles,

who recalled his biases of the time by noting that he would travel to New York via Newark, a course that "went through the garment district and I would arrive at the Committee meetings feeling a bit anti-Semitic. Rabbi Wise was Chairman and I always thought of him as a bit of a fraud." Achilles, p. 248. See also Pell to Moffat, March 8, 1939, President's Secretary's Files, Confidential, FDR, Box 46, f.3; Feis, pp. 158–159. Background on Pell is from David Bruce diary entry, January 19, 1951, DB, Box 1, f.13, and Achilles, p. 251. For a sample of Rublee's difficulties with the Germans, including defending himself against false charges of having non-Aryan blood, see his correspondence with Hugh Wilson, October 14, November 9, November 10, and November 13, 1938, in Wilson Papers, HHPL, Box 3.

49. Long to Berle and Dunn, June 26, 1940, BL, Box 211, f.9; Long diary, June 17, November 20, 1940, Box 5, f.2, and April 20, 1943, same box, f.3.

50. E.g., "Gibson and I had a long talk on the Jewish question, which is lamentably misunderstood in America and may become, along with communism, of vital importance to the world. It is not only the surge of Jewish emigration to America that is dangerous to us but the more subtle danger for the world is a misunderstanding of Jewish aims.... [I]t was Brandeis himself who tried to blackmail Gibson into lying about the situation [pogroms] by threatening that the Jews would prevent his confirmation as Minister to Poland. The Jews of Poland are an incubus on the state. They are not producers. They live on driving hard bargains, on usury. They clutter the streets, because they have nothing to do except to discuss the theology of the Talmud. They are dirty and harbingers of all diseases; immoral and servants of immorality; absolutely unpatriotic. This is true of the Jews as a mass everywhere but it can be understood only when they can be seen in compact masses as in Warsaw. They oppose a strong Poland. Is it possible that they are looking toward a Jewish state from Riga to Odessa, the Baltic to the Black Seas, which will levy toll on the trade of the world?" Castle diary, September 4, 1921, WRC, Vol. 2; see also entries for November 7 and 12, 1923, Vol. 4, for his views of the diplomat Lewis Einstein: "over-unctuous ... a little too complimentary to sound sincere."

51. HF, Box 3, f.2; Long diary, April 20, 1943, BL, Box 5, f.3; see also Weil, p. 91; Schacht to Foreign Ministry, May 6, 1933, No. 214, 9037/E632796-802, AA, Series C, Vol. 1, p. 390.

52. The words are ironic given the suspected rationale behind Steinhardt's own appointment to Turkey in 1942. When Roosevelt decided to appoint him, the president might have recalled the pledge once given to Atatürk that no more Jewish ambassadors would be sent to Turkey as some had been in Ottoman times, but also perhaps another story: President Cleveland's nominee to Vienna had been a Catholic Virginian with a Jewish wife who had previously made himself unpopular in Italy. Seeking to derail the nomination, the Viennese authorities used the excuse of his wife's religion to claim that she would not be permitted at court receptions. Secretary of State Thomas Bayard wrote to his opposite that the United States took no account of religion in ministerial nominations. The first secretary in Vienna at the time was the president's half brother, James Roosevelt Roosevelt. FDR probably would have heard stories of the episode as a child, and so, when it came time to nominate Steinhardt, he may have remembered Bayard's principle and went ahead. Allan Nevins, *Grover Cleveland: A Study in Courage* (New York: Dodd, Mead and Co., 1932), p. 209; Dodd to House, July 19, 1934, WED, Box 43, f.18; Long diary, November 28, 1941, Box 5, f.2.

53. Feis to Joseph Cotton, September 20, 1938, HF, Box 15, f.6; Long diary, October 3, 1940, BL, Box 5, f.2. Cf. "The History of Intervention on Behalf of the Jews," in Thayer Papers, HST, Box 3, f.4 (probably written by Thayer in 1938–1939).

54. "Memorandum for the Record, April 8, 1963," HF, Box 23, f.7; John Wesley Jones, "Miscellaneous Observations on 'Post-War Planning,'" RG59, Lot Files, Records of Leo Pasvolsky 1938–45, NARA, Box 2, f.2.

55. See Harley Notter, *Postwar Foreign Policy Preparation, 1939–1945* (Washington, D.C.:

Department of State, 1949), and Neil Smith, *American Empire: Roosevelt's Geographer and the Prelude to Globalization* (Berkeley: University of California Press, 2003). The French and British governments had similar planning directorates, although there has not appeared a systematic comparison of all three. Further details on the origins are in Hamilton Fish Armstrong, "Memorandum on first chapter (or section) of Notter book," letter, Hamilton Fish Armstrong Papers, Department of Rare Books and Special Collections, Princeton University Library, Princeton University, Princeton, NJ (hereinafter HFA), Box 47, f.23, and in Kenneth Weisbrode, "The Master, the Maverick, and the Machine: Three Wartime Promoters of Peace," *Journal of Policy History* 21, no. 4 (November 2009): 366-391.

56. "Memorandum for the State-War-Navy Coordinating Committee," November 13, 1945, JJM, WD1, f.6 (draft by "CHB"). For his part, Hull was almost totally in the dark about unconditional surrender, etc. Hull to Roosevelt, December 22, 1943, in HF, Box 53, f.6, although Hickerson had a minor part in pushing hard for a non-Carthaginian Peace. Hickerson to Matthews and Dunn, September 3, 1943, MH, Box 1, Reel 2. Cf. Memorandum of Conversation (Long and A. P. Beveridge), April 21, 1944, BL, Box 204, f.18. Matthews's account of the Morgenthau-Stimson-McCloy battle is in *FRUS Conferences at Malta and Yalta, 1945*, pp. 134-135: "Memorandum by the Deputy Director of the Office of European Affairs," September 20, 1944 740.0011 EW/9-2044; Stimson diary, April 4 and August 23-26, 1944, HLS, Reel 8, Vol. 47 and Reel 9, Vol. 48. For an interpretation of the State Department's role at the time as being little more than an auxiliary to the armed services, see Ernest R. May, "The Development of Political-Military Consultation in the United States," *Political Science Quarterly* 70, no. 2 (June 1955): 161-180.

57. Draft in MH, Box 3, Reel 17. For the European Advisory Commission and the problems with the British therein, see Winant to Roosevelt, January 26, 1945, John G. Winant Papers, FDR, Box 195, f.10; Communiqué, October 31, 1943, No. 50, CH, Box 82, f.351; Bellush, pp. 198ff.; Kennan, chap. 7; summary of work in MH, Box 1, Reel 4; Matthews on the bureau's disfavor, MH, Box 2, Reel 9.2; Kennan to Bullitt, April 23, 1944, WB, Box 44, f.1061; "The Work of the European Advisory Commission, January 1944–July 1945," July 12, 1945, Records of the Central European Division, 1944–53, RG59 Lot 55D374, NARA, Box 1, f.6. A summary from the perspective of the British delegate (who took the EAC a good deal more seriously) is in Strang, chap. 6. Cf. Hamilton Fish Armstrong to Harley Notter, January 5, 1949, HFA, Box 46, f.23; Oral Histories of E. Allan Lightner Jr., October 26, 1973, and James W. Riddleberger, April 26, 1972, HST. See also the next chapter.

58. Hickerson to Hugh Fullerton, December 28, 1944, MH, Box 1, Reel 4; Merchant to Labouisse, December 9, 1944, Livingston Merchant Papers, Department of Rare Books and Special Collections, Princeton University Library, Princeton University (hereinafter LM), Box 1, f.1; Plischke, pp. 302–307. Julius Holmes, by now "polished, polyglot and protocolaire"—who had once worked for an airline and mining company as well as serving as chief of protocol—was the architect of this reform during his brief tenure as assistant secretary for administration under Stettinius, who also came from the private sector. Holmes's son, Allen, would become a prominent diplomat in the 1980s. Achilles, p. 247, quoting Drew Pearson.

59. Makins, "Reflections on the Sforza Incident," December 7, 1944, RM, Box 521. N.b.: Makins's son, Christopher, was a British diplomat active in the 1970s and later president of the Atlantic Council of the United States.

60. Ibid.

61. Bullitt to Henderson, November 1, 1939, LH, Box 6, f.6; see also Bullitt to Roosevelt, January 29, 1943, President's Secretary's Files, Confidential, FDR, Box 24, f.6, in which Soviet power is described as an amoeba. According to Frankfurter, Stimson regarded Bullitt's bias as "anti-British, anti-Russian, anti-Roosevelt" and coming "from a mind essentially disloyal to this country." Cf. Wilson to Kirk, December 4, 1939, Wilson

Papers, HHPL, Box 3, f.9.

62. For wartime strains, see Steinhardt to Henderson, October 5 and October 20, 1940, LH, Box 1, f.3; cf. Halifax to Eden, June 19, 1944, 1320/3/44, No. 620, CAB 122/1035, National Archives (formerly Public Record Office), Kew, UK (hereinafter PRO); for tension with Steinhardt over the Harriman mission, see W. Averell Harriman and Elie Abel, *Special Envoy to Churchill and Stalin, 1941–1946* (New York: Random House, 1975), pp. 84–85, 96; David Mayers, *The Ambassadors and America's Soviet Policy* (New York and Oxford: Oxford University Press, 1985), pp. 132–133.

63. De Santis, pp. 122–123; Robert E. Sherwood, *Roosevelt and Hopkins: An Intimate History* (New York: Harper and Brothers, 1948), pp. 774–775; cf. Achilles, p. 336, reporting that Bohlen said in 1944, "[D]on't kid yourself that [the Russians] are our allies in any other sense." For a notoriously rosier view, see John R. Deane, *Strange Alliance* (New York: Viking Press, 1947), pp. 38ff.

64. The correspondence is in GK, Box 28, f.7, and in the Charles Bohlen Papers, Library of Congress, Washington, D.C. (hereinafter CB), Box 3, f.1; cf. Long to Roosevelt, July 12, 1944 (on Welles's *The Time for Decision*), BL, Box 89, f.12; Bohlen, pp. 175–177; Kennan, pp. 211ff.

65. Bullitt to Roosevelt, May 28, 1937, WB, Box 71, f.1792; Hull to Roosevelt (drafted by Bullitt), n.d. (July–August 1943), CH, Box 51, f.157. Cf. Wilson, *A Career Diplomat*, p. 80; Feis, *Seen from E.A*, p. 294.

5. Mastering Europe

1. James P. Warburg, n.d. (1946), W. Averell Harriman Papers, Library of Congress, Washington, D.C. (hereinafter WAH), Box 213, f.7; for EUR's draft of the Potsdam agenda, see "Memorandum July 6, 1945," in MH, Box 2, Reel 10. The final document appears in *FRUS 1945*, Vol. 1 (the Potsdam Conference), no. 177 (June 30, 1945), pp. 199–205.

2. Leahy diary, July 21, 1945, WLD, Reel 4; Matthews, pp. 292–295; George Allen to Loy Henderson, July 16, 1945, George V. Allen Papers, HST, Box 1, f.1. Joe Alsop said that Berlin reminded him of what he imagined Manila to be in 1904. Charles Kindleberger to J. K. Galbraith, October 30, 1946, Charles Kindleberger Papers, HST, Box 4, f.1. None, so far as it is known, helped himself to Hitler souvenirs, unlike others. George Elsey, *An Unplanned Life* (Columbia and London: University of Missouri Press, 2005), p. 87.

3. Bohlen to Berlin, n.d. (1945), IB, Box 112, f.213. Bohlen's recollections of the conference, including the twenty-four-foot red star made of geraniums planted by the Soviets in the palace garden, are in his memoir, pp. 225ff.

4. *Time*, March 2, 1959; memo by J. Anthony Panuch (presumably), n.d., J. Anthony Panuch Papers, HST, Box 7, f.4; "Performance Report, James W. Riddleberger, Foreign Service Officer, Class 1," January 5, 1951, JJM, Box HC 6, f.1; H. Freeman Matthews to Robert Murphy, July 9, 1947, in RDM, Box 58, f.51; OMGUS-3-D-11 March 4, 1949, James W. Riddleberger Papers, HST, Box 1, f.7.

5. Interview with Antonia Stearns; James Riddleberger to Amelie Riddleberger, July 24, 1945, in Riddleberger Papers, HST, Box 1, f.1.

6. Cf. the following reported exchange in 1946:

Winston Churchill: "Young man, I remember you." Chip Bohlen: "Yes, sir, we met when I was translating for President Roosevelt."

Churchill (growling): "One cannot be reassured when one remembers the Oder-Neisse line."

Bohlen (very calmly): "I feel sure you remember that it was not the United States that was responsible for the Oder-Neisse."

Churchill (blowing cigar smoke into the face of Mrs. Bohlen): "You are married to a brilliant young man, my dear."

Susan Mary Alsop, *To Marietta, from Paris 1945–1960* (New York: Doubleday and Company,

1975), p. 83. Alsop, formerly Patten and Jay, was the daughter of a diplomat and niece of a law partner of Henry Stimson's as well as a lover of the British statesman and biographer of Talleyrand, Duff Cooper, husband of Diana.

7. Robert Murphy, *Diplomat Among Warriors* (Garden City, NY: Doubleday and Company, 1964), pp. 225–226, 231; Herbert Feis, *From Trust to Terror: The Onset of the Cold War, 1945–1950* (New York: W. W. Norton and Company, 1970), p. 32; Feis to McCloy, December 9, 1944, HF, Box 30, f.1; Matthews, pp. 260, 270–274; Phil Mosely to Matthews, November 16, 1944, MH, Box 2, Reel 12; David Harris to Matthews, September 17, 1946, MH, Box 3, Reel 15; E. Alan Lightner Oral History, October 26, 1973, HST; James W. Riddleberger Oral History, May 29, 1981, James W. Riddleberger Papers, George Marshall Foundation, Lexington, VA (hereinafter JR), Box 3, f.4. Clayton's and Feis's occupation memos (March 22 and March 20, 1945) are in JJM, Box WD3, f.1 and f.2. Folders 4–6 contain McCloy's own working memos; for a plea to link German recovery with that of the rest of Europe, see Richard Bissell to Harriman, October 16, 1947, WAH, Box 238, f.1; Elbridge Durbrow Oral History, May 31, 1973, HST; James Riddleberger to Amelie Riddleberger, July 24, 1945, HST, Box 1, f.1; "Suggested United States Policy Regarding Poland" and "The Polish Problem," in Office Files of Ambassador Elbridge Durbrow State Department RG59 Lot 68D404 E1575, NARA, Box 3, f.6, on the Oder-Neisse line.

8. Riddleberger Oral History, JR, Box 3, f.1; Acheson to Dulles, January 16, 1953, General Correspondence and Memoranda Series, John Foster Dulles Papers, DDE, Box 3, f.8; "Telephone Conversation with Governor Adams," June 19, 1953, Subject Series, John Foster Dulles Papers, DDE, Box 6, f.13; Bruce diary, February 5, 1952, DB, Box 1, f.23.

9. Feis to McCloy, December 9, 1944, HF, Box 30, f.1.

10. "Minutes of an Informal Meeting of the European Advisory Commission," EAC Files RG59 Lot 52M64, File "Minutes—EAC Meetings—1 June 45 To" *FRUS 1945*, Vol. 3, p. 540; Philip E. Mosely, "Dismemberment of Germany: The Allied Negotiations from Yalta to Potsdam," *Foreign Affairs* 28, no. 3 (April 1950): 487–498. See also Kennan, chap. 7; Winant to McCloy, February 24, 1945, Winant Papers, FDR, Box 195, f.10; Clayton and Feis memos in JJM, March 1945, WD3, f.1, f.5; Breckinridge Long diary, June 26, 1944, BL, Box 5, f.3, indicating the split between the department and the Big Three; Hickerson to Matthews and Dunn, September 3, 1943, MH, Box 1, Reel 2; Memorandum of Conversation, Walter Lippmann and William Strang, December 4, 1947, WL, Reel 93. One American who seemed to take the EAC seriously was the geographer Isaiah Bowman, who had been involved heavily in the postwar planning committees. See Matthews, "Diary of a Mission to London, March 10th, 1944 to May 4th, 1944," MH, Box 3, Reel 14.

11. Harriman to Truman, June 9, 1945, WAH, Box 187, f.7; Memorandum by Harry Hopkins, June 13, 1945, HH, Box 6, f.31. According to Ted Achilles, Dunn was the primary "mastermind" both at San Francisco and in devising the formula of postwar conferences of foreign ministers. Achilles pp. 343, 346.

12. Many, like Elbridge Durbrow, regarded the "Yalta Charade" to have been over by May. Unpublished memoir, p. 133, EDD, Box 40, f.1; while Kennan went so far as to urge that the United States withdraw entirely from the agreements reached at Potsdam. Kennan to Carmel Offie, May 10, 1946, 740.00119 Control (Germany)/5-1046 *FRUS 1946*, Vol. 5, pp. 555–556; Leahy diary, April 23, 1945, WLD, Reel 4.

13. Matthews, p. 298; Riddleberger Oral History, April 26, 1972, HST; Riddleberger Oral History, March 7, 1980, JR, Box 3, f.1.

14. DeWitt Poole to Robert Murphy, May 8, 1946, and Poole speech, "The Future of Germany," January 19, 1946, in RDM, Box 59, f.15. A trusteeship plan is in a letter by Matthews, June 28, 1956, RDM, Box 58, f.41; Nicolas Nabokov to Robert Murphy, August 18, 1947, RDM, Box 59, f.1. Cf. Kennan, "Policy Questions Concerning a Possible German Settlement," August 12, 1948, Policy Planning Staff Files: Lot 64D563, Box 20029, Germany, *FRUS 1948*, Vol. 2, pp. 1287–1297. Notwithstanding a few dissenters, the acceptance by

most senior members of the department of a divided Germany, however temporary, would last another decade or at least as long as Europe itself remained divided. Cf. Lewis Pollack to Phillip Jessup, "Departmental Views on Germany," CF 662.001/4-252 *FRUS 1952-1954*, Vol. 7, pp. 194–199; and Hermann-Josef Rupieper, "American Policy Toward German Unification, 1949–1955," in Jeffry M. Diefendorf, Axel Frohn, and Hermann-Josef Rupieper, eds., *American Policy and the Reconstruction of West Germany, 1945–1955* (Washington, D.C.: German Historical Institute and Cambridge University Press, 1993), pp. 54ff.; Marc Trachtenberg, *A Constructed Peace: The Making of the European Settlement, 1945–1963* (Princeton, NJ: Princeton University Press, 1999), p. 21. For British ambivalence about the prospects of a "splitting" of Germany, see Frank Roberts's notes on a memo about Germany by Gladwyn Jebb, February 5, 1943, RM, Box 517; cf. Bohlen's views on the inevitability and desirability of division, mentioned in Brandon's diary, May 27, 1952, HB, Box 3, f.1.

15. This applied, of course, only to their generation. Among the older one of Grew, Dunn et al., anti-Soviet sentiment was common but had other antecedents that were less connected to the termination of war. Incidentally, Dunn, along with a then obscure intelligence officer named James Jesus Angleton, helped to save Italy from a Communist fate in 1948. He succeeded Alexander Kirk there as ambassador in 1946 and would remain popular in Italy until he moved to France in 1952. Matthews, p. 310; cf. Thayer to J. and M. Dunn, n.d., Thayer Papers, HST, Box 2, f.7: "Jimmy rushing from city to city, port to port, harassing the enemy and rallying our friends while Mary exhorted them at Villa Taverna dispensing courage with the cocktails, patience with the pasta and wisdom with the wine"; John Wesley Jones Oral History, HST, June 8, 1974; Achilles memoir, p. 456, crediting Walter Dowling with the Italian-American letter-writing campaign; Clare Boothe Luce Oral History, January 11, 1968, DDE (for Joe Kennedy's role); Achilles to Merchant, November 4, 1953, Bureau of European Affairs, Miscellaneous Office Files of the Assistant Secretaries of State for European Affairs, 1943–57, RG59 Lot 59D233 NARA, Box 25, f.12, for Hickerson's role in keeping pressure on the Italians. For the Clay meeting, see Riddleberger Oral History, HST.

16. Loy W. Henderson Oral History, July 5, 1973, HST; Acheson, p. 217. A similar version appears in Joseph M. Jones, *The Fifteen Weeks, February 21–June 5, 1947* (New York: Viking Press, 1955), pp. 3ff. See also pp. 148ff. on the State Department's role in the drafting of Truman's March 12, 1947 speech.

17. E.g., "Memorandum by Mr. Elbridge Durbrow, 'Certain Aspects of Present Soviet Policy,'" February 3, 1944, 761.00/2-344 *FRUS 1944*, Vol. 4, pp. 813–814, and Kennan, "Russia—Seven Years Later," September 1944, 861.00/2-1445. ibid., pp. 902–914. See also Kennan, pp. 226–230.

18. This was true almost immediately after Kennan articulated his containment policy. See Matthews, "Political Estimate of Soviet Policy for Use in Connection with Military Studies," April 1, 1946, SWNCC Files, *FRUS 1946*, Vol. 1, pp. 1167–1171; de Santis, pp. 175ff., for Matthews's and others' exuberant reaction to the Long Telegram.

19. Cf. Murphy to Dunn, June 29, 1944, RDM, Box 30, f.25. Riddleberger's reporting from Berlin during the 1948 crisis is in *FRUS 1948*, Vol. 2, pp. 868ff. For Kennan's underappreciated role in the transition, see Richard J. Bissell Jr. Oral History, July 9, 1971, HST.

20. See Lincoln Gordon, "Recollections of a Marshall Planner," *Journal of International Affairs* 41, no. 2 (Summer 1988): 233–245.

21. Livingston Merchant to Henry Labouisse, January 17, 1945, LM, Box 1, f.1; for a sample of similar divisions among Europeans, see Kohnstamm and von Staden Oral Histories, EU; interviews with Avis Bohlen, Karl Kaiser. For his part, Paul-Henri Spaak did not see any "conflict between European Union and Atlantic Union; but the stimulus for the latter must come from the United States." Lithgow Osborne to Kenneth Lindsay, February 21, 1951, Papers of the Atlantic Union Committee, Library of Congress, Washington, D.C.

(hereinafter AUC), Box 1, Atlantic Congress.

22. For origins, see Kennan to Riddleberger, June 13, 1944, GK, Box 28, f.6; Carolyn Eisenberg, *Drawing the Line: The American Decision to Divide Germany, 1944–1949* (Cambridge: Cambridge University Press, 1996), pp. 205ff., for the various disputes. Eisenberg's book is a revisionist study that criticizes McCloy, especially. Few in EUR would have endorsed her conclusion that the United States deliberately acceded to (let alone devised) the division of Germany in order to provoke the Soviet Union into a protracted war it would someday lose. Concerns about the Soviet Union and regret over partition, so far as the evidence suggests, were genuine at the time.

23. Charles Kindleberger to Sarah Kindleberger, August 4, 1946, and Kindleberger to John de Wilde, same date and August 15, 1946, Charles Kindleberger Papers, HST, Box 4, f.4; and Kindleberger to Sarah Kindleberger, March 12, 1947, ibid., Box 4, f.6; Kindleberger Oral History, July 16, 1973, HST; E. Allan Lightner to Robert Murphy, August 15, 1946, Records of the Central European Division 1944–1953, RG59 Lot 55D 374 NARA, Box 1, f.1; Riddleberger to Sec-State, July 20, 1946, same box, f.2. The Treasury Department by now had little to do with German recovery. J. Burke Knapp Oral History, July 24 and 30, 1975, HST; Perry Laukhuff Oral History, July 23, 1974, HST; E. Allan Lightner Oral History, October 26, 1973, HST; interview with William R. Smyser; Murphy, p. 291.

24. Woodruff Wallner to Douglas MacArthur, September 5, 1946, Records of the Office of Western European Affairs, Records of the French Desk 1941–51, RG59 Lot 53D246 NARA, Box 2, f.4; Riddleberger Oral History, March 7, 1980, JR, Box 3, f.1; A good friend of Brandt's was Eleanor Dulles, the sister of the secretary of state who held an analyst's job on the German Desk for many years after working for Leo Pasvolsky. Riddleberger appointed her, according to Drew Pearson, because she had made it clear that she could not wait until the Democrats were out of power, lest it appear like nepotism; in return, so it was said, Riddleberger got the embassy in Yugoslavia. *Drew Pearson Diaries*, January 23, 1958, p. 424. However, Riddleberger had most likely sided with Eleanor on principle against both her brother and Pearson when it was suggested that she go. Letter to the author from Peter Riddleberger.

25. Martin Hillenbrand, *Fragments of Our Time: Memoirs of a Diplomat* (Athens, GA: University of Georgia Press, 1998), p. 76; the moniker for McCloy was President Roosevelt's, who reportedly held up his hand in a Hitler salute when he issued it. John J. McCloy Oral History, February 19, 1971, DDE; for the formal relationship between HICOG and the State Department, see "Notes on the State Department Organization for the Administration of Germany," Records of the Office of Western European Affairs, Miscellaneous German Files 1943–54, RG59 Lot 55D371, NARA, Box 7, f.10.

26. Murphy to Department, August 19, 1949, RDM, Box 59, f.19.

27. Hickerson to Murphy, June 27, 1947, MH, Box 1, Reel 5; Coburn Kidd to Riddleberger and Lightner, "Conflicts in Our German Policy," May 12, 1947, Records of the Central European Division, Box 2, f.18 (probably misfiled). See also "Office of German Political Affairs: Functional Duties of Personnel," n.d., Martin Hillenbrand Papers 1950–75, RG59 Lot UP025, NARA (hereinafter MJH), Box 4, f.3; flowchart diagram drawn by Elwood Williams, n.d., same collection, Box 6, f.11.

28. This launched a long diplomatic career as a most candid and companionable ambassador to Egypt, South Africa, Burma, the Philippines, and Pakistan.

29. Including luminaries such as Elwood Williams, Martin Hillenbrand, Coburn Kidd, and Jonathan "Jock" Dean.

30. Interviews with Jonathan Dean, Thomas Simons, William Smyser. Other important German hands of the first generation included E. Allan Lightner and Arch Calhoun, and of the second, George Muller, Karl and Martha Mautner, and Joachim von Elbe; Hillenbrand, pp. 50ff., 111.

31. Ball Oral History, August 10, 1987, EU; interview with Arthur Hartman; see

also Theodore White, *Fire in the Ashes: Europe in Mid-Century* (New York: William Sloane Associates, 1953), pp. 60ff; Richard Bissell Jr. Oral History, HST.

32. Katz to Harriman, "From the Pen of a Britisher," n.d., WAH, Box 267, f.8.

33. Lincoln Gordon to Miriam Camps, September 5, 1991, Miriam Camps Papers, Mt. Holyoke College Archives and Special Collections, South Hadley, MA (hereinafter MC), Box 9, f.26; Milton Katz to Arthur Krock, June 15, 1948, WAH, Box 238, f1; Wayne Jackson to Arthur Kimball, summarizing Norman Armour's views, December 18, 1947, MH Box 1, Reel 3; "Policy With Respect to American Aid to Western Europe," May 23, 1947, MH, Box 3, Reel 18; interview with Lincoln Gordon; Oral Histories of Dean Acheson, Lucius Battle, William Clayton, Edmund Hall Patch, Joseph Johnson, Frederick Reinhardt, Willard Thorp, Tyler Wood, and John Hickerson, HST. (N.b.: Hickerson's father sold cotton to Clayton in Texas for many years.) Cf. Frederick Nolting's Oral History, HST, which contradicts the minimal role Hickerson claimed he played; James E. Webb to the President, November 10, 1947, "Organization to carry out European Recovery Program," Presidential Secretary's File: General File, HST, Box 102, f.12. For his part, Bohlen was known to interrupt meetings of the Marshall planners, chirping "ERP, ERP, ERP," "which he thought was funny." Lincoln Gordon Oral History, July 17, 1975, HST. For the contribution and perspective of some New York bankers, see Russell Leffingwell to Allen Dulles, September 12, 1947, RL, Box 1, f.32.

34. Joseph Alsop to Isaiah Berlin, n.d. (1947), IB, Box 278, f.37–39; cf. Kennan, "Notes on the Marshall Plan," GK, Box 23, f.50; David Bruce Oral History, March 1, 1972, HST.

35. Bohlen draft notes, "U.S. Policy and Western European Integration," WAH, Box 269, f.8.

36. Kennan to Bohlen (and replies), beginning October 6, 1949, GK, Box 28, f.10; cf. "Minutes of the Seventh Meeting of the Policy Planning Staff, January 24, 1950" (Kennan, Nitze, Bohlen et al.) RG59 840.00R/1-2450 in *FRUS 1950*, Vol. 3, pp. 617–622, and Gladwyn Jebb, *The Memoirs of Lord Gladwyn* (London: Weidenfeld and Nicolson, 1972), pp. 217–222. This exchange coincided with the OEEC crisis with the British (see below) and the "great integration debate." See Michael Hogan, *The Marshall Plan: America, Britain and the Reconstruction of Western Europe, 1947–1952* (Cambridge: Cambridge University Press, 1987), pp. 270–271; John Lamberton Harper, *American Visions of Europe: Franklin D. Roosevelt, George F. Kennan, and Dean G. Acheson* (Cambridge: Cambridge University Press, 1996), pp. 214ff.; Sally Dore, "Britain and the European Payments Union," in Francis H. Heller and John R. Gillingham, eds., *The United States and the Integration of Europe: Legacies of the Postwar Era* (New York: St. Martin's Press, 1996), p. 194n8, notes that for Harriman's deputy, Milton Katz, presumably stating a widespread view, "to say that the relationship was special was merely a truism, and the real question was what consequences flowed from it."

37. Interview with Roger Kirk.

38. "Myth and Reality in European Integration," *Yale Review* 45, no. 1 (September 1955): 83. Gordon's position has remained consistent since the 1950s; see his "Recollections of a Marshall Planner," pp. 241–242. According to him, the notion of the Marshall Plan as the primary and self-conscious engine of European unity derived too much from contemporary rhetoric, namely, of ECA director Paul Hoffman, and has since been overstated by historians, particularly Michael Hogan. Cf. Hogan's *The Marshall Plan*, pp. 26ff., and Greg Behrman, *The Most Noble Adventure: The Marshall Plan and the Time When America Helped Save Europe* (New York: Free Press, 2007), pp. 349–350, 400–402.

39. Raymond Vernon to Bruce, July 25, 1950, RG59 850.337-2550, in JMDS/74(2), EU. See also Camp to Perkins, December 29, 1950, on limiting ECA's direct involvement in the Schuman Plan negotiations, in the subsequent file. However, this did not stand in the way of pushing hard to generate public support for ratification, particularly in Germany.

40. Wilson to Moffat, March 7, 1938, Wilson Papers, HHPL, Box 3, f.25. The former view is stated clearly in Hogan, p. 27. It may not have been as true at higher levels, or

in the minds of its principal protagonists. Konrad Adenauer, according to one report, regarded "Acheson [as] the real instigator." Hays (Bonn) to SecState, May 10, 1950, RG59 850.33 Plan Schuman, in JMDS/74(1), EU. For his part, David Bruce was almost constantly worried about falling off course, viz., "If the British continue their present tactics there will be sharp and open friction that will tend to divide these now friendly nations into two blocs. Moreover, the disillusionment of our own people in the event that the Schuman Plan is torpedoed should not be disregarded. When such grand issues are at stake a forceful reiteration to the British of the American concern over Western unity might be salutary.... The French are in the throes of a political crisis, the British are sulking, but in a vocal way on their island, the Dutch and the Belgians are in effect arguing about how many angels can stand on the head of a pin, and if we do not make our position unmistakably clear to the British we run the risk that the only European integration will be a unification of all the elements opposed to a rapprochement between France and Germany." Bruce to SecState, July 5, 1950, 859.33/7-550, in JMDS 74 EU.

41. Finletter was a onetime protégé of Herbert Feis who would go on to become secretary of the air force and NATO ambassador as well as a successful banker; Zellerbach was a California paper and pulp tycoon; Douglas, noted below, was a politician from a rich Arizona mining family who was also John McCloy's college friend and brother-in-law; Chapin was a diplomat with a navy background—he attended Annapolis and his sister married Admiral Alan Kirk, the naval commander at D-Day and later ambassador to the Soviet Union and Belgium.

42. Caffery to SecState, October 28, 1948, RG59 851.5017/10-2848, in JDMS/64, EU; Phillips to Dulles, November 29, 1952, JFD, Reel 23, noting the "swarms" of Americans in Paris "where there are three other ambassadors besides Ambassador Dunn." See also note 82. Chapin to Riddleberger, September 26, 1950, RG59 Lot 57D694, Records of the Office of European Affairs, Records of the Office of the Executive Director, 1948–53, NARA, Box 1, f.13.

43. Interview with William Clayton by his daughter, Ellen Garwood, March 1947, William L. Clayton Papers, Hoover Institution on War, Revolution, and Peace, Stanford University, Stanford, CA (hereinafter WLC), Box 2, f.2; André Leprevost, September 22, 1944, no 825 B., Amérique, États-Unis 1944–1952 33 MAE; n.a., July 11, 1945, 1315 11.C7.455 Politique, ibid.; Bonnet to Min., May 30, 1947, No. 1183/AM, ibid.; Benson E. L. Timmons Oral History, July 8, 1970, HST; Joseph Alsop with Adam Platt, *I've Seen the Best of It* (New York: W. W. Norton, 1997), p. 287. Caffery may have kept his job for as long as he did in part because he was said to be well liked by Secretary Byrnes. C. L. Sulzberger, *A Long Row of Candles: Memoirs and Diaries, 1934–1954* (New York: Macmillan Company, 1969), p. 366. See also Susan Mary Alsop, p. 67, suggesting that Caffery's principal quality was shyness.

44. Richard M. Bissell Jr., *Reflections of a Cold Warrior: From Yalta to the Bay of Pigs* (New Haven, CT: Yale University Press, 1996), p. 50, and Bissell Oral History, HST. One suspects Dulles took special pleasure in denying Harriman a diplomatic passport a few years later. Loy Henderson to Jonathan Bingham, June 16, 1955, JFD, Reel 36.

45. Helen Woods to Paul G. Hoffman, April 12, 1951, Paul G. Hoffman Papers, HST, Box 22, f.5; cf. Henry Labouisse to Charles J. Little, July 30, 1947, Henry Labouisse Jr. Papers, Department of Rare Books and Special Collections, Princeton University Library, Princeton University (hereinafter HL), Box 3, f.18; Robert A. Lovett Oral History, July 7, 1971, HST; Charles Bonesteel to Lovett, "Summary Statement of Departmental Position on 'Marshall Plan' for European Recovery," August 26, 1947, Office of European and British Commonwealth Affairs, Historical Collection Relating to the Formulation of the European Recovery Program 1947–60, RG59 Lot 123 NARA, Box 42, f.19.

46. E.g., Achilles to SecState, August 6, 1952, RG59 850.33/8-652, in JMDS/74 (5), EU.

47. Ball to Lippmann, July 12, 1948, WL, Reel 45. He most likely used the term

pejoratively; Gordon Oral History, HST; interview with Lane Timmons and Harry Labouisse, Harry B. Price Interviews, HST.

48. A. P. Young to Ernest Bevin, August 23, 1949, Ernest Bevin Papers, Churchill Archives Centre, Cambridge University, Cambridge, UK, BEVN II 6/9.

49. Camp notes on State Department working paper, "Problems of European Reconstruction," n.d., MC, Box 9, f.14.

50. Stanley Cleveland Oral History, July 12, 1981, JM, p. 8. Cleveland was the brother of two prominent Atlanticists—Harlan and Harold, although he was known primarily as a Europeanist; Pascaline Winand, "European Insiders Working Inside Washington: Monnet's Network, Euratom, and the Eisenhower Administration," in Kathleen Burk and Melvyn Stokes, eds., *The United States and the European Alliance Since 1945* (New York: Berghahn Books, 1999), p. 207; Ball Oral History, EU, noting that Monnet's penchant for the "talk fest" was among his Americanisms. He also preferred, according to Ball, to think and speak colloquially in English, using phrases like "We'll railroad through" and "Where is the snag?" See also Bowie and Uri Oral Histories, EU; interviews with Richard Mayne and Arthur Hartman.

51. Schaetzel Oral History, March 24, 1982, JM.

52. Nathan Oral History, May 15, 1987, EU.

53. Background on McCloy is from Kai Bird, *The Chairman: John J. McCloy and the Making of the American Establishment* (New York: Simon and Schuster, 1992); on Swatland and another key figure in this milieu, Andre Meyer, see Tennyson Oral History, June 4, 1987, EU.

54. Sumner Welles to Grace Tully, December 18, 1942, Official File, FDR, F5207; Alan K. Henrikson, "Commentary on Papers Delivered at the Joint Session of the American Historical Association and the Society for Historians of American Foreign Relations: The United States and the 'United States of Europe,' 1941–50," December 28–30, 1980, pp. 1–2, COR3, f.61, JJM; interview with Richard Mayne; Robert Nathan and John McCloy Oral Histories, HST. For a glorified inventory of Monnet's achievements, see Bruce diary, September 30, 1962, DB, Box 4, f.18. For general views on European federalism, see Robert H. Ferrell, "The Truman Era and European Integration," in Heller and Gillingham, eds., pp. 25–43.

55. Peter Carington, *Reflect on Things Past: The Memoirs of the Lord Carrington* (London: Collins, 1988), p. 185.

56. Jean Monnet, *Memoirs*, trans. Richard Mayne (London: Collins, 1978), p. 270; Monnet to Bruce, January 21, 1952, AMG 28/2/6, JM.

57. Bruce diary, March 30, 1950, DB, Box 1, f.6.

58. W. Phillips diary, March 15, 1924, WP, Box 2, f.4.

59. Matthews, p. 348; Bruce to family, September 29, 1918, in David Bruce Papers, Virginia Historical Society, Richmond, VA (hereinafter VHS), Mss1 B8303 a10; interview with Timothy Dickinson.

60. Bruce notes, Paris "about 1950," Bruce Papers, VHS, Mss1 B803 a129. They continue in four pages of poetic renditions of French dishes (twenty lines alone on sole cardinal), then culminate: "As a wise man once said of strawberries, 'Doubtless God could have invented something better but very decidedly he never did.'"

61. Bruce diary, March 22, 1959, Box 3, f.20, June 5, 1949; Box 1, f.1, June 27, 1949; on Ridgway Knight's wife, Box 1, f.2, May 4, 1953; on Dolce Martinez de Hoz, Box 2, f.6, all DB.

62. Quoted in Nelson D. Lankford, *The Last American Aristocrat: The Biography of Ambassador David K. E. Bruce, 1898–1977* (Boston: Little, Brown and Company, 1996), p. 324.

63. This, according to Bruce, never actually happened, although both men were indeed on the scene. Bruce to Carlos Baker, December 13, 1965, Bruce Papers, VHS, Mss1 B8303

a15–16.

64. See Joan Mellen, *Privilege: The Enigma of Sasha Bruce* (New York: Dial Press, 1982); David Bruce (son) to Alsop, March 29, 1973: "[W]e are all estranged ... the results of their life-long selfishness are coming home to roost." JA, Box 138, f.4; cf. Iver B. Neumann, "To Be a Diplomat," in Olav F. Knudsen, ed., *Cultural Barriers, Cultural Bridges: Experience and Evidence from Diplomacy and Politics*, Conference Paper No. 34 (Stockholm: Swedish Institute of International Affairs, 2004), pp. 92–93.

65. Interview with Edward Streator; Lankford, pp. 201–202.

66. Cf. Edwin Martin to John Leddy, July 11, 1950, Records of the Office of European Regional Affairs, Miriam Camp Files 1946–53 RG59 Lot 55D105, NARA, Box 3, f.11. The policy planning staff (notably Robert Tufts, Leon Fuller, and Bob Joyce) also played such a role with regard to European policy: e.g., Robert Tufts, "The European Policy of the United States," April 19, 1950, in ibid., f.12.

67. J. Graham Parsons, "A Bit of the 'Creation'; EUR/RA-Washington, June 1951–July 1953," J. Graham Parsons Papers, Georgetown University Library, Archives and Special Collections (hereinafter JGP), Box 12, f.26, pp. 2–4, 9; interview with James Lowenstein.

68. John Leddy recollection in "Miriamiana," MC, Box 24, f.8 and Box 25 for photos; Myra MacPherson, "Miriam Camps: She Helps U.S. Look into Future," *New York Times*, August 23, 1968, p. 46.

69. Camps Oral History, August 31, 1988, EU.

70. MacPherson, MC, Box 24, f.1 for chronology.

71. Recollections from J. Robert Schaetzel, John and Margaret Leddy, Robert Asher, William Diebold, and Lincoln Gordon, in the collection "Miriamiana," MC.

72. Weil, p. 209.

73. Gordon in "Miriamiana," MC.

74. Randall to Perkins, October 11, 1950, RG59 850.33/10-1150, in JMDS/ 74(2), EU; Bissell Oral History, HST; Hartman Oral History, March 3, 1990, EU; Sherrill Brown Wells, "Monnet and the 'Insiders': Nathan, Tomlinson, Bowie, and Schaetzel," in Clifford P. Hackett, *Monnet and the Americans* (Washington, D.C.: Jean Monnet Council, 1995), pp. 204, 211; interview with Miriam Camps by F. Duchêne, November 22, 1989, in MC, Box 24, f.6; see also Duchêne, p. 212.

75. Hartman and Vernon Oral Histories, EU.

76. Interviews with Frank and Margot Lindsay and Lincoln Gordon; Hillenbrand, p. 90. The Harriman and the Bruce missions were actually in different buildings—the latter was at 4 avenue Gabriel. The Bruce personnel were more committed ideologically to Monnet and integration than the Harriman staff. Martin Hillenbrand was the only notable figure assigned to both (formally to the Bruce and NATO missions). Hartman, Hillenbrand Oral Histories, EU.

77. Hersh, p. 229; Achilles, p. 372; interview with Ben Bradlee; Bruce diary, December 15, 1951, noting 156 congressional visitors to Paris in one month. DB, Box 1, f.20. Offie would go on to help Monnet lobby in favor of the Schuman plan while drawing from Jay Lovestone's accounts at the AFL-CIO.

78. C. Tyler Wood Papers, George C. Marshall Foundation, Lexington, VA, Box 4, f.20.

79. C. Tyler Wood Oral History, June 18, 1971, HST.

80. Charles W. Thayer, *Checkpoint* (New York: Harper and Row, 1964), p. 3.

81. Bruce diary, May 14, 16 and June 4, 1949, DB, Box 1, f.1.

82. George Perkins Memorandum (drafted by Parsons), "Future Conduct of United States Relations with European Regional Organizations," January 5, 1953, Records of the Office of European Regional Affairs, Camp Files, NARA, Box 2, f.13; cf. Burgess to SecState, February 25, 1959, POLTO 2411, Records of Component Parts of the Bureau of European Affairs 1944–62, RG59 multiple Lot Files, NARA, Box 20, f.2; Bruce diary, September 30, 1952, DB, Box 1, f.29. Cf. White, p. 359: "In the year 1952, the American Embassy in Paris

was responsible for 2,500 American officials and employees in the Paris area, who, with their wives and children, made an overseas community of 7,500 Americans, all involved somehow in American policy in Europe."

83. Kennan, p. 450.

84. Parsons to James Penfield, July 2, 1952, JGP, Box 1, f.42.

85. Camps interview with Duchêne, November 22, 1989, MC; Camp, "Various Schuman Plan Questions," July 18, 1952, RG59 Records of the Office of European Regional Affairs, Camp Files, NARA, Box 3, f.12. See also Camp, "Draft Circular Telegram," October 24, 1952, PPS files, RG59 Lot 64D563 "Europe, 1952–53," in *FRUS 1952–1954*, Vol. 6, part 1, pp. 224–228: "If an enduring union of the Six Countries is to be established, it must be created because they want it, it must be European in concept and reflect their traditions, not ours."

86. Martin to Perkins, "Recent Developments on European Integration," October 6, 1949, RG59 Records of the Office of European Regional Affairs, Camp Files, NARA, Box 1, f.2; "Western European 'Integration,'" n.a., January 25, 1949 (handwriting appears to be Camp's), RG59 Records of Component Parts, NARA, Box 11, f.5; Labouisse to SecState (drafted by Camp and cleared by Achilles), January 12, 1949, "What Should the Department's Attitude be with Respect to 'Western European Integration'?" same folder. The policy included electoral interventions, Italy in 1948 being the best-known case. In most instances, the available evidence shows EUR viewing them as a last resort. See, for example, Merchant to Achilles, August 18, 1953, RG59 Lot 59D233, NARA, Box 24, f.7.

87. Interviews with David Acheson, Robert Bowie, and Antonia Stearns; Patrick Gordon-Walker diary notes, January–February 1959, in Gordon-Walker Papers, Churchill Archive, GNWR 1/13; Livingston Merchant Oral History, May 27, 1975, HST; Matthews, p. 352. Llewellyn Thompson Jr. to Dulles, October 12, 1954, Dulles to Achilles, April 13, 1955, Dulles to Bruce, May 6, 1955, all apparently drafted by Merchant, JFD, Reel 34. Merchant had gotten to know Dulles well soon after the war, when the latter oversaw the drafting of the Japanese peace treaty and Merchant was one of his deputies. Merchant Oral History, May 4, 1967, DDE; for his rankings of several officers, including Riddleberger, see Merchant to Dulles, March 12, 1954, John Foster Dulles Papers, Personnel Series 1951–59, DDE, Box 1, f.3.

88. William R. Willoughby, "The Eastern Hemisphere Division," War History Report, June 26, 1948, Records of the War History Branch, Drafts of Chapters for an Overall History of the Department of State During World War II, 1945–50, RG59 multiple Lot Files, NARA, Box 12, f.3; see also Box 39, f.3–6.

89. Interview with Fisher Howe.

90. Parsons, p. 6.

91. Bruce diary, May 20, 1959, DB, Box 3, f.22; Merchant, Oral History, DDE; Eisenhower to Merchant, December 28, 1960, LM, Box 6, f.18; Parsons to Martin, April 4, 1952, RG59 Lot 57D694, NARA, Box 1, f.5; Merchant to Sec-State, April 3, 1953, "Future of SRE in Paris," Records of the Office of European Regional Affairs, Files of J. Graham Parsons 1951–53, RG59 Lot 55D115, Box 1, f.11; interview with Fisher Howe.

92. Interviews with Anne Peretz and Lisa Farnsworth.

93. Parker McCollester to Dean Acheson, January 13, 1952, Dean G. Acheson Papers, HST, Box 35, f.2; Llewellyn Thompson to "Grandpa" (Hickerson), July 14, 1949, RG59 Lot 59D233, NARA, Box 22, f.3; minutes of the meeting of the Committee on European Recovery Program, June 25, 1947, RG59 Lot 123 NARA, Box 28 (notebook, pp. 4ff.); Paul R. Porter to Labouisse, June 24, 1948, RG59 Records of Component Parts of the Bureau of European Affairs, NARA, Box 11, f.1; Labouisse's first wife, who died in 1945, was an heiress to the Singer Sewing Machine fortune; Marjolin, p. 190.

94. *Los Angeles Times*, March 28, 1987.

95. Bruce diary, April 4, 1961, DB, Box 3, f.33.

96. Butterworth to Timmons, February 20, 1957, WWB, Box 4, f.1; A. J. Edden to Hood and replies, January 6, 1956, infra, FO 371/122022 1956; G. W. Harrison note, January 16, 1956, M 612/2 FO 371/150075 PRO; Roger Allen to Harold Caccia, M 611/14, January 24, 1956, ibid.

97. After a bad airplane crash. "Statement Made by H. R. Labouisse at Memorial Service in the Princeton University Chapel on Saturday Afternoon, May 3, 1975," HL, Box 1, f.7; interview with Arthur Hartman. Additional views of Butterworth appear in the next three chapters.

98. Leddy in "Miriamiana"; Paul J. Porter Oral History, November 30, 1971, HST; Raymond Vernon Oral History, July 19, 1973, HST; John M. Leddy Oral History, June 15, 1973, HST; Vernon Oral History, EU.

99. Parsons to Martin, April 4, 1952, RG59 Lot 57D694, NARA; Martin, "Memorandum of Conversation with Linc Gordon on Spaak Appointment, November 5, 1949," Records of the Office of British Commonwealth and Northern European Affairs (BNA), 1941–53, RG59 Lots 54D225 and 59D559, NARA, Box 1, f.13; Miriam Camps, "Talk to G. Goodwin Graduate Seminar, LSE May 1976," MC, Box 8, f.6; Memorandum of Conversation: Acheson, Spaak, Silvercruys, January 19, 1950, Acheson Papers, HST, Box 66, f.4; Memorandum of Conversation: Acheson, Franks, Perkins, January 20, 1950, ibid.; Franks Oral History, June 27, 1964, HST; Bissell, Harriman, and Plowden Oral Histories, HST; Perkins (MacArthur) to SecState, September 9, 1949, RG59 Lot 55D105, NARA, Box 3, f.1; H. H. Smith memorandum, January 30, 1950, ibid.; Spaak to Paul van Zeeland, December 30, 1949, ibid. Spaak had been Harriman's top candidate, and he was only too happy to comply. E.g., Spaak to Harriman, November 23, 1948, D3526 Archives Paul-Henri Spaak, Fondation Spaak, Brussels, Belgium (copy in JM); Spaak to André Visson, February 24, 1949, D5198, ibid. The battle over him coincided with a very contentious set of negotiations over the European Payments Union, which ended suddenly in July 1950, when the Korean war necessitated a drastic reallocation of defense support—and budgets—throughout Europe for rearmament. Sorting it out fell largely to Gordon—who moved from the EPU negotiations to Charles Spofford's office at NATO and proposed the Wise Men's exercise of 1951. Gordon Oral History, July 17, 1975; Robert Marjolin Oral History, July 2, 1971, HST. The task of integrating German payments in the EPU (and ultimately, German membership in the OEEC), fell to Riddleberger. Oral History, HST. For an account of Harriman's difficulties with the British, especially Edmund Hall Patch, see Hall Patch to E. A. Berthoud, August 17, 1948, UR 2017, FO371/71915 PRO; Hall Patch to Harriman, August 18, 1948, ibid.; Hogan, pp. 158–160.

100. Bruce to SecState, October 22, 1949, CF 840.00/10-2249, *FRUS 1949*, Vol. 4, pp. 342–344, reporting the views of the ambassadors to Europe (Bruce, Douglas, Dunn, Alan Kirk, Harriman, and McCloy).

101. Dillon Oral History, September 21, 1988, EU; interview with John Tuthill, April 15, 1981, JM; W. Randolph Burgess Oral History, March 1, 1977, DDE; Dillon to President, August 19, 1959, White House Office of the Staff Secretary, Records 1952–61, International Series, DDE, Box 14, f.9; Hogan, pp. 344–349. See also chapter 8, below.

102. Edwin Martin to Merchant, April 22, 1952, RG59 Lot 55D105, Camp Files, reprinted in *FRUS 1952–1954*, Vol. 6, part 1, pp. 65–67.

103. Excerpt of a draft speech by Miriam Camps, August 16, 1976, MC, Box 1, f.5; "Record of Round-Table Discussion by Twenty-Four Consultants with the Department of State on 'Strengthening International Organizations' November 17, 18, and 19, 1949," EUR Office of European Regional Affairs, Records Relating to the North Atlantic Treaty Organization 1947–53, RG59 Lot 57D271, NARA, Box 3, f.4 and Lot 55D258, NARA, Box 1, f.35; "Points to Suggest to Mr. Merchant," n.d., n.a. (probably C. Burke Elbrick), RG59 Lot 55D115, NARA, Box 2, f.25; Wayne Jackson to Frances E. Willis, October 19, 1949, and reply, November 2, 1949, RG59 Lot 54D225, NARA, Box 1, f.13; Edwin Martin memoranda

of communication with Linc Gordon, November 7, 1949, ibid.; Acheson to Perkins, October 19, 1949, RG59 840.00/10-1949 in *FRUS 1949*, Vol. 4, pp. 469–472; "Memorandum of Conversation (Acheson, Spaak, Silvercruys)," January 19, 1950, Acheson Papers, HST; Camps Oral History, EU; see also Ernest B. Haas, *The Uniting of Europe: Political, Social, and Economic Forces, 1950–1957* (Stanford, CA: Stanford University Press, 1958), pp. 5ff., and Karl Deutsch et al., *Political Community and the North Atlantic Area* (Princeton, NJ: Princeton University Press, 1957).

104. Nitze to Dulles, November 16, 1957, John Foster Dulles Papers, 1951– 1959, General Correspondence and Memoranda Series, DDE, Box 3, f.5.

105. E.g., Achilles to Joseph H. Johnson, May 19, 1949, RG59 Lot 59D233, NARA, Box 22, f.3.

106. For Camp's putative invention of "integration," see Diebold in "Miriamiana," MC, and Note 103 above.

107. Bruce diary, July 16, 1958, DB, Box 3, f.9.

108. Ronald Steel, "Walter Lippmann and the Invention of the Atlantic Community," in Valérie Aubourg, Gérard Bossuat, and Giles Scott-Smith, eds., *European Community, Atlantic Community?* (Paris: Soleb, 2008), pp. 29ff.

109. Hickerson to Joseph Johnson, October 3, 1950, enclosing an excerpt from "Towards the Atlantic Community" by Lionel Robbins, *Lloyds Bank Review*, July 1950, RG59 Records of Component Parts of the Bureau of European Affairs, NARA, Box 10, f.2; Camp cast it as a three-way choice: "Western Union" without the United Kingdom; with the UK and Dominions; with the UK and without the Dominions, alongside a kind of Atlantic Community, including the United States. She preferred the third option. "'Unification' or 'Integration' of Western Europe," n.d. (1948), RG59 Lot 55D105, NARA, Box 2, f.1. A similar conception is in the report by the Policy Planning Staff, "Review of Current Trends in U.S. Foreign Policy," PPS/23 February 24, 1948, *FRUS 1948*, Vol. 1, part 2, pp. 510ff.; Gordon, "Myth and Reality," p. 97.

110. Richard Bissell Jr. Oral History, July 9, 1971, HST; Henri Bonnet Oral History, June 29, 1970, HST.

111. Camp to Leddy, draft paper on U.S. commercial policy, 1955, MC, Box 2, f.3. An interdepartmental committee on European integration, including Tufts, Camps, Achilles, Labouisse, and others, sent its recommendations to the National Security Council in February 1950. Martin to Gordon, December 16, 1949, RG59 Lot 55D105, NARA, Box 3, f.16; Perkins (Ben T. Moore) to Sec-State, February 15, 1950, ibid., Box 1, f.2.

112. Frank Roberts Oral History, July 3, 1996, Churchill Archives Centre, Churchill College, Cambridge University, Cambridge, UK; interview with Robert Bowie.

113. Castle diary, March 9, 1936, WRC, Vol. 30; see also June 2, 1935, Vol. 28. Achilles recalled him as "a delightful person ... [who] courtly as ever, received me as if he had nothing else to do." Achilles, pp. 121, 141, 190, 220; interview with David Acheson. "Crash operation" comes from G. Frederick Reinhardt Oral History, June 13, 1970, HST. See also G. Bernard Noble, draft paper, "The Origins of the North Atlantic Treaty Organization: A Brief Sketch," December 8, 1952, RG59 Lot 67D271, NARA, Box 8, f.12.

114. Achilles, pp. 1–5.

115. "In Memoriam: Theodore C. Achilles 1905–1986," *The Federator* (pamphlet), Washington, D.C., Supplement, 1986, in JGP, Box 9, f.52; Achilles, pp. 142, 167.

116. Interview with David Acheson.

117. Theodore Achilles Oral History, November 13, 1972, HST; Hickerson's recollection of the Bevin/Marshall conversations is in his Oral History, November 10, 1972, HST. For his acquaintance with Senator Connally (another friend of his father), see Oral History, January 26, 1973, ibid. They were helped considerably by a young British diplomat and later ambassador to the United States, Nicholas "Nicko" Henderson, who joked that the pride of authorship should go to Achilles "if he claimed it." Interview with Nicholas Henderson.

Cf. Alan Henrikson, "The Creation of the North Atlantic Alliance," in John F. Reichart and Steven R. Sturm, eds., *American Defense Policy* (Baltimore: Johns Hopkins University Press, 1982), pp. 298–305.

118. "Record of a Meeting Between Lord Ismay and the Foreign Ministers of France, the United Kingdom and the United States at Bermuda (Mid-Ocean Club) on Monday, 7th December, 1953," Hastings Ismay Papers, Liddell Hart Centre for Military Archives, King's College, London, 3.22.4a–k; Herbert Feis notes on Achilles Oral History, HF, Box 78, f.1; Harriman to President, attaching Eisenhower memo, "Points on Organization," Presidential Secretary's Files: General File, HST, Box 105, f.5; Memorandum of Conversation: Marshall, Lord Inverchapel, Henderson, Hickerson, January 19, 1948, RG59 Lot 59D233 NARA, Box 23, f.1. Senator Arthur Vandenberg, for his part, regarded the Rio Pact as a "model of futility." Vandenberg to Lovett, November 19, 1948, and Vandenberg to Lodge, n.d., Papers of Arthur H. Vandenberg, Bentley Historical Library, University of Michigan, Ann Arbor, MI, Reel 5; Memorandum of Conversation with Dulles, Vandenberg, Marshall, and Lovett, April 27, 1948, JFD, Reel 11; Achilles, pp. 234, 413–424.

119. After which Hickerson, Achilles, and a bystanding air force sergeant went and drank bourbons in the Willard Hotel bar. Achilles, p. 308; see also pp. 339, 425, 430, 450.

120. "Address Given by General Eisenhower at a Dinner Given in His Honor by the English Speaking Union," July 3, 1951, JFD, Reel 18. The Latin phrase, "hurry slowly," as applied to diplomacy appears in Neumann, p. 91. Cf. Kopp and Gillespie, p. 197.

121. Kennan's memoirs (pp. 404ff.) are misleading on this point. See Achilles Oral History, HST, and Achilles, p. 427; General Norstad, Memorandum for the Record, June 15, 1949, Lauris Norstad Papers 1930–87, DDE, Box 20, f.1. The truth was somewhere in between. He was an opponent in principle but helped in practice; by contrast, Bohlen was ambivalent at first but tried to undercut the treaty behind the scenes; Bohlen glossed over this in his memoir, p. 267; cf. Lippmann to Welles, February 3, 1949, WL, Reel 97.

122. Nicholas Henderson, *The Birth of NATO* (Boulder: Westview Press, 1983), pp. 9, 12, 60.

123. Kennan to J. A. Lukacs, October 31, 1955, GK, Box 31, f.1; cf. Kennan to SecState, August 8, 1950, Alfred Gruenther Papers, DDE, NATO Series, Box 1, f.1; and Kennan, "The Soviet Union and the Atlantic Pact," n.d. [1952] ibid., Box 3, f.47.

124. Bissell Oral History, HST. Harriman was one of the three "Wise Men" (the other two being Monnet and Edwin Plowden), or Temporary Council Committee, who laid the groundwork for the Lisbon conventional forces goals of 1952 and the establishment of NATO headquarters at Paris. As noted above, the Wise Men's exercise was proposed initially and staffed by Linc Gordon. Gordon interview; Monnet memorandum AMI 10/1/31, JM; Bruce diary, February 13, 1952, DB, Box 1, f.23. See also Labouisse to Harlan Cleveland, March 7, 1952, EUR Office of European Regional Affairs, Subject Files Relating to European Security 1950–55, RG59 Lots 55D273, 55D243, NARA, Box 2, f.6; Lord Ismay, *NATO: The First Five Years, 1949–1954* (Utrecht: North Atlantic Treaty Organization, 1954), pp. 44–45.

125. Brandon diary, August 9, 1949, and January 29, 1957, HB, Box 1, f.3 and Box 4, f.3; Bonnet to Min., May 26, 1950, No. 2492/SGL B-Amérique 1944– 1952, États-Unis 115 MAE; a comprehensive statement of the policy is in Merchant to SecState, July 7, 1953, CF 740.5/7-753, *FRUS 1952–1954*, Vol. 5, part 1, pp. 427–432. Thomas Simons, who joined the foreign service in the early 1960s, recalled the longer-term effects: "I was never much of an Atlanticist, and yet found a productive and even happy home in this Atlanticist EUR.... At one point [in the mid-1980s] our in-house EUR policy planner Richard Haass delivered himself of a particularly breathless memo about the danger that Soviet maneuvering would damage our fundamental strategic interest in keeping the Alliance (I was always tempted to write The Alliance) strong, and I remonstrated mildly that I guess I had had the wrong priorities, since I had always thought The Alliance was there to ward off the Soviet

threat, and now I learned that our concern about the Soviets was just a function of our fundamental interest in The Alliance. He took my point a little sheepishly, I thought, and went on about his business." Simons, letter to the author.

126. Hillenbrand Oral History, October 6, 1988, EU.

127. Bowie Oral History, May 12, 1987, EU; Acheson to McCloy, July 13, 1951, and enclosures, McCloy's handwritten notes on EDC, and McCloy to Acheson, March 25, 1952, all in JJM, HC1, f.1; Franks and Gordon Oral Histories, HST; Bruce diary, October 4 and 24, 1950, DB, Box 1, f.11. McCloy to Sec-State August 3, 1950 CF 740.5/8-350, *FRUS 1950,* Vol. 3, pp. 180–182; *Pearson Diaries,* p. 213; Alphand Oral History, April 20, 1988, EU; Pascaline Winand, "Dulles and Eisenhower," in Hackett, ed., p. 104. Bohlen and Matthews also had a hand in it, as well as Ted Achilles, whose claim to have originated the plan in a dinner conversation with Harriman and Gruenther cannot be substantiated. Achilles, p. 470. See also Sulzberger, p. 610. The record of Byroade's memoranda is in Thomas Alan Schwartz, *America's Germany: John J. McCloy and the Federal Republic of Germany* (Cambridge, MA: Harvard University Press, 1991), p. 348; see also pp. 223–224; Bird, pp. 340, 372.

128. Hillenbrand Oral History, EU; Makins to Ivone Kirkpatrick, September 25, 1954, RM, Box 27, Official 11: "[T]he United States has three main objectives in Europe: restoration of German sovereignty, a German defence contribution and European unity—listed in that order"; Aide-mémoire de la délégation Néerlandaise, January 8, 1952, Série CED, Box 160, Document D/22, MAE; "Erklärung von Mr. Dulles," October 1954, B14(211).76, AA.

129. Riddleberger Oral History, George Marshall Foundation; Schwartz, pp. 143ff.; cf. Lippmann to Dorothy Thompson, March 15, 1953, WL, Reel 94.

130. Byroade to McCloy, October 10, 1949, JJM, HC1, f.2; Acheson to Schuman, June 20, 1949, Robert Schuman Papers, 3/1/3 JM; Bonnet to Min., November 30, 1951, No. 5361/EU B-Amérique 1944–1952, États-Unis 102 MAE; Achilles, pp. 473, 479. Another person operating more or less on his own but actively with the French was Tony Biddle, by then a major general. MacArthur to Perkins, October 19, 1952, EUR files RG59 Lot D233 "Letters—France, Sept–Dec. 1952," in *FRUS 1952–1954,* Vol. 6, part 2, p. 1259.

131. Makins to Eden, May 21, 1954, RM, Box 526, Official 10; Harriman to René Mayer, October 25, 1951, and Labouisse to Gordon, November 14, 1951, WAH, Box 275, f.7; Ismay to Gruenther, December 2, 1953, Ismay Papers, Liddell Hart Military Archive, King's College, London, 4/15/8; Acheson Oral History, HST. One other person who played an interesting role in the wings was the State Department's man on Indochina—Abbot Low Moffat—brother of the late J. Pierrepont. For his animus toward EUR, see Moffat to Dulles, August 21, 1954, John Foster Dulles Papers, Personnel Series 1951–59, DDE, Box 2, f.1. On Lodge's activities, see Lodge to Dulles, April 22, June 11, and October 5, 1954, Henry Cabot Lodge Jr. Papers II, Massachusetts Historical Society, Boston, MA (hereinafter HCL) P-373, Reel 4, and confidential journal in Reel 17; James Bonbright to Mac Godley, August 16, 1951, RG59 Lot 59D233, NARA, Box 25, f.8. The earlier views of Dunn and others on Indochina are in Dunn to Phillips, May 15, 1945, Lot 54D246, NARA, Box 2, f.15. FE's version of the story is told by Mark Atwood Lawrence, *Assuming the Burden: Europe and the American Commitment to War in Vietnam* (Berkeley: University of California Press, 2005), esp. pp. 69–74, 218ff.

132. Acheson, p. 557.

133. Henry Brandon, *Special Relationships: A Foreign Correspondent's Memoirs from Roosevelt to Reagan* (New York: Atheneum, 1988), p. 28.

134. Merchant Oral History, DDE; Merchant handwritten notes, LM, Box 2, f.7; Sulzberger, p. 964. Bruce's recollection was roughly equivalent: "Dulles looks like an antique Cretan bull; Bidault like a rather fat elfin creature; Eden a fin de siècle, languid aristocrat; Molotov an unsympathetic caricaturist's dream of right angles. By all odds our front row—Chip, Livy, Foster, Doug [MacArthur] and Jim [Conant]—are the most

distinguished-looking single group, worthy of Calvert Whisky advertisements." Bruce diary, January 30, 1954, DB, Box 2, f.17. For some time "walking into the office with a copy of *Pravda* under one's arm was quite prestigious. That stopped with Dulles." Interview with William Smyser; Merchant, "The Berlin Conference" presentation at the National War College, March 12, 1954, pp. 2, 5–9, LM, Box 2. Another lively account is in C. D. Jackson to Marie McCrum, February 10, 1954, DDE, C. D. Jackson Papers, in *FRUS 1952– 1954*, Vol. 7, part 1, pp. 1031–1034. Merchant's tough memo (February 9, 1954 RG59 Lot 60D627, 215) calling for an end to the conference is reproduced in the same volume, pp. 1005–1007. For the animus between Dulles and Eden, see, inter alia, Kevin Ruane, *The Rise and Fall of the European Defence Community: Anglo-American Relations and the Crisis of European Defence, 1950–55* (London: Macmillan, 2000), pp. 41, 87–88. Anti-Eden sentiment was long-standing in the department; for earlier episodes, see Castle to Moffat, March 28, 1936, JPM, Vol. 10; Moffat to Wilson, March 21, 1938, and Wilson's reply, ibid., Vol. 14; Wilson to Hull, May 18, 1936, CH, Box 39, f.90.

135. Dulles to Michael Gibson, December 13, 1954; Hugh Gibson to Dulles, March 4, 1954, JFD, Reel 31.

136. Robert Joyce to Merchant, January 11, 1954, RG59 Lot 59D233, NARA, Box 26, f.1; Merchant, "The Berlin Conference," pp. 13–14; see also the thinly fictional account by the Australian expatriate Godfrey Blunden, *The Looking-Glass Conference* (New York: Vanguard Press, 1956), esp. pp. 152ff.

137. "Transcript of Secretary Dulles Press Conference, London, October 2, 1954," JFD, Box 331.

138. "Ouin-Ouin" (Woodruff Wallner) to Bonbright, February 12, 1952 (with notation by Matthews: "I agree"), RG59, Lot 59D233, NARA, Box 25, f.10; Pascaline Winand, *Eisenhower, Kennedy, and the United States of Europe* (New York: St. Martin's Press, 1996), p. 50; Ruane, pp. 12, 193. The thrust of Ruane's book is to prove that "British policy ... [was] largely designed to ensure that the Americans [namely, the Congress more than Dulles] were denied an excuse or justification for making good their threat." For his part, Churchill "had always loathed the EDC." Ibid., pp. 54, 103; Achilles, p. 518.

139. Interview with Arthur Hartman; Vernon A. Walters Oral History, April 21, 1970, DDE; Dillon Oral History, EU. Roger Makins described Dulles then as "an awkward old buster" with "pachydermatous qualities" but nevertheless "a more forceful and positive character than the President himself.... I still think he wants to be friends." Makins to Eden, June 18, 1954, RM, Box 527, Official 11; cf. "Memorandum of Conversation with Livingstone [*sic*] Merchant, November 30, 1966," HF, Box 84, f.2. Other good summaries of the EDC are in Butterworth to Merchant, September 1, 1954, WWB, Box 2, f.4, and Achilles, "Post-Mortem on the Rejection of the EDC Treaty," September 16, 1954, Embtel 554 Paris (drafted by Martin Herz), Martin Herz Papers, Georgetown University Library, Archives and Special Collections Washington, D.C. (hereinafter MFH), Box 1, f.25, and Bruce diary, September 25, 1954, and infra, DB, Box 2, f.22.

140. Dillon to Dulles, November 14, 1953, John Foster Dulles Papers, General Correspondence and Memoranda Series, DDE, Box 2, f.7; Lodge to Bruce, February 14, 1974, Bruce papers, VHS, Mss 1B 8303a, 233–34; MacArthur to Dillon, November 5, 1953, and Memorandum of Conversation: Henri Bonnet, Daniel Mayer, Dulles, MacArthur, November 2, 1953, RG59 Lot UP-253 Records of Douglas MacArthur II 1951–62 NARA, Box 2, f.6. For more on Bruce's passion for the European army, see Martin F. Herz, *David Bruce's "Long Telegram" of July 3, 1951* (Washington, D.C.: University Press of America, 1978), pp. 7ff. Some British insisted that the French "still honestly believed Germany to be a greater threat than the Soviets." Oliver Harvey, ambassador to Paris, quoted in Ruane, p. 19.

141. Bruce to Merchant, July 19, 1954, DB, Box 2, f.21; secret memo on the future reorientation of Germany, March 29, 1954, DB, Box 2, f.18.

142. Charles Cogan, *Oldest Allies, Guarded Friends: The United States and France Since 1940* (Westport, CT: Praeger, 1994), p. 86.

143. Dillon and Max Kohnstamm Oral Histories, EU. According to Dillon, Dulles "felt he understood the French far better than the people who were advising him ... "; Dulles to Bruce, August 31, 1954, John Foster Dulles Papers, General Correspondence and Memoranda Series, DDE, Box 2, f.15. Alphand's case was especially interesting. Many of his colleagues in Quai d'Orsay—Christian Jacquin de Margerie and Alexandre Parodi, for example—were well-known opponents of the EDC. Only a couple of years earlier, Alphand himself expressed horror at the thought that Germany would reconstitute an army and that the costs for it would be figured into Marshall Plan calculations. Interview with Lincoln Gordon. Cf. Bonnet to Min., August 10, 1950, No 3814/CE B-Amérique 1944–1952, États-Unis 166 MAE; Hillenbrand, p. 100; Nora Beloff, *The General Says No: Britain's Exclusion from Europe* (Harmondsworth, UK: Penguin Books, 1963), p. 62; Ruane, p. 38, noting that because of the war in Indochina, the "projected French contribution to the EDC had been reduced from 14 divisions to a maximum of ten.... The implication was plain, at least to French minds: potential German military and political dominion...."

144. Hillenbrand Oral History, EU; Dunn to Matthews, December 10, 1952, RG59 Lot 59D233, NARA, Box 25, f.9; Lucius D. Battle Oral History, June 23, 1971, HST; Camp, "Significant Points Set Forth in the Meeting on NATO Non-Military Objectives," October 3, 1951, RG59 Lot 55D105, NARA, Box 2, f.16; telephone call to Gov. Adams, August 23, 1954, John Foster Dulles Papers, Telephone Series, DDE, Box 10, f.7; Bruce diary, July 10, August 31, October 25, and December 20, 1954, DB, Box 2, f.21–23; C. W. Adair Jr. to Parsons, December 31, 1952, RG59 Lot 55D115, NARA, Box 4, f.8 and infra; Ben T. Moore, "U.S. Position on Alternative to EDC," attachment to memo from Merchant to SecState, September 10, 1954, Conference Files Lot 60D627, CF 359 *FRUS 1952–1954*, Vol. 5, part 2, pp. 1164–1167; Achilles, p. 526; Aufgaben der Interimistischen NATO-Vertretung, October 29, 1954, 223-110E 1023/54 B14-301 Band 34 AA. For British reactions, see Ruane, pp. 111ff, 132–135, 150–151, including the refutation of Eden's claim that he came up with the post-EDC solution to German rearmament "while taking a bath in his Wiltshire cottage."

145. Cogan, p. 79; Burin de Roziers Oral History, April 28, 1999, EU.

146. Achilles, p. 502; a summary of the reporting is in Achilles, "Postmortem," p. 2; cf. Ruane, pp. 66–69.

147. Achilles, p. 528; Mendès-France instructions, July 2, 1954, No. 9I17/I8 AM 1952–1963 États-Unis 349 MAE.

148. Sulzberger, p. 952; Achilles, pp. 519, 528, for the implied disingenuity of the "agonizing reappraisal."

149. "Note by Lord Ismay," December 8, 1953, Ismay Papers, King's College, 3.22.4a-k.; cf. Ruane, p. 99.

150. Sulzberger, p. 599 ("Who's loony now?").

151. Brandon diary, October 31, 1950, HB, Box 2, f.2. Nitze by then had replaced George Kennan as director of the Policy Planning Staff, to be followed by Bob Bowie. EUR's support for the staff's NSC 68 document, which provided a new rationale for the Truman administration's Cold War rearmament program, is in Hickerson to SecState, April 3 and April 5, 1950, Policy Planning Staff Files in *FRUS 1950*, Vol. 1, pp. 214–217. See also Alsop to Berlin, n.d. (1952), IB, Box 239, f.61; Kirkpatrick to Makins, September 20, 1954, RM, Box 527, Official 11; Acheson, Achilles, and Byroade Oral Histories, HST; McCloy, "The Godkin Lectures: The Challenge to American Foreign Policy," JJM, Box SP1, f.57; Acheson to James Warburg, December 22, 1950, Acheson Papers, HST, Box 45, f.2, and Acheson to McCloy, October 15, 1951, ibid., Box 67, f.6; interview with Robert Bowie for views of Department of Defense; cf. Schwartz, pp. 123–124.

152. Kennan, pp. 257–258, 446, and *Memoirs, 1950–1963* (Boston: Little, Brown and Company, 1972), pp. 227ff. Kennan noted here that he was suffering from a bad flu and

poor working conditions, which may have impaired his judgment. Some colleagues saw Kennan's reversal as having begun as early as 1948. See, for example, Schwartz, p. 35; Brandon diary, April, 15, 1949, HB, Box 2, f.1; Murphy to Clay, March 10, 1949, RDM, Box 57, f.25; Offie to Murphy, September 14, 1948, ibid., Box 59, f.6; Murphy to Riddleberger, March 10, 1949, ibid., Box 59, f.19. Cf. Bonbright to Bohlen, August 7, 1951, RG59 Lot 59D233, NARA, Box 22, f.10; Lippmann to Kennan, February 1, 1949, and replies, WL, Reel 70; Acheson to Dulles, January 15, 1958, JFD, Reel 49.

153. Interview with William R. Smyser. The public rebuke of Kennan was orchestrated behind the scenes by Christopher Emmet of the American Council on Germany and C. D. Jackson. Emmet to Jackson, January 31, 1958, CE, Box 80, f.23, and Samuel Reber to Emmet, April 13, 1958, enclosing an angry complaint from Kennan, ibid., Box 95, f.13:

.... I did not advocate "the neutralization of Germany ..."

I did not "warn against strengthening nato" [sic]

I did not "urge our nato [sic] allies to do or not to do anything at all"

I did not say that Germany should be "without the 12 promised German divisions" or any other number of divisions

I didn't say that a Europe from which the US and Soviet forces had been withdrawn should be "a virtual military vacuum" ...

I did not propose any "atom-free zone"

I did not advocate that we reduce tensions by placing our trust in the promises of the leaders of the Kremlin.

At no time did I urge anybody "to accept the finality of Soviet control of Eastern Europe."

I have not spoken of any "offer" ...

I did not use the word "appeasement."

For Acheson's views on rearmament, see Acheson to McCloy, July 12, 1951, JJM, HC1, f.1; Acheson to Kennan, November 4, 1958, Dean G. Acheson Papers, Sterling Memorial Library, Yale University, New Haven, CT (hereinafter DAY), Box 17, Reel 11, f.222; Bruce diary, December 10, 1957, and April 3, 1958 (for Adenauer's suspicion that there was collusion with the British Foreign Office), DB, Box 3, f.2, f.7; see also Robert L. Beisner, *Dean Acheson: A Life in the Cold War* (Oxford: Oxford University Press, 2006), pp. 627–628.

154. Not even a $100 million loan to the Coal and Steel Community in April 1954, in addition to still-classified covert funds, was able to make the difference. Winand, *Eisenhower, Kennedy and the United States of Europe*, p. 54; Elmer B. Staats, Memorandum for the Record, May 10, 1954, National Security Council, OCB Board of Project Approvals, 1953–1955, *FRUS, 1950–1955, The Intelligence Community*, p. 497.

155. Achilles Oral History, HST; Merchant to Ridgway Knight, March 12, 1954, RG59 Lot 59D233, NARA, Box 24, f.7; John C. Hughes to Gruenther, January 18, 1954 and enclosure, Gruenther Papers, DDE, Box 3, f.42; several sources note the similar change of heart (at least publicly) of Hervé Alphand; Achilles, pp. 479, 520. The one person whose views on the EDC may have been both negative and decisive were Dunn's, in Paris as ambassador until March 1953; although, apart from a vague reference in the Eisenhower Presidential Library to a deliberate leak on his part, there is almost no evidence to suggest that he had a role in sabotaging it. Thayer Oral History, June 12, 1972, DDE; interview with Arthur Hartman. For other instances of Dunn's suspicious carelessness with memoranda, see Michael Creswell, *A Question of Balance: How France and the United States Created Cold War Europe* (Cambridge, MA: Harvard University Press, 2006), p. 96; Benjamin C. Bradlee, *A Good Life: Newspapering and Other Adventures* (New York: Simon and Schuster, 1995), p. 136. His replacement, Doug Dillon, was "never wholly sold on it but tried loyally to urge it." Achilles, p. 520.

156. Interview with Arthur Hartman.

157. A central point of Creswell's book.

158. Henry Cabot Lodge Jr., "Memorandum of Conversation with Prime Minister Pleven," n.d. (1952), HCL, Reel 17; Andrew J. Goodpaster Oral History, September 21, 1990, Nuclear Age, Liddell Hart Centre for Military Archives, King's College, London; MacArthur to Perkins, October 27, 1952, and Dunn to Bruce, November 18, 1952 (with Dunn's concerns), RG59 Lot 59D233, NARA, Box 25, f.9; Perkins to SecState, March 31, 1952, RG59 740.5/3-3152 *FRUS 1952–1954*, Vol. 5, part 1, pp. 631–634 ("Do we now have to protect EDC against itself?").

159. He and Monnet would continue to be "most emphatic" about maintaining such an approach toward European integration. Martin to Timmons, November 10, 1955, "U.S. Policy on European Integration," *FRUS 1955–1957*, Vol. 4, pp. 346–348; cf. Maurice Couve de Murville, *Une politique étrangère, 1958–1969* (Paris: Plon, 1971), p. 50.

160. John E. Gray quoted in Melvin Small, "The Atlantic Council—The Early Years," unpublished paper, June 1, 1998, p. 65, 53n; Joseph Alsop to David Sulzberger, February 24, 1967, JA, Box 77, f.8.

161. This culminated in the signing of the Paris agreements in October 1954 establishing the Western European Union. The following year, West Germany would join NATO as a full member. The British diplomat Christopher "Kit" Steel was the unsung hero at this stage. See Hillenbrand, p. 104, and Roberts, pp. 158, 169–170, noting that he, Steel, and Michael Palliser had prepared what became known as the Eden Plan well before, but had kept it secret.

162. Becker (German consul in Cairo) enclosing clipping from *Egyptian Gazette*, May 10, 1955, J.-Nr. 1591/55 B14-301 Band 33 AA; Merchant Oral Histories, DDE, HST; Merchant to SecState, draft memo to the president, June 1, 1954, December 11, 1954, February 5, 1955, RG59 Lot 59D233, NARA, Box 25, f.7.

6. Winds of Change

1. Kirkpatrick to Makins, November 22, 1955, RM, Box 525, Official 9.

2. James Bonbright Oral History, ADST; interview with Antonia Stearns; Achilles, p. 150. A variation on this story was told by Nicholas Henderson, with O'Shaughnessy having been exiled to Chicago, resulting in "a great swathe of Chicago that really got to know Cézanne and Botticelli." Interview with Nicholas Henderson; MacArthur to O'Shaughnessy, May 3, 1951, RG59 Lot UP-253, NARA, Box 2, f.1; for his relations with Caffery, see Susan Mary Alsop, p. 98. Achilles's version has him going to Texas to work in the oil fields.

3. Matthews to Gruenther, April 5, 1958, Alfred Gruenther papers, DDE, Box 3, f.54. MacArthur's pleas were received with "what is commonly called 'mixed feelings'"; cf. C. H. Bonesteel III, "NATO and the Underdeveloped Areas," March 1953, EUR Office of Regional Affairs, Office Files of Leonard Unger 1951–56, RG59 Lot 57D321-4, NARA, Box 4, f.23.

4. Hickerson to Bonbright, February 4, 1947, MH, Box 2, Reel 8; "British Commonwealth: Colonial and Imperial Policy," March 19, 1945 (notes a hardening of policy), MH, Box 2, Reel 11; Bonbright and Raymond Hare to Hickerson, June 30, 1950, RG59 Lot 53D246, NARA, Box 1, f.2; Central Intelligence Agency Intelligence Memorandum No. 231, "Consequences of Communist Control of French Indochina," October 7, 1949, SMOF: National Security Council Files, Box 1, f.4, HST; Matthews, p. 363 (on taking the side of the Dutch in Indonesia); Charles Yost Oral History, September 13, 1978, DDE; cf. Nolting Oral History, HST, pointing out differentiated policies stemming from domestic politics in Europe; McCloy to Bowie, January 19, 1952, JJM, HC5, f.28; Marjolin Oral History, July 2, 1971, HST; Dillon address to the diplomatic press, March 20, 1956, HCL II, Reel 4; Lodge to SecState, January 12, 1959, ibid., Reel 5 (on Cyprus and Algeria); David Raphaël Zivie, *La Guerre d'Algérie vue par un diplomate américain: documents diplomatiques rédigés par Francis de Tarr* (Paris: University de Paris X, 1998).

5. Dodds-Parker to Makins, "Co Co Colonialism," June 18, 1956, RM, Box 525, Official

9. In reply, Makins urged patience and understanding: "We are more Machiavellian than you might suppose." Makins to Dodds-Parker, n.d., ibid.

6. Kirkpatrick to Makins, May 25, 1954: "I think I should let you know that some of your telegrams and letters have been arousing some resentment here because they seem to be rooting for America and critical of H.M.G." RM, Box 527, Official 11; Roger Makins Oral History, February 6, 1990, Suez Oral History Project, Liddell Hart Centre for Military Archives, King's College, London; see also Oral Histories of Archibold Ross and Denis Wright in the same collection; cf. Hood to Caccia, December 3, 1956 and enclosure, JE1422/295 1956 FO371/119058 PRO; interview with Michael Palliser; Brandon, pp. 125–126.

7. Susan Mary Alsop, p. 294.

8. Thayer Oral History, DDE; Hickerson to Bonbright, February 4, 1947, MH, Box 2, Reel 8; Brendan Bracken to Lewis Douglas, January 25, 1957, Brendan Bracken Papers, Churchill Archives Centre, Cambridge, UK, BBKN 4(1) and infra; Winthrop W. Aldrich, "The Suez Crisis: A Footnote to History," *Foreign Affairs*, April 1967; see Acheson to Frank Altschul, October 4, 1956, DAY, Reel 1, Box 1, f.9; Ball, p. 331.

9. Makins to Eden, April 3, 1953, RM, Box 525, Official 9. N.b.: The American ambassador in Cairo then was none other than Jefferson Caffery. He would be replaced presently by Hank Byroade.

10. Bob Murphy, for example, sent his deputy, Bob Blake, back to Murphy's old stomping ground in North Africa to liaison with the National Liberation Front (FLN). Interview with Robert O. Blake; Blake Oral History, ADST; Martin Herz report on Algeria, MFH, Box 1, f.1, pp. 18ff. Dulles to Julius Holmes, July 13, 1955, John Foster Dulles Papers 1951–59, Subject Series, Box 6, f.12, DDE; Matthew Connelly, *A Diplomatic Revolution: Algeria's Fight for Independence and the Origins of the Post–Cold War Era* (Oxford: Oxford University Press, 2002), pp. 162–163; Achilles to Joe Satterthwaite, September 4, 1953, Records of Joseph C. Satterthwaite 19530û72, RG59 Lot 72D232, NARA, Box 1; and Tuthill, pp. 103–104 for dissent within the Paris embassy.

11. Brandon diary, January 27, 1957, HB, Box 4, f.3; Yost to Achilles, December 19, 1949, RG59 Lot 53D246, NARA, Box 3, f.1; Robert A. Lovett Oral History, June 17, 1964, George Marshall Foundation, Lexington, VA; an exception was in Congo.

12. Robert Bowie and Pierre Gallois, September 24 and 17, 1990, Oral Histories, Nuclear Age Collection, King's College, London.

13. Andrew J. Goodpaster Oral History, September 21, 1990, ibid.; interview with Arthur Hartman.

14. They included the American Committee on United Europe, the American Council on NATO, the Atlantic Union Committee, the Bilderberg Group, and several others (see the next chapter).

15. William R. Tyler to George Ball, February 3, 1964, National Security File, Country File, Europe, Lyndon B. Johnson Presidential Library, Austin, TX (hereinafter LBJL), Box 169, f.7; cf. Couve de Murville, pp. 33–34. See also Couve's speech to the French National Assembly, April 14, 1966, for the lasting effects, in Maurice Couve de Murville Papers, Sciences Po, Paris (hereinafter CM), CM2.

16. Robert Kleiman, *Atlantic Crisis: American Diplomacy Confronts a Resurgent Europe* (New York: W. W. Norton and Company, 1964), p. 38. Relations with de Gaulle were already difficult, not only because of Roosevelt's earlier treatment of him but also because of more recent snubs, including one at the hands of Jefferson Caffery. By the time Dillon arrived as ambassador in 1953, no American ambassador had met de Gaulle in seven years. The meeting was difficult to arrange, with Dillon finally resorting to the CIA and its colleagues in the French government to set it up at a private location. Dillon Oral History, EU; interview with Charles Cogan.

17. Murphy to Dunn, March 19, 1954, RDM, Box 88, f.19. Acheson's views on Wriston

and his predecessors (Hoover and Rowe) are in *Present at the Creation*, pp. 244–245.

18. Paul Mendelsohn, "Foreign Service Examinations (1948–1950) and Foreign Service Personnel Policies," unpublished paper, Princeton University, January 1976, p. 3, JCG, Box 39.

19. Eugene H. Dooman to Joseph Grew, January 25, 1954, Eugene H. Dooman Papers, Hoover Institution for War, Revolution, and Peace, Stanford University, Stanford, CA, Box 2, f.18; interview with Fisher Howe; Battle Oral History, HST; "F.S.O." (anonymous letter) January 9 (1955?), MFH, Box 1, f.26; Joseph C. Green to Selden Chapin, June 29, 1948, Examination file 1925–52 RG59 Lot 52D337, NARA, Box 15, f.3; "Preliminary Comments on Those Portions of the Report of the Hoover Commission Which Relate to the Foreign Service," February 25, 1949, ibid., Box 16, f.5; A. Montague to Humelsine, January 26, 1953, Personnel Policy Files, RG59 Lot 56D286, NARA, Box 1, f.15.

20. Cf. J. Carney Howell to John Peurifoy, n.d. (August 1950), Melbourne L. Spector Papers, HST, Box 2, f.1. Between 1945 and 1946 the size of the department nearly doubled, then again in 1950. By 1953, 32,000 out of 42,000 State Department employees were posted overseas. Statement by Donold B. Lourie before the House Committee on Government Operations, June 22, 1953, JFD, Reel 29.

21. Kennan to Henderson, January 24, 1955, LH, Box 2, f.11; cf. Kennan to Elim O'Shaughnessy, October 29, 1952, GK, Box 29, f.6; Howe Oral History, HST. The reform was part of a government-wide effort under the auspices of the two Hoover Commissions, the second of which was called "Little Hoo." It was based initially on a suggestion by Joe Alsop to Henry Cabot Lodge. William Pemberton to Henry Cabot Lodge Jr., March 3, 1975, and infra, HCL, Reel 1; Andrew J. Goodpaster et al., Oral History, June 11, 1980, DDE; James L. McCamy, *The Administration of American Foreign Affairs* (New York: Alfred A. Knopf, 1950), pp. 68–73. Joseph Green, introduced earlier as the longtime head of examinations (until he was driven out of the department by Dulles) suspected that Wriston's hostility to the existing system stemmed at least in part from "an unfortunate experience of one of his sons" who had applied to the foreign service. Green to Kennan, June 29, 1955, GK, Box 38, f.10. Green, incidentally, once taught Kennan, Merchant, and several other future officers at Princeton. Peurifoy, whose career in the department began as an elevator operator, had once been his clerk. For details on Green's reaction to Wristonization, see Mendelsohn in JCG. A summary of the various reform efforts after 1949 (the Rowe, Wriston, and two Hoover Committees) is in Plitschke, pp. 453–456.

22. Nitze to Linc Gordon, January 4, 1956, DAY, Reel 15, Box 23, f.295. The Kennan-Wriston exchange (Kennan's portion appearing initially in *Foreign Affairs* and Wriston's in the *Providence Evening Bulletin*) was reprinted in the *Foreign Service Journal* (September 1955): 22–23, 45–56. Bohlen also considered it "a great mistake." Bohlen Oral History, November 20, 1968, LBJL. Kennan depicted the decline as having been the product of a long-standing anti–foreign service bias on the part of Acheson and others: "a tragic thing because they had many good officers and they could have made a great service out of it." See his Oral History, February 17, 1959, George Marshall Foundation, Lexington, VA.

23. Interview with Margaret Beam; Dulles to Eisenhower, October 26, 1954, John Foster Dulles Papers, Personnel Series 1951–59, DDE, Box 1, f.9; John J. Harter, "Mr. Foreign Service on Mossadegh and Wristonization," *Foreign Service Journal* (November 1980): 19.

24. WPG (?) to Henry Luce, December 2, 1954, C. D. Jackson Papers, DDE, Box 46, f.19.

25. Acheson Oral History, October 2, 1957, George Marshall Foundation, Lexington, VA. Lovett was another pillar of the foreign policy establishment. He helped to create the postwar air force, was the person who sold the North Atlantic Treaty to the Joint Chiefs (after having been converted to it himself), and for years thereafter made regular trips to Europe to survey conditions, report back to old friends and former deputies, and watch over policies. A lifelong hypochondriac, he died in 1986 at age 90. Interview with David

Acheson; Walter Issacson and Evan Thomas, *The Wise Men: Six Friends and the World They Made* (New York: Touchstone Books, 1988).

26. Often overlooked is Acheson's background as the department's former head of congressional affairs and international conferences under Secretary Stettinius—an experience that proved very useful given the number of multilateral and other matters on the horizon. Interview with David Acheson. See also Acheson, p. 89.

27. Oliver Franks Oral History, June 27, 1964, HST; Michael F. Hopkins, *Oliver Franks and the Truman Administration* (London: Frank Cass, 2003), p. 106.

28. Cf. Alsop: "His staff is so bad that both the Under Secretary and the Asst. Sec. in charge of West European Affairs (an incredibly dim man called Perkins) begin all conversations with the statement—'Of course, I know nothing about foreign policy'—which led Chip to say 'At least they're honest.' And partly because Dean depends on these dubious creatures and has let Chip, George and the other professionals go, but mainly because he is always trying now to appease Congress and protect himself ..." Alsop to Berlin, n.d. (1951), IB, Box 239, f.54. Perkins had been with the Marshall Plan in Paris and then went on, after his tenure as Assistant Secretary, to become ambassador to NATO. Cf. Alsop to Acheson, November 30, 1949, JA, Box 5, f.2; Alsop to Felix Frankfurter, January 6, 1950, ibid., f.4; Alsop to Robert Cutler, February 12, 1953, ibid., Box 8, f.8; Llewellyn Thompson to Board of Governors, Chevy Chase Club, September 23, 1949, RG59 Lot 59D233, NARA, Box 22, f.2; "FW" (probably Francis Williamson) to Jeff Parsons, "[D]on't *ever* tell Draper that Perkins is a Republican," ibid., Box 25, f.9 his emphasis.

29. Interviews with Roger Kirk and Fisher Howe; Hickerson Oral History, HST.

30. Couve interview with Philip A. Crowl for Dulles Papers, Princeton, June 19, 1964, in CM, CM1, emphasis in the original.

31. Debating points, n.d., JFD, Box 279.

32. Kidd to Merchant, January 13, 1956, JFD, Reel 40.

33. Alsop, p. 347; for Dulles's roles during the Truman administration, see Memorandum of Conversation, Dulles, Truman, March 16, 1945, JFD, Reel 6; Hillenbrand Oral History, EU.

34. Not including his periodic service as an official envoy, representative, and negotiator.

35. J. F. Dulles to Allen Dulles, January 19, 1950, JFD, Reel 15, on why he "strongly favor[s] European Union" but not "Atlantic Union"; Achilles, p. 537, who advised him in this vein, "You could promote a lot more unity if you would pull rather than push"; Monnet to Dulles, November 11, 1958, JFD, Reel 52. Dulles and Monnet had known each other since World War I and worked closely together during the 1920s. See Bowie Oral History, EU.

36. "Memo of Conferences Had in Germany," July 1923, and "The Young Plan in Relation to World Economy," record of a discussion between Dulles and Hjalmar Schacht, October 20, 1930, at the Foreign Policy Association, JFD, Reel 2; telegram from Dulles to Henri Bonnet, November 26, 1952, JFD, Reel 20. The standard account of these years is in Leonard Mosely, *Dulles: A Biography of Eleanor, Allen, and John Foster Dulles and Their Family Network* (New York: Dial Press/James Wade, 1978). See also Max Warburg, *Aus meinen Aufzeichnungen* (Glückstadt: J. J. Agustin, 1952); Thomas W. Lamont, *Across World Frontiers* (Privately printed, 1950), p. 174.

37. The two were not close, although Bruce was a longtime friend and OSS colleague of Dulles's brother, Allen. Monnet and General Gruenther prevailed upon Eisenhower (who needed some persuading, but only for political reasons) and Dulles to make use of Bruce. He had also been the department's chief liaison during the transition period. Lodge to Bruce, February 14, 1974, Bruce Papers, Mss. B8303b, f.233, VHS; Eisenhower to Gruenther, December 24, 1952, Alfred Gruenther Papers, Eisenhower Correspondence Series, DDE, Box 1, f.2; Winand, *Eisenhower, Kennedy and the United States of Europe*, pp. 38–40.

38. The Thursday lunch group was a regular table at Washington's Metropolitan Club,

usually presided over by Nitze, which had met since about 1947 to work through the complexities of European policy. Edwin M. Martin, Oral History, July 6, 1970, HST.

39. Merchant to Dulles, February 9, 1953, JFD, Reel 27; Memorandum of Conversation: Dulles, McLeod, Tappin, O'Connor, Hanes, Leonard Hall, Chauncey Robbins (Republican National Committee), January 18, 1954, John Foster Dulles Papers, Personnel Series 1951-59, DDE, Box 2, f.11; Hanes to Sec-State, March 18, 1953, ibid., f.10; Dulles to Eisenhower, January 27, 1953, John Foster Dulles Papers, 1951-59, Subject Series, DDE, Box 6, f.14.

40. MacArthur to Merchant, January 22, 1959, LM, Box 5, f.11. More on "MacMerBo" is in MacArthur's Oral History, ADST. Another person whom Dulles respected and listened to seriously on the subject of Europe was Bill Tyler. Interview with Roger Kirk.

41. Makins to Kirkpatrick, January 23, 1956, RM, Box 527, Official 11.

42. Matthews, p. 354; Charles E. Bohlen Oral History, December 17, 1970, DDE; Francis Wilcox Oral History, February–June, 1984, DDE; Thurston B. Morton to SecState, September 20, 1954 and enclosure, John Foster Dulles Papers, Personnel Series, DDE, Box 1, f.1; Blake Oral History, ADST; "appeasement" is from U. Alexis Johnson diary, Tape 9, U.A. Johnson Papers, LBJL, Box 1, f.1.

43. Handwritten notes on birds at Luna Plantation, March 27–31, n.d., John W. Hanes Jr. Papers, DDE, Box 4, f.23; interview with Jonathan Dean.

44. Data from Conrad E. Snow Oral History, July 2, 1973, HST. This does not include the eighty-one mainly junior clerks and typists dismissed for suspected homosexuality. By the 1960s, some 1,000 people lost their jobs in the so-called Lavender Scare. David K. Johnson, *The Lavender Scare: The Cold War Persecution of Gays and Lesbians in the Federal Government* (Chicago: University of Chicago Press, 2004), pp. 76, 130. See also Robert D. Dean, *Imperial Brotherhood: Gender and the Making of Cold War Foreign Policy* (Amherst: University of Massachusetts Press, 2001), chaps. 4–6. Chapter 5 treats the Thayer and Bohlen cases extensively; see below.

45. Acheson, p. 354; Brandon diary, April 8, 1953, HB, Box 3, f.2.

46. They might have expressed themselves differently if they had not still been in official service. Cf. "Backing Our Diplomats," letter to the editor of the *New York Times*, January 17, 1954, from Norman Armour, Robert Woods Bliss, Joseph Grew, William Phillips, and G. Howland Shaw.

47. Holmes to Murphy, September 6, 1945, RDM, Box 58, f.19; phone conversations with Winthrop Aldrich and Dulles, April 6, 1956, Dwight D. Eisenhower Papers, Ann Whitman File, Administration Series, DDE, Box 2, f.1; Memoranda of Conversation, August 22, 1958, January 12, 1959, John Foster Dulles Papers, General Correspondence and Memoranda Series, DDE, Box 1, f.7; Memorandum of Conversation, May 18, 1956, ibid., Personnel Series, DDE, Box 1, f.10.

48. Hints appear in Reber's file in Murphy's papers (RDM, Box 90, f.15), most of which remain classified. Additional background on Reber from interviews with Margaret Beam and Jonathan Dean; Joseph Harsch to Dulles, September 4, 1956, John Foster Dulles Papers, General Correspondence and Memoranda Series, DDE, Box 2, f.9; Robert Dean; Reber to Walter Hallstein, August 6, 1953, Nachlass Walter Hallstein, Band 18, AA; Bonnet to Min., No.800 EU April 9, 1947, Série B, Amérique 1944–1952, États-Unis 101 MAE; and Mosely, pp. 313–314. Reber served in Brussels under Hugh Gibson and went on to join the delegation to the Geneva Disarmament Conference in the early 1930s, then served in North Africa during the war. His brother, Miles, incidentally, was a major general who was chief of congressional liaison during the Army-McCarthy hearings. The quotation is from Robert Bendiner, *The Riddle of the State Department* (New York: Farrar and Rinehart, 1942), p. 195; Matthews to Acheson, February 6, 1947, MH, Box 2, Reel 10. Another German hand who was reportedly threatened was Perry Laukhuff. Riddleberger's daughter, Antonia Stearns, recalled many long visits to their house in the early 1950s accompanied by many tears. Interview with Stearns.

49. Bradlee interview and memoir, pp. 140–142; Thayer and Yost Oral Histories, DDE; Bruce diary, March 7 and 22, 1954, DB, Box 2, f.18.

50. Labouisse tribute to Butterworth, May 3, 1975, HL. Yet another was Miriam Camp, who convinced Dulles to sign a series of letters telling McCarthy to stop pestering her colleagues, namely Leddy, who defended the department's refusal to punish the British for trading with China, one of McCarthy's many pet issues. Leddy in "Miriamiana," MC; for a less flattering view of Butterworth, see Achilles, pp. 253, 294, 892, and Kohnstamm Oral History, Jan–July 1986, EU, noting his "nationalistic fits." Butterworth had once been a favorite of Pierrepont Moffat. Moffat to Atherton, May 11, 1935, JPM, Vol. 8.

51. Press Statement, March 20, 1953, JFD, Reel 24; John W. Ford, "The McCarthy Years Inside the Department of State," *Foreign Service Journal* (November 1980): 12; Drew Pearson also had been accused of having a hand in spreading the rumors. *Pearson Diaries*, p. 314.

52. Louis Halle, "The Davies Case," February 4, 1955, WL, Reel 65; A. R. Forest to Bohlen, March 28, 1953, CB, Box 29, f.1; Grew to H. Alexander Smith, March 26, 1953, ibid., Box 30, f.9 (re. his defenders—Grew, Armour, and Gibson); interview with Henry Owen; Bohlen to Eisenhower, July 29, 1959, Dwight D. Eisenhower Papers, Ann Whitman File, Administration Series, DDE, Box 7, f.11; for Dulles's stance, John W. Hanes Jr. to W. W. Rostow, February 20, 1981, Eleanor Dulles Papers, DDE, Box 20, f.14, and for Eisenhower's see Bohlen Oral History, DDE. Bohlen's memoir (pp. 313ff.) barely mentions the substance behind the attacks on him or on Thayer.

53. Alice Longworth quoted by Marion Frankfurter, Frankfurter to Berlin, (July?) 2, 1950, IB, Box 122, f.123.

54. Charles W. Thayer, *Diplomat* (New York: Harper and Brothers Publishers, 1959).

55. E.g., efficiency report for Thayer, August 1, 1936, WB, Box 40, f. 945; interviews with Frank and Margot Lindsay.

56. Thayer to John Paton Davies, November 5, 1954; Thayer to Nicolas Nabokov, March 27, 1953; Thayer diary, March 23, 1953, and infra, Thayer Papers, HST, Box 2, f.6, Box 4, f.6, Box 7, f.6; See also Dean's *Imperial Brotherhood,* a reconstruction based largely on Thayer's unpublished novel, "An Officer and a Gentleman"; E. Allen Lightner Jr. Oral History, October 26, 1973, HST.

57. Joseph Alsop to Evangeline Bruce, March 5, 1959, JA, Box 14, f.2; Alsop to Chip Bohlen, September 6, 1958, ibid., Box 14, f.4; for the role of Frank Wisner and Allen Dulles in the Thayer case, see Hersh, pp. 305–306.

58. Joyce to Charles Saltzman, November 26, 1954, HCL II, Reel 3; for similar thoughts, see Bill Tyler to Thayer, May 3, 1953; Jake Beam to Thayer, April 2, 1953, Thayer Papers, HST, Box 1, f.7; Box 4, f.16; interview with Wendy Hazard.

59. Above it, in the margin, he noted, "und wie!" Ibid., Box 2, f.4 (appears to have been misfiled among Thayer's papers from interwar Germany).

60. Susan Mary Alsop, p. 204.

61. MacArthur to Dulles, August 28, 1953, JFD, Reel 32. To top it off, he gave the secretary a Yale fish to join the Harvard and Princeton fishes in his aquarium. Ibid., February 27, 1956, Reel 41.

62. Kitchen to Acheson, October 18, (1957?), DAY, Reel 11, Box 17, f.227; telephone conversation, Dulles and Herbert Brownell, June 12, 1953, John Foster Dulles Papers, Telephone Series, DDE, Box 1, f.6; Bruce diary, June 17, 1953, DB, Box 2, f.7; White, pp. 376–377; cf. Jonathan Dean memorandum, "Establishment of a Channel for Submitting New Ideas and Projects to the Department," September 8, 1959, MH, Box 2, f.13.

63. A. E. Weatherbee to Scott McLeod, June 9, 1953, RG59, Lot 56D286, NARA, Box 1, f.7.

64. Max V. Krebs to Mrs. Anne Schenck Huxley, October 9, 1958, Christian A. Herter Papers, 1957–61, DDE, Box 6, f.1.

65. Interviews with James Lowenstein and Roger Kirk; Raymond Hare Oral History,

June 15, 1972, DDE; Frederick Flott Oral History, ADST.

66. E.g., Nancy Matthews (the daughter-in-law of Doc), "Foreign Service Wife: A Study in Motion," *Foreign Service Journal* (January 1981): 41ff. The formal practice lasted until 1972. Kopp and Gillespie, p. 21. An interesting British parallel, noting that the Diplomatic Service Wives Association was the "Foreign Office's secret weapon," is in Jane Ewart-Biggs, *Pay, Pack and Follow: Memoirs* (London: Weidenfeld and Nicolson, 1984), pp. 102ff. I am grateful to Toni Stearns for this reference.

67. Details of Dulles funeral from memoranda, May 27, 1959, JFD, Reel 55. Acheson's undocumented statement is part of Washington lore.

68. Bruce diary, January 5, 1967, DB, Box 5, f.25; Schaetzel Oral History, May 18, 1987, EU.

69. Except, perhaps, for Maurice Couve de Murville, with whom his correspondence in mid-1959 is extremely tense, e.g., Herter to Couve, May 2, 1959, and Alphand to Couve, November 27, 1959, quotes Herter, "Nous en avons assez de M. de Gaulle," CM7, CM. Emmet profile from *Die Zeit*, January 10, 1957, his translation, Christian A. Herter Papers, Houghton Library, Harvard University (hereinafter CAH), AM 1829, Series I, f.19; interview with Fisher Howe.

70. Bohlen, p. 259; Jeff Parsons to D. K. Adams, n.d., JGP, Box 9, f.18; Hillenbrand, p. 135.

71. Interview with Richard Mayne.

72. Notable troubleshooters in the Trieste dispute were Llewellyn Thompson, James C. Dunn, Elbridge Durbrow, and Robert Joyce as well as Robert Low, the *Time* correspondent in Italy. Joyce to Dillon, October 23, 1953, RG59 Lot UP253, NARA, Box 2, f.6; Joyce excerpts from draft memoir, Robert Joyce Papers, private collection; Matthews, p. 304; Philip E. Mosely, "The Treaty with Austria," *International Organization* 4, no. 2 (May 1950): 219–235; Durbrow draft memoir, ED, chap. 41. Durbrow was serving as deputy to Ambassador Clare Boothe Luce, who claimed a good deal of the credit for herself: e.g., Luce Oral History, January 11, 1968, DDE. The officers charged with paving the way for normalizing relations with Spain were Outerbridge Horsey and Jack Morgan. Interview with George Vest. A summary of the Saar negotiations is in Schwartz, pp. 87–89.

73. Andrew J. Goodpaster Oral History, October 11, 1977, DDE; Francis Deak to Merchant, January 21, 1953, RG59 Lot 57D321-4, NARA, Box 4, f.28.

74. Bruce diary, April 24, 1958, February 20, 1959, DB, Box 3, f.7, f.20; Laukhuff to Hillenbrand, May 5, 1953, Bernard Gufler to SecState, August 3, 1959, MJH, Box 6, f.11, and Box 4, f.5 for photos. I am grateful to David Klein for identifications.

75. Merchant had also been on the list but his promotion was postponed for reasons of seniority, which reportedly upset Eisenhower so much he refused to sanction another class. Briggs, p. 383.

76. Harrop Oral History, ADST.

77. Louis J. Halle Jr. to Acheson, October 7, 1953, DAY, Reel 10, Box 15, f.189. Cf. Bob Joyce: "I think that historians in the future will agree that this short period of 1947–49 represents, at least in international affairs, 'our finest hour'.... The decay started in 1950." Robert Joyce Papers, private collection; interview with Arthur Hartman; Merchant, "Summary of Remarks at Conference on U.S. Foreign Policy, June 4 and 5, 1953," JFD, Reel 27.

78. See Henry James, "The Question of Our Speech" (1905), reprinted in Pierre A. Walker, ed., *Henry James on Culture: Collected Essays on Politics and the American Social Scene* (Lincoln: University of Nebraska Press, 1999), pp. 42–57.

79. Jenkins, p. 2.

7. The Ambivalence of Dean Acheson

1. Achilles to Rusk, May 8, 1962, White House Staff Files, Ralph A. Dungan Papers, John F. Kennedy Presidential Library, Boston, Massachusetts (hereinafter JFKL), Box 2,

f.13. The cover note was written by Roger Jones, a political appointee.

2. Zbigniew Brzezinski, *Alternative to Partition: For a Broader Concept of America's Role in Europe* (New York: McGraw Hill Book Company, 1965), p. vii.

3. Arthur M. Schlesinger Jr., *A Thousand Days: John F. Kennedy in the White House* (Boston: Houghton Mifflin Company, 2002 [1965]), p. 435.

4. Interview with Francis Bator.

5. Schlesinger, pp. 138–141; Joseph Alsop, pp. 431–433. Reportedly, Kennedy had said that if Stevenson only had asked him for the secretaryship, he would have found it very hard to say no. Interview with Carl Kaysen.

6. Walter Lippmann was also a top source of advice. Interview with Francis Bator; Ball to Lippmann, December 5, 1960, WL, Reel 45.

7. Acheson to Kennedy, July 17, 1960, President's Office Files, JFKL Box 27, f.1.

8. Alsop to Kennedy, June 21, 1963, President's Office Files, JFKL, Box 27, f.3; Lankford, p. 298; David Brinkley, *Dean Acheson: The Cold War Years, 1953–71* (New Haven, CT: Yale University Press, 1992), pp. 113–115. Nitze became an occasional ally of Bundy's. See Bundy, Memorandum for the Record, March 13, 1963, Bundy Papers, JFKL, Box 32, noting that Nitze "can write just about twice as fast as the Department of State and can coordinate much more effectively." For his part, Bruce claimed to be utterly opposed to taking the job of secretary. Bruce Oral History, December 9, 1971, LBJL.

9. For its modest status before, see R. N. Magill to Margaret Tibbetts, November 7, 1958, EUR Office of European Regional Affairs, Records of the NATO Advisor 1957–61, RG59 Lot 62D370, NARA, Box 2, f.12.

10. Following some miscommunication about it being Rome. Cf. Kenneth Downs to Bruce, January 9, 1961, Bruce Papers, VHS, Mss B8303b 190; Alsop to Polly Wisner, December 30, 1960, JA, Box 17, f.7; Bruce diary, n.d. (1961), DB, Box 3, f.33; Lankford, p. 300.

11. Interviews with Thomas Hughes and David Acheson. Other nominees for the number two slot were Arthur Dean and Robert Bowie (Bundy to Kennedy, July 7, 1961, President's Office Files, JFKL, Box 62, f.14), and Richard Bissell for number three. Bundy to Kennedy, February 25, 1961, President's Office Files, JFKL, Box 62, f.13.

12. E.g., Bohlen, p. 476.

13. Livingston T. Merchant Oral History, Spring 1965, JFKL.

14. Jack Anderson, "Washington's Curious Caste System," from *Washington Exposé* (1967), quoted in Gottlieb et al., p. 694.

15. Bruce diary, September 30 and December 19, 1962, DB, Box 4, f.18, f.20; see also Bundy, Memoranda for the Record, April 16, 1963 (on Bohlen), and February 25, 1963 (on Bruce), Bundy Papers, JFKL, Box 32. The British caught on quickly. Immediately after the election, Harold Caccia advised Derick Hoyer Millar, "[I]t will be fatal if we give the impression to Kennedy that we are impatient of innovation.... We must not seem to him to represent a repetition of the generation of whom he wrote his first book with the title *Why England Slept*." Caccia to Hoyer Millar, November, 14, 1960, CAB 21/4411, PRO.

16. Dean Rusk Oral History, July 28, 1969, LBJL; Robert M. Beaudry Oral History, ADST.

17. Richard E. Neustadt, *Report to JFK: The Skybolt Crisis in Perspective* (Ithaca, NY: Cornell University Press, 1999), p. 120; Geoffrey Kabaservice, *The Guardians: Kingman Brewster, His Circle, and the Rise of the Liberal Establishment* (New York: Henry Holt and Company, 2004), p. 110. See also Christian Nünlist, *Kennedys Rechte Hand: McGeorge Bundys Einfluss als Nationaler Sicherheitsberater auf die amerikanische Aussenpolitik, 1961–63* (Zurich: Center for Security Studies, 1999). Bundy's brother William, also a government official, was the son-in-law of Dean Acheson.

18. Isaiah Berlin to Maurice Bowra, October 27, 1962, IB, Box 246, f.91–92; John P. Leacacos, *Fires in the In-Basket: The ABC's of the State Department* (Cleveland: World Publishing Company, 1968), pp. 159–160.

19. Bundy, "Principles and Policy in U.S. Aid to Europe," July, 13, 1949, Bundy Papers, JFKL, Box 1, f.19; cf. Russell Leffingwell to Hamilton Fish Armstrong, March 6, 1949, HFA, Box 40, f.21.

20. Bruce diary, January 7, 1964, DB, Box 4, f.28.

21. Bundy to Kennedy, September 20, 1962, Bundy Papers, JFKL, Box 31, f.14.

22. Robert R. Bowie and Richard H. Immerman, *Waging Peace: How Eisenhower Shaped an Enduring Cold War Strategy* (Oxford: Oxford University Press, 1998), pp. 258–289; cf. I. M. Destler, *Presidents, Bureaucrats, and Foreign Policy: The Politics of Organizational Reform* (Princeton, NJ: Princeton University Press, 1972), pp. 98–99, 155; Leacacos, pp. 6, 46–47.

23. A glimpse is offered by Smith Simpson's *Anatomy of the State Department* (Boston: Houghton Mifflin Company, 1967), an ode that begins by dissecting the causes of immense "dissatisfaction." Cf. Schlesinger, p. 431, quoting John Davies on the foreign service: "Purged from the right under Dulles, now purged from the left under Kennedy.... How can you expect these men to do a good job?" See also Henry S. Villard, *Affairs at State* (New York: Thomas Y. Crowell Company, 1965).

24. The story is told by Schlesinger, pp. 383–384, and refuted by Hillenbrand, pp. 176–177, claiming that it had been the White House that had twice misplaced the State Department memoranda.

25. Baldrige to Bromley Smith, n.d., National Security Files, JFKL, Box 71, f.8.

26. Bruce diary, December 4, 1962, DB, Box 4, f.19.

27. U. Alexis Johnson, tape transcript 14, U. Alexis Johnson Papers, LBJL, Box 1, f.2; U. Alexis Johnson Oral History, June 14, 1969, LBJL. About the only person who said the SIG system worked well was Nicholas Katzenbach. Katzenbach Oral History, November 23, 1968, LBJL; Rusk Oral History, July 28, 1969, LBJL.

28. Interviews with Francis Bator, Timothy Dickinson, Brandon Grove; Bruce diary, September 28, 1961, DB, Box 4, f.2; Steve Dryden, *Trade Warriors: USTR and the American Crusade for Free Trade* (New York: Oxford University Press, 1995), p. 41. Cf. Ball: "I think, quite frankly, I had a hell of a lot of influence." Ball Oral History, EU.

29. Bruce diary, May 17, 1966, DB, Box 5, f.11; interview with Thomas Hughes; for Ball's disdain of the traditional foreign service, with the partial exception of EUR, which he considered "an extremely competent professional shop," see Telcons Dungan/Ball, May 31 and July 5, 1962, George Ball Telcons, JFKL, Box 7, f.1; Myer Rashish Oral History, September 11, 1967, JFKL.

30. Quoted in James A. Bill, *George Ball: Behind the Scenes in U.S. Foreign Policy* (New Haven, CT: Yale University Press, 1997), p. xiv. Dean Acheson added, "Keep on making sense; you have the field to yourself."

31. Interviews with Richard Mayne and Rosalind Springsteen; David L. DiLeo, "Catch the Night Plane for Paris: George Ball and Jean Monnet," in Hackett, ed., p. 147.

32. Ball's appointment came by way of his affiliation with Stevenson but mainly by his drafting of a long briefing paper on European policy, called the "bible," which impressed Kennedy. See, for example, Kohnstamm Oral History, EU.

33. According to Robert Bowie, quoted in Henry Owen and John Thomas Smith II, eds., *Gerard C. Smith: A Career in Progress* (Lanham, MD: University Press of America, 1989), p. xiii. Henry Brandon diary, quoting Francis Bator with reference to the de Gaulle crisis, August 3, 1966, HB, Box 7, f.2; George Ball Oral History, April 12, 1965, JFKL; William Tyler Oral History ADST (noting that, according to Rusk, "talking with the British was like putting on an old shoe"); interview with Ed Streator.

34. Schaetzel Oral History, EU; interview with Francis Bator (who disagreed with the latter element).

35. Interview with Arthur Hartman; Hartman Oral History, ADST.

36. Kennedy, quoted in Brinkley, p. 2. N.b.: In early 1963, Kennedy asked Bruce to undertake a systematic review of U.S.-European relations in order to prevent "the whole

post-Nassau machine" from grinding to a "halt." Telcons Bundy/Ball, February 4 and 6, 1963, Ball Telcons, JFKL, Box 2, f.15; Joseph Kraft, "The White House Versus State," *Washington Evening Star*, February 15, 1963; Bundy, Memorandum for the Record, February 4, 1963, Bundy Papers, JFKL, Box 32; see also note 15, above.

37. Hillenbrand, p. 178.

38. His staff assistant was a young foreign service officer (and future secretary of state), Lawrence Eagleburger, who would be hired subsequently by Francis Bator in the White House, and then by Henry Kissinger. For his part, Kissinger worked for a time as a consultant and roving emissary for Kennedy's NSC, billing over $10,000 for salary, travel, telephone, safe and alarm installation, etc. EUR struggled to distance the U.S. government from the various remarks he made to European officials. David Klein to Bromley Smith, July 9, 1962, National Security Files, JFKL, Box 321, f.1; Tyler to ambassadors, January 17, 1963, ibid., f.2; Telcon Kaysen/Ball, June 18, 1962, Ball Telcons, JFKL, Box 1, f.12; Telcon Rostow/Ball August 3, 1966, George W. Ball Papers, LBJL, Box 5, f.18. Kissinger's own negative reaction to Acheson's report is in Kissinger to Bundy, July 14, 1961, National Security Files, JFKL, Box 81A, f.14, and Kissinger, "Some Reflections on the Acheson Memorandum," August 16, 1961, ibid., Box 82, f.10–11.

39. Camps to James Huntley, February 18, 1960, MC, Box 1, f.6; Camps to Schaetzel, October 9, 1961, ibid., Box 13, f.6. This debate was wrapped up in an ongoing one over the identity of NATO as a purely military organization or one with broader, political, economic, and social missions. See, for example, Leon Fuller to George McGhee, "Agenda for the Bilderberg Meeting, April 21–23," March 28, 1961, McGhee Papers, Georgetown University Archives and Special Collections (hereinafter GMM), Box 1, f.8. A few tried to square the circle, with middling success. See, for example, Jack Tuthill's speech as the new ambassador to the EC, replacing Walt Butterworth, which noted "the challenge ... in reality a great and historic opportunity—that of evolving together, for our common well-being and prosperity, a dynamic and flexible concept of partnership ..." BAC003/1978-187/3, EU.

40. David Calleo, *The Atlantic Fantasy: The U.S., NATO, and Europe* (Baltimore: Johns Hopkins University Press, 1970), p. 145.

41. Interview with Richard Mayne; Timothy W. Stanley, "NATO's Nuclear Debate: Washington's View," *Reporter*, July 5, 1962, p. 19. Stanley was a deputy to Nitze and later a longstanding supporter of the Atlantic Council.

42. Achilles to Will (Clayton), July 30, 1964, Papers of the Atlantic Council of the United States, Archives of the Hoover Institution on War, Revolution, and Peace, Stanford, CA (hereinafter ACUS), Box 33, f.13.

43. For a hint of where the policy arm of the Pentagon stood, see Henry Rowen to McNamara, April 14, 1962, Re. Basic National Security Policy, in *FRUS 1961–63*, Vol. 8, pp. 264–265.

44. Ronald Steel, *Pax Americana* (New York: Viking Press, 1967), chap. 4.

45. Martin Herz to James Penfield, "Conclusions from the Supplementary Chapter on the Congo," March 9, 1961, MFH, Box 1, f.1; Grove, Matlock, Smyser, and Stearns interviews. N.b.: Among several foreign service officers to serve in the Congo who later became notable European hands were Ray Seitz, Jock Dean, Frank Carlucci, Bob Blake, Monty Stearns, and Ed Streator. Within the department, Ball and George McGhee (the undersecretary for political affairs who became ambassador to Germany) vied with the African bureau under G. Mennen "Soapy" Williams, J. K. Galbraith, and others, with Harlan Cleveland and Bill Tyler playing referee with regard to that conflict, where "just about everything ... is uncivilized." Harriman to Bruce, July 26, 1967, WAH, Box 439, f.4; Harriman to Ball, December 14, 1961, ibid., Box 434, f.6; Bruce diary, October 2, 1967, DB, Box 5, f.30; Telcons Ball/McGhee, December 12, 1961, Tyler/Ball, September 26 and 28, 1962, Ball Telcons, JFKL, Box 2, f.17, and Box 3, f.1; and Ball Oral History, February 16, 1968, JFKL for his regrets. For EUR's status in 1961, see Chester Bowles to Kennedy, July

28, 1961, NSF, Department and Agencies Series, JFK in *FRUS 1961–63*, Vol. 25, pp. 69–70, noting that EUR is "the best *administered* bureau of the Department," despite having "no fresh blood."

46. It was unlikely that Bundy ever regarded Ball as a rival: "It would have been news to him." Interview with Carl Kaysen.

47. Kaysen to John Macy, December 17, 1964, Office Files of John Macy, LBJL, "Leddy, John M."; Myerson Oral History, July 9, 1987, EU.

48. Bill, p. 68. Additional background from Schaetzel press release, September 21, 1966, Office Files of John Macy, LBJL; Achilles Oral History, HST.

49. Kennedy's so-called Grand Design was largely the invention of journalist Joseph Kraft. See his *Grand Design: From Common Market to Atlantic Partnership* (New York: Harper and Brothers, 1962); and David L. DiLeo, "George Ball and the Europeanists in the State Department, 1961–1963," in Douglas Brinkley and Richard T. Griffiths, eds., *John F. Kennedy and Europe* (Baton Rouge: Louisiana State University Press, 1999), p. 263. When asked about it, Dean Acheson joked that it probably "comes from the Press Club bar.... I believe the psychiatrists call this rationalization." Kleiman, p. 12; Marjolin, pp. 336ff.

50. Kurt Birrenbach to Adolph Schmidt, letter referred to in Richard Wallace to Clayton, August 14, 1964, ACUS, Box 19, f.4; Pierson Dixon to Foreign Office, December 5, 1964, No. 902, PREM 13/027, PRO; interview with Timothy Dickinson.

51. Ball Oral History, EU.

52. Ibid.; cf. Acheson, *Present at the Creation*, pp. 382–384.

53. Acheson to Henry Owen, April 25, 1966, in J. Robert Schaetzel Papers, DDE, Box 1, f.12; Acheson, "Europe: The Hinge of Fate," essay in ibid., Box 1, f.6. A later version of the essay appeared in *Foreign Affairs*.

54. C. David Heymann, *The Georgetown Ladies' Social Club: Power, Politics, and Passion in the Nation's Capital* (New York: Atria Books, 2003), p. 53.

55. Leahy diary, January 15, 1942, WDL, Reel 3.

56. Wilhelm G. Grewe, "Konrad Adenauer and the United States of America," The Konrad Adenauer Memorial Lecture 1987, St Antony's College and Konrad Adenauer Stiftung, 1995, p. 7. Kennedy would demand his recall after a leak scandal. Bundy, Memorandum for the Record, May 5, 1962, National Security Files, JFKL, Box 75, f.5; Frederick Holborn to Bundy, May 21, 1962, ibid.; Foy D. Kohler Oral History, October 1964, JFKL; Profile of Grewe, January 1961, n.a., President's Office Files, JFKL, Box 117, f.5 (noting that Grewe's university thesis carried the title "Law and Mercy—a philosophical and juridical interpretation of the concept of mercy in Shakespearian drama"). Grewe's side of the story is in Nachlass Grewe, Band 83, AA. See also *Time*, May 18, 1962; Achilles, p. 469.

57. *The Mid-Atlantic Man and Other New Breeds in England and America* (London: Weidenfeld and Nicolson, 1968), esp. pp. 50ff. Cf. Edmund Wilson, *Europe without Baedeker* (New York: Noonday Press, 1966), p. 17; and Ludovic Kennedy, *Very Lovely People* (New York: Simon and Schuster, 1969), pp. 196ff. Cf. "As Kennedy was a European version of an American, Johnson is being turned by Europeans into a caricature of an American ..." J. Robert Schaetzel, "Double Error or Myths Compounded," talk at Chatham House, May 11, 1965, in Schaetzel Papers, DDE, Box 4, f.5. De Gaulle reportedly held similar views.

58. Bruce diary, November 12, 1965, DB, Box, 5, f.1.

59. Interview with Timothy Dickinson.

60. Interview with Frank and Margot Lindsay; Katharine Graham in Gottlieb et al., p. 186. See also, in the same volume, the essay by Russell Baker, "It's Middletown on the Potomac," from *New York Times Magazine*, 1965, describing life in the city then as "urbanely dull ... perhaps the last great city in which a middle income [family] can afford a house, a tomato patch and a canopy of dogwoods within fifteen minutes of the office" (p. 47).

61. Robert Joyce to Henry Labouisse, September 1, 1964, HL, Box 3, f.5; Heymann, pp.

33ff., 70–83.

62. Lippmann to Brand, March 2, 1951, WL, Reel 48; Wilson to Moffat, March 5, 1935, JPM, Vol. 9; Achilles, pp. 329, 715; AUC, Board of Governors Biographies, Box 3; Stimson diary, November 7, 1931, HLS, Reel 4, Vol. 19. Additional inspiration may have come from a loose-knit group of British interwar figures who argued that the future of the empire required a close alliance with the United States. See Michael G. Fry, *Illusions of Security: North Atlantic Diplomacy, 1918–1922* (Toronto: University of Toronto Press, 1972), pp. 6ff. N.b.: Donovan's group was seen as too close to the U.S. government for comfort. Monnet, for example, ordered his Washington representative, Leonard Tennyson, to "have nothing to do with this organization under any circumstances." Tennyson Oral History, EU.

63. Memos on fieldwork and agenda, Papers of the Declaration of Atlantic Unity, Rare Book and Manuscripts Library, Columbia University (hereinafter DAU), Box 17A, f.1; Bruce diary, November 24, 1952, DB, Box 1, f.32, for role of Royall Tyler, Bill's father, in Committee for a Free Europe. Lists of the various Atlantic organizations are in the memo by Joseph E. Johnson, July 13, 1962, GMM, Box 1, f.8; and in the memo of the Atlantic Institute, August 17, 1961, DAU, Box 4, f.4. See also notes 64, 65 and 68, below.

64. Moore to Livingston Hartley, August 3, 1961, DAU, Box 20, f.9; Valérie Aubourg, "*L'Atlantic Union Committee*, un groupe de pression internationaliste dans l'Amérique de la guerre froide, 1949–1962," in Jean Garrigues, ed., *Les groupes de pression dans la vie politique contemporaine en France et aux États-Unis de 1820 à nos jours* (Rennes: Presses universitaires, 2002), p. 300. Moore's principal interest was in pressing for the regular congressional passage of "Atlantic Resolutions," the first of which passed in 1960, largely through the efforts of then secretary of state Herter. It would lead to the establishment of the Citizens' Committee on NATO, the forerunner of the Atlantic Council. See Winand, *Eisenhower, Kennedy and the United States of Europe*, p. 197. Another summary of the various groups is in Aubourg, "Organizing Atlanticism: The Bilderberg Group and the Atlantic Institute, 1952–1963," in Giles Scott-Smith and Hans Krabbendam, eds., *The Cultural Cold War in Europe* (London: Cass, 2003), pp. 92–108, and, by the same author, "Creating the Texture of the Atlantic Community: The NATO Information Service, Private Atlantic Networks and the Atlantic Community in the 1950s," in Aubourg et al., eds., pp. 404ff.

65. Summary of Board of Directors meeting, April 24, 1951, Papers of the American Committee on United Europe, Georgetown Library Special Collections (hereinafter ACUE), Box 2, f.91. The origins and backing of the ACUE are discussed in Richard Aldrich, "European Integration: An American Intelligence Connection," in Anne Deighton, ed., *Building Postwar Europe: National Decision-Makers and European Institutions, 1948–63* (London: St. Martin's Press, 1995), pp. 159–177.

66. Background from CE, Box 1, f.1, on the American Council on Germany, in Box 4, f.8, and on the Atlantik-Brücke, Box 14, f.11; interview with Richard Hunt; background on ACUE is in ACUE, Box 1, f.5; a list of members of the Committee for the Marshall Plan, one of the earliest of such groups, is in HF, Box 29, f.8.

67. Annual Report of Activities, April 10, 1958, Ralph C. M. Flynt Papers, HST, Box 2, f.4.

68. Memorandum of Conversation, July 24, 1961, "Voluntary Organizations in the Atlantic Field," ACUS, Box 27, f.4; Edward Cooper to Walden Moore, July 27, 1961, HCL, Box 37, and Herter to Moore, July 26, 1961, CAH, AM 1829, Series A, f.13 (for a correction of the record). The only person who seemed unhappy with the new arrangement was Wally Moore, who objected to the inclusion of the "extreme, but very powerful, right wing" of the Atlantic Treaty Association and what he might have presumed to be his own eventual exclusion. "I am all in favor of Dean Rusk calling together the various Atlantic groups," he wrote to his friend, the writer, retired diplomat, and onetime former assistant to Joseph Grew, Lithgow Osborne, "but I think it *most* important that we retain ... our informal character and ... our freedom of decision and action." Another friend and backer, Justin

Blackwelder, chimed in, "[I]t is perfectly obvious what the [American Committee on NATO] has to gain by a merger, but no-one has explained to me what we stand to gain by it." Justin Blackwelder to Walden Moore, August 3, 1961, ACUS, Box 27, f.4; cf. Ben Moore to Allen Siebens, January 20, 1958, DAU, Box 1.

69. Speech by Lauris Norstad to the Atlantic Council, January 14, 1963, President's Office Files, JFKL, Box 116, f.12. Norstad had just retired from the air force and as supreme allied commander of NATO. For an interpretation of Norstad's retirement as a repudiation of Allied strategic policy, see Trachtenberg, p. 302. Cf. "Long-term Planning: Political Consultation, Summary," TYP(61)13, April 7, 1961, Archives of the North Atlantic Treaty Organization, Brussels.

70. "Policy Statement," n.d., ACUS, Box 1, f.3; cf. similar Spenglerian language in the "Manifesto of Atlantic Union," AUC, Box 1, Atlantic Congress, 1951; Frank Munk, *Atlantic Dilemma: Partnership or Community?* (Dobbs Ferry, NY: Oceana Publications, 1964), p. 2; Robert Strausz-Hupé et al., *Building the Atlantic World* (New York: Harper and Row, Publishers, 1963), pp. 15ff. For the history of the Atlantic idea emphasizing World War II and postwar trends, see Bernard Bailyn, *Atlantic History: Concept and Contours* (Cambridge, MA: Harvard University Press, 2005), pp. 4ff.

71. The conspiracy literature on such groups is too vast to cite. A good example, from the Left, is Kees van der Pijl, *The Making of an Atlantic Ruling Class* (London: Verso, 1984). A recent nonpolitical history of the Bilderberg Group is by Thomas Gijswijt (unpublished Ph.D dissertation, Heidelberg University, 2007).

72. Interview with Richard Mayne.

73. Bruce diary, July 5, 1951, DB, Box 1, f.17; Achilles proposal for an Atlantic Institute of Technology, ACUS, Box 1, f.7; George Franklin Jr. to McCloy, February 14, 1969, Papers of the Council on Foreign Relations, Department of Rare Books and Special Collections, Princeton University Library, Princeton University, Princeton, NJ, Box 2–11, f.5; AUC, Box 1, Atlantic Award 1952; Deane Hinton to John Leddy, October 22, 1965, EUR Office of OECD, European Community and Atlantic Political-Economic Affairs, Records Relating to Economic Matters 1953–75, RG59 Lot 88D259, NARA, Box 23, f.5; Slater to Shepard Stone, April 4, 1960, Unpublished Reports 010753, FF. The assembly's principal promoter was J. Allan Hovey, who wrote his dissertation about it. EUR/RPE, NARA Box 4, f.3. See also Oliver Schmidt, "Toward an Atlantic Society: U.S. Cultural Diplomacy, German-American Visitor Programs, and the Return of Transnational History After 1945," in Frank A. Ninkovich and Liping Bu, eds., *The Cultural Turn: Essays in the History of U.S. Foreign Relations* (Chicago: Imprint Publications, 2001), p. 172.

74. Lithgow Osborne to Gerald B. Henry, March 22, 1963, DAU, Box 21, f.8, followed by a letter from Walden Moore that includes an ideological breakdown of leading "Atlanticians"; Bruce diary, January 7, 1964, DB, Box 4, f.28; cf. "[the Atlantic Institute] has too much money and not enough brain about how to use it." Hartman to Schaetzel, February 24, 1966, Records of the Deputy Assistant Secretary of State for European Affairs (Schaetzel), 1961–66, RG59 Lot 66D439, NARA, Box 1, f.5.

75. Leonard Tennyson, "Comments on European Regional and Atlantic Area Studies in U.S. Universities and Colleges," March 18, 1966, Joseph Slater Files, Ford Foundation Archives, New York, NY (hereinafter FF), Box 27, f.286. For most of its existence, the *Quarterly* was edited by Edna Rostow, wife of Gene and sister-in-law of Walt.

76. For the essential involvement of Sam Reber in this project, see Bruce diary, October 12, 1967, DB, Box 5, f.30; "1968 Program," Commission for the Atlantic Colleges, Inc., December 6, 1967, Flynt Papers, HST, Box 3, f.3.

77. The idea for it dated from the mid-1950s. See Huntley's memoir, *An Architect of Democracy: Building a Mosaic of Peace* (Washington, D.C.: New Academia Publishing, 2006), pp. 111–112, 123ff., 169–172, 175ff.; and "Historical Summary: The Atlantic Institute," n.d., n.a., HCL, Box 37. Huntley was a persistent opponent of the dumbbell theory. See

ibid., pp. 118–121, 151–155. He also worked for the U.S. Information Agency, the Atlantic Council, and the Ford Foundation. The institute's record was mixed. Its first director-general, Henry Cabot Lodge Jr., seemed more interested in using the institute to maintain his close ties to French officialdom, which had initially offered him a headquarters in the Palace of Versailles until he was named by Kennedy to become ambassador to South Vietnam. After a brief stay in Milan, the institute set itself up in Paris at the Hôtel Crillon. Huntley, p. 197; Bruce diary, April 21, 1961, DB, Box 3, f.33; William Y. Elliott to Herter, December 6, 1957, EUR Records of the Director of the Office of European Regional Affairs, RG59 Lot 61D252, NARA, Box 1, f.6. Lodge's own statement of mission is in "Operation of the Atlantic Institute," n.d., HCL, Box 37. According to Lodge, Rusk had asked him to take the job. Lodge to Bohlen, May 31, 1962, HCL II, Reel 2; Rusk correspondence, ibid., Reel 14. The institute would later be run by Jack Tuthill and Martin Hillenbrand. Hillenbrand Oral History, EU.

78. See "Proposal to Transform the Atlantic Institute into an Institute for International Policy," in Pierre Uri Papers, PU-99, 1963–1978, Institut atlantique, and letter from Uri to Walter Dowling, n.d. (September 1968), EU.

79. Although here, too, the philosophical divisions created problems, with some lamenting Schaetzel's insistence that "Atlantic" and "Western European" were synonymous. See Huntley to E. V. Rostow, March 23, 1965, Joseph Slater Files, FF, Box 27, f.286; Schaetzel, "Long-range Organizational and Personnel Program for the Atlantic Community Affairs," October 3, 1962, EUR/RPE Records Relating to European Integration 1962–66, RG59, Lots 67D33, 68D27, 69D73, NARA, Box 1, f.6; Joel W. Biller to Christopher Van Hollen, April 17, 1963, nominations of officers for Atlantic specialization, ibid., Box 1, f.7; for example, in 1962, the Johns Hopkins University's Bologna Center changed its course title from "European Integration" to "The Atlantic Community and European Integration." Richard Neustadt Papers, JFKL, Box 10, f.14.

80. Uri to Tuthill, August 8, 1969, and March 1, 1974, Uri Papers, EU; "almost impossible" comes from Henry Cabot Lodge quoted in Achilles, p. 734; Uri was a brilliant but difficult, calculating man of whom Jean Monnet once reportedly said, "[I]f asked how many shoes were under the table, he would count the number of people and multiply by two." Interviews with Henry Owen and Richard Mayne. Cf. Monnet to McCloy, November 10, 1966, AMK C 26/4/385, JM; John Tuthill Oral History, ibid.; figure on giving is in "Brief Description and List of Prior Ford Foundation Grants in Support of Activities in the Atlantic Area (1950–1963)," FF, Reports 010732, n.d. Stone was a major promoter and watcher of Germany since his time there as a student in the 1930s. See Fritz Stern, "Shepard Stone: Witness and Actor in Fifty Years of German-American Relations," in *Ein Buch der Freunde: Shepard Stone zum Achtzigsten* (Berlin: Siedler, 1988), pp. 296ff., and Volker R. Berghahn, *America and the Intellectual Cold Wars in Europe: Shepard Stone Between Philanthropy, Academy, and Diplomacy* (Princeton, NJ: Princeton University Press, 2001).

81. Tuthill to Ball, January 17, 1961, John W. Tuthill Papers, USDOS/JT 11, JM.

82. Walden Moore to William Draper, May 21, 1963, DAU, Box 16, f.4; interview with David Acheson; Schaetzel to Van Hollen, October 18, 1963, National Security Files, JFKL, Box 221, f.3. Herter was skeptical about the administration's acceding to the idea of a commission. Herter to Achilles, September 26, 1963, CAH, Series A, f.3.

83. "Record of Meeting, November 7, 1963," with Rusk, Norstad, Herter, Clayton, Schaetzel, and Achilles, Lauris Norstad Papers, DDE, Box 126, f.2, and Achilles to Norstad, November 12, 1963, ibid.: "[T]his seemed like a real brushoff ..."; see also Achilles to Walter Dowling, November 8, 1963, and Randolph Burgess to Norstad, January 10, 1964, ibid., f.3. For its part, the White House regarded the council as little more than "a speakers clearing house." Selma G. Freedman to Klein, August 29, 1962, Bundy Papers, JFKL, Box 31, f.14. Cf. "The essential problem is to keep Norstad on our side without getting involved in this Rube Goldberg device that someone has hatched.... The Atlantic Council clearly is in need

of a job and should be invited to come forth with ideas without being given any promise of full-time federal employment.... This, of course, is easier said than done." Klein to Bundy, November 1, 1963, National Security Files, JFKL, Box 222, f.1; Bundy to Kennedy, November 23, 1961, ibid.; W. Y. Smith to Bundy, July 25, 1963, President's Office Files, JFKL, Box 63a, f.4; EUR essentially agreed. Tyler to Rusk, drafted by Schaetzel, April 17, 1963, ibid., noting that it "seem[ed] unwise to rebuff" the council. General William Y. Smith after his retirement would also become a long-serving member and treasurer of the organization.

84. Schaetzel to Rusk, November 8, 1963, RG59 Lot 66D439, NARA, Box 2, f.1.

85. Achilles, pp. 738 (his emphasis), 905; Memcon with McCloy (who disagreed), August 22, 1967, Norstad Papers, DDE, Box 127, f.2. McCloy resigned as the chairman of the Atlantic Institute over it. Birrenbach to Norstad, June 22, 1967, ibid. See also Livingston Hartley to Richard Wallace, September 22, 1962, complaining about the popularity of dumbbellism in "EEC circles," ACUS, Box 23, f.3.

86. March–May 1964, February 13, 1967 (several letters), AMK C 26/6/12326/6/150, JM.

87. Janet Flanner quoted in Bruce diary, January 9, 1959, DB, Box 3, f.12.

88. For a detailed chronology, see Hillenbrand, "The Berlin Problem in 1961," National Security Files, JFKL, Box 81, f.8.

89. Birrenbach to Hillenbrand, July 16, 1984, MJHH, Series 3, Box 1, f.10; Bundy to Kennedy, May 29, 1961, President's Office Files, JFKL, Box 126, f.1; Bohlen, "Line of Approach to Khrushchev," June 1, 1961, ibid.; cf. Monnet to Acheson, November 23, 1962, AMK C 23/1/9, JM; Hillenbrand to John Ausland, September 20, 1966, MJH, Box 5, f.1; Hillenbrand, pp. 206–207, on the prolongation of the Berlin crisis beyond the Cuba events; Couve de Murville, speech to the NATO Parliamentary Assembly, November 12, 1962, CM1, CM.

90. William Tyler, David Ormsby-Gore, and George McGhee Oral Histories, JFKL; Henry Kissinger had been among the first in 1961 to advise making the trip. Kissinger to Kennedy, April 5, 1961, President's Office Files, Box 117, f.5. Bundy's account of the visit, noting the "paleness" of the foreign service officers in Germany, is in his Memorandum for the Record, July 4, 1963, Bundy Papers, JFKL, Box 32.

91. He answered "no" to both. Nitze to Walter Lippmann, October 26, 1959, DAY, Reel 15, Box 23, f.295, and in WL, Reel 83.

92. Bundy Oral History, September 24, 1990, Nuclear Age, Liddell Hart Military Archive, King's College, London; cf. Llewellyn Thompson to Rusk, June 19, 1961, National Security Files, JFKL, Box 81A, f.3; Hillenbrand, p. 175. Hillenbrand also recalled the state banquet in Vienna when, due to an oversight by the caterers, the entire meal was served "stone cold" (p. 174).

93. Tyler to Bruce, December 4, 1959, in Bruce Papers, VHS, Mss. B8303b; see also letter of November 29 expressing similar concerns about the work of the Berlin planning under way in Washington.

94. Loy Henderson to Herter, October 28, 1959, and Herter to Dillon, May 13, 1959, Herter Papers, DDE, Box 21, f.4–5; Hillenbrand, p. 169; Davis Eugene Boster, Thompson Buchanan, Constance Ray Harvey, and Walter B. Smith II Oral Histories, ADST.

95. Kennedy to Rusk, September 12, 1961, National Security Files, JFKL, Box 82A, f.8; L. J. Legere to Bundy, November 1, 1962, ibid., Box 85, f.3; "The Berlin Task Force and the Operations Center," n.a., April 16, 1962, Office of the Executive Secretariat, Records Relating to the Berlin Crisis, 1961–62, RG59 Lot 66D124, NARA, Box 1, f.6; Memorandum of Conversation, William Tyler and Heinrich Knappstein, March 6, 1964, MJH, Box 1, f.2, and John C. Ausland, "Six Berlin Incidents, 1961–1964," ibid., Box 1, f.1; Hillenbrand to Merchant, January 21, 1959 and Hillenbrand to Kohler, January 23, 1959, RG59 Lot 64D291, NARA, Box 3, f.1. In April 1964 the task force was "institutionalized" in EUR.

Ausland to Hillenbrand, April 30, 1964, ibid., f.2; AP wire report, July 21, 1962, in ibid., Box 3, f.9; Alfred Puhan to Hillenbrand, January 16, 1965, Box 5, f.18. Karl and Martha Mautner Oral Histories, ADST; cf. Lilienfeld to Ministry, July 25, 1962, no. 2145 B12 Band 1678, AA.

96. The high point was reached in 1955, with about 430,000 American troops in Western Europe, about half of them in Germany. Gregory F. Treverton, *The Dollar Drain and American Forces in Germany* (Athens: Ohio University Press, 1978), p. 4. See also pp. 33ff. for a chronology of the offset negotiations and pp. 99–100 for the "status quo" views of EUR; and Hubert Zimmermann, "The Quiet German: The Vietnam War and the Federal Republic of Germany," in Christopher Goscha and Maurice Vaïsse, eds., *La guerre du Vietnam et l'Europe, 1963–1973* (Brussels: Bruylant, 2003), p. 56.

97. Interview with Francis Bator. Bator feared another Skybolt (see below). Bator to Johnson, February 23, 1967, National Security File, Country File, Europe, LBJL, Box 187, f.5; McCloy to Birrenbach, May 10, 1966, JJM, Box NA1, f.16; Telcon Fowler/Ball, April 11, 1961, Ball Telcons, JFKL, Box 1, f.12; Telcon Kaysen/Ball, August 20, 1962, ibid., f.13. See also Joachim Arenth, *Johnson, Vietnam und der Westen: transatlantische Belastungen, 1963–1969* (Munich: Olzog Verlag, 1994), pp. 51ff. and Francis Gavin, *Gold, Dollars and Power: The Politics of International Monetary Relations, 1958–1971* (Chapel Hill: University of North Carolina Press, 2004).

98. Memorandum of Conversation with LBJ, McCloy, W. Rostow, Bator, March 2, 1967, Francis M. Bator Papers, LBJL, Box 18, f.3; detailed discussion of the relationship between this issue and the Vietnam War is in Thomas Alan Schwartz, *Lyndon Johnson and Europe: In the Shadow of Vietnam* (Cambridge, MA: Harvard University Press, 2003), pp. 87ff.

99. Ball Oral History, March 29, 1968, JFKL.

100. Both George Ball and Bill Tyler got heavily involved with the latter, balance of payments question, as did Acheson; Kennedy asked Acheson to chair a special task force on it. Additional help came from Dillon, Leddy, Nitze, Bator, Phil Trezise and Anthony Solomon of the State Department, Francis Deming, and perhaps most critically, Robert Roosa of Treasury. See cartoon of monetary policy on a tightrope in President's Office Files, JFKL, Box 64, f.3; Telcons Bundy/Ball February 6, 1963, Kaysen/Ball February 25, 1963, and Dillon/ Ball May 17, 1963, Ball Telcons, JFKL, Box 1, f.14 and Box 9, f.7; Nitze Oral History, May 22, 1964, JFKL; Telcon Heller/Ball, December 4, 1963, George W. Ball Papers, LBJL, Box 1, f.10; Bator to Johnson, August 24, 1966, National Security File, Name File, LBJL, Box 1, f.2; Fowler to Johnson, July 18, 1966, National Security File, Office File, LBJL, Box 12, f.4. A good, long summary of the offset negotiations is in "The Trilateral Negotiations and NATO," in National Security File, National Security Council Histories, LBJL, Box 40, f.1. See also, in same folder, Leddy to Rusk, August 23, 1966. Among other things, it reveals that Leddy was the person who linked offset effectively to the nuclear nonproliferation issue and conventional force levels in Europe by way of a trilateral approach.

101. Memorandum of Conversation with Harriman, Macmillan, McNamara, and Sir Patrick Dean, January 15, 1968, WAH, Box 486, f.7; cf. Ball to Fowler, July 28, 1965, Records of Under Secretary George W. Ball, RG59 Lot 74D272, NARA, Box 23, f.6, urging full commitments in both places; Harold Watkinson to David Ormsby-Gore, May 9–10, 1962, DEFE 13/335, PRO; Brandon, pp. 214–216.

102. "It was a pile of junk.... It would have no military utility. We cancelled it. Thank God." Robert McNamara Oral History, September 23, 1990, Nuclear Age, Liddell Hart Military Archives Centre, King's College, London; Peter Hennessy and Caroline Anstey, *Moneybags and Brains: The Anglo-American "Special Relationship" Since 1945* (Strathclyde Analysis Papers, No, 1, 1990, University of Strathclyde), p. 11. The principal opponents at the Pentagon were Paul Nitze, who became a strong advocate of a French national deterrent, and Charles Hitch. See Memorandum of Conversation, Alphand, Nitze, December 7, 1962,

National Security File, JFKL, Box 71A, f.14. On the other side of the French nuclear question was Foy Kohler. Memorandum of Conversation, John Newhouse, Foy Kohler, Stephen Low, May 6, 1967, Chronological Files of Deputy Under Secretary for Political Affairs Foy D. Kohler 1966–67, RG59 Lot 66D229, NARA, Box 1, f.2; Neustadt, p. 42; John Newhouse, *De Gaulle and the Anglo-Saxons* (London: Andre Deutsch, 1970), pp. 22, 88, 155; Alphand to Couve, March 23, 1961, No. 509/AM, Amérique 1952–1962, États-Unis 356 9-4-1 MAE.

103. Bundy Oral History, Nuclear Age, Liddell Hart Military Archives Centre, King's College, London.

104. Lawrence Freedman and John Gearson, "Nassau and the British Nuclear Deterrent," in Burk and Stokes, eds., p. 196.

105. Memorandum of Conversation with William Tyler, June 1 and June 14, 1963, Richard E. Neustadt Papers, JFKL, Box 2, f.4; Neustadt, p. 79; Ball, p. 268. The reasons for Rusk's absence remain obscure; his excuse was a diplomatic dinner in Washington. Bruce was one of several people who said it was a mistake for him to be away. C. L. Sulzberger, *The Last of the Giants* (New York: Macmillan Company, 1970), p. 967.

106. Tyler memcons, Neustadt Papers, JFKL. A memo drafted by Bundy to Adenauer on the offer, which he presumably passed along to de Gaulle, mistaking "same" and "similar" regarding the weapons system, did not make that much of a difference. Memorandum of Conversation with Paul H. Nitze, June 19, 1963, Neustadt Papers, JFKL.

107. N. Beloff, p. 159.

108. Bohlen, pp. 500–501; Newhouse, p. 255; Bundy to Kennedy, Draft Instructions to Chip Bohlen, December 31, 1962, Bundy Papers, JFKL, Box 33; Macmillan to Kennedy, July 18, 1963, Macmillan Papers, Bodleian Library, Oxford University, Box 357, f.122–124; Couve, pp. 70ff., and Couve to Alphand, n.d. (April 1963), CM8, CM (noting the role of Bobby Kennedy and little in the way of initiative on the part of Bohlen).

109. Hillenbrand Oral History, EU; Jackson quoted in Owen and Smith, eds., p. 29.

110. Rusk to USRO Paris, TOPOL 1526 April 25, 1961, Norstad Papers, DDE, Box 90, f.5; EUR/RA "Issues of U.S. Policy Regarding the Defense Posture of NATO" November 9, 1959, ibid., f.10; for general summaries of this plan, and of the MLF, see John D. Steinbrenner, *The Cybernetic Theory of Decision: New Dimensions of Political Analysis* (Princeton, NJ: Princeton University Press, 1974), chaps. 6–8; Trachtenberg, pp. 211ff.; Alastair Buchan, *The Multilateral Force: An Historical Perspective*, Adelphi Paper 13 (London: The Institute for Strategic Studies, October 1964).

111. "The North Atlantic Nations: Tasks for the 1960s," in RG59 Lot 66D439, NARA, Box 3, f.5; cf. Memorandum of Conversation with Paul-Henri Spaak et al., "NATO Long-Range Planning," June 13, 1960, Staff Secretary Records, DDE, in *FRUS 1958–1960*, Vol. 7, Part I, pp. 591–596; Memorandum of Conference with Bowie, Goodpaster and Eisenhower, August 16, 1960, Whitman File, DDE, in *FRUS*, same volume, pp. 611–614.

112. Memoranda of Conversation with Henry Owen, May 25, 1963, George Ball, May 24, and July 2, 1963, and John F. Kennedy, April 27, 1963, Neustadt Papers, JFKL, Box 22, f.4; Bowie and Bundy Oral Histories, Nuclear Age, Liddell Hart Military Archives Centre, King's College, London; Telcon Kennedy/ Ball January 29, 1963, Ball Telcons, JFKL, Box 2, f.15.

113. Bundy had earlier advised against having Bowie work for Kennedy on the grounds that their views on Europe were too different. Telcon Bundy/Ball July 9, 1963, Ball Telcons, JFKL, Box 9, f.7. Ball later denied having been a committed supporter of the MLF, which he termed "a manifestly absurd contrivance." Ball, p. 274. Though he fought hard for it, he was probably less attached to it ideologically than were Owen, Smith, and Schaetzel. Interview with Arthur Hartman.

114. Jenkins, p. 359.

115. Interview with Henry Owen. Owen had been educated in Switzerland, generally spoke with Europeans in fluent French or German, was a devoted supporter of Monnet and

the European idea, and married an Austrian. Smith, the son of an executive at General Motors, was a lawyer who went on to become a public enemy of Richard Nixon following Smith's resignation as chief negotiator of the first Strategic Arms Limitation Treaty.

116. Hillenbrand, p. 227.

117. Neustadt, p. 9; Memorandum of Conversation in the President's Office, February 18, 1963, National Security File, JFKL, Box 217, f.4. For a sampling of European reaction to the Merchant mission, see Merchant to Rusk, March 20, 1963, National Security File, JFKL, Box 372, f.8; Ormbsy-Gore Oral History (with Neustadt, n.d.), JFKL; "Brief for the Prime Minister, Visit of Mr. Livingston Merchant, March 12–13," PREM 11/4587, PRO.

118. Known later as the International Institute for Strategic Studies, or IISS. Schaetzel to Hartman, October 19, 1963, and Schaetzel, Memorandum for the Record re. Schelling, October 5, 1963, Records of the Multilateral Force Negotiating Team, Subject Files 1963–66, RG59 Lots 68D301 and 66D55, NARA, Box 16, f.2. Others enlisted in the campaign were Shep Stone (who secured Ford Foundation support for the founding of the ISS), Bob Murphy, and William Draper, with mixed success. Same folder, memoranda for meetings with Stone and Draper, and Murphy to Merchant, March 7, 1964.

119. Walden Moore to Thomas Finletter, October 28, 1965, DAU, Box 17A, f.3; Tuthill to Ball, June 21, 1963, RG59 74D272, NARA, Box 26, f.8; Walter Dowling to Gerard Smith, September 29, 1961, in Records of Multilateral Force Negotiating Team 1961–65, RG59 Lots 69D297 and 66D366, NARA, Box 6, f.12; Foreign Office Paper for New Government, July 11, 1964, esp. pp. 27ff., W UN 1193/296, FO371/179029; P. Dixon to Foreign Office, November 6, 1964, No. 814, W UN 1193/432, FO371/179032; and Peter Ramsbotham to E. J. W. Barnes, July 21, 1964, W UN 1193/226 FO 371/179027, PRO; Alphand to Ministry, October 23, 1964, No. 6362–65, Amérique 1964–1970, États-Unis 575 9-4-1 MAE. Bundy noted that in Germany, "enthusiasm" for the MLF was "strongest among those concerned with diplomacy, and weakest among those concerned with money, with the military not far behind in caution." Memorandum for the Record, July 4, 1963, Bundy Papers, JFKL, Box 32; Wilhelm Grewe, "NATO Today and Tomorrow," lecture at the NATO Defense College, January 15, 1965, Nachlass Grewe, Band 86, AA; cf. Zbigniew Brzezinski, "Moscow and the M.L.F.: Hostility and Ambivalence," *Foreign Affairs* 43, no. 1 (October 1964); "On the Fence with MLF," *Time*, June 7, 1963.

120. Hillenbrand to Schaetzel, March 10, 1964, RG59 Lot UP-025, NARA, Box 5, f.20.

121. Bundy to Rusk, "New Steps on the MLF," July 11, 1963, RG59 Lot 68D301 and 69D55, NARA, Box 1, f.1; Steinbrenner, pp. 292ff. For a hint of Nitze's views, see Christopher Emmet to Nitze, November 12, 1963, CE, Box 92, f.35; Bundy, Memorandum for the Record, July 4, 1963, Bundy Papers, JFKL, p. 21.

122. Memorandum of Conversation, Johnson, Rusk, McNamara, Ball, Bundy, Bruce, Neustadt, December 6, 1964, Neustadt Papers, JFKL, Box 21, f.9.

123. Nicholas Henderson, *The Private Office Revisited* (London: Profile Books, 2001), p. 80.

124. Neustadt to Bundy, January 8, 1965, National Security File, Name File, LBJL, Box 7, f.3, his emphasis; "Memorandum of Conversation with Professor Neustadt" (with Healey et al.), November 25, 1964, PREM 13/026, PRO; "Considerations Involving Germany and France Which Are Pertinent to Modification of the US Position on MLF," November 4, 1964, Multilateral Force Documents, RG59 Lot 66D182, NARA, Box 3, f.4, for the infamous memo by David Mark that Bundy used to kill the plan; Bundy, Memorandum for Rusk, McNamara, Ball, November 25, 1964, RG59 Lot 74D272, NARA, Box 27, f.4, contradicting NSAM No. 318 of November 14, 1964; the MLF proposal would survive, but only in name (as MLF and ANF, or Atlantic Nuclear Force) for another year. For Neustadt's role and the divisions it imposed on EUR, see Ronald Spiers Oral History, ADST. For the president's role, see Bundy Oral History, LBJL, January 30, 1969.

125. Interview with Michael Palliser; Eric Roll, *Crowded Hours* (London: Faber and

Faber, 1985), p. 110.

126. Denis Healey Oral History, February 5, 1990, Nuclear Age, Liddell Hart Centre, King's College, London; Bruce diary, November 25, 1964, DB, Box 4, f.34.

127. Klein, letter to the author.

128. Neustadt to Bundy, June 18, 1963, National Security File, JFKL, Box 217A, f.5.

129. Bowie Oral History, EU; interview with Henry Owen; Livingston Merchant, "Overall Thoughts on the MLF Enroute from Ankara to Naples," 2nd draft, April 29, 1963, in LM, Box 10; for his part, Bowie insisted that the MLF was less about Germany than about making sure the British and French national deterrents would not threaten the strength of the Alliance. Moreover, the navy assured him that it would work just fine. Interview with Robert Bowie and Bowie Oral History, September 24, 1990, Nuclear Age, Liddell Hart Centre, King's College, London; "Dr. Bowie's Proposal" RG59 Lots 69D297 and 66D366, NARA, Box 2, f.8; and Bowie to Rusk, July 31, 1964, ibid., Box 4, f.1. Cf. Tuthill to Margaret Tibbetts, April 19, 1966, Tuthill Papers, USDOS/JT53, JM; Ball Oral History, EU.

130. See Gavin, esp. pp. 154ff.; Bird, p. 586; cf. Bundy to Lippmann, August 13, 1963, WL, Reel 49; Kohnstamm Oral History, EU.

131. W. W. Rostow to Johnson, January 16, 1967, National Security File, Country File, Europe, LBJL, Box 187, f.4. The idea of the nuclear planning group was circulated quietly behind the scenes by State Department official Ron Spiers, who also discussed it and other possible outcomes with British officials before the MLF had been shelved. Denis Greenhill to Sammy Hood, June 6, 1964, W UN1193/140, and J. A. Thomson to E. J. W. Barnes, June 26, 1964, W UN 1193/166, FO 371/179026; K. B. A. Scott to E. J. W. Barnes October 1, 1964, W UN 1193/359 FO 371/179030, PRO. For his part, Spiers—who was the first director of the new Bureau on Political-Military Affairs—said he supported the idea of the MLF but objected to the way it was handled bureaucratically. Letter to the author from Ron Spiers; Jeffrey Kitchen, "MLF Alternative," n.d., National Security File, JFKL, Box 217A, f.2; Spiers to Leddy, October 18, 1965, RG59 Lot 74D272, NARA, Box 29, f.4; Spiers Oral History, ADST. For the saga of the Germans and the Non-Proliferation Treaty, see Robert C. Creel to Hillenbrand, February 23, 1967, MJH, Box 5, f.4 ("the bête noire in our relationship"); Hillenbrand to SecState, August 13, 1965, National Security File, Country File, Europe, Box 186, f.1; Bator to Johnson, April 4, 1966, "A Nuclear Role for Germany: What Do the Germans Want?" ibid., f.3; Msge for Mr. Rostow from John Roche, July 7, 1967, ibid., Box 188, f.2; Spurgeon M. Keeny Jr., "The Non-Proliferation Treaty," December 24, 1968, National Security File, National Security Council Histories, LBJL, Box 55, f.1; Memorandum of Conversation between Harriman and McCloy, January 22, 1966, WAH, Box 486, f.4; Schaetzel to Leddy, March 7, 1967, RG59 Lot 88D259, NARA, Box 22, f.12 (for role of Monnet), and Schwartz, pp. 157–165, 208–209.

132. Interview with Thomas Hughes; Camps to Schaetzel, January 4, 1964, RG59 Lots 67D33, 67D27, 69D73, NARA, Box 5, f.2.

133. Achilles, p. 760; Bruce diary, December 27, 1962, DB, Box 4, f.20; The turn to the MLF after de Gaulle's rejection of the British application was notable. See also Patrick Gordon-Walker diary, May 31, 1963, Gordon-Walker Papers, Churchill Archive Centre, Cambridge University, Cambridge, UK, GNWR 1/15; Schaetzel, "United States Policy Towards Europe and the Atlantic Partnership," March 21, 1963, National Security File, JFKL, Box 214, f.1.

134. Quoted in Bundy to Kennedy, March 30, 1961, President's Office File, JFKL, Box 62, f.13; interview with Michael Palliser; Newhouse, "Weighing the Risks in the MLF," March 20, 1964, AMK C 23/7/45, JM; Merchant, "The MLF and the Atlantic Community," December 3, 1964, LM, Box 11, f.14.

8. *La Période Texane*

1. Thompson to Rusk, February 27, 1963, National Security File, JFKL, Box 213A, f.3;

cf. Kennedy to Thompson: "Well Tommy, I suppose we'll end up with the Berlin solution which you proposed." Thompson Oral History, March 25, 1964, JFKL. Gene Rostow was another who said "De Gaulle's diplomatic bombshell" was "a blessing in disguise." Rostow to Ball, January 29, 1963, AMK C 23/1/166, JM.

2. Crane Brinton, *The Americans and the French* (Cambridge, MA: Harvard University Press, 1968), p. 226; cf. Couve, pp. 81–82; Alphand to Ministry, November 2, 1964, NR 6584/87, Amérique 1964–1970, États-Unis 575 9-4-1 MAE; Grewe handwritten notes on conversation with Finletter, July 1965, Nachlass Grewe, Band 88, AA.

3. See, for example, the prescient memo by Turner Cameron to Herter, sent under Merchant's signature, May 5, 1959, Project Cleanup, DDE, in *FRUS 1958–1960*, Vol. 7, part 2, pp. 207–212. For French insistence on the important distinction between the Alliance and the Organization—including persistent pledges of loyalty to the former—see, inter alia, Couve de Murville, speech to the Seventh Annual Conference of NATO Parliamentarians, November 13, 1961, CM1, CM, Couve interview with CBS, February 21, 1965, CM2, interview with RTF, March 16, 1966, and radio interview, April 6, 1966, same folder. Couve's own edits to memoranda at the time suggest considerable deliberating over tone and content. See, for example, the aide mémoire of March 11, 1966, CM8.

4. Cf. Telcons Kuchel/Ball, January 30, 1965, Mansfield/Ball, March 3, 1966 and Collins/Ball, March 10, 1966, Papers of George W. Ball, LBJL, Box 3, f.15; George C. Denney Jr. to Rusk, REU-31, May 1, 1964, RG59 Lot 66D439, Box 1, f.12; Bohlen to Achilles, January 14, 1965, copy in possession of author; Hervé Alphand, *L'étonnement d'être: Journal, 1939–1973* (Paris: Fayard, 1977), p. 473. Cf. Achilles, p. 819. For his part, Russ Fessenden read the whole episode as part of a long-term game whose end, for de Gaulle, was to "obtain mastery over the Germans." Fessenden to Schaetzel, May 25, 1966 in RG59 Lot 66D439, NARA, Box 3, f.7.

5. Bohlen to Rusk, March 3, 1966, National Security File, Country File, Europe, LBJL, Box 174, f.2; Central Intelligence Agency Memorandum No. 0591/68, "If De Gaulle Resigns," May 29, 1968, ibid., Box 174, f.3.

6. Interview with George Vest; John M. Leddy Oral History, ADST; Brinkley, pp. 189ff.; Walter W. Rostow, "Some Reflections on National Security Policy," February 1965, S/S-NSC Files: Lot 70D265 in *FRUS 1963–68*, Vol. 10, p. 223. Cf. McGeorge Bundy Oral History, March 19, 1969, LBJL.

7. Bruce diary, May 19, 1966, DB, Box 5, f.11.

8. Acheson to Anthony Eden, June 29, 1966, DAY, Reel 6, Box 8, f.117; Morton H. Halperin, *Bureaucratic Politics and Foreign Policy* (Washington, D.C.: Brookings Institution, 1974), pp. 284–285.

9. Interview with Francis Bator; Schwartz, *Lyndon Johnson and Europe*, p. 109; Bator noted that Bruce got the depiction wrong in his diary. According to Bator, the president was calm throughout. Cf. Neustadt's recollection in his oral history, LBJL, consistent with Bruce's, noting that Johnson simply "had a streak ... of just liking to pull the wings off flies." For the parallel views of Tyler, Bruce, and Bohlen on how to handle the crisis, see Tyler to Rusk, March 7, 1966, National Security File, Country File Europe, LBJL, Box 177, f.4; Memorandum of Discussions, March 6, 1966 (McNamara, Vance, McNaughton, Rusk, Ball, Leddy, Meeker), ibid.; Bruce to SecState, March 6, 1966, in Bruce diary, DB, Box 5, f.10; Neustadt Memorandum of Conversation with Charles E. Bohlen, Neustadt Papers, JFKL, Box 22, f.4.

10. Bundy to Kennedy, June 17, 1962, Neustadt Papers, JFKL, Box 20, f.2; cf. Bohlen: "It is always easier to say what should *not* be done in regard to de Gaulle than what should be done." Bohlen, "Reflections on Current French Foreign Policy and Attitudes Toward the United States and Recommendations," n.d., National Security File, LBJL, in *FRUS 1963–68*, Vol. 12, p. 80; Lyndon Baines Johnson, *The Vantage Point: Perspectives of the Presidency, 1963–1969* (New York: Holt, Rinehart and Winston, 1971), p. 305. The American ambassador

to NATO, Harlan Cleveland, did much to smooth the transition to Brussels, helped by George Vest, who had worked previously for Dirk Stikker at NATO. Interviews with Vest and Ed Streator. For the role of Eisenhower, see A. J. Goodpaster, Phone Conversation with General Eisenhower, March 21, 1966, White House Confidential File, LBJL, Box 58, f.22.

11. Interviews with James Lowenstein, Claude-Gerard Marcus, and Charles Cogan; "Transcript of Senator Church Meeting with President de Gaulle," May 4, 1966, National Security File, Country File Europe, LBJL, Box 172, f.8; for his part, Lippmann claimed to have lunch with Ball once a week and fight about de Gaulle: "It's too hard to stay mad at Ball," he said. Telcon Bundy/Ball December 14, 1964, Ball Papers, LBJL, Box 5, f.4. A good, short summary of his views is in *Western Unity and the Common Market* (Boston: Little, Brown and Company, 1962), a book dedicated, ironically, to Jean Monnet.

12. N. Beloff, p. 20; Schaetzel to Acheson, December 11, 1967, Schaetzel Papers, DDE, Box 1, f.8; Ball, p. 96; Kleiman, p. 30; Bowie Oral History, EU. To some extent, Macmillan was regarded in a similarly romantic fashion. See Kohnstamm Oral History, EU.

13. Dulles, "The Relation of France to a Program of World Reconstruction," n.d. (1927), JFD, Box 279.

14. Emmet to Hillenbrand, November 21, 1964, MJH, Box 5, f.7, his emphasis.

15. Kleiman, p. 111; Roberts, p. 54.

16. Walden Moore to Monnet, enclosing a letter from Moore to Herter, January 3, 1963, AMK C 26/6/108, JM; Acheson speech, "Europe: Kaleidoscope or Crowded Crystal," March 13, 1963, in George W. Ball Papers, Department of Rare Books and Special Collections, Princeton University Library, Princeton University, Princeton, NJ (hereinafter GB), Box 1, f.9; Livingston Hartley, "Atlantic Partnership—How?" *Atlantic Community Quarterly* 2, no. 2 (Summer 1964): 176–177.

17. Interviews with François de Rose, Andrew Goodpaster, and Alexander Haig; Davignon Oral History, November 9, 1998, EU (noting the critical role of both de Rose and André De Staercke); Alphand to Ministry, March 18, 1965, NR 1660–64, Amérique 1964–1970, États-Unis 576, and Lucet to Ministry, May 24, 1966, No. 3044-46 577 9-4-1 MAE; Frank Church speech, National War College, May 15, 1963, AMK C 26/9/247, JM; of the various EUR hands, only Tyler and C. Burke Elbrick, who served briefly as assistant secretary at the end of the Eisenhower administration, were known to be drawn to Gaullism. Interview with George Vest; cf. Bohlen in Neustadt Memorandum of Conversation, Neustadt Papers, JFKL, Box 22, f.4; de Rose in Bohlen to SecState, April 19, 1963 in ibid., Box 20, f.13; Kissinger, Memorandum of Conversation with de Rose, January 11, 1963, National Security File, JFKL, Box 214, f.4.

18. There was also an obscure but tough fight over something called the NATO Military Payments Union. This was a proposal that originated with Richard Cooper, Ed Fried and Anthony Solomon to recast the offset problem on a multilateral basis. EUR was mildly supportive, but it died with McNamara and the White House. Treverton, pp. 115–117; Deane Hinton, letter to the author; interview with Francis Bator.

19. Telcons Tyler/Ball, March 14, 1963, and Kitchen/Ball January 18, 1963, Ball Telcons, JFKL, Box 6, f.7, f.9. Another office to question the desirability of the MLF was the Bureau of Intelligence and Research. Its main European hands, William Hitchcock and Anton de Porte, were against it, but their opposition was tolerated by Ball because he may have liked having INR on his side in the debates over Vietnam policy. Interview with Thomas Hughes. For Monnet's strong objection to providing nuclear assistance to the French, see Fessenden, Memorandum for the Record, December 15, 1961, National Security File, JFKL, Box 220A, f.4; cf. Couve, pp. 96–97.

20. Klein, letter to the author.

21. Jeff Parsons to Ellis Briggs, November 13, 1967, JGP, Box 6, f.1; cf. the view of Martin Hillenbrand: "Katzenbach referred to the State Department as 'the only non-operational agency ... whose ... business is policy formation.... I do find his premise to

reflect a continuous error about the Department ... which indicates general ignorance ..."
Diary January 13, 1969, MJHH, Series II, Box 2. f.17.

22. Interview with Thomas Hughes.

23. Telcon Rostow/Schaetzel, February 23, 1961, Ball Telcons, JFKL, Box 5, f.20;
Bator biography, National Security File, Name File, LBJL, Box 1, f.2; John S. Odell, *U.S. International Monetary Policy: Markets, Power, and Ideas as Sources of Change* (Princeton, NJ: Princeton University Press, 1982), p. 131.

24. Bundy to Century Association Committee on Admissions, n.d. (1966), WL, Reel 49.

25. "Europe's Assistant," *The Economist*, September 16, 1967, p. 995.

26. Interview with Bator; Deane Hinton, letter to the author. Abe Katz, who headed RPE and worked closely with Leddy, disputed the characterization of Leddy, noting that his devotion to Ball was too great for anything like a back channel to have existed. Interview with Abe Katz.

27. Interview with Bator; Robert C. Brewster and Theodore L. Eliot Oral Histories, ADST. There was some resentment expressed at the State Department, of course. George Ball was reported to have said, upon learning that the mission in Outer Mongolia had become available, "Wouldn't it be nice to send Francis Bator to Ulan Bator?" Interview with Thomas Hughes.

28. The leading alternative was Gerry Smith. See Winand, *Eisenhower, Kennedy and the United States of Europe*, p. 345.

29. Constance Ray Harvey Oral History, ADST.

30. Descriptions and background from H. Freeman Matthews to John Peurifoy and Christian Ravndal, June 5, 1947, MH, Box 2, Reel 10; Bruce diary, March 19, 1958, DB, Box 3, f.6; interview with Kenneth Thompson; press release, July 18, 1962, President's Office Files, JFKL, Box 88, f.9; Neustadt, p. 14.

31. Bruce diary, June 25, 1959, and September 22, 1962, DB, Box 3, f.22 and Box 4, f.18; interviews with Roger Kirk, Brandon Grove, and Ben Bradlee; additional background from Tyler Oral History, ADST; Moffat to Wilson, September 2, 1938, Moffat to Bliss, September 13, 1939, Tyler to Moffat, May 22, 1940, JPM, Vols. 15–18.

32. Tyler Oral History, ADST.

33. Tyler to Bruce, September 19, 1964, in Bruce diary, DB, Box 4, f.33. Cf. Tyler: "I thought that we must be prepared to work with whatever kind of Europe the Europeans themselves fashion.... our policy toward Europe must be based on an empirical and not a doctrinal approach." Tyler to Bundy, June 19, 1963, Bundy Papers, JFKL, Box 32. For the meeting of minds between Bundy, Tyler, and Klein, see, for example, Bundy, Memoranda for the Record, April 11, 1963, and June 21, 1963, ibid., Box 32.

34. Klein, Memorandum of Conversation, January 26, 1965, National Security Files, Country File Europe, LBJL, Box 162, f.3; The image of Europeans as recalcitrant children appears several times in Ball's memoranda and conversations: e.g., Meeting at U.S. Embassy, Paris, May 31, 1963 (Ball and U.S. ambassadors et al.), in WAH, Box 434, f.6; cf. Alphand, pp. 448–449, and James Schlesinger: "Europe now behaves like the perennial adolescent." Brandon diary, November 19, 1973, HB, Box 8, f.8.

35. E.g., Telcon Tyler/Ball, September 26, 1963, Ball Telcons, JFKL, Box 6, f.7; Joseph J. Wolf to Gerard Smith, September 26, 1961, RG59 Lots 59D297 and 66D366, NARA, Box 6, f.12.

36. Interview with Kenneth Thompson; material on Tyler's career in the Netherlands is in Giles Scott-Smith, *Networks of Empire: The U.S. State Department's Foreign Leader Program in the Netherlands, France, and Britain, 1950–70* (Brussels: P. I. E. Peter Lang, 2008), pp. 280–285, 330–331.

37. Bator, "The Politics of Alliance: The United States and Western Europe," in Kermit Gordon, ed., *Agenda for the Nation* (Washington, D.C.: Brookings Institution, 1968), p. 342.

Cf. Hillenbrand to Richard Vine, May 10, 1965, MJH, Box 5, f.23.

38. James Huntley to Walden Moore, August 12, 1959, DAU, Box 11, f.1. Dillon's family owned the château and vineyards Haut Brion. He was known in France as "l'Ambassadeur vigneron." Achilles, p. 506. His father, a Jewish immigrant from Poland, had founded the Dillon Read investment bank, which had once employed Paul Nitze and James Forrestal. Dillon Senior had an apartment in Paris where the family would spend every spring; their network of French friends and acquaintances went far and wide. Dillon Oral History, EU.

39. Interview with Francis Bator. The Regional Affairs (RA) Desk was subdivided in early 1962 into RPE and RPM. When the Bureau of the Budget suggested that EUR had too many functionalists distributed in its ranks, EUR later noted the value of overlapping: "We do not ... equate overlapping with duplication." Idar Rimestad to Assistant Secretaries, May 16, 1967, and enclosure, RG59 Lot 88D259, NARA, Box 28, f.5. Both RPE and RPM contained over a dozen functionalists, namely economic officers and military advisers, respectively. Even the embassy in Bonn had two "RA" officers. For a brief period the successor office to RA was called the Office of Atlantic Affairs. U.S. Department of State, Bureau of Administration, "Changes in Administration January 1961– January 1963," April 23, 1963, RG59 Lot 74D272, NARA, Box 1, f.4.

40. "The Kennedy Round Crisis April–June 1967," National Security Council Histories, LBJL, Box 52, f.1.; Bator to Johnson, January 3, 1967, National Security File, Name File, LBJL, Box 1, f.3. Blumenthal was a Jewish refugee from Germany who found his way to Shanghai, and then to the United States; Roth was an heir to a California shipping fortune. Frederick G. Dutton, Memorandum to Mr. Ralph Dungan, May 9, 1963, Dungan Papers, JFKL, Box 2, f.9; Dryden, pp. 69, 73.

41. Jenkins, p. 557.

42. Interview with Francis Bator.

43. Acheson to Schaetzel, May 16, 1967, Schaetzel Papers, DDE, Box 1, f.8; Bator, however, regarded its importance as overrated. Interview with Francis Bator. Rusk to Roth, May 15, 1967, Bator Papers, LBJL, Box 13, f.3. The secret codeword for all Kennedy Round–related cables was "potatoes." See also "The Kennedy Round Crisis April–June 1967," National Security Council Histories, LBJL, Box 52, f.1; Dryden, p. 102.

44. According to Hinton, it was "EUR's greatest accomplishment" of the 1960s. Hinton, letter to the author. For his part, Jean Monnet was no great fan of transatlantic trade liberalization, at least not right away. See Monnet to Ball, January 22, 1962, AMK C23/1/155, JM.

45. Ball to JFK, May 10, 1961, and Memorandum of Conversation, Ball/Couve, May 21, 1962, RG59 Lot 74D272, NARA, Box 21, f.7; Acheson to Adenauer, January 18, 1963, DAY, Reel 1, Box 1, f.6.

46. Telcons Ormsby Gore/Ball December 12, 1962, Dillon/Ball April 7, 1961, Rostow/Ball April 8, 1961, Ball Telcons, JFKL, Box 2, f.14, and Box 1, f.19; Memoranda of Conversations, Ball/Hallstein, December 8, 1962, Ball/Macmillan April 6, 1961, Fessenden to Kohler, April 3, 1961, EUR Office of Atlantic and Military Affairs, Records Relating to UK Negotiations for Membership in EEC 1961–62, RG59, Box 1, f.1.

47. Butterworth to Edwin Martin, July 8, 1960; Tyler to Dean Dent (U.S. Tariff Commission), October 9, 1961; Telcon Ball/Bundy, May 3, 1961, Hartman to Rusk, May 2, 1961, and Greenwald to Schaetzel, May 9, 1961, all in Records Relating to UK Negotiations, ibid., Box 1, f.1, f.3, f.8; cf. D. A. H. Wright, brief on European integration, January 11, 1956, FO 371/122022, PRO; Bruce diary, November 30, 1961, Bruce to Ball, inserted after July 27, 1962, DB, Box 4, f.4, on keeping up the "low profile" and the "public image ... of a benevolent onlooker"; Alphand to Ministry, October 17, 1961, No. 5856-68, Amérique 1952–1963, États-Unis 356 9-4-1 MAE; Ball, p. 213. Supporting the view of Anglo-American culpability is Oliver Bange, The EEC Crisis of 1963: Kennedy, Macmillan, de Gaulle and Adenauer in Conflict (London: Macmillan, 2000). Opposing it is Nigel Ashton,

Kennedy, Macmillan and the Cold War: The Irony of Interdependence (London: Palgrave, 2002), pp. 132–134. For Greenwald's opposition, see his Oral History, ADST.

48. Quoted in Kleiman, p. 48; N. Beloff, pp. 7, 164ff.; Tuthill Oral History, May 20, 1987, EU.

49. Robert Rothschild (Belgian aide to Paul-Henri Spaak), noting impressions of Walt Rostow, Bill Tyler, inter alia, in Rothschild, *Un phénix nommé Europe: mémoires, 1945–1995* (Brussels: Éditions Racine, 1977), p. 284.

50. Telcon Bundy/Ball January 3, 1962, Ball Telcons, JFKL, Box 1, f.19; Memoranda of Conversations with Michael Butler, July 15, 1963, and Timothy Bligh, July 31 and August 1, 1963, Neustadt Papers, JFKL, Box 22, f.5; Brandon diary, January 7, 1963, HB, Box 6, f.3, and Butler, Ramsbotham, and O. Wright Oral Histories, Churchill Archives Centre, Cambridge, UK; Burin de Roziers Oral History, EU, "Macmillan a plaidé, bien plaidé." For Macmillan's (and others' sustained) mistrust of Ball, see Macmillan diary, May 6, 1962, Ms Macmillan dep. d. 45, f.118–123, Macmillan Papers, Bodleian Library, Oxford; Derek Mitchell to Wilson, July 11, 1968, PREM 13/2450, PRO. Bligh claimed that Macmillan could not be honest with Kennedy about what de Gaulle had said to him at Rambouillet because he feared it would leak to the press. Macmillan also reportedly told de Gaulle at the same meeting that he would ask for Polaris at Nassau. Henry Brandon Oral History by David Nunnerley, n.d., JFKL. Cf. Ormsby-Gore history of Skybolt, June 1964, National Security File, Subject File, LBJL, Box 45, f.4; Kleiman, pp. 48–49; Couve, pp. 367ff., 395–400; 410–411.

51. "I gave [Karl] Carstens the ultimatum, and said, 'I don't know how you're going to do this, but you've got to fix this damned thing up.'" Ball Oral History, EU; see also Hillenbrand's Oral History in the same collection, noting that the only senior American on hand at the time in Berlin was the chargé, Brewster Morris. Despite repeated questions, Hillenbrand denied knowing whether or not any Americans "dictated" the preamble; Ball Oral History, September 24, 1990, Nuclear Age, Liddell Hart Centre; Stanley Cleveland to Ball, November 20, 1964, GB, Box 70, f.15; interview with Charles Cogan; Huntley to Slater, February 26, 1963, Slater Files, FF, Box 27, f.286; Bundy to Monnet, October 6, 1962, AMK C 23/2/183, JM; Egon Bahr to Kaysen, May 17, 1963, National Security File, JFKL, Box 77, f.3 (for the putative role of Egon Bahr); Monnet, *Memoirs*, pp. 468–469; Birrenbach to Herter, February 18, 1963, CAH, Series A, f.65; Kurt Birrenbach, *Meine Sondermissionen: Rückblick auf zwei Jahrzehnte bundesdeutscher Aussenpolitik* (Düsseldorf: Econ Verlag, 1984), pp. 169–172; cf. Tim Szatkowski, *Karl Carstens: Eine politische Biographie* (Cologne: Böhlau, 2007), pp. 89–96. Tuthill and Ball later recalled their reactions as being more severe than they seemed at the time. See Bange, pp. 132–133, 178–179; Tuthill Oral History, ADST (noting also the indifference of Bohlen and other suspected Gaullists); Bundy, Memorandum for the Record, February 25, 1963, Bundy Papers, JFKL, showing wishful thinking on the part of some Germans: "von Hassel made a very good show of believing that the real meaning of the Franco/German treaty was that it gave the Germans the means of pulling the French nearer to NATO"; see also Bundy, "Possible Comment on Franco-German Treaty," January 23, 1963, ibid.; Tuthill, p. 72; the verdict of Couve ("un aboutissement plus qu'un commencement"), in *Le monde en face: entretiens avec Maurice Delarue* (Paris: Plon, 1989), p. 55; and Couve speech to the National Assembly, June 12, 1963, CM1, CM.

52. *Britain and the European Community, 1955–1963* (Princeton, NJ: Princeton University Press, 1964).

53. Camps to Leddy, October 15, 1959, MC, Box 1, f.2 and Camps to Slater, February 17, 1960, ibid., Box 1, f.3; Camps, pp. 239, 268ff.; interview with Abe Katz.

54. Not to be confused with the European Free Trade Association (EFTA). Camps to Schaetzel, October 16, 1961, MC, Box 13, f.6; Max Kohnstamm to Ball and Schaetzel, October 26, 1960, AMK C 23/1/121, and Monnet to Ball, December 19, 1960, AMK C

23/1/122, JM; Memorandum of Conversation with Jean Monnet and John W. Tuthill, November 12, 1958, CF 840.00/11-1458, *FRUS 1958–60*, Vol. 7, part 1, pp. 72–76; Schaetzel to Kohnstamm, October 24, 1960, AMK C 23/9/48, JM, regarding the need for "a common economy" for the Atlantic Community; Owen Oral History, June 30, 1981, JM; Camps and Leddy Oral Histories, EU. The initial proposal for an OECD came in 1959 from the State Department's Jack Tuthill, another largely forgotten figure appearing in previous chapters, who was well regarded and influential in the 1950s and 1960s. Following a brief career in banking (starting as a teller) and as an academic, Tuthill joined the foreign service in 1940, working for Pierrepont Moffat in Canada and then for Bob Murphy. He would go on to become the first ambassador to the OECD, then would run the Atlantic Institute and the Salzburg Seminar. His ties to other Europeanists went back to the war, and he was also a friend and fellow boxing enthusiast of Art Buchwald, Ben Bradlee, and others. Tuthill to Ball, June 11, 1982, GB, Box 93, f.3; Hinton, letter to author; Note verbale 17 August 1962, BAC003/1978-187/2, EU; Winand, *Eisenhower, Kennedy and the United States of Europe*, pp. 131–137, 151 (noting that the Paris offices of Tuthill and Monnet were next door to each other); Tuthill, pp. xi, 26–27; Dillon Oral History, June 18, 1970, JFKL; Herter to Eisenhower, November 24, 1959, *FRUS, 1958–1960*, Vol. 4, pp. 58–59; Memorandum of Conversation, Leddy, Seydoux, Wormser, n.d. (February 1960), B20-200 Band 383, "Reorganisation der OEEC," and Karl Carstens, "Rationalisierung der europäischen Institutionen," February 14, 1959, Band 492, AA; L. C. Holliday, "Future of the O.E.E.C.," January 1, 1960, M 551/19 FO 371 150075, PRO; Thomas W. Fina and John W. Tuthill Oral Histories, ADST; interview with Abe Katz.

55. N. Beloff, p. 86. Hervé Alphand noted that the OECD was created simply because the Americans were convinced that the British would always veto European action in the OEEC. Alphand Oral History, EU; de Gaulle to Couve de Murville, January 8, 1960, in CM7, CM.

56. Myerson Oral History, EU; when that proved elusive, Monnet "lost interest in it." Tuthill Oral History, EU.

57. Not to mention window glass, tobacco, cut flowers, kitchen articles, tomato concentrates, oil seed and cake, and lard. Camps to Schaetzel, October 16, 1961, MC; BAC 3/1978 and No. 927/1 1968–69 and 1970–72 No. 7/1, EU. The Atlantic Council's Richard Wallace, for instance, promoted a "three way partnership between the United States, EEC and EFTA." Wallace to Will Clayton, August 14, 1964, ACUS, Box 19, f.4.

58. C. Heidenreich, January 7, 1969, BAC3/1978 No. 927/2, EU.

59. A point made by Deane Hinton. Note d'information (Memorandum of Conversation with Dahrendorf, Samuels, Mansholt, Hinton, et al.), October 29, 1971 XI/254/71-F, BAC 3/978 1971 No 931/2, EU.

60. Dillon to Eisenhower, August 19, 1959, White House Office of the Staff Secretary, Records 1952–61, International Series, DDE, Box 15, f.9.

61. Schaetzel to Monnet, March 2, 1967, AMK C 23/9/67, JM.

62. Bator to Johnson, July 26, 1966, in National Security File, Country File Europe, LBJL, Box 209, f.2.

63. Telcon Fulbright/Ball April 7, 1961, Ball Telcons, JFKL, Box 1, f.19; Schaetzel to Tuthill, March 6, 1962, USDOS/JT 14 Tuthill Papers, JM; Monnet to Ball, October 27, 1961, GB, Box 42, f.14; for debates over enlarging the membership, see "Some Thoughts on How to Make the OECD a More Useful Organization," n.a. (probably Leddy), n.d. (1963), RG59 Lot 88D259, NARA, Box 30, f.7; Tuthill to Schaetzel, March 6, 1962, and Stanley Cleveland to Schaetzel, with attachments, April 25, 1962, in RG59 Lot 66D439, NARA, Box 3, f.16; Schaetzel to Ben Moore, April 6, 1960, Schaetzel Papers, DDE, Box 2, f.20; W. W. Rostow, *View from the Seventh Floor* (New York: Harper and Row, 1964), pp. 60–61.

64. John Leddy called them "spear head[s] to try to break up the European Community." Leddy Oral History, August 18, 1987, EU; interviews with Abe Katz and Karl Kaiser;

Memorandum of Conversation with Harold Caccia, David Pitblado, Ball, Schaetzel, and Richard Vine, May 12, 1961, National Security File, JFKL, Box 170, f.3. An exception was Miriam Camps, who did not fully share the bias. Camps to Bator, June 6, 1967, Bator Papers, LBJL, Box 13, f.1; Schaetzel to Hinton, March 10, 1967, RG60 Lot 88D259, NARA, Box 22, f.12.

65. Interview with Richard Gardner; cf. Monnet to Ball, March 4, 1966, AMK C 23/1/193, JM, for Tuthill's insistence that success with the Kennedy Round took precedence to British admission to the Common Market; Gordon-Walker diary, Saturday April 6 (1963), Gordon-Walker Papers, Churchill College, Cambridge, UK, GNWR 1/15.

66. Memoranda of Conversations with Richard Vine, May 28, 1963, and Edward Heath, July 26, 1963, Neustadt Papers, JFKL, Box 22, f.4 and f.5; Bundy to Kennedy, April 24, 1962, National Security File, JFKL, Box 170, f.17, for Bundy's views. Vine also noted that there was a great deal of discussion in EUR, and opposition to their nominal number two, Schaetzel, more than appears in the written record.

67. The fear of failure led some officials to urge less rather than more linkage. See Stanley Cleveland to Ball, November 20, 1964, GB; cf. Tom Fina and Tom Enders, "European Integration and the Kennedy Round," RG59 Lots 67D33, 68D27, 69D73, NARA, Box 18, f.2; Leddy to Rusk, May 10, 1967: "Failure would be profoundly divisive of the political fabric of the western world." RG59 Lot 88D259, NARA, Box 29, f.10.

68. Cf. Christopher Emmet to Henry Kissinger, March 20, 1964, CE, Box 83, f.15; Bundy to Kennedy, January 30, 1963, Bundy Papers, JFKL, Box 32: "British entry into the Common Market, while important and desirable, has never been the first object of our policy in Europe nor even a matter in which we could expect to have decisive influence. Our first concern in the last two years has been with the specific defense of Berlin and the general defense of NATO, both in the primary context of the Soviet threat." Cf. N. Beloff, pp. 38–39.

69. Telcon Kennedy/Ball, January 29, 1963, Ball Telcons, JFKL, Box 2, f.15; interview with Francis Bator; cf. Franz Josef Strauss, "The Threshold of a New Era," translated text from *Rheinischer Merkur*, December 23, 1961, pp. 4–5, in National Security File, JFKL, Box 74A, f.3. At the time of his 1961 Chicago speech, Bundy was said to entertain the idea of having a German relationship replace the one between the United States and Britain; Grewe to Ministry, December 8, 1961, No. 3551, B12 Band 1678, AA; cf. Jeffrey Glen Giauque, *Grand Designs and Visions of Unity: The Atlantic Powers and the Reorganization of Western Europe, 1955–1963* (Chapel Hill: University of North Carolina Press, 2002), p. 3.

70. Telcons Bator/Ball, June 10, July 12, 1966, Ball Papers, LBJL, Box 3, f.9.

71. Remarks of the President at the National Conference of Editorial Writers, October 7, 1966, in Bator Papers, LBJL, Box 21, f.1; Ausland to Hillenbrand, January 16, 1964, MJH, Box 1, f.2.

72. Bator, p. 348; cf. Hillenbrand, p. 228, Brzezinski, pp. 82–88, 121ff.

73. Interviews with Francis Bator and Henry Owen; Brzezinski and Owen Oral Histories, LBJL, and Brzezinski, letter to the author. Others who contributed to the speech besides those on Bator's staff included Bob Bowie, Gene Rostow, and John Leddy. Owen to Bator, October 5, 1966, in Bator Papers, LBJL, Box 3, f.9; Bator, "Lyndon Johnson and Foreign Policy: The Case of Western Europe and the Soviet Union," in Aaron Lobel, ed., *Presidential Judgment: Foreign Policy Decisionmaking in the White House* (Hollis, NH: Hollis Publishing Company, 2001), p. 76n2. For Brzezinski's own contemporary views on the "unnatural" divisions of Europe, see his *Alternative to Partition*.

74. "Excerpt from Memorandum to I-Mr. Murrow," October 1, 1963, EUR/SOV Economic Affairs Section, US/USSR Trade Relations and Economic Subject Files 1933–81, RG59 Lots 81D176, 84D223, NARA, Box 4, f.11; Schwartz, *LBJ and Europe*, pp. 133–136, 210ff.; Thomas Hughes to Acting Secretary, October 21, 1966, and Nathaniel Davis, lunch with Vitaly Petroussenko, October 17, 1966, Bator Papers, LBJL, Box 21, f.1; Bator, "Note

on Origins of President Johnson's October 7, 1966, Speech on Europe" (n.d., 2001), ibid., Box 40, f.4.

75. Livingston T. Merchant, "U.S. Relations with the Atlantic Community," in Francis O. Wilcox and H. Field Haviland Jr., eds., *The Atlantic Community: Progress and Prospects* (New York: Frederick A. Praeger, 1963), pp. 108–109.

76. E. V. Rostow to Ball, January 26, 1962, AMK C 23/8/92, JM.

77. Tyler to Hillenbrand, September 12, 1966, and Hillenbrand, "America and Its Responsibility Toward Europe," October 16, 1965, MJH, Box 5, f.21, and Box 6, f.10.

78. Tyler to Bundy, June 19, 1963, Bundy Papers, JFKL, Box 32. Cf. Bange, p. 7; Halperin, pp. 12–13; Alastair Buchan, *Europe's Futures, Europe's Choices* (New York: Columbia University Press, 1969).

79. These are two of the five types of bureaucratic actors popularized by Anthony Downs, the others being "climbers," "advocates," and "statesmen." See his *Inside Bureaucracy* (Boston: Little, Brown and Company, 1967), pp. 5–23, 88–91; Calleo, p. 116.

80. The one major exception was Gerry Smith, who, as already noted, became Nixon's ill-fated chief negotiator of the Strategic Arms Limitation Treaty; Bruce diary, February 6, 1967, DB, Box 5, f.25.

81. Giauque, p. 124.

9. The Ordeal of Helmut Sonnenfeldt

An earlier version of this chapter and the next was presented to an academic conference at the Roosevelt Center in Middelburg, the Netherlands, in 2007 and has been published in the proceedings, edited by Valérie Aubourg and Giles Scott-Smith (Paris: Soleb, 2009).

1. Deniau Oral History, November 3, 2003, EU; Schaetzel to Dean Acheson, May 6, 1968, Schaetzel Papers, DDE, Box 1, f.2; Theodore Achilles to Walden Moore, July 5, 1969, DAU, Box 1, f.2.

2. Thomas J. Hughes to the secretary, "Soviet Intervention in Czechoslovakia: Another Nail in the Coffin of the World Communist Movement?" August 27, 1968, Czechoslovak Crisis Files 1968 RG 59 Lot 70D19, NARA, Box 3 f.1; Ambassador Jacob Beam, on the scene in Prague, later said the crackdown, along with U.S. reversals in Vietnam, would "bring about a kind of enforced rapprochement." He would then head to Moscow as ambassador. Jacob D. Beam, *Multiple Exposure: An American Ambassador's Unique Perspective on East-West Issues* (New York: Norton, 1978), p. 212.

3. The former title was still "special assistant to the president for national security;" interview with Rozanne Ridgway.

4. This step was accomplished by placing himself instead of the undersecretary of state at the head of the Senior Interagency Group (SIG), a highly valued spot.

5. Sutterlin to Martin Hillenbrand, December 5, 1968, MJH, Box 6, f.5. He added: "I went to a seminar yesterday that Kissinger and Stanley Hoffmann usually conduct jointly. Neither was there, Henry being at the Pierre [Hotel in New York] and Stanley being at the current meeting of towering intellects from around the world at Princeton. The British guest professor started things off rather nicely by saying that Kissinger was making Nixon safe for the world and Hoffmann was making the world safe for Nixon."

6. Interview with Kempton Jenkins.

7. Brandon diary, June 8, 1969, HB, Box 7, f.7. Brandon also noted a telling poster in Kissinger's office: "When I want your opinion I beat it out of you." January 17, 1975, Box 9, f.3; letter to the author from James Goodby.

8. Background from Brandon diary, July 23, 1970, HB, Box 8, f.1.

9. Helmut Sonnenfeldt, "Major U.S. Interests and Objectives in Europe, Including the U.S.S.R.," speech delivered at the National War College, August 16, 1972, p. 2, Records of Helmut Sonnenfeldt 1955–77, RG59 Lot 81D286, NARA (hereinafter HS), Box 10, f.28; Thompson Buchanan Oral History, ADST.

10. E.g., "I had worked a good deal with Tommy Thompson, Foy Kohler, Chip Bohlen

and most of the others. There was always mutual respect." Interview with Helmut Sonnenfeldt.

11. Longtime Soviet ambassador Anatoly Dobrynin, among others, called him "Kissinger's Kissinger." Anatoly Dobrynin, *In Confidence: Moscow's Ambassador to America's Six Cold War Presidents* (Seattle: University of Washington Press, 2001), p. 271.

12. Sonnenfeldt to Kissinger, January 27, 1965, HS, Box 2, f.8.

13. Sonnenfeldt to Morris Rothenberg, April 10, 1957, HS, Box 1, f.9; Sonnenfeldt to Marshall D. Shulman, May 22, 1961, HS, Box 1, f.17.

14. Interviews with Jonathan Dean, Henry Owen, and Helmut Sonnenfeldt; Sonnenfeldt, "Evening Reading," May 10, 1968, HS, Box 2 f.12, and miscellaneous INR memos, f.14; Brandon diary entries for April 10 and October 4, 1968, HB, Box 7, f.4, f.5; Mayers, p. 160.

15. Sonnenfeldt to Thomas L. Hughes, June 27, 1968, HS, Box 2, f.12.

16. Richard Reeves, *President Nixon: Alone in the White House* (New York: Simon and Schuster, 2001), p. 49.

17. Bruce diary, February 22, 1969, DB, Box 6, f.19.

18. Hersh, *Price of Power: Kissinger in the Nixon White House* (New York: Summit Books, 1983), pp. 85, 114–115, 322n, for Kissinger's humiliations of Sonnenfeldt; Henry Kissinger, *White House Years* (Boston: Little, Brown, 1979), p. 78. For Hillenbrand's views on the relationship, see Stephan Fuchs, *"Dreiecksverhältnisse sind immer kompliziert": Kissinger, Bahr und die Ostpolitik* (Hamburg: Europäische Verlagsanstalt, 1999), pp. 113–114.

19. Kissinger, *White House Years*, p. 74.

20. Alsop to Kissinger, February 27, 1969, JA, Box 132, f. 9; interviews with Margot Lindsay and Timothy Dickinson; Bruce Mazlish, *Kissinger: The European Mind in American Policy* (New York: Basic Books, 1976), p. 142; Peter Ramsbotham to Isaiah Berlin, April 12, 1976, IB, Box 202, f.170; Memorandum of Conversation with Gerald Ford, Kissinger, and Brent Scowcroft, July 17, 1975, National Security Adviser, Memoranda of Conversations, Gerald R. Ford Presidential Library, Ann Arbor, MI (hereinafter GFPL), Box 13, f.40.

21. Henry Kissinger, *The Troubled Partnership: A Re-appraisal of the Atlantic Alliance* (New York: McGraw-Hill for the Council on Foreign Relations, 1965), p. 232.

22. Calleo, pp. ix–x.

23. Statement from the Board of Directors meeting of April 10, 1974, ACUS, Box 2, f.9.

24. Sonnenfeldt speech to the National War College, August 16, 1972, HS.

25. Achilles, excerpt after p. 35.

26. Kissinger, *White House Years*, pp. 85–86.

27. "The Secretary's Principals and Regionals Staff Meeting, Tuesday, April 23, 1974– 3:00 P.M," Transcripts of Secretary of State Henry Kissinger's Staff Meetings 1973–77, RG59 Lot 78D443, NARA (hereinafter HK), Box 3, f.8; additional memoranda in Sonnenfeldt's papers suggest the latter had a greater hand in changing Kissinger's mind by arranging a compromise: "Mr. Secretary: I think Art is right in suggesting that we should have some sort of line on our attitude regarding European unity.... Art's proposed line.... is one way to do it; another would be to say that we have always supported unity but of course must ask ourselves what the purpose of unity is ... The unity we support ... is one in which Europe will work [then referring Kissinger to the language in Hartman's memorandum]: confidently and cooperatively with the United States, directly and within the framework of the Atlantic Alliance." Sonnenfeldt to Kissinger, April 24, 1974, HS, Box 4, f.1. One of the few people to whom Kissinger confided his ambivalence about the Common Market and related subjects appeared to be the journalist Henry Brandon, even though he was not known as the most truthful raconteur among the Washington press corps. See Brandon diary, July 8, December 25, 1969, HB, Box 7, f.7, 8; interview with Francis Bator. Cf. Joseph Kraft, "Kissinger Goes 'European,'" *Washington Post*, December 11, 1973, p. A25; for a description of Kissinger's feelings about senior staff meetings, see Mazlish, pp. 230–231.

28. Schaetzel to Acheson, February 26, 1969, Schaetzel Papers, DDE, Box 1, f.3;

Acheson, "A Letter to the Editor of *Interplay*," January 22, 1969, ibid., Box 1, f.8; Schaetzel to Henry Owen, January 24, 1969, ibid., Box 2, f.7.

29. McCloy to Monnet, April 8, 1969, AMK C 26/4/409, JM.

30. Vernon A. Walters to Kissinger, December 31, 1968, Henry A. Kissinger Administrative and Staff Files, Richard Nixon Presidential Papers, Washington, D.C. (hereinafter RN), Box 1, f.20.

31. Maurice Schumann Oral History, September 17, 1990, Nuclear Age, Liddell Hart Centre for Military Archives, King's College, London; excerpts from a meeting between Richard Nixon and de Gaulle, June 8, 1967, Amérique 1964–1970, États-Unis 578, rélations politiques 9-4-1 MAE; interview with Robert Blake. Blake, who was then deputy chief of mission in Paris, also came from Whittier, California. His father had once been Nixon's campaign treasurer, and the first lady, Pat Nixon, had been his high school teacher. Blake was the American to whom André Malraux first confided that de Gaulle would stage a phony referendum in order to step down from power. He was also the brother-in-law of Charles Whitehouse, a foreign service officer whose father had been close to Theodore Marriner and ran the embassy in Paris for Myron Herrick. Blake's son also became a foreign service officer and ambassador.

32. Mayne Oral History, July 23, 1988, EU. The chronology of rapprochement is refuted only partially by the popularity of Ambassador Sargent Shriver, who remained in Paris for the first year of the Nixon administration. Hervé Alphand, "Relations franco-americaines de 1958 a mars 1969," No. 156/AM, Amérique 1964–1970, États-Unis 580 rélations politiques 9-4-1 MAE. Cf. debate between Couve de Murville and Altiero Spinelli, in *Pouvoirs*, April 1977, in CM5, CM.

33. See clippings and photos in MJH, Boxes 2 and 3, including duplicated letters sent to his three children; and "Power and Morals: Reflections of a Professional Diplomat," January 23, 1964, in Box 4, f.6, a synopsis of his published dissertation (New York: Columbia University Press, 1949).

34. Bruce diary, April 24, 1958, DB, Box 3, f.7. Hillenbrand, chaps. 2–4; Bernard Gwertzman, "State Department's Expert on Europe: Martin Joseph Hillenbrand," *New York Times*, May 22, 1972, p. 21; personnel file for Martin J. Hillenbrand, DF, RG59 Lot 123 1940–44, NARA, Box 453, f.10.

35. Bruce diary, April 24, 1958, DB. See also December 26, 1957, same box, f.2.

36. Schaetzel to Acheson, February 26, 1969, Schaetzel Papers, DDE, Box 1, f.3; letter from David Klein to the author; Hillenbrand diary, January 24–26, 1969, MJHH, Series II, Box 2, f.17.

37. Hillenbrand diary, January 1, 1970, ibid.

38. Interview with Arthur Hartman. See also John H. Kelly Oral History, ADST: "Their relationship was complicated and tangled, but marked by mutual respect and mistrust."

39. J. F. O. McAllister quoted in "Lawrence S. Eagleburger," *Biography Resource Center Online* (Gale Group, 2002).

40. Eagleburger's retort reportedly was, "[P]erhaps but I found his ego too big to alter." Eagleburger was known to keep in touch with former associates but sometimes by pay phone because "things are a little difficult around here." Interviews with Rosalind Springsteen, Edward Streator, James Goodby, and Francis Bator.

41. Interview with a foreign service officer.

42. "Points Made by Assistant Secretary for European Affairs Hillenbrand in discussion with Walden Moore and Livingston Hartley on January 12, 1970," DAU, Box 2, f.7.

43. Interview with Roger Kirk.

44. Hillenbrand, p. 269.

45. Cf. Acheson, "The Eclipse of the State Department," n.d. (later published in *Foreign Affairs*, July 1971), Schaetzel Papers, DDE, Box 1, f.4; Wilfrid L. Kohl, "The Nixon-Kissinger Foreign Policy System and U.S.-European Relations: Patterns of Policy Making,"

World Politics 28, no. 1 (October 1975): 1–43.

46. Peter Rodman, "U.S. European Policy: The Impending Choice," n.d., Henry A. Kissinger Administrative and Staff Files, RN, Box 15, f.2. Cf. Roger Seydoux telegram, Brussels, November 15, 1968, Europe fonds EU 2-3-1 2012 Organismes internationaux 1966–1970, MAE, f.2.

47. Rogers to Nixon, "Memorandum for the President. Subject: Whither Post–de Gaulle France," April 29, 1969, NSC Subject Files, RN, Box 674, f.3. De Gaulle had resigned the day before. A cover letter from Kissinger to Nixon urged the president to pass along an appreciative word to Hillenbrand.

48. Hillenbrand, p. 281.

49. See David C. Geyer and Bernd Schaefer, eds., "American Détente and German Ostpolitik, 1969–1972," *Bulletin of the German Historical Institute*, Supplement No. 1 (2004): 90, 146–147, 156–157; Hillenbrand, p. 287; and James S. Sutterlin and David Klein, *Berlin: From Symbol of Confrontation to Keystone of Stability* (New York: Praeger Publishers, 1989), chap. 7. Documentation on the origins of the German back channels is in *FRUS 1969–1976*, Vol. 40, p. 103. See also note 55, below.

50. Cf. "In light of the impression that subsequently gained currency that linkages originated with Henry Kissinger, as truth with God, it is well to note that the first linkage (between acceptance of the GDR ... and improvements in Berlin) was proposed by Brandt and the second (tying a European security conference to successful negotiations on Berlin) originated in NATO on the basis of instructions from foreign ministries and the Department of State." Sutterlin and Klein, p. 86; Hyland to Kissinger, August 25, 1970 (comments on NSSM-83, Longer-Term Perspective on European Security), *FRUS, 1969–1976*, Vol. 40, pp. 302–304, and subsequent verbal duel between Kissinger and Hillenbrand, pp. 309–316; Oliver Bange, "An Intricate Web: *Ostpolitik*, the European Security System and German Unification," in Bange and Gottfried Niedhart, eds., *Helsinki 1975 and the Transformation of Europe* (New York: Berghahn Books, 2008), pp. 25, 33. For Kissinger's earlier views on the need to "separate the Berlin issue from that of European security ... ," see Kissinger to Murphy, February 16, 1959, JFD, Reel 56.

51. Nixon and Kissinger were not of the same mind, however, with Nixon being less condescending, though probably no less dismissive or discomfited, toward Brandt and *Ostpolitik*. See Sutterlin and Klein, pp. 84–85.

52. Kissinger, *White House Years*, pp. 409ff.; cf. Dennis L. Bark, *Agreement on Berlin: A Study of the 1970–72 Quadripartite Negotiations* (Washington, D.C.: American Enterprise Institute and the Hoover Institution for War, Revolution, and Peace, 1974), pp. 33, 57.

53. Acheson to Schaetzel, telegram, July 31, 1970, Schaetzel Papers, DDE, Box 1 f.4; cf. Schaetzel to Acheson, July 20, 1970, Schaetzel Papers, DDE, Box 1, f.9; (unknown) to Rush, September 11, 1970 (on Schaetzel's views of *Ostpolitik*), Records of Ambassador Kenneth Rush, 1969–74, RG59 Lot 74D430, NARA, Box 12, f.3; Bark, p. 64.

54. Kissinger, *White House Years*, p. 825; Rush would go on to become deputy secretary of state and then would be passed up for the top job—for which he campaigned—in favor of Kissinger. He later served as ambassador to France and then as chair of the Atlantic Council of the United States. For the views of his Soviet counterpart, who appreciated the back channel, see Ed Djerejian to Rush, July 23, 1979, Kenneth Rush Papers, Hoover Institution for War, Revolution, and Peace, Stanford, CA (hereinafter KR), Box 33, f.2.

55. Kissinger, *White House Years*, pp. 807ff. It involved not only a "secret" communication channel run by the U.S. Navy out of Frankfurt, thereby avoiding both State Department and CIA channels, but also featured meetings between the two at Cape Kennedy during the moon launch and at a meeting of the Bilderberg Conference in Woodstock, Vermont. The German foreign ministry, like its American counterpart, was not as unaware of the back channels as Bahr and Kissinger seemed to believe. James Sutterlin, letter to the author. Other accounts are in Egon Bahr, *Zu meiner Zeit* (Munich: Karl Blessing Verlag, 1996), pp.

344–371, and Dobrynin, pp. 229–230.

56. "Speech Given by Joe Sterne of the *Baltimore Sun* at the Press Farewell Luncheon for Ambassador Rush, at the Maternus Restaurant on February 11, 1972, Top Exclusive Secret (i.e., never to be read by anyone ever again)," RG59 Lot 74D430, NARA, Box 10, f.3: "[W]e have co-ambassadors in Bonn, co-Amb. Klein and co-Amb. Dean." Cf. Rush to Rogers, September 9, 1971, ibid., NARA, Box 16, f.8; Fuchs, pp. 223–227; Owen B. Lee Oral History, ADST.

57. Letter to the author from a foreign service officer; interview with Reginald Bartholomew.

58. Hillenbrand, p. 287.

59. Interview with a foreign service officer.

60. Robert Bowie to Lodge, April 9, 1968, HCL, Box 38, f.3; Lodge to Dean, November 25, 1969, HCL II, Reel 8; interview with Jonathan Dean.

61. Interview with Jonathan Dean.

62. Hillenbrand, p. 293.

63. W. R. Smyser, *From Yalta to Berlin: The Cold War Struggle over Germany* (New York: St. Martin's Press, 1999), p. 244.

64. A detailed reconstruction of the negotiations and the treaty is found in Bark.

65. Dean to Rush, "Overall Situation on East-West Negotiations" July 3, 1970, Records Relating to the Four Power Talks and Quadripartite Agreement 1961–87, RG59 Lot 91D341, NARA, Box 4, f.8. Examples of such plans are Hillenbrand to Merchant, January 21, 1959, "Possibilities for New Initiatives on German Reunification and European Security," Records of the Office of Soviet Union Affairs 1949–60, RG59 Lot 64D291, NARA, Box 3, f.1; and Dean to Robert Creel, December 30, 1957, "An Outline Settlement for Central and Eastern Europe," MJH, Box 2, f.13. Cf. Henry Kissinger, "Some Reflections on the Acheson Memorandum," August 16, 1961, National Security Files, JFKL, Box 82, f.11; "Soviet Negotiating Interest on Berlin" March 11, 1969, *FRUS, 1969–1976*, Vol. 40, pp. 51–55: "In short, there has never existed a common basis for negotiations on Berlin." See also note 95 in chapter 7, above.

66. Charles E. Bohlen, "The United States and Europe," speech delivered at the National War College, January 29, 1971, CB, Box 3, f.2; Schaetzel to Acheson, July 20, 1970, Schaetzel Papers, DDE; Chalmers M. Roberts, "Acheson Urges Brandt's 'Race' to Moscow Be 'Cooled Off,'" *Washington Post*, December 10, 1970, p. A8; lines on ambiguity are from Thomas L. Hughes, "Thoughts on the Causes of the Present Discontents," remarks to the convention of the Virginia State Bar Association, January 17, 1969, JR, Box 3, f.14. Differences over the nature and scope of East-West relations, particularly détente, were nothing new. See, for example, the speech by Maurice Couve de Murville, October 27, 1959, to the French National Assembly, CM1, CM.

67. George W. Ball, "Un punto di vista americano," *Affari Esteri* 3, no. 9 (January 1971): 28–46. For Acheson's reaction, see Acheson to Ball, December 24, 1970, GB, Series 1, Box 1, f.8.

68. Haig to Kissinger, February 6, 1971, Henry A. Kissinger Administrative and Staff Files, RN, Box 60, f.5: "Sonnenfeldt has gleaned on this like a leach [*sic*] on a hippo's belly. He is, of course, convinced that you are the source of the problem ... also emphasized that he was the source of the CDU's information.... I think it would be helpful for you to set Hal straight."

69. "Policies of Putative Brandt Government (Memorandum of Conversation with Bahr, Kissinger, Sonnenfeldt, and Hillenbrand)," October 13, 1969, NSC Subject Files, RN, Box 682, f.2; Acheson to Kissinger, R07165BZ February 7, 1971, Henry A. Kissinger Administrative and Staff Files, RN, Box 58, f.1; Robert Gerald Livingston to Kissinger, August 29, 1972, NSC Subject Files, RN, Box 687, f.2.

70. Memorandum of Conversation with Bahr, Guenther Van Well, Rush, and Dean,

December 9, 1970, Records Relating to the Four Power Talks and Quadripartite Agreement 1961–87, RG59 Lot 91D341, NARA, Box 5, f.2. For additional differences and tensions between Bonn, Berlin, and Washington, see Sutterlin and Klein, pp. 103, 109, and 116–117; Klein to Embassy Bonn, Secret Berlin 1304 041831Z, September 5, 1970; Nelson Ledsky to Embassy Bonn, Secret State 135459 August 25, 1970, ibid, Box 4, f.1; Dean to Sutterlin, June 3, 1970, ibid., Box 3, f.6; Brewster Morris to Russell Fessenden, January 21, 1970, ibid., Box 2, f.3.

71. Dean to Sutterlin, June 3, 1970, ibid.

72. Lawrence S. Eagleburger to Dean, October 6, 1970, RG59 Lot 91D341, NARA, Box 5, f.5. "The NATO business" refers to the CSCE, his emphasis. It was also believed that the Soviets linked success in the Berlin negotiations to ratification of the German-Soviet treaty signed the previous August. See also Geyer and Schaefer, p. 84, and Memorandum of Conversation with David Klein and Egon Bahr, October 23, 1970, RG59 Lot 91D341, NARA, Box 4, f.11.

73. Kissinger to Rush via Special Back Channel, June 28, 1971, Henry A. Kissinger Administrative and Staff Files, RN, Box 58, f.6.

74. Unpublished eulogy of Kenneth Rush by Jonathan Dean, in the author's possession. For Nixon's and Kissinger's alarm over the speed of the negotiations, see telephone transcript, June 7, 1971, appearing in footnote 2, *FRUS, 1969–1976*, Vol. 40, p. 729.

75. Hillenbrand diary, September 1, 1971, MJHH, Series II, Box 2, f.20; he added the next day, "Despite all, it is an agreement with which we can live—perhaps comfortably...."

76. Sutterlin and Klein, pp. 110, 114–115. They also point out that Kissinger only involved himself in the talks in February 1970, over six months after Brandt and the State Department had set the process in motion. Ibid., pp. 89–92. One of several cables on the draft treaty, highly marked up by Sonnenfeldt, suggests that a great deal more to-and-fro had taken place. Embassy Bonn to Secretary of State 1156, 301530Z, January 30, 1971, Henry A. Kissinger Administrative and Staff Files, RN, Box 58, f.4, f.5: "totally inadequate."

77. Sutterlin and Klein, p. 121; cf. Willy Brandt: "Kissinger saw Europeans as pawns in the great game of the superpowers." Brandt, *My Life in Politics* (London: Hamish Hamilton, 1992), p. 175.

78. The phrase is commonly translated to mean "change through a coming together."

79. They would also acquiesce reluctantly to the so-called differentiation policy, which required closer ties with some states, like Romania, and more frigid relations with others, like the GDR. See Thomas P. H. Dunlop Oral History, ADST; Timothy Garton Ash, *In Europe's Name: Germany and the Divided Continent* (New York: Vintage Books, 1993), p. 178; and the next chapter, below.

80. Birrenbach to Eleanor Dulles, June 1, 1973, Eleanor Dulles Papers, DDE, Box 20, f.1; "West Europeans Still Fear 'Finlandization,'" *Chicago Tribune*, August 20, 1972, p. A4.

81. Wolfgang Klaiber et al., eds., *Era of Negotiations: European Security and Force Reductions* (Lexington, MA: Lexington Books for the Atlantic Council of the United States, 1973), p. 95. The coeditor of this volume, James Sattler, was later uncovered as an East German spy. Other reactions are in the Minutes of the Board of Directors Meeting, Atlantic Council of the United States, Inc., January 13, 1970, William C. Foster Papers, George C. Marshall Foundation, Lexington, VA, Box 24, f.10.

82. Sonnenfeldt to Kissinger, October 5, 1970, NSC Subject Files, RN, Box 684, f.1; see also Brandt, pp. 167–168; and Berndt von Staden, *Ende und Anfang: Erinnerungen, 1939–1963* (Vaihingen/Enz: IPa, 2001), pp. 229–230.

83. Garton Ash, pp. 34ff.; cf. George Kennan, "I have never liked the word itself, which I find confusing and somewhat misleading ... [but] ... [the Soviets] represent a relatively old regime.... Let us, then, take what we can get while we can get it ..." Address to the Smithsonian Institution luncheon, December 11, 1974, National Security Adviser, Presidential Name File, 1974–1977, GFPL, Box 2, f.5.

84. Memorandum of Conversation with Gerald Ford, Henry Kissinger, Arthur Hartman, Helmut Sonnenfeldt, Aldo Moro, Mariano Rumor, Raimondo Manzini, and Francesco Vallauri, August 1, 1975, National Security Adviser, Memoranda of Conversations, 1973–1977, GFPL, Box 14, f.21; Peter Ramsbotham to Secretary of State for Foreign and Commonwealth Affairs, June 21, 1974, FCO 28/2573, PRO.

85. See the discussion in Chapter 11 regarding the Committee on the Present Danger.

86. Alsop to Anthony Astrachan, September 18, 1973, JA, Box 138, f.3.

87. Andrew J. Goodpaster, "NATO and U.S. Forces: Challenges and Prospects," manuscript prepared for *Strategic Review*, Andrew J. Goodpaster Papers, George C. Marshall Foundation, Lexington, VA, Box 37, f.24, his emphasis; "NATO Chief Urges Caution on Détente," *New York Times*, September 16, 1970, p. 5.

88. Fessenden to Hillenbrand, July 11, 1969, Records Relating to the Four Power Talks and Quadripartite Agreement 1961–87, RG59 Lot 91D341, NARA, Box 1, f.2.

89. E.g., Fessenden to Hillenbrand, December 2, 1969, RG59 Lot 74D430, NARA, Box 12, f.14; Hillenbrand to Fessenden, February 7, 1970, in *FRUS, 1969–1976*, Vol. 40, pp. 145–146.

90. Emmet to Richard Hunt, June 8, 1971, CE, Box 80, f.3; interview with Helmut Sonnenfeldt. See also Kissinger to Nixon, April 8, 1969, "The Recent Warsaw Pact Proposal for a European Security Conference," *FRUS, 1969–1976*, Vol. 39, pp. 5–6, and memorandum from Sonnenfeldt to Kissinger, October 2, 1969, with a noteworthy title: "European Security and Forthcoming NATO Meetings—The Bureaucratic Steamroller Pushes Irresistibly Forward," ibid., pp. 8–9. In these memos Hillenbrand appears as an early skeptic, too.

91. Secretary's Staff Meeting, December 9, 1974, HK, Box 5, f.4; cf. Kissinger: "[C]an you explain this Basket III crap to me? ... And here our solution is to sneak in a reference to peaceful change in some other place in a way acceptable to the Germans. And the problem is that horse's ass Scheel now wants to get more out of CSCE than he got in his treaty with the Soviets." Memorandum of Conversation with Kissinger, Robert McCloskey, Helmut Sonnenfeldt, Arthur Hartman, William Hyland, Brent Scowcroft, Lawrence Eagleburger, Jan Lodal, and Dennis Clift, March 22, 1974, HS, Box 8, f.7.

92. Memorandum of Conversation with Michel Jobert, Henry Kissinger, John N. Irwin II, and Peter Rodman, June 8, 1973, Henry A. Kissinger Administrative and Staff Files, RN, Box 56, f.6.

93. See Jacques Andréani, *Le piège: Helsinki et la chute du communisme* (Paris: Odile Jacob, 2005), pp. 6–9, 27–29, on the Gaullist roots, and p. 29 for impact of the Budapest appeal. The author, later a French ambassador to the United States, was closely involved with the CSCE talks. He noted a Belgian origin of the humanitarian language, which was then hitched to a Dutch, Italian, and British bandwagon (p. 47). Cf. Daniel C. Thomas, *The Helsinki Effect: International Norms, Human Rights, and the Demise of Communism* (Princeton, NJ: Princeton University Press, 2001), pp. 39ff., and Michael Cotey Morgan, "The United States and the Making of the Helsinki Final Act," in Fredrik Logevall and Andrew Preston, eds, *Nixon in the World: American Foreign Relations, 1969–1977* (Oxford: Oxford University Press, 2008), pp. 164–182.

94. R. Seydoux to Foreign Ministry, Brussels, March 27, 1968, NR 432/34 MAE Europe fonds EU 2-3-1 2012 Organismes internationaux 1966–1970, f.2; cf. George Vest to Secretary of State, USNATO 4390 October 22, 1971, RG59 Lot 74D430, NARA, Box 15, f.6. Cf. Andréani, pp. 49–50.

95. Bill Safire quoted in Brandon diary, October 15, 1972, HB, Box 8, f.6.

96. Hillenbrand diary, December 4, 1969, MJHH, Series II, Box 2, f.14. This section is based largely on the unpublished account of James Goodby, who was present for much of the negotiations. Other versions of his story appear in Goodby, *Europe Undivided: The New Logic of Peace in U.S.-Russian Relations* (Washington, D.C.: United States Institute of Peace Press,

1998), chap. 2, and in an address to the Eighty-fifth Annual Meeting of the Organization of American Historians, April 3, 1992. A rendition of the story was published recently by Stephan Kieninger as "Transformation or Status Quo: The Conflict of Stratagems in Washington over the Meaning and Purpose of the CSCE and MBFR, 1969– 1973," in Bange and Niedhart, eds., pp. 66–82. My own reading of the events suggests less of a clear-cut strategic conflict than bureaucratic opportunism on the part of foreign service officers in NATO and in EUR, and halfhearted dismissal, then embrace of these policies by their superiors when convinced that the policies would go forward regardless. I am grateful to both Kieninger and Bange, and to Ambassador Goodby, for shaping my understanding of the subject.

97. "Suggested Talking Points, Conference on Security and Cooperation in Europe, CSCE," Richard Cheney Files, 1974–77, GFPL, Box 155, f.9.

98. Eagleburger to Kissinger, "The United States and Europe," n.d. (January 1970), HS, Box 2, f.15. The memo included a cover note from Eagleburger to Sonnenfeldt: "Hal—I gave the attached to HAK last week. I don't think you will agree with it too much. P.S. Thanks for lunch, ping-pong, etc. Kiss your wife for me." Cf. Hillenbrand to Rogers, April 10, 1970, RG59/Subject Numeric Files 1970–73, NARA, Box 2264, f.5; Lord Cromer to Thomas Brimelow, March 31, 1972, FCO 41/1069, PRO; "Remarks by Ambassador Rush on MBFR and CESC" December 7, 1971, RG59 Lot 74D430, NARA, Box 13, f.7; interview with Karl Kaiser.

99. Memorandum of Conversation with Ambassador Adrien Meisch, Helmut Sonnenfeldt, and Katherine Shirley, November 29, 1974, HS, Box 3, f.2.

100. Rogers to all European diplomatic posts, December 23, 1971, RG59 Lot 74D430, NARA, Box 15, f.6; Stoessel to Secretary of State, Moscow 10342, 241627Z, July 1975, Country Files for Europe and Canada, GFPL, Box 20, f.20; "Helsinki/CSCE," n.d., National Security Adviser, Staff Assistant Peter Rodman Files 1974–77, GFPL, Box 1, f.14.

101. Ellsworth to Nixon, November 30, 1968, et seq., Henry A. Kissinger Administrative and Staff Files, RN, Box 1, f.18. Ted Achilles possibly played some role in securing the job for Ellsworth. Achilles, p. 814; interviews with Robert Ellsworth and Edward Streator.

102. Ellsworth to Nixon, November 30, 1968, ibid. When interviewed in 2007, he did not recall the reason.

103. Interviews with Robert Ellsworth and François de Rose.

104. Sonnenfeldt to Kissinger, "US Pushes Ahead on 'European Security,'" November 25, 1969, NSC Subject Files, RN, Box 667, f.2; Kosciusko-Morizet to Ministry, Brussels, February 4, 1970, 9-4-1 PR, NR 170/171 Amérique 1964–1970 590 MAE. For Eagleburger's views, see Goodby Oral History, ADST, and Goodby letter to the author. The other principal officers involved were Leo Reddy, Ed Streator, Jack McGuire, and Arva Floyd.

105. Interview with Thomas Niles. This aspect was known unofficially as the "Helsinki Tea Party."

106. Interview with Thomas W. Simons Jr.; Goodby, unpublished manuscript, p. 4.

107. Goodby, unpublished manuscript, p. 4; a Sonnenfeldt memo from 1966 foreshadowed the approach of using NATO for collective approaches to the East. Sonnenfeldt to Schaetzel, "East-West Matters in NATO," June 30, 1966, HS, Box 2, f.11; interview with Tom Niles.

108. John J. Maresca, To Helsinki: The Conference on Security and Cooperation in Europe, 1973–1975 (Durham, NC: Duke University Press), 1985, pp. 43–44, 64–65; Guy E. Coriden Jr. Oral History, ADST.

109. Goodby, unpublished manuscript, p. 18; "Interim Report on the Inter-Agency Task Force on CSCE," National Security Council Institutional Files, Policy Papers 1969–1974, National Security Decision Memoranda, RN, Box H-233, f.1 (NSDM 162). See also comments by Crispin Tickell and Jacques Andréani at the Center for Security Studies at ETH, Zurich, "At the Roots of the European Security System: Thirty Years Since the Helsinki

Final Act," September 8–10, 2005. Cf. Jonathan Dean, *Watershed in Europe: Dismantling the East-West Military Confrontation* (Lexington, MA: Lexington Books, 1987), p. 115.

110. "US Attitudes Towards the Conference on European Security (CSCE): Note of a Meeting Held on 14 March [1972]," FCO 41/1069, PRO. Appended to this is a "piece of paper given to Sir T. Brimelow by Mr. Galloway (US Embassy) on 14 March." Cf. Andréani, pp. 49–50.

111. N.a., Note, November 24, 1970, Organismes internationaux O.T.A.N. No. 50/E.U. des Pactes, Organismes internationaux, Europe fonds EU 2014, 23-1 MAE; Note from the Director for Europe, April 29, 1971, Europe fonds EU 2900 Organisation du Traite l'Atlantique Nord, 1971–Juin 1976, Eu 2-3-1; see also Schumann Oral History, Nuclear Age, Liddell Hart Centre, King's College, London.

112. "Konferenz über die Sicherheit Europas (KSE)," November 26, 1970, B20, Band 1601, AA; "Die wirtschaftliche Zusammenarbeit zwischen Ost und Westeuropa und die europäische Integration," January 11, 1971; "Europäische Gipfelkonferenz der Zehn," June 26, 1972, both in B20, Band 1891, AA; Cromer, Secret Washington 242352Z, March 24, 1972, FCO 41/1069, PRO (on the role of Hillenbrand in reassuring the Germans, et al.); Andréani, p. 48.

113. Cabinet meeting, August 8, 1975, National Security Adviser, Memoranda of Conversations, 1973–77, GFPL, Box 14, f.34; Memorandum of Conversation with Bruno Kriesky, Hannes Androsch, Gerald Ford, Henry Kissinger, and Brent Scowcroft, November 12, 1974, ibid., Box. 7, f.11.

114. Maresca, pp. 45–47; interview with George Vest; Vest to Secretary of State, USNATO 5329, January 12, 1972, RG59 Lot 74D430, Box 15, f.6; Andréani, p. 90. Vest's inquiry followed hearing from the West German delegates, who had heard from the East Germans, who themselves had heard from the Russians, that Kissinger had told Dobrynin that Vest was being too tough. ADST Oral History and interview with Vest.

115. Vest Oral History, ADST.

116. By contrast, the third volume, appearing in 1999, devoted a full chapter and retrospective to it, beginning with the lines, "Rarely has a diplomatic process so illuminated the limitation of human foresight." Henry Kissinger, *Years of Renewal* (New York: Simon and Schuster, 1999), p. 635.

117. Interview with James Lowenstein.

118. Interview with Thomas W. Simons Jr.; Brandon diary, July 18, 1973, HB, Box 8, f.7. Sections of the Arms Control and Disarmament Agency and the Joint Staff were also purged. See also Robert G. Kaufman, *Henry Jackson: A Life in Politics* (Seattle and London: University of Washington Press, 2000), p. 256.

119. Maresca, pp. 114–116; Sonnenfeldt, Hartman, and the German diplomat Berndt von Staden collaborated heavily in refining the treaty language. "CSCE: von Staden's Comment's on Peaceful Change Language," State 029569, February 5, 1975, Country Files for Europe and Canada, GFPL, Box 6, f.12.

120. Garton Ash, p. 84.

121. Kissinger, *Years of Renewal*, p. 638; Richard Davy, "Helsinki Myths: Setting the Record Straight on the Final Act of the CSCE 1975," *Cold War History* 9, no. 1 (February 2009): 1–22. Actually, the French would take the lead in opposing linkage of the conference to the MBFR talks. For the United States, the linkage would continue well into the Carter administration with SALT II. See Schmidt to Carter, March 12, April 2, 1979, Aaron to Carter, March 6, 1979, Germany, Federal Republic of: Chancellor Helmut Schmidt, 2/77–8/80, Zbigniew Brzezinski's President's Correspondence with Foreign Leaders Files (NSA3), Jimmy Carter Presidential Library, Atlanta, GA (hereinafter JCPL), Box 6, f.1–5/79.

122. Andréani, pp. 38–39, noting that Monnet regarded the Prague events as the forerunner of a drive for "serious negotiations" with the West.

123. Goodby, letter to the author.

124. "Secretary's Staff Meeting, October 29, 1973," HK, Box 1, f.9; "The Secretary's Principals' and Regionals' Staff Meeting, Wednesday, December 5, 1974," ibid., Box 5, f.8; cf. Sonnenfeldt in 1974: "[CSCE] negotiations have become a tangled web of nationalistic positions that have only marginal interest for the US.... [W]e and the Soviets are not the main protagonists...." Sonnenfeldt to Kissinger, November 14, 1974, HS, Box 5, f.9.

125. Interview with David Acheson.

126. Kissinger staff meeting, December 5, 1974, HK, ibid.; Maresca, p. 48; Terry O'Donnell trip memoranda, Helsinki visit, Richard Cheney Files, 1974–77, GFPL, Box 155, f.8, and also in same collection, White House Central Files, Box 57, f.15.

127. Maresca, p. 198. The author pointed out on page xii that the CSCE was both "a surrogate World War II peace treaty" and a "continuing European institution." In 1992, it was renamed the Organization for Security and Cooperation in Europe and still functions out of headquarters in Vienna.

128. "The Secretary's Principals' and Regionals' Staff Meeting, Wednesday, July 7, 1976," HK, Box 9, f.7; Douglas P. Bennett to Richard Cheney, October 12, 1976, Richard Cheney Files, 1974–77, GFPL, Box 2, f.4.; Hartman to Robert McCloskey, November 5, 1975, White House Central Files, Subject File, Box 216, f.4.

129. Hartman to Kissinger, October 1, 1975, "CSCE Implementation: Overall Concept," National Security Adviser, NSC Europe, Canada, and Ocean Affairs Staff: Files, General Subject File: Conference on Security and Cooperation in Europe 1974, GFPL, Box 44, f.7; interview with James Goodby; for opposition to EUR's program, see Winston Lord to Kissinger, November 19, 1976, HS, Box 11, f.12.

130. Goodby, letter to the author. See also William Korey, *The Promises We Keep: Human Rights, the Helsinki Process, and American Foreign Policy* (New York: St. Martin's Press, 1993), pp. 167–170. The bilateral visits would continue under Deputy Secretary of State John Whitehead in the Reagan administration. The title of Korey's book came from the final line of President Ford's speech at Helsinki, "History will judge this Conference not by what we say here today, by what we do tomorrow—not by the promises we make, but by the promises we keep." It was drafted by Hartman's deputy Jim Lowenstein and sent to the president by way of Eagleburger. Lowenstein Oral History, ADST.

131. Bobbie Greene Kilberg to Bud McFarlane, September 28, 1976, National Security Adviser, NSC Europe, Canada, and Ocean Affairs Staff: Files, General Subject File: Conference on Security and Cooperation in Europe 1974, GFPL, Box 44, f.8–10. In the margin, probably in Scowcroft's handwriting, are the words "amateur night."

132. Interviews with Arthur Hartman and Helmut Sonnenfeldt: "[O]h yes, 'my' doctrine. There was no such thing."

133. State 024976, in National Security Adviser, Presidential Name File, 1974– 1977, GFPL, Box 2, f.17.

134. Joe Alsop's comment on this event was telling: "Any fool ought to be able to see that Mr. Rumsfeld is a highly successful intriguer.... Any fool ought to be able to see, too, that although a successful intriguer, he is not a very wise man, for he has greatly damaged the President's chances of reelection by his coup ..." Alsop to Babe Paley, November 10, 1975, JA, Box 229, f.6.

135. Interview with Helmut Sonnenfeldt. The leaker, according to Sonnenfeldt, was W. Scott Thompson, an academic serving temporarily in the Pentagon as a White House fellow. He happened at the time to be the son-in-law of Paul Nitze and would soon join him in founding the Committee on the Present Danger.

136. Memoranda of Conversation, March 30, October 11, October 18, and November 23, 1976, National Security Adviser, Memoranda of Conversations, 1973–77, GFPL, Box 18, f.40, and Box 21, f.18, f.24, f.29. See also "U.S. Policy Toward Eastern Europe," GFPL, Box 1, f.1; Sonnenfeldt notes on Evans and Novak column, Robert J. McCloskey to Kissinger,

March 31, 1976, HS, Box. 9, f.9; see also William Safire, "Henry's Private Scorn," *New York Times*, October 18, 1976, p. 28.

137. Memorandum of Conversation with Kissinger, Sonnenfeldt, Brezhnev, and Gromyko, October 26, 1974, HS, Box 5, f.8, f.9; for an additional anecdote involving Brezhnev's swindle of Sonnenfeldt's expensive Swiss watch, see Dobrynin, pp. 273–274.

138. Mike Bowker and Phil Williams, "Helsinki and West European Security," *International Affairs* 61, no. 4 (Autumn 1985): 617.

10. Frayed Edges

1. White House Central Name Files, GFPL, "Stoessel, Walter." The film also features Cicely Tyson, Nadezhda Pavlova, Oleg Popov, and Margarita Terekhova.

2. Oatsie Charles quoted in Heymann, p. 100; interview with Margot Lindsay.

3. Peter Ramsbotham to Isaiah Berlin, April 12, 1976, IB, f.170.

4. Brandon Grove, *Behind Enemy Walls: The Life and Times of an American Diplomat* (Columbia: University of Missouri Press, 2005), p. 189; Alsop to David Bruce (son), April 4, 1973, JA, Box 138, f.4.

5. Grove, p. 185: "Winston Lord, head of the Policy Planning Staff at the State Department, told me Kissinger had asked him to expedite Cooper's departure for East Germany to 'get that woman off my back.'"

6. Grove, pp. 189, 198; Lorraine Cooper Papers, Schlesinger Library, Radcliffe Institute for Advanced Study, Harvard University, MC 393, Box 1, f.4, f.6, and photo files.

7. Memorandum of Conversation with Kissinger, Shultz, and Scowcroft, March 29 (1973), National Security Adviser, Memoranda of Conversations, 1973–77, GFPL, Box 1, f.26; Arthur Veysey, "How Europe's Fear Turned to Anger over U.S. Alert," *Chicago Tribune*, December 3, 1973, p. 1; "The Situation in the Mediterranean, June–November 1973," Action Sheet C-M(73)117 (Revised), February 6, 1974, Subject Files, North Atlantic Treaty Organization Archives, Brussels (on the lack of repercussions of October War upon the CSCE talks).

8. "Personal Summary Washington July 18 to July 23, 1971," Schaetzel Papers, DDE, Box 2, f.7; the claim about 1968 is in Jeremi Suri, *Power and Protest: Global Revolution and the Rise of Détente* (Cambridge, MA: Harvard University Press, 2003).

9. Kissinger: "Malaise! What causes the malaise? I have tried for a year to strengthen the Alliance and it is worse every day." Memoranda of Conversation with Kissinger, Robert McCloskey, Helmut Sonnenfeldt, Arthur Hartman, Winston Lord, William Hyland, Lawrence Eagleburger, and George Springsteen, March 11, 1974, HS, Box 4, f.1; cf. Kissinger, *White House Years* (Boston: Little, Brown and Company, 1979), pp. 81ff.

10. Memorandum of Conversation with Michel Jobert, Kissinger, John N. Irwin II, and Peter Rodman, June 8, 1973, Henry A. Kissinger Administrative and Staff Files, RN, Box 56, f.6; Memorandum of Conversation with Ford, Kissinger, and Scowcroft, September 29, 1974, National Security Adviser, Memoranda of Conversations, 1973–77, GFPL, Box 6, f.14, and October 8, 1974, f.26.

11. Secretary's Staff Meeting, January 21, 1974, HK, Box 2, f.3.

12. *Foreign Service Journal* (November 1968), part 2. The figures are not inclusive of the U.S. Information Agency and U.S. Agency for International Development; U.S. Department of State, *Foreign Service List*, February 1972.

13. Interview with Kempton Jenkins.

14. Richard Fox Beigel Oral History, ADST; cf. Michael A. G. Michaud, "Communication Re. Confessions of a Glopee," *Foreign Service Journal* (March 1977): 5ff.; "Secretary's Staff Meeting, October 29, 1973," HK, Box 1, f.9; interviews with Tom Niles and Chas. W. Freeman Jr.

15. Interviews with Jack Matlock, Tom Niles, and Nicholas Henderson; Mayers, pp. 224–225. Kissinger's fondness for Stoessel may also have had something to do with

Stoessel's role as an intermediary with the Chinese while he was ambassador to Poland and with their past association at Harvard's Center for Foreign and International Affairs. For his part, Hillenbrand became ambassador to the Federal Republic in 1972 and subsequently retired at the end of the Ford administration, disappointed that a bureaucratic oversight (or the pique of Henry Kissinger, it is not clear which) had prevented him from receiving the rank of career ambassador and disclosed the news of his retirement before he had announced it himself. As noted above, he went on to head the Atlantic Institute in Paris, where he lived in the same building as Jean Monnet. Hillenbrand to Kohler, January 21, 1977, and Hillenbrand to George Landau, September 30, 1976, paraphrasing Dr. Johnson, in several similar letters that follow, "[T]here is nothing that so wonderfully concentrates the mind as the prospects of bureaucratic execution." MJHH, Series III, Box 8, f.3; Duchêne Oral History. See also Hillenbrand, "The Foreign Service: Ten Years from the Outside," MJHH, Series II, Box 4, f.25.

16. Interviews with Roger Kirk and Tom Niles; Dobrynin to Kissinger, October 7, 1974, HS, Box 8, f.4; Dennis Clift to Kissinger, "Funding for New U.S. Embassy in Moscow," June 30, 1975; David Elliot to Brent Scowcroft, "Memorandum from John Egar re. Moscow Radiation Hazard," April 1, 1976; and Kissinger to Embassy Moscow, State 029350, all in Country Files for Europe and Canada, GFPL, Box 17, f.15, Box 19, f.2, and Box 20, f.13.

17. Interview with E. Wayne Merry.

18. Bruce to Rusk, July 28, 1965, in Bruce diary, DB, Box 4, f.36, and entry for October 18, 1968, Box 6, f.9.

19. Profile of Arthur Hartman, FCO 82/497, PRO. For Shultz, see section on Library Group, below.

20. Ball to Acheson, March 3, 1970, GB, Box 1, f.8; Kissinger's reaction is in a memorandum he wrote to Nixon, December 29, 1969, NSC Subject Files, RN, Box 667, f.2; cf. Hyland to Rodman, n.d., Henry A. Kissinger Administrative and Staff Files, RN, Box 15, f.2.

21. Ball to Acheson, ibid.

22. Don Oberdorfer, *Senator Mansfield: The Extraordinary Life of a Great American Statesman and Diplomat* (Washington, D.C.: Smithsonian Books, 2003), pp. 387ff.

23. John W. Finney, "Nixon Firm in Fight to Bar U.S. Troop Cut in Europe," *New York Times*, May 14, 1971, p. 1; Arthur Siddon, "How Nixon Reduced Big Troop Cut in Senate," *Chicago Tribune*, September 29, 1973, p. W1; the standard work on the Mansfield legislation is Phil Williams, *The Senate and U.S. Troops in Europe* (New York: St Martin's Press, 1985). For a premonition, see Alphand to Couve, August 19, 1960, in CM7, CM.

24. Oberdorfer, p. 390; interview with James Lowenstein; Memorandum of Conversation with Rolf Pauls, Carl Lahusen, Martin Hillenbrand, and Kenneth N. Skoug Jr., December 10, 1970, RG59 Subject Numeric Files 1970–73, NARA, Box 2264, f.6.

25. Interview with Tom Niles.

26. James Goodby, letter to author; Jonathan Dean, p. 103.

27. For a full description of the interrelationship of SALT, CSCE, and MBFR, see Stanley Resor to Sonnenfeldt (and attached memo by Avis Bohlen to William Shinn), September 10, 1974, HS, Box 11, f.3.

28. Interview with Jonathan Dean; editorial note in *FRUS, 1969–1976*, Vol. 39, p. 999.

29. Interviews with W. R. Smyser, Avis Bohlen, and Thomas W. Simons Jr.

30. Interview with Reginald Bartholomew.

31. Defense Department position on MBFR (Laird), March 29, 1972, and Laird to Nixon, May 13, 1972, National Security Council Institutional Files, Policy Papers, 1969–1974, RN, Box H-233, f.1 (on assuaging the Pentagon); "Minutes, National Security Council Meeting, Thursday, January 23, 1975," National Security Adviser, NSC Meeting File, 1974–77, GFPL, Box 1, f.7; Robert C. Hill to Secretary of Defense, "Overview of Your Meeting with Lord Carrington," n.d. EUR Office of Northern European Affairs, Records

Relating to the UK, 1962–74, RG59 multiple Lot Files, NARA, Box 6, f.4 (on assuaging the British); Dean to Rush, October 26, 1971, RG59, Lot 74D430, NARA, Box 15, f.5 and passim (on assuaging the Germans); Sonnenfeldt to Kissinger, May 3, 1975, HS, Box 3, f. 5; Hartman to Sonnenfeldt, October 22, 1975, HS, Box 3, f.6; William Shinn to Sonnenfeldt, October 21, 1975, HS, Box 3, f.6; Sonnenfeldt's handwritten notes of talks at Vladivostok with Brzezhnev and Kissinger, Box 5, f.8 (on assuaging the French).

32. Interviews with Alexander Haig and Andrew Goodpaster; Sonnenfeldt to Kissinger, February 26, 1970, NSC Subject Files, RN, Box 676, f.5, and Embassy, Paris to Secretary of State, 5321 141091Z, "Koven Article on Alleged U.S.-French Nuclear Discussions," ibid., Box 674, f.1; Don Cook, "France's Attitude Toward NATO Begins to Warm," *Washington Post*, February 12, 1971, p. A27.

33. Richard H. Ullman, "The Covert French Connection," *Foreign Policy* 75 (Summer 1989): 3–33; from French chargé in London to Schumann, "Eventuelle cooperation nucleaire franco-britannique," No. 993/EU July 31, 1969, Europe fonds EU 2-3-1 2012 MAE, f.4; Sonnenfeldt to Kissinger, August 3, 1970, NSC Subject Files, RN, Box 677, f.1. The secret was not as closely guarded as Ullman claimed, however. Officials in the Departments of Defense and State, and throughout the Atomic Energy Commission, were aware of it; the same was true in France. Interviews with Helmut Sonnenfeldt, Arthur Hartman, and Claude-Gerard Marcus. Another possible impetus for maintaining the program was to counterbalance French resentment over the Nixon-Brezhnev Agreement on the Prevention of Nuclear War issued as part of the deeply unpopular Year of Europe. The agreement reportedly was drafted by the British diplomat Thomas Brimelow and others in secret at the behest of Kissinger, without the knowledge of the State Department. In response, NATO issued the so-called Ottawa declaration, which was the first of its kind to mention that national nuclear deterrents contributed to the "global deterrent." It was negotiated by Goodby and his French counterparts, and sold by de Rose to the NATO Council once Jobert made it clear to him that "he did not want to have two quarrels at once with the Americans." An eleventh-hour push by the then U.S. ambassador to NATO, Donald Rumsfeld, made it happen. Interviews with de Rose and Goodby; letter to the author from Victoria Coates. See also Jonathan Haslam, *The Soviet Union and the Politics of Nuclear Weapons in Europe, 1969–87* (London: Macmillan, 1989), p. 48; letter from Roger Jackling to Kathleen Burk, cited in Burk's *Old World, New World: The Story of Britain and America* (London: Little, Brown, 2007), p. 614; Keith Hamilton and Patrick Salmon, eds., *The Year of Europe: America Europe and the Energy Crisis, 1972–1974, Documents on British Policy Overseas*, Series 3, Vol. 4 (London: Whitehall History Publishing/Routledge, 2006), pp. 5–6 and supporting documents (on "Operation Hullabaloo").

34. "Secretary's Staff Meeting, Monday, December 9, 1974," HK, Box 5, f.8; Memorandum of Conversation, December 19, 1973, Quai d'Orsay, in Walter Stoessel Papers, Georgetown University Archives and Special Collections (hereinafter WS), Box 2, f.11b. According to François de Rose, the bad blood was exacerbated by Jobert's feeling that Kissinger did not appreciate all he (Jobert) had done for him regarding Vietnam. Whether there would have been any bad blood at all is an open question; the two personalities were probably bound to clash. Interview with de Rose.

35. Memorandum of Conversation with Ford, Kissinger, Rumsfeld, and Scowcroft, November 26, 1975, National Security Adviser, Memoranda of Conversations, 1973–77, GFPL, Box 16, f.48; for negative reaction, see (n.a.) to John McCloy, March 27, 1969, AMK C 26/4/409, JM; and Schaetzel to Acheson, December 31, 1968, Schaetzel Papers, DDE, Box 1, f.2.

36. Interviews with Arthur Hartman and Alexander Haig; Sonnenfeldt to Kissinger, February 26, 1970, RN; the State Department official charged with following the program was Sonnenfeldt's assistant John Kelly. See ADST interview and Brent Scowcroft to Col. (?) Oveson, June 29, 1976, HS, Box 6, f.1.

37. Interview with Arthur Hartman.

38. Story told to the author by Donna Hartman (wife of Arthur). In July and August 1974, Turkish forces invaded Cyprus and occupied nearly half the island in order to protect the rights of Turkish Cypriots against those who sought unification with Greece. Because the Cyprus conflict had long been under the purview of the Bureau of Near Eastern Affairs, and remained fairly well contained, it is not treated here in detail. Essentially, the State Department would manipulate Kissinger into a more balanced handling of the Greek government of Constantine Karamanlis, which, for all its faults, had legitimate grievances against Turkey. The crisis is described in Kissinger, *Years of Renewal*, chap. 7. Kissinger favored the Turkish position, having known Turkish premier Bülent Ecevit since Harvard days and reportedly having gained respect for him for, among other things, translating T. S. Eliot's "The Cocktail Party" into the Turkish language. The persistent anti-Americanism among large sectors of Greek public opinion also grated upon Kissinger and his staff, while the pro-Greek sentiment within the State Department, and in particular among former NEA Desk officers like Thomas Boyatt, who drafted a famous dissent, grated upon him even more. Hartman inherited the crisis, devoted himself to a crash course in Cypriot politics, and did a great deal to ease emotions on all sides. Interviews with Arthur Hartman and James Lowenstein. A summary of State's position is in the memorandum of the Cyprus Task Force, July 22, 1974, *FRUS, 1969–1976*, Vol. 30, pp. 366–374; Hartman to Joseph Sisco, "Your Meeting with Ambassador Dimitriou," December 5, 1974, Records Relating to Cyprus, 1969–74, RG59 Lot 77D34, NARA, Box 1, f.21; P. H. S. Stoddard to Thomas Boyatt, March 28, 1973, ibid., f.29; Boyatt to Hartman, May 6, 1974, ibid., f.34; Hartman to Kissinger, "Assessment of Cyprus Task Force: Lessons for the Future," August 2, 1974, HK, Box 4, f.10, for lessons learned. The handling of the Cyprus question under the previous administration fell principally to George Ball and Cyrus Vance.

39. Mário Soares, the embattled head of the Portuguese Socialist Party, made it clear that Portugal was "more like" Northern Europe, perhaps being aware of EUR's bias in favor of Northern Europeans as being reliable and Southern Europeans as volatile and unpredictable. Memorandum of Conversation with Mário Soares, João Hall Themido, Rui Mateus, Kissinger, Sonnenfeldt, Lowenstein, and Robert Barbour, January 26, 1976, HS, Box 7, f.7; interview with Monteagle Stearns.

40. Dennis Clift to Kissinger, April 3, 1975, Country Files for Europe and Canada, GFPL, Box 1, f.5.

41. Memorandum of Conversation with Ford, Kissinger, and Scowcroft, March 27, 1975, National Security Adviser, Memoranda of Conversations, 1973–77, GFPL, Box 10, f.25; Memorandum of Conversation with Nelson Rockefeller, Kissinger, Scowcroft, and President's Foreign Intelligence Advisory Board, August 7, 1975, ibid., Box 14, f.33; Memorandum of Conversation with Kissinger, James Schlesinger, Major General John Wickham, and Brent Scowcroft, February 8, 1975, ibid., Box 9, f.18, calls for a "brutal" and "unexpected" response; "Secretary's Staff Meeting Monday, January 20, 1975," HK, Box 6, f.3; Kissinger, *Years of Renewal*, p. 630; Clift to Scowcroft, December 30, 1974, Country Files for Europe and Canada, GFPL, Box 10, f.12.

42. Cf. Kissinger to Embassy, Lisbon, State 233020, October 22, 1974—a domino theory of Eurocommunism, Country Files for Europe and Canada, GFPL, Box 11, f.6; cf. Alsop to La Contessa Anna Maria Cicogna, May 12, 1975, JA, Box 228, f.11; "Secretary's Staff Meeting, Thursday, July 1, 1976," HK, Box 10, f.6; Meeting with Interns, August 17, 1976, ibid., Box 11, f.2.

43. N.b.: Most Portuguese did not regard their Communists as being allied fully with other Eurocommunists, but this made little difference to Kissinger. I thank Luis Nuno Rodrigues for this point.

44. Frank C. Carlucci, "The View from the U.S. Embassy," in Hans Binnendijk, ed., *Authoritarian Regimes in Transition* (Washington, D.C.: Foreign Service Institute, U.S.

Department of State, 1987), p. 209; Richard Bone, "Eurocommunism—Does It Exist?" July 1977, FO 972/6, PRO.

45. Interview with Monteagle Stearns; two other noteworthy officers who followed the Zanzibar route were Jack Matlock and Thomas Pickering.

46. He would go on to become deputy director of the CIA, national security adviser, and secretary of defense under Ronald Reagan.

47. This was not the case initially because a few people in the bureau saw the appointment as political, even though Carlucci spoke Portuguese, served in Brazil, and knew a good deal about African decolonization, which was top of the agenda for the Portuguese government. Interview with Carlucci. For Rumsfeld's role in the Portuguese affair, see Scowcroft to Ford, "Secretary Rumsfeld's Visit to Portugal," Country Files for Europe and Canada, GFPL, Box 10, f.12, and subsequent memos; letter to author from Victoria Coates noting that the policy was not designed primarily on Soares's behalf.

48. Interview with Arthur Hartman.

49. Interview with Frank Carlucci.

50. Robert V. Keeley, ed., *First Line of Defense: Ambassadors, Embassies, and American Interests Abroad* (Washington, D.C.: The American Academy of Diplomacy, 2000), p. 40; Carlucci to Kissinger, June 24, 1976, Lisbon 4229 241408Z, Country Files for Europe and Canada, GFPL, Box 11, f.10; Bonn 0965 April 18, 1975 (especially for impact of Portuguese troubles on CSCE, etc.), B212, Band 111522, AA; Clift to Kissinger, "Willy Brandt's Role in Current Portuguese Situation," March 22, 1975, Country Files for Europe and Canada, GFPL, Box 5, f.13, and subsequent memos; Memoranda of Conversation with Brandt, Ford, von Staden, Kissinger, and Scowcroft, March 27, 1975, National Security Adviser, Memoranda of Conversation, 1973–77, GFPL, Box 10, f.24; Record of a Conversation with British and Portuguese Prime Ministers, June 25, 1974, PREM 16/241, PRO; letter to the author from Berndt von Staden. Another ally was the new supreme allied commander for Europe, General Alexander Haig, as well as Valéry Giscard d'Estaing. Barbour/Kissinger to Carlucci, State 279594, November 14, 1975, Country Files for Europe and Canada, GFPL, Box 4, f.8; Kopp and Gillespie, p. 65.

51. Quoted in Binnendijk, ed., p. 210; cf. Carlucci to Kissinger, "1976 Annual Assessment," Lisbon 1336, National Security Adviser, Outside the System Chronological File 1974–77, GFPL, Box 4, f.6.

52. Kissinger, *Years of Renewal*, pp. 631–632; the original statement is in Binnendijk, ed., p. 210.

53. Richard Gardner, *Mission Italy: On the Front Lines of the Cold War* (Lanham, MD: Rowman and Littlefield Publishers, 2005), and Zbigniew Brzezinski, *Power and Principle: Memoirs of the National Security Advisor, 1977–1981* (New York: Farrar, Straus, and Giroux, 1983), pp. 311–312. Cf. Frank R. Barnett to Brzezinski, February 6, 1979, with attachments, Public and Congressional Correspondence Files (NSA-14), JCPL, Box 5, folder Eurocommunism 2/79 (OA 6187); Brzezinski to Carter, May 31, 1978, "Information Items ... Problems and Prospects for Eurocommunism," Declassified materials, NLC-1-6-48-2, JCPL. For the impact of the Portuguese events on Italian politics, see Springsteen to Scowcroft, Memorandum for the President, "Your Meeting with Italian Foreign Minister Mariano Rumor, September 23, 1975," Country Files for Europe and Canada, GFPL, Box 8, f.3; cf. John Volpe to Hartman, June 25, 1975, Rome 9113 2516272Z, ibid., Box 8, f.15.

54. Interview with Richard Gardner; Tarnoff did not recall the episode when asked about it in 2009.

55. An early example is in a memorandum of conversation between John Foster Dulles and Francisco Franco (along with Livingston Merchant, Henry Cabot Lodge Jr., and Spanish foreign minister Martin-Artajo), November 1, 1955, John Foster Dulles Papers, 1951–1959, General Correspondence and Memoranda Series, DDE, Box 1, f.5. Some credit for imparting the nuances of differentiation to Dulles probably went to James Riddleberger,

then serving as American ambassador to Yugoslavia. Interview with Antonia Stearns. For the Nixon administration see, inter alia, Sonnenfeldt to Kissinger, October 18, 1972, "Relations with Eastern Europe," *FRUS, 1969–1976*, Vol. 29, pp. 45–51. There would be a hiccup in Yugoslavia, where a political appointee, Ambassador Laurence Silberman, waged a one-man campaign against Tito. Silberman would go on to become a well known judge in the District of Columbia. Interview with James Lowenstein; Memorandum of Conversation with Kissinger, Rumsfeld, Marsh, and Scowcroft: "Obviously we need to corral this Silberman," February 21, 1975, National Security Adviser, Memoranda of Conversations, 1973–77, GFPL, Box 9, f.28; Memoranda of Conversation with Ford, Kissinger, and Scowcroft, June 15, 1976, ibid., Box 19, f.47; Silberman to Sonnenfeldt, March 22, 1975, HS, Box 3, f.7; Sonnenfeldt to Kissinger, June 17, 1976, and Hartman to Kissinger, June 15, 1976, ibid., Box 3, f.8; John Montgomery to Sonnenfeldt, November 9, 1976, ibid., Box 11, f.12; and Silberman to Sonnenfeldt, Eyes Only, Belgrade 367 270745Z, April, 27, 1976: typical Silberman language, here to Sonnenfeldt at the time of the "Doctrine" affair (see above): "We are going out of our way to support you personally in light of predictable goy tactics. This is not time to crawl in hole. As my English headmaster used to say 'keep your pecker up.'" Ibid., Box 10, f.27.

56. Interview with Arthur Hartman.

57. Walters, *Silent Missions* (Garden City, NY: Doubleday, 1978), pp. 551ff., and Binnendijk, ed., pp. 193–194. See also Ellsworth to U. Alexis Johnson, February 13, 1970, RG59 Subject Numeric Files 1970–73, NARA, Box 3146, f.3, for Ellsworth's two-track plan to reintegrate Spain with NATO. The irony was that Kissinger defended his misreading of the Portuguese situation by its potential for replication in Spain. Memorandum of Conversation with Helmut Schmidt, Hans-Dietrich Genscher, Ford, Kissinger, Scowcroft, and Sonnenfeldt, May 29, 1975, National Security Adviser, Memoranda of Conversations, 1973–77, GFPL, Box 12, f.8; Memoranda of Conversation with Gaston Thorn, Pierre Wurth, Paul Helminger, Ford, Kissinger, and Hartman, May 29, 1975, ibid., f.15; Sonnenfeldt to Kissinger, "Spain and NATO," March 28, 1975, HS, Box 3, f.3; interview with H. Freeman Matthews Jr.; W. J. Lehmann to George Landau, July 16, 1971, EUR Office of Western European Affairs, Records Relating to Spain, 1963–76, RG59 multiple Lot Files, NARA, Box 12, f.2; John Leddy to the Under Secretary, January 28, 1969, ibid., Box 7, f.17; "Possible Spanish Relationship in NATO," December 20, 1968, State 290321, included in DB, Box 6, f.10.

58. Interview with Abe Katz: Soon after the announcement, European Commissioner Sicco Mansholt came to Washington with Ralf Dahrendorf to complain and to ask if Secretary of the Treasury John Connolly or anyone else had had taken the Alliance into account. The reply from Deputy Secretary of Defense Jack Irwin, as reported by Rolf Pauls, then German ambassador to the United States, was "why? It was an economic matter." Cf. David Hannay Oral History, British Diplomatic History Programme, Churchill Archives Centre, Churchill College, Cambridge. For suggestion of a silver lining, see Monnet to McCloy, December 28, 1971, AMK C 26/4/422, JM.

59. Katz should not be confused with another prominent economic adviser, Jules Katz, who worked out of the undersecretary's office. The hidden hand of RPE is suggested by Robert Hormats to Kissinger, December 18, 1972, a lengthy memo on European consultations that echoes many of RPE's priorities without ever mentioning the office. NSC Subject Files, RN, Box 322, f.5. It appeared that leadership on economic policy had well left the State Department, although some of it would shift back under Carter. See Hillenbrand, "The Foreign Service: Ten Years from the Outside."

60. Jacob Myerson to W. Walton Butterworth, March 14, 1973, WWB, Box 2, f.5; another factor affecting the French position might have been their own assessment of divisions within the U.S. government. See Kosciusko-Morizet to Ministry, November 11, 1970, NR 3467–74, Amérique 1964–70, États-Unis Relations politiques avec la France

580 MAE, f.1; Bernard Gwertzman, "Nixon Cautions the Arabs Not to Attach Conditions to Lifting of Oil Embargo," *New York Times*, March 16, 1974, p. 64; Richard F. Janssen, "Shifting Loyalties: As U.S. Intensifies Aid to Israelis, Europeans Move Closer to Arabs," *Wall Street Journal*, October 22, 1973, p. 1. Cf. Couve de Murville, "Devons nous prendre des gants avec les Américains?" *Réalités* (June 1972), draft in CM4, CM. See also Note 7, above.

61. Interview with Michael Palliser.

62. Henry Kissinger, *Years of Upheaval* (Boston: Little, Brown and Company, 1982), pp. 896–934; Secretary's Staff Meeting November 20, 1973, HK, Box 1, f.11.

63. Interview with Abe Katz; Firestone to Sonnenfeldt and Hartman, Brussels 8536 041581Z, November 14, 1974, Country Files for Europe and Canada, GFPL, Box 1, f.19. Much of the credit also went to Thomas Enders. Joseph Kraft, "A Shakeup in Oil Diplomacy," *Los Angeles Times*, August 21, 1975, p. C7.

64. Shultz rated the Library Group as one of his proudest achievements, even though it had since become "ridiculous, a circus." Interview with Shultz; Ford to Helmut Schmidt, December 26, 1974, National Security Adviser, Presidential Name File, GFPL, 1974–77, f.13; Schmidt, *Menschen und Mächte* (Berlin: Siedler, 1987), pp. 193–199; for origins, see Sonnenfeldt to Scowcroft, November 24, 1973, NSC Subject Files, RN, Box 688 f.1; Casey to Rogers, March 30, 1973, KR, Box 14, f.2.

65. E.g., speech by Schaetzel to the Deutsche Gesellschaft für Aussenpolitik, February 12, 1970, BAC 3/1978 1969–1970 No. 928/3, EU.

66. Interview with Abe Katz. One notorious case took place in 1969 when the French proposed another directoire to the British; Harold Wilson liked the idea, but it was leaked by Katz's opposite number in the Foreign Office, John Robinson. The reaction from the smaller European states was fierce, and the idea died. See Karl E. Meyer, "Soames Affair: Rift Widens," *Washington Post*, February 25, 1969, p. A1; Bruce diary, March 6, 1969, DB, Box 6, f.20. Katz claimed to have been responsible for making sure the U.S. government stayed out of the dispute. See also Harold Wilson, *The Labour Government 1964–1970: A Personal Record* (London: Weidenfeld and Nicolson, 1971), pp. 610ff.; Lucet to Ministry, March 5, 1970, NR 1499/500, Amérique 1964–70, États-Unis Relations politiques avec la France 580 MAE, f.1. For other White House consideration of "alternatives" to the EC, see C. Fred Bergsten to Kissinger, December 11, 1970, NSC Subject Files, RN, Box 322, f.1; Sonnenfeldt to Kissinger, April 27, 1972, ibid., f.2.

67. Kissinger, *Years of Upheaval*, pp. 152–153. Cf. Hannay Oral History, Churchill Archive; Kissinger to de Rose, July 25, 1975, HS, Box 3, f.4.

68. Interview with Charles Cogan; handwritten notes by Walter Stoessel, June 12–13, 1973, WS, Box 1, f.5bii, and Memorandum of Conversation with François Puaux, June 14, 1973, Box 2, f.9f; Lord Powell of Bayswater, Oral History, Churchill Archives; Kissinger to Ford, "Meeting with Edward Heath," September 10, 1974, Country Files for Europe and Canada, GFPL, Box 15, f.1; "European Reaction to Kissinger April 23 Speech," May 27, 1973, n.a., notes from the ATA Meeting at Norfolk, VA, ACUS, Box 2, f.6; Couve de Murville, Speech in the French National Assembly, November 12, 1973, in CM4, CM; Hennessy and Anstey, p. 17. Cf. Carington, *Reflect on Things Past*, p. 387.

69. Kissinger, *Years of Upheaval*, p. 192; Memorandum of Conversation with Jobert, Kissinger, John N. Irwin II, and Peter Rodman, June 8, 1973, Henry A. Kissinger Administrative and Staff Files, RN, Box 56, f.6; Memorandum of Conversation with Kissinger, Emiel van Lennep, and Robert Hormats, July 27, 1973, NSC Subject Files, RN, Box 322, f.4; Kissinger speech to the Atlantic Treaty Association, September 10, 1973, ibid., Box 409, f.4.

70. Schumann Oral History, Nuclear Age, Liddell Hart Centre; much of the Atlantic Declaration was drafted and negotiated by James Goodby. See Note 33, above. Cf. "Europe Circles Kissinger's April 23rd Speech," July 2, 1973, Schaetzel Papers, DDE, Box 5, f.3; and François de Rose, Wilhelm Grewe, and Denis Healey Oral Histories in Nuclear Age, Liddell

Hart Centre; State 179141, "Belgian Views of 'Year of Europe,'" September 7, 1973, NSC Subject Files, RN, Box 409, f.4; Sonnenfeldt to Kissinger, "von Staden on Year of Europe Problems," August 2, 1973, ibid., Box 687, f.4; Hormats to Kissinger, May 14, 1973, ibid., Box 679, f.2.

71. Binnendijk, ed., p. 192; on the Monnet meeting, see Kissinger, *Years of Upheaval*, p. 139; "L'affaire Watergate deviant grave. Jusqu'où ira-t-elle?" May 18, 1973, AMK C 23/6/259, JM; Kissinger to Monnet, March 30, 1971, NSC Subject files, RN, Box 685, f.1. Monnet's Action Committee would cease work in 1975, and he would die four years later.

72. Memorandum of Conversation with Nixon, Rogers, Elliot Richardson, Schlesinger, Kissinger, James Farley, Rumsfeld, Admiral Thomas Moorer, Rush, and Scowcroft, April 12, 1973, National Security Adviser, Memoranda of Conversations, 1973–77, GFPL, Box 1, f.29; Memorandum of Conversation with Nixon, Kissinger, Shultz, William Simon, and Scowcroft, February 9, 1974, ibid., Box 3, f.23. Some exceptions were Alec Douglas-Home and Hans Dietrich Genscher. Kissinger: "Mr. [German diplomat Günther] Van Well was a student of mine." Genscher: "I am the only German who wasn't!" Memorandum of Conversation with Genscher, Van Well, von Staden, Ford, Kissinger, and Scowcroft, September 26, 1974, ibid., Box 6, f.12.

73. "Talking Points: America and Europe on the Eve of the 1970s," MJH, Box 6, f.6.

74. Arthur Schlesinger Jr. to Isaiah Berlin, September 2, 1971, IB, f.213 (on Thompson); Lemnitzer to Chip Bohlen, February 6, 1968, CB, Box 30, f. 4 (on Lemnitzer); eulogy of Tommy Thompson, ibid., Box 31, f.1; Schaetzel to Acheson, December 31, 1968, Schaetzel Papers, DDE, Box 1, f.2 (on Shriver). Cf. a more positive French view: Lucet to Ministry, NR 1434–40, March 11, 1968, Amérique 1964–70, États-Unis 571 MAE; Evangeline Bruce to Monnet, May 14, 1977, AMK C 23/2/172, JM; Philip M. Kaiser to Evangeline Bruce, December 6, 1977, Kaiser Papers, HST, Box 18, f.5 (on Bruce); Bruce to Ford, January 16, 1976, White House Central Files, Name Files, Bruce, David, K. E.; Bruce diary, February 26, 1969, DB, Box 6, f.20 (on Tyler); and March 19, 1969, ibid.: "Secretary Rogers generously asked us to attend a little ceremony in the Thomas Jefferson Room. In the course of it we were given Diplomatic Passports valuable for life. Speeches were made by the Secretary, Dean Acheson, Dean Rusk, and Averell Harriman. Thus ended, as far as I can foresee, my diplomatic career."

75. The initial plan had been to name Haig army chief of staff, but the army objected to the job being given to so young and inexperienced an officer. Goodpaster, by contrast, was only a few months short of retirement and learned of his replacement indirectly, an oversight that probably never would have occurred under any previous administration. Interviews with Alexander Haig and Andrew J. Goodpaster; Sonnenfeldt to Kissinger, "Goodpaster-Haig," September 10, 1974, HS, Box 5, f.4; Memorandum of Conversation with Ford, Kissinger, and Scowcroft, December 17, 1974, "Goodpaster is being a shit," (Kissinger) National Security Adviser, Memoranda of Conversations, GFPL, Box 7, f.45, and multiple memos in National Security Adviser, Presidential Name File, 1974– 77 GFPL, Box 1, f.30; Alexander M. Haig Jr., *Inner Circles: How America Changed the World* (New York: Warner Books, 1992), p. 520; Don Cook, "Haig for NATO Irks Europeans," *Los Angeles Times*, September 22, 1974, p. H1; cf. Office of White House Operations, Alexander M. Haig, Assistant to the President Files, 1973–74, August 20, 1974, GFPL, Box 1 (on possible candidacy of Patrick Buchanan for NATO ambassador).

76. "Pension Rise Lures Many Senior Aides in State Department," *New York Times*, December 8, 1972, p. 9.

77. Huntley to Adolph Schmidt, April 10, 1971, DAU, Box 21, f.9; Benjamin H. Read to Robert D. Murphy, December 6, 1968, Henry A. Kissinger Administrative and Staff Files, RN, Box 2, f.11.

78. Cf. Dean Acheson, "Meeting at the White House," December 7, 1970, Schaetzel Papers, DDE, Box 1, f.9; Kissinger, *White House Years*, pp. 938ff.

79. Memorandum of Conversation with Kissinger, Robert Ingersoll, Sonnenfeldt, Lord, Hyland, John Newhouse, Mark Palmer, and Robert Blackwill, July 30, 1974, HS, Box 3, f.1.

80. "Conversation avec M. Robert Blake," April 16, 1970, AMK C 26/1/136, JM.

11. The Last Dance

1. Although she was nominally head of a bureau and was one of the most feared bureaucrats in the history of the department, Shipley was never an assistant secretary, nor was Camps. Shipley, incidentally, began her career as Wilbur Carr's office secretary.

2. Ridgway Oral Histories, ADST.

3. "Remarks at Retirement Ceremony Rozanne L. Ridgway, June 23, 1989," in Don Oberdorfer Papers, Department of Rare Books and Special Collections, Princeton University Library, Princeton University, Princeton, NJ (hereinafter DO), Box 2, f.30. Willis herself had barely made it into the foreign service, rescued, it seems, by William Castle. His diary for May 19, 1927, noted:

> There was only one bad row in the [personnel] board and that was when I insisted on admitting a lady. She was by far, at least in her intellectual equipment, the best candidate we had examined and she was, furthermore, very presentable, obviously efficient and calm. Carr and Norton insisted on marking her way down because they do not want women in the Service. I pointed out that this seemed to me entirely dishonest, that, furthermore, it was breaking the law ... Carr said they never did come up to the standard and that, therefore, we should always throw them down. I asked him whether he thought it was fair to let the regulations stand as they are, to let women spend a year or two studying for the Service when there was absolutely no chance of their getting in. He admitted it was not fair, but that there were the higher interests of the Service to be considered. We had a pretty hot discussion about the matter and finally the Civil Service man... switched over and agreed with Joe and me so we won out. (WRC, Vol. 11)

4. Interview with Mark Palmer, March 30, 1990, DO, Box 2, f.23.

5. Interview with Thomas Simons, July 6, 1989, DO, Box 3A.

6. Brzezinski, *Power and Principle*, p. 11; for Brzezinski's admiration of de Gaulle, see his *Alternative to Partition*, pp. 104ff., where he takes care to point out that "although de Gaulle had a vision, he still did not have a policy."

7. Brzezinski, Richard Gardner, and Henry Owen to Carter, November 3, 1976, Cyrus R. Vance and Grace Sloane Vance Papers, Sterling Memorial Library, Yale University, Box 9, f.19.

8. Brzezinski, *Power and Principle*, p. 5.

9. Ibid., pp. 7ff.

10. Interview with David Aaron.

11. Interviews with David Aaron and Paul Henze. Aaron had much experience in Europe. He served in the Paris embassy during the 1966 crisis, traveled extensively to Europe during subsequent tenure at the Arms Control and Disarmament Agency, and then specialized in arms control and the MBFR while on Kissinger's White House staff. Cf. Brzezinski, *Power and Principle*, p. 76.

12. Interviews with James Goodby and George Vest.

13. Interview with James Goodby. For his part, Brzezinski "saw [it] as [a] nonstarter ... too complicated a process, with too many participants, to yield any tangible results." Brzezinski, *Power and Principle*, p. 172n and interview; Brzezinski to Carter, May 31, 1979, Germany, Federal Republic of ... , Box 7, f.6–10/79, JCPL.

14. Vladimir Lehovich, "Some Thoughts on Europe and the U.S.," in WS, Box 1, f.5dii; Hillenbrand, "European Cultural Pessimism and the Conduct of Affairs," August 1977, MJHH, Series II, Box 4, f.7; Philip H. Trezise, *The Atlantic Connection: Prospects, Problems, and Policies* (Washington, D.C.: Brookings Institution, 1975), pp. 92–93; George P. Shultz,

Leaders and Followers in an Age of Ambiguity (New York: New York University Press, 1975).

15. Schmidt to Carter, September 7, 1977, Carter to Schmidt, September 19, 1977, Germany, Federal Republic of ... , Box 6, f.1–5/79; Carter to Schmidt, April 29, 1977, ibid., f.2–4/77; Schmidt to Carter, June 22, 1977, ibid., f.5–12/77, JCPL.

16. To which Robert Marjolin later added, "Well, he must be a rather lonely man indeed if Valéry is his only friend, because Valéry is nobody's friend but his own." Quoted in Jenkins, who described Schmidt as "deeply offended" and "superficially irritated" by Carter, pp. 68–69, 137, 225. Despite being on a first-name basis with Schmidt, Vest lacked the high-level backing at home to make a difference. Interview with Vest; see also Stoessel to Haig, January 7, 1981, in WS, Box 2, f.5bii. Vest was assisted by his "kind of secret ally," Robert Hunter, then on the NSC Staff. Goodby Oral History, ADST. Description of Carter comes from Brzezinski, *Power and Principle*, pp. 22, 26. For Schmidt's strident views on Carter and Brzezinski, see Schmidt, pp. 222, 229, on Giscard, p. 249; and Klaus Wiegrefe, *Das Zerwürfnis: Helmut Schmidt, Jimmy Carter und die Krise der deutsch-amerikanische Beziehungen* (Berlin: Propyläen, 2005).

17. Brzezinski, *Power and Principle*, pp. 291ff.; interviews with Vest and Joseph Wippl.

18. For the reputed Francophilia of Vance's deputy, Peter Tarnoff, see the previous chapter. For Brzezinski's fondness for Valéry Giscard d'Estaing and French foreign policy, see Brzezinski, *Power and Principle*, pp. 24–25, 313ff.

19. John Kornblum, quoted by Tom Simons, letter to the author.

20. Interviews with E. Wayne Merry, Tom Simons, and Jack Seymour.

21. Interviews with E. Wayne Merry, Tom Niles, Jack Matlock, and Tom Simons.

22. Dobrynin, p. 430; Jeffrey Herf, *War by Other Means: Soviet Power, West German Resistance, and the Battle of the Euromissiles* (New York: Free Press, 1991), p. 51; Haslam, pp. 58–59.

23. Interview with Reginald Bartholomew; James Dobbins Oral History, ADST. The neutron bomb, or Enhanced Radiation Weapon, was a controversial system that the United States had decided to deploy, only to have Carter abandon it following criticism in the press and, according to Brzezinski, his own moral misgivings. The botching of the issue, which infuriated Schmidt, led directly to Carter's decision to assuage the Europeans with the Euromissile deployments and the Joint Chiefs with development of the MX. See James E. Goodby, *At the Borderline of Armageddon: How American Presidents Managed the Atom Bomb* (Lanham, MD: Rowman and Littlefield Publishers, 2006), pp. 116–118; Herf, p. 62; Haslam, p. 100; Brandon, pp. 334–335; Goodby Oral History, ADST; Brzezinski, *Power and Principle*, pp. 301–306; Schmidt, pp. 257ff.

24. Schmidt, pp. 223–225, 230–232; cf. Robert M. Gates, *From the Shadows: The Ultimate Insider's Story of Five Presidents and How They Won the Cold War* (New York: Touchstone Books, 1997), p. 262. Hal Sonnenfeldt, present at the speech, reportedly played a significant role in spreading the word back in Washington. Schmidt to John Chipman, March 28, 2008, read by Chipman at the Guildhall, London, April 3, 2008, as published on the Web site of the IISS, www.iiss.org. Arguing against the case for inevitability is evidence of mounting public pressure since the mid-1970s to respond to Soviet advances in theater nuclear weaponry. In addition to Nitze's Committee on the Present Danger (see below), the work of another group, the European-Atlantic Workshop, headed by Albert Wohlstetter and including Rick Burt, was also significant. See Haslam, p. 65, and the statement by the Committee on the Present Danger, "Is America Becoming Number 2?" in Charles Tyroler II, ed., *Alerting America* (McLean, VA: Pergamon-Brassey's, 1984), pp. 39ff.; Haslam, p. 87; Gelb memorandum, November 10, 1977, WS, Box 2, f.5E; and Goodby Oral History, ADST.

25. Herf, p. 54. Cf. Brzezinski, *Power and Principle*, pp. 308ff.

26. Dean, pp. 150–151; for Carter's apparent change of heart, see, for example, Carter to Schmidt, June 1, 1979, Brzezinski to Carter, May 31, 1979, "Correspondence with Chancellor Schmidt on TNF," draft letter from Carter to Schmidt, October 11, 1979,

Germany, Federal Republic of ... , Box 7, f.6–10/79. The staff work on the NSC at this point fell to David Aaron and Robert Blackwill, with additional help from James Thomson.

27. Herf, p. 64.

28. William Hyland, "The Struggle for Europe: An American View," in Andrew J. Pierre, ed., *Nuclear Weapons in Europe* (New York: New York University Press for the Council on Foreign Relations, 1984), p. 21. Surveys of European opinion are in Herf, pp. 115ff., and in Jacquelyn K. Davis, Charles M. Perry, and Robert L. Pfaltzgraff Jr., *The INF Controversy: Lessons for NATO Modernization and Transatlantic Relations* (McLean, VA: Pergamon-Brassey's, 1989); interview with Reginald Bartholomew.

29. Haslam, p. 92.

30. Interview with Reginald Bartholomew.

31. For instance, Roy Jenkins, who described him as "an agreeable and interesting man, maybe, as some people say, rather a politicians' general, but so for that matter was Eisenhower." Two years later, however, he had become "a strange man, with a simple manner and very right-wing views, very critical of Carter, full of political ambition and I think rather overrating his chances.... [H]e may have a great political future, but he is not to my mind remotely a great man." Jenkins, pp. 121, 387, 437.

32. One European who seemed pleased was Kurt Birrenbach. He wrote to Stoessel and, overlooking his actual origins, congratulated him on providing some "East Coast thinking" to the administration. Birrenbach to Stoessel, January 14, 1982, WS, Box 3, f.21.

33. Interview with Tom Simons. See also Strobe Talbott, *Deadly Gambits: The Reagan Administration and the Stalemate in Nuclear Arms Control* (New York: Alfred A. Knopf, 1984), pp. 13–14, 50–51, 108.

34. Interview with Rick Burt.

35. Interview with a foreign service officer.

36. Interview with George Vest.

37. Interview with David Gompert. Burt somewhat disputed the characterization, noting that Eagleburger was not deeply interested in specific aspects of the negotiations, leaving them to PM to oversee. Interviews with Rick Burt and James Goodby.

38. Interview with Burt; cf. John H. Kelly Oral History, ADST, claiming that the rivalry was occasionally exaggerated for public consumption. Shultz later co-opted Perle by including him in the superpower summits, though ordering him to defer to Ridgway. Shultz interview, July 11, 1989, DO, Box 3, f.2; Ray Seitz to Shultz, June 26, 1984, Charles Hill Papers, Hoover Institution for War, Revolution, and Peace, Stanford University, Stanford, CA (hereinafter CHH), Box 3, f.11; interview with foreign service officer.

39. Interviews with Avis Bohlen, David Gompert, Rick Burt, James Dobbins.

40. Interviews with David Aaron, Rick Burt, and Reginald Bartholomew; Steven K. Smith and Douglas A. Wertman, *US-West European Relations During the Reagan Years* (London: Macmillan, 1992), p. 248, and esp. charts on pp. 55–56, 74–75.

41. Interview with James Dobbins.

42. Among other founding members of the Committee on the Present Danger were Ted Achilles, Jake Beam, W. Randolph Burgess, C. Douglas Dillon, Red Dowling, Andrew Goodpaster, Foy Kohler, Lyman Lemnitzer, George McGhee, Charles Saltzman, and Francis Wilcox.

43. Interview with Rick Burt. See also his Oral History, October 20, 1987, and that of Helmut Schmidt, 5/10, Nuclear Age 11/21, Liddell Hart Centre. Cf. Raymond Garthoff, *The Great Transition: American-Soviet Relations and the End of the Cold War* (Washington, D.C.: Brookings Institution, 1994), p. 511; Talbott, pp. 162ff. For German reaction, see Herf, pp. 140–141.

44. Interview with Rick Burt; Haslam, pp. 124, 140. Nitze's version is in his memoir, *From Hiroshima to Glasnost* (New York: Grove Weidenfeld, 1989), pp. 375ff.

45. Hyland p. 36; Dean, p. 93; Garthoff, pp. 326–327, 551–553.

46. The closest would be Acheson, although he did not make use of the foreign service and the regional bureaus as much as Shultz did.

47. Shultz, *Turmoil and Triumph*, p. 523.

48. Hill to Shultz, December 10, 1984, CHH, Box 20, f.3; Hill, letter to the author, noting that "no one paid much attention to it."

49. Interview with Tom Simons; Gates, p. 279. For Shultz's Eurocentrism, see interview with Eagleburger, September 16, 1989, in DO, Box 2, f.13.

50. Shultz, *Turmoil and Triumph*, p. 268; Simons letter to the author; Jack F. Matlock Jr., *Reagan and Gorbachev: How the Cold War Ended* (New York: Random House, 2004), p. 3. Cf. Garthoff, pp. 49–50, 107, 161–162; Don Oberdorfer, *The Turn* (New York: Touchstone Books, 1992), p. 71.

51. Interviews with David Gompert and Rozanne Ridgway; Charles Powell and Percy Craddock Oral Histories, Churchill Archives Centre, Cambridge University, Cambridge, UK.

52. Shultz, *Turmoil and Triumph*, p. 377; Smith and Wertman quote David Abshire: "[T]he final battle of the Cold War ... was won in 1983 when NATO stayed together on the INF deployment" (p. 51).

53. Other attendees included Attorney General Ed Meese, Ken Dam, and Jeremy Azrael from the State Department, and one or two lower-ranking officials from the NSC and Defense Department. Saturday Group Notes, Matlock Files, Ronald W. Reagan Presidential Library, Simi Valley, CA (hereinafter RRPL), Box 34. See especially notes of meetings on November 19, 1983, December 3, 1983, and "Suggested Policy Framework." Reagan's reaction to one of the early speech drafts, according to Michael Deaver as reported to Jack Matlock, was, "No news. No new ground. Pedestrian." Ibid.

54. "U.S.-Relations: The Next Year," ibid. Attached are handwritten notes, presumably by Matlock, listing "bait," "possible bait," and the "need" for "contingency planning on how to handle" a "probe."

55. Jack F. Matlock Jr., *Autopsy on an Empire: The American Ambassador's Account of the Collapse of the Soviet Union* (New York: Random House, 1995), pp. 8–9.

56. Interview with Matlock; Matlock, *Reagan and Gorbachev*, pp. 190–191.

57. Oberdorfer, *The Turn*, p. 110.

58. Ibid., p. 121; Matlock, *Autopsy*, pp. 73–74; letter from Simons to the author.

59. Memorandum of Conversation, Dinner, November 20, 1985, Matlock Files, RRPL, Box 54. And for his part, Gorbachev noted that he and Reagan "should bear in mind that the world did not belong to the two of them." Memorandum of Conversation, Reagan-Gorbachev Meetings in Geneva, First Private Meeting, November 19, 1985, ibid.; Ridgway, letter to the author. Matlock noted the "pleasant surprise" of the American delegation. Matlock, *Autopsy*, p. 92; Oberdorfer, *The Turn*, p. 139.

60. These included, inter alia, important steps toward raising emigration quotas for Soviet Jews. Interview with Rozanne Ridgway; cf. Oberdorfer, *The Turn*, pp. 96, 181. According to Shultz, Ridgway was "a real professional, tough minded, a very good negotiator ... who knew the essential part of negotiating—to look to your base all the time and make sure they're with you." Interview with Shultz. Shultz identified the base in this case as being the NATO allies, prompting a retort from Ridgway: "The bureau's job is to explain US interests by way of the importance of the Alliance, that is, the US interests that are at play in Europe." Interview with Ridgway; cf. Shultz, pp. 572, 689. One is reminded of Monnet's dislike for the interference of small countries, for example, the Norwegians, "who always stand up and say, 'fish!'" Camps Oral History, EU.

61. Regan quoted in Matlock, *Reagan and Gorbachev*, p. 216; see also Matlock, *Autopsy*, pp. 96–98; Garthoff, p. 285; Tom Simons interview, DO, Box 3A; SecState 010725Z, October 1, 1986, and Amembassy Moscow to SecState, 011603Z October 1, 1986, Reykjavik Summit Cables, Jack Matlock Files, RRPL, Box 57; Rodney B. McDaniel to Tony Dolan, October 3,

1986, European and Soviet Affairs Directorate, National Security Council Records, Box 90907, ibid.: "Essentially a private meeting between the two leaders.... Anticipate no substantive agreements per se.... We should avoid overblown expectations."

62. Matlock, *Reagan and Gorbachev*, pp. 238, 249–250; cf. Goodby, p. 149, Garthoff, p. 290; interview with Arthur Hartman, May 23, 1990, DO, Box 2, f.16.

63. CHH, Box 20, f.6; Michael D. Schneider, acting associate director, USIA, to Matlock, October 10, 1985, "Western European Attitudes on the November 18–19 Geneva Meeting: October 1–8, 1985," Matlock Files, RRPL, Box 51.

64. Interview with Arthur Hartman; Shultz, *Turmoil and Triumph*, p. 755. Shultz's narrative of the "marathon" is at pp. 762–780. Ridgway's job was to brief the allies at various stages. See her interview, DO, Box 2, f.30.

65. Interview with Rozanne Ridgway.

66. Tom Simons interview, July 6, 1989, DO, Box 3A; Brzezinski, *Power and Principle*, pp. 149, 297, 300.

67. Rozanne Ridgway interview, January 19, 1989, DO; Garthoff, pp. 578–582.

68. Matlock, *Reagan and Gorbachev*, p. 209. Cf. Garthoff, pp. 590–593; Talbott, pp. 239, 261–264, 286, 327–330 (for Goodby's work with Burt on START).

69. For a summary of the CDE negotiations, see Jonathan Dean, chap. 8, pp. 185ff.

70. Haslam, p. 140; Rozanne Ridgway interview, DO; cf. Bureau of Intelligence and Research (State Department), Analysis, March 27, 1985, European and Soviet Affairs Directorate, National Security Council Records, 1983–1989, Box 91036, RRPL.

71. E.g., "How to Maximize Your Leverage," October 2, 1986, and "Gorbachev's Position on the Eve of the Summit," in European and Soviet Affairs Directorate, National Security Records, 1983–1989, Box 90907, RRPL.

72. Interviews with Ridgway and Shultz; Philip Zelikow and Condoleeza Rice, *Germany Unified and Europe Transformed: A Study in Statecraft* (Cambridge, MA: Harvard University Press, 1997), pp. 20, 25–27; Michael R. Beschloss and Strobe Talbott, *At the Highest Levels: The Inside Story of the End of the Cold War* (Boston: Little, Brown, 1993), pp. 19–20; Matlock, *Autopsy*, p. 16; G. Jonathan Greenwald, *Berlin Witness: An American Diplomat's Chronicle of East Germany's Revolution* (University Park: Pennsylvania University Press, 1993), pp. xii–xiv, 14, 37–38, 77ff., 109, 278–279. For Ridgway's and Simons's specific objections to the Eastern European initiative proposed by Henry Kissinger involving a path toward greater liberalization—described by Zelikow and Rice on pp. 27–28—see Andrew Carpendale to Zelikow, January 9, 1995, Zelikow-Rice Papers, Hoover Institution for War, Revolution and Peace, Stanford University, Stanford, CA (hereinafter ZR), Box 1, f.2; also Baker to Dennis Ross, December 16, 1988, terming Ridgway's views "more of the same" and a "strait-jacket." Box 1, f.3, and f.7 for handwritten notes about shooting down the Kissinger plan. For Matlock's objections, see Matlock, *Autopsy*, p. 190.

73. Interviews with Tom Simons and Frank Carlucci.

74. Baker insisted that this was not the case and that the picture drawn in his memoir was exaggerated. Interview with Baker. According to Tom Niles, a later assistant secretary of EUR, the relevant point was that Baker may have come in saying he was "the president's person in the State Department, not the State Department's person in the White House" but left office both indebted and devoted to the foreign service, having learned to use it well. Interviews with Niles and Robert Hutchings; cf. Hutchings, *American Diplomacy and the End of the Cold War: An Insider's Account of U.S. Policy in Europe, 1989–1992* (Washington, D.C.: Woodrow Wilson Center/The Johns Hopkins University Press, 1997), pp. 25, 155–156.

75. Credit for inventing that phrase went to Alexander Haig's former speechwriter, Harvey Sicherman. See Carpendale memo to Zelikow, ZR; and Sicherman, letter to the author.

76. See Walter LaFeber, "An End to Which Cold War?" in Michael J. Hogan, ed., *The End of the Cold War: Its Meaning and Implications* (Cambridge: Cambridge University Press,

1992), pp. 13–19; Hutchings, pp. 1–2, 340ff.

77. Interview with Avis Bohlen; Hutchings p. 93.

78. Interview with Arthur Hartman; Matlock, *Reagan and Gorbachev*, pp. xiii–xiv.

79. E.g., Carington, p. 389.

12. Coda

1. Tony Judt, *A Grand Illusion? An Essay on Europe* (London: Penguin, 1996), pp. 3–4.

2. This program was designed mainly by the Defense Department's Office of International Security Affairs, with considerable assistance from the Atlantic Council (author's recollection).

3. "Talking Points on the Geneva Meeting," November 8, 1985 (enclosure), Matlock Files, RRPL, Box 45.

4. Interview with A. Elizabeth Jones.

5. Hillenbrand to Schaetzel, February 14, 1994, MJHH, Series 3, Box 1, f.14.

6. James Dobbins, "Friends Again?" in Marcin Zaborowski, ed., *Friends Again? EU-US Relations After the Crisis* (Paris: Institute for Security Studies, 2006), pp. 22–23.

7. Cf. Stephen M. Walt, "The Ties That Fray," *National Interest* 54 (Winter 1998–1999): 3–31, and my response in the subsequent issue. For a more empirical look at one important aspect of the post–Cold War transatlantic relationship, see Christopher J. Makins, *The Study of Europe in the United States* (Washington, D.C.: German Marshall Fund and the Delegation of the European Commission to the United States, 1999).

8. A suggestion is in James E. Goodby, *Europe Undivided*. I am grateful to Graham Avery for sharing his thoughts on this question.

9. Garrett Mattingly, *Catherine of Aragon* (New York: Vintage Books, 1941), p. 3.

10. I am indebted to the work of the geographer Carl Sauer for this point and for many others throughout this book.

11. Kornblum to Hillenbrand, March 11, 1975, with enclosure (Kornblum to Lord, November 1, 1974), MJHH, Series 3, Box 1, f.7.

12. Interview with Chas. W. Freeman Jr.

13. Interviews with Rozanne Ridgway and Kempton Jenkins.

14. Bailyn, pp. 4ff.; Marco Mariano, "The U.S. Discovers Europe: *Life* Magazine and the Invention of the 'Atlantic Community' in the 1940s," in Vaudagna, ed., pp. 161–185.

15. Address by Dulles before the American Club of Paris, November 18, 1948, JFD, Box 296.

SOURCES

PRIMARY SOURCES
(INCLUDING ABBREVIATIONS USED IN THE NOTES)

Amherst College, Amherst, Massachusetts
John McCloy Papers (JJM)
Dwight Morrow Papers (DM)

Association for Diplomatic Studies and Training, Arlington, Virginia
Oral History Collection (ADST)

Auswärtiges Amt, Berlin, Germany (AA)
R 56. Deutsche Friedensdelegation Versailles bzw. Versailles/Paris 1919–21
R 85. Akten der deutschen Delegation zur Dawesplan-Konferenz Juli–August 1924
R 91. Akten der deutschen Delegation, Reparationsfrage 1929–1930
R 106. Bernstorff, JH Graf von
R. 111. Davidsen, Hermann
R. 166. Schubert, Carl von
R. 168. Simon, Hugo
Botschaft Washington 1908–1931
IV. Politische Abteilungen
  B14–301 NATO, Pleven Plan, etc.
  B14 211
  B14 301
  B14 Pleven Plan
  B15 Schuman Plan
  B20 200/IA2 Laufzeit 1949–1972
  B27 Konferenzsekretariat 1952–62
  B28 212 Fragen der allgemeinen Ost-West Beziehunge (KSZE)
  B64 245
  VII. Kulturabteilung B90 600 Laufzeit 1958–1997
Nachlass Wilhelm Grewe
Nachlass Walter Hallstein
Nachlass Ago von Maltzan
Nachlass Gustav Stresemann

Bentley Historical Library, University of Michigan, Ann Arbor, Michigan
Arthur H. Vandenberg Papers

Bodleian Library, Oxford University, Oxford, United Kingdom
Isaiah Berlin Papers (IB)
James Bryce Papers
Stafford Cripps Papers
Eyre Crowe Papers
Paul Gore-Booth Papers
Lord Inverchapel Papers
Harold Macmillan Papers (HM)
Roger Makins Papers (RM)
Horace Rumbold Papers

British Library, London, United Kingdom
Arthur Balfour Papers
Robert Cecil Papers
Andrew Browne Cunningham Papers
Paul Emrys-Evans Papers
William Gladstone Papers

Jimmy Carter Presidential Library, Atlanta, Georgia (JCPL)
National Security Files
Zbigniew Brzezinski Files

Churchill Archives Centre, Cambridge University, Cambridge, United Kingdom
Ernest Bevin Papers
Brendan Bracken Papers
Thomas Brimelow Papers
Alexander Cadogan Papers
Duff Cooper Papers
Winston Churchill Papers
Patrick Gordon-Walker Papers
Gladwyn Jebb Papers
Philip Noel-Baker Papers
Eric Phipps Papers
Frank Roberts Papers
Selwyn Lloyd Papers
Cecil Spring-Rice Papers
William Strang Papers
Robert Vansittart Papers
Diplomatic Oral History Collection
    Antony Acland; Michael Butler; Percy Craddock; Dennis Greenhill; David Hannay; Nicholas Henderson; Douglas Hurd; Christopher Mallaby; Michael Palliser; Charles Powell; Peter Ramsbotham; Frank Roberts; Oliver Wright; Patrick Wright

Rare Books and Manuscripts Library, Columbia University, New York
Carlton Hayes Papers (CJHH)
Papers of the Declaration of Atlantic Unity (DAU)
J. Theodore Marriner Papers (JTM)

Deutsche Gesellschaft für Auswärtige Politik, Berlin
Nachlass Wilhelm Cornides

Dwight D. Eisenhower Presidential Library, Abilene, Kansas (DDE)
W. Randolph Burgess Papers
Eleanor Dulles Papers
John Foster Dulles Papers
    Chronological Series
    General Correspondence and Memoranda Series
    Personnel Series
    Gerard Smith Series
    Special Assistants Chronological Series
    Subject Series
    Telephone Conversations Series

Alfred Gruenther Papers
John Hanes Papers
Bryce Harlow Papers
Christian Herter Papers
Julius Holmes Papers
C. D. Jackson Papers
Lauris Norstad Papers
J. Robert Schaetzel Papers
Gerard Smith Papers
White House, Office of the Staff Secretary Files
    International Series
    Subject Series
Ann Whitman File
    Administration Series
    Dwight D. Eisenhower Diary Series
    Dulles-Herter Series
    NSC Series
    Ann Whitman Diary Series
Oral History Collection
    Winthrop Aldrich; George V. Allen; Charles Bohlen; Wiley Buchanan; William Burden;
    W. Randolph Burgess; William Draper; Eleanor Dulles; Andrew J. Goodpaster; Alfred
    Gruenther; John Hanes; Raymond Hare; Amory Houghton; Lyman Lemnitzer; Robert
    Lovett ; Clare Boothe Luce; John McCloy; Livingston Merchant; Lauris Norstad; Roderic
    O'Connor; G. David Schine; Timothy Stanley; Charles Thayer; Vernon Walters; Francis
    Wilcox; Henry Wriston; Charles Yost

Archives of the European Union, Florence, Italy (EU)
Papers of the European Commission
François Duchêne Collection
Pierre Uri Papers
Oral Histories
    Hervé Alphand; George Ball; Robert Bowie; Miriam Camps; Claude Cheysson; Bernard
    Clappier; Étienne Davignon; François Deniau; Étienne Burin de Roziers; C. Douglas
    Dillon; Arthur Hartman; Martin Hillenbrand; Étienne Hirsch; Max Isenbergh; Max
    Kohnstamm; John Leddy; Roger Makins; Richard Mayne; Jacob Myerson; Robert
    Nathan; Émile Noël; Michael Palliser; John Pinder; Eric Roll; J. Robert Schaetzel;
    Gerard Smith; Leonard Tennyson; Christopher Tugendhat; John Tuthill; Pierre Uri;
    Raymond Vernon; Berndt von Staden; Edmond Wellenstein

Ford Foundation, New York (FF)
Joseph Slater Files
Unpublished Reports

Gerald R. Ford Presidential Library, Ann Arbor, Michigan (GFPL)
Country Files for Europe and Canada
Richard Cheney Files, 1974–77
Robert T. Hartmann Papers
National Security Adviser
    Memoranda of Conversations, 1973–77
    NSC Europe, Canada, and Ocean Affairs Staff: Files
    NSC Meeting File, 1974–77
    Outside the System Chronological File 1974–77

Presidential Name File 1974–77
Staff Assistant Peter Rodman: Files (1970) 1974–77
Office of White House Operations; Alexander M. Haig, Assistant to the President: Files, 1973–74
White House Central Files
    Diplomatic Consular Relations
    Name Files
    Subject Files
Oral History Collection
    Patrick Buchanan; Robert Ellsworth; Bryce Harlow; Anthony Lake; Daniel
    P. Moynihan; Donald Rumsfeld; Brent Scowcroft; Helmut Sonnenfeldt

Georgetown University, Archives and Special Collections, Washington, D.C.
American Committee on United Europe Papers (ACUE)
Homer Byington Papers
Martin Herz Papers (MFH)
Harry Hopkins Papers (HH)
Robert F. Kelley Papers (RFK)
Cecil Lyon Papers
Edwin W. Martin Papers
George McGhee Papers (GMM)
J. Graham Parsons Papers (JGP)
Walter Stoessel Papers (WS)

Herbert Hoover Presidential Library, West Branch, Iowa (HHPL)
William Castle Papers
Joseph Green Oral History
Hugh Wilson Papers

Hoover Institution for War, Revolution, and Peace, Stanford University, Stanford, California
Papers of the Atlantic Council of the United States (ACUS)
W. Randolph Burgess Papers
William Clayton Papers (WLC)
Eugene Dooman Papers
Elbridge Durbrow Papers (EDD)
Christopher Emmet Papers (CE)
Hugh Gibson Papers (HG)
Joseph C. Green Papers
Charles Hill Papers (CHH)
Stanley Hornbeck Papers
James Huntley Papers
Tracy Kittredge Papers (TK)
Franklin Lindsay Papers
Jay Lovestone Papers
Robert Murphy Papers (RDM)
Kenneth Rush Papers (KR)
Laurence Silberman Papers
Frances Willis Papers
Zelikow-Rice Papers (ZR)

Houghton Library, Harvard University, Cambridge, Massachusetts
William Castle Diary (WRC)
Ellis Loring Dresel Papers (ED)
Joseph Grew Papers (JG)
Christian Herter Papers (CAH)
J. Pierrepont Moffat Papers (JPM)
William Phillips Diary (WP)

L'Institut d'Études Politiques, Paris
Maurice Couve de Murville Papers (CM)

Lyndon B. Johnson Presidential Library, Austin, Texas (LBJL)
White House Central File
National Security File (NSF)
    Country Files
    Subject Files
    Agency Files
    Committee on Nuclear Proliferation
    Miller Committee
Office Files: Francis Bator, McGeorge Bundy, Spurgeon Keeny, Walt W. Rostow
    Name file
    NSC meetings file
    NSC histories
WHCF Confidential File (CO)
Papers of Lyndon Baines Johnson, President, Meeting Notes File
Papers of George Ball
Papers of Francis Bator
Papers of Henry Fowler
Papers of U. Alexis Johnson
Papers of John Wesley Jones
Papers of John Macy
Papers of William Roth
Papers of Anthony Solomon
Oral Histories
    Gardner Ackley; Joseph Alsop; George Ball; Lucius Battle; Keyes Beech; Charles Bohlen; David Bruce; Zbigniew Brzezinski; McGeorge Bundy; Harland Cleveland; Chester Cooper; Frederick Deming; C. Douglas Dillon; Elbridge Durbrow; Thomas Finletter; Henry Fowler; Ed Fried; Andrew Goodpaster; Lincoln Gordon; W. Averell Harriman; U. Alexis Johnson; Nicholas Katzenbach; John Leddy; Lyman Lemnitzer; John McCloy; George McGhee; Robert McNamara; Karl Mundt; Richard Neustadt; Paul Nitze; Drew Pearson; Stanley Resor; Eugene Rostow; Dean Rusk; Anthony Solomon; Paul Warnke; Frank Wisner

John F. Kennedy Presidential Library, Boston, Massachusetts (JFKL)
George Ball Papers
McGeorge Bundy Papers
Harlan Cleveland Papers
Ralph Dungan Papers
Christian Herter Papers
Richard Neustadt Papers
Arthur Schlesinger Jr. Papers
President's Office Files

NSC Files
Central Files, FO
Oral Histories
   Dean Acheson; Stephen Ailes; Hervé Alphand; Joseph Alsop; George Ball; Walworth
   Barbour; Lucius Battle; Prince Bernhard of the Netherlands; Charles Bohlen; David
   Bruce; Lucius Clay; Harlan Cleveland; Maurice Couve de Murville; C. Douglas Dillon;
   Thomas Finletter; Kay Halle; Lord Harlech; W. Averell Harriman; Outerbridge Horsey;
   U. Alexis Johnson; George Kennan; Alan Kirk; Foy Kohler; Lyman Lemnitzer; George
   McGhee; Livingston Merchant; Myer Rashish; G. Frederick Reinhardt; Llewellyn
   Thompson; Walter Thurston; William Tyler; Charles Yost

League of Nations Archives, Geneva, Switzerland
Letters of Huntington Gilchrist

Library of Congress, Washington, D.C.
Papers of the Atlantic Union Committee (AUC)
Joseph and Stewart Alsop Papers (JA)
Charles Bohlen Papers (CB)
Henry Brandon Papers (HB)
Wilbur Carr Papers (WJC)
William Dodd Papers (WED)
Herbert Feis Papers (HF)
Felix Frankfurter Papers
W. Averell Harriman Papers (WAH)
Leland Harrison Papers
Loy Henderson Papers (LH)
Cordell Hull Papers (CH)
Harold Ickes Papers
William D. Leahy Papers (WDL)
Russell Leffingwell Papers
Breckinridge Long Papers (BL)
Clare Boothe Luce Papers
Leo Pasvolsky Papers
Elihu Root Papers

Liddell Hart Centre for Military Archives, King's College, University of London, United Kingdom
John Dill Papers
Hastings Ismay Papers
Nuclear Age Series and Interviews
   Egon Bahr; George Ball; Robert Bowie; McGeorge Bundy; Richard Burt; François
   de Rose; Pierre Gallois; Andrew Goodpaster; Wilhelm Grewe; Denis Healey; Roger
   Makins; Robert McNamara; Pierre Messmer; Frank Roberts; Helmut Schmidt; Maurice
   Schumann; Thomas Simons
Suez Oral History Project

George C. Marshall Foundation, Lexington, Virginia
W. Walton Butterworth Papers (WWB)
Lucius Clay Papers
William Foster Papers
Andrew J. Goodpaster Papers
George Marshall Papers

James Riddleberger Papers (JR)
C. Tyler Wood Papers
Oral History Collection
    Dean Acheson; George Kennan; Robert Lovett; John McCloy

Massachusetts Historical Society, Boston, Massachusetts
Henry Cabot Lodge Papers
Henry Cabot Lodge Jr. Papers (HCL)

Ministère des Affaires Étrangères, Paris, France (MAE)
Série Correspondance politique et commerciale 1914–1940
    Sous série États-Unis 1918–1929
    Sous série États-Unis 1930–1940
Série Guerre 1939–1945 Vichy
    Sous série: Amérique
Série Z: Europe 1944–
    Tranche 1966–1970
Série Z: Europe
    Sous série: Généralités 1944–
Série Communauté Européenne de Defense Série Correspondance politique et commerciale,
    Guerre 1939–1945, Londres-Alger
Serie B: Amérique 1944–1952
    Sous série États-Unis Série B: Amérique 1952–63 Sous série États-Unis
Série B: Amérique 1964–1970
    Sous série États-Unis
Henri Bonnet Papers
Henri Hoppenot Papers
Jules Jusserand Papers

Fondation Jean Monnet pour l'Europe, Lausanne, Switzerland (JM)
Jean Monnet Papers
    Series: C, E, F, G, I, K, M
Robert Marjolin Papers
Robert Schuman Papers
Paul-Henri Spaak Papers (copied from the Fondation Paul-Henri Spaak, Belgium)
John Tuthill Papers (copied from U.S. National Archives)
Oral Histories
    Max Kohnstamm; Henry Owen; Eugene V. Rostow; J. Robert Schaetzel; Shepard Stone;
    John Tuthill

Mount Holyoke College, Archives and Special Collecions, South Hadley, Massachusetts
Miriam Camps Papers (MC)

National Archives, Kew, United Kingdom (PRO)
CAB (Cabinet): 1, 21, 12, 122, 123
DEFE (Defense Ministry): 13
FCO (Foreign and Commonwealth Office): 28, 32, 41, 69, 82, 972
FO (Foreign Office): 81, 371, 800, 801, 953, 954
PREM (Prime Minister's Office): 11, 13, 15, 16
T (Treasury): 194

Richard Nixon Presidential Papers, College Park, Maryland (RN)
Henry A. Kissinger Administrative and Staff Files
National Security Council Institutional Files
National Security Council Subject Files

North Atlantic Treaty Organization Archives, Brussels, Belgium
Subject Files

Department of Rare Books and Special Collections, Princeton University Library, Princeton University, Princeton, New Jersey
Norman Armour Papers
Hamilton Fish Armstrong Papers (HFA)
George Ball Papers (GB)
Jacob Beam Papers
Papers of the Committee for Defending America by Aiding the Allies (CDAA)
Papers of the Council on Foreign Relations
John Foster Dulles Papers (JFD)
Walter Edge Papers (WEE)
Joseph C. Green Papers (JCG)
George Kennan Papers (GK)
Arthur Krock Papers
Henry Labouisse Papers (HL)
Robert Lansing Papers
Lincoln MacVeagh Papers
Livingston Merchant Papers (LM)
Don Oberdorfer Papers (DO)
Benjamin Strong Papers
J. Butler Wright Papers (JBW)
Charles Yost Papers

Private Collections
Theodore Achilles Memoir (S. Victor Papacosma)
H. Freeman Matthews Memoir (Nancy Matthews)
Robert Joyce Papers (Wendy Hazard)

Ronald W. Reagan Presidential Library, Simi Valley, California (RRPL)
National Security Council Records
Jack Matlock Files

Franklin D. Roosevelt Presidential Library, Hyde Park, New York (FDR)
Adolph Berle Papers
John Cudahy Papers
Harry Hopkins Papers
Tyler Kent Papers
R. Walton Moore Papers
Robert Pell Papers
Roosevelt Presidential Papers
    Map Room File
    Official File
    Presidential Personal File
    President's Secretary's File
Myron Taylor Papers

Sumner Welles Papers
John Winant Papers

Richard B. Russell Library, University of Georgia, Athens, Georgia
Martin Hillenbrand Papers (MJHH)

Schlesinger Library, Radcliffe Institute, Harvard University
Lorraine Cooper Papers
Caroline Phillips Diary (CP)

Sterling Memorial Library, Yale University, New Haven, Connecticut
Dean Acheson Papers (DAY)
Chester Bowles Papers
William Bullitt Papers (WB)
Edward House Papers (EH)
Russell Leffingwell Papers (RL)
Walter Lippmann Papers (WL)
Henry Stimson Papers (HLS)
Cyrus and Grace Sloane Vance Papers

Harry S. Truman Presidential Library, Independence, Missouri (HST)
Dean Acheson Papers
George V. Allen Papers
John Allison Papers
William Batt Papers
Lucius Battle Papers
Papers of the Committee for the Marshall Plan
Nathaniel P. Davis Papers
Emile Depres Papers
Thomas Finletter Papers
Ralph C. Flynt Papers
Abbott Gleason Papers
Paul Hoffman Papers
Philip Kaiser Papers
Milton Katz Papers
Charles Kindleberger Papers
Robert Lovett Papers
    (copied from the New York Historical Society)
George McGhee Papers
J. Anthony Panuch Papers
James Riddleberger Papers
Melbourne Spector Papers
Myron Taylor Papers
Charles Thayer Papers
White House Central Files
    Confidential File
    NSC File
    Official File
    President's Personal File
    President's Secretary's File
Oral History Collection
    Dean Acheson; Theodore Achilles; Konrad Adenauer; Willis Armstrong; Edward

Barrett; Lucius Battle; Jacob Beam; Richard Bissell; Donald C. Blaisdell; Henri Bonnet; David Bruce; W. Walton Butterworth; Henry Byroade; Lucius Clay; Emilio Collado; William H. Draper Jr.; Elbridge Durbrow; Thomas Finletter; Henry Fowler; Oliver Franks; Lincoln Gordon; Edmund Hall-Patch; W. Averell Harriman; Loy Henderson; John Hickerson; Philip Hoffman; Fisher Howe; Benjamin Hulley; Joseph E. Johnson; U. Alexis Johnson; John Wesley Jones; Philip Kaiser; Milton Katz; W. John Kenney; Charles Kindleberger; J. Burke Knapp; Perry Laukhuff; John Leddy; E. Allan Lightner; Robert Lovett; Roger Makins; Robert Marjolin; Edwin Martin; H. Freeman Matthews; George McGhee; Livingston Merchant; Paul Nitze; Frederick Nolting; Roger Ockrent; J. Graham Parsons; Edwin Plowden; Paul Porter; G. Frederick Reinhardt; James Riddleberger; Charles Saltzman; Joseph Satterthwaite; Conrad Snow; Dirk Stikker; Willard Thorp; Benson E. L. Timmons; Philip Trezise; Raymond Vernon; Alexander von Süsskind-Schwendi; C. Tyler Wood

United States National Archives and Records Administration, College Park, Maryland (NARA)

Record Group 59: Department of State
> Central Files
>> Decimal Files 250 1920–29; 1930–39; 1940–44; 1945–70
>>> 111 Administrative Series
>>> 123 Personnel
>> Subject Numeric Files 1963–70; 1970–1973
> Foreign Relations of the United States (various) (FRUS)
> Lot Files
>> Bureau of European Affairs, Miscellaneous Office Files of the Assistant Secretaries of State for European Affairs, 1943–57
>> Bureau of European Affairs, Office of Eastern European Affairs, Miscellaneous Office Files 1952–60
>> Chronological Files of Deputy Under Secretary of Political Affairs Foy D. Kohler 1966–67
>> Czechoslovak Crisis Files 1968
>> Diaries of David K. E. Bruce 1949–74 (DB)
>> Diplomatic exams 1906–23
>> Diplomatic exams 1909–24
>> Draft histories of Dept. 1943–49
>> EUR Office of Atlantic Political and Military Affairs, Records Relating to NATO 1957–64
>> EUR Office of Central European Affairs, Berlin Desk, Records Relating to the Four Power Talks and Quadripartite Agreement 1961–87
>> EUR Office of European Regional Affairs, Office Files of Leonard Unger 1951–56
>> EUR Office of European Regional Affairs, Records of the NATO Advisor 1957–61
>> EUR Office of European Regional Affairs, Records Relating to the North Atlantic Treaty Organization 1947–53
>> EUR Office of European Regional Affairs, Subject Files Relating to European Security 1950–55
>> EUR Office of OECD, European Community and Atlantic Political-Economic Affairs Records Relating to Economic Matters 1953–75
>> EUR Office of Northern European Affairs Records Relating to the UK 1962–74
>> EUR, Office of Western European Affairs, Records Relating to Spain 1963–76
>> EUR Office of Western European Affairs, Subject Files of the Officer in Charge of German Political Affairs, 1946–56
>> EUR Office of Western European Affairs, Subject Files Relating to Italian Affairs,

1944–56

EUR, Records of Component Parts of the Bureau of European Affairs 1944–62

EUR Records of the Director of the Office of European Regional Affairs, Subject files 1959–60 and Correspondence 1955–59

EUR, Subject Files Relating to European Defense Arrangements, 1948–54

EUR/RPE (OECD, European Community and Atlantic Political Economic Affairs), Records Relating to European Integration 1962–66

EUR/RPM, Records Relating to NATO Affairs 1959–66

EVR/RPM, Records Relating to Political Affairs, 1957–66

EUR/SOV, Economic Affairs Section, US/USSR Trade Relations and Economic Subject Files 1933–81

EUR UN Adviser, Subject Files 1955–65

Exam questions 1913–24

Examination file 1925–52

Files of Ambassador Charles E. Bohlen, 1942–1970

Foreign Service School Program Policy Files of the Director

General records of the Board of Examiners 1873–1947

History of Posts 1943–47

History of State Dept. 1945–50 (HLG)

INR Office of Research and Analysis for the Soviet Bloc, Records Relating to Soviet Foreign Policy 1947–61

Miscellaneous Subject Files 1951–55

MLF Sub-Group and Paris Working Group Files 1963–65 Subject Files (MLF) 1963–66

Multilateral Force Documents 1960–65

Office of Eastern European Affairs, USSR Section 1917–41

Office of European and British Commonwealth Affairs, Historical Collection Relating to the Formulation of the European Recovery Program 1947–60

Office of the Executive Secretariat, Records Relating to the Berlin Crisis 1961–62

Office of Western European Affairs, Records Relating to France 1944–60

Personnel Policy Files 1953–54

Records of Amb. Joseph C. Satterthwaite 1953–72

Records of Amb. Kenneth Rush 1969–74

Records of Ambassador-at-Large Llewellyn E. Thompson 1961–70

Records of Central European Division 1944–53

Records of the Deputy Assistant Secretary of State for European Affairs (Schaetzel) 1961–66

Records of Douglas MacArthur II 1951–62

Records of Helmut Sonnenfeldt 1955–77 (HS)

Records of Martin J. Hillenbrand 1950–75 (MJH)

Records of Multilateral Force Negotiating Team 1961–65 Chronological Files (MLF) 1963–65

Records of the Office of British Commonwealth and Northern European Affairs, 1941–53

Records of the Office of European Affairs 1948–51

Records of the Office of European Affairs (Matthews-Hickerson File) (MH)

Records of the Office of European Regional Affairs, Files of J. Graham Parsons 1951–53

Records of the Office of European Regional Affairs, Miriam Camp Files 1946–53

Records of the Office of Western European Affairs, Miscellaneous German Files 1943–54

Records of the Office of Western European Affairs, Records of the French Desk

1941–51
Records Related to the Berlin Crisis 1961–62
Records Relating to Equal Opportunity Employment and Minority Employment in the Department of State 1943–66
Records Relating to UK negotiations for membership in the EEC 1961–62
Records of State-JCS meetings 1959–63
Records of Under Secretary of State George W. Ball 1961–66
SOV 1949–60
Subject files of the Officer in Charge of Economic Organization Affairs, 1947–55
Transcripts of Secretary of State Henry Kissinger's Staff Meetings 1973–77 (HK)
Working papers-history of units 1938–49

Virginia Historical Society, Richmond, Virginia (VHS)
David Bruce Papers

Author's Interviews and Correspondence
David Aaron; David Acheson; Avis Bohlen; James Baker III; Reginald Bartholomew; Francis Bator; Lucius Battle; Margaret (Peggy) Beam; Robert Blake; Robert Bowie; Benjamin Bradlee; Zbigniew Brzezinski; Richard Burt; Michael Calingaert; Frank Carlucci; Victoria Coates; Charles Cogan; Jonathan Dean; François de Rose; Timothy Dickinson; James Dobbins; Robert Ellsworth; Lisa Farnsworth; Chas. W. Freeman Jr.; Richard Gardner; David Gompert; James Goodby; Andrew J. Goodpaster; Lincoln Gordon; Brandon Grove; Alexander Haig; Arthur Hartman; Wendy Hazard; Waldo Heinrichs; Nicholas Henderson; Paul Henze; Charles Hill; Deane Hinton; Fisher Howe; Thomas L. Hughes; Richard Hunt; James R. Huntley; Robert Hutchings; Kempton Jenkins; A. Elizabeth Jones; Karl Kaiser; Abraham Katz; Carl Kaysen; Roger Kirk; David Klein; Franklin and Margot Lindsay; Winston Lord; James Lowenstein; Claude-Gerard Marcus; Jack Matlock; Gary Matthews; H. Freeman Matthews Jr.; Richard Mayne; E. Wayne Merry; Helen Chapin Metz; Thomas Niles; Henry Owen; Michael Palliser; Ann Peretz; Christopher Phillips; Thomas Pickering; Peter Riddleberger; Rozanne Ridgway; Jack Seymour; Harvey Sicherman; William R. Smyser; George Shultz; Thomas Simons Jr.; Helmut Sonnenfeldt; Ronald Spiers; Rosalind Springsteen; Monteagle and Antonia Stearns; Edward Streator; James Sutterlin; Peter Tarnoff; Kenneth Thompson; Gwenyth Todd; George Vest; Berndt von Staden; Joseph Wippl; Ellis Wisner

For a complete list of books and other secondary sources, please visit:
www.NortiaPress.com/Atlanticists

ACKNOWLEDGMENTS

I MOST SINCERELY THANK, for providing shelter and sustenance, Harold and Judy Wittman, Warren Coats, Ito Briones, the Weiss family (Arlene, Pam, Eleanor, Margo, Richard, and Jack Courtright), Keir and Susan Whitson, Martie and Paul Henze, Yael Heller, Amitai Touval, Louise Mellor, Peter McDermott, Ruth Trapnell, Patrick Cohrs, Erica Benner, Joanna Kidd, Robin Markwica, Frank and Margot Lindsay, Lauren and Marc Linowitz, Sam Ewing, Rex Baker, Pablo Ros, Matt Montemayor, Jeffrey Yip, Ellen Sutherland, Luciano Burgalassi, the John Winthrop House, and the Biblioteca Marucelliana. For financial support, the John Anson Kittredge Fund; the George Kennan Institute at the Woodrow Wilson Center for International Scholars; the Franklin D. Roosevelt, Dwight D. Eisenhower, Lyndon B. Johnson, and Gerald R. Ford Presidential Libraries; the George C. Marshall Foundation; the Massachusetts Historical Society; and, at Harvard University, the Charles Warren Center for Studies in American History, the Minda de Gunzburg Center for European Studies, the Graduate School of Arts and Sciences, the Department of History, the Graduate Student Council, and the Center for American Political Studies. For ideas and encouragement, David Acheson, Valérie Aubourg, Graham Avery, Oliver Bange, Klaus Becher, Henry Catto, Sahr Conway-Lanz, Kathleen Dalton, Evan Dawley, Jaap Dronkers, Drew Erdmann, Yonatan Eyal, Niall Ferguson, Nate Fick, Thomas Gijswijt, Neva Goodwin, Patricia Hass, James Huntley, K. C. Johnson, Hal Jones, Rob Karl, Alexander Keyssar, Nino Luraghi, David Mayers, Bruce Mazlish, Michael McCormick, Priscilla McMillan, Edward Miller, Virginia Mulberger, David Nickles, Christian Nünlist, Jason Rockett, Luis Nuno Rodrigues, John Romano, Daniel Sargent, Philippe Schmitter, Giles Scott-Smith, Jonathan Stevenson, Nicholas Thompson, Brian Villa, and Jessica Wardhaugh.

I am additionally grateful to Susan Pedersen for sharing copies of letters and diaries of Huntington Gilchrist from the archives of the League of Nations; Karl Kaiser and the staff at the Deutsche Gesellschaft für Auswärtige Politik for their hospitality in Berlin; Valeria Brunori for a memorable tour of the Villa Taverna; Ellis Wisner for a journey around the Georgetown of his childhood; Wendy Hazard for permitting me access to the papers of Robert Joyce; the late H. Freeman Matthews Jr. and Nancy Matthews for allowing me to view the privately published memoir of Doc Matthews; the late Christopher Phillips for sharing a day of excellent conversation and his collection of Italian books and photographs; S. Victor Papacosma, for loaning the unpublished memoir of Theodore Achilles; Sahil Mahtani, Pamela Coleman Nye, Kat Shirley, Jennifer Mandel, and Anne-Marie Smith for research assistance; the many former officials and members of their families who granted interviews; the indispensable archivists and librarians who obtained materials as well as the distinguished occupant of Widener 783, Professor Oscar Handlin, for the inspiration of his scholarship and work ethic; and Sally Makacynas for her many efforts, large and small.

Eric and Hugh Van Dusen, Alexander Hoyt, Robert Pigeon, Renee Caputo, and Michele Wynn supplied the necessary faith, advice, and good offices to ensure that this story would see the light of day.

Kiran Klaus Patel, Stefano Bartolini, Mei Lan Goei, and colleagues at the Robert Schuman Centre for Advanced Studies of the European University Institute provided an ideal environment in which to complete the final stages of research and writing.

Francis Bator, James Goodby, Waldo Heinrichs, Akira Iriye, Carl Kaysen, Ernest May, Frank Ninkovich, Thomas Schwartz, Thomas Simons, and Allen Wells read parts or all of the manuscript in draft. I thank them for their generous contributions of time, ideas, and common sense. Of course I alone bear responsibility for any errors.

I am much indebted to my former colleagues and mentors at the Atlantic Council of the United States, especially Dick Nelson, Éliane Lomax, Helen Soderberg, and the late John Gray and Donald Guertin, for providing invaluable instruction in "the way things are done."

Finally, to Phyllis, my deepest thanks for making a life.

INDEX

Metternich, Klemens von 161
Millikan, Max 141
Mitchell, John 165
Mitterrand, François 194
MLF. *See* Multilateral Nuclear Force
Moffat, Jay Pierrepont 32, 35, 41-42, 43, 45, 89
Molotov, Vyacheslav 93
Molotov-Ribbentrop Pact 39, 65
Mondale, Walter 205
Monick, Emmanuel 52
Monnet, Jean 54, 74, 75-76, 80, 81, 82, 83, 84, 86, 87, 88, 91, 94, 104, 111, 114, 116, 119, 120, 125, 126, 127, 128-129, 134, 139, 142, 143, 144, 145, 147, 149, 150, 160, 176, 188, 198, 202, 216
Monnet's Action Committee 94, 125, 127, 128
Monroe Doctrine 20
Moore, Ben 80
Moore, John Bassett 36
Moore, R. Walton "Judge" 27, 28-29, 33
Moore, Walden "Wally" 125, 128-129, 199
Morgenthau, Henry 57, 58, 135
Morrow, Dwight 18-19
Moscow 34, 36, 39, 40, 51, 61, 66, 102, 107, 108, 130, 148, 156, 174, 175, 187, 189, 194, 207
Multilateral Nuclear Force (MLF) 94, 95, 133-136, 137, 140, 142, 147, 149, 173, 177, 191, 207, 208
Munich Conference (1938) 56
Munich Security Conference 126
Murphy, Robert 39, 43, 47, 52, 53, 54, 63, 67, 68, 101, 102, 107, 110, 112, 125
Mussolini, Benito 33, 44, 55
Mutual and Balanced Force Reduction Talks (MBFR) 177, 179, 188, 189-190, 191, 206, 215
Mutual Security Agency 85
Myerson, Jacob 195

Nassau meeting 132, 133, 139, 144
Nasser, Gamal Abdel 100
Nathan, Robert 82
National Security Council (NSC) 116-117, 118, 123, 136, 140, 141, 152, 164-165, 170, 205, 209, 212, 216
NATO. *See* North Atlantic Treaty Organization
Navy Department 34
Nazism 7, 35, 36, 39, 52, 54, 56, 62, 69-70, 153, 167
Nazi-Soviet Pact. *See* Molotov-Ribbentrop

Pact
Near Eastern Affairs Division (later Bureau) 8, 66, 192
"Negative guidance" 191
Netherlands 36, 57, 73, 143, 157
Neustadt, Richard 116, 134, 135
New Deal 24, 30, 31, 40, 57, 63, 82, 106
New Diplomacy 9, 17
New Frontiersmen 121, 123-124, 128
Nicolson, Harold 108
Nitze, Paul 76, 82, 85, 95, 102, 104, 115, 118, 119, 130, 140, 175, 201, 210, 213-214
Nixon, Richard 116, 136, 149, 150, 151, 152, 154, 155, 156, 157, 160, 161, 162-163, 164, 165, 167, 170, 175, 182, 184, 186, 188, 190, 195, 197, 198, 199, 200, 208, 210
Nixon Doctrine (Guam Doctrine) 188-189, 190
Norstad, Lauris 126, 128, 133
North Atlantic Treaty 4, 7, 67, 68, 84, 86, 89-91, 92, 94, 100, 101, 111-112, 113, 120, 131, 132, 133, 136, 138, 139, 145, 146, 148, 150, 151, 155, 156, 157, 160, 163, 177, 179, 185, 190, 191, 192, 193, 198, 200, 205, 208, 212, 219
North Atlantic Treaty Organization (NATO) 76, 85, 86, 87, 88-89, 90, 91, 92, 95, 96, 97, 99, 100, 101, 106, 112, 113, 122, 123, 125, 126, 131, 133-134, 136, 137-140, 146, 150, 163, 164, 165, 169, 171, 172, 173, 174, 175, 176, 177-178, 182, 185, 189, 190, 191, 192, 193, 195, 199, 200, 203, 204, 206, 207, 208, 209, 210, 219, 220, 221
Norway 149, 203
Novak, Robert 182
NPT. *See* Nuclear Non-Proliferation Treaty
NSC. *See* National Security Council
Nuclear Non-Proliferation Treaty (NPT) 135-136
Nuclear Planning Group, NATO 136
Nunn-Lugar Programs for Safe and Secure Dismantlement 176

O'Connor, Roderic 106
October War (Arab-Israeli War) 192, 195-196
OECD. *See* Organization for Economic Cooperation and Development
OEEC. *See* Organization for European Economic Cooperation
Office of European Affairs. *See* Bureau of European Affairs